POLITICA AETERNA

Politica Aeterna

POLITICAL PLATONISM &
THE DARK ENLIGHTENMENT

ALEXANDER DUGIN

The Fourth Political Theory vol. III

ARKTOS
LONDON 2024

ARKTOS

🌐 Arktos.com 👤 fb.com/Arktos ◐ ◉ arktosmedia ✖ arktosjournal

Copyright © 2024 by Arktos Media Ltd.

All rights reserved. No part of this book may be reproduced or utilised in any form or by any means (whether electronic or mechanical), including photocopying, recording or by any information storage and retrieval system, without permission in writing from the publisher.

ISBN
978-1-915755-49-0 (Paperback)
978-1-915755-50-6 (Hardback)
978-1-915755-51-3 (Ebook)

Editing
Constantin von Hoffmeister

Layout & Cover
Tor Westman

CONTENTS

Preface: *Politica Aeterna* — Topology, Theory, Method xiii
    The Political Dimension of Eternity xiii
    Philosophy and Politics: The Nature of the Unbreakable Bond xvii
    Politica Aeterna and the Fourth Political Theory xix

I. Political Platonism

1 The Essence of the Political. Plato and his Cave 1
Our Subject Matter 1
Uniting the Philosophical and the Political 2
Homologies: The History of Kingdoms and the History of Ideas Are
    Indistinguishable from Each Other 3
In the Image and Likeness 4
Politics and the Political (*Das Politische*) 5
The Philosopher King. Plato as Synonymous with All Philosophy 6
Politeia and the Doctrine of Ideas 8
Tri-Functionality 10
The Cave. Anodos and Kathodos 12
Rulers Are Those Who Define the Philosophical Paradigms of Government 14
Layers of the *Politeia* 15
The Dog Metaphor 17
Guardians and Philosophy 19
Stratification of the *Politeia* 19
Chthonogenesis 20

2 Ontology of the Ideal State (Kallipolis) 23
The Political: Implicit and Explicit 23
Every One of Plato's Philosophical Ideas Has a Political Dimension 24
The Ontology of the *Timaeus* and the Three States: the Ideal, the Phenomenal,
    the Material 24
The Metaphor of the Father: A World of Paradigms 25
The Ideal State Is a State Which Is Eternal 26
The True and the Visible 27
The Metaphor of the Son: Icons, Symbols 28
Phenomenon as Icon 30
Time According to Plato Is a Copy of Eternity 31
The Ideal and the Phenomenal State 32

The Woman and Bastard Logos 33
The Chariot of the Soul. 35
The Dialectic of Parmenides 36
Three Types of Political Ontology in the *Timaeus* 38
Plato's Ideal State: The Philosoper King 41
The Phenomenal State — the Warrior State 42
Pacifistic Warriors Are Abnormal 42
Providing for Thinkers and Warriors 43
Plato's Stages of State Degradation: Timocracy, Oligarchy, Democracy, Tyranny 44
The Anti-King. 46

3 The State of the Son. Aristotle 49
Politics According to Aristotle 49
Three Philosophies of Politics 51
Polity of the Father and Polity of the Son 52
Two Masculine Philosophies 53
Logos Apophatikos and the Demonstrative State 53
Aristotelian Philosophy Denies Not Only Plato's Higher World of Ideas, But Also the
    World of the Mother 55
Two Philosophies 56
Aristotle as an Apologist for Slavery. 56
First a Warrior, Then a Philosopher 60
The Paradigm of the Three Types of Governance 62
The Good State 63
The Bad State 67

4 Sacred Politics and Religion 69
Religion and the Three Types of Society 69
The Sacred: The Light and Dark Sides 70
Religion According to Guénon 73
Creation and Manifestation 73
Creator-God as a Personality 76
Religious and Profane Societies 76
Experiencing the Death of the Individual 79
Secularism 79
When Religion Becomes an Individual's Private Affair, It Ceases to Be a Religion . . . 80

II. Monotheistic Religions and Types of Political Theology

5 The Political Philosophy of Judaism 85
Judaism and Politics. Israel as an Idea 85
At the Heart of Judaism Is a Covenant with the Creator 87
Judaism and Platonism 87
The Philosopher Samuel and King Saul 89

Babylonian Captivity 90
Israel and Aristotle 91
Israel as a Political Praxis. Zionism. The King Mashiach 93
An Argument about Timing and Methods 94

6 The Political Philosophy of Christianity 97
Christianity and Rome. The Withholder (Katechon). 97
Christianity Already Has a Political Component, Even When It Does Not Yet
    Speak of It 105
The Doctrine of the Four Kingdoms and the 'Political Antichrist' 106
The Devil's Political System 108
Byzantium. A Symphony of Powers 108
The 'Unholy Politics' Model 110
The Papacy. Usurpation of the Empire by Charlemagne. 112
Two Political Philosophies: Orthodox and Catholic .114
Wandering Rome Reaches Moscow 115
Glimmers of the Katechon 117
Protestantism and Democracy 118
Protestantism — a Revolution against Vertical Thinking 119
The Three Political Philosophies of Christianity and the Assumption of a
    Fourth Model 120

7 The Political Philosophy of Islam 123
Radical Creationism 123
Shirk 124
The Political and Religious Anthropology of Islam. People of the Book
    and Their Status 125
Jihad: Either Islam or Paganism 126
Attitudes towards Jews and Christians 127
A Global Islamic Political Empire 129
Islam and Christianity in Architecture 129
The Absence of Priesthood in Islam 130
Islam and Politics: Dispute is War 132
The Caliphate 133
House of Islam and House of War 134
Shiism and Its Philosophy 136
Mahdi and the Culture of Waiting 138
Shiism and Iranian Influences 139
Sufism — the Secret 'Religion of Love'. 140
Madhhabs and States 141
The Political Landscape 142
Salafism and Wahhabism 143
Contemporary Shiism 144
Traditional Islam 146

The Sufi Empire of the End. 148
The Islam of the Constitution of Medina 149
Islam in Russia 150

III. The Political Paradigm of Modernity. The War of Concepts

8 The Political Philosophy of Atomism   155
    A Generalised Paradigm of the Political in the Premodern 155
    The Centrality of Hierarchy in Traditionalism .158
    The Third Origin in the *Timaeus* 159
    From Democritus to Democracy 160
    The False Logos. 167
    The Mortality of the Gods, the Attraction of Hell and Democracy 169
    The Formula 'Out of Many, One' 170
    Epicurus: The Ancient Liberalism of the 'Garden' 171
    Ockham's Nominalism 173
    The New Age. The Paradigm of Modernity. 177
    Protestantism is Based on a 'Religious Atom'. 179
    Rebellion of the Third Estate. 181
    Man as a Producer and Trader. 183
    Theomachy and Democracy 184
    Secularisation: A Society Which Kills God 185
    New Age Swineopolis. 187
    Regicide Is a Fundamental Gesture of Modernity 188
    Present-Day Modernity 189

9 Protestantism and Its Secularisation   193
    A Third Christianity 193
    Abolition of Sacred Tradition 194
    Against Celibacy 197
    Against Empire 197
    Wealth as a Virtue 199
    Protestantism as the Foundation of Modernity. 202
    The Secularisation of Calvinism Produces Liberalism 204
    The Secularisation of Lutheranism Produces Bourgeois Nationalism 205
    The Secularisation of Anabaptism Produces Communism 206
    Three Ideologies. 207

10 The Founding Fathers of Modern Political Philosophy   209
    Niccolò Machiavelli: Autonomy of the Political 209
    The Prince: The Tyrant as a Force from Below 210
    Machiavelli's Two Moralities. 211
    Machiavelli's Paradox: The Purpose of Power Is Power 214

The Prince as Tyrant and Antichrist.................................... 217
Hobbes and the Idea of Absolutised Original Sin 218
Spencer: Atomism and the Struggle for Survival in a Liberal Society.......... 222
The Primordial Nature of the Social Contract and Pan-Egoism............. 225
Jean Bodin and the Notion of Sovereignty 230
Eliminating the Power of the Pope 231
The King's Musketeers against the Cardinal's Guards 232
Towards the Westphalian World Order................................. 233
Inside the Leviathan 235
The Politics of the Third Begininng.................................... 236

11 Individualism as the Basis of New Age Political Philosophy 239
The Foundation of Protestantism Is the Social Contract................... 239
Paradoxes of the Atom — The Nihilistic Undercurrent of Modern Ontology 241
An Idiot Is a Man without Qualities..................................... 244
The Idiot as the Norm and Individual-Objects 246
The Goat-Stag and Pseudologic 251

12 Liberalism (the First Political Theory). John Locke and His Legacy 255
The Common Metaphysical Denominator of the Three Poltical Ideologies
 of Modernity.. 255
The Three Types of Social Contract and Hobbes' Universality 258
John Locke: Anthropological Optimism 261
From Wolf to Blank Slate... 264
The Relativisation of Leviathan 266
Sacred Private Property 268
Adam Smith: Trade vs. War 269
The Roadmap to Global Capitalism.................................... 272
The Infinite Accumulation of Wealth 273
The Middle Class and Endless Growth 276
Replacement of the 'Third Estate': Bourgeois Usurpation 278
The Marginalisation of the Peasantry and the Political Science of Mystery 281
Kant: The Foundations of Constructivism and the Prototype of Artificial Intelligence 283
The 'Lockean Heartland' 286
'Civil Society' as an Ideological Slogan 289
Jeremy Bentham: Utilitarian Deontology............................... 294
John Stuart Mill: The Negativity of Freedom 296
The Austrian School: Mises the Founder 299
Hayek: Neoliberalism.. 299
Karl Popper: The 'Open Society'....................................... 301
George Soros: Liberalism Becomes Aggressive.......................... 303
Voegelin: Gradualism of Order, Political Religions and Totalitarian Heresies 303
Leo Strauss: The Need to Lie... 309
Francis Fukuyama: The 'End of History' Thesis 312

The First Political Theory: Liberalism. 314

13 Communism (the Second Political Theory) 319
The Second Political Theory. 319
Campanella: The Rational City 322
Francis Bacon: Atlantis of Scientists. 323
Baruch Spinoza: Substantialism 325
Jean-Jacques Rousseau: Direct Democracy 327
Political Materialism: Matter as Being. 328
The Living Matter of Communism 331
Marxism as Post-Capitalism 332
Declinations of the Atom: The Individual and Fate 333
Prometheus' Titanic Rebellion. 334
Marx Is the Modern 336
The Dialectic of the 'World Inside Out'. 339
The Immanent Eschatology of the Proletariat 342
The Splintering of Class and Ontological Antagonism. 344
Class Definition and the Battle of the Concepts 346
The Genesis of the Proletariat 350
The Concept of the Proletarian: The Minimum Man 353
Value as the Basis of a Revolutionary Narrative 356
Ideology as False Consciousness. 361
Antonio Gramsci: Autonomy of the Superstructure 364
The End of History in the Second Political Theory. 368
The Significance of Political Thought and Its Price. 371

14 Classical and Revolutionary Nationalism (the Third Political Theory) 375
The Genesis of the Third Political Theory. 375
Bourgeois Nationalism and Revolutionary Nationalism. 377
Countries and Estates in the Feudal System 379
The Nation as a Bourgeois Concept 381
The Nation as a Product of Nationalism 383
An Imagined Community 386
A Limited Body of 'Idiots' as the Ideal of Nationalism. 387
Nationalism, Hobbes and Anthropological Pessimism 389
Mercantilism as Economic Nationalism. 391
German Romanticism Changes the Perception of the Nation. 392
Herder: History as the Story of Nations. 393
Fichte: The 'Great Self' of the German Nation and the Closed Mercantile State. . . . 395
Hegel: Philosophical Empire. 397
Gentile: The State as Philosophy. 405
Nietzsche: A Political Philosophy of Life 408
Pareto: Being Elite Is the True Meaning of Politics. 417
Carl Schmitt: Friend/Enemy and the Structure of the Pluriverse 421

Revolutionary Nationalism: The Limits of Ideology 428
Italian Fascism: Futurism and Conservatism. 432
Guido De Giorgio's Sacred Fascism 436
Julius Evola: Fascism and Criticism from the Right 440
German National Socialism: From Left to Right 441
Racial Ideas in Germany 443
The Conservative Revolution: Against the Subject of Modernity 445
Ernst Jünger: The Gestalt of the Worker 448
Arthur Moeller van den Bruck: The Third Reich on the Other Side of Hitler 450
Werner Sombart: Against the Spirit of Capitalism 455
The Atypicality of the Third Political Theory. 456

IV. The Political Philosophy of the Postmodern

15 Postmodern Political Philosophy   461
The Paradigms of Tradition and Modernity Exhaust (Almost) All Forms
   of the Political. 461
Games of the Lying Logos on the Lower Frontier of Matter. 463
The Subject and Object of Materialism: The Singular and Its Property. 465
Postmodernism Is Not Satisfied with the Achievements of Liberalism. 467
Dissipation of the Individual and Dissociation of the Object: Towards the Fractal . . 472
The Cancer of Civilisation 474
The Search for the Authentic Individual: Towards Transhumanism 478
Postmodern Political Philosophy: Three Key Theories. 482
Lacan's Three Orders 483
Lacan's Political Ontology 488
Foucault: Freedom to Madness! 491
Foucault's Three Epistemes. 493
Biopower and Biopolitics. 494
Gilles Deleuze: The Will to Nothingness 495
A Body without Organs: The Political Doctrine of Humpty Dumpty. 496
Splitting the Object: Chaosmos 497
Splitting the Subject: The Rhizome 498
The Rhizomatic Topology of Consciousness and the Desire Machine 500
Liberating the 'Black Depths' 501
Schizomass 502
Micropolis and Micropolitics 503
Realism and Liberalism of Desire 508
Microglobalism. 511
Property Erosion 512
The Anti-State. 516
Negri and Hardt: 'Empire' as a Global Anti-State 517
The United States and Alterglobalism. 520

    Overcoming from within. 520
    The Multitude Counter-Attacks: The Triumph of the Disabled, Perverts and Viruses. 522
    Underground Civil Society. 524
    A Postmodern Reading. 525

16 The Dark Enlightenment   527
    Object-Oriented Ontology: Nihilism and Its Objects 527
    Graham Harman: Understanding the Object by Killing the Subject 528
    The Abolition of *Dasein* and the Immortality of the Machine. 530
    Singularity and the Mystery of the Bastard Logos 532
    Bruno Latour: Hybrids and the Constitution. 533
    Democracy of Objects and Sovereignty of Matter 535
    The Political Philosophy of Mould. 538
    Nick Land: The Dark Enlightenment 540
    Lucifer's Political Physics. 542
    Soros' Soup: A Metaphor for Butchers 547
    Postmodernism Goes Dark 549
    At the Line 552

17 The Fourth Political Theory   555
    The Political Meaning of the Twentieth Century. 555
    The Universality of the West and Dark Modernisation 559
    Questions about the Alternative 564
    The Fourth Political Theory Begins from a Critical Distance 566
    Against Liberalism, but Also Communism and Fascism 568
    Rejecting Liberalism Is Not Enough. 569
    The Totality of the Time of the Woman. 571
    The Rupture of Pseudo-logic and the Experience of Eternity 573
    Metaphors of Bird and Stone: Awakening in the Fall. 575
    The Dialectic of Shadows. 579
    Rejecting the Hypnosis of the Mother. 581
    Political Eschatology 583

Bibliography   585
    Works by Alexander Dugin 585
    Works by Other Authors 588

PREFACE

POLITICA AETERNA — TOPOLOGY, THEORY, METHOD

The Political Dimension of Eternity

THIS BOOK IS BASED ON edited lectures from a course on 'The Philosophy of Politics' given at the Department of Sociology at Moscow State University in 2014. However, some of the topics touched upon there have been elaborated on considerably, and some sections are re-written. Thus the clear language of the lectures is combined with a more rigorous philosophical overview. At the same time, the core message of the course remains unchanged. The aim was to show the *synchronic* structures of the political *Logos* in their relation to philosophy, metaphysics and ontology, and only then to outline the *diachronic* unfolding of these structures in political history. It was precisely this synchronicity of the structural description that was the decisive argument for the choice of the title — *Politica Aeterna* or 'Eternal Politics', but it can also be understood as 'The Political Dimension of Eternity' or 'The Politics of Eternity'. *Politica Aeterna* approaches the examination of the Political first as a timeless structure, and only then as processes of historical transformation. The eternal explains time, which itself adds nothing to the structure of the philosophical city (*polis*), but may well take something away from its fullness. However, this completeness, whose momentary insights we find in the philosophical systems of the greatest geniuses — Plato, Aristotle and... Democritus — generally represented in the classical teachings of

Antiquity, many of which have direct analogues also outside of Mediterranean civilisation — in India, Iran, China, etc. — still in turn has some less fully described and interpreted aspects. This concerns above all the materialistic interpretation of the Political, which was in general deeply alien to the very spirit of Greco-Roman culture and indeed traditional civilisation as a whole. Yes, the ancient materialists Leucippus, Democritus, Epicurus, Lucretius, and schools and trends close to them, had already outlined the main lines of their interpretation of the political *Logos*, but it probably took the political philosophy of modernity to fully clarify them, as the New Age allowed political materialism and nihilism proper to be explored much more thoroughly than in traditional society, where they were marginal and 'heretical' (from the philosophical point of view) phenomena. Thus, *Politica Aeterna*, static in some of its patterns, can only fully explore the range of its structures in the course of historical processes which actualise what previously lay dormant as potential. In contrast, the foundations of the Political which dominated traditional society, in turn, become potential, virtual, and gradually as marginal and 'heretical' as the earlier materialist models — democracy, individualism, economics, etc.

Politica Aeterna, therefore, is somewhat enriched by the analysis of political modernism, which, while not adding anything to the eternal structure, nevertheless clarifies some border territories of the political *Logos*, making explicit its darkest aspects associated with the structures of nothingness, matter and the figure of the Great Mother. And at the same time, referring to the political *Logos* of traditional society as the basic content of *Politica Aeterna*, we are reminded that its relation to the past has a symbolic and contingent meaning, which should not overshadow the eternal relevance of patriarchal — Platonic and Aristotelian — models of the vertical and hierarchical organisation of society. Therefore, what was obvious and evident — truly — in traditional society, in modern times has become potential, blurred and considered 'something overcome', 'thrown off', and hence irrelevant and in the extreme 'incomprehensible'. Conversely, the marginal and peripheral representation of the Political in traditional society, which in turn had been 'incomprehensible', 'eccentric' and 'extravagant', became self-evident in modern age Europe. This tension in the polar interpretation of the Political over the course of history is organised in such a way that at first one pole, being well aware of itself, approximates or even falsely describes the opposite pole, and then the same thing happens on the opposite pole. The political philosophy of Plato and Aristotle communicates the truth of the vertical *Logos* of Tradition, but political materialism is represented distortedly and very approximately. The political philosophy of modernity moves towards the comprehension of its nihilistic essence gradually, reaching it only when modernity is finally defeated and the transition to postmodernism and speculative realism begins. Here the truth of political nothingness is revealed, but the understanding of the *Logos* of Tradition is lost completely. Thus, in both cases we are dealing with a partial truth of the structure of the political *Logos*, which is an inevitable aberration of time and probably constitutive of the very nature of history. It is precisely time — political time — that prevents us from correctly assessing the metaphysical foundations of the Political in its entirety, since we are forced to take a position in time, that is, in a particular phase of political history, which predetermines our gaze and simultaneously the object on which it falls and which it seeks to discern. In modernity, and especially in postmodernity, we are close to political nothingness, to the lowest limit of the Political, to political matter itself, and so we are able to discern its details on a quantum level. But the price for this detail is the loss of the comprehension of the whole, the complete, the perfected entirety. The price for discovering the truth of nothingness is the loss of being.

In traditional society, and especially in its most complete and perfect forms, being reigns supreme, but at the cost of ignoring nothingness, of putting nothingness beyond attention, at the cost of a lack of detail. While in traditional forms of the Political — empire, theocracy, monarchy, aristocracy, etc. — the deficit is nothing (only the knowledge of what is nothing is missing here), and in political modernity, on the contrary, the knowledge of nothingness is achieved by the total oblivion of being, it is still important for the completeness of the political *Logos* to connect the diachronic picture into a synchronic model which will take into account not only completeness and perfection (lost in modernity and even more so in postmodernity), but also matter, distortion, dissolution, poverty, nothingness and Nothing itself. This is what constitutes the content of *Politica Aeterna*, supplementing the traditional conception of the Political with the nihilism and motifs of the Dark Enlightenment, but at the same time reminding the nihilistic period of political history in which we are living of something that not only *was*, but which is *eternal*, and thus may be in the future, beyond the modern and its attempts to overcome tradition by sinking ever deeper into its own essence (that is, into the postmodern). Platonism's vertical political structure and Aristotle's normal state (i.e. monarchy) always exist and are always possible. But there is also always the existence and possibility of a political modern and postmodern, realised today, but already fully comprehended and lived through by Democritus.

Taken together, these constitute the general topology of *Politica Aeterna* as a system of political philosophy that does not recognise the decrees of political history as something irreversible or fatal and opens up the field of political thought to the absolute vertical. The ancient Greeks or Hindus could have chosen materialism, scepticism, nihilism or democracy. And sometimes they actually did choose such an option. But then that choice was overturned and the decision shifted to monarchy, aristocracy or theocracy. That vertical politics prevailed is the basic definition of traditional society: in it the vertical and the sacred predominate and the ever possible outbursts of materialism are the exceptions. In modernity, on the contrary, materialism, egalitarianism, democracy and atomism (individualism) are the most common, and attempts to return to sacred politics are the exceptions. *Politica Aeterna* draws a fundamental conclusion from this observation: political time, while having its own logic, is not an irreversible fate. It may appear to be so, but this is an illusion. Every political system — traditional and modern — is based on a decision. Turning to 'political eternity' we can choose any area thereof. Some of them seem more distant and difficult to reach, others, on the contrary, are close and almost obvious. This is precisely what political history determines. But *Politica Aeterna* asserts a perpendicular relation to this history.

It has to be taken into account and has to be reckoned with, but *there is always a choice*. This is the revolutionary substance of *Politica Aeterna*: it makes the decision free, restoring the dignity of human (and non-human) thought. Choosing in the context of *Politica Aeterna* we are dealing with the present, that is, with what *is* and is *here and now*. Another matter is the degree of intensity of this presence. It varies. But even this is not fatal, because no matter how shaky the truth may seem, in the end it will prove firmer than any metal.

Philosophy and Politics: The Nature of the Unbreakable Bond

From the description of the essence of *Politica Aeterna* it is possible to move in different directions. First, one can go deeper into developing the thesis of the profound unity of philosophy and politics, or the Philosophical and the Political. This is almost theoretically obvious, but we often forget it when we delve into the realm of political analysis and especially applied political science. And yet, no other field lies as close to philosophy or depends on it so much as does politics. It is philosophy that institutes the Political and all its proportions and structures, which in turn affect science, society, education, economy, and life. This totality of the Political is recognised by everybody from Plato to Deleuze, but politicians themselves and those who try to think of politics more systematically (political scientists) very often overlook this, reducing politics to a number of technologies or solutions to practical questions connected with power, its acquisition, its retention, and its application, and all those purely instrumental practices connected with it. For individuals or entire groups of society, the question of power is indeed central and paramount. But the context of the acquisition and application of this power is much more important than it is usually assumed. Everything fundamental in society depends on the political *Logos*, and a particular ruler, party, group, dynasty, etc., is only capable of influencing it to a very small extent. A tyrant, a dictator or, on the contrary, a benevolent humanitarian in power can change virtually nothing about its structures. At the origin of the most serious political transformations are prophets and philosophers, often with no direct connection to a particular power, but who have a profound understanding of the very nature of the political *Logos*. It is the *Logos* that rules, and those who realise this are closer to the element of power than those who occupy central positions in it. Power is a philosophical category and it is connected with the depths of metaphysical Decision. Those who are not aware of this element of Decision do not rule, but only play a role, representing the true power which is then somewhere else.

In traditional society, this fact was openly acknowledged: the ruler was a priest, a philosopher, the main figure of a public — spiritual — cult. Power was sacred and therefore the ruler should be as close to the realm of the sacred as possible. In the modern age, democratisation processes were aimed at desacralising power. But this did not abolish the sacred altogether (as this would abolish power altogether), it concealed it. In this sense, the German political philosopher Carl Schmitt spoke about two types of power: *Potestas Directa* (direct power) and *Potestas Indirecta* (indirect power). True power is sacred, metaphysical and based on the decision made in the context of the general synchronic structure of *Politica Aeterna*. In traditional society, *Potestas Directa* (direct power) was overtly sacred, and therefore the only one. Sometimes only two sides of it were represented by the pair of king and priest (like King Arthur and the wizard Merlin of medieval legends) or the Emperor and the Patriarch (as in the Byzantine symphony of powers). Both king and priest were *Potestas Directa*. In modernity, the *Potestas Directa* is stripped of its sacred content, hence the principle of separation of powers, transparency, etc. But this power without a connection to the political Logos would be unstable and would quickly collapse. That is how the 'shadow power', *Potestas Indirecta*, comes into being. It also keeps a connection with the sacred, but in a hidden way, not directly, through parallel hierarchies and closed structures like lodges, clubs etc. *Potestas Directa*, then, may indeed remain profane and ignorant in the sphere of political philosophy, as the care of the political Logos is taken over by *Potestas Indirecta*. In such a case, the philosophical incompetence of the ruler does not create problems: he thinks he rules, whereas, in fact, others rule for him. And if the *Potestas Indirecta* also pursues mundane technical goals, this means only one thing: it is not the real *Potestas Indirecta*, but its simulacrum. Political ontology itself is such that it is inseparable from philosophy and depends on it directly.

But in any case, *Politica Aeterna* draws attention to the fundamental and decisive importance of philosophy in relation to politics, which is sometimes overlooked.

Politica Aeterna and the Fourth Political Theory

Politica Aeterna is also fundamental in another context: in the search for an alternative to modern and postmodern political philosophy. We call the move beyond the modern political paradigm a generalised 'Fourth Way' or 'Fourth Political Theory'.[1] This direction aims to overcome the three dominant political philosophies of modernity — liberalism, Communism and nationalism — and to build an alternative political theory to them beyond the currently prevailing political paradigm. Gradually, interest in this is growing and, accordingly, more and more detailed arguments are required both in criticising the political modern, and especially its dominant version today — liberalism — and in justifying an alternative political Logos — its content, its structures, its proportions and forms.

The Fourth Political Theory includes first and foremost what was discarded by modernity — political Platonism and Aristotelianism. Platonism is included through its most radical and revolutionary version in the form of twentieth-century traditionalism, which declares ontological and epistemological war on the modern. And as such, one can consider the Fourth Political Theory as a logical continuation of traditionalism. But the reference to *Politica Aeterna* significantly expands the idea of political Platonism, placing it in a broader context and clarifying its relationship with other political paradigms — above all with political Aristotelianism.

However, since the Fourth Political Theory applies not only to the elites, but also to the masses, to people as such, its focus is on the individual, though taken apart from secondary historical and social superstructures. It is therefore proposed that *Dasein*, the central concept of

---

[1] Alexander Dugin, *The Fourth Political Theory* (London: Arktos Media, 2012).

Martin Heidegger's philosophy, should be taken as the subject of the Fourth Political Theory. This opens the way to phenomenology as a whole, which makes the Fourth Political Theory not just a call for sacred restoration, but also a way of constructing a particular existential ontology. This is part of the avantgarde character of the Fourth Political Theory, which is not reducible exclusively to traditionalism. In the context of *Politica Aeterna*, the area of phenomenology corresponds precisely to the teaching of Aristotle, whose influence was crucial for the development of phenomenology — for Brentano, Husserl and Heidegger himself. Moreover, Heidegger's reading of Aristotle established a metaphysical affinity between Aristotle's philosophy and phenomenology, contrasting with Platonism.

The combination of a political reading of Plato and Aristotle, or in modern terms of traditionalism and phenomenology (existentialism), constitutes the metaphysical basis of the Fourth Political Theory. Combining it with the context of *Politica Aeterna* further clarifies its structure and its essence.

At the same time, *Politica Aeterna* allows for a correct interpretation of speculative realism and object-oriented ontology as an expression of the terminal stage of the entire political modern and the concluding chord of the postmodern. Speculative realists close the page on the rhetorical humanism under which modernity concealed its essential nihilism — at one time revealed only by its critics (such as Nietzsche and Heidegger) — and recognises this as its essence. Hence Nick Land's Dark Enlightenment thesis, accelerationism and 'transcendental nihilism' (R. Brassier). This truth about political materialism, which only finds its justification and topological purpose in *Politica Aeterna*, is also the most important argument of the Fourth Political Theory. Political Platonism and Aristotelianism did not know the truth of matter, denied the very possibility of its Logos. Modernism created a political reality which was impossible and inadmissible in the structure of the ontological hypotheses of sacred vertical politics. It thus insisted on its own Logos, fully manifested precisely in a speculative realism that pushed the most daring intuitions of the postmodern to the limit. The Fourth Political Theory, being thus in opposition to liberalism, Communism and nationalism, metaphysically first of all rejects the political modern in its entirety. But the essence of this political modernity — political materialism and nihilism — in the field of philosophy is precisely the 'Dark Enlightenment'. Dark Enlightenment no longer conceals the essence of modernity, and openly proclaims war on man and even life in favour of the Radical Object. This is precisely what the Fourth Political Theory opposes, not merely rejecting the Logos of Matter, but henceforth — and precisely because of modernity — knowing its truth. The Fourth Political Theory does not simply reject nihilism, not wishing to know anything about it (like Plato and Aristotle), but overcomes it by first knowing it. And this overcoming, based on prior knowledge, is another distinctive feature of the Fourth Political Theory. It does not simply combine traditionalism with phenomenology (*Dasein*), but takes up the challenge of the Dark Enlightenment, offering an answer to the problem of the Radical Object of the speculative realists. This answer is the Radical Subject,[2] but this topic is already beyond *Politica Aeterna*, although it remains deeply connected to it.

---

2   Александр Дугин, *Радикальный Субъект и его дубль* (Moscow: Евразийское движение, 2009). [Alexander Dugin, *The Radical Subject and its Double.*]

PART I
POLITICAL PLATONISM

CHAPTER 1

THE ESSENCE OF THE POLITICAL. PLATO AND HIS CAVE

Our Subject Matter

FIRST OF ALL, let us look at the nature of the discipline known as *political philosophy*. If we turn to the history of philosophy and the history of political systems, we find the following pattern — from the beginning, philosophy and politics have developed not just side by side, but inseparably from each other. Among the first Seven Sages, who are considered to be the founders of the philosophical tradition of the Pre-Socratics, are many of those famous for writing political laws and regulations (notably Solon). In essence, they were political figures representing their cities, political entities. Therefore, from the very beginning of the history of philosophy, we see an *inextricable link between philosophy and politics*.

Thus, politics as a separate phenomenon, detached from philosophy, is an entirely different approach. Political philosophy is a much deeper discipline, which looks at both philosophers who have written about politics and politicians who have grounded their laws, designed their political system, on philosophical principles.

In fact, at the birth of philosophy and at the birth of politics, these things were not separated from each other at all. Thus, the subject matter of political philosophy is that primordial sphere which united philosophy and politics into a common and unified direction.

My point is that there are no such separate phenomena as 'philosophy' and 'politics', which we artificially conflate by using philosophy to study politics. This is not just a question of the political philosophy of a particular movement, period, culture or civilisation. When we talk about *political philosophy*, we are, on the one hand, talking about the *nature* of politics, about what makes politics into *politics*, and, on the other hand, about the political nature of philosophy, which makes philosophy into *philosophy*. However, note that there is still a difference — philosophy dominates here, because *politics without philosophy is impossible altogether*.

Politics is a form of applied philosophy, the application of philosophy to a certain sphere of human life. And philosophy without politics *is* possible. That is, there is a philosophy that does not deal with politics. But there is no policy that is not based on philosophy.

Uniting the Philosophical and the Political

Political philosophy studies not only the philosophical foundations of politics, but also the political aspects of philosophy itself, because politics is not a private and incidental application of philosophy, but *the most fundamental*, though still applied, element of philosophy. As soon as a philosophy emerges, it necessarily applies to politics first; and all politics derives from philosophy. Between the two there is not an equilibrium but a deep, organic connection. Where this initial unification of the Philosophical and the Political occurs, all possible political systems are born and philosophical knowledge crystallises.

Theoretically, there is a philosophy that is free of politics and deals with non-political questions. But in fact even such free, non-political philosophy is in one way or another connected with politics (because philosophy and politics have common roots). If a philosophy deals with aesthetic, historical, and cultural issues, yet says nothing about politics, that does not mean that such a philosophy is a completely separate — non-political — phenomenon.

Every philosophy has a political dimension: in some cases explicitly (Solon, Pre-Socratics, Plato, Aristotle), in others implicitly (when philosophy says nothing about politics, but the very fact of having a philosophical paradigm implicitly contains the possibility of a political dimension). There is therefore a very deep connection between philosophy and politics — a connection at the level of their origins. The study of philosophy in isolation from politics vastly impoverishes or weakens the very meaning of philosophy.

On the other hand, the study of politics without philosophy is not credible at all. A man who does not know philosophy cannot engage in politics.

Homologies: The History of Kingdoms and the History of Ideas Are Indistinguishable from Each Other

Strictly speaking, the history of philosophy and the history of politics reproduce the same pattern. There is an absolute homology between the two. When philosophy moves in one direction, politics moves with it in the same direction and cannot move otherwise. If something has changed in philosophy, something is bound to change in politics. But if something has changed in politics, it means that something (before or simultaneously) has changed in philosophy, which has predetermined this change.

In fact, there is no autonomy of politics from philosophy. From the perspective of political philosophy, political history is a slice of the history of philosophy, dependent on this history in an absolute way. No politician is free from philosophy, and no philosopher can be seen in isolation from the implicitly political dimension of his work. In other words, the narrative of history, history itself — the rise of kingdoms; the fall of kingdoms; the building of a particular civilisation; the demise of a civilisation; the conflict of civilisations, states or peoples; dynastic changes; political revolutions; changes in the balance of urban and rural populations; etc. — a philosophical dimension exists underneath all of this (though not always obvious, not always explicitly realised). But the task of those people who study political philosophy is to reveal the totality of this homology.

What does *homology* (Greek ὅμοιος, 'similar'; λόγος, 'word', 'law') mean? It means equivalent; meanings are shared. The meaning of history, whether political-philosophical or philosophical-political, is the same. History has two sides: on the one hand, it is the history of kingdoms, states, peoples; on the other, it is the history of ideas. *The history of kingdoms and the history of ideas are not different from each other.* They are one and the same history.

So if we record a change in the field of philosophy, for example from subjective idealism to objective idealism, it is necessarily accompanied by a similar political change. In the transition from subjective idealism to objective, we transition from one political model to another. The shift from idealism to materialism entails a different change; changes in the configuration of religions radically alter the content of the political processes within the society where that philosophy is prevalent. This homology between the Philosophical and the Political can be examined from all sides, but it is explained by the unity of a common semantic core.

In the Image and Likeness

This homology can be likened to the Father and Son figures. Philosophy — the realm of ideas — is the Father's realm. It is always at the top. From this follows a certain autonomy for philosophy in relation to politics — that is, the fact that philosophy can contain politics both explicitly and implicitly. Politics is always and in all cases a projection of the Philosophical.

However, the relationship between Father and Son or Idea and Kingdom cannot be represented in a strictly linear way. The Father, who creates the Son, reproduces in him what is *common to both*, which is usually called *reproductive*. There is no more generativity in the Father than in the Son, in spite of a certain hierarchy and logical and chronological succession. In some cases the Son may reproduce more extensively than the Father, in which case he is more the Father than the Father himself.

This can be represented in a diagram.

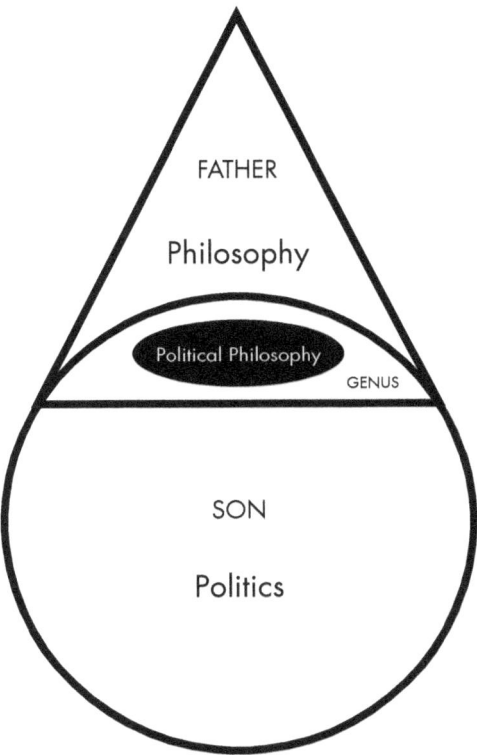

Figure 1. Relationship between the Philosophical and the Political.

Thus the homology between the Philosophical and the Political has to be conceived from the point of view of a generative unity, and not as a mechanical application of philosophy to politics. After all, generativity is equally primary in relation to both the Father and the Son, though not chronologically but ontologically, metaphysically.

Politics and the Political (*Das Politische*)

In order to study political philosophy, we start with a kind of axiom — the absolute homology between the Political and the Philosophical. A definite distinction can be found here between politics and the Political. One of the greatest political philosophers, Carl Schmitt (1888–1985), separates politics and the Political (*das Politische*).¹ The latter should not be seen as an adjective, but as a noun. By 'politics' Schmitt means the application of the Political to a specific social and historical situation. That is, *politics is a concretisation of the Political*.

What, in turn, is the Political? *Das Politische* is the point where the Son/Politics connects with the Father/Philosophy. This is the domain of the generative. The Political is the sphere of the political-philosophical, the point of homology where we are no longer speaking of politics, but not yet of philosophy. Thus, the realm of the Political is the realm of pre-concepts. And when we study pre-concepts, we study the homology that was talked about earlier.

The point is that there is a certain field where the plurality of philosophy intersects with the plurality of politics, and between them there is that which belongs to both the former and the latter circle — a certain segment which is the Political, the main subject of political philosophy.

The Philosopher King. Plato as Synonymous with All Philosophy

Plato (circa 427–347 BC) is believed to be the creator of the first fully fledged philosophical system. He most completely articulated the philosophical agenda that predetermined the entire ancient history of philosophy, the entire Middle Ages, to a large extent Renaissance philosophy, foreshadowing the philosophy of the New Age. There is no thinker today in the twenty-first century more famous and relevant, but at the same time less comprehended, less understood, than Plato.

Plato is the whole of philosophy. All the most brilliant thinkers, from the fourteenth to the twentieth century, turn to Plato. We still have not outlived his agenda. To this day, every word of Plato's is hotly debated. Some geniuses rise to overthrow Platonism,² others to re-establish it. All Christian dogma is based on Plato; there is not a single thesis in Christian

---

1   Carl Schmitt, *The Concept of the Political*, trans. George Schwab (Chicago: University of Chicago Press, 2007).
2   These geniuses included Friedrich Nietzsche (1844–1900), whose philosophy was, in his own words, 'inverted Platonism', and Martin Heidegger (1889–1976).

theology which does not have a Platonic dimension. In Islamic theology, too, everything is built solely on Platonism. That is why Plato is regarded as the Philosopher King, whose realm — within philosophy — no one has yet been able to adequately assail. Thousands of times it has been announced that Plato's empire has fallen, but such claims have been reduced to mere 'marginal hallucinations'. It stands.

Plato is the king of philosophy. We either dispute this (and then raise a slave revolt) or unequivocally accept it. The idea that the history of philosophy has brought something additional to Plato is completely unfounded. Even those considered to be the epitome of modern philosophy — Henri Bergson (1859–1941), Karl Popper (1902–1994), Bertrand Russell (1872–1970) — have turned to Platonism. At times even positivist philosophers like Whitehead (1861–1947) were inspired by Plato.

Plato is everything. If one reads Plato, one encounters not one philosopher, not one author, not one school — one encounters philosophy as such, because all philosophy is nothing but the movement between Plato's theses, their development, their comparison or opposition, their rejection and their renewed acceptance. Plato created all philosophy at once. We may say that the study of philosophy is the study of Plato's philosophy. Everything else is, in fact, as Whitehead said, 'a series of footnotes to Plato'.

Accordingly, we must pay attention to the fact that philosophy is only Plato, and if we do not understand Plato, we do not understand the 'fundamental language' of philosophy. The study of philosophy begins with the study of Plato's works, continues through the study of Plato's works, and ends also through the study of Plato's works. There is no philosopher who does not *know* Plato.

Thus, if we want to get to know the matrix on the basis of which the Political (*das Politische*) is built, i.e. the sphere of that homology we are talking about, if we want to understand where politics comes from, what its structure is and how it is manifested through the Political, we need to study Plato. Consequently, for the political philosophy course the primary author is Plato.

Politeia and the Doctrine of Ideas

Let us take a look at where Plato formulates his doctrine of ideas in the clearest form. The key to understanding Plato's entire work in this sense is the dialogue *Republic* (*Politeia*, Greek Πολιτεία; in Latin *Respublica*). Plato's *Republic* is not just a 'republic' in our sense of 'republic', 'state' or 'power'. It could be said that *Politeia* is the Political itself. Πολιτεία is translated both as 'state' and 'republic', but the Greek word has a deeper meaning. It means any political entity. In essence, *Politeia* is what Carl Schmitt calls *das Politische*. It is the Political which is most often embodied in the state; the state itself finds its meaning in the Political. *The Politeia is primary in relation to the State.*

The question arises: is it a coincidence that Plato formulates his philosophy in its most systematic form in a work called the *Politeia*, the Political? The answer is no. Therefore, it is Plato's dialogue *Republic*, the principal work of the principal philosopher, that provides us with a starting point for understanding the philosophy of politics.

Every philosopher has an inner connection and an inner commitment to truth. The philosopher is not free from the truth. Every text, every phrase, every call to the public, is a principled statement in the face of a most monstrous authority, no less terrifying and irreversible than death.

As Heidegger puts it, *the philosopher thinks in the face of death.* He who does not think in the face of death, does not think at all. Every word of the philosopher is his last word.

Note the dialogue *Phaedon*, which describes the last days and last speeches of Socrates. The words Socrates utters before drinking the cup of hemlock are philosophy. What does Socrates say in this dialogue? He says: What have I been doing all my life, my friends? I have been philosophising all my life on the brink of death. Will I, after drinking the poison, comprehend a new state? All my life I have been here — facing death. This cup of hemlock has accompanied me from the moment I felt my calling to philosophy.

Alcibiades, in the *Symposium*, says how bravely Socrates retreated during the war. He was involved in hostilities in which the Athenian army was defeated and its members fled. Those who ran away in cowardice were the first to be pursued by their enemies. Alcibiades says: How well Socrates retreated. He retreated thoughtfully, calmly, and the enemies, seeing his leisurely pace, did not dare to throw a spear at him or strike him with a sword. According to Alcibiades, Socrates retreated with *dignity*. Alcibiades says:

> Furthermore, men, it was worthwhile to behold Socrates when the army retreated in flight from Delium; for I happened to be there on horseback and he was a hoplite. The soldiers were then in rout, and while he and Laches were retreating together, I came upon them by chance. And as soon as I saw them, I at once urged the two of them to take heart, and I said I would not leave them behind. I had an even finer opportunity to observe Socrates there than I had had at Potidaea, for I was less in fear because I was on horseback. First of all, how much more sensible he was than Laches; and secondly, it was my opinion, Aristophanes (and this point is yours); that walking there just as he does here in Athens, 'stalking like a pelican, his eyes darting from side to side,' quietly on the lookout for friends and foes, he made it plain to everyone even at a great distance that if one touches this real man, he will defend himself vigorously. Consequently, he went away safely, both he and his comrade; for when you behave in war as he did, then they just about do not even touch you; instead they pursue those who turn in headlong flight.[3]

Plato's title *Republic* cannot be a coincidence. His doctrine of ideas is thus of direct relevance to politics. The *Politeia* is the basic document of political philosophy or the philosophy of politics. There we are dealing with the transition boundary between philosophy (for Plato it is the doctrine of ideas) and politics as the organisation of the polis in its purest form. Between philosophy and politics lies the *Politeia*.

Note that in Plato's *Republic*, the Philosopher King is the figure of the Political.

Plato did not manage to build the political system described in the *Republic* during his lifetime, and it is entirely possible that it could not be built at all, but he did manage to found the Political, the 'philosopher's state', the ideal state or Kallipolis (Καλλίπολις — from Greek Κάλλος, 'beautiful' and πόλις, 'city'). If we understand what Plato was leading to (and he was leading to philosophy of politics, not politics), if we realise

---
3 Plato, *Symposium*, 220d–221c.

that all his statements are not concepts, but pre-concepts (in other words, that from which specific political concepts are derived), then we will realise that in fact the ideal state (Kallipolis) and that Political, which Plato justified in his *Republic*, are the meaning of almost all subsequent history — both history of thought and history of action.

In fact, in his ideal state he did not simply present some covenant, plan or project that is either implemented or not — he raised and showed the foundation of what all politics stands on in its concrete incarnations.

Plato wanted to bring a whole range of specific forms of politics into a single matrix, and he succeeded in doing so. Plato's *Republic* is therefore what is most realistic in the entire history of politics.

We live in Plato's republic, we have always lived in Plato's republic and we are moving towards building Plato's republic — from Plato's republic to Plato's republic, but only by going through the technical possibilities, the historical and political concepts of this 'republic', which all converge to the pre-concepts of Kallipolis.[4]

Tri-Functionality

Plato says that the structure of the Political is divided into three castes: philosophers (guards), warriors (helpers) and all others (mainly peasants, but also craftsmen and artists) involved in the production of material goods. If we look at the history of the Indo-European civilisation, reconstructed by Georges Dumézil (1898–1986), we see that these three functions have driven the structures of the Indo-European societies for millennia, from the ancient Scythians and nomads, who lived in Eurasia from time immemorial, to Rome, Greece, Iran, India, all over the Mediterranean. Everywhere we find these three types: divine kings (or priests), warriors and peasants.[5]

---

4 In modern sociology this corresponds to the concept of the 'ideal type' (German: *Idealtypus*) put forward by Max Weber (1864–1920).

5 Georges Dumézil, *Les dieux souverains des Indo-Européens* (Paris: Gallimard, 1986); Georges Dumézil, 'L'idéologie tripartite des Indo-Européens', *Latomus (Revue des études latines)* 31 (1958).

Plato described to us the principle matrix of what was and is. The whole Middle Ages, the whole Roman Empire was built strictly according to this principle: at the top — sacred monarchs (Philosopher Kings, or a division into king and philosopher, emperor and high priest); then, noble warriors (Russian aristocracy is also part of this second estate), which, according to Plato, function as guards; below, the main population — peasants (and craftsmen). We see exactly this model in Greece, Rome, Iran, India, etc.

It is widely believed that Plato's state did not materialise and that the philosopher himself was a 'failure' who devised a non-viable system; that all his attempts to involve the tyrant Dionysius in that system proved futile, after which Plato was sold into slavery, then ransomed and later never engaged in politics again. This is a banal — and utterly false — account of Plato's failures to build an ideal state.

The true account of Plato's fate is this: Plato built that great state — which was, is and will be — in that he substantiated ontologically and metaphysically a system of pre-concepts of political structure. The three-functional model that Georges Dumézil (1898–1986) discovered in twentieth-century sociological research on the organisation of Indo-European societies is none other than another retelling of Plato's *Republic*. The entire Middle Ages, with its three estates, is a *realisation* of Plato's ideal state (Kallipolis).

We see these estates in most societies. Therefore, Plato is one of the most successful political philosophers in the world, because the model he founded is in fact prevalent in different historical eras (with variations of one kind or another). It should be understood that *Plato was concerned with the philosophy of politics*, not politics:

- his ideas are presented as a pre-concept;

- it is the construction of matrices, within which different names and relations can be fixed and variously arranged;

- he outlined the most general structure of what is political; all political forms which follow are concretisation, transition of the pre-concept into the concept.

Plato has nothing accidental, nothing trivial and nothing peripheral.

The Cave. Anodos and Kathodos

Let us turn to Plato's fundamental image in the *Republic*. That is the image of the cave. The story told by Plato is as follows: in the depths of the cave, people (believed to be slaves or prisoners) are sitting and looking at the wall on which shadows are moving; the attention of this whole group is completely fixed on the shadows, they believe that this is life.

What does the philosopher do at this point? He realises that something is not right; he begins to look for some other explanation for what is happening. The philosopher turns his head in a different direction; *he turns around*. In this way he separates himself from the other people, who are still contemplating the shadows (looking straight ahead). He commits a risky action; he goes against the current.

And what does the philosopher see? He sees an elevation, and a procession of people carrying statues. Of course, we are talking about the Dionysian procession. The priests of Dionysus are walking there. Everyone in the cave looks only at their shadows.

Then the philosopher makes a second gesture — he rises from his seat and heads towards this procession. This is followed by a third — the philosopher does not stay with the bacchants and maenads, but looks for the source of light which casts its rays on them so that they in turn cast their shadows. Thus the philosopher reaches the entrance of the cave and for the first time beholds the real world. Socrates says that the philosopher must do this at night, because his eyes must first become accustomed to the weak light of the stars, for if he immediately jumps out, the revelation of the sun will blind him. First the philosopher must look at the multitude of stars, the world of ideas, and only then should he look at the sun, which is the source of these ideas. The ascent to the exit of the cave Plato calls *anodos* (Greek ἄνοδος, 'the way up').

Thus, the philosopher takes three steps: he turns his head, joins the bacchants[6] and goes out to the source of the cave to see the real world,

---

6   In the *Phaedo*, Socrates calls true philosophers bacchants, counting himself among their number: 'There are indeed, as those concerned with the mysteries say, many who carry the thyrsus but the bacchants are few. These latter are, in my opinion, no other than those who have practised philosophy in the right way. I have in my life

where at first he contemplates a multitude of ideas (in the form of stars) and then the main idea, the idea of the Good (in the form of the sun; a black sun, according to some interpretations[7]).

The philosopher is the one who has taken these three steps, and who has emerged from the cave to see the true form of those things whose shadows satisfy the ordinary man. That is, the philosopher transcends man twice:

1) he passes from shadows to reality and

2) he passes from reality to an understanding of the forms.[8]

Thus he accomplishes the fundamental ascent, *anodos*.

But what follows is *kathodos* (Greek κάθοδος, 'the way down'). Having realised how everything is arranged in the world of ideas, the philosopher makes a *descent*. In this descent he returns to those who contemplate the shadows and becomes their king. The philosopher becomes a philosopher through *anodos*/ascent, and a politician through *kathodos*/descent.

Philosophy is ascent, politics is descent. So we come to the main connection between philosophy and politics, to the structure of that homology we were talking about earlier. This is how pre-concepts are formed. The philosopher comes with knowledge that is inaccessible to everyone else and begins to open the eyes of the prisoners. He says that freedom is better than slavery, that rationality is better than stupidity, that volition and control is better than blind obedience, that truth is much more interesting and sweeter than delusion, that light is much more meaningful and exciting than this game of shadows in the eternal twilight, that breathing

---

left nothing undone in order to be counted among these as far as possible, as I have been eager to be in every way. Whether my eagerness was right and we accomplished anything we shall, I think, know for certain in a short time, God willing, on arriving yonder.' Plato, *Phaedo*, 69d.

7   The Neoplatonists emphasised the apophatic character of the Good, identifying it with the supra-being, the One from Plato's dialogue *Parmenides*. On the black sun, see Stanton Marlan, *The Black Sun: The Alchemy and Art of Darkness* (College Station: Texas A&M University Press, 2005).

8   Translator's note: the Forms are abstract, perfect concepts or ideals that transcend time and space, unsullied by the shortcomings and decay of life.

the real air of being is incomparably more pleasant than suffocating in this nightmarish stench of the cave.

Next (often) he is killed. Killed because everything he says is totally at odds with the conventional view, and he simply gets in the way of watching the spectacle that is cast on the wall by the shadows of the Korybantes. But in some cases (as an exception) he is not killed, and then he convinces the prisoners that even if not all of them are ready for the three philosophical actions, at least they are able to face the truth — to look around, to look in a different direction. Others may go up to the bacchants and take part in the feast of Dionysus. If someone wants to follow on, the philosopher takes them by the hand and leads them to the exit of the cave.

Rulers Are Those Who Define the Philosophical Paradigms of Government

We have this whole integral political programme in front of us: to rise up, but then to descend, so as not to leave people behind, to lift up those who can still be awakened. We have to put politics *under* the Political, i.e. under political philosophy. Then the philosopher is King, and only the philosopher has the right to power. All others are usurpers. Only the one who accomplished the two acts — *anodos* and *kathodos* — can be an adequate philosopher and adequate ruler.

Of course, the question arises: why descend? Socrates answers that this is a sacrifice. A genuine philosopher must go up, but if he does not go down, he will show that he is powerless in the face of the filth he has left behind him. He will be too squeamish a philosopher. The real need is precisely to descend into the cave, to reach the bottom of it and clean out all the rubbish that is there, to awaken people from their sleep.

True politics, therefore, is the politics of philosophical awakening. Only that political system is adequate which directs all its citizens towards awakening, towards acquiring spiritual self-awareness. If politics does not pursue such a goal, it is false politics, a politics of evil, a politics of usurpation.

All power has a philosophical dimension, and it is always the philosopher who rules. It is those who determine the philosophical paradigms of government, those who are concerned with political philosophy and not with politics, who rule. And political philosophy, as we said, presupposes the realisation of two actions — the ascent to philosophical contemplation (*anodos*) and the sacrificial descent in order to awaken the peoples (*kathodos*).

In this parable, in Plato's cave, where the doctrine of ideas is introduced, the most complete idea of political philosophy appears for the first time. The metaphor of the cave is the essence of political philosophy. For Plato, philosophy becomes fully fledged when the one who has known the highest comes down to the lowest, when the one who has seen the truth brings it to those who have gone astray and are sitting below (but this is possible only through political means). A philosopher truly becomes a philosopher when he becomes King.

Layers of the *Politeia*

In his *Republic*, Plato gives a description of an ideal City. Its fundamental feature is the vertical organisation, a hierarchy corresponding to the vertical structure of Plato's ontology — that is, of existence as a whole.

The Philosopher King stands at the top of the social hierarchy of the politeia. He is totally non-materialistic, ascetic, devoted only to contemplation of the Good, and performs all other functions only under the influence of the contemplated idea. The Neoplatonist Plotinus (204/205–270 AD) described this as the philosopher's 'overflowing' with rays of the One (ἕν), which requires an outpouring of these contemplated rays onto the rest of society. The philosopher thus fulfills the function of saviour, and power acts as a soteriological instrument which dispenses the genitive (from Greek ἕνας 'genada', 'belonging to the One') of belonging to a transcendent origin.

The main function of the philosopher is *knowledge*, so in the human soul royalty and aristocracy correspond to the capacity for higher forms of thought — theory (θεωρία, 'contemplation').

At the opposite end, at the bottom of society, are the peasants, herdsmen, tradesmen, merchants, artists, foreigners and slaves. They are divided vertically (slaves are the lowest) and horizontally (Plato recognises the division of labour and therein sees that people engaged in particular professions do not have the capacity to rule the whole of society). This is the basic composition of the *politeia*, interacting with the realm of the material and corporeal by necessity. The inclination towards material things is predetermined by the quality of the soul of the commoners; they are dominated by cravings for material pleasure, food, bodily comfort, and below that for lust, debauchery, baseness, meanness, etc. Here the key instrument is money as the antithesis of philosophical thought. All that is noble, sublime, refined, perceptive and upward-looking is drawn towards philosophy. All that is flawed, ignorant, base, brutal, banal and consumed by a multiplicity of carnal sensations is drawn towards money. The soul of the lower class is so arranged that it is dominated by an attitude of production (ποίησις).

Above the main mass of materially driven citizens focused on production are the 'guardians' (φύλαξ) and their assistants. 'Guardians' are in some cases identified as the philosophers themselves, while the assistant guardians are identified as the warriors. The warrior type is driven by *thumos* (θυμός — spiritedness). The warriors are called upon to defend the citizens of the City against external threats. In the structure of Platonic *politeia*, the guards and warriors play a key role. They are seen as carriers of a special character, dominated by gold and silver, whereas the lower classes are dominated by copper and iron. It is the guards who represent the elite of the City and are the primary focus of Plato's attention. They are the 'political class' and the quality of their condition and upbringing directly determines the entire politeia as a whole.

The possession of 'spiritedness' vividly distinguishes warriors from other types. Plato interprets rage as *that which restrains the natural animal need*: primarily the need for production. The spirited man seeks honour and glory, i.e. builds his existential strategy on overcoming and excelling. Here, according to the theories of the Neoplatonists, politics proper and 'political virtues' begin.

The political virtue differs from other virtues (e.g. ethical virtues) in that it rigidly regards the body as an instrument of the soul. The soul is fierce, that is, the part of the self which to the greatest extent is the soul and not the body, i.e. an autonomous entity unfettered by matter, a source of movement and the focus of life. It is spirited where it is full, where it is 'overflowing' with life, surging over the edge. Spiritedness manifests itself freely in war, in defending the Motherland and people from external threats. And it is there that warriors realise the fullness of their nature.

The Dog Metaphor

At one point Plato comes to a very important problem: if rage is the main virtue of the warriors (auxiliary guards), will they not extend it towards each other, and will this not lead to chaos and discord within the politeia itself?

Here Plato's attention falls on the dog (incidentally, many have wondered why Socrates repeatedly swears by the dog in his dialogues). And it is the dog that Plato calls the philosophical animal, the beast that has the primal qualities for philosophy. Of what do they consist?

In the Second Book of the *Republic,* Plato addresses this in the following way:

> (…) you know that well-bred dogs are perfectly gentle to their familiars and acquaintances, and the reverse to strangers.
>
> Yes, I know.
>
> Then there is nothing impossible or out of the order of nature in our finding a guardian who has a similar combination of qualities?
>
> Certainly not.
>
> Would not he who is fitted to be a guardian, besides the spirited nature, need to have the qualities of a philosopher?
>
> I do not apprehend your meaning.
>
> The trait of which I am speaking, I replied, may be also seen in the dog, and is remarkable in the animal.
>
> What trait?
>
> Why, a dog, whenever he sees a stranger, is angry; when an acquaintance, he welcomes him, although the one has never done him any harm, nor the other any good. Did this never strike you as curious?

The matter never struck me before, but I quite recognise the truth of your remark.

And surely this instinct of the dog is very charming—your dog is a true philosopher.

How is this?

Why, because he distinguishes the face of a friend and of an enemy only by the criterion of knowing and not knowing. And must not an animal be a lover of learning who determines what he likes and dislikes by the test of knowledge and ignorance?

Most assuredly.

And is not the love of learning the love of wisdom, which is philosophy?[9]

The ability to control the inherent spiritedness of the guardian is rooted only in wisdom, i.e. in theory, in philosophy. Therefore, a dog capable of abstract notions of 'friend' ('my own', even if he has done the dog no good) and 'enemy' ('stranger', even if he has done him no evil) represents the initial stage of abstract philosophising, of identifying the forms of 'my own' and 'stranger' as predetermining rigid attitudes of behaviour (affectionate play/threatening barking). In this way, the dog becomes a symbol not only of loyalty to its master (as the guardian is loyal to the *politeia*), but also a symbol of wisdom, as it is able to mobilise the higher aspects of its soul—precisely those where wisdom is rooted and where the ability to contemplate ideas is located. From this we can deduce the importance of the symbolism of the dog. The dog can relate to the caste of warrior-philosophers or warrior-priests, which refers us to the Ghibelline Emperor, symbolised by the hound (veltro), to the Catholic order Dominecanes (dogs of the Lord), as well as to the use of dog heads in the symbolism of the Russian *oprichnina* [TN: bodyguard corps] under Ivan the Terrible (1530–1584), the character of Russian history who stood closest to the figure of the Philosopher King.

---

9   Plato, *Republic*, 375e–376b.

Guardians and Philosophy

The guardians' ability to control their temperament gives them entry into philosophy. The nobility of their souls is such that the best of them can become philosophers, and a philosophical education in their case should complement the physical and martial ones. Strength of body and subtlety of feeling must be crowned with proficiency in theoretical knowledge. Therefore the guardians become the framework which holds together the whole politeia: from this framework the most worthy and wise become philosophers and maybe kings, while others maintain the philosophical level from generation to generation through education, upbringing and a kind of caste hygiene (encouragement of selection — heroes and wise men should have as many children as possible, weak and mean as few as possible). The other portion of the guardians, whose philosophical abilities are limited, remain in the rank of 'helpers'. Helpers interact with the main population, oversee order and the enforcement of rules and laws, and take part in military operations.

All guardians are forbidden to have private property, money or families. Equality and simplicity of character, as well as contempt for materiality and corporeality, flourish among them. Their whole human nature is carefully cultivated: the body is shaped by physical exercise; the soul and the sense of beauty by mastering the arts and music (in the *Laws*, Plato insists that residents constantly lead sacred roundels in honour of rulers and gods, singing and dancing, and this should be the duty of citizens); wisdom by contemplation and dialectics — the highest of sciences. Here it is important to underline the direct association of power with asceticism and material minimalism, of the subordination of material well-being and wealth. Noble modesty rules over voluptuous wealth.

Stratification of the *Politeia*

In the *Republic*, two forms of vertical division of society can be found: dyadic and triadic. In one, there are commoners and guardians; and the most philosophically gifted watchdogs are brought up to become philosopher-rulers. Both of these models can be adopted simultaneously, because the triadic structure corresponds exactly to the triadic structure of the basic qualities of the soul: lust, spiritedness and rationality (which gives us commoners, guardians and philosophers), while the dyadic structure draws a watershed between the noble elite (guardians, including philosophers) and the masses (all the rest). Meanwhile, all strata of the society are thought of as a single organism, in which the soul and mind are related to the higher, and the body and organs to the lower.

The upbringing of the guardians is the main task of the politeia. In order to achieve this goal, Plato proposes to censor mythology and poetry, preserving in them only those stories which describe the gods and heroes in a virtuous form.

Chthonogenesis

Plato expresses an important idea concerning the chthonogenesis of the citizens of the ideal state. Plato mentions the origin of human beings from the earth in his dialogue *Statesman*:

> *Stranger.* It is evident, Socrates, that there was no such thing in the then order of nature as the procreation of animals from one another; the earth-born race, of which we hear in story, was the one which existed in those days — they rose again from the ground.[10]

Plato proposes to instil in the citizens of the *politeia* that they have been produced by the earth and not by other people (he thus proposes a return to the original time, the 'golden age'). For this purpose, families are abolished so that children do not know their parents and attribute their birth to the state and its earth, and a chthonic genealogy is taught from childhood. Plato writes:

> I propose to communicate gradually, first to the rulers, then to the soldiers, and lastly to the people. They are to be told that their youth was a dream, and the education and training which they received from us, an appearance only; in reality during all that time they were being formed and fed in the womb of the earth, where they themselves and their arms and appurtenances were manufactured; when they were completed, the earth, their mother, sent them up; and so, their country being their mother and also their nurse, they are bound to advise for her

---

10 Plato, *Statesman*.

good, and to defend her against attacks, and her citizens they are to regard as children of the earth and their own brothers.[11]

And he continues:

> Citizens, we shall say to them in our tale, you are brothers, yet God has framed you differently. Some of you have the power of command, and in the composition of these he has mingled gold, wherefore also they have the greatest honour; others he has made of silver, to be warriors; others again who are to be laborers he has composed of brass and iron. And as you are all akin, though for the most part you will breed after your kinds, it may sometimes happen that a golden father would beget a silver son and that a golden offspring would come from a silver sire and that the rest would in like manner be born of one another. So that the first and chief injunction that the god lays upon the rulers is that of nothing else are they to be such careful guardians and so intently observant as of the intermixture of these metals in the souls of their offspring, and if sons are born to them with an infusion of brass or iron they shall by no means give way to pity in their treatment of them, but shall assign to each the status due to his nature and thrust them out among the artisans or the farmers. And again, if from these there is born a son with unexpected gold or silver in his composition they shall honor such and bid them go up higher, some to the office of guardian, some to the assistanceship, alleging that there is an oracle that the state shall then be overthrown when the man of iron or copper is its guardian.[12]

Plato specifies here that if real properties of a member of this or that caste do not correspond to the ideal, their caste can be changed — if a child of peasants is found to have an aptitude for war and philosophy, it means that there is gold and silver in his soul; and if an aristocrat is distinguished by cowardice, meanness, lust, greed, falsehood or love of money, copper or iron prevails in him and he must be expelled from his caste.

By these means, patriotism is also fostered: all citizens have grown up from the Hellenic earth (as if Plato is perpetuating Xenophanes of Callophon's mystical idea of the primordiality of the earth) and thus its protection is their direct natural duty.

Here it is important to emphasise that this structure — the citizens of the City growing directly out of the earth under the influence of a

---

11   Plato, *Republic*, 414d–e.
12   Plato, *Republic*, 415a–c.

heavenly Logos without the mediation of men — corresponds to the phase when the cosmos is governed directly by God. Birth from humans and, consequently, the institution of the family belong to that historical phase when the cosmos becomes autonomous and begins (falsely) to think of itself as self-created, autogenous. Within the cosmos, individual parts also begin to think of themselves as autonomous and autogenous. Therefore the artificial myth of the origin of men from the earth, which Plato proposes to introduce as an element of the education of the guardians, is in fact more consistent with the truth than the birth of man by man. Man is made man by Logos, acting upon matter.

CHAPTER 2

ONTOLOGY OF THE IDEAL STATE (KALLIPOLIS)

The Political: Implicit and Explicit

CONSIDER PLATO'S CLASSICAL notion of political philosophy. Three of his dialogues are specifically devoted to the problems of political philosophy: *Republic, Statesman*, and *Laws* (and its supplement, *Epinomis*). However, we will not focus exclusively on them. While it is in these dialogues that Plato's conception of the philosophy of politics is given as fully as possible, this conception is inextricably linked with Plato's philosophy in itself. Therefore, based on the homology between the Political and the Philosophical, we can locate and consider the political dimension not only in those dialogues devoted to the philosophy of politics, but also in the dialogues devoted simply to philosophy.

This is a very important element. Plato's philosophy is something whole: partly he talks about politics and partly he does not. But even where he does not speak of politics, a political variation can be found. In any, even the most abstract and off-hand, philosophical statement from Plato we can find some equivalent of the Political — in that *intermediary multitude* where the homology between philosophy and politics is constructed, i.e. in the sphere of the Political.

This does not mean that all philosophy is reduced to politics, it just means that all philosophy has the possibility of political interpretation. Philosophy, as we said, is more than politics. Philosophy contains within itself the whole of politics. Therefore, from the entirety of philosophy we can derive the entirety of the Political. Plato's dialogues, listed at the very beginning of the lecture, are an example of this. They make explicit the basic philosophical origins of the Political.

Every One of Plato's Philosophical Ideas Has a Political Dimension

In the dialogues devoted to the Political directly, Plato says: take philosophy, apply it to politics and we get the domain of the Political. In other cases, he himself does not carry out this operation of translating the Philosophical into the Political.

But does this mean that Plato's other dialogues should be considered exclusively in the realm of philosophy? Certainly, they can be considered as philosophy in isolation from politics (this is a perfectly legitimate exercise), but in fact, not exclusively and not necessarily; in other words, any philosophical idea of Plato has its political dimension.

In one case this dimension is explicit, i.e. overt and obvious, and in the other it is implicit (this means that Plato himself did not apply this or that philosophical idea to the sphere of politics, but this does not mean that those who follow him cannot do so). Does this mean that the very application of a philosophical idea in this sphere is called into question? No, it does not. If Plato himself did not draw political conclusions from his philosophical ideas, this does not mean that this should not be done or that it is impossible to do so. Consequently, to understand the completeness of Plato's Political we may involve both dialogues explicitly devoted to the philosophy of politics, and those dialogues in which nothing is said on the subject.

Accordingly, Plato's entire philosophy can be seen as either explicitly or implicitly containing political philosophy.

The Ontology of the *Timaeus* and the Three States: the Ideal, the Phenomenal, the Material

In this regard, we should pay attention to the following dialogue, which is strictly necessary to understand the scope of Plato's thought in its entirety. This is the *Timaeus*. In it Plato talks about the structure of the cosmos, ontology and metaphysics, and says nothing about politics. Nevertheless, proceeding from what we have reasoned already, we can do that operation which Plato did not do. That is to apply his philosophical, cosmological, ontological and metaphysical views to the sphere of politics. He does something similar in the *Republic*.

The *Timaeus* is a large, extended dialogue, most likely a Platonic exposition of Pythagorean cosmology. What is important for us is this: what is set out in the *Timaeus* is entirely consistent with the whole structure of Plato's thought and, in particular, with the picture we have discussed of the metaphor of the cave — firstly where it deals with shadows, then with physical objects, and then with the search for the source of light. This ascent (ἄνοδος) of the philosopher to the source of light and his descent/return (κάθοδος), on the one hand, describes a kind of vertical journey of philosophy and, on the other, the vertical structure of politics, because at the centre of the Political, according to Plato, stands the Philosopher King who has returned from his metaphysical journey. If he has not made this journey, his power is *metaphysically illegitimate*.

The philosopher returned from his transcendent journey embodies legitimacy, validity, normality, ideality in this power structure. This is the King. He returns with the memory of contemplating the supreme origin. Thus, the vertical ascent and descent which underlies the basic scenario of normative political philosophy is clarified in the subject matter of the dialogue *Timaeus*.

The Metaphor of the Father: A World of Paradigms

What does the *Timaeus* dialogue say at its most fundamental level? It says that there are three natures, three main kinds of all things. All of existence can be divided into three ontological categories.

The first category, which Plato generally calls the Father, is the *world of paradigms* (Greek παράδειγμα, 'model'). This corresponds exactly to the concept of a *form* (Greek ἰδέα, 'prototype', 'kind'). A form is almost the same as a paradigm. The world of paradigms is the world of the spirit, the world of the Mind, Νοῦς. The world in which the originary seeds of things, ideas or *eidos*, reside.

Accordingly, this world is truly real. It is, in the full sense of the word, *real*. It is neither a representation nor a projection of human consciousness. On the contrary, it is human consciousness that is the projection of these ideas.

It is important to note that in the beginning, according to Plato, lies that which can be contemplated (νοητῶς), and only then the contemplation of it (νοερῶς). In the beginning there is the world of the forms, containing within itself the prototypes according to which everything else is arranged. This world is active, and it is the concentration of all being.

Though the Greek ἰδέα can translate to 'idea', Plato's conception of a form is not something nebulous in the mind, it is not something we make up; a form is something which truly is. The form is that which is contemplated. It is a paradigm, παράδειγμα. ἰδέα is the visible, παράδειγμα is the model.

These two concepts are very important because their meaning and identification show us how Plato's philosophy (Platonism) and virtually all idealist philosophy is constructed. When we speak of ἰδέα, of παράδειγμα, we are describing philosophy as such, in its original, unchanging, eternal structure, characteristic of philosophy today.

Today's philosophy is a shrill attack on Plato—that is, an attack of time on eternity, of stupidity on intelligence, of delusion on truth. In reality, however, all there is is Plato and his enemies (and, of course, the notes in the margins of his writings).

Everything is Plato. This is why it is so important to understand *what* Plato is. And if we talk about the philosophy of politics, we must constantly refer to Plato. Plato was, is and will be. It is the only thing with which people who study the philosophy of politics begin, and, more often than not, the only thing they end up with. Everything else is, at best, good commentary. A reading of the dialogues *Republic, Laws, Statesman*, but also *Timaeus* will give us some idea, even if only distant, of Plato. Without this, it is impossible to engage in political philosophy. If Plato is not revealed and these works are not read, our knowledge of political philosophy will be notably incomplete.

The Ideal State Is a State Which Is Eternal

Thus ἰδέα is παράδειγμα, the visible is the exemplary. This means that the form/paradigm/world of the Father is that which *is*. *How* does the form exist? It exists *eternally*. So the idea was, is and will be. The form is primary in relation to time. The form contains all of its possible incarnations. The world of forms is the world of paradigms (models). This is the world of the Father.

Note: when we say 'ideal state', we are not talking about the kind of state we should aspire to, nor are we talking about the kind of state we have dreamed up. We are talking about *the state that is* — the form of the state. And to the extent that the existing state resembles that ideal state, *to that extent* it is.

The ideal state is the state that eternally exists and is the model for all historically existing states. And all historically existing states are nothing but reflections — temporary and incidental — of this ideal state. Accordingly, we speak of the ideal state not as something that could be, should be or was invented by somebody, but as a state that really is.

We can say the following about the state we live in: to the extent that it resembles the ideal state, it also truly is. Similarly: to the extent that it does not resemble the ideal state, to the extent that it is non-ontological, non-being, fictitious, transient, unstable, false and non-existent. That is, it does not exist in essence, but is a distorted parody of true being, a pseudo-state.

The True and the Visible

Greek philosophy, as far back as Parmenides (c. 540–c. 470 BC), distinguished between the True (ἀλήθεια, Greek 'unhidden', 'truth') and the Visible (Greek δόξα, 'opinion', 'imaginary'). The world that is given to us is the imaginary world. The real world is hidden behind the imaginary world, just as truth (ἀλήθεια) is hidden behind opinion (δόξα). What we see is the imaginary, containing within itself the truth — simultaneously hiding and revealing it. But not all of what we see, perceive and know is true; very much of it is only imaginary, seeming. This is how the imaginary deceives us, pretending to be but not being.

The ideal state is that state which completely corresponds to the form of the state; that state which exists forever in the structure of the paradigm. So we can say that it is a paradigmatic state, or a state of ideas/the state of paradigms. Accordingly, the conception of the ideal state as the

Father State, based on the logic described by Plato, is eternal; it is true, it is. Everything else combines 'is' and 'is not' within itself. Anything which is distinguishable from the ideal state is an *imaginary state*.

The Metaphor of the Son: Icons, Symbols

In order to understand the ontology of everything else besides the Father's world and to move on to the second nature discussed in the *Timaeus*, we turn to the metaphor of the Son. This is the second world.

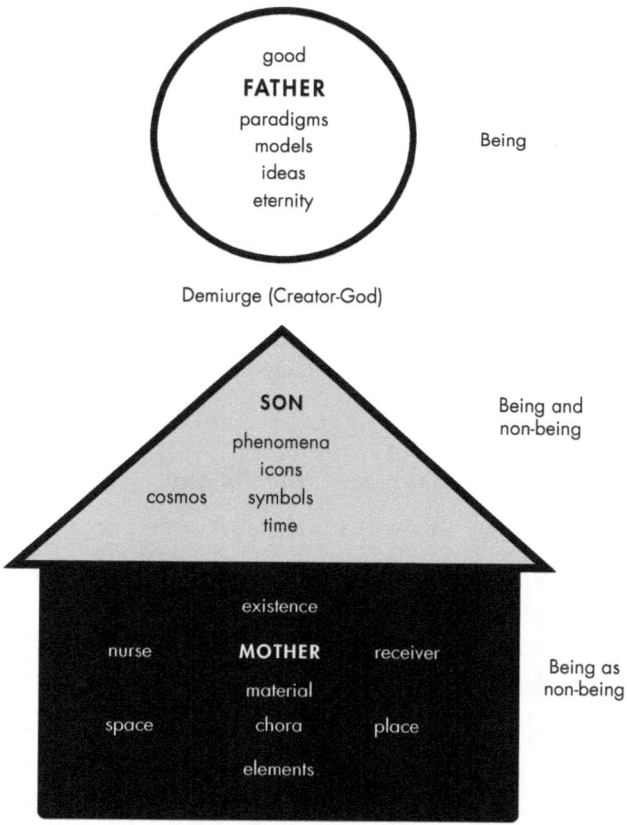

Figure 2. Structure of the *Timaeus*.

Who is the Son? The Son is both the Father, as he is created by the Father, and different from the Father. And because the Son exists in the Father and not the Father in the Son, he is in some ways similar to the Father and in other ways different from him. The Son is in some way worse than the Father. He cannot be better than the Father, otherwise, in terms of the forms, he himself would be the Father.[1] The Father-Son relationship in the patriarchal Greek model is a symbolic relationship, a relationship of fullness and part (inheriting something from fullness). So, the metaphor of the Son, that is the first thing.

The second is the icon (cf. Greek εἰκόνα from the Greek εἰκών, 'image', 'representation'). The world of the Son consists of icons or images. Images are not models; images are copies. The second world is the iconic or symbolic world, the world of symbols (σύμβολον).

What do the symbols symbolise? They symbolise the forms. The forms are that which is, but symbols… do they exist or not? *They both do and do not*. The forms are consistent within themselves. They are the very thing that they are. And symbols *refer* to these forms.

That is, symbols are partly there insofar as they refer to an idea, but partly they are not — as there is no such thing in isolation from the ontological act of referring. If the formula A=A is valid for a form (a form is a form), then the symbol is much more complexly related to being; it is there because it is not itself (A≠A); the symbol symbolises not itself, but something else, and without the other it loses its meaning in being, disappears. It exists so long as it refers to something other than itself.

But the symbol itself is not that to which it refers. It is not a form and not a model. A symbol is not a paradigm, but an icon, a copy. Accordingly, as A=A, it does not exist.

The existence of a symbol is not the same as the existence of a form. The existence of the symbol is both valid and invalid. It is a *combination of being and non-being in one*. In reference to a form (which truly is), the symbol is. In isolation, it is not. What is a mirror? In reality, a mirror *by itself* is contentless. It attains contents when it reflects something. But what does a mirror that reflects nothing reflect? Nothing. That is to say, there is no being in this mirror. If we imagine the symbol as a mirror

---

[1] This is possible, however, if we consider the primordial nature of the concept of kinship in relation to both the Father and the Son.

reflecting some being, we will say that we do see in it some being, and therefore this mirror is there.

In Stéphane Mallarmé (1842–1898) the image of a mirror lying on the floor of a dark room at night is repeated, and the poet asks, in what sense is this mirror there? This mirror does not reflect anything. The meaning of a mirror is to reflect. But if the mirror does not reflect anything, is this a mirror?

From the idea of a mirror left in an empty room at night comes the idea of pure possibility, which is described by Plato in the *Timaeus* as the third genus or order of being.

Phenomenon as Icon

However, before we move on to an explanation of the ontology of matter, I would like to draw attention to another name for the second order, the world of copies or the iconic world. Plato calls it *phenomenon* (from the Greek φαινόμενον, 'appearing', 'phenomenon').

It is important to note that a symbol, an icon, a copy is a *phenomenon* of a form. Through the Son the Father is manifested, through the copy the paradigm is manifested, through the phenomenon the idea is manifested. The meaning of the phenomenon is its double being. On the one hand, it — φαινόμενον, the phenomenon — is (because something appears in the phenomenon), and, on the other hand, it does not exist in itself. This is a very important philosophical concept. Hence the term 'phenomenal' or the 'phenomenology' field in philosophy. A phenomenon is that which can be perceived, but is not identical to itself. A phenomenon always has an essence, that is, something that is manifested through it.

The world of phenomena, the world that is given to us by direct experience, is the world of the apparition of forms. That is, the forms are manifested through our world, hence our world is not identical to itself. The world we perceive is an imaginary world, a world of opinions. Not a single thing here refers to itself, not a single thing here is self-referential. Every object and every phenomenon of nature, from the point of view of Platonism, is a symbol, i.e. an indication of another. It is not the truth itself, but its phenomenon.

Time According to Plato Is a Copy of Eternity

But in this phenomenon there is that which is like a form (therefore the world is fundamentally beautiful) and there is also that which is not like a form (therefore the world is essentially perishable, mortal). The law of the second world, the world of the Son, is γένεσις (origin) and φθόρος (annihilation); it is also time.

If in the world of models/paradigms there are eternal ideas, in the world of copies there is time. What is time, according to Plato? *It is a copy of eternity.* That which in eternity is simultaneous, in time is sequential.

In eternity we are unborn, young, adult, old and dead simultaneously.[2] The idea of us is eternal and unchanging, but in our world it is given to us sequentially: we appear from nowhere, come into the world of phenomena and disappear into nowhere.

But according to Plato, this 'nowhere' — the world of death and the world before birth — is *ourselves*. Our death is fundamentally ontological. It is our *form*. We come from our form and we return to our form. And this idea of self exists in itself to a greater extent not when we are, but when we are not.

Plato describes this through the notion of the eternity of the *soul* (ψυχή). The soul is our form. We ourselves are phenomena, so we live in time. In time our form becomes a phenomenon, our ideal selves become phenomenal, we are manifested through ourselves. *We are a copy of ourselves.* Note: this introduces the notion of the dialectic of the world of the Father and the world of the Son, the world of the original and the world of the copy.

---

2   In this sense, Empedocles (c. 490–c. 430 BC), who taught about the four elements (roots) of reality, stated that he was *simultaneously* a child, a bush, a fish and a bird. With this he wanted to show that his inner self, his subject or *daimon*, is inherently unchanged, no matter what elements he was clothed in. It is interesting that in Empedocles the human figure (the child) corresponds to the element of fire or the sun. M. R. Wright, *Empedocles: The Extant Fragments* (New York, London: Yale University Press, 1981). The Neoplatonist Plotinus (204/205–270 BC) had a similar conception of the eternally unchanging soul.

The Ideal and the Phenomenal State

We can apply the second principle to the state: there is the ideal state and the phenomenal state (symbolic state, iconic state, state of copies). Of what is the phenomenal state a copy? The ideal. If an ideal form-state exists, then what is the ontological status of the phenomenal state?

One the one hand, the phenomenal state is (because it reflects, represents the ideal state), and, on the other, it is not (because it has a diminished—and ultimately no—ontology in and of itself). We can say that the ideal state (Kallipolis) is the state of the *soul*, where its citizens are eternal forms, while the phenomenal state is a state of becoming (it arises and then inexorably it perishes). Its citizens are human beings.

The ontological status of the ideal state and the phenomenal state through the *Timaeus* help us understand the metaphor of the cave. The upward movement of the philosopher (ἄνοδος) and the downward movement of the philosopher (κάθοδος), the exit from politics through the Political into the Philosophical, and next—the establishment of ideal politics through the Political upon return are in fact precisely this *dialectic of the transition from the Father to the Son*. When the Political emerges, the philosopher (the Son, the phenomenal man) returns to his own soul (the Son returns to the Father) and descends again to himself, but now he is *changed*. It is one thing for the Son to be simply *born*, and quite another for the Son to *know the Father*. At first the Son realises that he is *only* the Son, that this phenomenal world, the world of opinion (δόξα), is only a copy just like he himself. Having realised what he is a copy of, i.e. comprehending the Father through consideration of himself, he becomes a *different* Son; a Son who accentuates similarity to the Father rather than difference, unity with the Father rather than opposition. The Son understands that he is not himself alone, but a symbol. He is no longer a victim of the delusion that the world we are given is everything. The Son understands that this world is not real. What is real about this imaginary world? That it symbolises the real world. So by the method of cataphaticism (from the Greek καταφατικός, 'affirming'), the method of likeness, we can arrive at *what* is in the phenomenal. It is not the phenomenon itself that is in the phenomenon. Note how the phenomenal state relates to the ideal state:

the phenomenal state is a phenomenal state, a copy, and to the extent that this copy reflects the ideal state (Kallipolis), this state is. Similarly: to the extent that it does not reflect it, that state does not exist.

Philosophy of politics argues that *politics cannot be studied by political methods*. The content of politics is not politics. The content of politics is philosophy. Politics is the realm of phenomena and philosophy is the realm of forms. Each element of the Political is nothing but a *political phenomenon*, a manifestation. *What* is in this phenomenon is a question to be studied.

One last remark, we have to pay attention to what a norm (Latin *norma*) is. *Norma* means almost the same thing as 'form' or 'ideal'. 'Being normal' and 'being ideal' are roughly the same thing. The norm is never a given; the norm is an ontological content or paradigm/image against which we measure the phenomenal. Therefore Plato's ideal state is the normal state. Moreover, any phenomenal state is normal only insofar as it is ideal or resembles the ideal state. What then are the states we have to deal with in history? By definition, they are abnormal states, and the only difference is the scale and varieties of this abnormality.

The Woman and Bastard Logos

The third kind in the *Timaeus* is 'chora' (χώρα). This term literally means 'space' or 'place'. Plato calls χώρα 'Mother', 'Receiver' or 'Nurse' and equates space with the feminine principle, while describing this as the sphere where the primary elements (στοιχεῖον) are found.

This third feminine principle, from Plato's point of view, cannot be understood by the mind, because in the pure feminine everything is meaningless. Woman is comprehended by means of a special Logos, the bastard Logos ('illegitimate'). Everything in woman that is purely feminine is comprehended not by the mind, but by the pseudo-mind.

In contrast, that pertaining to the Father and the Son is comprehended by the normal Logos. Therefore Plato does not pay too much attention to the bastard Logos. The Greek for 'illegitimate' is λόγος νόθος.

Plato describes it thus:

> And there is a third nature, which is space, and is eternal, and admits not of destruction and provides a home for all created things, and is apprehended without the help of sense, by a kind of spurious reason, and is hardly real; which we beholding as in a dream, say of all existence that it must of necessity be in some place and occupy a space, but that what is neither in heaven nor in earth has no existence. Of these and other things of the same kind, relating to the true and waking reality of nature, we have only this dreamlike sense, and we are unable to cast off sleep and determine the truth about them. For an image, since the reality, after which it is modelled, does not belong to it, and it exists ever as the fleeting shadow of some other, must be inferred to be in another [i.e. in space], grasping existence in some way or other, or it could not be at all.[3]

It should be noted that at this point in the *Timaeus* Plato's previously crystal-clear speech loses its transparency, and he begins to speak with vague images, losing the metaphysical certainty that is unshakeable when he describes the first and second kind of being. This may be likened to the gaze of a celestial god reaching the surface of the earth, the lower boundary of the world of copies, and here, encountering its limits, seeing something that defies clear discernment. At the boundary of the day flickers the region of night and dreams. Plato therefore confines himself to a few indications and postulates 'chora', χώρα (space), as a flat boundary beyond which there is nothing, which cannot be understood, since there is nothing to understand in it as such.

The legitimate Logos is the Logos of the Father and the Son. Between them the whole political philosophy of the ideal state (Kallipolis) unfolds. The woman (χώρα), on the other hand, is only the Nurse; she feeds the Son without giving him anything substantial. The woman (χώρα) merely gives him a kind of *phenomenal materiality*. In fact, the woman (χώρα) brings to the world only the *imaginary*. She is the mother of pure 'doxa', that is, the direct opposite of truth.

When does the phenomenal approach the ideal? When the second kind (the Son) approaches the first (the Father), breaking away from the third (the Mother, the Nurturer). What does woman, from Plato's point of view, give to the soul? A body. But the body is a kind of meaningless

---

3   Plato, *Timaeus*, 52a.

burden, transforming the eternal into the temporal, transparent into semi-transparent, etc.

The Chariot of the Soul

Plato asserts the same fundamental triad in the very structure of man. In the *Phaedrus* he likens the human soul to a chariot pulled by two horses. This chariot is involved in the race of the gods across the firmament. And only when the chariot gets off course and breaks away from the company of the deities, it enters the body, where it seeks release and return to its divine companions and leaders.

In the structure of the soul (chariot — Greek ὄχημα) there are

1) a charioteer (Greek κυβερνήτης, i.e. λόγος, νοῦς, 'mind'),
2) a white horse with a black eye (spiritedness — Greek θύμος) and
3) a black horse with a white eye (lust — Greek ἐπιθυμία).

The chariot of the soul, driven by the charioteer, has three beginnings: the charioteer and the two horses.

The charioteer himself is the philosopher, the most noble part of the soul. He who cultivates the mind, develops the highest principle in himself. He does not just live by the powers of the soul, but makes life subject to thought, contemplation, that is, seeks to give life meaning and purpose. The charioteer represents the most divine side of the soul.

The white horse with the black eye is spiritedness (θύμος), the desire for murder, for violence, but also for courage, for defending the fatherland. Fury is a masculine quality, the soul's desire for expansion. It is the turbulent beginning of the soul, connected with pride, vanity, the will to power, the desire to master others, to conquer. But at the same time, this desire leads the soul away from the corporeal world — into finer worlds.

The black horse with the white eye is lust (ἐπιθυμία), which binds man to material things, thereby constituting them, because it is the focus on material expansion that gives rise to the materiality and corporeality of things. According to Plato, this horse must be subdued first, the other must be tamed, and the charioteer must be nurtured, because it is our 'higher self'.

Thus, Plato identifies three fundamental levels in the structure of man.

The Dialectic of Parmenides

The dialogue *Parmenides* is also important for understanding Plato's thought as a whole. In it a hierarchy of dialectical statements is built up, reflecting the relation between the One and the Many. Later Neoplatonists, in particular Plotinus,[4] Iamblichus[5] (245/280–325/330 BC), and especially Proclus[6] (412–485 BC) and Damascius[7] (458/462–after 538 BC), used this dialogue as a basis for constructing a detailed and wide-ranging system which united theology, cosmology, ethics and physics.[8] Proclus and Damascius distinguish nine hypotheses in the *Parmenides*. The first five hypotheses are centred on the recognition that the One (Ἕν) exists. For the Platonists, this recognition is fundamental; if the One (Ἕν) exists, then so does everything else, so does the Many. The first hypothesis immediately clarifies the nature of the One (Ἕν): the One (Ἕν) does not exist just like everything else; it is radically different. In a sense, if one takes for granted that everything else exists, then the One (Ἕν), which is qualitatively superior to everything else, does not exist. This is what the first hypothesis claims: the One (Ἕν) is radically superior to being. And it is only by being acknowledged in this way that being itself begins to exist. Being has a pre-existence (super-existence) cause. In the theological system of Christianity, this has been called 'apophatic mysticism'.[9] Similar concepts are found in Islamic Sufism, Jewish Kabbalah, Hinduism and Buddhism.

So the first five hypotheses are as follows:

1) ἕν (the One),

2) ἕν πολλά (the unified Many),

---

4   Plotinus, *The Enneads*.
5   Iamblichus, *Commentaries on Plato's Dialogues*.
6   Proclus, *Commentary on Plato's Parmenides*.
7   Damascius, *Commentary on Plato's Parmenides*.
8   Александр Дугин, *В поисках темного Логоса* (Moscow: Академический проект, 2014). [Alexander Dugin, *In Search of the Dark Logos*.]
9   [Translator's note: a negative approach to theology that seeks to explain what God is by identifying that which cannot be said about him.]

3) ἕν καὶ πολλά (the One and the Many),

4) πολλά καὶ ἕν (the Many and the One) and

5) πολλά (the Many).

All of the first five hypotheses of *Parmenides* come from the One (Ἑν), so all the worlds they describe exist. The second, third, fourth and even fifth hypotheses become valid only because the first hypothesis has been confirmed.

The other four hypotheses, from the sixth to the ninth, discussed in the same dialogue, proceed from the non-One. These are purely speculative logical constructions, which for the Platonists have no ontological basis.

The sixth hypothesis states that *the One does not exist, only the Many exists, therefore, the Many can, under certain circumstances, be combined into a 'One'*. This 'One' will be composite, collective, artificial, i.e. it will not have the primordiality of the true one (with the denial of which the second series of hypotheses begins). Some Neoplatonists say that such an assumption is simply a reasoning game. Others (like Damascius) say that this is a way to contemplate unity from the approach of the body. In other words, such a unity is the possibility of adding a multitude of atomic (individual) parts into some secondary whole.

The seventh hypothesis states: There is no One, but Many exists as an entity left to itself, i.e. it *cannot* be combined into 'One'.

The eighth hypothesis: *There is no One, but there is a lot of the Many*. That is individual atoms exist through interaction with each other.

At last, the ninth hypothesis: There is not One, *but there is also not the multiples for the Many.*

This dialectic of the One/Many generates another kind of hierarchy, quite homologous to the general structure of Plato's ontology, and clarifies some of its most important points.

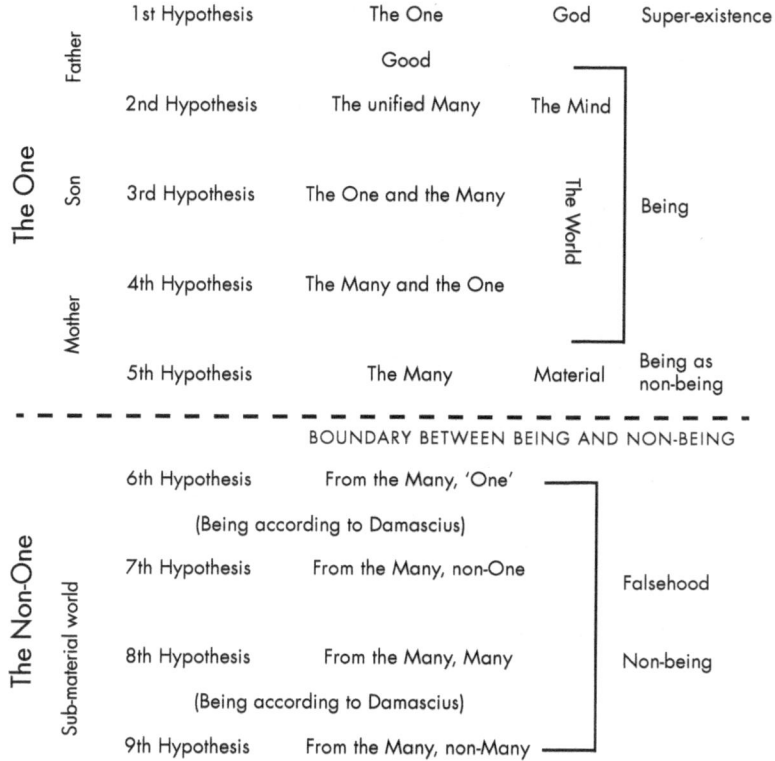

Figure 3. Metaphysical and ontological hierarchy of the One/Many in Plato's *Parmenides*.

Three Types of Political Ontology in the *Timaeus*

Thus we come to three types of political ontology. Accordingly, there is:

- The ideal world of Forms, the paradigmatic, the realm of the Father; that which truly is.

- The phenomenal, the iconic, the realm of the Son; it does and does not exist; it exists as a symbol. Thus there are two states: the ideal and the phenomenal.

- Χώρα is the place where the State exists; where the corporeality of the State, the primordial matter of the State, is present. To the extent that

Χώρα is itself, is only a woman, it does not exist; however, to the extent that the matter is affiliated with the Son, it does exist; the Mother herself exists through the Son.

According to Plato, a woman is nothing but a vessel to nurture and bear that which is *other* than herself. And the physical entity of statehood only acquires being (including political being) when the woman begins to act as primordial matter *for the state phenomenon*.

So, we can envisage three ontologies of political philosophy:

- The State of the Father: the eternal, ideal, paradigmatic State, which eternally is;
- The State of the Son: the phenomenal state — the projection of the ideal state of forms into the realm of phenomena, which partly is and partly is not; combining being and non-being, emerging and disappearing, and which can be likened to ourselves, the living.
- The material aspect of the state. In its purest form it is not-being. It is a kind of burdening of the state. A non-existence, a false state.

We get the shape of a triangle, where three sectors can be outlined:

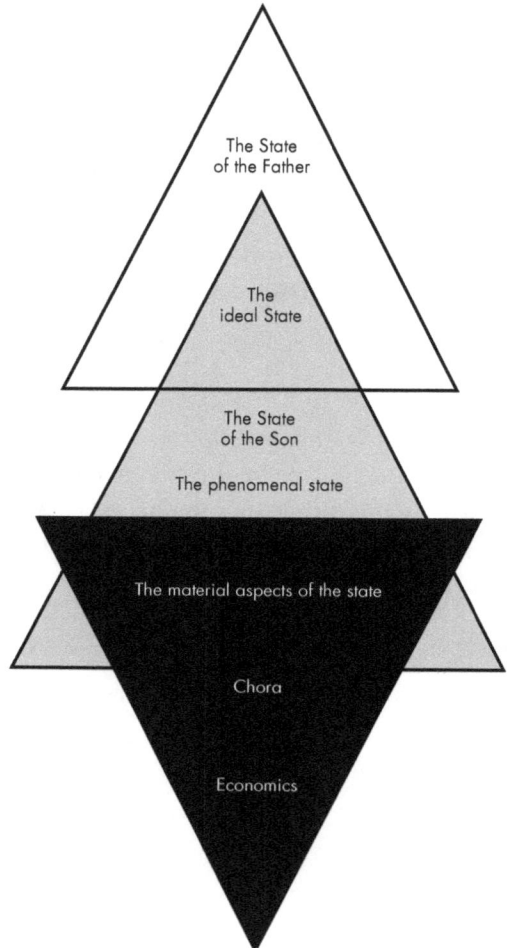

Figure 4. Three ontological levels of the Political.

Economics appears here as a sub-politics, or the politics of 'bovine humanity' (according to Plato); this is the lower aspect.

A multitude of positions and a multitude of schools will fit into this triangle, into this Platonic picture of political philosophy. Whatever philosophy of politics, whatever state and whatever political system we adopt, we will have to find its place in this Platonic picture. Beyond this schema, there can be neither politics nor the thought of politics.

Plato's Ideal State: The Philosoper King

It is now possible to correlate these three parts of the general ontology of the *Timaeus*, the three types of state (ideal, phenomenal and material) and the three classical castes of Plato's ideal state.

With what does the ideal state correspond? The Philosopher King. Plato also adds: the aristocracy. At the head of Plato's ideal state (Kallipolis) stand the representatives of the first caste (philosophers, kings, aristocrats, guardians). This is monarchical rule as well as philosophical rule and aristocratic rule. For Plato, the *best* (ἄριστος) is none other than the philosopher. Any state must be ruled by those who know what the ideal state is. And even in the case of a phenomenal state, the best should rule.

What is a monarch? A monarch is someone who has most thoroughly probed his soul. For him, the whole state is himself, not the sum of others. The monarch lives everything personally; accordingly, the Political in him reaches its peak of intensity at the moment of power. He represents the most concentrated expression of the Father.

And the fourth element (along with the three already named: philosopher, king, aristocrat) is the guardian (φύλαξ). The guardian is not just a watchman, *he is awake when everyone else is asleep.*

Recall how the philosopher behaved in the metaphor of the cave? Everyone was satisfied with the state of the imaginary, but he wanted the truth. Everyone was asleep; he woke up. Everyone was looking in one direction; he looked in the other. Night falls and everyone sinks into sleep. Everyone, but not the guardian. He walks alone through the city with his baton, while everyone is asleep. Surrounded by watchful owls and gods, the guardian walks around the Greek *polis*. He separates his fate from others. He lives in the night. Not only does he guard these sleeping people, but to a greater extent he guards the gods (sometimes from the people themselves). The guardian keeps watch over the sacred, the being, the ideal state. He is the guardian of the Other. That which truly is.

The Phenomenal State — the Warrior State

The second level is the phenomenal state. In the Platonic hierarchy, it corresponds to the *assistant guardians*. They are also warriors whose virtue is courage.

What is most important in the world of phenomena? Plato says that another virtue dominates here — not the direct contemplation of ideas, not the guarding of being, not the view of the paradigm, but *courage*. If the philosopher enters the world of death, approaching its depths, then the warrior or helper of the philosopher constantly interacts with this death from the outside. The warrior inflicts death on others, i.e. he is bound to kill, and he is prepared to sacrifice himself for his state and for the Political itself.

Accordingly, they are the second warrior caste, the helpers and protectors of the philosophers, aspiring to glory and courage; they are also the disciples of the philosophers. They have a totally different structure — they are *people of the phenomenal world*; they give birth, kill and die, they do not exist in eternity, but in temporality. If the first caste is the philosophical, ontological caste of the Philosopher Kings, the second caste is the phenomenal caste.

The phenomenal is not the concern of the philosopher. Unlike him, members of the second caste are concerned with what is apparent. In this sphere *spiritedness* (θύμος) reigns. According to Plato, this is a positive drive. Certainly spiritedness hinders philosophising, yet it is very useful in other cases, as it is the peak of vitality.

Thus we arrive at an understanding of the phenomenal state, or warrior state (akin to the Hindu *Kshatriya*), in which valour (αρετή) and spiritedness (θύμος) dominate.

Pacifistic Warriors Are Abnormal

The *Statesman* dialogue speaks of how to tame warriors who live by spiritedness. Since a warrior is incapable of pure contemplation, being left to his own devices, he may find himself prone to ὕβρις (Greek for 'insolence', 'pride'), an immense belligerence (under its influence one does not just kill an enemy, but, for example, mutilates his corpse). Sufficient examples can be found in the *Iliad* and the *Odyssey*. Under the influence of ὕβρις, the spiritedness of the warrior transcends its justifiable boundaries.

Plato considers spiritedness to be necessary, but a balance must be found. It is precisely the philosopher that tames the warrior. In order to pacify them, warriors must be eager to fight. Without a doubt, pacifist warriors are abnormal. Warriors should be fierce, they should love to kill like hound dogs, they should smell blood and revel in it, but there has to be a limit. Thus the problem of the phenomenal state is balancing rage with *the limiting of rage*. In other words, the phenomenal state is created by warriors; they constitute the warrior caste.

Providing for Thinkers and Warriors

The third element is associated with χώρα, the Nurse. As the Nurse nourishes the child, so the peasantry and craftsmen nourish the warriors and philosophers. The task of the peasant is to ensure that the warrior is satiated when he gallops off to chop off someone's head. Accordingly, the resource economic state is placed under the warriors.

Mother and Nurse (χώρα) correspond to the third caste, the caste of producers and peasants. They are in the realm of the spatial, χώρα; they work in the countryside: they plant and reap the harvest. Their role is to give a visible material background to the state, to be the place in which the state manifests itself.

In *Laws*, Plato talks a great deal about what the ordinary citizens of the state should do. They should do roundels (circle-formation dances introduced by the state as a duty). Plato elaborates on how the roundels should be arranged, suggesting that they should be divided into three circles — according to age. The circles reproduce the rotation of the celestial bodies and planets. Therefore, through the cycles of work and festive roundels, the basic population of the ideal state also partakes of eternity — the world of ideas.

The philosophers think, the warriors fight, the rest work and dance. This is the ideal model of political philosophy.

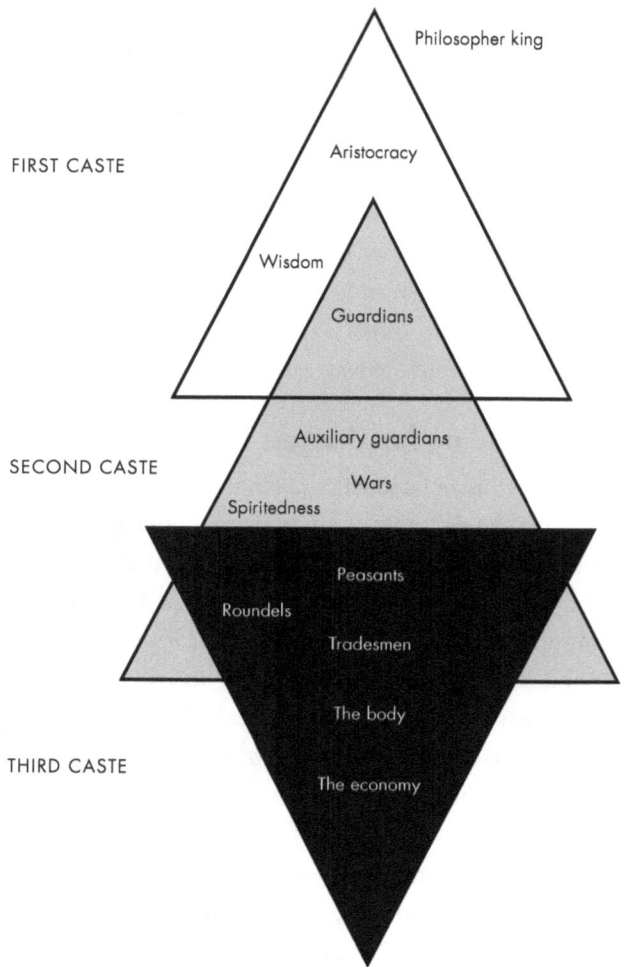

Figure 5. The Three Castes of Kallipolis.

Plato's Stages of State Degradation: Timocracy, Oligarchy, Democracy, Tyranny

In the *Republic*, Plato talks about perverted types of state. So, there is the ideal state (Kallipolis), which we have described, and there are perversions or deviations from this paradigmatic model. Plato names four types of statehood which should not exist, but which unfortunately do: *timocracy*, *oligarchy*, *democracy* and *tyranny*.

1) *Timocracy (τιμοκρατία) or Timarchy (τιμαρχία)*. Plato links this to the Spartan model, which is dominated by the military (rather than by philosophy). That is to say, there is less emphasis placed on the philosophical element and more on the military. The focus shifts from guardians to the auxiliary guardians. There are still philosophers in a timocracy, but they are not as powerful as they should be. Spiritedness as a property of the warriors, a second-level virtue, begins to dominate wisdom — a first-level virtue. This is not yet a complete seizure of power from the philosophers, but only the initial state, the first symptoms. Here, the sages are already given less heed, and valour is elevated to an absolute rather than a relative good. Spartan *gerousia*, warrior nature, militarism become the dominant values.

   Plato does not regard timocracy too harshly, saying it is not yet the worst case. Nevertheless, timocracy is a perversion. It is very important to note that once the warrior has become distracted from philosophy — that is, ceased to be a spiritual warrior, assistant to the guardians of being — he begins to be attracted to materiality. He begins to use his nature not only to fight, but also to grab more trophies. As the realm of phenomena concentrates on itself, it becomes more and more material and less of that which *is*. When the warrior caste becomes interested in the material elements, it is approaching its own demise.

2) *Oligarchy (ὀλιγαρχία)*[10]. This type of government arises when a few degenerate, influential military rulers, or their respective groups, together with the townspeople who have become rich, form a society in which wealth and power are concentrated in a few people, the oligarchs. This is a group of large material-political figures who, by truth and falsehood, by force and cunning, have gained power and rule the city (state). Plato considered this to be a very bad system. It is a transition to an even lower stage — between a phenomenal state and an

---

10 Greek ὀλιγαρχία (*oligarchia*) — 'the power of the few', from the Greek ὀλίγος (*oligos*) — 'the few' and the Greek ἀρχή (*arche*) — 'power'.

outright economy. Oligarchy is a decisive step from the order of the Son to the order of the Mother.

3) *Democracy (δημοκρατία)*[11]. Plato believed that this political system represented a complete perversion and decay, and essentially meant the transition of the phenomenal state into a material *sub-state*. Here, oligarchic power is distributed among a large number of townspeople, each of whom selfishly thinks only of his own material well-being.

For Plato, the death of Socrates was the death of the Philosopher King at the hands of a frenzied democratic mob. This was Plato's revolution against the society in which he lived. He argued that we are in the third, nearly the worst form of perversion, and that in order to return to a normal state we must turn away from the democratic mobs and take a step towards the ideal model. Thus, Plato, as a representative of the aristocratic Athenian family (one might say the oligarchical family), challenges the state and says that we need to correct this perversion and from the material sub-state χώρα return to the ideal model.

4) *Tyranny (τυραννία)*. This, according to Plato, is the worst and last form of statehood. It is an inverted parody of the rule of the Philosopher King. The Philosopher King is the best of men who rule, while the tyrant is the worst. Any democracy ends in a dictatorship, i.e. a tyranny, a seizure of power. It is clear that sooner or later, the dim-witted democratic society will choose (or have imposed upon it) the very worst of its representatives. Or, out of horror at the chaos and lack of order, it will itself hand over power to the usurper.

The Anti-King

This is how Plato describes the four stages of degradation of the ideal state (Kallipolis). In the beginning we have a departure from the norm, then an increasing retreat, and finally a complete parody, for a tyrant parodies a Philosopher King. A tyrant is the anti-king, the anti-philosopher. It is the

---

[11] The Greek δημοκρατία, 'power of the people', from δῆμος, 'people' and κράτος, 'power'.

stupidest and most despicable of men, purporting to rule over the rest. It is the cowardly man who pretends to lead an army. It is the thief and corruptionist who says he can make life comfortable. Tyranny embodies *antipolitics*. Starting with democracy we enter the realm of the sub-state.

The whole picture we have described will only be clear if we have understood what the ideal state (Kallipolis) is. The ideal state always *is*, it remains unchanged, which cannot be said of its projections, phenomena. The ideal state can appear slightly distorted in timocracy, more distorted in oligarchy, even more distorted in democracy, and as a parody, as its own opposite in tyranny. Accordingly, the tyrant parodies the monarch, the dictator the philosopher, etc. Plato argues that all the worst that can be found in other types of statehood comes together in a tyranny. From the ontological perspective, *the tyrant stands even lower than matter*. Therefore the *being* of tyranny is minimal. There is nothing more ephemeral than tyranny. What in tyranny claims to be eternal tends to be temporary, transient and chimerical.

However, the cycle of degradation does not affect the nature and being of the ideal state. All distortions are distortions of the original, which remains unchanged in itself. Therefore, according to Plato, after tyranny the time of the Philosopher King comes again. Kallipolis, in its ideal immutability, sets the limits of its phenomenological manifestation. When the copy-state reaches the limit of dissimilarity with the model-state, i.e. when tyranny is established, everything returns to Kallipolis, restoring its normative proportions. That is why the Greeks considered the 'old tyrant' to be a miraculous phenomenon; tyrants usually did not live to old age.

CHAPTER 3

THE STATE OF THE SON. ARISTOTLE

Politics According to Aristotle

PLATO'S PHILOSOPHY provides the most coherent image of the essence of metaphysical, ontological, cosmological, political and anthropological issues. As we have said before, Plato represents the totality of all possible options and includes all possible types of worldview. When we talked about the *Timaeus*, we pointed out that there are three kinds of being—

1) paradigmatic,

2) phenomenological and

3) material

They correspond to three beginnings:

1) that of the Father,

2) the Son and

3) the Mother (Nurse, Receiver).

Theoretically, we can identify three philosophies in this cosmology of the *Timaeus*:

1) philosophy which emphasises *paradigms*,

2) philosophy which emphasises *phenomena* and

3) philosophy which emphasises *matter*.

These three levels of cosmos, being, ontology and metaphysics really correspond to three philosophical traditions. We encounter them in the modern world as much as we do in ancient Greece.¹ In fact, Plato and all that is called Platonic philosophy are inseparable from the first philosophy — the supremacy of the world of paradigms. In the first philosophy (in Platonism in the widest sense), ideas are endowed with being, and are considered to be fully and impeccably existing, while the phenomenon in that case becomes half-existing and half-not existing, while almost no attention is paid to the material side of being (hence the idea of matter as privation, shortage).

Matter is the *corporeality* of a phenomenon. Everything we see in the material world is due to the fact that it has some kind of *eidos* (εἶδος), a form, i.e. the *being* of a material object in no way derives from matter itself, which is only a 'receptor' of the *eidos*, but from its immaterial (supramaterial) nature.

Here we get a very clear picture: the world of paradigms *is* in the absolute sense, the world of matter/the corporeal *is not* in the absolute sense, and the phenomenal world between them is *a mixture of being and not-being*.

Platonic philosophy, and consequently Platonic political philosophy, is constructed strictly in this way. In this case there are

1) the ideal state (which is),

2) the phenomenal state (which partly is, partly is not) and

3) the lowest material 'state', preoccupied with purely material issues — concerns over population, desire for comfort, i.e. economy²

---

1 Александр Дугин, *Ноомахия. Три Логоса* (Moscow: Академический проект, 2014). This trend is consistently seen in all volumes of the Noomakhia project. [Alexander Dugin, *Noomakhia. The Three Logoi*.]

2 By 'economy' we mean the modern meaning of the term here, whereas in ancient Greece it was called *chrematistics*, χρηματιστική, 'enrichment', from χρήματα, 'money'. Significantly, etymologically the word χρήματα, 'money', comes from the verb χράομαι, 'to need something', 'to be in need'. This corresponds exactly to the Platonic understanding of matter as lack, scarcity, need. 'Economy' (from οἶκος, 'house', 'household' and νόμος, 'law', 'organisation of territory') was a more comprehensive

(such a state *is not*, or at least is not a state, not a polity (πολιτεία), but something else — for example, a 'civil society' or a 'market').

From Plato's point of view, that political system which focuses on the third caste of producers and merchants (oligarchy and democracy) is anti-political and destructive of the political ideal.

Three Philosophies of Politics

It is theoretically possible to consider other types of philosophy. Plato describes all of them at once, but we may also outline the consideration of phenomenological philosophy (in the twentieth century this philosophy is partly constructed by Husserl (1859–1938) and to a considerable extent by Heidegger) and of materialistic philosophy (materialism appears already in ancient Greece — Democritus, Epicurus). Thus, three philosophies of politics can be distinguished within the Platonic complex (*Timaeus*):

- Platonic,
- phenomenological and
- materialist (which reduces politics to economics).

Examples of modern materialism with a developed political component are well known — liberalism, Marxism and (partly) nationalism. The materialists of the ancient world did not succeed in definitively constructing their political system. Plato built it (and we can see how complete, holistic his philosophy of politics is). It should be noted that the materialist Democritus was the first to engage in speculation (pure chremasticism) in his city of Abdera; he bought up stocks of grain, and then resold them when they went up in price. Yet, the Greeks did not create a materialistic philosophy of politics which would be directly and explicitly linked to the third kind of being — the Mother and the *chora*.

---

concept of ordering life and living space, that is, 'home-making' or 'housekeeping', which was by no means reduced to increasing comfort, much less the pursuit of money and profit.

Polity of the Father and Polity of the Son

Now we come to the philosophy that was developed in Greece, yet differed significantly from Plato's philosophy. This is the political philosophy of Aristotle (384–322 BC).

To begin with, Aristotle was a disciple of Plato and had listened to the whole course of Platonic teaching. Therefore, whether he liked it or not, he was fundamentally 'programmed' by the basic maxims of Platonism.

If you like, Aristotle's consciousness is moulded by Platonism. This thinker is within the Platonic topicality. When one says 'Plato and Aristotle', one must essentially understand it as 'Aristotle is Plato's "Son"'. What Aristotle has that is most essential and reasonable is taken by him from the 'Father'.

But Aristotle decided to construct a philosophy of the Son, that is, a kind of prototype of what in the nineteenth to-twentieth centuries would be called 'phenomenology'. Earlier we spoke of three worlds or origins: the world of ideas, the world of phenomena and the world of matter. *Plato's philosophy is based on the first order, while Aristotelian philosophy is based on the second order*. It is a *phenomenological political philosophy*.[3]

Aristotle constructs the philosophy of the Son partly like that of the Father and partly not. As we said, the Son has in himself something of the Father and something not of the Father. Or, from Plato's point of view, he has in himself something of being and something of not being. Similarly, Aristotle: he has something of Plato, something not of Plato. What he has from Plato predetermines his resemblance to Platonism. But Aristotle also has something else — a critique of Plato.

Aristotle, being a Platonist, sets himself the task of criticising Plato. It is a critique of the Father by the Son. To the extent that the Son follows the Father, he is the same as the Father. To the extent that he opposes the Father, he falls, in Platonist terms, into 'sin'.

---

3   This can be compared with the sociological theory of the 'normal type' (German: *Normaltypus*) put forward by Ferdinand Tönnies (1855–1936). In this interpretation, Max Weber's 'ideal type' relates to Tönnies' 'normal type' in the same way that Plato's ideal state relates to Aristotle's actual (normal, phenomenal) state.

Two Masculine Philosophies

Aristotle's philosophy is partly the same as that of the Father and partly directed against him. To the extent that it is directed against the Father, it is not. To the extent that it perpetuates the Father, it is. Therefore Aristotle himself is the spiritual 'Son' of Plato, and together Platonism and Aristotelianism cover all the possibilities of masculine philosophy (philosophy of the first two genera). That is, a man thinks either as Father (and then he is a Platonist) or as Son (and then he is an Aristotelian). Where the third order/materialism prevails (in particular the economy), the masculinity disappears, is eliminated, and what may be called the philosophy of the Mother or the philosophy of *chora* begins.[4] There ends statehood (as politeia, πολιτεία), the idea of the classical Greek Indo-European order disappears, the dominance of the two castes (the philosopher caste and the warrior caste), which correspond to the two philosophies of the Father and the Son, is eliminated.

There are two male philosophies: Platonism as a fully male philosophy (Plato did not admit women to his lectures, but some of them slipped in anyway, dressed as men; among them there were some pupils so faithful that after his death they created the oracle of Plato, promoted his teaching and proved their philosophical merit) and Aristotelianism as the revision of Platonism from the point of view of the Son. Plato and Aristotle inhabit the same philosophical space: one looks at ideas and positions himself as Father (philosophy of Zeus, Apollo), the other looks away from ideas and positions himself as Son (philosophy of Dionysus).[5]

Logos Apophatikos and the Demonstrative State

So, if Plato develops the theme of the *ideal* state (i.e. the one that *is*) in terms of the world of ideas, and believes that the phenomenological state (i.e. the state that is apparent to us) is nothing other than the relative manifestation of the eternal in the temporal, the absolute in the transient, then Aristotle establishes another state — the phenomenal (phenomenological)

---

4 Alexander Dugin, *Noomakhia. The Three Logoi.*
5 *Ibid.*

state itself. It is the state that exists here and now and has to be understood as a given, as a phenomenon. We can call it, in the spirit of the Aristotelian doctrine, the *apophantic state* (from the Greek ἀπόφφανσις, 'manifestation', 'declaration'), parallel to the way Aristotle uses the notion of apophatic speech (λόγος αποφαντικός). The apophantic state is what the state is in isolation from what it should be or what it is in the transcendent world of ideas. Here we see the transition from the political philosophy of the Father (paradigms) to the political philosophy of the Son (phenomena).

Now, if we remember the *Timaeus*, it will become clear to us that as soon as we put ourselves in the position of the Son, we say, 'The Son is everything. And the Fatherly in him is the Son, and the non-Fatherly in him is also the Son.'

But while the Platonist would argue that the part in the Son which is non-Father is incidental and illusory, the Son who builds an autonomous philosophy argues otherwise and says, 'The Son is what is, and the Father and the Nourisher are not, but are only the boundaries of the Son.'

In other words, the Son puts himself at the centre and constructs politics, the state, philosophy, cosmology, theology on the basis of this *central position*. Therefore, if Plato's philosophy is divine, Aristotle's philosophy is divinely godless. To the extent that the Son is like the Father, his philosophy is divine. To the extent that there is a critique of the world of ideas, it is a godless philosophy.

But this is so only from Plato's point of view. From Aristotle's point of view, this is most certainly not the case. On the contrary, Aristotle asserts that his philosophy is true, correct in both its directions. There is neither the material nor the paradigmatic, only the phenomenal. What is, is that which is apparent, λόγος αποφαντικός.

It is fundamentally important that for Aristotle the phenomenon is precisely real (as for Plato there is the idea from which all else stems); that is why he attacks Plato's doctrine of ideas. At the same time, Aristotle does not assert things (in their corporeality) instead of ideas, he asserts something else — instead of ideas, for him there is an *eidos* (εἶδος), a universal commonality that objects share. For Plato, *eidos* (εἶδος) and idea (ἰδέα) are almost the same thing. Aristotle argues that ideas do not exist apart from phenomena, but that phenomena are eidetic, since every phenomenon has within it μορφή (form), which is *eidos* (εἶδος), and ὕλη (matter, wood). While Plato spoke of χώρα (space), Aristotle spoke of ὕλη. Incidentally, the word 'matter' (māteria) is not derived from the word 'mother', as many believe, but from the word for ship timber, of which masts in particular were built. We are essentially dealing with a tracing of the Greek word ὕλη, meaning 'wood', 'timber'.[6]

Aristotelian Philosophy Denies Not Only Plato's Higher World of Ideas, But Also the World of the Mother

So, according to Aristotle, there are no ideas, but there are *eidos* (εἶδος). Phenomena are always constructed in this way: they have a primary component (*eidos*, εἶδος) and a secondary component (matter, ὕλη); there is a substantiality (content, form) and a subject (substance), i.e. that in which this substantiality manifests itself (material). Unlike Plato, Aristotle believed that matter does not exist by itself. In Plato, matter, χώρα, the Nurturer, is called the third kind of being. This kind of being, which is non-being, still exists in itself, in its non-being. Aristotle says: there is no matter just as there are no ideas, but there is a material and an ideal eidetic *horizon of phenomena*. Aristotelian philosophy denies not only Plato's higher world of ideas, but also the world of the Mother. It claims that there is only and exclusively the world of the Son. Who is the Father? It is the Son's hypothesis of his origin. Who is the Mother? It is the material cause of the Son speculating about its origin. In other words, Aristotle reduces everything to the Son, to the intermediate level, to the world of phenomena, where there are two horizons, the ideal and the material. But what is a *horizon* (Greek ὁρίζων — literally 'limit', 'limitation', from the root ὁρίζω, 'to divide')? It is the outermost limit of the thing itself. And Aristotle implies that there is *nothing* beyond the horizon of the Son, on the other side of that limit. The philosophy of the Son is made absolutist, which clarifies the fundamental difference between Plato's use of 'ideas' (ἰδέα) and

---

6   In some Latin authors, the Aristotelian term ὕλη was not translated as māteria, but as 'mast timber', 'ship timber', and *selva* simply as 'forest' or 'wood'.

Aristotle's '*eidos*' (εἶδος). Aristotle conceives of the *eidos* (εἶδος) as the upper horizon and ὕλη (matter) as the lower horizon. These are the boundaries *within* the Son himself. Beyond these boundaries nothing exists. This is why Aristotle has no concept of the 'transcendent', of the 'beyond'. In this respect Aristotle's philosophy is certainly not Platonism and is built on the basis of total immanence.

Two Philosophies

Thus two philosophies emerge: the transcendental philosophy of Plato and the immanentist philosophy of Aristotle. Whereas Plato's theology, later developed by the Neoplatonists, in particular Proclus[7] (412–485 BC), is concerned with a *transcendent* God, a God beyond, Aristotle's God is quite different — it is an *immanent* God ('unmoved mover' — Greek ὃ οὐ κινούμενον κινεῖ). Plato's God is God the Father, while Aristotle's God is God the Son. These are essentially two views of the divine.

According to Aristotle, the totality of things moves invariably around the 'unmoved mover', and all things aspire to it, but matter, mingled with these things, does not allow them to merge with God. They remain at a certain distance. The rotation of the celestial spheres, the daily rhythms, the cycle of the year and the elements show us how this happens. Everything revolves around the point of the 'unmoved mover', around the pure Son, and only the Aristotelian philosopher can approach God enough to become that God. Aristotle considered himself a god, and his disciple Alexander the Great (356–323 BC) also considered himself a god. They (the former in terms of philosophy, the latter in terms of politics) were closest to the 'unmoved mover'. In this sense, Aristotle is divine, but divine *immanently*.

Aristotle as an Apologist for Slavery

Aristotle constructed a complete, thorough, developed, phenomenological, immanentist ontology, philosophy, cosmology, physics and political

---

7   Proclus, *On the Theology of Plato*.

science. These things are necessary to know in order to understand the meaning of Aristotle's treatise *Politics*.[8]

Like Plato, Aristotle talks about politics, applying his philosophy to the political sphere. And, like Plato, Aristotle states that the practice of politics and the practice of philosophy are two kinds of occupation of a noble, superior man. Any person who is not involved in philosophy and politics, from the point of view of Aristotle, is a slave. However, Aristotle treats this slave very well, because the slave is supposed to work, learn technical professions, and be able to cope well with the community. Accordingly, those people who are engaged in technical things (production, management, etc.) are inferior for Aristotle. He even said that people who produce things with their own hands should not be given freedom. People who are connected with matter, with corporeality, must be slaves; otherwise they will try to bring their totally unnecessary economic considerations into politics, which is the business of warriors, and into philosophy, which is the business of sages. Aristotle was an apologist for slavery.

On the one hand, Aristotle rebelled against Plato, saying that one should not submit to a higher transcendental principle. But at the same time he retained many of Plato's principles, believing that a strict hierarchy should be introduced within the framework of the phenomenal (*apophatic*) state. At the head of the apophatic state (of the Son) we find again three Platonic types: guardians (philosophers), auxiliaries and producers. Aristotle taught that at the head there should be philosophers (though not Platonists, but Aristotelians; priests of the 'unmoved mover'; clerics of the immanent deity), next to them should be soldiers (well-armed, strong, courageous and willing to sacrifice their lives) and below should be everybody else.

Aristotle posed a practical problem, asking the question: how is it possible to have philosophers rule over warriors? This was solved by an ethical system that prioritised nobility and refinement. People who think, of course, are more noble and refined than those who fight. In turn, those

---

8   Aristotle, *Politics*.

who fight are nobler and more refined than those who labour, dealing with corporeality, matter and their inherent heaviness and coarseness.

For all his differences from Plato, Aristotle retains his threefold structure of the vertical organisation of society. Thus, in the *Nicomachean Ethics*[9] he speaks of three types of life and the hierarchy that exists between them. These types are as follows:

1) βίος θεωρητικός (the *contemplative* life, its aim being to comprehend the essence of the human element as such within oneself and the truth),

2) βίος πολιτκός (the *political* life, its aim being the attainment of glory, *tīmḗ*[10] — τιμή) and

3) βίος ἀπολαυστικός (life for pleasure, that is, hedonism).

These three forms of life correspond to the three capacities of the human soul:

1) mind (νοῦς),

2) striving, desire, lust (ὄρεξις)[11] and

3) feeling (αἴσθησῐς).

Here we see the same triadic scheme that Plato sets out in the *Phaedrus*. Accordingly, the types of life are methods of prioritising the development of this or that part of the soul. Once again, like Plato, Aristotle elevates this triad to the three human types:

1) the ideal man,

---

9   Aristotle, *Nicomachean Ethics*.
10 The prevalence of this type of life in Plato is the basis of 'Timocracy'.
11 The term ὄρεξις is derived from the verb ὀρέγω, 'to stretch out', meaning horizontal expansion. Its etymology is related to the Indo-European root *h₃reǵ-, from which the fundamentally important Indo-European terms associated specifically with the second caste (warrior caste) are derived in Sanskrit (element of fire, related to the middle — warrior — part of the soul — *rajas*, whence *raja* — 'king', 'ruler'), Iranian tradition (*khrajr*, also 'king', 'ruler') and Latin (*rex*, 'king' and *rego*, 'I rule'). From the same root (*rehtaz*) concepts meaning 'right', 'straight direction', 'order' are formed in the Germanic languages.

2) the hero and

3) the commoner.

He who has the most developed mind and strives for a contemplative life is, according to Aristotle, the ideal man (τέλειον). Such a man, through the practice of philosophy, attains complete self-sufficiency (αυτάρκης). Thus it is thought that makes man truly free and independent of all external conditions and circumstances. Self-sufficiency derives from the fact that it is only through contemplation that the good is apprehended as the highest goal of being. And it is precisely in the course of the contemplative life that the good becomes the inner content of the thinker (from which self-sufficiency arises).

Heroes, according to Aristotle, also seek to make goodness internal and inseparable from themselves (δυσαφαίρετον) through glory, but they are still dependent on some external conditions — albeit not on nature, but on society.

A third category of people lives by the senses and seeks bodily and emotional pleasures. They constitute the commoners' class.

The commoners are predominantly engaged in 'homemaking' (economics, οἰκεῖον) and are totally dependent on the outside world, on society and nature.

In a normal society, the Philosopher King, the perfect contemplator, rules. He is the bearer and guardian of the *Logos*, hence the *polis*. According to Aristotle, man is defined by nature as the 'rational animal'[12] (ζῷον λόγον ἔχον) and simultaneously as the 'political animal'[13] (ζῷον πολιτικόν). Thought and politics constitute the essential aspects of the human being that separate him from other forms of life. Therefore, the most intelligent man (the philosopher, the thinker) is at the same time the most political, and the contemplative life is not opposed to politics, but is its origin and its centre. States are a form of thought. Therefore, the central place in a good state must be reserved for the wise.

---

12 λόγον δὲ μόνον ἄνθρωπος ἔχει τῶν ζῴων. Aristotle, *Nicomachean Ethics*. Aristotle, *Politics,* book 1, section 1253a.

13 ὁ ἄνθρωπος φύσει πολιτικὸν ζῷον. Aristotle, *Politics,* book 1, section 1253a.

The state is defended and guarded by warriors who love glory. If the philosopher is focused on truth (ἀλήθεια), the warrior is focused on phenomena, that is, on approaching the truth, which the Greeks defined as δόξα. The meaning of the term δόξα is multifaceted and goes back to the verb δοκέω, 'to think', 'to appear', 'to suppose', 'to imagine'. In Slavic, δόξα is in some cases translated as 'glory', from whence ὀρθοδοξία, 'orthodoxy', meaning 'right opinion'. Thus warriors, driven by the pursuit of glory, on the one hand seek the truth, and on the other hand they translate what they have been able to comprehend into life, thereby ordering it, bringing an orthodox vector into life. This vector is the existential drive (ὄρεξις) of heroism.

All other citizens of Aristotle's phenomenal state live quiet and measured lives, focused on pleasure and bodily goods. They belong to the lower spectrum of being and have an indirect relation to truth, and even to orthodoxy, through the ordering of the world of things and the senses. They also contribute to politics, but only in the most pragmatic and practical matters of organising the corporeal world.

As ordinary citizens cultivate the inferior — sensual — side of the soul, they should play a subordinate role in politics as well.

First a Warrior, Then a Philosopher

Regarding the structure of the soul, Aristotle generally accepts the Platonic division into three parts — the rational, the spirited and the lustful, and accordingly the metaphor of the chariot of the soul, consisting of the charioteer (reason), the white horse (spiritedness) and the black horse (lust). Depending on which element prevails in man we get the philosopher-sage, the warrior or the lustful toiler. How can one build a hierarchy between them? Aristotle believed that the clever and strong would necessarily establish dominance over the 'materially oriented segment of the population'. Aristotle asks the following question: how is society organised in the majority of Greek polities, in Lacedaemon (Sparta), Attica, Epirus, Magna Graecia, Ionia, as well as in other countries, for example, Phoenicia or Thrace? It is set up in precisely that manner. It has never been otherwise. The foolish, the weak and the materially preoccupied are always under the boot of the clever and the bold.

The question is how to make a powerful warrior with a sword submit to a philosopher without a sword, whose thoughts are lofty, astute and true but whose spiritedness is tamed. That is, how do you make a mighty horse submit to a charioteer?

According to Aristotle, the problem of the philosophical and the bellicose can only be solved if we consider such a situation: when there is *difference* and simultaneously *sameness* (i.e. he simply violates the first law of his own logic). In order for us to be able to subordinate warriors to philosophers, they must be *the same people*. The same, but different. For that we have to divide the life of a nobleman into two parts — young and old, before 50 and after 50. Before 50 he is a warrior, after 50 he is a philosopher. That is, during the first part of his life a man fights for the state, and during the second part he lives as a philosopher. So a man (warrior) is subordinated not to another, but to himself (philosopher), embodied by an older man. According to Aristotle, a noble man is a warrior-philosopher (who is first a warrior and then a philosopher).

Both types — philosopher and warrior — are considered aristocracy by Aristotle and Plato. Aristotle said that in some societies aristocrats are born, in others they become aristocrats, and in others they are both born and become aristocrats. The philosopher believed that if a man came from a noble family, and if his ancestors fought for Greece, he would probably be a good man and have good offspring. People born with inferior attributes, according to Aristotle, should be killed, as only those who improve rather than degrade society should live.

Aristotle himself was not a citizen of Athens, i.e. a Metic (Greek μέτοικος), he even had restrictions on owning his own school — the Lyceum (Greek Λύκειον). He was born in Stagira. He did not resent this. He who brought up the great Emperor nevertheless possessed, by virtue of law, certain restrictions of citizenship. Aristocracies therefore do not always have to coincide with the highest administrative positions in the polis. As with Plato, Aristotle is primarily concerned with the aristocracy of the soul.

The Paradigm of the Three Types of Governance

What types of state does Aristotle establish in his *Politics*? He differs somewhat from Plato in enumerating these types, but he still partly agrees with him. Aristotle says that there are in principle three types of government, which can be examined positively and negatively or authentically and falsely. There is the rule of one — the rule of a king. There is the rule of a few — this is the rule of an elite. There is the rule of the majority — the rule of the many. Aristotle sees these three forms in all political systems. In Sparta he identified all three of these named types and therefore (along with Plato) he sympathised with this part of Greece and its political system, being sceptical about Athenian democracy.

The three outlined models create a kind of matrix, a topology of political systems, which has not changed to this day. Accordingly, just as Plato set the global framework of political philosophy, so the Son's philosophy of Aristotle also delineates the fundamental types of the Political. Unlike Plato's categorisation, these types are not built on the model of the eternal-temporal and the ideal-perverted. Aristotle looks at the situation from a phenomenological perspective. In actuality, there is either the rule of one, the rule of a few, or the rule of many — and in various combinations. One can draw a triangle of Aristotelian politics, where the rule of one is at the top, the rule of a few inside and the rule of many at the bottom.

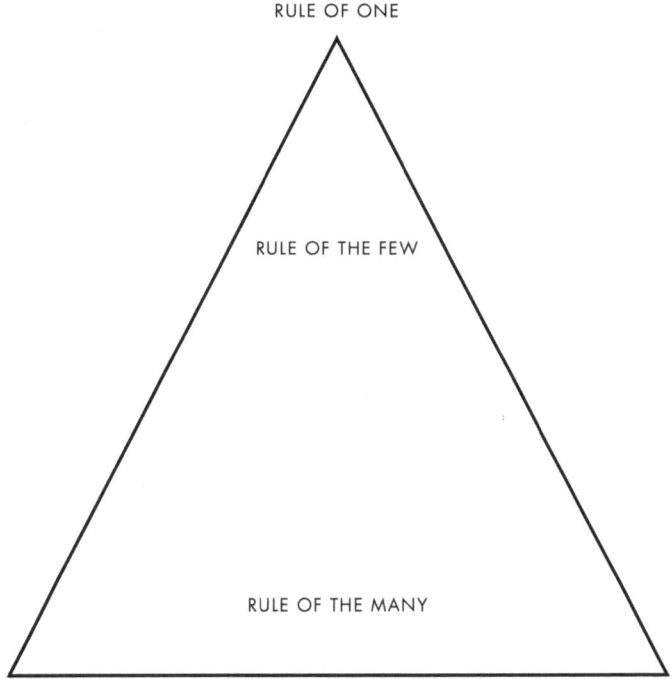

Figure 6. General schema of Aristotle's political types.

This triangle should be used to analyse any political system, both ancient and modern. It is a general law of political science, or political philosophy.

The Good State

Aristotle goes on to say that there is a good rule of one, a good rule of a few and a good rule of many, and there is a bad, perverse rule of one, a rule of a few and a rule of many. In other words, a double of this schema is created. Not one triangle, but two triangles.

The proper triangle would represent:

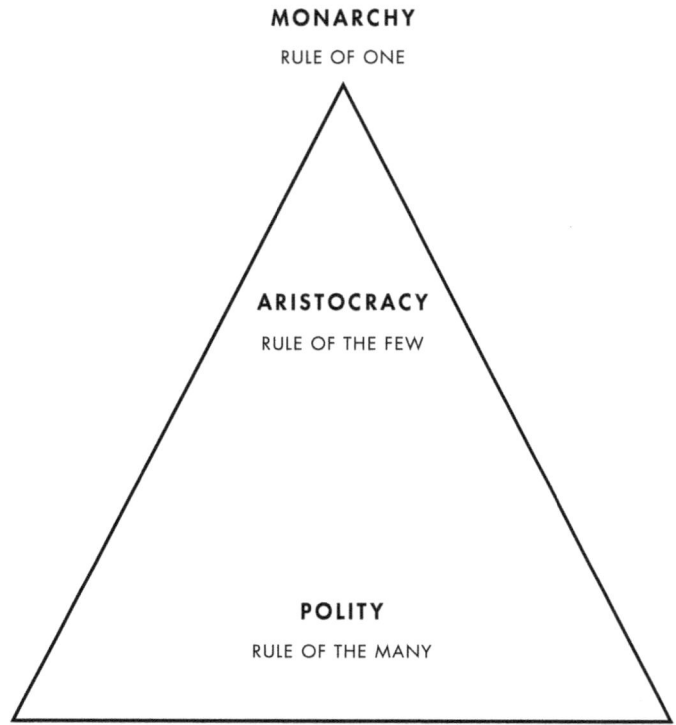

Figure 7. Positive types of government, according to Aristotle.

These three systems of government are considered by Aristotle to be the correct ones:

1) monarchy (μοναρχία),

2) aristocracy (ἀριστοκρατίᾱ) and

3) polity[14] (πολιτεία).

---

14 Aristotle uses the term πολιτεία in a slightly different sense from Plato. For Plato it means any politically organised community, independent of government, while for Aristotle it means a particular type of government where power is distributed among all the free citizens of a town or village. Therefore we render for the same Greek word πολιτεία two English transcriptions — 'politeia' in Plato's case and in his interpretation, and 'polity' in Aristotle's case to denote a positive version of what is generally understood as 'democracy' or 'organic democracy'.

Various combinations and blends are possible between the three, which are also theoretically positive.

Monarchy: The monarch is a noble philosopher, a sage and a person who is truly guided by the public good. The monarch is the embodiment of the political good. His power should be as reasonable, unselfish and exalted as possible. This is precisely how Aristotle tried to raise the son of Philip of Macedon (382–336 BC), Alexander, who indeed became the greatest of the Greek rulers.

Aristocracy: the embodiment of political dignity, possessing the virtues of courage, bravery, heroism, sacrifice. Aristocrats are above all noble warriors. At the head of their value system are courage, honour, dignity and no fear of death.

Polity: a body of mentally competent, responsible, well-meaning people of benevolent will. This majority is qualified to make laws and rule itself. Usually Aristotle says that we are talking about a kind of village where everyone knows each other. Polity is the least good rule, much worse than the rule of warriors, aristocrats and especially of the monarchy. But it is not bad either.

Aristotle also introduces a spatial principle to classify the types of the Political. Monarchy is best suited to large territorial states. Aristocracy is for medium-sized states, and polity is most effective on a small scale — in villages, hamlets, small towns, where people know each other and can assess the qualities of those elected more or less responsibly.

If we mix all these levels — monarchy, aristocracy and polity — we get a positive image of a state that is not ideal, but *good*. Aristotle does not say that there is such a state. He says that it can be and it must be. It is that 'unmoved mover' for which we reach. It is that *natural place* of politics to which all processes are directed. In any state there must be an intelligent king who cares about the public good, there must be the best aristocratic warriors who have proved by their actions, courage and skill that they are entitled to power, and there must be a responsible, kind, pious, rule-abiding people.

According to Plato, there is no doubt that there is an ideal state. According to Aristotle, there are such doubts, because a good state may or may not appear.

Consider how this political teaching transformed the consciousness of Alexander the Great. The Macedonians came from the north, captured Athens, and Aristotle told his disciple Alexander that all must be united, there must be one 'unmoved mover' at the centre; one should strive for a feasible creation of a state with a well-intentioned king, an aristocracy and a responsible population around him. Alexander considers — Alexander does. He listened to his teacher and a few years later the vast Greek world, which would never have been united otherwise, plus the vast territories all the way to northern India, the entire Middle East, and all of Iran, all come under one monarch.

This is what it means to be a good philosopher and what it means to be a good student. Alexander realised himself as that 'good king', dealt with his rivals, selected the best, formed a guard from their ranks and conquered the whole world. Aristotle's ontology of politics acquires the character of action, an active phenomenon. For something to appear, it needs to be manifested. The state comes into being when we create it. This is Aristotle's philosophical praxis.

Notice how political philosophy is transformed when we move from Plato to Aristotle, from a philosophy where contemplation completely dominates over action to Aristotle's 'contemplative action'. When we take this teaching seriously, we get an empire with a genuinely superior king, genuinely superior aristocrats and responsible citizens. It is the combination of monarchy, aristocracy and polity that made possible a feasible ideal of classical Mediterranean civilisation.

It was this idea that later laid the foundations of the Roman Empire. It was built on the template of Alexander the Great. It is an entirely Aristotelian Empire, dominated by three principles: Caesar (the holy Emperor), the Senate (aristocracy) and the Roman people (polity). Aristotle's eidetic goal, the natural seat of Aristotelian politics is possible, realisable, desirable, and the best are moving towards it.

The Bad State

If there can be a good state, there can also be a bad state. But even a bad state in all its versions can be reduced to the original typology of the Political. So we get a version of the same triangle, but one in which all the forms of government are negative.

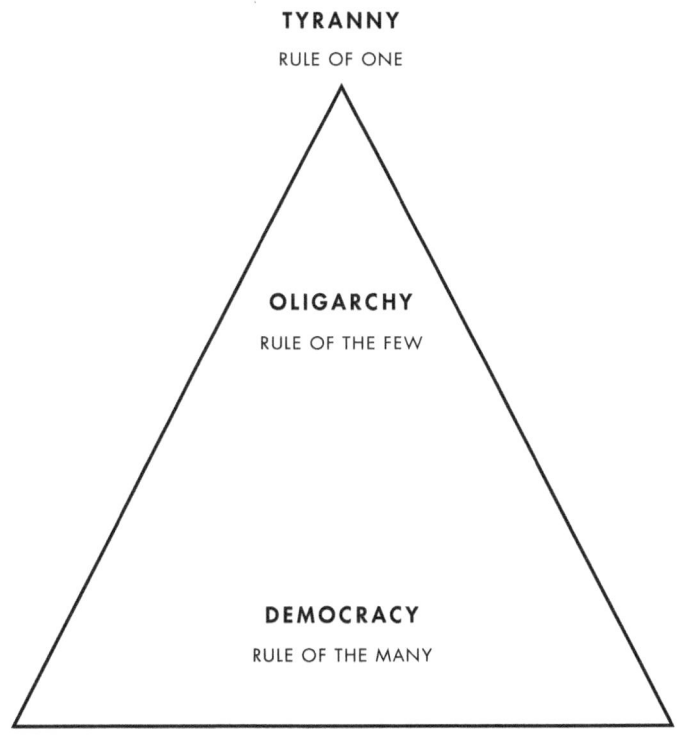

Figure 8. Negative types of political systems, according to Aristotle.

According to Aristotle, as well as Plato, the worst is tyranny, the rule of an idiot; Carl Schmitt calls it 'sovereign dictatorship'[15] (where the dictator acts only in the interest of himself as an individual). In the positive case, the rule of one is the best, and the same rule of one in the case of the

---

15 Carl Schmitt, *Dictatorship: From the Origin of the Modern Concept of Sovereignty to Proletarian Class Struggle* (Cambridge: Polity, 2013).

negative triangle is the worst. Accordingly, if the sole ruler is guided not by the public good but by his individual interests, he is the representative of the worst political system.

Slightly better than tyranny, but still a bad form of government, is oligarchy, the rule of a few. Oligarchy is the antithesis of aristocracy. A few of the best rule in the aristocratic form, a few of the worst rule in the oligarchical form.

The next level of the worst form of government is democracy. Democracy is a parody of polity. Whereas responsible citizens make responsible decisions in a polity, irresponsible citizens make irresponsible decisions in a democracy, moving in sporadic bursts of sleepy consciousness. That is, democracy is a parody of majority organisation, with the mob (ὄχλος) acting in the guise of majority. Moreover, Aristotle was excluding from such a democracy not only slaves, but also many workers.

Democracy was considered by the philosopher as a terrible rule of the mentally inferior masses. At the same time, he said that if tyranny differs radically from monarchy (as top from bottom) and oligarchy differs strongly from aristocracy, polity differs from democracy to a lesser degree. Appropriately, worse than democracy is oligarchy and worse than oligarchy is tyranny. On a par with the kingdom of Alexander the Great, it is possible to imagine an anti-empire, where a tyrant rules, supported by oligarchs, under the shelter of an unthinking majority.

Aristotle's analysis, with all its models, is absolutely applicable to any political system of any time.

CHAPTER 4

SACRED POLITICS AND RELIGION

Religion and the Three Types of Society

ALL TYPES of society can be reduced to the three most general groups[1]:

1) Premodern society (otherwise known as traditional society),

2) Modern society and

3) Postmodern society.

Religion is a distinctive (and central) feature of traditional society. Therefore, in order to study all aspects of any traditional society, and above all its political structure, it is necessary to thoroughly examine the religious premises on which it is based.

Any religion and, more broadly, any traditional teaching[2] puts at the head of its system of values an otherworldly, spiritual beginning, that is, something sacred, divine, sometimes framed in a strict theological system, sometimes presented in the form of myths, rites and rituals, sometimes existing as quite archaic beliefs (which is characteristic of the simplest types of societies).

---

1 Александр Дугин, *Постфилософия* (Moscow: Евразийское движение, 2009). [Alexander Dugin, *Postphilosophy*.]

2 There are many different definitions of religion. The distinction between religion and sacred tradition is dealt with later.

This is the most general concept of religion, encompassing all types of traditional societies, including archaic ones. Religion can be institutionalised in the form of the Church, a framework of dogmas, texts, laws. It can also have looser forms, embodied in mythology, rituals, a system of belief in spirits, gods, heroes, the souls of the dead, etc.

Characteristically, modern society is built on the denial of the axial supremacy of religion. Modernisation therefore includes secularism, i.e. placing religion on the periphery of the socio-political system; a rigid separation of religion from power, politics, education, and so on. Modern society is also defined by its attitude towards religion, but in this case this attitude is negative; if religion is allowed, it is only as a marginal phenomenon, and the choice of religion becomes, by law, an individual matter for each person. This is the fundamental difference between traditional/premodern society and modern society. The former is necessarily religious and religion plays a dominant role in it (including politically). The second denies religion this role, and either places it on the periphery or abolishes it altogether.

Postmodern society treats religion in a more complex way. It does not deny it outright, but rather parodies it, mocks it, and gives it grotesque features. The postmodern seeks to complete the course of modernity, but believes that this cannot be achieved by means of modernity itself. Therefore, atheism and secularism, dominant in the modern era, are seen by postmodernists as insufficient, and they resort to the methods of irony, parody and simulacra for the destruction of religion.

The Sacred: The Light and Dark Sides

Traditional society includes all types of societies centred on God, the divine and the spiritual. We can call this type of societies *sacred societies*.

The *Sacred*[3] is a very complex category. The Sacred is usually separated from the concept of the Holy, although it is formally very difficult to find

---

3 From the Latin *sacer*, 'sacred'. The sacral is ambivalent and includes not only the 'sacred', the 'pure', but also the 'demonic'. Mircea Eliade (1907–1986) also points this out: 'Commenting on Virgil's phrase *auri sacra fames*, Servius remarks quite rightly that *sacer* can mean at the same time accursed and holy. Eustathius notes the same double

an exact correspondence to the concept of the Sacred in Russian.⁴ It is both sacred and holy simultaneously. At the same time, it also includes something 'cursed' and 'demonic'. In any case, the Sacred inspires awe, reverence and establishes a distance between people and powers that are many times beyond human capabilities and human understanding.⁵

The notion of the Sacred is the most important sociological category and represents a certain supreme beginning that defies rational comprehension, preceding all types of myths, theologies and religious theories. This notion is lived in concrete experience — that experience which C. G. Jung's (1875–1961) depth psychology calls *numinous experience*.⁶

It is about man's encounter with something fundamentally higher than himself. So high that this encounter generates a twofold emotion: a sense of elation and a sense of horror. It is very important that the Sacred is not only an experience of the good; it is an experience not yet dissected into rapture and horror, into a consciousness of one's absolute nothingness and of the greatness of what is being discovered.

---

    meaning with *hagios*, which can express at once the notion "pure" and the notion "polluted". And we find this same ambivalence of the sacred appearing in the early Semitic world and among the Egyptians.' Mircea Eliade, *Patterns in Comparative Religion* (London: Sheed & Ward, 1958), 15.

4 [Translator's note: сакральное translated as 'sacred', святое translated as 'holy'.]

5 Rudolf Otto, *The Idea of the Holy: An Inquiry into the Non-Rational Factor in the Idea of the Divine and Its Relation to the Rational* (London: Oxford University Press, 1936).

6 The concepts of 'numinosity', 'numinous', *numinosum* (from Latin *numen* — 'deity', 'will of the gods') were introduced by German theologian Rudolf Otto (1869–1937) in his work *The Idea of the Holy* ('Das Heilige'). The numinous, according to Otto, had four main components: 1) the sense of insignificance (*Kreaturgefühl*), 2) the awe-inspiring mystery (*Mysterium tremendum*), 3) admiration (*Fancinans*), and 4) *the numinous sense of the value of the sacred (Sanctum als numinoser Wert)*. The foundation of all religions, according to Otto, is the same and is rooted in the experience of the numinous. See Rudolf Otto, *The Idea of the Holy. An Inquiry into the Non-Rational Factor in the Idea of the Divine and Its Relation to the Rational*. Following him, C. G. Jung believed that 'the idea of God originated with the experience of the numinosum. It was a psychical experience, with moments when man felt overcome. Rudolf Otto has designated this moment in his Psychology of Religion as the numinosum, which is derived from the Latin *numen*, meaning hint, or sign.' James L. Jarrett, ed., *Jung's seminar on Nietzsche's Zarathustra* (Princeton, NJ: Princeton University Press, 1988), 1038.

The Sacred has a dark, horrific side and a light side. The dark side is what terrifies the individual and therefore removes his personhood (in this respect, the sacred often comes in the form of death). In other words, the individual comes to an end in the experience of the Sacred.

The other, light side of the Sacred is that which brings man into delight, into infinite joy, into bliss; here again the individual is stripped away, but in a positive sense, the vanished man is replaced by the all-absorbing joy of luminous contemplation.

The Sacred is characterised by the fact that the terrifying and the delightful remain *undivided* within it. This is the common root of the two most powerful forms of experience. Thus, sacred is that society which places this very instance at the head [of the triangle]. It may be called 'God', 'spirit', 'Heaven', 'supernatural', but in every case we are dealing with something sacred. In some societies, sacred figures were leaders (the sanctification of power) who inspired terror and love in people.

The sacred ruler is the central figure of a religious society.

The fundamental element in the political philosophy of a religious society (if we understand religion in a broad sense) is the Sacred, and we are dealing either with a *sacred* society (and then it is religious), or with a *profane* one, that is, one that puts something other than the Sacred at the centre. Traditional society is sacred. Modern society is profane, i.e. non-sacred. Continuing to apply this criterion, we can say that the postmodern society is anti-sacred, parodied sacred or sacred in reverse.

The term sacred has been widely used in sociology and politics since Durkheim. Sacred sociology was founded in the late 1930s by Roger Caillois (1913–1978) and Georges Bataille (1897–1962).[7]

Religion According to Guénon

There is a narrower understanding of the term 'religion', in particular used by Protestant theologians[8], as well as by the French traditionalist René

---

7   Denis Hollier, ed., *The College of Sociology* (Minneapolis: University of Minnesota Press, 1988).

8   Hans Werner Bartsch, ed., *Kerygma and Myth: A Theological Debate* (New York: Harper Torchbooks, 1961).

Guénon (1886–1951). Guénon does not see religion as the whole sacred community, not as all types of the Sacred, but only as part of it. In his terminology, 'religion' in the full sense of the word can only be applied to those sacred institutions which believe that the sacred origin is strictly transcendent. René Guénon insists that the term 'religion' should be applied only within the group of monotheistic religious traditions formed by Judaism, Christianity and Islam. He also points out the difference between purely metaphysical thinking, corresponding to the Sacred in the most general sense, and theological thinking, i.e. religious thinking.[9]

Religion, according to Guénon, differs from other sacred systems by referring to its supreme sacred source as the transcendent God. This God is the Creator (hence creationism); he creates the world from nothingness, not from himself (in creationism there is an ontological divide between God and the world he has created). God is always and absolute while the world is created out of nothingness (the idea of creation *ex nihilo*). It is precisely the notion of creation, creation out of nothingness, that defines what is called religion in the narrow sense. From this view emerges strict monotheism, that is, the dogmatic assertion that God is not just one, but the one and only, and that between Him and the rest of the world (including humans) lies an insurmountable ontological abyss.[10]

Creation and Manifestation

Every term in philosophy, politics and science in general has to be explained in a certain way through the pairing of opposites. When speaking of the Sacred, we emphasise: the Sacred, *not* the profane. Speaking of the ideal, we contrast it with the 'normal' and the 'material'. Speaking of singular rule, on the opposite pole we assume the rule of the few and the rule of the many. The most important moment in philosophy is the precise selection of the concrete and positive meaning that comes into place in the process of negating an initial thesis, term or assertion.[11]

---

9   René Guénon, *The Essential René Guénon: Metaphysics, Tradition, and the Crisis of Modernity*, ed. John Herlihy (Bloomington: World Wisdom, 2009).

10 Alexander Dugin, *Postphilosophy*.

11 This is systematically studied by hermeneutics and in particular by A. Greimas (1917–1992), who developed a specialised semantic square. See A. J. Greimas, *Structural*

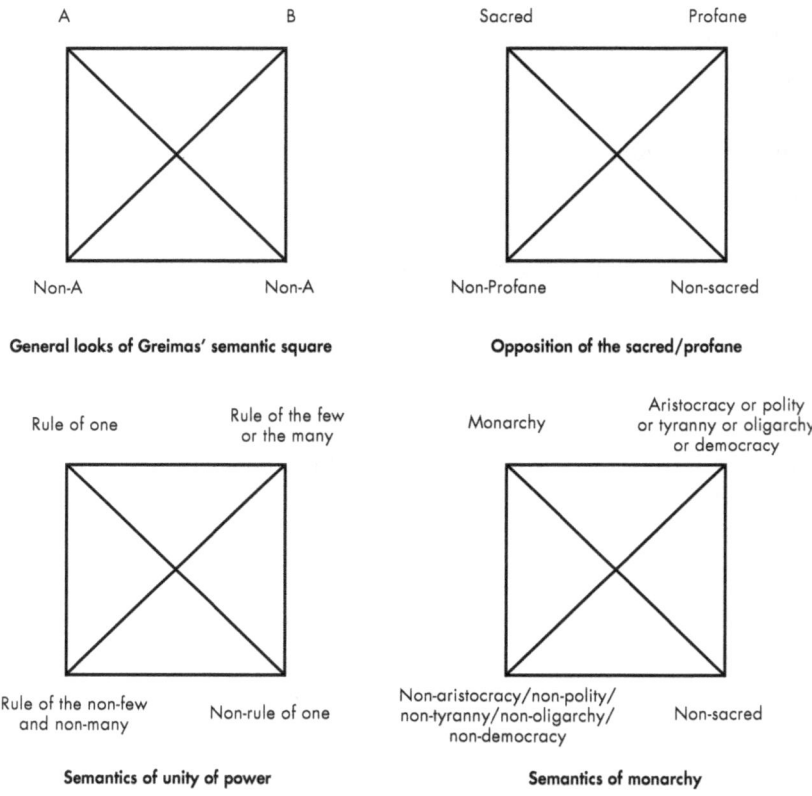

Figure 9. Examples of Greimas' semantic squares as applied to the basic terms of political philosophy.

What semantic pairing, what antonymic doublet does the term 'creation' have? It is the term 'manifestation'. Here lies the distinction between a *broad* understanding of the religious (which includes in the realm of religion both theories based on manifestation and theories based on creation) and a *narrow* understanding (which includes only those theories of the origin of the world which are based on the principle of creation).

Semantics: An Attempt at a Method (Lincoln: University of Nebraska Press, 1984).

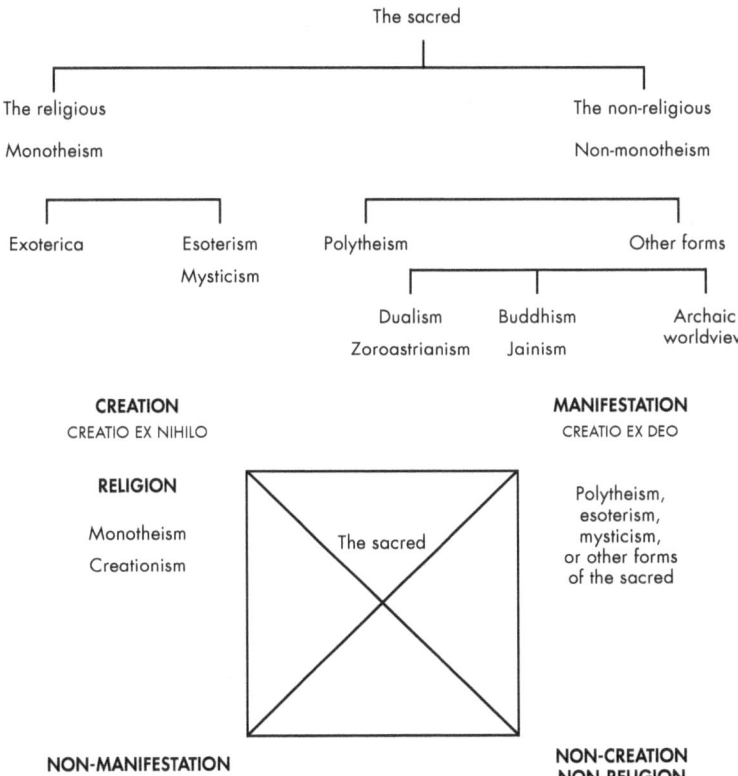

Figure 10. Semantics of the definition of religion and monotheism.

Creation means creation by God from nothingness (*ex nihilo*) and not from the Self (*ex Deo*). And so another pair of terms to the pair 'creation — manifestation' is '*creatio ex nihilo — creatio ex Deo*' ('creation from nothingness — creation from God'). *Creatio ex Deo* = manifestation. If God creates from Himself, then He is manifesting Himself in the world. There is no rigid ontological barrier between Him and the world, no strict transcendence.

Creator-God as a Personality

God the Creator is a personal God. He is, if you like, an individual who is in a 'contractual' relationship with other individuals. Hence the idea of the covenant as an agreement, a contract, a legal transaction formalised between one individual (transcendent, omnipotent, absolute, eternal, immortal and creative) and other individuals who are his antithesis; that is, they are individuals who are mortal, limited, temporal and ambiguous.

This conception of the individualisation of the Sacred is the second feature that defines a narrow understanding of religion. The God of religion in the narrow sense is always a personal, creative and transcendent God.

Religious and Profane Societies

Thus, we have divided the concept of the religious into a broad understanding and a narrow understanding. It is the second — narrow — understanding of religion that is characterised by such a phenomenon as theology.

The term 'theology' itself was introduced by monotheism to describe the construction of a philosophy of religion within this basic model: where God is the Creator and where God is an individual. Three monotheistic religions belong to the narrow understanding of religious societies:

1) Hinduism,

2) Christianity and

3) Islam.

If we take the broader concept of religion, then of course it includes all other kinds of societies except the profane society -- that is, the modern Western society or one built on its model.

Profane societies have been emerging in modern Europe since the sixteenth century. All other — non-European societies as well as European societies before the sixteenth century — were and are *broadly* religious.

Some societies of our time are also religious. Those are the Islamic states of Saudi Arabia, the United Arab Emirates, Qatar, Iran, etc.

Hindu civilisation is naturally sacred and religious in the broad sense (but not in the narrow sense!); apart from a few strands of Vishnuism, the bulk of Hindu religious belief corresponds to Manifestationism.[12] In Hinduism, God is impersonal, he creates the world from Himself (*creatio ex Deo*).

The Chinese civilisation is a sacred civilisation (perhaps before the Soviet period) and the peoples under its defining influence such as Korea, Vietnam, Japan and partly Indochina. Throughout its history, Chinese civilisation has been religious in the broad sense, but not monotheistic or creationist, because the Chinese tradition is farther removed than all other traditions from the idea of a personal deity.[13] Whereas in Hinduism, in some forms of Krishnaism and Vishnuism, there are instances of an individual God perceived as a person, nothing of the sort can be found in the Chinese tradition. This tradition has not even the remotest idea of a creative transcendent personality. It has the Tao, the will of Heaven, the sacred Emperor. It is a sacred civilisation in the full sense of the word, but in the narrow sense 'religion' is very poorly instilled there.

If we look at the world as a whole, we find that most political systems, most societies — both ancient and present — exist as sacred societies. Many people may be surprised by this because we are used to thinking that we live in the modern age (the Russians only half live in it), but this is only a small speck of profanity compared to the vast sea of sacredness. Yet modern society is extremely obsessive and intolerant, claiming universality though in fact even today, despite Westernisation, modernisation and globalisation, it is only a pretentious, aggressive, colonial, imperialistic island of profanity in the sea of sacredness. That sea has not dried up.

---

12 Александр Дугин, *Ноомахия. Великая Индия. Цивилизация Абсолюта* (Moscow: Академический проект, 2017). [Alexander Dugin, *Noomakhia. Great India. Civilisation of the Absolute.*]

13 Александр Дугин, *Ноомахия. Желтый Дракон. Цивилизации Дальнего Востока. Китай. Корея. Япония. Индокитай* (Moscow: Академический проект, 2017). [Alexander Dugin, *Noomakhia. The Yellow Dragon. Civilisations of the Far East. China. Korea. Japan. Indochina.*]

The Romanian intellectual Călin Georgescu, who was the UN special envoy to the Pacific, has said that the Marshall Islands were an absolute paradise, where everything was sacred until the 1950s. Then the Americans came and in just a few decades the heavenly islands were transformed into a living hell. The Americans set up a naval base there, set up tents with Coca-Cola and Pepsi, and gradually the people began to degenerate.

Organic relations between the tribes began to turn into competition, and life expectancy was drastically reduced. Nature was destroyed by underwater nuclear bomb blasts, everything was contaminated by radiation, the huge impoverished population, clustered in the new pseudo-Western cities, was forced to eat scraps.

This is how the taint of profanity reached the sacred Marshall Islands. In roughly the same vein we can look at the history of Western European civilisation, which first dismantled sacredness in its own territory and then began to spread around the world like a poisonous stain, reaching more and more distant territories from Europe.[14]

Therefore, when we want to have a clearer understanding of what is sacred society and what is profane society, and consequently what is sacred (religious) politics and profane politics, it must be kept in mind that although our education today is built on the *absolutisation of the profane*, the majority of humanity still lives in the world of the sacred. When we talk about sacred political philosophy, we are not talking exclusively about something that once was — today this characterises almost the entire Islamic world(!), and if we look at regions aside from Europe and North America, we see that sacred beginnings predominate there. Contemporary humanity is said to have been living in a modern society for several centuries. This is true only of Western Europe and North America. Outside their borders, elements of traditional society are still extremely stable and at times outright dominant.

It is a paradox: modern humanity is more sacred than profane, although the official (quite totalitarian) ideology of self-understanding of all our cultures and civilisations is precisely profanity.

---

14 Alexander Dugin, *Theory of a Multipolar World* (London: Arktos Media, 2021).

From this idea arises the notion that there is somewhere a pole of the 'purely profane'; this is contemporary Europe and the United States. For 500 years the West has been living with profane philosophy and profane politics. During these 500 years, religion has been gradually shifting from the centre of society to the periphery, from a public (and political) institution to a private institution.

Experiencing the Death of the Individual

The collective aspect of religion is a defining feature of sacred societies which prioritise not the individual, but that which *removes* the individual. When we experience the sacred, we experience the death of the individual. When we experience the sacred, we experience something that is bigger than us. So much bigger, brighter, more global that we dissolve before it and rejoice in that dissolution. Or we are horrified. Or we experience both together.

So we can say that at the basis of the *sacred philosophy* of politics lies the experience of death, the experience of the 'terrible' beginning, which is at the same time the 'good' beginning. And if we try to separate the good beginning from the terrible beginning, e.g. elation from horror, we would simply destroy the sacred because it is characteristic for it to have both of these sides *simultaneously*.

The sacred cannot *only* be holy. The sacred is necessarily also monstrous, i.e. it frightens, destroys, suppresses, makes you tremble. If the sacred does not make you tremble, it is not sacred, but only a surrogate, a simulacrum. The true sacred is different in that it precedes the division into the good and the terrible.

Secularism

A profane civilisation banishes the notion of the sacred and builds a completely different kind of profane politics. In this case, religion changes from a central institution of society to a peripheral one, from a generally binding model to a matter of private choice.

Accordingly, religion ceases to be religion, and even if it persists, it persists in these profane societies in a new capacity. Is there religion in the contemporary West? Of course there is. But it is a profane society, because religion is neither at the centre of social life, nor does it have a public dimension, nor is it a political institution. It exists, but from the socio-political point of view, it does not exist. It does not exist as an axis and core of the Political. And until the beginning of the modern age it was just that — a kind of 'measure of things'.

This is the idea of secularism and secularisation: the separation of Church and State, the separation of religion and society. In a sacred (religious) society this is impossible. Politics is subordinate to religious principles and has its origins in religion. In a profane society, politics is presented as something independent, also stemming from philosophy, but from a profane philosophy.

Thus, we can say that there is a religious philosophy of politics characteristic of sacred societies and a profane philosophy of politics characteristic of profane societies — that is, those which proclaimed the principle of secularism and made religion not a political or social matter but a personal and private matter for an individual.

When Religion Becomes an Individual's Private Affair, It Ceases to Be a Religion

The fact is that if religion becomes a private matter of the individual, it *ceases to be a religion*. When a Church or other institution moves from the sacred world to the profane world, *the nature of religion changes*. Religion presupposes an all-encompassing understanding of the world. The religious world cannot be the product of the 'self-development of matter' or the 'evolution of monkeys'. The world with which the religious worldview deals is either an expression of deity or a product of God's creation. In both the former and the latter case this world unconditionally possesses the beginning of holism, of wholeness. The whole precedes the parts, it is not made up of the parts, is not the result of their 'evolution'. God, thought, the spirit, the subject is there from the beginning.

Holism is opposed to the notion of individualism.[15] Thus we have two approaches to understanding (any)thing. The holistic understanding of a

---

15 Louis Dumont, *Homo Hierarchicus: The Caste System and Its Implications* (Chicago: University of Chicago Press, 1970); Dumont, *Essays on Individualism* (Chicago:

thing is given by Aristotle: the whole is greater than the sum of its parts. Individualistic understanding implies that the whole is an arbitrary combination of parts (i.e. the whole is equal to the sum of its parts, and if we regroup these parts we will create a different whole). From the point of view of holism, the whole possesses a quality that surpasses, defines and precedes the qualities of all its aggregate fragments. From the point of view of individualism, the whole is completely equal to its parts. The founder of sociology, Émile Durkheim,[16] understood society in an Aristotelian way, believing that society is primary in relation to the individual. This is a holistic approach.

Regarding the *religious* philosophy of politics, broadly speaking we can consider it as a combination of political Platonism and political Aristotelianism. All types of religious philosophy fit completely within Platonism and Aristotelianism. In fact, Islamic political philosophy, Christian political philosophy, Jewish political philosophy, and the political philosophy of India and China can all be explained in one way or another with the Platonic understanding of the world and the state (*polis*), and — provided something does not fit within this political Platonism — the principle of political Aristotelianism can also be applied.

Both Plato's philosophy of politics and Aristotle's philosophy of politics are *religious*. These types of political philosophy are sacred and correspond to a traditional society (and one with a highly differentiated social structure).

Another general observation should be made. As a rule, many archaic societies are not as symmetrically and vertically organised as the pictures that Plato and Aristotle paint. We have already said that both Plato and Aristotle distinguish three castes, three segments:

- priests/philosophers
- warriors
- producers

University of Chicago Press, 1986).
16 Émile Durkheim, *The Rules of Sociological Method* (New York: Free Press, 1982).

This schema corresponds to developed traditional societies where we see a high degree of social differentiation. We do not find such a strict triadic model in hunter-gatherer societies or in primitive agrarian collectives.

PART II

MONOTHEISTIC RELIGIONS AND TYPES OF POLITICAL THEOLOGY

CHAPTER 5

THE POLITICAL PHILOSOPHY OF JUDAISM

Judaism and Politics. Israel as an Idea

The political philosophy of Judaism is based on the religious principle of a covenant between a single personal God (the Creator) and a 'chosen people' (the Jews). This is called the Old Testament.[1] The Jews made a covenant with the Creator God to serve Him and not the other gods.

Out of the totality of the sacred, the Jews chose one figure. Here religion coincides with the people, and belonging to the people is determined by the fact of religion. He who believes in the one God of the Old Testament, he who inherits the covenant with him, is a Jew.

As the Jewish people had long lived in opposition to the other nations, they developed a distrustful attitude towards nations who also claimed to believe in gods and a sacred political order, but did so differently from them. Thus there was a gradual convergence between the ethnic and the religious.

Interestingly, from the point of view of Judaism's political philosophy, the optimal political system is the state of paradise (before the fall into sin). In this 'political' system there are no lords or labour, only Adam, faithful to God. This paradise on earth is the starting point of history, and

---

1   Александр Дугин, *Ноомахия. Семиты. Монотеизм Луны и гештальт Ва'ала* (Moscow: Академический проект, 2017). [Alexander Dugin, *Noomakhia. Semites. Monotheism of the Moon and the Gestalt of Va'al.*]

a spiritual model. Paradise in Judaism fulfils the same role as Plato's ideal state (Kallipolis).

It is important that the word 'paradise' (Heb. פרדס, *pardes*) itself comes from the ancient Iranian base *parādaijah-*, from which comes the Avestan *pairi-daêza-*, which meant 'a park surrounded by walls'.[2] Moreover, the most ancient meaning of the term was associated with walls (ancient Pers. *daêza*), and it was the presence of walls that was the main attribute of a city, πόλις, in ancient times.[3] Paradise (*pardes*) is the paradigm of life in the Jewish tradition.

All history is thought of as the expulsion of the forefathers from paradise, i.e. the departure from the ideal city, wandering and trials, and the restoration of paradisiacal conditions in the end times. Thus history itself is interpreted in a political-philosophical sense by the Jews as a journey from paradise (which lay at the beginning of history) to the final Messianic times, when the Mashiach[4] will come — that is, back to paradise.[5]

---

2   Александр Дугин, *Ноомахия. Иранский Логос. Световая война и культура ожидания* (Moscow: Академический проект, 2016). [Alexander Dugin, *Noomakhia. Iranian Logos. Light Warfare and the Culture of Waiting.*]
3   The fact that in Judaism such a fundamental term as 'Pardes' is an Iranian loanword is highly significant. After their return from the Babylonian captivity, the Jews incorporated many elements of Iranian religion in the context of their religious, political and cultural tradition. See Alexander Dugin, *Noomakhia. Semites. Monotheism of the Moon and the Gestalt of Va'al*.
4   Messiah — from Heb. מָשִׁיחַ, 'anointed one'. See Alexander Dugin, *Noomakhia. Semites. Monotheism of the Moon and the Gestalt of Va'ala*.
5   This religious and political philosophy of history, associated with the arrival at the end of time of a Saviour-King — and the term 'anointed', which refers specifically to a King 'anointed to the kingdom' — is also almost certainly of Iranian origin, since the Iranian tradition was originally built on a close connection between the structure of history, the destiny of the kingdom and the expectation of the coming Restorer-King (Saoshyant in the Mazdean tradition). At the same time, all these themes are absent from early Judaism and appear only in the later — post-Babylonian — wording. See Alexander Dugin, *Noomakhia. Iranian Logos. Light Warfare and the Culture of Expectation*.

At the Heart of Judaism Is a Covenant with the Creator

Accordingly, the various historical stages between the fall/expulsion of the forefathers from paradise and the restoration of the original fullness of paradise constitute the cycle of sacred history.

The Jewish people and the Jewish religion are directly connected to this sacred history. A Jew is one who lives in this history and is part of it. The Jew is the subject of history. All other peoples are demons, manifestations of the powers of the 'Other Side' (Hebrew אחרא סטרא — *Sitra Ahra*). Hence the idea arises that since the Jewish people are the subject of history, then from beginning to end all history is thought of and measured by the stages of the Jewish people's existence. A radical religious ethnocentrism emerges.

So at the heart of Judaism's political philosophy is the contractual axis between the Jews and the Creator of the world, the God of Abraham, Isaac and Jacob. In fact, the whole of history is a matter of faithfulness and betrayal towards their God.

The political organisation of the Jews relates to this vertical axis in different ways at different stages. Having received the Old Testament, the Jews begin to carry it. The most important idea becomes the organisation of society around the vertical axis of the Covenant: around religious leaders, judges, prophets, around the shrine of the Ark of the Covenant, which houses those Tablets of the Covenant that Moses received on Mount Sinai. Accordingly, Jewish society, politics and history are built around this sacred model, which is why Jews often refer to themselves as 'priestly people'.

Judaism and Platonism

If we now go back to the Platonic model of the cave and ask who is the legitimate ruler in the Jewish sense, we answer that it is the same Platonic philosopher who goes up from the cave (*anodos*) and down again (*kathodos*). The other peoples are either warriors or artisans, while the priestly people are a people of books, a people of thought, a people who make service to a higher deity their primary task (hence so many synagogues and Torah learners).

This approach forms a picture of the Jews' place among other nations. This is the place of philosopher-royalty, which was occupied by the Jews during the period when Abraham was given a place in the Promised Land for a future kingdom; this was followed by the Egyptian captivity, and then with Moses the Jews were able to return to the Promised Land to become rulers again, restoring their royal dignity.

The Promised Land was given by God to the Twelve Tribes of Israel, and they return to their land to become kings of the nations of Canaan living around them. A Canaanite centre emerges where the Jews control Israel, a vast territory by the standards of that time.[6] At first the organisation of the Jewish people, in relation to the division of the territory into twelve tribes, is uncertain: after the Messianic leaders (Moses, who led the Jews out of Egypt, and Joshua, who reclaimed the territory of Israel after completing his wanderings in the Arabian Desert), there comes the period of the Judges. All Jewish leaders constituted priests and sages who determined how the political and social model of ancient Israel should be justly organised on the basis of the Testament.

In the conquest of Canaan, however, it was military leaders, such as Joshua, who accomplished the religious task by military means. The Israelites were often at war with the surrounding nations, but in their eyes this war was *sacred* — a holy war. The imposition of Jewish authority over the 'Promised Land' was a religious mission, a kind of restoration of the conditions of the lost paradise. From this it is easy to see what place the territories of Palestine hold in the political philosophy of Judaism (both ancient and modern).

Property, livestock, slaves and everything else that the Jews seized from the defeated nations as a result of war was referred to by the special term *herem* (Hebrew חרם). This is a very interesting term, and is the basis of E. Durkheim's sociology of religion.

Why are the spoils taken by the Jews from other nations called *herem*? Herem, on the one hand, can be sacrificed to God, and on the other, it is something that the Jews themselves, being pure, cannot eat or take for

---

6   Alexander Dugin, *Noomakhia. Semites. Monotheism of the Moon and the Gestalt of Va'ala*.

themselves. Herem must either be sacrificed to God or destroyed, because other nations are 'stained with demons', polytheism, and what is taken from them is 'herem'. The term 'herem' corresponds exactly to the concept of 'sacred'. It is both too elevated (i.e. belonging to God) and too terrible, capable of causing their people irreparable harm. Here we see the duality of the principle of the sacred itself, which lies in the fact that the sacred transcends the human level—both upwards, towards God, and downwards, towards the 'demonic'.

We see that in the Jewish religion and sacred history of the 'Bible' there is from the outset a clear political philosophy which fits perfectly into the concepts of political Platonism, but instead of a Philosopher King here appears a chosen people, a 'king of all nations'. God says to the Jews: 'You shall rule over all nations'.[7] Not because they are kings, and not even because they want to. They will rule over other nations because they have ascended (ἄνοδος) to God, and God sends them to rule, sends them to sacrifice (κάθοδος) so that they will save their people and through them the whole world. Both the religious structure of Judaism and its political philosophy can be understood from a Platonic perspective. The *anodos* of the Jews is the Revelation received by Noah, Abraham, Jacob, Moses and other Jewish leaders, which became the axis of the Covenant or Law.

Tellingly, in Hebrew the 'Bible' is called 'Torah' (Hebrew תּוֹרָה), which literally means 'law', the socio-political and legal order governing the life of society. Again we clearly see the deep unity and common roots of religion, philosophy and politics.

The Philosopher Samuel and King Saul

During the reign of Saul, the idea of a Kingdom of Judah emerges. It is very interesting how the Bible describes its formation: the Jewish people feel that they cannot cope with the order based on the authority of the institution of judges that developed after Joshua, and they ask the prophet Samuel to appoint a king to rule over them.

---

7 'You will rule over many nations but none will rule over you'. Deuteronomy 15:6.

The prophet Samuel is very upset by this request, because the king of Israel is God, and if the people ask to have a king over them, as other nations have, it means that they want something that is lesser and worse for themselves.[8] The prophet Samuel tests the Jewish people by pointing out that if he puts a king over them, they will have to obey God not directly but *indirectly*. Samuel promises to anoint Saul as king, while at the same time warning the Jews that they will lose their best king (God) — by losing a *sacred* king, they will gain a *sacralised* king, that is only *partly* sacred.

By the decision of the Jewish people the prophet Samuel does indeed anoint Saul for kingship. Thus a new political system, a kingdom that receives blessing and ritual anointing from a priestly authority (a prophet), is instituted. The king of Israel becomes the 'firstborn of Israel'. Again we see here the figure of the Philosopher King, but now it is divided: there is the 'philosopher' Samuel and the 'king' Saul. And Saul, the king of Israel, is not just a warrior, not just the best and strongest. He becomes a sacred figure who belongs to the first and not the second caste. Beneath him is the Israelite nobility, and beneath the nobility (as in any system) are the toilers.

Babylonian Captivity

In the Age of Kings the nature of the relationship of the Chosen People to God changes, but the general model of the Political remains the same — we are dealing with a classical sacred political philosophy, but instead of the figure of the Philosopher King (as in Plato) here the patriarchs (Abraham, Isaac, Jacob), Messianic leaders (such as Moses, Joshua), then judges and then kings (Saul, David, Solomon etc.) succeed each other.

The Age of Kings is also based on sacred philosophy: the king is a sacred figure. Gradually, however, the warning of the prophet Samuel begins to come true and kings begin to deviate from the lofty ideals in the practical execution of their rule.

---

8   'And the LORD said to Samuel, "Obey the voice of the people in all that they say to you, for they have not rejected you, but they have rejected me from being king over them."' 1 Samuel 8:7.

The deviation begins with Saul, and even the prophet David had serious transgressions (taking Bathsheba as his wife and actually killing her husband 'Uriah the Hittite'). Under King Solomon, through his many wives taken from other nations, foreign motives, cults and practices infiltrated the religion itself.

The kingdom begins to decline somewhat, until there is a complete collapse, a division into Israel (north) and Judea (south) under the rule of separate dynasties and finally the invasion of Babylonians, the capture of Jerusalem, the destruction of the Temple and the Babylonian captivity. Thereafter the Kingdom of Israel no longer reaches its own high-water mark. It is punished by God for deviating from its ideal model, for the departure of the Jews from their destiny. The practical political execution deviates to a critical degree from envisaged political philosophy, from heavenly Israel, from the idea of Israel, from Israel as an idea, from the eternal paradigm of *pardes*.

Israel and Aristotle

The meaning of Israel, when it operates in history, can be reduced to Aristotelian politics. Recall the nature of Aristotle's 'unmoved mover' or his immanent God.

In Jewish political philosophy, the axis of the world — Jerusalem or the Temple, built by the third king Solomon — fulfils the function of the 'unmoved mover'.[9] All that is associated with Jewish history is the desire to preserve and protect the Temple, and after its destruction to rebuild the Temple (which was done during the construction of the Second Temple by Zerubbabel) and, finally, in our time (considered in Judaism as messianic, 'the Last') to build the Third Temple.[10]

---

9   But Jerusalem is already the fourth historical manifestation of the 'unmoved mover'. The original, first and eternal is 'paradise', the 'garden enclosed by flocks', the Kallipolis of Judaism. Then its role is transferred to the Promised Land at the centre of Canaan. Finally, under David, the ancient city of Jebus (from the name of the people of the Jebusites), later known as Jerusalem, becomes the final historical-mystical form.

10 Alexander Dugin, *Noomakhia. Semites. Monotheism of the Moon and the Gestalt of Va'ala*.

If the Platonic model represents an ideal and eternal Israel, which is always near to God, the Aristotelian model represents a phenomenal Israel. Such a phenomenal Israel can in some situations deviate from God, but it can (and must) by its own *efforts* return to Him. This is the Aristotelian effort. Not just the contemplation of a pure image of political philosophy, but a wilful, active, practical effort linked to the political metaphysics of the Temple. Hence the idea of a return to Jerusalem and the restoration of the Temple. Thus, on the spectrum of political Aristotelianism, Jewish political philosophy is linked to the restoration of the Temple, the defence of Jerusalem and the re-establishment of the State of Israel.

In a political sense, the dispersion which began in the era of Titus Flavius Vespasianus (9–79 AD) in 70 AD was God's final punishment of the Jews for unfaithfulness to Him, for departing from the divine commandments. And the Jews are sent into *galut* (Hebrew גלות, 'exile') in order to purify themselves. During this period, their politics are directed to the past and to the future; they have no political philosophy for the present. The Jews have been living under the influence of other (*goyim*) political systems for these 2000 years, which is their punishment. So those political philosophies, states and societies in which Jews have been present for 2000 years are in fact presented as anti-Jewish, and given to Jews to let them feel how bad it is to forsake God. This is some historical propaedeutics.

The peak of suffering is the mass extermination of the Jews, the Holocaust (Greek ὁλοκαύστος 'burnt-offering') or *Shoa* (Hebrew שׁוֹאָה, 'catastrophe', 'ruin'). In this purifying suffering, the next — the last — phase of Jewish history is being prepared: the return to the Promised Land, the proclamation of Jerusalem as the capital of Israel, the building of the third Temple on the Temple Mount and, finally, the coming of the King of the Jews, the Mashiach. This will be the restoration of the 'unmoved mover' as the axis of the world and the founding of the 'good kingdom', which in turn will restore a direct connection with the transcendent and be a return to paradise (the ideal state).

Israel as a Political Praxis. Zionism. The King Mashiach

How does the political philosophy of Judaism enjoin Israel to act during the time of the galut? The main thing is to strive to return to the Promised Land, that is, to restore the past (but essentially the eternal) in the future. Hence the messianic-political idea of returning by any means to Palestine, to rebuild the State of Israel again, to recreate it where it was. It is effectively a desire to return to what Aristotle calls the 'natural place'. And the 'natural place' of the Jews, in religious terms, is the Temple of Jerusalem. This aspiration forms the basis of the politics of the galut during that period.

However, how and when the Jews should return to Palestine from the galut was a matter of fierce controversy in the Jewish Diaspora. At the same time, there was a strict prohibition in the Talmud against making this return ahead of time — that is, *before the coming* of Mashiach.

The first outburst of Zionism, that is a return to Zion (where Jerusalem is located) to its 'natural place', is the appearance in Jewish history of the 'pseudo-Mashiach' — Sabbatai Tzvi[11] (1626–1676). Sabbatai Tzvi announced to his followers that the end of times had come, that he himself was the Messiah, and that it was necessary to follow him to the Promised Land. The first active emigration of Jews to Palestine begins. In terms of Jewish philosophy of history, the end of the world will be the arrival of the King Mashiach. Note: the Messiah for the Jews is a *king*,[12] a benevolent righteous king, by whom the fullness of the political philosophy of Judaism is restored in both its Platonic and Aristotelian versions.

In the Platonic sense, this eschatological Israel becomes ideal Israel, and in terms of wilful intention, it is embodied in the Messiah King (it is very important that the Messiah for the Jews is not God, but a king, a messenger of God, and this is their fundamental difference from Christians). This king wilfully — in Aristotelian terms — returns his

---

11   Alexander Dugin, *Noomakhia. Semites. Monotheism of the Moon and the Gestalt of Va'ala*.
12   On the Iranian roots of this idea, see. Alexander Dugin, *Noomakhia. Iranian Logos. Light War and the Culture of Waiting*; Ibid. *Noomakhia. Semites. Monotheism of the Moon and the Gestalt of Va'ala*.

people to the Promised Land; and here the action of the phenomenal world, subject to time, enters into resonance with the structures of the unchanging eternal world; the immanent pole, which is the Jerusalem Temple, and the transcendent beginning are coming together, locking the circuit. This is the end of history, and it is the political project of contemporary Judaism.

An Argument about Timing and Methods

The process of implementation by Jews of their historical political programme of many thousands of years does not happen in a vacuum. It unfolds in the context of the collapse of Western traditional civilisations, de-Christianisation and the establishment of a secular political paradigm of modernity, where religious factors are not taken into account at all. Modernity also affects Zionism, which in the nineteenth century takes the form of a nationalism copied from the European bourgeois type (but within the Zionist movement, of course, the religious political philosophy is invigorated).

Israel today existing, having been created in 1947, is a sign of the beginning of the Messianic era. The Jews are already living in the Messianic Age. The Jews return to Israel, the Promised Land from their galut, only in the Messianic Age (not on the eve of it).

Thus there is a closure of this horizontal phenomenal philosophy of politics — to a vertical philosophy of politics. And this is happening now. This explains such an acute confrontation with the Muslims in Jerusalem. The Muslims control the territory where the Temple was located, and the Temple, as we have said, is the 'unmoved mover' of Jewish politics, the historical-political and religious target.

Most Jews, both those who have returned to Israel and those who remain outside, accept the general model of Zionism in one way or another, either in its religious form, in its secular form, or as a mixed model. Only a minority of religious Jews, in particular from the Neturei Karta movement, reject Zionism as contrary to the traditions of the Talmud and the entire logic of the Jewish religion. For them, the creation of Israel before the coming of the Mashiach, relying on force, nationalism and political intrigue, is a travesty and a sacrilege, akin to the actions of the pseudo-Mashiach Sabbatai Tzvi. While the Neturei Karta proceed from a strictly identical political philosophy as the Zionists, they radically diverge from them on the method and time for returning to Palestine. To return from the *galut* before the arrival of Mashiach is tantamount in their eyes to 'political and religious "Satanism"', since in this event people ascribe to themselves the characteristics of God and God's messenger.

The political philosophy of Judaism, inscribed in sacred history, in the Old Testament religion, in Judaism as a body of religious and legal ideas, is not merely a shadow of some distant past. Even today the texts of the Torah are constantly read, the prayers are incessantly offered, the commentaries and the Talmud are invariably studied, and this is one continuous process of the political philosophy of Judaism, which at the present stage, the final stage for the Jews, puts an end to the Testament that the Jews made with their God in ancient times.

The philosophy of politics as applied to religion is something extremely topical. And it is not the past — it is what is happening today and allows us to adequately decipher those news items that concern the Israeli-Palestinian conflict or American-Israeli relations, for example. Thus, the political philosophy of religion is a functioning factor in the tangible politics of today, explaining the past and predetermining the future.

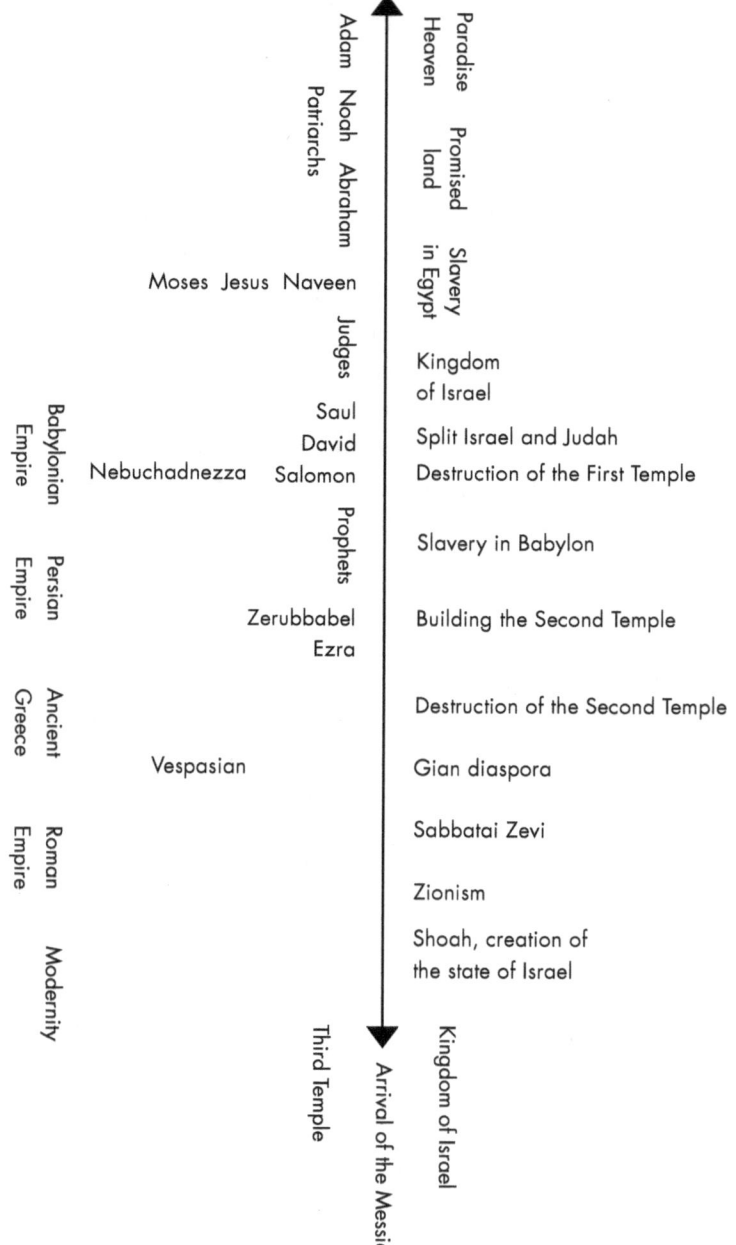

Figure 11. Structure of the historical process in the context of Judaism.

CHAPTER 6

THE POLITICAL PHILOSOPHY OF CHRISTIANITY

Christianity and Rome. The Withholder (Katechon)

The Christian political philosophy is made up of several factors. Firstly, from the particular theological model of Christianity. Christianity is a specific religion which is partly derived from Judaism and therefore adopts its basic ideas of monotheism and a creationist perspective. However, the idea of the incarnation of God, unimaginable in Judaism and contrary to any logic of Jewish religious theology, finds itself at the centre of the Christian religion. Christianity, therefore, is both a continuation of Judaism and at the same time its theological overcoming or refuting. In this sense, Christianity is in a difficult position with regard to Judaism. The fact that Christian theology is quite specific in the context of other versions of monotheism (Judaism and Islam) affects *Christian political philosophy* as well.

Apart from the specific theology based on the New Testament and on the basic Christian idea of the incarnation of God in man, there is another very important factor — the succession of Christianity to the Roman Empire.[1]

The philosophy of the Roman Empire tended to combine all three types of positive models from Aristotelianism. The Roman Empire is

---

1 Александр Дугин, *Ноомахия. Латинский Логос. Солнце и Крест* (Moscow: Академический проект, 2016). [Alexander Dugin, *Noomakhia. Latin Logos. The Sun and the Cross.*]

more akin to the Aristotelian philosophy of politics than to the Platonic; and to a large extent the Roman Empire saw itself as a repetition (in Latium, in Italy) of the state-building exploits of Alexander the Great, who was a disciple of Aristotle. This empire sought to embody the three best aspects of the Aristotelian understanding of politics and proposed to establish a positive monarchy (hence: the emperor as a sacred figure, in fact a living deity). The emperor was also called *pontifex*, 'bridge-builder' — the bridge between the world of men and the world of the gods, between earth and heaven, between life and death. Therefore the sacred king, the emperor, is at the centre of this sacred monarchy of the Roman Empire.

The next level of authority is the *aristocracy*: it is the Roman Senate, the Roman patricians, the high-ranking noble citizens of Rome, who represent the second layer of the Aristotelian model.

And finally, the Roman *polity*, i.e. the people of Rome, who also act as a political authority in significant cases. The Roman people support or overthrow the emperor; they stand on the side of the aristocratic patrician families or, on the contrary, contradict them; and in the Roman Empire they sometimes even organise systems of self-government based on the *qualified* majority (as opposed to democracy).

Thus in the Roman Empire we see a combination of all three types of Aristotle's political model:

1) a sacred emperor (*pontifex*) who corresponds to a monarch,
2) the aristocracy in the form of the Senate and
3) Roman citizens, *Populus Romanus Quiritium* — the members and basis of Roman polity.

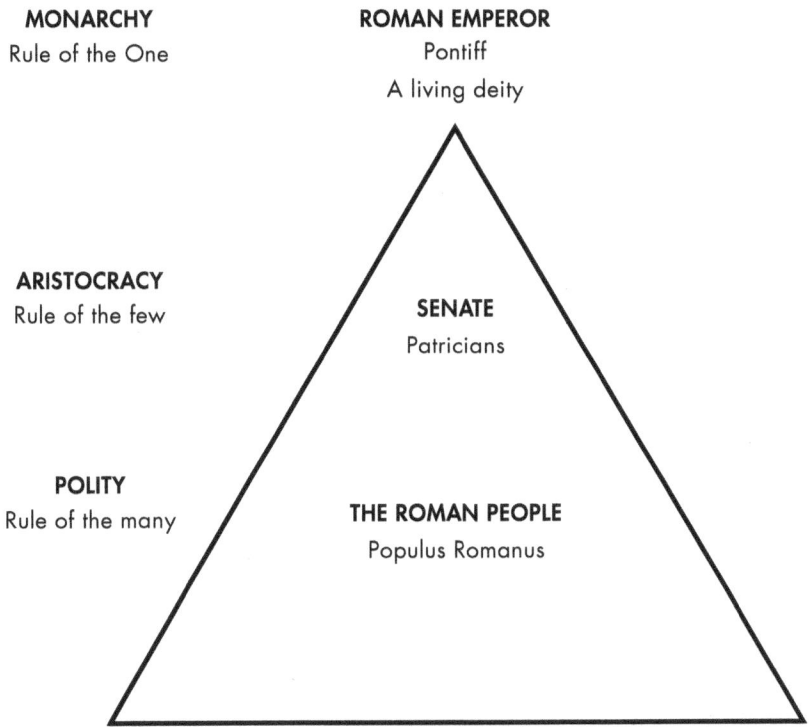

Figure 12. Structure of the Political in the Roman Empire and the 'good' governments of Aristotle.

Note how Aristotle divides power between these forms of government:

1) a large territory gravitates towards monarchy,
2) the middle one towards aristocracy and
3) the small one to the polity.

Accordingly, as the Roman Empire was vast, it was ruled by monarchs or emperors. At a more limited level of the regions of the Roman Empire, power belonged to the aristocracy; finally, in small villages, towns or localities, the polity prevailed.

When Christianity was established in the Roman Empire, there was a very important theoretical identification of the figure of the emperor with the image from the Second Epistle of St. Paul[2] to the Thessalonians. This is the point which defines the essence of Christian political philosophy.

In the prophecy of St. Paul, it is said that the son of perdition, i.e. the Antichrist, is already at work, 'but the one who now holds it back will continue to do so till he is taken out of the way.'[3] This enigmatic phrase has been interpreted in different ways. The classical Orthodox (and to a large extent Catholic) medieval interpretation was to identify the image of the 'withholder' with the emperor.[4]

The Apostle Paul's prophecy of the 'End Times' states that the 'son of perdition', i.e. Antichrist, will not come into the world until the one who now holds him back is taken out of the way — in Greek it is *katechon* (ὁ κατέχων, 'the one who withholds'). The word *katechon*, usually translated as 'withholder'[5] means literally 'one who has under him' (Greek κατ, 'under', and ἔχω, 'to have'), that is 'one who rules', 'one who possesses'.

In the Greek text of the Gospel, the passage from Paul's epistle — 'And now you know *what* is holding him back, so that he may be revealed at the proper time' — includes an important concept that is missing in the Synodal translation: 'И ныне удержавающее весте, во еже явитися ему в свое ему время'[6] — 'удерживающее', in the neutral gender — in Greek τὸ κατέχον. This suggests a thing, a place which contains the withholder

---

2   The Apostle Paul, who lived at the time of the first apostles, first acted as a persecutor of Christ, then was converted and became the most prominent preacher of Christianity.

3   'Let no one deceive you in any way; for that day will not come until first the apostasy comes and the man of sin is revealed, the son of perdition, who opposes and exalts himself above all that is called God or holiness, so that in the temple of God he sits as God, proclaiming himself God. Do you not remember that I told you this when I was still with you? And you know what is restraining him now so that he may be revealed in his time. For the secret power of sin is already at work; but the one who now holds it back will continue to do so till he is taken out of the way.' Second Epistle to the Thessalonians by St. Paul. Ch. 2:3–7.

4   Александр Дугин, *Ноомахия. Византийский Логос. Эллинизм и Империя* (Moscow: Академический проект, 2016). [Alexander Dugin, *Noomakhia. Byzantine Logos. Hellenism and Empire.*]

5   удерживающий

6   In the original Greek: καὶ νῦν τὸ κατέχον οἴδατε εἰς τὸ ἀποκαλυφθῆναι αὐτὸν ἐν τῷ ἑαυτοῦ καιρῷ.

himself. It is this 'withholding place' that St. John Chrysostom (c. 347–407), the undisputed bearer of Christian orthodoxy, identifies as the 'Roman State'. Let us cite this entire passage because of its fundamental importance for the very fabric of Christian political philosophy:

> One may naturally enquire, what is that which *withholds*, and after that would know, why Paul expresses it so obscurely. What then is it that withholds, that is, *hinders him from being revealed*? Some indeed say, the grace of the Spirit, but others the Roman empire, to whom I most of all accede. Wherefore? Because if he meant to say the Spirit, he would not have spoken obscurely, but plainly, that even now the grace of the Spirit, that is the gifts, withhold him. And otherwise he ought now to have come, if he was about to come when the gifts ceased; for they have long since ceased. But because he said this of the Roman empire, he naturally glanced at it, and speaks covertly and darkly. For he did not wish to bring upon himself superfluous enmities, and useless dangers. For if he had said that after a little while the Roman empire would be dissolved, they would immediately have even overwhelmed him, as a pestilent person, and all the faithful, as living and warring to this end. And he did not say that it will be quickly, although he is always saying it — but what? that he may be revealed in his own season, he says.
>
> [...] So indeed he also says here. *Only there is one that restrains now, until he be taken out of the way*, that is, when the Roman empire is taken out of the way, then he shall come. And naturally. For as long as the fear of this empire lasts, no one will willingly exalt himself, but when that is dissolved, he will attack the anarchy, and endeavor to seize upon the government both of man and of God. For as the kingdoms before this were destroyed, for example, that of the Medes by the Babylonians, that of the Babylonians by the Persians, that of the Persians by the Macedonians, that of the Macedonians by the Romans: so will this also be by the Antichrist, and he by Christ, and it will no longer withhold. And these things Daniel delivered to us with great clearness.
>
> *And then*, he says, *shall be revealed the lawless one*. And what after this? The consolation is at hand. *Whom the Lord Jesus shall slay with the breath of His mouth, and bring to nought by the manifestation of His coming, even he whose coming is according to the working of Satan*.
>
> For as fire merely coming on even before its arrival makes torpid and consumes the little animals that are afar off; so also Christ, by His commandment only, and

Coming. It is enough for Him to be present, and all these things are destroyed. He will put a stop to the deceit, by only appearing.[7]

Christianity emerges in a premonitory sense of the coming of the Antichrist and this defines the Christian philosophy of history. The Christian religion claims that Christ comes at the 'End Times', saves the world, then an era of apostasy (Greek ἀποστασία) follows and finally the Antichrist appears. In contrast to Judaism, Christ is not the King of Israel, but the King of all being, with 'his kingdom not of this world'. Consequently, the understanding of political history is also different from Judaism: it is not limited to the Jewish people (as the subject of history), but extends to all humanity. However, it is the Church of Christ which becomes the real subject. It is founded by Christ and the Third Person of the Holy Trinity, Holy Spirit, after Christ's Resurrection and Ascension. And since Christ is God to Christians, the Old Testament history ends and a new history, the New Testament history, begins. This is the history of the Church. In this history semantic poles arise — the exemplary time is not so much 'heaven' as the time of Jesus Christ's presence on earth among men, and the opposite pole is the coming of the Antichrist. Christianity therefore thinks of the Political differently, bringing into it a 'transcendental' dimension — the Kingdom of Heaven, which is expressed in the Church.

Christian doctrine is eschatology, the doctrine of the 'end of the world' (from Greek ἐσχατον, 'the end', 'the limit'). Christ comes in the last days before the arrival of the Antichrist, and the Christian worldview can be described as the worldview of people waiting for the end of the world. This end of the world has the following scenario: first comes the Antichrist (Αντίχριστος), which can mean both the one who is *against* Christ and the one who comes *before* Him. Then the Second Coming of Christ takes place and the Antichrist is defeated by the Heavenly Host.

---

[7] St John Chrysostom. *Homilies on Second Thessalonians*, Homily 4. Translated by John A. Broadus. From *Nicene and Post-Nicene Fathers*, First Series, Vol. 13. Edited by Philip Schaff. (Buffalo, NY: Christian Literature Publishing Co., 1889.) [Emphasis author's own.]

The First Coming is Christ suffering, crucified. The Second Coming is the 'Saviour in Power'.[8] The Second Coming is Christ coming no longer as man, but as God, and He puts an end to the kingdom of the Antichrist. The kingdom of the Antichrist thus lies between the First Coming and the Second.

Christian philosophy of history states: Christ came, saved the world, was crucified, in his blood and flesh the Church was formed as a new subject of history (this New Testament Church moves in history, realising the mission of world salvation), then eventually the coming of the Antichrist, apostasy and finally the Second Coming which will end the apostasy. Accordingly, by saying that 'until the withholder is taken out of the way' the son of perdition (the Antichrist) will not appear, St. Paul is indicating that after the worldwide spread of Christianity and its victory there will be a certain historical period, during which the coming of the Antichrist will *not yet* take place. In other words, there is the following structure to the Christian logic of history.

---

8   This is also the name of the central icon in the traditional Russian iconostasis. 'The Saviour in Power' is an image that expresses the appearance of Christ the Saviour at the end of time in glory and power. Christ will descend to earth in the name of the fulfilment of God's Providence, uniting under Christ's head the heavenly and the earthly.

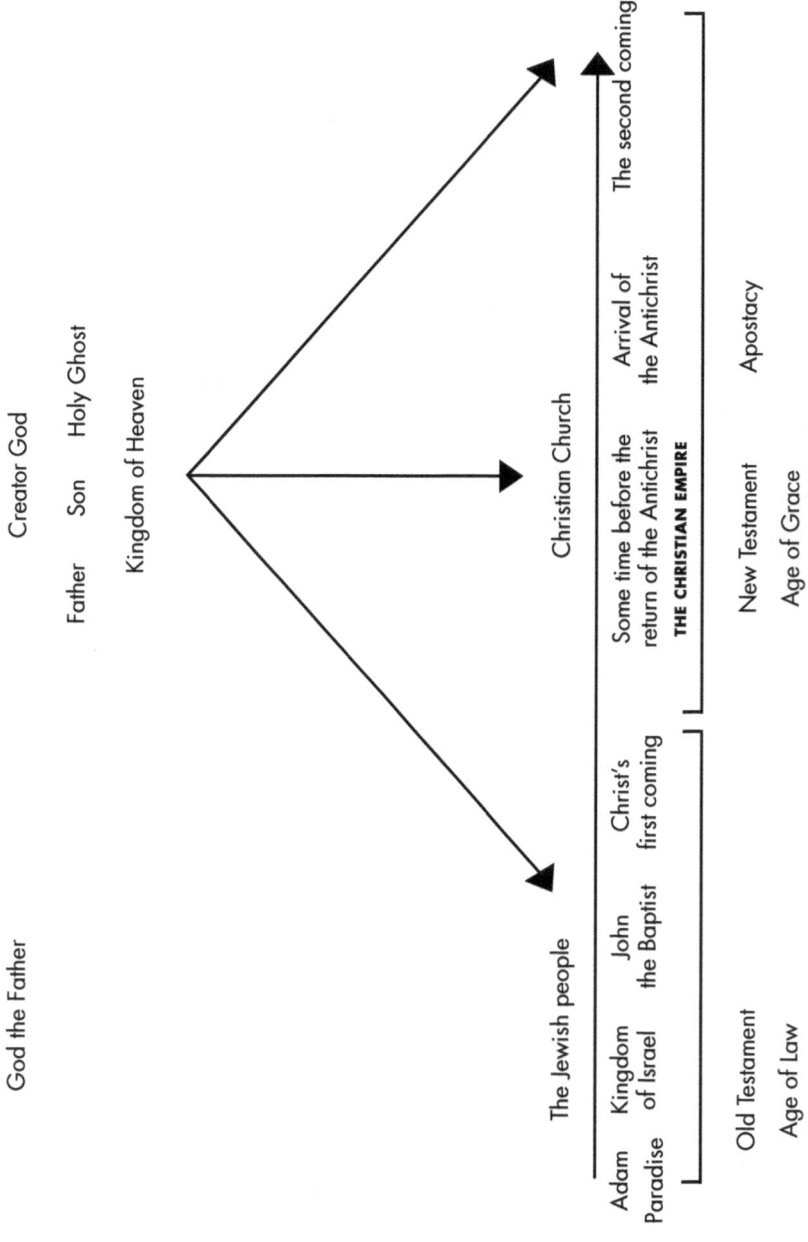

Figure 13. Structure of the Christian understanding of history.

After the age of Christ follows a unique period when the Antichrist is yet to come — in the Apocalypse it is described as the time when the dragon, the ancient serpent, is confined for a thousand years.

> And I saw an angel descending from heaven, who had the key of the abyss and a great chain in his hand.
>
> And he took the dragon, the serpent of old, which is the devil and Satan, and chained him for a thousand years,
>
> And he cast him down into the abyss and sealed him and set a seal upon him, that he might not again ensnare the nations till the thousand years should come to pass; but after that he must be set free for a little while.[9]

And furthermore:

> And when the thousand years is over, Satan shall be released from his prison, and shall go out to deceive the nations which are in the four corners of the earth, Gog and Magog, and to gather them unto war; their number is as the sand of the sea.[10]

The serpent (Satan) is released from prison precisely at the moment when 'the withholder is taken out of the way'. This is the Christian view of history.

Christianity Already Has a Political Component, Even When It Does Not Yet Speak of It

The first community built at the time of Christ was a community of equality; it was not yet a political system, but an organisation of society, fully immersed in the fact of the divine incarnation and in the comprehension of the 'Good News'.

But already in the first generation, with St. Paul in particular, there is some insight into the form in which Christianity will exist until the next period, when it is destined to be spread throughout the whole earth. *The prophecy of the Katechon is the key to the whole formula of Christian history and political philosophy.* The Withholder referred to in St. Paul's letter has

---

9   Revelation of St John the Evangelist. Chapter 20: 1–3.
10 Revelation of St John the Evangelist. Chapter 20: 7–8.

been interpreted by Orthodox teachers — including St. John Chrysostom — as the Roman Emperor.

Thus, long before Christianity became the official religion of the Roman Empire, there was already a certain prophetic understanding of the coming Christianisation of the empire and the religious mission of its ruler, the emperor. Already in the first apostolic period, which was an era of persecution and oppression (from the empire as well), the early Christians believed that in a certain time Christianity (as a community without any political dimension) would change its catacomb nature and become a doctrine with a *political dimension*.

So we see that Christianity already contains a political component, even when it is not yet explicit about it and appears to be completely detached from politics. In the notion of the Withholder we are dealing with an image, rare in the early Christian context, which has a political dimension; it is from this point that the whole political philosophy of Christianity is born.

The Roman Empire (Aristotle's political model) is further seen as the providential vessel (the kingdom prepared by God's Providence) for the reception of Christianity. Thus already the first Christians, in an astonishing way, believed that the Roman Empire was created for them, and that the fact of Christ's birth in this very empire is endowed with tremendous prophetic meaning. Thus this empire, according to the early Christians, was to have a very important religious function connected with the coming of the Antichrist. As long as there is an empire, as long as there is an emperor (the Withholder), the Antichrist cannot come. Notice what a fundamental religious burden the Roman state appears to bear in Christian political philosophy.

The Doctrine of the Four Kingdoms and the 'Political Antichrist'

In Christianity there was a doctrine of the Four Kingdoms. The first kingdom was Babylonia, the second was Persia, the third was Greece (Alexander the Great's kingdom) and the fourth was the Roman Empire. Each of these kingdoms had a corresponding metal: gold for Babylon, silver for Persia, copper or bronze for Alexander's kingdom and iron for the Roman Empire. This symbolism was based on the story of Nebuchadnezzar's dream, in which he saw a colossus made of four metals standing on clay feet, and on the interpretation of this dream by the prophet Daniel.

It is very important that the empire in this sense is not just an ordinary state. It is thought of as a *world kingdom*, a kind of absolute state, a metastate, a super-state which included many states and smaller polities (πολιτεία). The emperor was not just a king, but a 'king of kings' — a figure, sacred, divine.

It is precisely because of its sacred nature that the empire is able to unite such diverse individual states, peoples, principalities and other political forms. The only legitimate entity, from a Christian perspective, is the Christian Roman Empire. It is the political homeland of the Christian. This empire is the direct heir to the previous three kingdoms, and after it there can be no legitimate organisation of political space on a world scale. When Rome falls, the Antichrist will come. It will happen when the Roman Emperor, the 'Katechon', the 'Withholder' will be 'taken out of the way'. The fall of the empire will mean the coming of the End Times and the arrival of the Antichrist.

Here a very interesting point arises — the possibility of giving the Antichrist a political or historical-political dimension. In a sense one could speak of a 'political philosophy of the Antichrist'. That which destroys the normative (good) kingdom, that which replaces the only correct and acceptable political form of the Christian state is the *political Antichrist*. The political Antichrist is generally all that is the *enemy of the empire*. The doctrine of the political philosophy of the Antichrist is the doctrine of any political organism which denies the fundamental soteriological (from Greek σωτήρ, 'saviour') and eschatological function of the Christian Roman Empire. Thus the conscious opponent of the empire, the opponent of the 'Katechon', appears in the context of the political philosophy of Christianity as the bearer of the political philosophy of the Antichrist.

The Devil's Political System

The end of the Roman Empire, the fall of Rome, the removal of the 'Withholder' brings the Christian into the world of an *illegitimate political system*. Any non-imperial, non-Christian political system is illegitimate for the Christian, and that which is not just yet to be included in the empire, but comes after its end or in its place, contributing to its destruction, is an *active* form of the political Antichrist. It follows that the Christian is obliged to oppose the Antichrist not only on the religious level, but also on the political level. A political system built around a secular non-Christian (anti-Christian) ruler and *any* non-Katechonic (and especially anti-Katechonic) political ideology is the *political system of the devil* or of the Antichrist.

When the heathen Emperor Constantine (288–337) issued the Mediolanian decree forbidding the persecution of Christians, and soon afterwards moved the capital to the newly-built Byzantium and proclaimed Christianity as the official religion of the Roman Empire, St. Paul's prophecy from his Second Epistle to the Thessalonians came true, and the *Katechon* (Withholder) became a concrete political and historical reality.

Thus a Christian Roman Empire was established in practice, the purpose of which was to keep the devil, the ancient serpent, in chains for a thousand years and to prevent the coming of the Antichrist. Constantinople receives the name New Rome, but now the Orthodox Empire is seen as a continuation of the same Fourth Universal Kingdom.

Byzantium. A Symphony of Powers

In the beginning, the Roman Empire united East and West, but gradually they begin to separate, because the Western Roman provinces withdraw from the control of New Rome.

There is thus a difference in the political fortunes of the two halves of the Christian world. That classical point we have been talking about — the doctrine of an orthodox empire, of a *Katechon*, of Rome, of an emperor preventing the coming of the Antichrist — is fully established in the Eastern part of the Roman Empire (much later to be called the 'Byzantine' Empire).

Here also emerges the political doctrine of a normative 'symphony of powers', whereby the Orthodox emperor, a sacred figure endowed with the function of preventing the coming of the Antichrist, stands at the head of the holy state, and with him together is the patriarch (or several patriarchs) as the head of the Church. The emperor bases his rule on a collaboration with the head of the Church. The religious and imperial authorities, represented by the patriarch and the emperor, act in perfect harmony because the Church is not just some addition to the empire, but that force which changes the very essence of the empire. Thus we again encounter the Platonic figure of the Philosopher King, the sacred ruler, only in this case this figure is divided into two 'inseparable and unmerged' (like the two natures in Christ) poles, constituting the essence of the 'symphony of powers'.

In its turn, the empire is not just an instrument of the Church, it is something transformed by the rays of faith in Christ; a space where 'sacred' ('sacral') politics is established. From the Christian point of view, imperial politics is sacred; in its context, every person who carries out the political instructions of a superior is doing not just a civic duty, but a *religious* one.

When the Church becomes inseparable from the state, the state itself becomes part of the Church. Therefore political decisions and political institutions are not simply rational mechanisms — they become moral soteriological instruments. A man who governs well or a man who governs badly does not simply pass a technical examination of his competence, much less exercise his personal will to power — he either sins or exercises virtue. At the same time, the scale of the emperor's sins and virtues far exceeds that of ordinary citizens — the emperor is granted much, but much is also asked of him. Therefore the very rule of the empire takes on a cosmic and, moreover, spiritual dimension. The Christian emperor acts in the earthly world on behalf of Christ's Heavenly Kingdom, carrying out the will of Heaven on earth.

In the east of the Roman Empire the idea of holy politics is preserved in its original form. In the west, from the first centuries of the Byzantine Empire, a gradual retreat from this standard began. This occurs against the background of the increasing political autonomy of the western lands, their distance from the capital of the empire and the gradual takeover of these territories by the pagan peoples. The Western Roman Empire begins to tremble and crumble under the blows of the barbarians.

The barbarians are establishing a completely different political system there. Its main difference is that the barbarians do not build an empire, but ordinary states, totally detached from soteriology, eschatology, the katechonic mission and the doctrine of the universal kingdom. In each part of the fragmented Western Roman Empire appears its own king, whose polities (πολιτεία) are arranged according to the traditions of the bellicose — above all Germanic — tribes and tribal alliances. Here there is no figure of the emperor. These peoples still nominally recognise the Byzantine emperor as the supreme ruler, but they are already building an entirely different political system. It is qualitatively different from the katechonic Byzantine system. Each ruler finds himself in his polity as a sovereign lord, and acts in the interests of his power and the ruling class, on which he relies. Politics here ceases to be sacred, at least in the sense in which it was sacred in Rome — before and after the adoption of Christianity.

In the new political system, the unity of the Western Roman Empire is no longer ensured by the emperor (as in the Eastern Roman Empire), but by the pope.

The 'Unholy Politics' Model

Thus an entirely new model of 'unholy politics' takes shape, the precursor of which can be seen in the theory of the 'two cities'[11] of St. Augustine (354–430). Instead of the Aristotelian idea of a phenomenal empire, St. Augustine proposes a theory more reminiscent of Plato. He formulates the doctrine of 'two cities', the city of heaven and the city of earth, which are at war with each other. The earthly city lies in evil, the heavenly city is the city of the saints at war with the city of the damned.

---

11 St. Augustine, *City of God*.

In this we can see the origin of a very different political philosophy from the Byzantine sacred (symphonic and katechonic) politics. Here, a holy ideal city and an unholy dark earthly city are established, between which there is not harmony, symphony, i.e. 'harmony' (as in Byzantium), but opposition. It is this teaching of St. Augustine that forms the basis of the political system which is familiar to us as Catholic political philosophy.

Initially, the Christian political philosophy which we spoke of earlier also prevailed in the west of the Roman Empire, but gradually, as the destinies of the western and eastern parts of the Roman Empire diverged, it survived only in Byzantium, where it existed until its end, while in the west a new political philosophy based on the *opposition* between Church and State was formed. While a *synthesis* was established in Byzantine political philosophy, Catholic political philosophy saw a *separation* of the two.

In such a situation, the pope, who was the only authority ensuring the ideological and cultural unity of the Western Roman Empire, begins to be identified as the earthly representative of the 'city of saints', the heavenly city, while secular kings, princes and other rulers, as well as the polities (πολιτεία) created by them on the ruins of the Western Roman empire, find themselves positioned as the 'city of the damned'. This is how the idea of a spiritual war between Catholicism (the Roman throne) and the political systems of the barbarian rulers emerges.

Thus in the dualism of the 'two cities' appears something that goes beyond the classical Roman tradition — there appears a political phenomenon that is itself devoid of sacredness, i.e. 'unholy'. And in order to give this phenomenon legitimacy, it is necessary to subordinate it to the will of the pope and the Catholic Church as the institution that provides the link with the 'city of heaven'. In the Eastern Empire, 'sacrality' is inherent in imperial politics as such. In the western part of the Empire, this sacredness disappears, and only a non-political institution — the Catholic Church — can restore it, albeit only partially.

The Papacy. Usurpation of the Empire by Charlemagne

This is how two political philosophies gradually emerged in the once united Christian world (the Christian ecumene):

1) a core 'katechonic' philosophy which continues to exist in Byzantium, in the eastern part of the Roman empire and

2) a new dualistic philosophy of 'two cities', systematically taking root in the realm of the gradually disintegrating Western Roman Empire.

If we look at these models from the point of view of the philosophical-political paradigms we analysed earlier, we can say the following: initially, Christianity is dominated by the Aristotelian idea of the Roman Empire, but the Western Roman Empire gradually adopts a dualistic political Platonism, where the models are set against their copies (the earthly city against the heavenly city).

In history, this has been called 'Caesaropapism'[12] and 'Papocaesarism'.[13] Caesaropapism is the Eastern, Byzantine model, in which the emperor is not just a political, secular ruler, but also a spiritual authority preventing the arrival of the Antichrist. Papocaesarism is a Catholic model in which, by contrast, any political figure is seen as a strictly secular, non-sacred, and even a knowingly 'sinful' ruler, above whom stands the sinless and holy pope.

Aristotelianism and Platonism thus take on somewhat antagonistic implications within Christian political philosophy. This continues from the fourth to the early ninth century.

But since there is only one emperor (nominally recognised even by the West) in the Christian ecumene until the ninth century, it can be said that during this period the entire Roman Empire still formally exists as a single political-religious space with a common political philosophy. At a certain point in Byzantium, Empress Irene (c. 752–803) comes into power, while in the West important changes occur — a mighty king from the Carolingian dynasty, Charlemagne (748–814) unites under his rule numerous

---

12 Also Caesarepapism — from Latin caesar and Latin papa, 'pope'.
13 Formed of the same words in reverse order.

Germanic tribes and becomes almost the sole ruler of the previously fragmented lands of the Western Roman Empire.

So simultaneously in the East the dynastic power ends up in the hands of a woman (which was unusual for patriarchal Roman society), and the western, previously fragmented, half of the Roman Empire is united under the powerful and courageous king of the Franks. In this situation Charlemagne decides to become emperor. According to some sources, he first wanted to achieve this through a dynastic marriage with the Byzantine Empress Irene. The plan was that if he married Irene, he would become sovereign emperor of both East and West, and the Roman Empire would be recreated in its ecumenical unity. Charlemagne sends emissaries to Irene, but the empress refuses. Following her fatal decision, Charlemagne announces that he denies her the imperial title and is prepared to proclaim himself emperor. The pope anoints Charlemagne to the throne according to the ancient practice by which the patriarchs of Constantinople anoint the Byzantine emperors. The coronation of Charlemagne takes place.

Thus, in the space of the still nominally united Christian empire, two katechons, two emperors, arise at once—Charlemagne in the Western Roman Empire and Empress Irene in the Eastern Roman Empire.

Constantinople does not recognise the coronation of Charlemagne.

Significantly, in parallel with his claim to imperial status, Charlemagne goes on to recognise *Filioque* (the dogmatic addition to the Niceno-Constantinopolitan creed of a formula concerning the Third Person of the Trinity, the Holy Spirit, as 'proceeding from the Father and the Son').[14] By introducing Filioque and crowning Charlemagne as emperor, Western Christianity had separated itself from Constantinople. This is how a second katechon emerged in the Christian ecumene.

---

14 In the Orthodox version, the Holy Spirit comes only from the Father. The addition to the creed of the formula 'also of the Son' (Latin Filioque) gave the impression to Orthodox theologians that the West had adopted the model of subordinationism, that is the hierarchical subordination of the Persons of the Holy Trinity, which was rejected as heresy.

Byzantium rejected both, declaring Filioque a heresy and not recognising the imperial status of the Carolingian king. From the perspective of Byzantine political philosophy, a usurpation took place. Here the tension between the Christian East and the Christian West, which had been building up well before, reached its limits, leading to a final schism in 1054.

It should be noted that in the case of Charlemagne, the West acted according to the original and common view of Christian *political philosophy*. The Carolingian ruler was well aware that the only legitimate political form for Christians (and the Franks were among the first to embrace Orthodox Christianity)[15] was the Holy Roman Empire. One can only be the political ruler of all Christians as emperor, however vast the power of one or another ruler may be. The Franks were able to retain their imperial status even later, which Constantinople — and Orthodoxy in general — never recognised. Charlemagne's state later came to be known as the Holy Roman Empire by the Germanic nations.

Two Political Philosophies: Orthodox and Catholic

In 1054 the final division of the churches took place, after which an excommunication happened: the Catholics called the Orthodox 'Eastern schismatics' and the Orthodox declared the Catholics to be representatives of the 'Latin heresy' or 'papal heresy'.

Strictly from this point on, there are two political forms — two political philosophies that prevailed in the two parts of the once united Christian world. On the one hand was the Orthodox philosophy of the Political, on the other, the Catholic one. These two models continued to dominate for many centuries, and in part retain their influence in Western and Eastern Christianity up to the present day. One could say that political Platonism in its dualistic, rigidly antagonistic version, opposing the City of Heaven (the Church) and the City of Earth (the state and its ruler), became dominant in Western Europe. This was finally consolidated for the West in the victory of the Guelph party (the Papocaesarist side) in opposition to the Ghibellines, supporters of imperial power (the heirs of

---

15   Many other Germanic tribes — above all the Goths — were inclined towards Arianism, a heresy already rejected at the First Council of Nicaea.

Charlemagne and above all of the Hohenstaufen dynasty). Thus the West became the territory of Papocaesarism. In the East the original Caesaropapist, katechonic imperial principle of Christianity remained unchanged, and remained predominant until the end of the Byzantine Empire. From the latter it passed on to the other Orthodox peoples — the Bulgarians, the Serbs and finally the Russians, who at various stages declared themselves continuers of the Byzantine Empire (from which the ideology of Moscow, the Third Rome, derives).

Thus two political philosophies emerged within the unified Christian religion: the Orthodox and the Catholic. The first predetermined the normative structure in the politics of the Eastern Church, the second in the politics of the Western Church.

Wandering Rome Reaches Moscow

In 1452, the history of Byzantium comes to an end. The Byzantine Empire falls to the Ottoman Turks and is replaced by the Ottoman Empire, where Islam and its corresponding political philosophy become the predominant religion. At different points in time, a number of Orthodox nations already had the intention of succeeding Byzantium. This was the case during the golden years of the First and Second Bulgarian kingdoms.[16] In the fourteenth century, the Serbian rulers grew considerably stronger, establishing a powerful state that successfully competed with the weakening Byzantine Empire. Thus the Serbs also dreamt of becoming the Third Rome. These claims by Slavic Orthodox rulers, as they reached power and prosperity at various moments, were based on the concept of a 'wandering Rome'.

The idea was this: in the historical and geographical context of the Fourth Universal Kingdom (the Roman Kingdom of Iron), the centre of the Empire (i.e. Rome) could shift. It is important that the First Rome is not the Catholic Rome of the popes, but Rome as the capital of the pre-Christian Roman Empire, the seat of the emperor. With the acceptance of

---

16 Александр Дугин, *Ноомахия. Восточная Европа. Славянский Логос: балканская Навь и сарматский стиль* (Moscow: Академический проект, 2018). [Alexander Dugin, *Noomakhia. Eastern Europe. Slavic Logos: Balkan Navi and Sarmatian style.*]

Christianity, this Rome moved to the Second Rome, or New Rome, which became Byzantium. Therefore, the status of 'Rome' could move again as Byzantium weakened — to those Orthodox peoples who proved to be worthy of it.

This idea of a 'wandering Rome' became particularly relevant when Byzantium finally fell to the Ottoman Turks. Accordingly, the notion that this time Rome had 'migrated' to those Orthodox nations and states which had remained independent was inescapable.

Among all the Orthodox kingdoms at this point only one managed to retain its imperial scale, independence and Orthodox faith — that of the Russian state, Muscovite Russia.[17] It was then that the Russians declared themselves the Third Rome, while the Bulgarians, Serbs and even Romanians, who had previously claimed this status, found themselves under the rule of the Ottoman Empire. Moscow, as the Third Rome, assumed the mission of katechon. The doctrine of a normative political system was transferred to Muscovite Russia. Perhaps that is why Aristotle, the brightest thinker of the 'real empire', is depicted on some of the ancient frescoes in Russian churches. Sacred politics moves to the Third Rome, and Russian rulers, beginning with Ivan the Terrible (1530–1584), become not just grand dukes, but *vasilevs* (Greek Βασίλειος), emperors. Awareness of the new significance of Muscovite Russia began as early as under Ivan III (1440–1505), when the doctrine of 'Moscow as the Third Rome'[18] was finally formulated. During the reign of Ivan IV, the Byzantine ritual of anointing the Russian tsar was adopted. Since then, the Russian tsar became a katechon, the Russian Empire a 'Rome', and the Russian people a part of a holy politics, where — at least according to religious and political philosophy — every action of every individual acquired a soteriological character. This found expression in the theory of the 'draught state'.

---

[17] Александр Дугин, *Ноомахия. Русский историал. Народ и государство в поисках субъекта* (Moscow: Академический проект, 2019). [Alexander Dugin, *Noomakhia. Russian Historial. The People and the State in Search of a Subject.*]

[18] It was written by the monk Philotheus of the Pskov-Pechersk Monastery (c. 1465–1542).

Glimmers of the Katechon

The end of the Muscovite period is associated with processes of desacralisation, which culminated in an ecclesiastical schism. The official Church and state followed the countries of the West, which had already entered the New Age, into the paradigm of modernity. The Old Believers[19] were the most consistent proponents of the Moscow as Third Rome ideology, but they were defeated and found themselves in the position of a persecuted minority. The Old Believers clung to the norms of Old Russia, which predetermined their total rejection of religious reforms that were later followed by political innovations.

This was most clearly felt during the reign of Peter the Great (1672–1725), who began to restructure the political and church system along the lines of Western European — above all Protestant — monarchies.

Although he departed from the basic Orthodox political philosophy embodied in the principle of the symphony of powers (Peter abolished the patriarchate by transferring power over the Church to a secular official, the chief procurator of the Synod), distant echoes of Eastern Christian politics have survived in later eras. This was especially noticeable in the nineteenth century, when Russian tsars and the intellectual elite (primarily Slavophiles) once again put the mission of defending Christian truth at the centre of their attention and rethought the role that the theory of Moscow as the Third Rome had played in Russian history. Alexander the First (1777–1825) proclaimed the 'Holy Alliance', an attempt to give politics a sacred — Christian — dimension in order to unite the Christian nations in the face of advancing secularism, atheism, and political Modernity in general.

The shadow of sacred politics — the idea of the empire as a mission, the religious function of the Russian state, the Russian tsar acting as the Withholder, the one who prevents the coming of the 'son of perdition' — lies right up to the Soviet period of Russian history.

---

19 Alexander Dugin, *Noomakhia. Russian Historial. The People and the State in Search of a Subject.*

It may be noted that, for an Orthodox person, the only legitimate form of political existence is precisely a sacred Christian empire. The Catholics have a somewhat different view: for them — in accordance with the political philosophy of Catholicism — the most important thing is obedience to the pope.

From the point of view of a fully-fledged Christian politics (both Orthodox and Catholic), the idea of the separation of Church and State is inherently anti-Christian and even symbolic of the Antichrist. Political modernity, which attempts to build its political philosophy on the denial of the sacred character of the empire, and of politics as a whole, can be nothing but an 'anomaly', an unnatural, perverted form of state, a 'bad state' in the eyes of the Christian. The worst examples of a state, according to Aristotle, are democracy and tyranny.

Protestantism and Democracy

In Western Christianity the Reformation began in the sixteenth century and led to another form of Christian political philosophy, the phenomenon of Protestantism.[20] Protestantism, standing in opposition to Catholicism, is at the same time an entirely Western phenomenon and inherits all the features that have historically divided Catholicism and Orthodoxy. Protestantism stands even further from Orthodoxy than Catholicism, although in the first phase of the Reformation some Protestant leaders sought an alliance with the Orthodox rulers, but these attempts did not achieve any further development.

How does Protestant political philosophy oppose its Catholic counterpart? For Catholics, the ultimate authority, as we have already noted, is the pope as the spiritual head of the Western Christian world. The Protestants in turn reject this authority, abolish the doctrine of the two cities, attack Saint Augustine and political Platonism, and for the first time in history

---

20 Александр Дугин, *Ноомахия. Германский Логос. Человек Апофатический.* (Moscow: Академический проект, 2015) [Alexander Dugin, *Noomakhia. The Germanic Logos. Apophatic Man.*]; Ibid., *Ноомахия. Англия или Британия? Морское могущество и позитивный субъект* (Moscow: Академический проект, 2015). [*Noomakhia. England or Britain? Maritime Power and Positive Subjectivity.*]

introduce an entirely new model of political system based on the *individual*, which had not previously existed in Christendom.[21]

Protestantism within the Western Christian Church substantiates the doctrine of democracy — i.e. the worst and lowest type of government (according to Aristotle). In Protestant ecclesiastical democracy, the clergy, the celibacy of the monks, the authority of the priests and the transmission of the apostolic blessing, i.e. all those sacred components which in the West are still preserved in Catholicism, are denied. Believers themselves are able to create any denominations based on a contractual acceptance of this or that interpretation, which completely abolishes the very idea of the Church as created from the top down — from God to men, from heaven to earth.

Out of the vertical model emerges a kind of horizontal religiousness, where there is a transcendent God and an individual who builds his personal model of a relationship with this God, ignoring all mediating institutions. In fact, such a view of religion brings to the forefront the human rationality, the human individual who is by himself outside the Church (unlike Catholics) and outside the empire, outside sacred politics (unlike the Orthodox) and takes it upon himself to judge what is right and wrong, that is, to 'establish' the Church and, accordingly, to create a political regime that meets his needs and interests. This is an act of radical desacralisation of Christian teaching as a whole, including its political dimension.

Protestantism — a Revolution against Vertical Thinking

Protestantism represents an unprecedented step in Christian history in a direction sharply divergent from both Platonism and Aristotelianism, from Catholicism and from Orthodoxy. It is in fact a break from the whole tradition of Christian politics, which continues, as we have seen, the Greco-Roman patterns. There is neither explicitly sacred politics (Caesaropapism) nor religious Platonic politics (Papocaesarism).

---

21 Louis Dumont, *Essays on Individualism* (Chicago: University of Chicago Press, 1986).

Protestantism represents a religious revolution against the authority of the Church. In fact, it denies the thesis of the Church as a community of the elect, whose pastors have direct apostolic succession.

Directed primarily against the pope, Protestantism carries with it a fundamentally new political philosophy. This political philosophy has to do with the self-organisation of separate individual groups.

Protestantism begins a struggle simultaneously with the empire (Western) and with the Catholic Church. It is essentially a rejection of both political Platonism and political Aristotelianism. It is a revolt of the matter, of the plebs, a revolt of the mob against the qualified majority, against the clergy, against the priesthood, and against the nobility and aristocracy.

This is the bourgeois revolution, or Protestant ethics.[22] In fact, this is how an entirely new *bourgeois political philosophy* emerges, which is a direct product of the Protestant religious reform. Capitalism and the bourgeois order grow in Protestant Europe as a direct consequence of it. Protestantism as a religious phenomenon carries with it the political idea of an anti-sacral, anti-imperial and anti-church democracy, where all decisions are made on the basis of individual reflection of a single member of society.

Thus, a new subject emerges — not a chosen people (as in Judaism), not the Church, and not the Christian Empire (as in Catholicism and Orthodoxy), but the individual, who henceforth becomes the source and measure of legitimacy in religious and political matters.

The Three Political Philosophies of Christianity and the Assumption of a Fourth Model

So, we have briefly considered three types of Christian political philosophy:

1) the political philosophy of Orthodoxy (Caesaropapism, symphony of powers, catechism, the Holy Empire),

---

22 See Max Weber, *The Protestant Ethic and the Spirit of Capitalism*.

2) the political philosophy of Catholicism (Papocaesarism, two cities, supremacy of the Holy See over 'sinful' politics) and

3) the political philosophy of Protestantism (which denies superhuman authority and considers the individual, capable of determining his relations with God and the people around him, as the main criterion).

Here it is appropriate to recall that Christian thought theoretically allows for a fourth type of political philosophy, which is in direct opposition to Christianity altogether. We could nominally call it the 'political philosophy of the Antichrist'. Such a philosophy can be found in that state or other form of political organisation where the truth of Christianity is denied and the separation of Church and politics is normatively justified. In the eyes of the Christian, such a political system represents an anomalous eschatological phenomenon, leading to the assumption that the coming of the 'son of perdition', to which the traditional political model has been an obstacle, has taken place.

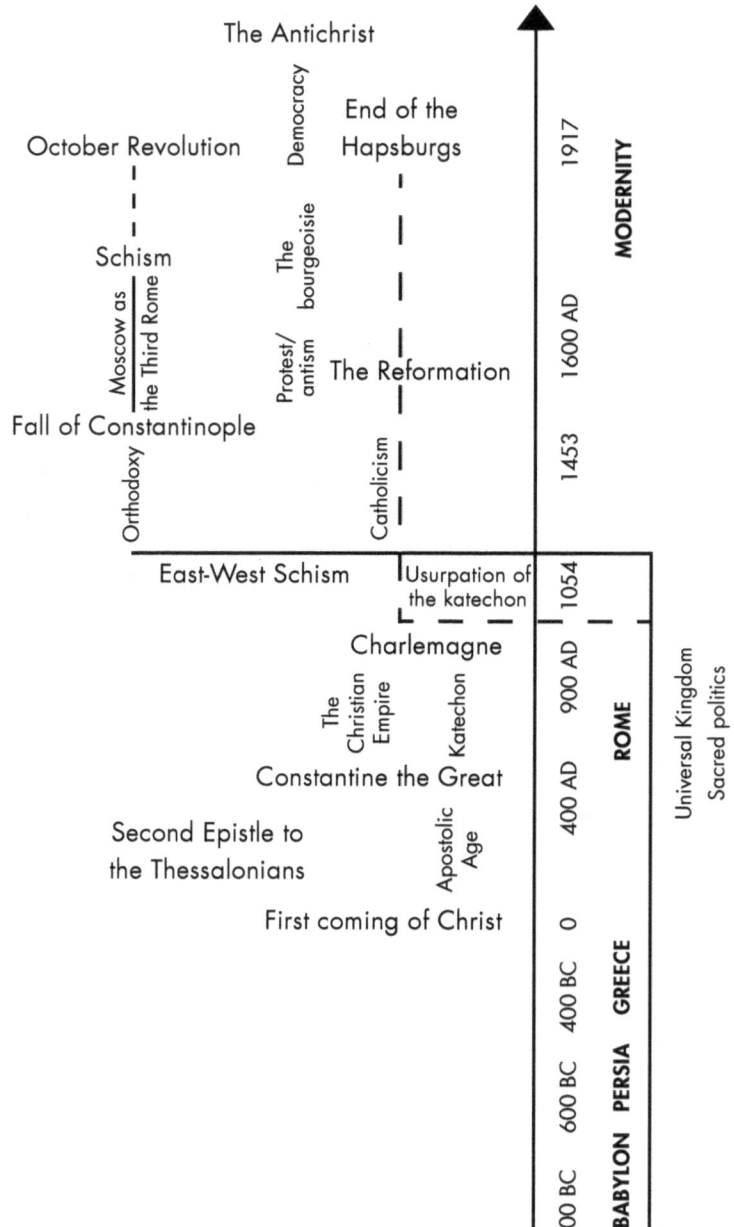

Figure 14. Christian history and the contexts of Christian political philosophy.

CHAPTER 7

THE POLITICAL PHILOSOPHY OF ISLAM

Radical Creationism

THE ISLAMIC RELIGION is based on the principle of radical creationism, embodied in the notion that there is no intermediary between God and the world (man). This is the essence of Islam. The central meaning of Islam is: 'God will not forgive the sin of considering something equal to Him.'[1] The act of establishing a co-creator of God, i.e. the denial of pure monotheism, is called *Shirk* (Arabic شرك, 'paganism', 'polytheism') in Islam, which is not only a religious, but also a *political* (within the Islamic system) crime of the utmost significance.

The point of Islam's strict creationism is that there is no intermediary and thus a relationship emerges of absolute domination of God over men: God appears as the unconditional, sole Lord of the world and men, a Lord who has no common ground with his slaves.

The term Islam (Arabic الإسلام) itself means 'submission' (to God), total humility before the Lord (Arabic بَر) and recognition of one's own nothingness before Him.[2] Thus, God and the world (man) are radically different metaphysical entities. God is All and man is nothing. God acts as the absolute scythe of death in relation to the world — God kills the world

---

1   Quran. Verse 4:116.
2   Alexander Dugin, *Noomakhia. Semites. Monotheism of the Moon and the Gestalt of Va'al.*

because the world is nothing in relation to God.[3] Between these two poles — insignificant man and absolute God — there is no middle ground. This is the fundamental meaning of the Islamic religion: one cannot put anyone or anything in any way between the absolutely insignificant man and the absolutely complete God.

Here we see a particular version of the transcendental relationship between God and man, more broadly between Creator and creation.[4] This relation is heightened to the extreme and represents an opposition: God is opposed to man and the world as a radical alternative, and all creation is forced to make a fundamental choice between submission to the Other or solidarity with that which is provided — with the fact of existence. Thus the Platonic dualism of the 'ideal state' takes on a conflicted character here, and the two poles, the paradigmatic and the phenomenological ontology of the *Timaeus*, find themselves in profound opposition.

This is the basis of Islam's critique of what is called *jahiliyya* (Arabic جاهلية), or 'polytheism'.[5]

Shirk

Polytheism implies 'considering something equal to God', the assertion of some equal or *intermediate* instances between God and the world (man), and therefore for Islam polytheism represents a metaphysically completely false model of philosophy and ontology.

The main thrust of Islamic philosophy is directed against paganism and polytheism. Those who recognise the oneness of God are correct, true, submissive to a transcendent God (Muslims). Those who oppose the oneness of God, this absolute Personality that removes any possibility of autonomous ontology, are the bearers of evil, the rebels against God.

What evil, to what extent is it evil? Islam is clear: to the extent of the absolute necessity of the physical destruction of the polytheists.

---

3 Гейдар Джемаль, *Революция пророков* (Moscow: Ультра.Культура, 2003). [Geydar Dzhemal, *The Revolution of the Prophets*.]

4 Alexander Dugin, *Postphilosophy*.

5 Translator's note: The term more closely translates to 'Age of Ignorance', and is used to refer to the time before Islam in Arabic culture.

In the Quran, such a call exists explicitly:

> And kill (infidels) wherever you find them, and drive them out from whence they drove you out, and *fitnah* (heresy) is worse than slaughter by your hand.[6]

Elsewhere, this call is literally repeated as:

> They long that ye should disbelieve even as they disbelieve, that ye may be equal with them. So choose not friends from them till they forsake their homes in the way of Allah; if they turn away, then take them and kill them wherever ye find them.[7]

A person who does not recognise the oneness of God must be put to death. This is the norm in Islamic tradition. At least that is how the normative (Islamic) society should be.

The Political and Religious Anthropology of Islam. People of the Book and Their Status

Islamic theology is based on the idea of genocide according to the religious principle: all people who do not recognise the oneness of God (Allah) must be exterminated. An exception is made only for those called 'people of the Book' (Arabic الكتاب اهل — *Ahl al-Kitāb*) — Jews and Christians. From the Muslim perspective, Jews and Christians worship the same God as the Muslims themselves. This is the One God, the transcendent God, the creationist God. Jews and Christians are neither considered to be polytheists nor, therefore, guilty of *Shirk*, i.e. 'considering something equal to God'; accordingly, the people of the Book have the right to live.

And yet the Quran contains a substantial criticism of Jews and Christians, based on this most basic principle of the Islamic religion. Those who are pure pagans blatantly acknowledge equals of God. In turn,

---

6 Quran. Verse 2:191.
7 Quran. Verse 4:89. [Translator's note: The English translations have been chosen for their equivalence to Dugin's original text, and so they do not strictly follow one translation of the Quran but rather multiple.]

the 'People of the Book' ('Abrahamic traditions' — Judaism, Christianity and Islam) recognise the oneness of a transcendent God.

The Prophet Muhammad (571–632) is considered by Muslims to be the last prophet and the 'Seal of the Prophets'[8] (خَاتَمَ النَّبِيِّينَ), closing the cycle of prophets. Why, from a Muslim perspective, is the last Revelation of the monotheistic cycle necessary? Muhammad restores the fullness of the original Revelation, so we can say that Islam has always existed as an archetype (as pure paradigmatic monotheism): in the original form of the ancient Revelation, then in the form of Judaism, then in the form of Christianity, then Revelation was again restored to its fullness through the prophet Muhammad.[9]

Jihad: Either Islam or Paganism

Continuing this line of radical purification of the transcendent God from all intermediaries, insisting that the transcendent God and the immanent world (and man) have nothing in common and nothing transitional, the norm of religious genocide of polytheists (which is the leitmotif of Islamic history) is justified. We are talking about holy war, *jihad* (from Arabic الجهاد, 'effort', 'struggle') against the pagans, i.e. those who 'consider something equal to God'. All of Islamic history has been and continues to be marked by this.

Thus, religious philosophy in Islam is directly expressed in politics, as *jihad* appears as an expression of an underlying metaphysical truth. 'Why is it necessary to go to war with the pagans?' 'Because they deny the philosophical religious truth of the *oneness* of God.'

From the Muslim perspective, the pagans are wrong theologically, which means they must either submit to the Muslims and accept their views as correct, or be destroyed. This radical approach to religious philosophy has guided the political practice of Islam throughout its history.

The oneness of God (Allah) is directly linked to the theme of authority. Acknowledging the One God means acknowledging his authoritative

---

8   Quran. Verse 33:40.
9   Alexander Dugin, *Noomakhia. Semites. Monotheism of the Moon and the Gestalt of Va'al*.

status. To be a 'Muslim' (that is, literally 'humbled' in the sight of Allah) means not only to acknowledge God as the Creator of the world, but also as the supreme ruler. The Islamic religion at its very core already includes a *political* dimension, since power is first and foremost a political concept.

Where polytheism or other forms of society exist that refuse to recognise God (Allah) as the bearer of absolute power, there is a socio-political and cultural environment that is radically incompatible with Islam. It is either Islam or paganism (*Shirk, jahiliyya*). If Islam comes into contact with paganism, someone has to die (so from the point of view of a Muslim, but not from the point of view of a pagan, who does not take away a Muslim's right to believe in the only God while reserving the right to believe otherwise).

How, then, do Muslims view such a figure as Christ, i.e. the God-man (the mediator between the purely transcendent God and the world)? And what is their attitude towards the community of Israel, the Jewish people, who also regard themselves as the mediator? These two points — about the incarnation of God in Christian theology and the special sacred function of the chosen people in Judaism — are what the Quran accuses Christians and Jews of, distinguishing them fundamentally from Muslims. These groups recognise no gods other than the One God, so they are recognised as human, but they, from the Muslim perspective, violate precisely the purity of radical transcendentalism with these theological postulates, and hence are *between* heretics/polytheists and pure Islam. Jesus Christ is regarded by Muslims as one of the chain of prophets who preceded Mohammed, while the Jews are seen as one of the peoples who received the revelation, on an equal footing with others, but they are not considered 'the chosen' and are not fundamentally different from anyone else.

Attitudes towards Jews and Christians

Islam denies the dogma of the Holy Trinity, the incarnation of God in Christ — in whom Muslims see only a man, a prophet — and the belief of the Jews that they are a chosen people (Islam has no such concept as 'a people' at all). Jews and Christians are, from the point of view of Islam, 'non-Muslims' and consequently 'non-citizens', so in the political system they are subject to additional taxes (*jizya* — جِزْي), considerable restrictions on the exercise of certain functions in the state and various kinds of prohibitions on religious worship (for example, some Islamic countries prohibit crosses on Christian churches and virtually all Islamic countries do not allow the use of bells). In the political system of Islam, the 'people of the Book' have the status of *dhimmi* (Arabic ذمي), literally 'under protection', 'protected'. Similar formulas are applied in political philosophy to the category of people restricted in their rights, but not totally deprived of them.

Note the importance of theology here: the gradation of the three types of people in Islam (Muslims, 'non-Muslims', pagans), linked to the structure of the religious worldview, receives a purely political expression and predetermines the socio-political status.

A belief in the absolute transcendence of God constitutes a Muslim, which in Islamic politics guarantees full-fledged political status and citizenship. Recognition of the transcendence of God with some elements of mediation in the form of the incarnation of Christ or the concept of a chosen people puts *dhimmi* on a lower level (people who are 'under protection' of others, i.e. full citizens). Polytheists in general fall outside the entire political system, finding themselves in the position of outcasts — they are offered either to accept Islam or be destroyed. In practice, Muslims have not always been so harsh with polytheists, sometimes having to compromise and give them the 'right to live' in a marginal area of society. This was the case with Hindus and Buddhists in India, with Zoroastrians in Persia, with some archaic tribes in Africa that came under Muslim rule, etc. In terms of the full-fledged political philosophy of Islam, however, such 'softness' is already a deviation from the strict standard of exclusive monotheism.

The legal and juridical system of Islam thus reflects three precepts of the metaphysical relationship between the world and God.

A Global Islamic Political Empire

Islamic theology shapes not only the domestic politics of Islamic society, but also its foreign policy. This was originally the driving force behind Islamic expansion, when a small religious community of nomadic Arabs from the Arabian Peninsula spread its influence on a global scale, creating a huge centralised state, the Caliphate, built on the principles of Islamic religious philosophy.

Why should Muslims rule the world? Because the world is *already* ruled by the one transcendent God (Allah). Muslims' belief in this purely transcendent God, and moreover the recognition of Him as the only valid and legitimate Lord, entitles them to global planetary rule, moreover, makes it an obligation.

Christians and Jews are under the guardianship of Muslim rule until they become Muslims themselves.

At whose expense is this global Islamic political empire being built? At the expense of pagans (as well as materialists, atheists, agnostics) who must either be destroyed or converted to Islam. This is why Islamic religious philosophy carries inherently political universalism and justification for political expansion.

Of course, having found themselves in the context of other — non-Islamic — societies, built on principles different from Islamic philosophy, Muslims adapt to the existing conditions. But from the point of view of the completeness of the Islamic worldview, such a state of affairs is 'temporary', a kind of political (and even partly religious) compromise, which has easily observable limits.

Islam and Christianity in Architecture

Let us turn our attention to other aspects of the Islamic tradition. Architecture, for example. In *Understanding Islam*, Frithjof Schuon[10] (1907–1998), a Swiss traditionalist philosopher who embraced Islam in its mystical version (Sufism), describes the particularities of Islamic architecture. The concept of not presenting anything as equal to God is embodied

---

10 Frithjof Schuon, *Undestanding Islam* (Bloomington, Indiana: World Wisdom, 1998).

in the absence of roofs on Islamic buildings. The idea of flatness, of horizontality, which has no common measure with the vertical, is expressed in the very structure of the Islamic city. If we look at a traditional Islamic city, we see flat roofs, low buildings occasionally cut by tall, slender minarets (towers dedicated exclusively to God). This model of the Islamic polis reflects the essence of both Islamic religion and Islamic political philosophy.[11]

With God everything is vertical, with man everything is horizontal. There is no unity between the temple and the house. In the Christian tradition, on the contrary, the structure of the temple and the structure of the house are always linked in the roofs (there is a gradual and slow ascent from the horizontal to the vertical). The triangular roof of an ordinary dwelling (both rural and urban) symbolises the ascent of the many to the One. The very phenomenon of the roof (above all its shape, ridge, carved patterns, etc.) represents the deepest metaphysical element of the Christian world. In essence, every house is a little temple, a little church. The church is the big house and the house is the little church. And both aim towards heaven.

A completely different picture is presented when we consider Islamic architecture with the flat roofs of dwellings for ordinary people and the minarets pointing up into the sky. Two different metaphysics, two different architectures, two different societies.

The Absence of Priesthood in Islam

In Islamic teaching, all human beings are fundamentally equal. This equality leads to the Islamic tradition's abrupt refusal to recognise the

---

11   Reza Negarestani, a contemporary American philosopher (of Iranian origin) and supporter of 'speculative realism', gives a similar theological and political interpretation of the aversion of modern radical Salafist Muslims, who preach a return to original Islam, to all vertical structures and objects in general. In the spirit of Negarestani's own philosophy, he interprets this as a longing for the subterranean realms, the interior of the earth, the heart of ultimate poverty, nothingness, as the main property of the creation in the Islamic version of creationism — the most radical among other versions of monotheism. Reza Negarestani, *Cyclonopedia: Complicity with Anonymous Materials* (Melbourne: Re.Press, 2008).

status of priests.¹² In Islam there are no priests, there is no consecration to the priesthood, and the *mullah* whom we sometimes mistakenly perceive as a priest is none other than a scholarly Muslim who has only received special training. This is in stark contrast to the Christian priesthood, where the priest receives the special ordination of the Holy Spirit that comes from the Apostles, and is in fact considered to be a person endowed with a special status.

For a Muslim, there is no difference between a common believer, a political leader of Islam and a mullah. They are all ordinary people. And if someone says that he has greater reason to suppose that he is closer to God than others, he will find himself in the position of one who considers God to have an equal (i.e. himself) and thus becomes a bearer of shirk and thereby brings a death sentence on himself.

There is a fundamental equality among Muslims; Islam rejects any anthropological caste differentiation. It is important to note that, for Muslims, even Muhammad, whom they hold in high esteem — along with the other prophets — is merely human. Muhammad is neither God nor angel, but only a human being, though chosen amongst other human beings to receive the revelation of the absolute transcendence of God.

That is why the landscape of Islam is only flat roofs, only dust, only decay, only death. The Islamic world is a world of principled death.¹³ Everything that happens in Islamic society is a movement *within the realm of death*, because only God is alive and only God is an individual (while everyone else is not an individual, they are not alive, they do not possess being, and at most they can be submissive). What is a Muslim? He is a submissive, bowed down, prostrate man. He sees himself neither as God, nor as a son of God. He is only a creature, but unlike other creatures he possesses the knowledge of the existence of the absolute God, the creator of heaven and earth and humbly accepts His absolute power.

Such a model departs from the traditional pyramidal state structure described by Plato and Aristotle. The radicalisation of the relationship

---

12   Geydar Dzhemal, *The Revolution of the Prophets*.
13   Гейдар Джемаль, *Дауд vs Джалут (Давид против Голиафа)* (Moscow: Социально-политическая мысль, 2011). [Geydar Dzhemal, *Daud vs Jalut (David vs Goliath).*]

between Creator and creation gives rise to a different model of the political Islamic state as a state based on anthropological equality (in contrast to Plato's ideal state with the dominance of the Philosopher King or Aristotle's phenomenal empire, where various forms of power or a combination of several types are permitted).

Islam and Politics: Dispute is War

In Islam we can trace the lack of distinction between religion and politics more clearly than anywhere else. Islam does not think of itself as *only* a religious or *only* a political phenomenon. Islam makes no distinction between religion and politics. If the power belongs to God, then those who *correctly* revere this God should rule. The struggle for faith in a theological dispute and the struggle of Muslims against non-Muslims in a military sense are strictly *one and the same*.

There is no separation between theological dispute and war. Dispute is war, war is dispute. *Muslims see the affirmation of their metaphysics in concrete political action.* Theology and politics are one and the same. In the Quran we find not only explanations about heaven and hell, the creation of the world and man, sacred history and religious norms, but also advice about the orderly organisation of human life, relations in the community (*Ummah*, أمة), the handling of livestock, hygiene and so on.

In this way the Quran is fundamentally different from the Gospel. The Gospel says nothing about how to organise the political and social spheres (Christians took their socio-political model from the Roman Empire). The Quran presents a completely different picture — it is full of political, social, economic, moral and even everyday attitudes that predetermine both the political system and the government, the norms of the organisation of the community and the forms of warfare. Here we see the complete unity of the religious and the political.

It is therefore totally unacceptable for a real Muslim to consider Islam only as a religion. This is the meaning of *Sharia* (Arabic شريعة), which originally meant 'manner of action', but in Islam has acquired the meaning of a legal framework for society. Sharia is a legitimate model of the Political that organically combines the theological norms, the structures of obligatory religious practice, the foundations of the political system, and the principles of economy, morality, culture and everyday behaviour that are deemed necessary to comply with. Religion and socio-political structure are regulated in Sharia with equal rigidity and unambiguity. For a Muslim, only Sharia is an acceptable and justifiable form of social organisation, which, in addition to religious worship, necessarily includes everything else.

The Caliphate

In its purest form, *Islam recognises no society other than Islamic society*, and the entire history reflected in the Quran, and indeed the entire history of Islamic conquests, is linked directly to this. In the beginning there was the struggle of Mohammed and the community of those loyal to him against the Arab pagans.[14] This later developed into the planting of Islam among the surrounding peoples. The impulse to combine religion with politics, the unconditional assertion that Muslims must rule over all non-Muslims, and the call for the destruction of polytheists — all this had a huge explosive effect in the era of Mohammed, in the late seventh and early eighth centuries. And in the course of just a few decades, during the eighth century, a giant Islamic empire was formed. In this empire everyone either accepts Islam, finds themselves in the position of dhimmi ('People of the Book'), or is destroyed. We see the building of the first Arab Caliphate as a complete, brutal assertion of the foundations of Islamic theology, reflected in the Quran and derived from the main tenet of Islamic religion (the absolute transcendence and oneness of the Creator).

The first Arab Caliphate, founded during Muhammad's lifetime, was a model for the practical application of Islamic teachings and their realisation. Throughout the centuries that followed, this was considered the norm for Muslims. History then, of course, threw Muslims into new circumstances. By no means have they been able to behave as rigidly and consistently (aggressively) everywhere and at all times. Nor have they

---

14 Alexander Dugin, *Noomakhia. Semites. Monotheism of the Moon and the Gestalt of Va'al.*

succeeded in always following their original line flawlessly. But wherever such an opportunity arose, this approach prevailed: a fusion of religion and politics and a direct implementation of creationist metaphysics, embodied in the political power of Muslims, without any intermediary instances.

Thus, Islamic history in its internal — paradigmatic — dimension represents the *eternal* struggle against *jahiliyya* ('polytheism', *Shirk*), the *eternal* capture of Medina and Mecca by those loyal to Mohammed (which symbolically means the struggle against pagans, against all non-Muslims), and the establishment of Islamic power in all historically accessible territory. It is a model, a kind of 'ideal type' of society (according to Max Weber), which under favourable historical circumstances also becomes 'normal' (according to Ferdinand Tönnies). The notion of the Islamic religion, embodied in the Islamic political system and historically fixed in the Arab Caliphate, is for Muslims the *absolute height of the Political*.

House of Islam and House of War

Modern Islamic theorists (mainly theorists of pure Islam)[15] have proposed the theory of the 'three houses'. Where the rules which we have spoken of are observed, i.e. where Shariah law is established, there is the 'house of Islam' (Arabic: *Dar al-Islam*, دار الإسلام). That area where there is no Dar al-Islam is called *Dar al-Kufr*[16] (دار كفر), 'house of disbelief' or 'house of shaitan' (دار شيطان) — because any non-Islamic society is a 'Satanic society'. A Muslim who lives in the house of Islam must be peaceful, law-abiding and humble. He is in his own territory, and any deviation from Sharia law is both a moral sin and a social crime, which must inevitably be punished accordingly.

In contrast, a Muslim who lives in a house of disbelief should turn that house into a 'house of war' (*Dar al-Harb* — دار الحرب). Thus, if a Muslim

---

15 According to the Iraqi scholar Majid Khadduri (1909-2007), this theory took its basic shape around 732, following the defeat of the Umayyad Caliphate at the Battle of Poitiers, which halted the advance of the Islamic conquests in Europe. See Majid Khadduri, *War and Peace in the Law of Islam* (Baltimore: Johns Hopkins Press, 1955).

16 The term *kufr* (كفر) means 'disbelief', 'concealing (the truth)', etc. Hence *kafir* — 'disbeliever', 'one who does not believe'.

lives in an Islamic society, he is a good and law-abiding citizen. Once that same Muslim is transferred to a non-Islamic society, he becomes a centre of terrorist activity and turns the house of shaitan into a house of war — in order to sooner or later destroy polytheists (*jahiliyya*) or subdue People of the Book (because Christians and Jews — normally — must also be in a subordinate position to Muslims, that is, have the status of dhimmi under 'protection').

Of course, most Muslims today do not think this way and do not adhere to such courses of action, but throughout world history there have been Islamic tendencies that have returned again and again to the original Islam and sought to build the same caliphate and to reproduce the same logic. Today it is a minority of Muslims; nevertheless, the basis of the Islamic religion itself, the basis of the religious philosophy and theology of Islam, and the basis of the political system of Islam contain this very principle. Therefore, there is always the possibility that some group of Muslims will decide to return to the original model and turn the house of lies (Dar al-Kufr) into the house of war (Dar al-Harb). From this arises a corresponding system of action against societies that do not coincide with Islamic norms.

In the full sense, such a strict ideology did not dominate for long. Muslims lived under such a law for several decades, during the era of the formation of the first Arab Caliphate.[17] There were no hereditary rulers of the Ummah at that time — the most courageous and gifted were chosen from Muhammad's followers; there were no national states and no priesthood. It was a society of radical, militant and religious egalitarianism, the *jamaat* (Arabic جماعة, 'society', 'collective', 'community'), men's fraternities essentially engaged in warfare with atheists, polytheists and Christians (at that time the Jews were not an independent political force). However, this idea received theoretical formulation at the next stage, during the Umayyad Caliphate,[18] when some departures from the original model of the Muhammadan military-religious community had already taken place.

---

17 Alexander Dugin, *Noomakhia. Semites. Monotheism of the Moon and the Gestalt of Va'al.*

18 Majid Khadduri, *War and Peace in the Law of Islam.*

In general, the 'three houses' theory is now widely used by theorists and practitioners of Salafism and Wahhabism, radical fundamentalists and other groups. This is the basis for political projects of extremist organisations such as al-Qaida (القاعد), Hizb ut-Tahrir (حزب التحرير), the Islamic State (also known as Daesh — داعش),[19] etc.

Shiism and Its Philosophy

Under the third caliph, Uthman ibn Affan (574–656), a *fitna* (Arabic فتنة, 'turmoil') begins, a civil war within Islam. At this point there is a division into two profoundly different tendencies in Islam — Sunni and Shiite. During this civil war, an alternative pole emerges — the cousin of the Prophet Mohammed, married to his daughter Fatima (605–633) — Ali (599–661). A separate *Shia* party (Arabic شش) is beginning to form around him. شِيعَةٌ — literally 'party', 'group of adherents'. As politics in Islam is inextricably linked to religion, the struggle for power in the Arab Caliphate was inextricably and organically intertwined with theological issues and the problem of interpreting the Quran and the Islamic tradition in general.

This is how Shiism emerges as a particular strand of Islam. Shiism asserts that all the fundamental Islamic theses accepted by the Muslim *Ummah* (community) by this point are completely correct. Except for one fundamental thesis concerning legitimate political authority in Islamic society and, at the same time (inseparably from it), the question of supreme authority in the interpretation of Muhammad's legacy. The Shia, supporters of Ali, proclaimed that in addition to the figure of the prophet, Nabi (Arabic نبي), Muhammad, there is another fundamental figure — the interpreter, Wali (Arabic ولي, 'interpreter', 'protector', 'friend of God') who has the ultimate divine knowledge of the Quran and fundamental religious principles. Ali, the Prophet's cousin, is such an interpreter. Accordingly, the fundamental principle of equality on which Islamic philosophy is based is here violated or rather substantially corrected.

---

19 These organisations are officially banned in Russia and most states as terrorist organisations.

Thus a model of a completely different theology, a different religious philosophy, emerges, where another entity emerges between God and the world. Islam eliminates all instances between God and the world, while Shiism, recognising the adequacy of this elimination in relation to polytheists, and in part to Christians and Jews, again establishes some entity which appears to be more important than the common man. This is further developed in the theory of the *Imamat* (Arabic إمامة), which is an institution of rulers and loyal followers (Shiites), founded by the 'first Imam' Ali and later by his descendants, the 'holy Imams'.[20]

Thus Shiism establishes anthropological, ontological, soteriological, epistemological and political *inequalities*. 'All people are equal', the Shi'a argue, 'except the "holy Imams"'. All human beings are equal except the house of the Prophet Muhammad through his cousin and his daughter Fatima. Holy Imams are mediators between God and men, and only they know how to interpret the Quran and Islam correctly. That is, only they hold the keys of true interpretation, and only their interpretation is authentic. In a religious sense, a new authority arises. When asked how to understand the Suras of the Quran, how to understand the Hadith, the Shi'a answer is, 'As the holy Imams tell us'. Accordingly, the authority in a full-fledged Islamic society should belong to them. This community was founded by the prophet, the Nabi, who is considered the last in Islam. Therefore, he can have successors among the prophets, whose chain ends at Mohammed. In their place comes the chain of Wali interpreters, i.e. the Imamate.

Ali's opponents, the followers of Uthman, rejected the claims of the Shiites in both theology and politics. And military force was on their side. Thus a division developed between the Shiites, supporters of Ali and the Imamate, and the Sunnis, who relied on the interpretation of the Quran and the Sunnah (سنة — the sacred Islamic tradition). The Umayyad

---

20 Alexander Dugin, *Noomakhia. Semites. Monotheism of the Moon and the Gestalt of Va'al.*

caliphate was a Sunni caliphate and the supporters of Ali were a persecuted minority.[21]

Mahdi and the Culture of Waiting

Shiism is a deeply elitist ideology which permeates Islam and changes many aspects of it.[22] 'Elitist' in this case means that all people are equal, but there are those who are higher than all these equals — the holy Imams. Hence the idea of the political power of the Imams — only the Alids (Arabic العلويين), the Imams, can rule, and if there are none, the representatives of the holy Imams, who mediate no longer simply with God, but with the Imams as well, must rule. It is believed that the Last Imam (the Seventh Imam for the Ismailis, the Twelfth Imam for the Shiites) did not die, but went into hiding and will return at the end of time.

Hence a political 'culture of waiting' emerges. The Shiites wait for the coming of the Imam, and while he is gone, they are in the persecuted minority. They build their political system on the return of the holy Imam Mahdi. A new principled hierarchy, denied by Sunni Islam, is emerging, hence the dynastic succession of the Alids and the notion that religious interpretation should be based on the authority of the holy Imams.

An opposition arises between the status quo, in which the Sunnis have political and theological superiority, and the ideal state of the Shiites. It is resolved through the arrival of the Last Imam and his representatives. At the same time, waiting for the Mahdi must not be passive: his arrival must be brought closer by the struggle for Shiite truth — both religious and political. On this principle was founded the Fatimid Caliphate (909–1171), which for a time united under Shiite rule the Maghreb and Middle East, the Qarmatian state, and later Safavid Iran, founded in 1501 by Shiites, and the modern Islamic Republic of Iran.[23]

---

21 Alexander Dugin, *Noomakhia. Semites. Monotheism of the Moon and the Gestalt of Va'al.*

22 Henry Corbin, *Histoire de la philosophie islamique* (Paris: Gallimard, 1964).

23 Alexander Dugin, *Noomakhia. Iranian Logos. Light Warfare and the Culture of Waiting.*

Shiism and Iranian Influences

Thus, two parties emerge in the Islamic world, the *Sunnah and the Shi'a*. One (the Sunnis) stands for the original version of Islam, although since the Umayyad era it has undergone certain changes, which became even more evident in the Abbasid Caliphate (with Baghdad as its capital), while the other stands for the Shiite version.[24] Thus, a certain pole of *alternative metaphysics* emerges in Islam, which is immediately projected into *alternative politics*. Moreover, since we have seen that in Islam theology and politics are not separated, if the theological orientation is altered slightly (as in Shiism), the political structure changes as well.

These principles are true both for understanding the history of Islamic states in the period of traditional societies (premodernity), but in many respects they also influence the current state of affairs in the politics of Islamic societies. For example, modern Iran is in the full sense a Shiite state, and the modern leadership of Syria is also Shiite (the Alawites are one of the branches of Shiism).

There were two other fundamental elements that changed Islamic metaphysics and politics. The second element, along with Shiism, was a movement known as *spiritual Islam* or *intellectual Islam*. This movement began to develop during the Abbasid Caliphate and was centred almost exclusively on Iranians.[25]

The Muslim Arabs, the bearers of the first ideology (extreme Sunni), took over the Persian Sassanid Empire, carried out a genocide of the Zoroastrians and converted all those who remained to Islam. Thus, huge masses of a completely different Iranian culture, which had nothing in common with the Arabs and represented a different metaphysics, based on the principle of confrontation between Light and Darkness,[26] came under the Islamic influence (having accepted Islam, they immediately began to rethink it, based on their own deep philosophical models). An Iranian stratum was immediately formed around the first Shiites,

---

24 Ibid.
25 Henry Corbin, *Histoire de la philosophie islamique*.
26 Alexander Dugin, *Noomakhia. Iranian Logos. Light Warfare and the Culture of Waiting*.

supporters of Ali. The Iranians supported the Shiite version with great enthusiasm, because they saw in it many more similarities with their own pre-Islamic tradition. Gradually, Shiism became to a large extent almost a purely Iranian phenomenon.

Sufism — the Secret 'Religion of Love'

In Sunni Islam, another current developed in parallel, *Sufism*, which radically reinterpreted Islamic tradition in the spirit of Platonism and dualistic Iranian gnosis of light.[27] It was a very different Islamic philosophy. In essence, Islamic philosophy itself was created by Iranians.[28] For example, two of the greatest representatives of Islamic philosophy — Al-Farabi[29] (870–950) and Avicenna (980–1037) — were Iranians.

Iranian philosophy and Sufism represented a metaphysics based on the *metaphysics of mediation*. We have already ascertained that Islam categorically *denies* mediation. In turn, Sufism and spiritual Islam *affirm* mediation. For example, it is claimed that before Muhammad there was an eternal Light of Muhammad (Arabic نور محمدى), which resided between God and men and which manifested itself in the historical Muhammad. Accordingly, this Light connected God and the world, and those who partake of this Light are special beings, 'friends of God'. Again an anthropological differentiation emerges, dividing people into two types on grounds very similar to Platonism. 'Friends of God' are those who contemplate his Light, rising above the prejudices of the blind majority satisfied with only contemplating the play of shadows on the wall of the Platonic cave.

---

27 Henry Corbin, *The Man of Light in Iranian Sufism* (Omega Publications, 1994).
28 Alexander Dugin, *Noomakhia. Iranian Logos. Light Warfare and the Culture of Waiting*.
29 Al-Farabi is the author of a series of treatises on the 'ideal state', which generally repeat Plato's main line. In Islamic philosophy it was he who most comprehensively described the Kallipolis model. Al-Farabi, *On the Perfect State* (Oxford: Clarendon Press, 1985). In so doing he proposed building Islamic societies on this basis in specific political-historical circumstances, i.e. by harmoniously combining Plato's 'ideal type' with Aristotle's 'normal type'. Al-Farabi, *The Political Writings. Selected Aphorisms and Other Texts* (Ithaca: Cornell University Press, 2001).

Sufism is less politically explicit than Shiism. Sufis do not have a uniform doctrine of who should have power. They have not created their own political doctrine, but they do have the notion that Sufi sages, sheikhs, should direct political power. This can apply equally to Sunnis and Shiites. Consideration of the inner dimension of being, on which Sufis insist, is extremely useful if power is to be just, harmonious and spiritual. Also, for Sufis, there is no great problem with Muslims residing outside Islamic society. By following their own — internal — interpretation of the Islamic religion, they can adapt in any society, finding reflections of the one Truth everywhere. Thus Ibn Arabi[30] (1165–1240), the greatest philosopher of Sufism, wrote of a special 'religion of love', meaning the teachings of the Sufis:

> My heart has become capable of every form: it is a
>
> pasture for gazelles and a convent for Christian monks,
>
> And a temple for idols and the pilgrim's Kaaba and the
>
> Tables of the Torah and the book of the Quran.
>
> I follow the religion of Love: whatever way Love's
>
> Camels take, that is my religion and my faith.[31]

Madhhabs and States

Already in the Umayyad Caliphate, and the Abbasid Caliphate that followed it, the idea of dynastic succession of caliphs gradually began to take root, which was some deviation from the original egalitarianism of the Ummah. There was also a gradual infiltration of different ideas and attitudes into Islamic culture from those peoples who were under the power of Arabs, but who gradually strengthened their influence on the Arabian top. This is how juridical schools, madhhabs (Arabic مذهب), began to actively form in the Abassid Caliphate.

---

30 Alexander Dugin, *Noomakhia. Semites. Monotheism of the Moon and the Gestalt of Va'al.*

31 Ibn al-Arabi, *The Tarjumán al-Ashwáq: A Collection of Mystical Odes by Muhyiddīn Ibn al-'Arabī* (London: Royal Asiatic Society, Oriental. 1911).

The most widespread was the Hanafi madhhab (Arabic حنفية), which included local ethnic beliefs as one of the sources of law, something completely unthinkable for early Islam. Other madhhabs — above all the Hanbali (Arabic الحنبلي) — reflected attitudes more appropriate to specifically Arab nomadic societies. The Shiites created their own madhhab, the Ja'fari madhhab (Arabic جعفرى), which incorporated the political-religious ideas of the Imamate.[32]

Parallel to this was the pluralisation of a single Islamic space: various separate states began to emerge where Islam and Sharia law formally dominated, but local customs — including political and social structures — continued to hold importance to a large extent. The initial extreme metaphysical radicalism of the early caliphate increasingly succumbed to various local tendencies. In the Abbasid Caliphate, which succeeded the Umayyad Caliphate[33], these tendencies gained some foothold. Although the state was thought of as a religious ummah, it was, for the most part, becoming an independent entity.

The Political Landscape

The political history of Muslim societies is intimately linked to theology. Theology and politics are inseparable components of a single Islamic worldview. This fully confirms the basic thesis that politics is only one dimension of philosophy if we understand philosophy broadly to include religion and its inherent metaphysical worldview, i.e. theology. The political philosophy of Islam is shaped by how the Islamic religious worldview emphasises, understands or treats the relation of the world (man) to God, how radical or non-radical it is in pursuing the idea of no mediator, or conversely, how it expresses and describes an intermediate instance between God and the world. The entire political history of Islamic societies is inextricably bound up with theological attitudes within Islam. The same principle applies here as in the features of Islamic architecture noted by

---

[32] Alexander Dugin, *Noomakhia. Semites. Monotheism of the Moon and the Gestalt of Va'al.*

[33] Remnants of the Umayyad state survived, however, in north-west Africa and on the Iberian peninsula, where they persisted for several more centuries.

Shuon — the pattern of the political history of Islamic peoples and states is constructed according to the structures of metaphysical interpretation of the deepest and most fundamental theological questions. The nature of the attitude towards God, the interpretation of sacred texts, and this or that version of the sacred determine the way events, wars, conflicts, dynastic collisions, popular uprisings and social protests unfold. It should be noted that when we deal with Islamic society, we are in the paradigm of Tradition (premodern), and accordingly the transcendental dimension underlying Islamic religion and dogma should be considered as the most important and influential factor.

In order to understand what is happening in the Islamic world and how we should build relations with Muslims today, it is necessary to operate on theological principles.

Salafism and Wahhabism

In general, today we have several versions of political Islam:

- radical Islam, Salafism (and, as its extreme form, modern Wahhabism),
- political Shiism and
- a wide range of versions of traditional Islam.

Salafi Islam (from Arabic سلفية, 'predecessors') calls for a return to the ideals and norms of the first Arab Caliphate, the era of Muhammad himself and his followers. The political agenda here consists of a literal repetition of early Islamic history, including an uncompromising attitude towards 'infidels', a tightening of the application of Sharia law, the rejection of flexible forms of legal interpretation, and an implacable struggle against internal Islam (Sufism) and Shiism. The Salafists differ from the representatives of traditional Islam precisely because they view virtually all periods of Islamic history, with the exception of the earliest era, with suspicion. They see a departure from the 'ideal' ('norm') already under the Abbasids, not to mention the later periods.

In the eighteenth century an even more radical version of Salafism emerged in Saudi Arabia which denied any madhhabs at all (most Salafis do recognise the legitimacy of established Islamic legal forms — except for

Shiite ones): Wahhabism. Its founder was the preacher Muhammad ibn Abd al-Wahhab (1703–1792), who called on his followers to reject any interpretation of the Quran and the Sunna, taking everything strictly literally and returning to the era of the sixth-seventh centuries, down to the clothing, everyday life and every last detail.[34] With the Wahhabis, Salafist tendencies towards the 'purification of Islam' reached their logical limit, and the entire history of traditional Islam was subjected to radical criticism, being recognised as an aberration and hidden 'idolatry' (i.e. *Shirk*). An alliance of Wahhabi reformers with the political leaders of the Saud dynasty, who were the traditional rulers of the Arabian city of Ad Diriyah, laid the foundation for the future state of Saudi Arabia, which emerged with the support of the British on the wreckage of the Ottoman Empire.

Saudi Arabia and a number of neighbouring Arabian states are still strongholds of radical Salafism and its corresponding political philosophy. Ideologically similar to this current are such movements as the 'Muslim Brotherhood', which emerged in Egypt. In its extreme forms, this version of Islam is a justification for terrorism and various forms of political-religious extremism, which stem from a literal application of the 'three houses' principle. The Islamic State is one striking example of such a politico-religious model.

Contemporary Shiism

Modern Shiism is prevalent in the Islamic Republic of Iran, where a particular form of Shiite rule, called the 'state of the enlightened' (Arabic الفقيه ولاية — Wilayat al-Faqih), was established after the overthrow of the Shah's regime. It assumes that while the Last Imam is still in hiding, Shia sages are to rule on his behalf, constituting a hierarchy based on their depth of religious experience and breadth of Islamic knowledge. The highest rulers are the ayatollahs (آية الله, the highest rank among the interpreters of religion and law), among whom the Alids, descendants of different branches of the Ali family, are particularly prominent. Taken together, the Alids

---

34 Alexander Dugin, *Noomakhia. Semites. Monotheism of the Moon and the Gestalt of Va'al.*

constitute *Ahl al-Bayt* (أهل البيت), i.e. 'People of the House', meaning the descendants of Muhammad and Ali.

The Wilayat al-Faqih system is oriented towards the coming of the End Times, when the Last Imam should return to the world and engage in a final battle with the armies of Darkness (which the Shi'a primarily understand to mean modern Western civilisation — materialist, atheist, colonialist and hegemonic). This should be accompanied by the spread of Shiism and a series of political victories.

The Wilayat al-Faqih model and theories of an Islamic (Shiite) revolution were developed in the twentieth century by Shiite intellectuals — most notably Imam Khomeini (1900–1989), who eventually led the 1979 Iranian Revolution.[35] But similar ideas have been espoused by the Shiites of Iraq (who make up about 70 per cent of Iraq's population) and by the Lebanese Shiite movement Hezbollah. There are also Shiite populations in other countries — in Syria, in Yemen (where Shiite Hosays are now fighting other political groups), in Bahrain, in Turkey (Alevis), in some countries in the Middle East, the Maghreb and Central Asia. Shiism has some spread in Africa, as well as in the USA (mainly among African-Americans). There are also Shiites in Saudi Arabia and Pakistan.

The Shia, who have always been persecuted, have a principle called *taqiyya* (Arabic التقية, 'prudence', 'circumspection', 'caution'), i.e. the principle of hiding one's identity under difficult circumstances. Thus, Shiites do not always say that they are Shiite. And on those occasions when they encounter aggressive opponents of Shiism, they may refer to themselves as Sunni. In a sense, Shiism is a tradition of a parallel Islam. Shiism has almost always lost historic battles, the first Imams were all killed.[36] Therefore, it is very difficult to determine the exact number of Shiites in the world.

---

35 The Shia Revolution in Iran took place between January 1978 and February 1979. (1357 according to the Iranian calendar).

36 Abu Hasan Rida is reported to have said: 'All the eleven Imams after the Prophet were killed. Some were killed by the sword, like the Leader of the Faithful and Husayn, and others were poisoned.' Mahdi Muntazir Qa'im, *Jesus through the Qur'an and Shi'ite Narrations* (NY: Tahrike Tarsile Qur'an, 2007).

Shiism is a tradition of suffering and pain, a culture of waiting. But this waiting should be *active*. Currently, Shiite authorities explicitly identify the signs of the End Times and the proximity of the coming of the Mahdi, the Last Imam.[37] This significantly affects the current political map of the Middle East and parts of Central Asia. The confrontation between contemporary Iran and Israel on both sides is also interpreted in religious and eschatological terms. For Shiites, the Israeli state, which emerged on territories previously inhabited by the Islamic population and which is preparing to destroy the Al-Aqsa Mosque (the second most important holy site for Muslims after Kaaba) in order to start building the Third Temple in its place, embodies the power of pure evil — the principle of *Dajjal* (الدجال), 'Deceiver', an analogue of the Antichrist in Christian political philosophy, an eschatological enemy. The support for Israel from the West, and especially the US, further convinces the Shiites of the correctness of this analysis (the West = Dajjal, or 'Big Shaitan', to quote Khomeini). In response, the Israelis identify in Iran a force that obstructs the coming of the Mashiach and seeks to prevent the fulfilment of the prophecies for the restoration of the Third Temple.

Traditional Islam

It remains to briefly consider traditional Islam. As a rule, this is understood to mean the Abbasid-Ottoman versions of adapting Islam to local conditions. In other words, 'traditional Islam' is Sunni Islam, but not fundamentalist, not Salafi, not Wahhabi Islam. Such an Islam at the theological level tends to soften the relationship between the world and God. The theological and metaphysical point of traditional Islam is to soften the opposition between the immanent existence given to us and the transcendent Beginning (Allah). As soon as this opposition is softened, we are dealing with traditional Islam.

And where this traditional Islam reaches the highest possible level of intellectual comprehension, we deal with the Sufi *tariqats* (Arabic طريقه, 'the way', 'the path'), the representatives of *tasawwuf* (Arabic تصوّف).

---

37 Alexander Dugin, *Noomakhia. Iranian Logos. Light Warfare and the Culture of Waiting*.

Sufism, continuing the line of Ibn Arabi and his 'religion of love', reinterprets the exclusive oneness of God into inclusive unity, which allows Muslims to find a place even outside the Sharia context, and to be quite open to various religious forms in Islamic societies — primarily monotheistic, but not exclusively (as Asian Sufism shows in relation to the polytheistic tradition of Hinduism or Buddhism). Politically, this is projected into the fact that traditional Islam formally rejects Salafism and recognises the legitimacy of very different periods of Islamic and world history, trying to find a key to their dialectical interpretation. Therefore, for traditional Islam, the interpretation of the Quran is always relevant and should not be shut down at one stage or another or rejected altogether (as with the Wahhabis).

At the same time, supporters of traditional Islam, to which the vast majority of Muslims in all countries belong, do not have a unified political ideology. Such Islam naturally gravitates towards upholding the norms of Sharia, insisting on the implementation of religious obligations and the rule of Islamic law. Wherever possible, it prioritises the establishment of an Islamic social order based on the principles of the Quran and the Sunnah. But here the harshest precepts of Islam are interpreted allegorically. Thus, among the two versions of *jihad*,[38] 'holy war', priority is given to the 'great jihad', in which the believer must wage war against his own flaws and weaknesses, while the 'little jihad', 'war against the infidels', is interpreted as confronting the enemies of the fatherland, that is, in the spirit of generalised patriotism.

Consequently, traditional Islam and its most intellectual core (Sufism) contrast with the more distinctly Salafist and Shiite models (in both theological and political spheres), but they do not represent something coherently unified and allow for multiple interpretations.

---

38 This interpretation dates back to the Arab jurist and theologian of the Abbasid period, al-Khatib al-Baghdadi (1002–1071), whose authority the Salafis generally deny.

The Sufi Empire of the End

The political ideas expressed by Ibn Arabi in his major work *The Meccan Revelations*[39] have much in common with Shiite eschatology. For example, Ibn Arabi describes a regime to be established at the end of time by the Mahdi and his loyal viziers as an exemplary state. The Mahdi here is the eschatological version of the 'perfect man' (*al-insān al-kāmil* — الكامل الإنسان), who is generally described by Ibn Arabi as the mediator between God and the world, as the divine vice-regent. At the beginning of time, the 'perfect man' is represented by Adam, at the end by the Mahdi. The Mahdi, like the Jewish Mashiach, is presented as the 'perfect ruler'. During the Mahdi's reign, the restrictive aspects of external Islam and a number of legal interpretations will be abolished, as the Mahdi will know spiritual truth directly. The Mahdi's viziers are described as spiritual beings capable of penetrating the divine mysteries and, together with the Mahdi, bringing the external material world into conformity with the divine plan and light archetypes. Ibn Arabi specifies that none of the Mahdi's helpers will be ethnic Arabs, although they will all speak only Arabic. Some passages of Ibn Arabi suggest that Mahdi's viziers, endowed with superhuman qualities, would be not just his servants but also his guides, direct guides of the divine will, a kind of incarnated angels, while he would be only a sword, i.e. a willed instrument. This again refers us to the reign of Plato's philosopher guardians of Kallipolis. Mahdi (*al-Mahdi* — ٱلْمَهْدِي) literally means 'guided' (meaning 'guided by God'), but his viziers are called 'leading' (*al-hudat* — الهُداة). According to Ibn Arabi, there should be nine such 'leaders'.

Importantly, the Sufi vision of the End Times Empire includes a power component. The Mahdi himself is repeatedly referred to as 'the sword' and various fragments of the Meccan Prophecies emphasise that he will defeat his opponents by force.

At the same time, one of the most important features of the Mahdi's rule must be the equitable distribution of wealth and honours. If injustice

---

39 Morris J. W., Chittick W. (ed.), *Ibn 'Arabī: The Meccan Revelations* (NY: Pir Press, 2002).

reigns in the present world, the Mahdi Empire will overturn existing arrangements and restore the divine order that has been lost over time. This is the socialist character of political Sufism, attributed, however, exclusively to the prospect of the end of the world, in anticipation of which Sufis propose to focus on the inner spiritual path and quietly accept the injustices and lawlessness prevailing in the world. In this, the Sufi view of society differs profoundly from the Salafi creed, which insists that the observance of Sharia is already a sufficient condition for justice and that it must be insisted upon immediately, without waiting for a particular time.

Sufi sheikhs — including the highest of them — have the status of 'pole' (*al-qutb* — القطب), and as a rule avoid direct involvement in politics, limiting themselves to the spiritual tutelage of those leaders who appeal to them for it. But in the perspective of the End Times, Sufi doctrine (and hence the inner core of traditional Islam) acquires pronounced political features, and the scenario of the Mahdi fighting his opponents, and even his name 'Great Imam' (*al-Iman al-Akbar* — الأمام الأكبَر) is entirely consistent with Shiite eschatology. The only difference is that the Sufi scenario of the restoration of the 'ideal state' under the 'perfect man' is not directly linked to the descendants of Ali, and accordingly the Sufi Mahdi is seen outside (at least explicitly) the connection with the 'hidden Imam'.

The Islam of the Constitution of Medina

However, there is another version of traditional Islam which differs from the Sufi version. In this interpretation the emphasis is not so much on metaphysics as on ascertaining what constitutes the normative structure of society. In this case, the focus is on the state of the Islamic Ummah that prevailed during Muhammad's own lifetime. Back then, his followers formed a traditional tribal community of Arabian nomads, where the laws of military democracy reigned, but in the case of Muslims the head of this community was the prophet. It is likely that the Jews constituted a similar community in the time of Abraham, as well as the time of Moses and right up to the time of the Judges, which was displaced by the establishment of the kingdom under Samuel and Saul. In the corpus of

Islamic *Hadith*, evidence of how this very early community was arranged is found in the so-called Constitution of Medina.

Proponents of this interpretation of traditional Islam also reject Salafism, which considers as unconditional dogma the structures of Islamic society that developed after Mohammed under the first caliphs (i.e. 'salafs', 'followers'), when the foundation of the state as it is understood by the Sunnis was laid. In the Umayyad, Abbasid and eventually Ottoman Caliphates, many extraneous elements were added. The Shiites and Sufis further saturated Islamic culture with various mystical motifs, moving even further away from Mohammed's nomadic Arab community than the first caliphs and salafs. If traditional Islam is understood in this way, it may well provide a religious justification for the tribal system in combination with Islamic tradition, and serve as a paradigm for the preservation or even artificial revival of tribal communities. For some Islamic peoples who have preserved clan institutions (such as the Chechens and their *teips*), such an interpretation of traditional Islam may be relevant. This explains why one of the leading theorists of such traditional Islam is the Chechen social activist Khozh-Ahmed Noukhayev.[40]

The same is true for some ethnic groups in Afghanistan, Pakistan and Malaysia, and likely also for the Bedouin who have maintained a nomadic lifestyle, some Berber tribes and peoples of Africa who have converted to Islam.

Islam in Russia

In modern history, and in Russian society in particular, as well as in Europe, America and the rest of the world, these theological and consequently political models are still in force and predetermine a great deal.

Among Russian Muslims, Sunni Islam has traditionally been dominant (only the Azerbaijanis are Shiite).

In Sunni Russian Islam, in turn, there are two poles, two political philosophies:

---

40 Хож-Ахмет Нухаев, *Ведено или Вашингтон?* (Moscow: Арктогея-центр, 2001). [Khozh-Ahmed Noukhayev, *Vedeno or Washington?*]

1) traditional Islam, oriented mainly towards Sufi tariqats, and
2) radical Salafi and Wahhabi Islam, imported relatively recently and predominantly from Saudi Arabia.

Radical Islam, as we have seen, is guided by a metaphysics of violent opposition between man and God. It is essentially a terrorist ideology which turns any Muslim (if he is in a non-Islamic society) into a bearer of *Dar al-Harb*, the 'house of war'. If he is in an Islamic but still non-Salafi society (e.g. in a Shiite society or among traditional Islam), he must again rebel against the 'incorrect' (i.e. non-Wahhabi) Islam. Supporters of such a radical version unite in *jamaats* (Arabic جماعة), paramilitary politico-religious structures that turn to terrorist activities on a regular basis. Members of traditional Islam, particularly the authoritative Sufi sheikhs, are often the targets of acts of murder and terrorism. For the Salafists it is above all important to get rid of the ideological opponents in the Islamic Ummah itself.

Representatives of traditional Islam in Russia (including Sufi circles), for their part, are not unconditional supporters of the Russian political system. Historically some Sufi tariqats became the nucleus of resistance among the mountainous Islamic peoples of the Russian Empire — as was the case, for example, in Shamil's revolt (1834). However, these versions of Caucasian Sufism already had some features of Salafist ideology, aimed primarily against the local Caucasian ethnic customs quietly accepted by traditional Islam. Nor can traditional Islam, for all its inclusiveness, accept the legitimacy of atheistic, materialistic and hedonistic attitudes, as well as social models, which run directly counter to the norms of Islamic tradition. This applies both to some aspects of the political modern and — as is particularly evident — to the postmodern. Supporters of traditional Islam are, as a rule, the bearers of Traditional values — religion, ethics, justice, morality, family, etc. In fact, Russia owes the success of the Second Chechen campaign to the appeal to traditional Islam for support in combating radical Islam (Salafism), when Akhmat Kadyrov (1951–2004), the sheikh of the Sufi tariqat, became Moscow's main ally in Chechnya.

There is an irreconcilable enmity between the two poles of Islam, the traditional and the Salafi. Although the representatives of both poles are Muslims, their metaphysics, their political views, their social attitudes, their ideas about normative society and their attitude towards other peoples and other religions are polar opposites.

PART III

THE POLITICAL PARADIGM OF MODERNITY. THE WAR OF CONCEPTS

CHAPTER 8

THE POLITICAL PHILOSOPHY OF ATOMISM

A Generalised Paradigm of the Political in the Premodern

WE NOW MOVE from the political philosophy of traditional societies (premodern) to the political philosophy of modern societies. In order to understand the political-philosophical essence of this transition, it is necessary to refer again to the map of the types of the Political, constructed on the basis of Plato's *Timaeus*. The meaning of the modern and the whole spectrum of political doctrines inherent in it will remain absolutely unclear if we do not constantly keep in mind in what context it originated and what system of axioms, principles and basic postulates lay the foundation modernism sought to negate. Modernism is the negation of Tradition. But as it spread and deepened, what it initially and programmatically denied became hidden behind the horizon line or distorted beyond recognition in the biased and obsessive interpretations of modernism itself. Therefore, in order to understand how the Political came to be conceived and constructed in the modern age, and on what foundations its hermeneutics was based, one should always refer to this schema which the modern itself tried to bring down, deny and abolish.

Thus, the Political in traditional society is reducible to a general schema, described by Plato and Aristotle, which remained unchanged in principle right up until the modern age.

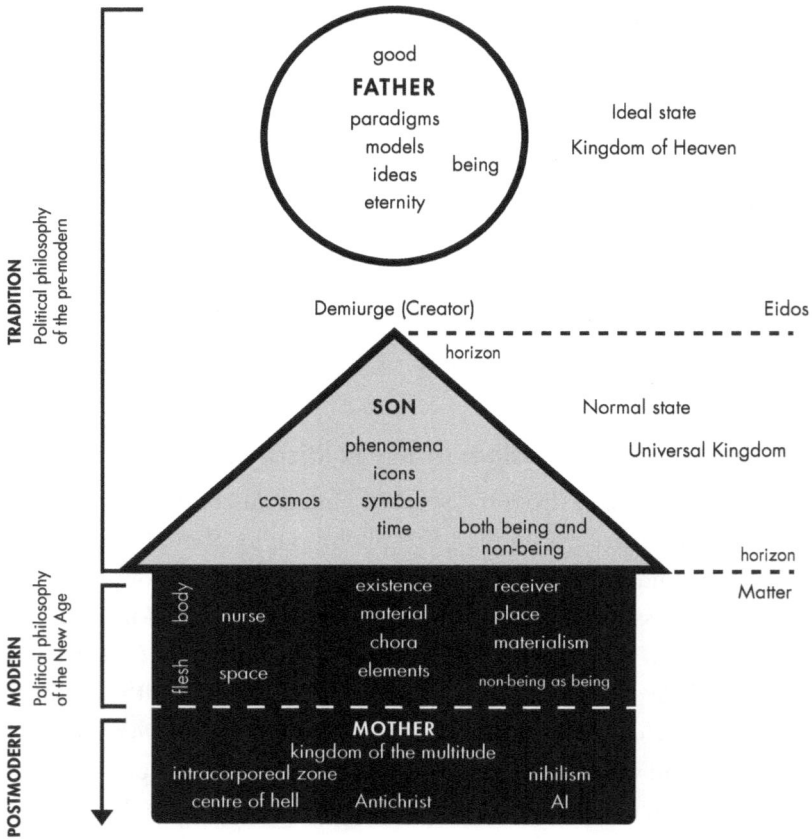

Figure 15. Structure of the *Timaeus* and types of political philosophy.

All types of political philosophy within traditional society are based on the first two principles. In turn, they can be divided into a political philosophy of the Platonic type, centred on the figure of the Father and the model of the earthly world imitating the world of heaven, and a political Aristotelianism (the political philosophy of the Son), centred on the world of phenomena, which is divided into an upper horizon (*eidos*, εἶδος) and a lower horizon (matter, ὕλη).

It is characteristic of premodern political philosophy to reduce all positive ('good') political systems to these two principled paradigms: the political philosophy of the Father and the political philosophy of the Son.

In relation to the political philosophy of the monotheistic religions we have discussed, we define in each case where more is drawn from the paradigm of the Father and where from the paradigm of the Son, how they combine and how their balance changes in the course of historical transformations, reforms and collisions.[1]

Let us also recall the division into three socio-political strata (milieu of castes) that we find in the most common models of traditional societies (also found in Plato and Aristotle).

Figure 16. Hierarchy of political strata in Plato and Aristotle.

---

[1] It is only in Protestantism that we encounter, for the first time, elements of a different political system beyond these two fundamental paradigms of the Political that are characteristic of traditional society. Some elements of democracy are also found in the Salafist interpretation of Islam.

These two types dominate the political philosophy of Tradition. In other words, they are either monarchical or aristocratic societies. A special case is the 'theocracy', θεοκρατία, in which the emphasis falls on the domination of the priests specifically, which does not change the general schema (the dominance of the contemplative life), but gives the higher caste a special quality.[2]

The Centrality of Hierarchy in Traditionalism

In a traditional society, there is necessarily a *vertical hierarchy*: radically vertical when it comes to the Father, or relatively vertical when it comes to the Son.

The Greek word ἱεραρχία is formed from the two roots ἱερός, 'sacred', and ἀρχή, 'rule', that is 'priestly rule' or 'priesthood'. One may wonder why '*priestly* rule'; why does the term ἱερός appear in this system of government? The point is that the political system reflects a system of theology (if we speak of monotheistic religions) or ontology (in the case of pre-monotheistic religions). In other words, the political system of traditional society is sacred; it is based on the principle of sacredness. This is the most important distinctive feature of a traditional society.

Vertical organisation is inextricably linked to sacrality, since it believes that the origin of hierarchy is not simply a quantitative criterion — strength, wealth and the ability to subjugate others by any means. Such a hierarchy would not be 'sacred', that is, it would not be a 'hierarchy'. Power has an otherworldly origin. It has its origin in heaven, in the realm of the eternal and the divine. And it is this relationship with the divine (however it is interpreted) that determines the legitimacy of power.

---

2   The opinions of two fundamental theorists of Traditionalism — René Guénon and Julius Evola (1898–1974) — differed on the primacy of priests or sacral kings in the traditional society. Guénon insisted on the supremacy of the priests (the Indian Brahman caste). See René Guénon, *Spiritual Power and Temporal Power* (Sophia Perennis et Universalis, 2004). Evola (in the spirit of Ghibelline ideology) defended the principle of supremacy of sacral kings. Julius Evola, *Revolt against the Modern World* (Vermont: Inner Traditions, 1995); Julius Evola, *Mysteries of the Grail* (Vermont: Inner Traditions, 2018).

The Third Origin in the *Timaeus*

In Plato's *Timaeus* and *Republic*, as well as in Aristotle, there is another, third beginning. In the *Timaeus* it is called *Chora* (χώρα), 'Mother', 'Nurse', 'Receiver'. In *Parmenides* it corresponds to the ontological concept of the many (πολλά). In Plato's ideal state (Kallipolis) this third element corresponds to the peasants or artisans.

In Aristotle's description of the physics of the world we find the principle of 'matter' (ὕλη — 'wood'). In politics it corresponds to democracy as the power of representatives of the lower — third — class.

Accordingly, the political philosophy of traditional society follows this model: the political philosophy of the Father and the Son can argue with each other, priests and warriors can argue with each other, just as aristocracy and monarchy can argue with each other — and this is within the limits of tolerance.

The third element in traditional society almost never acquires full power. It is a material, maternal, peasant and artisanal beginning. But purely theoretically, just as there is a political philosophy of the Father and the Son, there is also a potential, but unrealisable within traditional society, *political philosophy of the Mother*. This form of government exists only as a hypothesis; from Plato's point of view it is the ultimate degradation of the ideal state (democracy and tyranny) and from Aristotle's point of view it is the worst system of government. We are talking about third-origin power.

In philosophy this hypothesis corresponds to the zone of Mother, matter or space. The sacred politics of traditional society is constructed on a higher level, but the overall picture of the levels of ontology and types of political systems reserves a special place for such a political philosophy. This place is beyond the limits of the Traditional (premodern) paradigm and for many millennia has remained a purely theoretical possibility, only to be realised when normative forms of politics decay and reach the critical line of their degeneration.

From Democritus to Democracy

However, already in Antiquity we meet some thinkers who tried to ground the world not in the traditional Greek way — where everything comes from the Father or is contained in the living synthesis of the Son — but from the bottom-up, pushing away matter, bodies and the direct fact of being. In the dialogue *Sophist*, Plato speaks about a 'gigantomachy in relation to essence', i.e. about the dispute between those who admit the world of ideas and consider it primordial and autonomous (as Plato himself) and those who, on the contrary, accept only corporeal things as existent. Plato likens it to a battle between gods and titans (giants) — the position of gods corresponds to the carriers of the classical tradition, and titans are just the first representatives of the most ancient materialism. The protagonist of the dialogue *Sophist* says the following about them to his listener Theaetetus:

> They are the ones who take everything from the heavens and from the unseen to the earth, as if they were holding oaks and rocks with their hands. They hold on to all such things, as if there is only that which is touchable, and they regard bodies and being as one and the same, while they scorn all those who say that there is something immaterial, and no longer wish to hear anything but body.[3]

To which Theaetetus reasonably remarks:

> I have often met with such men, and terrible fellows they are.[4]

Plato is referring here to the teachings of the atomists — and above all to Democritus (c. 460–c. 370 BC). Democritus was one of the first to attempt to build a philosophical model based on the bottom-up principle. This includes early thinkers such as Leucippus, who is considered Democritus' teacher.[5] Later, similar ideas were developed by Epicurus (342/341–271/270 BC) and his follower, the Roman philosopher Lucretius (c. 99–55 BC).

---

3   Plato, *Sophist*.
4   Ibid.
5   Many thinkers in Ancient Greece (e.g. Epicurus) already questioned the existence of Leucippus, believing that Democritus himself was the creator of atomism.

Leucippus and Democritus put forward the thesis of 'isonomy' (ἰσονομία), anticipating the later modern ideas of isotropic space and more broadly of all existence (principle of contingency[6]). This thesis, often attributed to Leucippus, is 'the one no more exists than the other' (Greek — μηδὲν μᾶλλον τοιοῦτον ἢ τοιοῦτον εἶναι).[7] It stems from the notion of the infinity of the phenomenal world (which is strictly opposed to both Plato and Aristotle, since the world in their systems is limited and finite, though for different reasons — for Plato by virtue of its subsidiarity position to the paradigm, and for Aristotle by virtue of its harmonious structuring around a fixed centre[8]). Thus, everything becomes relative and any order turns out to be only a particular instance of chaos, and moreover, something random and transient. Thus the semantic verticality of the world, which turns out to be a purely material phenomenon, collapses completely because in Greek thought 'infinity' was synonymous with matter.

The principle of 'isonomy' established a kind of equality not only between the one and the other, but also between the existent and the non-existent, equating being with non-being, that is, 'something *is* no more than it *is not*' (Greek οὐδὲν μᾶλλον τὸ ὄν ἢ τὸ μὴ ὄν εἶναι).

---

6   Copernicus' astronomy, Galileo's and Newton's physics were built on this principle, and in the postmodern era contingency has been elevated to the highest principle in object-oriented ontology. See Quentin Meillassoux, *After Finitude: An Essay on the Necessity of Contingency* (London: Continuum International Publishing Group, 2009).

7   S. Y. Lurie, *Democritus. Texts. Translation. Research* (Leningrad: Science, 1970), p. 207.

8   The Roman philosopher Cicero (106–43 BC) transmitted Democritus' doctrine about isotropic space as follows: 'Democritus believes that those bodies which he calls atoms, i.e. indivisible, because of their hardness, are moving in an infinite void, where there is neither the highest, nor the lowest, nor the middle, nor the farthest, nor the extreme point, they are moving in such a way that they bind together, and as a result all those things appear which exist and which we see; this movement of atoms must be thought of as not having any beginning, but being made for infinite time'. S. Y Lurie, *Democritus. Texts. Translation. Research* (Leningrad: Science, 1970), p. 251.

Democritus, following Leucippus, put forward the idea that *atoms* exist.[9] An atom (ἡ ἄτομος) is literally 'something indivisible', 'something which cannot be dissected'. The atomists also used another term for indivisible particles — ἀδιαίρετα.[10] The corresponding term *amera* (Greek ἀμερῆ), literally 'that which has no parts', was proposed in the fourth century BC by the sophist and dialectician Diodorus Cronus. Democritus considered 'atoms' to be 'dense' ('complete', 'perfect' — Greek πλήρης, ναστός). Thus Democritus completely overturns the Platonic conception of being, placing being not at the top, in the realm of ideas and the divine One, but at the bottom. However, atoms were identified with being only by Democritus' interpreters. He himself apparently did not use such a category as being to describe them. Atoms were opposed to *emptiness*[11] (τo κενόν), infinity (ἀπειρία) or nothingness (οὐδέν), but precisely as a mirror opposition. Their not-emptiness, not-infinity and not-nothingness does not yet mean that they *are*, that they represent being. It is only a concept, and it is no accident that Democritus avoids ontological definitions in his philosophy. The distinction between emptiness and atoms is speculative, purely conceptual, as are emptiness itself and atoms themselves. The 'being' of atoms is evidenced only by human thought, but according to Democritus this thought is secondary, derived from a moment of random play of atoms. Thought is an accident of cosmic chaos. Therefore its conclusions as a whole are also accidental. Democritus does not have anywhere near the emphasis on reliability of thought that Plato and Aristotle put into their conclusions. These conclusions are truer than the hallucinations of sensuous forms, but still only relative. Therefore the existence of atoms is also relative. They are not so much the ontological foundations of everything as the concept of such foundations. Hence one

---

9   The Stoic Posidonius (139/135–51/50 BC) reports that the Phoenicians, in particular Mochus of Sidon, who lived before the Trojan War, were the first to formulate the theory of atoms. Isaac Newton (1642–1727), who identified Mochus with Moses, was convinced of the same. See Alexander Dugin, *Noomakhia. The Semites. Monotheism of the Moon and the Gestalt of Va'al.*

10 The term is attributed to a disciple of Democritus, Metrodorus of Chios.

11 Synonymous with 'emptiness' is also the important philosophical term 'absence'. (Greek στέρησις, Latin *privatio*).

can say of atoms that they are not emptiness, but one can hardly strictly say that they *are*.

Democritus was deeply interested in epistemology and ontology, that is, the meditation on the basis on which he himself claims the existence of atoms and emptiness and how these claims relate to sensory experience. The emphasis on this distinction has probably served to make Democritus sometimes regarded as continuing the line of the Eleatics, who, following Parmenides, based their philosophy on the distinction between opinion (δόξα) and truth (ἀλήθεια), with sense experience affecting only opinion and truth being hidden deep within and accessible only to the intellect. This epistemological attitude was most fully developed in Plato. In contrast, Democritus' whole system of looking at the world, opposed to the One of Plato and Parmenides, proceeds from the many, and from emptiness. But at the same time, Democritus bases his metaphysical judgements on sense experience, considering it of secondary, distorted and unreliable value. The Great Void and the atoms are postulated by thought, but by a thought fundamentally different from the classical Greek interpretation. It is not the Logos, nor the Nus (Νοῦς), nor Sophia, which are divine, universal and belong to the transcendental philosophy of the Father. This thought, νοερός, is the product of the mental activity of the individual being. In modern philosophy this is usually called *conceptum* (Latin, from the verb *capere*, which literally means 'to grasp'). The instance that grasps the concept is not the divine mind, but the human intellect.[12] But this 'grasping intellect' is distinct from the information that the senses communicate. Essentially, Democritus was the first to establish a thoroughly original conception of thinking, a particular epistemology, which wonderfully anticipated modern times, where major judgements were made on the basis of the same concept — human (mainly individual) reason — the *bon sens* of French rationalist Descartes (1596–1650) or common sense of Scottish realists — Thomas Reid (1710–1796), Adam Ferguson (1723–1816), etc. But it was John Locke (1632–1704) who in

---

12 Democritus had this to say: 'When we clearly comprehend something, we know nothing of what it is, but each of our opinions represents a different version of the form (of things).' Lurie, *Democritus. Texts. Translation. Research*, p. 219.

modern times offered the most complete formulation of thought as a product of reasoning, and we will speak of him later. Democritus' epistemology, as well as his vacuo-atomist ontology, were therefore completely unprecedented for classical Greece. Truth was the result of the activity of the individual mind, that is, the concept, while being (or not being, nothingness, emptiness, etc.) was conceived as the fruit of a rational conclusion. The truth itself, however, he regarded as inaccessible, hence his famous expression 'truth in the abyss' (Greek ἐν βυθῶι γὰρ ἡ ἀλήθεια[13]).

According to Democritus, atoms are like small dust particles that can be seen in the sun's rays, but which remain otherwise invisibly scattered in the air. However, it is not a question of man being able to see atoms, but only a metaphorical indication that something invisible in some circumstances can become visible in others. The Christian author Bishop Jerome of Stridon (Hieronymus, 342–419 or 420), in his commentary on the book of Isaiah (40:12), dwelt specifically on this passage:

> Who hath measured the waters in the hollow of his hand, and meted out heaven with the span, and *comprehended the dust of the earth in a measure*, and weighed the mountains in scales, and the hills in a balance?

In the expression 'dust of the earth', 'ashes', he saw an indication of another Hebrew word *daq* (דק), which in turn he compared with Democritus' 'atoms'. From this remark a number of important parallels can be drawn between grains of sand, the smallest particles of matter, and the atomist theory. A similar view was shared by the Islamic Ash'arite school, which also identified the smallest particle of matter, the 'atom' (Arabic ذرة — dhara[14]), with the fundamental basis of existence. For the Ash'arians every 'atom' of matter, every point of space and every moment of time is created by God. In the materialistic vision of Democritus, Leucippus and other atomists, these dust particles are not created by anyone, but have arisen by themselves and are not subject to any law other than chance. Therefore,

---

13   Lurie, *Democritus. Texts. Translation. Research*, p. 38.
14   ذرة — *dhara* literally means 'grain', which refers to an entirely different symbolic chain associated with agrarian societies and their concepts.

worlds are created and perish by the arbitrary play of clashing and disengaging atoms.[15]

Atoms, material particles, are what make up the cosmos. It arises from atoms colliding chaotically with each other, clumping together and disintegrating to form a *vortex* (δῖνος).

Democritus clearly did not want to explain whether atoms or emptiness came first, but the description of the emergence of a vortex as a flow of atoms cannot avoid this problem. This is what he says about the birth of a vortex:

> A vortex of various forms separated from the universe.[16]

These words are attributed to Democritus by the Neoplatonist Simplicius (c.490–560). This is how Epicurus puts it:

> The world is a part of space separated from infinity.[17]

---

15 This theme has been developed by contemporary speculative realist philosophers, supporters of object-oriented ontology, who at this new stage seek to justify the existence of matter and the sub-material dimensions. Thus the theme of 'sand' and 'memory of particles' is given great importance by the contemporary philosopher Reza Negarestani, linking sand and dust as the root of matter to particular Middle Eastern cultures and even directly to Islamic civilisation. See Reza Negarestani, *Cyclonopedia: Complicity with Anonymous Materials* (Melbourne: Re.Press, 2008). 'The memory of atoms' was also a central theme of the Russian cosmists, Nikolai Fyodorov and Konstantin Tsiolkovsky. According to Fyodorov, matter contains the atoms of dead ancestors, who must be resurrected by scientific methods. Nikolai Fedorov, *Собрание сочинений: в 4-х т.* [Collected Works in 4 Volumes] (Moscow: Progress-Tradition; Evidentis, 1995–2004). Tsiolkovsky believed that each atom of matter was once a part of a living organism (for Tsiolkovsky life could not be a random phenomenon present on just one planet but had to represent a universal phenomenon, hence his belief in the existence of life in other worlds, galaxies and planets). Therefore the atom contains a euphoric quantum of being (the memory that a particle of matter was a constituent element of a living organism instils it with happiness). Konstantin Tsiolkovsky, *Космическая философия* [*Cosmic Philosophy*], Moscow: IDLi; Sphere, 2004). Also see Dugin, *Noomakhia. Patterns of Russian Thought. The Solar Tsar, the Glare of Sophia and Russia Underground*.
16 Lurie, *Democritus. Texts. Translation. Research*, p. 274.
17 Ibid., p. 275.

In the first case the verb ἀποκρίνω is used to mean 'to separate', and in the second Epicurus uses the verb ἀποτέμνω, where the root is the same as in the word 'atom', indicating 'sectioning', 'cutting'. The vortex, consisting of indivisible particles, initially separates from the void (infinity), which becomes the beginning of the movement of atoms in the void. But here one should pay attention to the fact that to separate from emptiness one must first be merged with it, united, undivided. And although Democritus and Epicurus tend to attribute the property of eternity to both atoms and emptiness, and thus eternal separation from each other, the very description of the appearance of a vortex of atoms points to some state prior to this separation, because the appearance of the vortex is described as an event, the meaning of which is to separate. And obviously the primordial state preceding the appearance of the vortex must be the non-existence of atoms as such and their fusion with emptiness. This suggests a shadow side of atomist ontology (more accurately meontology, nihilistic ontology), to which Democritus himself probably refers when he describes it as 'the abyss in which truth resides'.

Putting aside this highly problematic cosmogeny (ontogeny), the cosmological description of an already existing cosmos in which vortices whirl is as follows. Voids exist between atoms, and motion (including the cycle of births and deaths) is explained by the random coupling (ἐπάλλαξις) and uncoupling of atoms among themselves. The world itself, according to Democritus, represents at its core the Great Void (τὸ κενόν[18]), infinity (ἀπειρία[19]) or 'nothingness' (οὐδέν[20]). Atoms move chaotically in this emptiness, creating worlds that arise and become annihilated.

> The atoms are floating around in the void; colliding with each other spontaneously due to their disorderly aspiration and intertwining due to their variety of forms, they catch on to each other and thus create the world and everything in it, or rather, the infinite worlds.[21]

---

18 Latin *inanitas*.
19 Latin *infinitas*.
20 Latin *nihil*.
21 Lurie, *Democritus. Texts. Translation. Research*, p. 276.

These worlds consist of forms (εἴδωλα[22]). Democritus denies the existence of ideas (unlike Plato) and that every thing has a purpose (unlike Aristotle). Therefore, the only way to explain *things* becomes the identification of cause. Existence without a purpose or higher eternal meaning becomes, on the one hand, accidental and, on the other hand, mechanically predetermined by causal law, i.e. material necessity.

The False Logos

We saw that Plato, in the *Timaeus*, claimed that matter is comprehended by a special 'bastard Logos'. This bastard Logos is the form of conceptual thinking by which Democritus grasps the existence of emptiness (τὸ κενόν) or nothingness (οὐδέν). The Neoplatonist Plotinus, reflecting on the nature of the bastard Logos (λόγος νόθος), concludes that Plato's third kind of being, the incomprehensible *chora* (χώρα) 'is grasped by reflection, not coming from the mind, but from the void'.[23]

The enigmatic, empty, bastardised, illegitimate Logos is not emptiness in itself, for it is still a definite property, but *emptied thought*. This is the conceptual thinking of the individual, which later became the normative form of consciousness of the modern age.

According to Plotinus, matter is a 'phantasm', that is, a purely pseudological category. Plotinus writes:

> (...) some find matter empty (identify it with emptiness). But I say that it is a ghost (phantasm) of mass (heaviness), φάντασμα ὄγκου, because the soul, which is (extremely) close to matter, cannot (clearly) distinguish anything (distinguish, ὁρίσαι, 'define', 'place in limits or in borders'), it begins to tremble

---

22 The choice of the term εἴδωλον for form as opposed to ἰδέα, εἶδος by Plato or μορφή by Aristotle is significant. The Greeks used this word to denote something apparent — a ghost, a spectre. The concept of 'idol' came from this same term. It is not a vision of the substance of a thing, but on the contrary, its false appearance. There is nothing of essence hidden in the *eidolon*, the 'idol', the ghost; it is a shadow devoid of the body that casts it. This is what the atomist universe is like — it is a ghost. In postmodernity this theme was developed in such direction as 'hauntology', 'the science of ghosts'. Jacques Derrida, *Spectres of Marx* (Oxfordshire: Routledge, 1994); Buse P., Scott, A. (eds.), *Ghosts: Deconstruction, Psychoanalysis, History* (London: Macmillan, 1999).

23 ἀλλὰ λογισμῷ οὐκ ἐκ νοῦ, ἀλλὰ κενῶς. Plotinus, *Second Ennead*.

(frantic, worried) in uncertainty, and it does not have the strength to grasp something with its gaze (to shape, outline, recognise *eidos*, eidetic features, define) or to come to (identify) the sign (meaning), because this would be the same as distinguishing (and this is exactly what it cannot do).[24]

This phrase develops the idea that weight is a state of the soul rather than a property of matter, that weight is born out of the demoniacal, obsessive state of the soul, which falls and tries desperately to stop its fall — though not through flight, but through black and ungodly manipulations, eventually constituting materiality — as a mark of the deepest degeneration of the mind.

There is no matter itself, but there is a 'Logos' that perceives it. It is the 'false Logos'.

The atom, according to Plotinus, is the limit of the descent of the Mind, splitting, dividing any object of thought into two halves.

The mind seeks out duality, for it produces division until it reaches a simplicity that can no longer divide itself. As long as it can, it will advance into its own abyss. Each man's abyss is matter; therefore it is altogether dark, as light is the Logos.[25]

Accordingly, the cessation of division, i.e. reaching the atom, is the moment of the Mind's complete extinguishing. But if the Mind has faded away, it does not exist. It can exist after its end only as a phantasm, as an utterly weakened parody of itself, unable to perform what is the main characteristic of the Mind — *discernment*. The non-discerning mind is a paradox, but it is the epistemological instance that operates on the concept of the atom.

This observation by Plotinus is extremely important for *Politica Aeterna* because it allows us to better understand the metaphysical foundations of modernism. Modernity is based on pseudologia; it is a generalisation of the 'false Logos'. And the first to formulate the false Logos as central and singular was precisely Democritus, the most modern of modern thinkers.

---

24   Plotinus, *Second Ennead*. [Recreation of Russian translation]
25   *Ibid*.

The Mortality of the Gods, the Attraction of Hell and Democracy

Democritus taught that there is nothing eternal, and even the gods prove to be only more longevous (enduring) than humans, but sooner or later they too perish. It is telling that various sources indicate Democritus wrote a work entitled *On the Things in Hades*, which claimed that the dead could feel something. On this basis he suggested preserving corpses (in honey) so that they could be resurrected under certain circumstances.[26] All this shows Democritus' heightened interest precisely in that subterranean realm, which in the traditional ontologies of classical Greece[27] was placed at the lowest level of being.

Democritus did not build an original political philosophy and he mainly taught about the structure of the world, but as we have pointed out many times, any philosophy necessarily has a political dimension. Therefore, if we apply Democritus' principle to society, we get the germ of a *theory of democratic society*. The philosophy of atomism, being projected into the sphere of politics, gives us the basic idea of *democracy*. As confirmation of this we find a brief fragment by Democritus himself:

> Poverty in a democracy must be preferred to what is called a happy life in a monarchy.[28]

When we project the notion of the atom onto the political system, we get a certain notion of the 'social atom'. The Greek term atom, ἄτομος, means 'indivisible', 'that which cannot be dissected'. In Latin, there is a direct translation of the term: *individuum*, 'indivisible'. From this it is easy to deduce logically the notion that the totality of individuals (political atoms) creates and establishes the political state. Thus, in the most general

---

26 This theme anticipates not only the modern, but partly the paradigm of the postmodern, where in the context of posthumanistic theory and technological development the question of achieving physical immortality becomes one of the main interests. It is possible to relate this aspect of Democritus' teachings to the philosophy of 'Russian cosmologists'. See Nikolai Fedorov, *Собрание сочинений: в 4-х т.* [*Collected Works in 4 Volumes*] (Moscow: Progress-Tradition; Evidentis, 1995–2004).

27 Dugin, *Noomakhia. The Hellenic Logos. The Valley of Truth*.

28 Lurie, *Democritus. Texts. Translation. Research*, p. 361.

terms, the philosophy of democracy is born, filling the hypothetical third place assigned to it in the complete three-part model of the Platonic and Aristotelian conception of the nature of the Political.

The Formula 'Out of Many, One'

Democritus is an atomistic philosopher and his philosophy, which describes a world made up of material atoms (he considered even the gods to be material), is the doctrine of democracy. This doctrine may be described by the following formula: out of the many may arise the 'one'. This is the 6th hypothesis from Plato's dialogue *Parmenides*. Tellingly, the Latin version of this expression *E pluribus unum*, (Latin for 'out of many one') is the motto placed on the Great Seal of the United States.

This is the philosophy of that third beginning, which, in fact, simply does not exist in the ancient traditional world, in the world of sacred politics. Plato called for Democritus' books to be burnt because, from the point of view of the Father- and-Son-orientated Greeks, the idea of the Mother 'philosophy from below', that the mob will determine for itself what is true, can only inspire disgust and horror. For those thinkers who stood on the side of the gods in the 'gigantomachy of essence', the phenomenon of democracy or the philosophy of Democritus (atomism) is the ultimate form of degradation.

As long as we are dealing with a religious society, we always remain in the paradigm of the Father or the Son, and the attempt to build a political system based on the multitude (individuals, political atoms) is impossible in such a traditional society. And although democracy was somewhat known in ancient Greece, it could hardly be elevated to a political doctrine in its own right, to a political philosophy. Democracy was rather considered a product of deterioration of more perfect forms of political order. But the example of Democritus (as well as Epicurus and Lucretius) shows that the possibility of building a philosophical doctrine on the basis of the third — material, matriarchal — beginning was still partly realised. Yet the traditional model of the sacred hierarchy steadily prevailed in the culture of Greece, Rome, and then throughout the European Middle Ages (as well as in the Islamic world and other civilisations) up to the modern age.

The situation only begins to change with the onset of the modern era. It is only then that this political philosophy, the philosophy of the third order, gradually comes to the fore, until it becomes dominant.

Epicurus: The Ancient Liberalism of the 'Garden'

Another Greek materialist philosopher, Epicurus, lived after Democritus and entirely adopted his idea of atoms and emptiness. While accepting the cosmology of Democritus with his atomistic metaphysics, he had a much greater trust in sense perception, and it was this that he regarded as the basic criterion of truth. Assuming the basis of real existence to be the data obtained from the senses, Epicurus developed a sensualist ontology, which, however, rested on a more fundamental foundation — the conceptual philosophy of Democritus, to which Epicurus turned every time he needed to draw a more solid conclusion than sense experience allowed. Thus, by the cohesion of atoms Epicurus explains the existence (and at the same time mortality) of the soul and even the gods. The gods of Epicurus live in the voids between the worlds (Greek μετακοσμία), which are again a magnification of Democritus' inter-atomic void.

If in the ontology of the third kind — Mother, *chora*, the multitude — Epicurus does not bring anything fundamentally significant,[29] and his sensualism is in a sense a step backwards from the conceptual materialism of Democritus, he does justify several social and ethical theories, which — like everything materialistic and individualistic — would be adopted in the modern era. For example, Epicurus considers the human desire for pleasure (Greek ἡδονή — from which we get 'hedonism') as the core of ethics. Here we easily identify the third origin of the soul in the metaphor of the chariot in Plato's *Phaedrus*. In Plato the inferior — third (in direct analogy with the third genus, the Mother-Receiver) — force of the soul is called precisely 'desire' or 'lust' (Greek ἐπιθυμία), and Epicurus

---

29 An exception is his assumption of deviation (Greek παρέγκλισις) of the atom from rectilinear motion, which was later pointed out by Karl Marx. The theme of deviation gained particular relevance in postmodern philosophy.

reduces the structure of man to this very quality. Man is governed only by desires, which constitute the supreme purpose of his existence. In turn, all desires can be categorised, but what desire as such gravitates towards is precisely *pleasure*. Such directness in glorifying the inferior — the least noble — property of the soul was rare in Hellenic culture, but in turn anticipated the ethics of the modern age — above all the 'utilitarianism' of Jeremy Bentham (1748–1832).

Even more insightful — in the same vein of pre-modernity — was Epicurus' theory of the origin of society. From his point of view, society and the state emerge from the bottom up, as a result of the *'social contract'*. Unlike Plato and Aristotle, for whom the whole precedes the parts, Epicurus deduces the whole from the parts. He considers the subject matter of the 'social contract' to be the provision of maximum pleasure and minimum violence, which is the antithesis of pleasure. People unite into society not because it has any special ontology, mission or purpose, but only as insurance against causing trouble to one another. On the whole, Epicurus saw the optimal life as more or less secluded, devoted to the pursuit of pleasures, which he regarded as sensual experiences of all kinds — from eating and drinking to talking with friends. This right to enjoyment constituted for Epicurus something natural, hence his theory of 'natural right' (φύσεως δίκαιόν) as the inherent and normative existence of the individual.

This is why Epicurus advised the sage to 'live secretly' (λάθε βιώσας), at a sufficient distance from society, not getting too involved in its spheres. He called his school, where he lived and taught his philosophy to others, 'The Garden'.

Epicurus' attitude towards death is very revealing. He regarded fear of death as superfluous, because he did not believe that the soul can outlive the body, and consequently between life and death (just as between atom and void) there was no continuity, no common dimension. When a person lives, he only lives, i.e. he is. And this presence of sentient existence is in a sense total. It is not limited by anything, because the onset of death does not affect the same being which enjoys life. Death is not experienced, not realised and does not represent a threat to life, because it does not exist during life, and after death also does not exist, because there is no subject who could witness his death and compare posthumous existence with life. In this Epicurus diverges from Democritus, who taught that the corpse has a residual faculty for feeling, and that the soul takes longer to decay than the body. On this Democritus based his ontology of Hades. For Epicurus, who bases everything on sensual experience, this distinction between the rate at which the body and the soul decay into atoms is meaningless, because it cannot be reliably deduced from experience. Again, this conception of death and of the absence of the soul corresponds exactly to the existential culture of modernity.

In fact, the ideology of Epicurus represents an almost complete *liberalism*, a millennium and a half ahead of philosophical thought in Europe.

The doctrine of Epicurus was first adopted during the Renaissance, where Pierre Gassendi (1592–1655) took a great interest in his atomism and sensationalism.

Ockham's Nominalism

The first approximation to modern atomism, in which some features of the doctrine of Democritus can already be identified, is the position of the nominalists in the medieval dispute about *universals*. This dispute was in fact an updated version of the 'gigantomachy regarding essence', renewed more than a millennium after Plato's time. The most consistent Platonism, i.e. following the philosophy of the Father, was the position of the 'idealists', the most prominent representative of which was the Irish mystic John Scotus Eriugena[30] (c. 810–877). The idealists fully subscribed to the position of Plato and the Platonists, asserting that ideas precede and exist independently of things. Idealists interpreted universals, i.e. generalising concepts, precisely as Platonic ideas and insisted on their autonomy and full ontological superiority. Such a position was defined as *universalia ante rem*. This position was rejected by Catholic dogmatics, although this did not prevent Platonism surviving in the Catholic Church, albeit predominantly in Catholic mysticism.

---

30 John Scotus Eriugena, *Periphyseon on the Division of Nature* (Eugene, Oregon: Wipf and Stock, 2011).

The position of the idealist-Platonists was opposed by the realists, who, on the basis of Aristotle, insisted that the *eidos* (but not the idea!) exists and has being only when it exists through a thing, within a thing (*universalia in re*). This construction was called 'realism' (from the Latin *res* — 'thing'), since only an existing thing was endowed with unconditional being. Here universalism was equated precisely with *eidos* or form, i.e. the philosophy of the Son and Aristotelian immanentism prevailed (but without materialism). This position was held by most of the scholastics and it was the one accepted by Catholicism as unconditional dogma.

But as early as the eleventh century, representatives of the third position emerged, who in fact laid the foundation for future materialism and individualism. They argued that the common conception was only a linguistic convention, and was not endowed with any kind of substance, being merely an 'empty sound' (*flatus voci*). Their position was defined by the formula *universalia post rem*. The term nominalism comes from the Latin *nomen*, 'name', 'title'. This meant that the nominalists believed that there was only a concrete thing and that its elevation to a generalising kind, to a *universalia*, was nothing more than an externally ascribed name, serving for the convenience of classification. The first representative of nominalism was the French scholast, the founder of nominalism, Roscelin of Compiègne (c.1050–c.1122). Roscelin's ideas and nominalism in general were condemned because they contradicted realism, which was accepted as a philosophical dogma.

In fact, the nominalists offer a model of the universe which corresponds to the third genus of Plato's *Timaeus* — that is, the Mother, the *chora*. The thing is thought of here as a primary given, whose basis is materiality and individuality. The nominalists argue that only the individual, the separate and particular *exists* in the full sense of the word. Attempts to give the same name to different — albeit similar — individual things, change nothing in the existence of each of them or all of them together. They continue to exist both together and separately just as individual objects, and the generality of names is ascribed to them by the human consciousness that simplifies its perception of the world through artificial operations that do not affect in any way the individuality — essentially the atomicity — of each particular thing. This means that for the nominalists there is no idea or *eidos*, i.e. no pattern (paradigm), no dual and inseparable structure where essence and matter necessarily exist and both are endowed with a full and distinctive being. By opposing the realists, the nominalists undermined the very basis of the worldview on which the medieval model of the world, dominated by Aristotle's ontology, was built.

In the spirit of nominalism, the model of one of the brightest representatives of late scholasticism, Duns Scotus (1265–1308), insisted that the most common element of existing things was matter, which was existence itself (an extreme anti-Platonic and anti-Aristotelian thought). At the same time, matter itself in its universality can only be known by God, and everything besides it that exists is an individual unit. Things for Duns Scotus are not a combination of form and matter, as with Aristotle and the realists, but individualities, which are the highest and final reality, *ultima realitas entis*. Duns Scotus' followers introduced a special term to refer precisely to this supreme individual reality — *haecceitas*, 'thisness'. According to Duns Scotus, the sign of being coincides not with what a thing is (*quidditas*, 'whatness'), but with the fact of the existence of precisely 'this' thing. Hence the recognition of being because of matter (though this truth is revealed only for God) and because of individuals, and this constitutes the truth in the final measure and the limit of cognition for man. Thus we see here both materialism (equating being with matter rather than with *eidos* or ideas) and individualism, that is, the refusal to recognise an independent being for the universals.

The final formulation of the nominalist philosophical paradigm came from another English thinker, the Franciscan William Ockham[31] (1285–1349). Ockham adopts most of Duns Scotus' ideas, but goes even further. According to Ockham, God by his will creates not matter (as in Duns Scotus), which then through a volitional impulse becomes individual objects, but individual things, individuals directly. Individual things, according to Ockham, exist entirely *outside* the mind, whether divine and human. But in God they have their origin as God's will, and in human

---

31 A compendium of Ockham's teachings: a translation of the Tractatus de principiis theologiae (St. Bonaventure, NY: Franciscan Institute, St. Bonaventure University, 1998).

beings, who are themselves pure individuals, the will is limited within certain bounds. Therefore, in any case, cognition is only the cognition of individuals and the individual. *God knows things through the process of their individual creation.* Man knows things through the individual experience of contact with individual things.

The experience of individual things, which alone possess being, corresponds in consciousness to two types of intensions, which form two classes of natural signs. The first intension is the *natural sign* of the mind, a concept (*conceptum*) corresponding to an individual thing. The second intension is even more contingent and, in turn, serves to denote 'natural signs'. These two intensions characterise the logical activity of cognitive reason. Finally, there are also *conditional signs* (*flatus voci*), which, by contrast, are used for the exchange of information about natural signs. Languages belong to this category. At the same time, according to Ockham, there are no 'universals' at all, and everything that serves to designate individual things is nothing but signs — of one sort or another.

Thus, Ockham's nominalism prepares the philosophical platform for the science and logic of the modern age. Being is given exclusively to the individual material corporeal thing, while its conceptual counterpart (first intension and second intension) is placed in the realm of human consciousness and treated as a convention.

Ockham's political ideas are highly symptomatic.[32] He was one of the first European writers to advocate the separation of church and state, formulating his ideal in terms of 'enlightened absolutism'. From his conception of the individual ontology of man and thing, he gave a metaphysical justification of absolute private property as a direct legal relationship between two individual instances — man and thing — which later became the basis of the economic philosophy of liberalism.

In general, Ockham is rightly regarded as the precursor of the later *bourgeois liberal-democratic ideology* based on philosophy, metaphysics and ethics extremely close to Ockham's views. Both the main currents in

---

32 Guilelmi de Ockham, *Opera Politica. 4 vols* (Manchester; Oxford: Manchester University Press; Oxford University Press, 1940–1997).

empirical science and modern analytic philosophy usually trace their origins to him.

Nominalism prepared the ideological ground for Protestant philosophy and for some currents of the Renaissance. In it we see two fundamental aspects of the political Logos of the modern age: materialism and individualism, which will be fully developed later in a different context — completely beyond the paradigm of Tradition. In principle, nominalism contains all the basic preconditions for such a political philosophy which is built strictly from the bottom up, contrary to those vertical models which dominated the Church and the state during the Catholic Middle Ages.[33]

The New Age. The Paradigm of Modernity

Here we come to what is the paradigm of the New Age.[34]

The New Age is an era that began with the sixteenth century in Western Europe and lasted until the end of the twentieth century, representing a completely unique historical period. In the same period of time in non-Western Europe there were still traditional societies built on the political philosophy of the Father and the political philosophy of the Son. The New Age is therefore a phenomenon localised not only historically but also geographically.

It can be said that the New Age is a particular type of philosophy, politics, culture, science and thinking characteristic of Western Europe from the sixteenth to the twentieth century. At first, its influence was partly felt in Italy,[35] where some scientific materialistic doctrines were formed, as

---

33 We should pay attention to the fact that in Orthodox culture nothing even remotely resembling nominalism existed nor exists, and the basic topology of thought remains in the context of the philosophy of the Father and the philosophy of the Son, never coming even close to equating being with matter or with individuality. In Orthodoxy, the philosophy of Aristotle, the most important points of which in the context of Orthodox theology are expounded by John Damascene (c. 675–c. 753), has retained its significance up to the present time. See Saint John Damascene, *Writings: The Fount of Knowledge*.

34 Dugin, *Postphilosophy*.

35 Dugin, *Noomakhia. The Roman Logos. The Sun and the Cross*.

well as in England[36] and France,[37] which became the two main poles of the spread of modernity both within Europe and beyond its borders. modernity then began to expand in 'circles' around the planet, spiralling — mainly through colonial conquests — around the world. In fact, the Age of Columbus coincides with the beginning of the modern age. In some societies, the New Age worldview penetrated as deeply as in Europe itself, where it reached some mineral roots of human culture, making the modern a natural, self-evident mental milieu.

While in Europe this movement was directed in depth (one can call it *intensive* modernity'), in colonial societies or in societies that were partially Westernised and Europeanised from outside, there was a surface overlay of these systems of thinking on deeper archaic and traditional models, in which case the extensive spread of the modern paradigm affected mainly the superficial aspects of society. Such superimposition of two paradigms — the paradigm of modern on the paradigm of Tradition which had not been fully exhausted — gave rise to a special sociological phenomenon: the *archaeomodern*.[38] In any case, since the sixteenth century this New Age paradigm has been gradually expanding, and today it is, in one form or another, dominant on a global scale.

What is the meaning of the New Age in terms of philosophy? Starting with Galileo Galilei (1564–1642) and Pierre Gassendi, the first theorists who laid the foundations for the scientific picture of the New Age,[39] this philosophy turns directly to Leucippus, Democritus, Epicurus and Lucretius. This marks a departure from a vertical worldview in the spirit of Plato and Aristotle and establishes a new view of the world — from the bottom up, from the perspective of matter, corporeality, and direct earthly presence. This is accompanied by radical attacks on Aristotle, who was regarded in the Middle Ages as the standard and infallible thinker in everything that concerned science and cosmology. The legacy of the atomists,

---

36 Dugin, *Noomakhia. England or Britain? Sea Power and Positive Subject Matter.*
37 Dugin, *Noomakhia. The French Logos. Orpheus and Melusina.*
38 Dugin, *Archaeomodern.*
39 Dugin, *The Evolution of the Paradigmatic Foundations of Science.*

which had existed in the margins of culture, is extracted from oblivion and gradually becomes a new scientific and philosophical dogma.

The direct predecessors of the atomists were the medieval nominalists, who were most influential in England. Later it was precisely England that would become the cultural milieu where the main points of this new paradigm would be developed earlier and, in a sense, more fully and vividly than in other European countries.

In terms of Plato's three levels of being, in modernity we are dealing with the philosophy of the Mother, matter, χώρα. The whole New Age scientific picture of the world by Galileo, Copernicus, and especially by Descartes and Newton (1642–1727) is based on the idea of Democritic atomism. In this way New Age philosophy is new because it overthrows both the principle of the Father and the principle of the Son; in parallel with this there is the overthrow of the Christian Middle Ages. Yet at the same time it rediscovers the basic tenets of that philosophical trend which in classical Greece was considered marginal and extravagant.

The New Age thought of itself as an alternative paradigm to the Middle Ages and set itself the task of overthrowing the verticality that had been the essence of the preceding worldviews, which had prevailed in Europe in both the Christian and pre-Christian eras. Henceforth, if scientists, who considered only knowledge based on rational judgement or physical experience to be reliable, still recognised God, it was only as a philosophical convention, as an abstract cause, necessary as an explanation of the fact of material existence. This current was called 'deism', i.e. the belief in God in isolation from religion, cult, full-fledged theology or a complete dogmatic worldview. Such faith was not thought of as a revelation from Heaven, but as a rational conclusion arrived at on the basis of consistent reasoning by a group of individual — atomic — personalities.

Protestantism is Based on a 'Religious Atom'

The most important moment of transition from the Traditional paradigm to the modern paradigm was the *Protestant Reformation* in Europe.

We have briefly described the model on which the Orthodox and Catholic interpretation of the Political was based, mentioning also

Protestantism. Here we should dwell on this in a little more detail, since it is with Protestantism that European civilisation transitions to the New Age.

In the sixteenth century, a new religious movement called Protestantism appeared in Europe. It rejected orthodoxy and Catholicism, establishing a new religious model based on a 'religious atom', not God, but man able to make his own judgement about God.

The Protestant Reformation — still formally within the Christian context — moves from a political theology of the Father and the Son to a political theology of the earth, which is no longer centred around God, but on man, the individual.[40] Protestants are united in congregations, communities, where they reason about God with the support of their own consciousness and make decisions about Him. They regard themselves as having the right to revoke aspects of tradition or to add new aspects. Religious dogma loses its meaning. The doctrine of the Church based on the supernatural presence of Christ and the Holy Spirit is replaced by a social constructivist interpretation. Thus, at the level of religion the hierarchy of verticality is completely lost and consequently the whole picture of the sacred world collapses. Protestants redefine Christianity on the basis of the individual. This was the main reform of Martin Luther (1483–1546) and his followers, which dealt a powerful blow to the medieval world image, to priesthood.

A new theology, a new philosophy of nature and, most importantly for us, a *new political philosophy* are emerging in the Protestant milieu. Almost all the classics of modern political philosophy were, in one way or another, from a Protestant background, because we are dealing with a common phenomenon — *a paradigm shift*, a transition from Aristotelianism and Platonism to an entirely new picture of the world. This time it is horizontal and even chthonic, and at its centre is not God, as before, but man. The concept of the world, of God, of the relationship between Creator and creation, is built not from the top down, but from the bottom up. The political system is organised in the same way, bottom-up; it is now seen as the product of a 'collective contract', a 'social contract'.

---

40 Dugin, *Noomakhia. The Germanic Logos. Apophatic Man.*

In principle, Democritus understood the essence of politics in a similar way, arguing that laws and states were invented by men and therefore there is nothing sacred about them; they can be reconstructed or abolished at any time.

Although Protestantism is still a religion, it essentially clears the way for the emergence of pure atheism. Here we can recall the words of the philosopher Friedrich Nietzsche (1844–1900): 'God is dead. It was we who killed him — you and I!'[41] In relation to political philosophy this tragic statement means that the essence of the New Age is the dismantling of the Platonic-Aristotelian conception of God and the shifting of everything to earth, to materiality, to economics, to the individual, to material and technological progress, to capitalism. Thus, the political philosophy of the New Age is nothing but a political slice of the new philosophical paradigm.

Rebellion of the Third Estate

In Plato, the philosopher rises from the cave and descends back into the cave; he separates himself from ordinary people who see only shadows; he then comprehends the truth and returns with new knowledge. In Aristotle we saw the 'unmoved mover', which is the immanent God around whom all beings revolve, striving to approach him. In Platonism, the subject is the transcendent God, and the whole politics of Platonism is built around God as the agent. In Aristotelianism God is no longer thought of as transcendent, but as inherent in the world; it is the idea of an 'unmoved mover' which stands at the centre of things, not above them.

On the third level, in New Age philosophy, *a new subject* (the bourgeoisie, the third estate) emerges, democratically organising its political system, acting as a socio-political atom and emphasising material things. This transformation is an act of rebellion by the third estate of European society against the two higher castes (priests and warriors). Such an act of rebellion constitutes the profound meaning of New Age philosophy.

---

41 Friedrich Nietzsche, *The Gay Science* (New York: Random House, 1974).

The political philosophy of the New Age presents society and politics as a *creation of human hands*. The state is presented as a product of human individuals and the idea of a social contract (a state that is based on a social contract) emerges.

Note the metaphysical and philosophical roots of this completely new idea. *The state becomes a product of the social contract only if the subject of politics is an individual* (i.e. an atom). Self-sufficient atoms unite into a group and launch the state, creating it.

Plato's conception of the state is quite different: the state is not created by anyone, its structure is not created by people, the state as Kallipolis always exists, while the state in the world of phenomena is an expression of being, of sacred being, built on the principle of sacred hierarchy.

Aristotle said that 'man is the political animal'. What does 'political animal' mean? It means that everything non-political in man is an animal, and if we take politics out of man, we get a beast. Elsewhere Aristotle says that man is 'the rational animal'. Here a man is defined through the state and through thought; the state and thought are not defined through man. In the classical version of vertical society, only a being ('animal') who has woken up to philosophy and politics is really a person. Aristotle and Plato believe that if a person is not engaged in politics, if he does not think and does not philosophise, then he does not exist. Thus, man is a derivative of the Logos, of the idea.

New Age philosophy completely overturns this definition. Here man himself produces both thought and state. From the eternal shining heavenly truth, the idea transforms into the result of the deduction of a single individual, whose normative character becomes the bourgeois, the philistine. Correspondingly, the state loses its sacred dimension, morphing into something akin to an *artel*[42], a trust or a commercial enterprise. The third estate brings its own philosophy with it — that of the body, feeling, matter, comfort, carnal pleasures, prosperity and security. Politics is henceforth

---

42 Translator's note: Artel (Russian артель) was a voluntary association of people to organise joint economic activities in the Russian Empire.

constructed in accordance with the philosophy not of priests, thinkers and heroes, but of merchants.[43]

Man as a Producer and Trader

New Age political philosophy regards thinking and political philosophy as an artificial construct of the individual. For the Platonists and Aristotelians, for people of traditional society, politics is just as much a given as the world is a given. For the New Age philosophers (as for Democritus) politics is a man-made phenomenon. Politics is as random as the cohesion of atoms. The state arose artificially, based on the contract and agreement of people and, accordingly, politics may as well not exist.

What then is man in this New Age philosophy? Man here is a creature who produces (*homo faber*) and trades (*homo mercatus*).

In the classical model, politics is an inherent part of the very nature of the philosopher and the warrior, but for a member of the third estate politics is fundamentally optional. Hence the idea that New Age political philosophy views the political dimension as artificial and contractual, i.e. not contiguous with the nature of the world or even the nature of man. Politics is here understood as an artificial construction, which is built by man, but which does not reflect human nature. Politics becomes optional.

What, then, reflects human nature? Food, commerce, comfort, security, pleasure, material activity, bodily reproduction. Politics and the state, unlike economic activity, are in New Age philosophy an entirely optional part of existence. From here emerges the idea of civil society as a community of autonomous individuals, who, in fact, do not need politics and are content with non-political forms of life.

This is how the economy, or political economy, gradually comes to the fore. For economic men (*homo economicus*), who have gradually supplanted political men (*homo politicus*), the economy has indeed become their destiny.

---

43 Werner Sombart, *Traders and Heroes* (London: Arktos Media, 2021).

Theomachy and Democracy

Gradually in modern times, political society (i.e. vertically organised — hierarchical) is replaced by civil society. 'Citizens' means ordinary city dwellers, townspeople, which implies that in their case there is no belonging to a higher class. The same meaning is held by the French term *bourgeois*, derived from the German *Burg*, meaning 'fortified town'. Civil society is the same as bourgeois society — that is, such a model where a member of the third estate represents the norm.

Civil society is, at its core, a radical, revolutionary, democratic and, at the extreme, a theomachist concept. It reflects the act of 'killing God' in the sphere of political philosophy. It is the rejection of the sacred dimension of politics, of the hierarchy, of the fact that the state is an ontological reality. It is the relegation of the Political to the economic, commercial and mercantile.

According to Plato, this is the ultimate degradation of Kallipolis to the level of oligarchy and democracy (approaching the edge of tyranny). And according to Aristotle, 'democracy' represents the worst model of government by many.

But in terms of the New Age paradigm, civil society is thought of as the 'natural state of man'. Hence the idea of the *non-obligatory nature of the state*. According to the classical theories of the modern age, the state can — and sooner or later *must* — be abolished. The various political ideologies of the modern age describe this with some differences. Liberals, for example, believe that a world market should emerge in place of the state. Communists believe that when the Communist state has fulfilled its historical function, it will be abolished and everyone will live in a 'united society of mankind'.[44] Why do liberalism and Communism as two typical philosophies of modernity deny the state? Because initially, from the

---

44 Vladimir Mayakovsky (1893–1930) wrote in his poem 'To comrade Nett, steamer and man': 'We live, clutched by an iron oath. For her — to the cross, and scratch with a bullet: it is for us to live as one human community in the world without Russia, without Latvia.' [Original Russian: 'Мы живём, зажатые железной клятвой. За нее — на крест, и пулею чешите: это — чтобы в мире без Россий, без Латвий жить единым человечьим общежитьем.']

point of view of the primordial conception of civil society as composed of atoms, the state is thought of as an artificial construct. And consequently, politics, although possible, does not constitute the essential dimension of the human being. With modernisation and 'progress', the state and politics have to be completely replaced by economics (hence the thesis: 'economy as destiny'). If the people have created the state themselves and it has nothing sacred in it, they may abolish it. This they will do, sooner or later, under the right circumstances.

Accordingly, politics is something temporary, contingent, intermediate, artificial and completely man-made; non-ontological, non-sacred, non-religious, non-natural, non-organic. Thus, in the transition to the modern paradigm, politics fundamentally changes its status, its being. It is no longer an obligatory feature inherent in every person, but something optional. From now on, it is no longer man created for politics (as a 'political animal'), but politics created for man.

Moving on to New Age political philosophy, we are dealing with a radically new philosophical picture of the world, with different philosophical foundations for thinking, science, culture and social organisation.

Thus the unity between the divine paradigm (Idea), man and the world is lost. Everything is now divided into the subjective and the objective (like Descartes): the state in this situation is thought of as something subjective, built by men, while nature and especially matter are thought of as something objective, something that needs to be learned and subjugated.

Secularisation: A Society Which Kills God

In traditional society, the idea of constructing a political philosophy on the basis of a material premise was impossible. Such a society had to deny God and the sacred in politics, to overthrow the hierarchical vertical, and this went against the whole structure of the worldview of Tradition.

A term that denies the dominance of religion and the sacred dimension in politics is 'secularisation'.[45] *Secular society is a society that has been desacralised. The very concept of secularism is a fundamental notion of New Age philosophy, implying that society is not created by God, not on the basis of Revelation or the Covenant, not by some supreme powers, but by human beings alone, by particular corporeal atomic individuals.*

Secular society is a society that kills God, a theomachist society, an anti-Christian society. A person who calls himself a supporter of the secular model is a supporter of the Antichrist. This is the meaning of the philosophy of Friedrich Nietzsche.

The hieromonk Seraphim Rose (1934–1982) said that the true enemy of Christ is not the one who is a great denier, but the one who is a small affirmer, who has Christ only on his lips and not in his heart.[46] He was referring precisely to Nietzsche. Nietzsche, who wrote about the death of God, does not kill God, he only states that the modern secular paradigm, the philosophy of modernity, is the Antichrist. Nietzsche does not call for the Antichrist; he sees the Antichrist in the Western, secular, modernist and scientific picture of the world. Nietzsche says that God was not killed by him personally; God was killed by Western European civilisation, which carried out the rebellion of the Earth against God the Father and God the Son. Nietzsche reveals that denial, that nihilism, which lies at the heart of the third version of political philosophy. Nietzsche is the great denier, but, from Seraphim Rose's point of view, the one who uncovers the monstrous essence of the modern world is not so terrible as the one who does not notice it, who is calm about everything that is going on around him. The truth about evil is not evil in itself.

45　We have seen that one of the first advocates of secularisation was the major nominalist William Ockham.

46　Seraphim Rose, *Nihilism: The Root of the Revolution of the Modern Age* (Forestville, California: Fr. Seraphim Rose Foundation, 1994).

New Age Swineopolis

All paradigms of New Age political philosophy are constructed within the fundamental model of the Mother (titanism, materialism[47]). As modernity strengthens, the upper hand in the battle between the gods and the giants shifts to the giants.

Modernity has radically changed human thinking. Europe, in both Antiquity and the Middle Ages, lived with inertia in the political philosophy of the Father and the political philosophy of the Son (in a traditional, sacred society). The New Age resolutely overturns these models: there is no Father and no Son, there is only the atomic individual who is left to himself, bound to his biological existence. And everything else is a construction of his, his projection, his creation. This is *homo faber*, 'man the creator', who has replaced *deus fFaber*, 'God the Creator'.

If Aristotle had seen the political history of Europe from the sixteenth to the twentieth century, he would probably have said, 'Look, these are not people! Their politics are secondary, their thinking is nebulous. Divine thought and contemplative life are no longer their highest values. Their souls are dominated not by wisdom, but by the animal spirit.' In fact, Socrates talked about something similar in the *Republic*, drawing the image of a 'city of pigs', 'swineopolis', inhabited by people interested only in food, individual comfort, recreational trips, etc. The following picture emerges in the dialogue:

> And Glaucon said: 'If you were founding a city of pigs, Socrates, what other fodder than this would you provide?'
>
> 'But what else is required, Glaucon?'
>
> 'What is customary', he replied, 'they must recline on couches and dine from tables and have the delicacies and dainties which men now have; that, in my opinion, is what is needed to avoid misery and deprivation.'[48]

---

47 Dugin, *Noomakhia. The Three Logoi.*
48 Plato, *Republic*, 372d-e.

To 'recline on couches and dine from tables' and have access to 'delicacies', 'to avoid misery and deprivation' — this is the ethical ideal of pig-like humanity.

New Age philosophy in all its dimensions falls under Socrates' notion of the 'city of pigs' or the Nietzschean idea of the 'Last Men' ('"We have discovered happiness", say the Last Men, and they blink'[49]).

Since Western European society and all societies under its influence have lived by this paradigm since the sixteenth century, it seems to us to be self-evident. In fact, all our education, all our social norms, all our culture, all our politics are built on the basis that the figure of the citizen and human rights are the main pillars, that the individual is the measure of things, that democracy is the only natural, acceptable, legitimate form of political order, that the state is a construct created by individuals and should be secular, and that the welfare and well-being of citizens, free trade and freedom of movement are the basic principles of the political system. For us, the political philosophy of modernity is a code which we are fundamentally incapable of questioning. But thereby other types of political philosophy remain completely inaccessible to us and we hold a very distorted view of them.

Taking 'swineopolis' for granted, we can already hardly imagine what politics was like in other eras, what it is for other cultures that have retained a connection to religion and Tradition, and what it could theoretically become again if we opt for a different paradigm — that of the Father or the Son.

Regicide Is a Fundamental Gesture of Modernity

In order to get an idea of what political philosophy is in its fullest form, of what *Political Aeterna* is, one has to realise how fundamental the shift from the Tradition paradigm to the modern paradigm has been. The modern picture of the world — with respect to both nature and society — is based entirely on Democritus' materialist principle. There can be no Platonic philosopher, no king, no aristocrat, no hero in the political

---

49 Friedrich Nietzsche, *Thus Spoke Zarathustra* (London: Penguin Classics, 1974).

philosophy of the modern. Moreover, within this model, *he who looks up*, he who strives to go beyond the cave and its spectacle, must be sacrificed — mauled, killed by the aggressive mob that *looks at the shadows* and predatorily destroys anyone who tries to show it otherwise.

Regicide can be called a fundamental principle of the political philosophy of modernity. The guardians of Plato's state, the priests and the aristocracy are also destined to be dismantled — the revolt of the bourgeoisie implies the elimination of the two higher estates, the priests and the warriors. The New Age is the embodiment and full realisation of the bourgeois caste, the third estate. The act of regicide was the culmination of three of the most symbolically significant revolutions in modern European history:

1) The English Revolution, when Charles I (1600–1649) was executed, which was the climax of radical Protestantism,

2) the French Revolution, when the Jacobins beheaded Louis XVI (1754–1793), establishing the bourgeois Republic and

3) the October Revolution, when the Bolsheviks executed the last Russian Orthodox tsar, Nicholas II (1868–1918), initiating the construction of the first ever socialist state based on radical materialism and theomachy.

These executions symbolised the breakdown of the vertical, because at each turn the revolutionaries dealt a crushing blow to the vertical organisation of society, to the sacred axis of hierarchy, to the foundations of Tradition's political philosophy. Moreover, each time the structure of society became — at least nominally — more and more horizontal, level, reduced to the lowest common denominator.

Present-Day Modernity

Today we are at the end of the full cycle of the establishment of the political philosophy of modernity — at the very bottom of this conceptual field, where individualisation and the movement towards materiality reach a stage of transition into the sphere of virtual dissipation and the final liquidation of the political beginning. The American political analyst Francis

Fukuyama wrote an important text on 'the end of history' in the early 1990s.[50] He had in mind the *end of political history*, the complete removal of the Political and the transition to trade. In his view, world politics was to be replaced by the world economy. And since history is always and foremost *political history*, the transition from politics to pure economics would also mean the end of history itself.

Although Fukuyama's prediction turned out to be somewhat hasty, his analysis is still broadly valid. Political modernity initially consisted of replacing hierarchical (sacred) politics with democratic and secular politics, and as democratisation progressed, politics itself was gradually to be abolished. In fact, Fukuyama declared that a 'swineopolis' was being built on a planetary scale, and in a sense, given the successes of civil society, liberalism and the market economy by the end of the twentieth century, he is not that far from the truth. In any case, there is no question that we are currently at the very last moment of the modern. This modern began in the sixteenth century and approached its conclusion at the beginning of the twentieth. Thus we are in a unique situation where we can look at the full cycle of the political paradigm of the modern. We know how and when it began, and we can trace its formation and roughly imagine how it will end, as this end is palpably close and absolutely inevitable.

Compared with the difference between the political philosophy of the Father and the political philosophy of the Son — between the two male political philosophies and ontologies — the transition to the Mother model of the third beginning was radically new. The New Age was indeed *new*. The shifts here were much more fundamental than in the transition from Platonism to Aristotelianism, all the more so because everywhere in the context of traditional society the political philosophy of the Father and the political philosophy of the Son coexisted quite harmoniously and often formed a unified structure.

Here, too, in the transition to the political philosophy of the Mother, χώρα, there has actually been a global revolution, a radical change of all proportions. In all the major philosophical axes, the vectors changed by

---

50 Francis Fukuyama, *The End of History and the Last Man* (London: Penguin Books, 2012).

180 degrees: in the structure of the world, in the structure of God, in the being of man, in the being of the Political, in notions of time and space, etc. It was a genuine revolution of the New Age, which becomes understandable only when it is properly juxtaposed with other political philosophies — those peculiar to traditional society.

Unless we understand how revolutionary, avantgarde, and innovative the philosophical assertions of the New Age were, we cannot understand the world we live in and the processes taking place within it. For if we look *only* at modern age philosophy as the basic, the only, and the optimal philosophy, we will be unable to comprehend what went on in the history of Europe, what is going on now in non-Western European societies, and what is more and more obviously coming over our contemporary culture in the form of the postmodern paradigm, which in many fields has already largely replaced the modern age.

To completely comprehend political philosophy, we should have in mind a complete frame of reference — we must understand the political philosophy of Platonism and the political philosophy of Aristotelianism in spite of the fact that they do not exist in their pure form in our society. This structure is necessary in order to understand more precisely the very nature of modernity (which is now in turn in a phase of transition to postmodernity), to interpret correctly the traditional societies remaining in the non-Western world, and to interpret complex variants of the archaeomodern — that is, such political systems in which modernisation has not penetrated deeply, giving rise to bizarre hybrid forms. This phenomenon is characteristic of some post-colonial countries (Asia, Africa, Latin America) as well as of Russia and China, which are forced to carry out defensive modernisation under external pressure from Western civilisation.

CHAPTER 9

PROTESTANTISM AND ITS SECULARISATION

A Phase Transition in the Structure of Political Theology

A Third Christianity

THE POLITICS of the New Age are closely linked to the Protestant religion. Protestantism emerged in the sixteenth century, with the reforms of Martin Luther, as well as other reformers Jean Calvin (1509–1564), Philip Melanchthon (1497–1560), etc. The leaders of Protestantism offered an entirely new model of Christianity. This model sharply broke with the paradigm of the Christian worldview that prevailed in Orthodoxy and in Catholicism during the Middle Ages. The Protestant interpretation of Christianity differed both from the Aristotelianism of the Scholastics (which had elements of Platonism, particularly evident in the teaching of the 'two cities') and from the ontology of Empire that prevailed in the Orthodox world (Byzantism).[1] Protestantism was based on a completely new approach to the interpretation of God, the world, the Church and man. At the heart of their theories was the Christian as an individual who determined his relationship to God on the basis of his reasoning.

Thus a new — third — Christianity emerges — beyond Platonic and Aristotelian Christianity, a Christianity which is democratic, 'Democritic',

---

1   Dugin, *Noomakhia. The Byzantine Logos. Hellenism and Empire.*

atomistic.[2] It is still a religion, that is, a doctrine which recognises the existence of God and a number of Christian dogmas, including the authority of the Old and New Testaments, the Revelation, the Trinity and the divinity-humanity of Christ. But there is already something emerging in it that fundamentally breaks with the age of the premodern, with the age of traditional European society.

Protestantism as a religion, theology and ethics prepares the paradigm of New Age philosophy in politics, in culture, in economics, and in other key areas of social life. It is precisely the Protestant worldview, the Protestant religion, the Protestant ideology that lays the foundations of the New Age paradigm. It is a transitional moment, because there is *still* a religion, but there is *no longer* a Church (as in Catholicism), *no longer* an Empire (as in Orthodoxy or the Habsburgs).

Abolition of Sacred Tradition

Luther proclaimed that it was necessary to return to the epochs of original Christianity, and to 'cleanse' religion of its historical burdens. Catholicism (as well as Orthodoxy) accepted as sources of unquestionable truth and supreme authority the Holy Scriptures (the Bible) and Holy Tradition, including traditional interpretations, institutions, customs, foundations, institutions, etc. Luther, Calvin and other leaders of Protestantism completely rejected Sacred Tradition. Though they still recognised the authority of Holy Scripture, they interpreted it arbitrarily, relying on reasoned analysis and personal spiritual experience.

The Catholic Church is built from the top down. There is Christ and His incarnation. There is the direct transmission of the grace of the rays of the Holy Spirit, the third part of the Holy Trinity, descending on the Apostles through the unbroken chain of the priesthood. On Pentecost the Holy Spirit *descends from above* upon the Apostles. The Apostles, through the power of the Holy Spirit, form the Church. The first of the Apostles, Peter, becomes the foundation (Greek Πέτρος, 'stone') of the Church, the

---

2   The immediate forerunners of this 'third' Christianity are the nominalists (materialists and individualists), who remained formally in the bosom of Catholicism, but prepared an entirely different worldview below the surface.

first Bishop of Rome, from whom the succession of popes proceeds. Everything is formed from top to bottom, from Christ to his Apostles, who as God ordains men, and the Holy Spirit descends on them at Pentecost. The Church is formed, strictly speaking, vertically, by condescension. In doing so it is eternal, and at the same time participates in history.

This dimension of eternity and this vertical symmetry is also fully inherent in Orthodoxy.

In Protestantism, however, things are different. There is an authoritative book, a text — the Bible. It is read by people. They comprehend, interpret, comment on the texts based on their own reasoning. Some may interpret a passage from Scripture in one way, others in another, still others in a third. Here everyone has the right and freedom to decipher, there is no obligatory tradition, no supreme unquestionable authority. Anyone can, relying entirely on his own reasoning, on his own reflection, interpret any passage of Holy Scripture. And when these interpretations satisfy others, they join together in a community, in a congregation, in a sect. That said, the term 'sect' in Protestantism is of a neutral and positive nature. Formally registered Protestant sects are called 'churches' or denominations.

This is not the case in Catholicism and Orthodoxy. Interpretation forms the basis of the Holy Tradition of the Church. The interpretation of the Gospel, the interpretation of the Old Testament, is transmitted in the Church as authoritative teaching, consolidated by the councils and the decisions of the pope. The Orthodox recognise the supreme authority of the First Seven Ecumenical Councils and the body of texts of the sacred patristic literature. Catholics also recognise later councils, but consider the opinion of the pope to be the ultimate authority in matters of religion. The pope has the final word in determining what is heresy and how to interpret this or that passage of Scripture. In Orthodoxy, this function is not carried out by the pope, but by the Orthodox tradition as a whole (the decrees of the Ecumenical Councils and the patristic writings of the Fathers). The two branches of Christianity, Catholicism and Orthodoxy, recognise both Scripture and Tradition. Tradition is passed down in

Church. In such a case, the personal, individual interpretation of religion and the main questions connected with it must be in conformity with that Tradition. Catholics add to this the binding nature of a decision officially pronounced by the pope.

Protestants object: No, we will interpret religion ourselves. As we think, so we will interpret it. Accordingly, an entirely new conception of power, of the source of authority, emerges. The church or its counterpart is *not created here from the top down, but from the bottom up*. On the basis of their own interpretations, people make judgements about God, about the world, about themselves.

In other words, a very different concept of authority emerges. The Church still exists while there is still a Christian community and while there is still Scripture endowed with supreme authority. But the whole interpretation, the whole constitution of Church, community and society in general, is constructed 'from the bottom up'.

The rejection of Sacred Tradition was at the heart of the Protestant Reformation, which demanded that only the text of the Bible should hold authority, questioning all other aspects of the living Christian tradition, from interpretation to ritual. Thus some versions of Protestantism rejected the Eucharist (communion), the liturgy, and the worship of icons, reducing the service to the joint singing of individual psalms and rather arbitrary sermons. Some currents — Calvinism, for example — abolished the institution of the priesthood. Most Protestant denominations deny icons. Some Protestant currents, such as the Hussite movement in Bohemia, deny the cross as a symbol of Christ's suffering. That is to say, even the cross ceases to be a symbol of Christianity here. Churches depict chalices as a symbol of this movement.

Many have questioned the fundamentals of the Christian faith, to the point where the most extreme Protestants, the 'Unitarians' or 'Socinianists',[3] have rejected the dogma of the Trinity.

---

3   Dugin, *Noomakhia. England or Britain? Sea Power and Positive Subject Matter.*

Against Celibacy

Protestant ideology, based on the individual, his reason and his personal will, destroys the very foundation of the idea of the Church's divine origin as it was understood by Catholics and Orthodox alike. Catholicism defined 'Church' as the clergy, that is, the totality of those ordained to the priestly rank. At the same time, for Catholics all priests had to remain unmarried and celibate.[4] According to Roman Catholic teaching, the Catholic clergy, that is, priests who have been ordained and are strictly observing celibacy, constitute the citizens of 'the City of God', i.e. the Church.[5] Ordinary Christians, on the other hand, have the right to marry through a special sacrament.

Luther and the other Reformers struck a blow to priestly celibacy, declaring that the clergy celibacy rules were a late 'fabrication' and decreed that from now on priests could be married. Luther himself was originally a monk, and by decreeing that monks could henceforth marry, set the example. Thus monasticism was abolished and the monasteries dissolved.

The authority of the pope, on which all Western European political philosophy had hitherto rested, was definitively rejected. The whole Catholic clergy — cardinals, bishops and priests — suffered the same fate. Some Protestant movements (Lutheranism proper) retained their hierarchy and a number of liturgical practices, while others (Calvinists) rejected both completely.

Against Empire

Parallel to the rejection of the former doctrine of the Church, the Reformation also rejected the very idea of the empire. At first the rulers of the Holy Roman Empire vacillated between supporting Rome or the Reformation, partly continuing the imperial tradition of the Ghibellines.

---

4   Orthodox tradition allows marriage for the diocesan clergy, but the highest ranks of the bishop require — as in Catholicism — celibacy.
5   From an Orthodox perspective, not only priests and bishops (clergy) but all baptised Orthodox Christians are included in the Church, which significantly broadens the concept of the Church and changes part of its substance.

Under Charles V, Holy Roman Emperor (1500–1558), the Protestant north and the Catholic south attempted to demarcate their powers within a common political system (the Peace of Augsburg). Nevertheless, a part of the Habsburgs, above all the radical Catholic Philip II (1527–1598), subsequently sided with Rome, and eventually the Austrian Habsburgs too were inclined towards this choice. This led to the secession of the Protestant countries of Holland, Sweden, Norway and Prussia. Together with England and France (which, although still Catholic, were fiercely opposed to the Habsburgs), this gave rise to an anti-imperial coalition of European powers.

In the place of empire (and its echoes of catechism) comes an entirely different politically normative idea: a nation-state created by the people (again from the bottom up) for security, protection and the optimal realisation of private material interests. Such a nation-state has no higher purpose or mission. It rejects both the Byzantine concept of catechumens and the Catholic interpretation of the doctrine of the 'two cities'. The empire had a sacred meaning and papal authority brought a transcendent dimension (also sacred) to medieval European politics. People were subject to God, the Earth to Heaven, and individual political entities to a higher unity. That is why the empire steadily bore the epithet 'Holy'. The Protestant state is not sacred in principle. It has no mission or higher objective. It performs technical functions, and can always theoretically be rebuilt, changed or even abolished. This was the principle used to build Protestant communities, from which anyone could leave at any time by changing their interpretation and joining a different sect. Bourgeois companies, firms, trusts and trading partnerships were also formed on this principle.

Thus, in this Protestant worldview we come to the concept of a *social contract*, which is fundamental to all New Age philosophy and politics. The Church is no longer a product of the condescension of an idea or the Holy Spirit radiating from above. It is the product of a *social contract*. And the state is no longer an empire endowed with a sacred mission, but an artificial creation of individuals aimed at resolving some private secular tasks.

Thus, the political philosophy of Protestantism overturned the very structure of the vertical organisation of the world, society and religion, which was common not only to Western and Eastern Christianity, not only to Byzantism and the doctrine of the 'two cities', but to the whole known history of Europe, from Antiquity to the Renaissance. This is the special significance of Protestantism: it prepared the transition to an entirely new model of looking at the world from the bottom upwards.

Wealth as a Virtue

The phenomenon of Protestantism as the basis of the New Age paradigm was thoroughly explored by the German sociologist, one of the founders of sociology itself, Max Weber in his work *Protestant Ethics*.[6] This work is one of the most famous classic works of sociology. In it, Weber shows how the Protestant worldview, Protestant theology, Protestant ideology and the ethics built upon it form the preconditions of bourgeois society, the system of values of capitalism born out of this Protestant approach.

Weber demonstrates that Protestantism justifies the supreme value of rational practical activity and elevates the merchant, the entrepreneur to the highest ideal — that is, the citizen, the bourgeois. Weber shows that the Catholic worldview as a whole is directed towards the spiritual world and wealth is never considered the highest virtue. Hence the cult of poverty in some monastic orders, first of all among the Franciscans. Protestantism, on the other hand, concentrated on earthly life, regarding material wealth as a sign of being 'chosen'. Calvin, in his theory of Predestination, declared that man can change neither his earthly nor his posthumous destiny and that wealth and success should be interpreted as the most visible form of virtue; wealth is the good and the sign of the elect, while poverty is a vice and a curse.

In Protestantism, such a thing as a posthumous reward disappears. It is believed that one does not receive a reward in the future, but in our lifetime. Therefore the thesis arises that God distributes good and evil, rewards the righteous and punishes the sinners in this life. Not afterwards,

---

6   Max Weber, *Protestant Ethics and the Spirit of Capitalism* (London: George Allen & Unwin Ltd, 1930).

not after death, but here and now. Thus the afterlife, which plays a huge role in Catholicism and Orthodoxy, actually loses its significance and the theme of judgement, punishment and retribution is transferred to earthly life.

Such an approach reverses all proportions. In Orthodoxy, in full accordance with Christ's Sermon on the Mount, it is those who are poor in spirit, those who weep, those who suffer, those who are hungry who are considered blessed.[7] That is, the beatitudes describe people who are deprived, people who suffer, who weep, who have nothing. And the second part of these symmetrical formulas gives the promise of the coming justice to be attained in the Kingdom of Heaven — for they shall be comforted, for they shall be sated, for they shall be called the sons of God… All the miserable, the unfortunate, the poor, the suffering, the deprived are the 'salt of the earth'. This, in Orthodoxy, is the norm of ethics. Poverty in Orthodoxy means likely to be good, honest. Rich means likely to be not so good. And it is more difficult for a rich person to enter the Kingdom of Heaven than for a poor person.[8] The poor man is promised an easy way into the Kingdom of Heaven, but the rich man has a difficult way. That does not mean it is closed; it does not mean that every poor person is good. But on the whole, the poor are better off than the rich. Because it is easier for the poor and the afflicted — they are deprived of much or even everything in this world, in the material corporeal universe. And this is not just a trial, but a driving impulse to seek truth and justice beyond the material world — to strive for the Kingdom of Heaven and Christ. The

---

7   'Blessed are the poor in spirit, for theirs is the kingdom of heaven. Blessed are those who weep, for they shall be comforted. Blessed are the meek, for they shall inherit the earth. Blessed are those who hunger and thirst for righteousness, for they shall be filled. Blessed are the merciful, for they shall be pardoned. Blessed are the pure in heart, for they shall see God. Blessed are the peacemakers, for they shall be called sons of God. Blessed are those who are cast out for righteousness, for theirs is the kingdom of heaven. Blessed are you when they shall revile and persecute you, and shall say all manner of evil against you falsely for my sake. Rejoice and be exceedingly glad, for great is your reward in heaven: thus were they that persecuted the prophets which were before you.' Gospel of Matthew 5: 3–11.

8   'It is easier for a camel to go through the eye of a needle than for a rich man to enter the kingdom of God.' Matthew 19: 24.

rich, on the other hand, are bound to an earthly existence, for it is said: 'Where your treasure is, there your heart will be also.'[9] Besides, one cannot serve God and mammon at the same time.[10] If the rich have riches in their hearts, they are not suitable for the other world and it is difficult for them to enter the Kingdom of Heaven. Of course, it is possible, if they give their wealth to the poor, if they serve the Motherland, the Church. But it is more difficult to do it. Pity for those who have gained a lot.

It is not quite the same in Catholicism as it is in Orthodoxy, but it is close. For example, St Francis of Assisi (1181 or 1182–1226) composed hymns to poverty, said that there is nothing more beautiful than the poor brethren, and the second thing he loves after Christ is poverty. He gives away everything. He completely sacrifices himself, absolutely everything. He walks barefoot in the winter, in just his shirtsleeves. His monasteries prosper but he lives only with the lowly, with the poor, settling for very little. Of course, this is by no means the whole of Catholicism, but to a large extent Franciscan ethics are considered to be the undisputed pinnacle of piety in Western Christianity. For all that is important and valuable is not here. 'My kingdom is not of this world.'[11] This is how the Orthodox and Catholic religions understand the world and ethics.

But this is not at all how Protestantism understands the world. On the contrary, from a Protestant point of view, rich means good, means chosen. The Last Judgement takes place here, and vengeance is also here. So the one who is poor is also bad. And, accordingly, the idea of enrichment takes on a religious sense. If a person works well, earns a lot, has gathered a lot of wealth, then he is almost a saint.

This idea that the rich are holy and the poor cursed is a crucial feature of Protestant ethics, a specific worldview. Notice how the ethical reference points change. Officially we are dealing with Christianity, but all the proportions are reversed, the whole structure of the worldview is almost the exact opposite.

---

9 Gospel of Matthew 6:21.
10 Luke 16:13.
11 John 18: 36.

Protestantism creates an entirely new scale of values within Christianity. Firstly, a Church which is not built from above, but from below. And, accordingly, can be dissolved and re-established. There is nothing, strictly speaking, holy about the Church. The Church becomes a matter of profane people gathering around the Scriptures in order to interpret them together, sometimes speaking in tongues (Pentecostals, modern Charismatics) — that is shouting incomprehensible words, sometimes shaking and making incomprehensible gestures, thinking that they are a vessel for the will of God (like the Shaker sect).

Protestantism as the Foundation of Modernity

It is from the Reformation movement that the political philosophy of modernity is born. The modern world carries Protestant attitudes at its core:

- religion here is a matter for the collective to determine by consensus whether or not there is a God, and how He should be interpreted;
- instead of a sacred Church founded by Christ and the Holy Spirit, there is a profane 'church', i.e. a sect;
- instead of a God-given and mission-bound Empire, a secular nation-state which is established on the basis of a social contract;
- instead of a focus on Christ and the Kingdom of Heaven, a total commitment to the material world;
- instead of a posthumous vindication and the Last Judgement, a predetermined destiny to poverty or wealth as an expression of earthly justice, the measure of which is material prosperity;
- instead of a sacred hierarchy, equality of opportunity;
- instead of priests, monks and warriors, the bourgeois;
- instead of the vertical, the horizontal;
- instead of universality, individualism and the glorification of absolute private property;
- instead of the heavenly, the earthly;

- instead of goodness and compassion, an ethics of profit and material prosperity.

This is precisely what Max Weber stresses: Protestantism, by shifting attention from the spiritual to the corporeal and from the heavenly to the earthly, has given the highest importance to wealth.

Protestantism breaks with traditional society and lays the foundations for modernity. Yet it is precisely a transition. Protestantism still maintains an appeal to God; the Church still exists; the authority of Scripture is still recognised; the existence of the state is still justified. The basis of these elements of religion and politics is henceforth the individual, but still some interpretation from the former paradigm of the Traditional world is retained. The axis of interpretation radically changes its direction — instead of a top-down gaze, the gaze is henceforth directed from the bottom upwards, but some distant connection with the vertical still remains.

If we secularise this Protestant theology, if we remove the reference to God and the Church, if we do away with the authority of the Bible altogether, and if we completely relativise the state (which for Protestants was necessary for protection from Catholics) — then we get the paradigm of the modern world, the modern in a full sense. Here instead of a 'church' (i.e. a sect), individuals unite into political parties, and parties constitute a parliament. Instead of freedom to interpret scripture, from now on one can interpret anything, and the authority of materialistic science completely supersedes the authority of religion. The individual is now free not only to decipher sacred texts, but to create his own, which in the context of a purely profane culture are given essentially equal status — private opinion. The state is disconnected now even from the task of defending Protestantism and becomes entirely an arbitrarily created Republic with strictly egoistic interests. Wealth is seen not as a sign of man's chosen status in some predetermined destiny, but simply as the highest value in isolation from any meaning whatsoever. Capital is henceforth the measure of things. This leads to capitalism, liberalism, secularism, civil society and, ultimately globalism.

Weber, as well as Louis Dumont (1911–1998), Werner Sombart (1863–1941), and others show that the Protestant Reformation led to just such a result, but that it was achieved only through overcoming Protestantism itself. The Reformation prepared the ground for the aodern age. But it was not yet modern in the full sense of the word, preserving in itself — albeit in an inverted and distorted sense — distinct echoes of traditional society.

The Secularisation of Calvinism Produces Liberalism

Protestant theology and Protestant ethics predetermine the foundations of New Age political philosophy. It should be noted that Protestantism can be divided into several quite different strands. Each of these strands can be seen as a matrix from which, in the course of further secularisation, one of the three main political ideologies of the modern age emerged.

The most ostensible line arising from the secularisation of Protestantism was capitalism, which is best reflected in the ideology of liberalism. It is liberalism that prioritises the individual as the measure of things in Protestant anthropology and considers the material state as the highest measure of the individual. Money in capitalism is an absolute virtue.

Among Protestant theologians, the Swiss Reformer Jean Calvin stands closest to this model. It was he who formulated the basic principles of an Individualist interpretation of religion, politics, society and culture. He was also the most consistent advocate of wealth as a sign of chosenness.

The Calvinists were the most radical opponents of Catholicism, denying hierarchy and the sacraments. In politics they held extreme democratic views. During the English Revolution from 1640 to 1660, the Calvinists and the different currents inspired by them formed the most extreme flank of the Protestant party, which insisted on the abolition of the monarchy (or the creation of a separate Fifth Monarchy) and a complete restructuring of society on the basis of bourgeois-democratic principles.

It is important to note that the Calvinists were the Founding Fathers who came by ship to New York when it was still a Dutch colony. The main nucleus of immigrants from England to North America, and from Europe as a whole, were from the most extreme Protestant groups of the Calvinist persuasion. It was they who laid the foundations of North American civilisation.

Calvin's Protestant doctrine of Predestination rejected the Christian thesis of free will (*liberum arbitrium*). This doctrine dramatically altered the very notion of the nature of time and the logic of history. Calvin believed that God's eternity necessarily contains all time. For God, time is synchronous, whereas for humanity it is experienced as a sequence. But in such a case the diachronic unfolding is incapable of changing anything in the content of history, for if it were otherwise, God would not be perfect. Consequently, Calvin concludes, free will does not exist; it is only the optical illusion of a mortal being whose horizon is fatally limited by time. In the view of Predestination, all history was deliberately predetermined and had a completed structure.

With the secularisation of this view and the removal of the 'God Hypothesis' from the equation, Calvinism — in its definitive modernist, materialist version — laid the foundations for an ideology of progress, that is, an interpretation of history in which all stages are deliberately predetermined. Calvinism passed on the ideology of progress to all the political ideologies of the modern age — liberalism, Communism and nationalism —, becoming one of the most important features of the Political in the context of the entire modern age. But on the whole, Calvinism influenced liberalism most of all. It could well be argued that *liberalism is a product of the secularisation of Calvinism*.

The Secularisation of Lutheranism Produces Bourgeois Nationalism

The ideas of Martin Luther, who is considered the main figure of the Reformation, generally placed the individual at the centre and had much in common with liberalism. Although Luther was politically supported by the German princes, who tried to leverage the Reformation to strengthen their political standing in opposition to the papacy and in part to the empire, he was, like Calvin, a spokesman for the third estate, what Plato ironically called 'swineopolis' in the *Republic*.

However, Lutheranism was not so rigid with regard to church traditions. It retained the idea of the priesthood (only now priests were allowed to marry), as well as some church sacraments — baptism, communion, marriage, etc. Lutherans categorically denied the authority of the pope, sometimes going so far as to identify him with the Antichrist. However, in their strict opposition to the Vatican, they recognised the legitimacy of national churches subordinate to secular — most often monarchical or princely — authorities. Thus, after the restoration of the monarchy, it was the Lutheran model which established itself as the main church in England, taking the shape of the Church of England with the King of England as its head.

A similar system developed in Scandinavia and Northern Germany, where Lutheranism became the philosophical basis of nation-states, where the vertical of monarchical power was combined with the ever-growing political influence of the bourgeoisie. A striking example of such a state was Protestant Prussia, which in the nineteenth century became the main initiator of the creation of Germany under the Protestant dynasty of the Hohenzollerns. An exhaustive description of the Lutheran Prussian political system — a kind of 'Prussian socialism or national socialism' — is convincingly described in the classic work *Prussianism and Socialism*[12] by Oswald Spengler (1880–1936).

Lutheranism may well be seen as the model which, in the course of secularisation and modernisation, gave rise to modern political nationalism (and in part National Socialism).

The Secularisation of Anabaptism Produces Communism

Within Protestantism there was also an extreme variant, most strikingly represented by the Anabaptist movement, of which Thomas Müntzer (c.1490–1525) was one of the leaders. The Anabaptists' adherents were predominantly peasants who held apocalyptic views. The Anabaptists shared similarities with the Christian Gnostics, who believed that an 'evil god' ruled the world and that the official Church and the nobility were his

---

12 Oswald Spengler, *Preußentum und Sozialismus* [*Prussianism and Socialism*] (London: Arktos Media, 2021).

servants.[13] The Reformation was seen by Anabaptists as the coming of the End Times, when the false church and its accompanying rule by the nobility would fall, and an era of universal equality would dawn.

Müntzer identified the Catholic Church with the Whore of Babylon, rejected Luther outright and likened the German princes who followed Luther to 'kings of the Apocalypse'. The Anabaptists called on all truly awakened Christians to rise up in a rebellion of the poor, who have Christ behind them, against the rich, who are enemies of the faith. Müntzer saw his own mission as that of John the Baptist, who came to call humanity to spiritual baptism.

Müntzer inspired the revolt of the Thuringian peasants, who were defeated in May 1525 at the Battle of Frankenhausen. He himself was captured and executed at Mühlhausen.

Here we see how, out of the rejection of Catholicism during the Reformation, an ideology is formed which is in many ways the antithesis of both Calvinism with its 'deification' of wealth and Lutheranism with its profound alliance with the princes and the nation-state. Marx (1818–1883) himself was clearly aware of the connection between his ideas and the Anabaptists, whom he saw as the forerunners of Communism.

Communism may well be regarded as the result of the secularisation of Anabaptism.

Three Ideologies

Thus Calvin, Luther and Müntzer can be considered as the figures of the Reformation who anticipated the three dominant political ideologies of the modern age — liberalism, nationalism and Communism. The roots of these respective versions of the Political are contained in Protestantism. Hence, we have the right to consider Protestantism as the historical paradigm of the political philosophy of the modern age. In Protestantism itself these three versions are not yet fully secular. We are still dealing with Christianity. Even Müntzer's Gnostic-revolutionary rebellion, very

---

13 Translator's note: This was a false or lesser god who had created the physical world. They also believed in the existence of a supreme God, who was separate from the flawed physical world.

similar to later communism, is still unfolding in anticipation of Christ's Second Coming. Calvin argues for the significance of wealth and prosperity as an expression of chosenness, of holiness, i.e. a consequence of Predestination. Meanwhile Luther insists that a nation-state must be established and maintained above all to protect Protestant interests against the Catholic Austrian Empire and the Roman throne.

These versions of the Reformation still retain a reference to the religious dimension. They are religious currents, and the politics which are based on them in the sixteenth and nineteenth centuries still retain something from Christianity and, consequently, from traditional society (the premodern paradigm). But in becoming secularised, divorced from theology, by bracketing the factor of God and scripture (in the course of what Nietzsche called the 'death of God'), they give us the three political theories that dominate the modern era (liberalism, Communism and nationalism). Geographically, the Germanic North of Europe becomes predominantly Protestant, while the Romanic South remains Catholic. At the same time, there is also a solid segment of Catholicism among the Germans — Austria, Bavaria, and more broadly Southern Germany. Furthermore, the Irish Celts remain faithful to Catholicism, in stark contrast to the Celtic Scots, who become the most radical bearers of Calvinism in the British Isles.

CHAPTER 10

THE FOUNDING FATHERS OF MODERN POLITICAL PHILOSOPHY

Thomas Hobbes, Niccolò Machiavelli, Jean Bodin

Niccolò Machiavelli: Autonomy of the Political

PROTESTANTISM represents a historical expression of the philosophy that contained the seeds of a concrete secular politics which became the norm of the New Age. It is now possible to consider how this philosophy of modern politics acquired its explicit features, formulated its programmes, and created its basic foundational texts.

The basis for the political philosophy of the New Age was laid first of all by three authors who are classics of modern political thought. These are the Italian Niccolò Machiavelli (1469–1527), the Frenchman Jean Bodin (1530–1596) and the Englishman Thomas Hobbes (1588–1679).

Niccolò Machiavelli is one of the three political thinkers who founded the concept of secular politics. There are still heated debates about how to interpret his thought. Some see Machiavelli as an extreme 'reactionary' and 'monarchist', a precursor of Fascism, others, on the contrary, as a 'progressive republican'.

Machiavelli's basic idea is that politics is an autonomous world, governed by laws peculiar to this domain. This was a perfect innovation for the fifteenth century. It was natural for people of the New Age to recognise that in politics there were certain laws, in morality there were others, in religion there were yet others. But for the medieval European Christian, the idea that there is one truth in politics, and another truth in morals, in religion, in ethics, was absolutely unacceptable and blasphemous. All spheres of knowledge were based on the same — universal, Christian — principles. The only area of medieval thought which partly anticipated this division into several truths was the philosophy of the Islamic thinker Averroes — Ibn Rushd (1126–1198) — whose followers, especially among Europeans, proposed to separate *theological truth* in the sphere of religion, based on the authority of the Scriptures, and *scientific truth* about the natural world, based on the conclusions of reason.

However, Machiavelli goes much further and proposes to consider the realm of the Political as an autonomous realm. He argues that politics is a completely self-contained thing. In his view, politics has no purpose or higher meaning. Power is a beginning and an end in itself. Therefore, the criteria to be applied to politics should not be taken from the realm of religion, morality, history, and so on. Politics is a completely self-contained world with its own inherent laws and rules, criteria and evaluations. Machiavelli proceeds from the premise that *the state has no purpose other than the exercise of power.*

The Prince: The Tyrant as a Force from Below

The personification of the state is the Sovereign, the Prince,[1] *il Principe.*

The Prince is not a person, it is not a particular ruler. It is a special instance, a figure that is the sum of politics, taken in isolation from all other levels of being. This is how the notion of an *autonomous self-referential sphere of politics* is formed. Politics is brought into an independent discipline, into an independent field. The figure of the Prince, who embodies the essence of politics, becomes the symbol of this politics.

Politics, meanwhile, is divorced from any higher meaning. Machiavelli completely and radically rejects the political philosophy of the 'two cities', proposing instead something completely new. He takes the 'city of heaven' out of the equation altogether and concentrates his attention entirely on the problems of earthly power, its preservation, reinforcement and the

---

1   Niccoló Machiavelli, *The Prince* (London: Penguin, 2003).

most effective use of it. Machiavelli deals henceforth only with the 'city of earth', which becomes the sole and self-sufficient object of political philosophy.

Machiavelli's sovereign is an *absolute individual* who rises to the heights of earthly power neither for a purpose (like Plato's Philosopher King) nor to fulfil a mission. He is elevated by the abundance and even excess of earthly power. It is *power* that, for Machiavelli, becomes the ontological basis of authority, and, moreover, power in its most direct and earthly sense. Everyone *wants* to rule, but only the strongest *can* rule. Therefore it does not matter in what way one becomes sovereign: if one becomes so, this in itself means that one is strong enough for it. If power is gained accidentally by someone who is not strong enough, he will quickly lose it to a powerful rival who is already rising from the chthonic depths to replace him.

On this Machiavelli builds his theory: the sovereign has no and can have no other goal than to hold onto the power he has, to strengthen it and, if possible, to increase its scope. In this theory we see the absolutisation of the 'city of earth' and at the same time the normalisation of the figure of the *tyrant*. According to Plato, the ruler who cares only about the realisation of his will and uses power only to achieve his egoistic goals is the epitome of a tyrant. Tyrannical traits were already characteristic of many Italian rulers in the Middle Ages, and in the Renaissance period examples of this type of government become even more frequent.

Machiavelli's Two Moralities

Machiavelli, developing his analysis of the figure of the Prince, comes to a crucial conclusion: there is not one morality, but two moralities:

- *the morality of the Sovereign,* which consists of the most effective retention of power, and
- *the morality of the general population*, the ordinary citizens, who must necessarily follow the prescribed ethical obligations and bear full responsibility for breaking the rules.

Machiavelli's idea that the sovereign requires a special morality, different from the morality of the masses, is entirely new. This morality must put power itself at the forefront. For the sovereign there is one good and one virtue: power, the stronger and the longer, the better. Everything else follows from it. Machiavelli argues that it is of no use if the ruler is kind, merciful, gentle and compassionate if he is unable to retain power — if he is unable to resist enemies both external and internal, to save citizens from distemper, to establish an efficient social and administrative system and to protect the state from opponents. And vice versa: what does it matter what personal sins — and even crimes — a ruler commits if he succeeds in the main task: ensuring the prosperity and stability of society, which is impossible without a strong government. Even the most bloodthirsty tyrant, by committing individual atrocities, cannot do much damage to society as a whole, not remotely comparable to the damage of rebellions or enemy invasions.

However, if public morality is violated by the masses, society will become confused, ungovernable; the sovereign's authority will be shaken and the state will descend into anarchy and collapse. The morality of ordinary people must be religious, ethical and in line with the perceptions of the social majority. As such, Christian morality is quite suitable. People who conform to moral-religious attitudes, aim at having a good reputation, saving their soul, maintaining social order, not breaking the rules — these notions of morality, from Machiavelli's point of view, are absolutely wonderful, beautiful and require adherence. By all, except the Prince. The Prince must first of all be guided by the *pure imperative of power*, which for him is the supreme and obligatory morality; he may follow that which is prescribed for the masses to a greater or lesser extent, but only as something additional and voluntary, and even then only if this does not interfere with the exercise of power functions.

Machiavelli does not directly oppose religion, the Church or tradition. He speaks only about the art of ruling and arranges his philosophy in a way that is as consistent as possible under the existing conditions.

A prince is a representative of the ruling authority. It is not necessarily an individual person. It can be a collective prince, it can be an individual one. It can be legal and legitimate, it can be illegal and illegitimate.[2] It makes no difference. The only important thing is that the one who stands at the head of society has to be guided by a fundamentally *different* approach to the evaluation of his acts than are ordinary citizens.

The notion that the people, the majority, and the Prince have two different moralities is an innovation of Niccolò Machiavelli. The morality of the Prince is that he is not responsible for himself personally and does not pursue his personal interests, but for the realisation of large-scale tasks which involve a large number of the population. For example, one of the Prince's tasks is to preserve the territorial integrity of the principality, the state in which he is ruler. To do this, the ruler can do anything: he can lie, threaten, disregard agreements, disguise his troops in the uniform of the enemy, organise provocations, send poisoners, invade the territory of others, take the relatives and loved ones of his enemies hostage — in short, violate all moral and ethical norms. According to Machiavelli, this is all moral and justifiable for a Prince, although for everyone else it should be strictly forbidden. Because if the majority act the same way, the state will soon collapse.

The opposite is also true: if a Prince is a good pious man who loves his neighbours, observes all moral precepts and meets the highest criteria of morality and piety, but at the same time cannot effectively resist the armies of his neighbour who invades his territory, plunders his lands, rapes and takes captive the locals, then even as a *good* man, he is a *very bad Prince*. He can be holy as a man, but utterly worthless as a Prince. But in the event that by deceit, cunning, meanness, force and sacrificing all Christian precepts the Prince is able to increase the size of his lands manyfold and strengthen the power of his duchy, then he is a great Prince.

The same applies to domestic politics. Here the main goal is calm, well-being, safety and satiety of the citizens, as well as the maintenance of order. If for this purpose the Prince eliminates his rivals, stirs enmity among his entourage, promotes to power not the most worthy, best or deserving, weaves intrigues, achieves his goals by deception, bribery and

---

2   Carl Schmitt, *Legality and Legitimacy; Law as Politics* (Durham, North Carolina: Duke University Press, 2004; 1998).

repression, as well as by any other methods, then again he is a good Prince. What is the use, Machiavelli argues, of a good and pious ruler avoiding such measures if chaos, disorder, distemper, famine and anarchy reign in the state? He may be able to save his own soul, but he will ruin the state he has been entrusted with.

So two logics are postulated. What is good for the Prince and what is bad for the common man. The goal is to provide a protected territory, a well-fed and satisfied citizenry, security, tranquillity and order. What you do meanwhile, Citizen Prince, is of no interest to anyone. What you do there, how you justify it, what's on your mind is your own business.

Machiavelli's Paradox: The Purpose of Power Is Power

Machiavelli bases his political philosophy on this. There is no justification for this state of affairs, no criticism and no satire, as Machiavelli's commentators sometimes think. It is simply a cold statement of the facts which the political philosopher sees around him and which he undertakes to describe systematically, as they are. If society is told about this openly, it will revolt, and indignation and chaos will ensue. But for the political science of the New Age, the founder of which may well be considered Nicollò Machiavelli, this is a basic truth. That is why Machiavelli himself is not addressing the masses. He writes for the Prince, for the political elite. Among Machiavelli's advice to the Prince is to conceal more of what he does, to use covert intrigue, to make everyone quarrel with everyone else, to prevent the rise of anyone who might pose a problem or become competition for that Prince. Not to let opponents know the real state of affairs. To use a variety of such political techniques.

The people are to think as they wish; they are only required to follow the established rules and obey them. This creates a special domain of the Political, where completely separate criteria apply.

From Machiavelli's point of view, the Prince has one overriding task — *to retain his power*. On the surface, this seems to be a completely selfish and immoral task. For a man it is, but for the Prince it becomes moral, because in order to hold on to it, he must meet all the requirements of power.

First, the Prince must have power. That is, he must get it, no matter by what means. This is the first condition. If someone manages to get power, this in itself, according to Machiavelli, is already a fundamental position. The Prince is only the one who has power, not the one who is born with it or wants to get it.

Secondly, he must have a state. There must be a people who do not overthrow him, who submit to him and thereby recognise him. It does not matter at all how they feel about the Prince — love him or hate him, accept him or simply tolerate him, respect him or simply fear him. It does not matter at all. If the Prince is in power, that alone is the decisive fact. And that means that the citizens are under him. He ceases to be the ruler only if he is overthrown — by rivals, opponents or his subjects. Then a new Prince takes his place and the cycle begins all over again.

For all the apparent simplicity of this analysis, it contains very serious points. After all, in order to gain and retain power, the Prince must preserve the territorial integrity and preferably even increase the territories of his polity. He needs a calm — submissive — people, observing discipline, obeying rules and regulations; no riots, revolts or conspiracies.

Hence the paradox of Machiavelli: the successful Prince, without setting any positive objective, totally unwilling to please his people, to leave a mark in history, to serve the Church, to promote the common good, thinking only of himself, of his power, following pure egoism and driven by power and the will to power, yet able to carry out brilliant historical acts and build states and societies where people flourish, temples are full, culture thrives, territories grow, grain is threshed, thought and science develop, people are free and happy. But above all this stands a sinister, selfish, jealous Prince, an aggressive and predatory 'political animal',[3] not allowing any figure or individual capable of competing with him to come close to his territory.

Such a princely egoism, because it operates on an entirely different scale from that of a private person, an ordinary citizen, is — but only and exclusively in the case of the Prince — more important than any altruism.

---

3   In a different sense from Aristotle's political animal.

It is important to note that we live in Machiavelli's world, because the current conception of power, of the political elite, fits fully into this Prince model (at least in those strands of political philosophy where realism predominates).

Although to a certain extent Machiavelli's views have influenced the very nature of the Political in modern times in general, the most consistent proponents of his approach have been the representatives of the neo-Machiavellian school, which has emerged in Italy since the late nineteenth century. The Italians Vilfredo Pareto[4] (1848–1923) and Gaetano Mosca[5] (1858–1941), as well as the German sociologist Robert Michels[6] (1876–1936) are the political philosophers normally associated with this school. Both were profoundly influenced by the ideas of the French economist Léon Walras[7] (1834–1910), who constructed a model of economic equilibrium. The theory of elites, constructed by these authors, actually develops the idea of the Prince in relation to the structure of society as a whole. From this perspective, all politics is reduced to the seizure and retention of power.

In other words, the elite is the collective definition of the Prince, and all political life is an aspiration to be in his place.

All representatives of the neo-Maciavellian school denied the independent significance of political ideologies as well as the religious influence on politics, justifying the field of the Political as a separate and independent sphere governed only by its inherent laws and rules. This technical and pragmatic attitude towards politics stemmed from Walrasian equilibrium and rejected the idea of progress, as well as any other linear and unidirectional change in society.

---

4   Vilfredo Pareto, *Compendium of General Sociology* (Minneapolis, Minnesota: University of Minnesota Press, 1980).
5   Gaetano Mosca, *Storia delle dottrine politiche* [*History of Political Doctrines*] (Bari: Laterza, 1937).
6   Robert Michels, *Soziologie als Gesellschaftswissenschaft* [*Sociology as a Social Science*] (Berlin: Mauritius, 1926).
7   Léon Walras, *Elements of Pure Economics* (Oxfordshire: Routledge Library Editions, 2010).

The various strands of realism in international relations are also based on this principle.[8]

The Prince as Tyrant and Antichrist

To say why a Prince, or why a political state, according to Machiavelli, is meaningless. It is equally impossible to determine whether it is 'holy' or 'unholy', 'good' or 'bad', leads to the salvation or perdition of the soul — all these questions are immaterial, totally irrelevant to the organisation of politics and to the study of its nature and its patterns.

Whereas in the Middle Ages the prevailing belief was that politics was a cross-section of philosophy, in Machiavelli the opposite happens. *Philosophy becomes an application to politics*. Politics takes on the character of absolute autonomy, and this is due to the very paradigm of the transition from top-down logic to bottom-up logic.

If we turn to the political philosophy of Plato and Aristotle, it is obvious that Machiavelli describes the worst form of government — *pure tyranny*. But unlike the classical vertical model of the ideal state or the normal state, where the tyrant is a purely negative image, turning the whole hierarchy upside down and asserting the worst in place of the best, in the New Age theoretical field such a titanic image becomes the new norm.

The ontology of the state itself also changes. The state of the Prince belongs to the dimension of the Mother; it is profoundly material because it is governed by materiality and accepts material criteria as primary. The Prince establishes a tyrannical ontology of the Political, introducing a new 'political theology' (according to Carl Schmitt), from which transcendence, mission, ideal and normativity are completely banished. The state of the Prince, his 'principality', is completely detached from the higher dimension. It represents nothing but itself. And in this sense, it is the antithesis of the Holy Empire, as there is nothing sacred and holy about it. Machiavelli gives the first fully profane description of the Political.

Importantly, he chooses the term 'Prince' to describe the main figure. Not a king, not a ruler, and still less an emperor; not a tsar, but precisely a

---

8 Dugin, *International Relations (Paradigms, Theories, Sociology)*.

prince, *il Principe*. In Latin, the devil in the Gospel is called *Princeps huius mundi*, 'prince of this world'. In this formulation, the reference is made to 'this' world, as opposed to 'that' world, which is the Kingdom of Heaven, the empire of Christ. Machiavelli's state belongs entirely to 'this world'; it has no higher meaning, no connection with heaven. That is why the image of the 'Prince' described by Machiavelli, with all his paradoxes, has so much in common with the typical honours embodied by the devil in religious tradition. Satan, who tempted Christ in the wilderness, also offered him power over the world. Christ rejected this as tempting the 'prince of this world'. Machiavelli accepts this as a fact, presenting such a diabolical version of the Political as the norm. In modern times it is indeed the norm.

Plato and Aristotle's political ontology is thus completely overturned and the worst form of government, tyranny, is not just granted the right to exist, but becomes the basic methodology in the analysis of the Political. In the Christian context, this could not but evoke direct associations with the devil, the 'prince of this world'.

Hobbes and the Idea of Absolutised Original Sin

The fundamental author who had a decisive influence on the political philosophy of the modern Age was the Englishman Thomas Hobbes. Hobbes was personally acquainted with such seminal figures of modern philosophy and science as Francis Bacon (1561–1626) and Galileo Galilei (1564–1642).

Hobbes authored a prominent book on the nature of the state, *Leviathan*.[9] Hobbes' radically materialistic and wholly immanent (secular) vision of politics predates political science by several centuries and has been adopted and practised by successive generations of English and French, as well as Europeans in general. *Leviathan* is the most fundamental work which lays down the basic underlying principles of New Age political philosophy. It gives an insight into human nature, the essence of the state, the meaning of ethics, the meaning of coercion and force, and

---

9   Thomas Hobbes, *Leviathan* (London: Penguin Classics, 2017).

the different states of civilisation as understood by the New Age. It is a fundamental political philosophy, providing answers to all principal questions.

Hobbes argues that humanity inherently resides in a natural state. At the same time Hobbes argues that man's nature is wicked; man is evil. Hobbes introduces the axiom 'man is wolf to man' (*homo homini lupus est*). In his natural state, Hobbes argues, man seeks only one thing: domination over another, the capture of prey, the satisfaction of his basest desires and instincts. In his view, man is an aggressive predator, a wolf who seeks only his own gain. If you leave man to his own devices, he will immediately begin to create violence, to subjugate others, to seize things and territories, not to reckon with anyone, to use everything that comes to hand for his own benefit. He acts this way out of sheer selfishness, because his nature is evil.

It is the idea of original sin, brought to the absolute in a political and anthropological way. Yes, Christianity claims that man is a product of original sin, but for Calvinist Protestantism the only way to be saved is to accumulate wealth, to become rich. Christianity and Catholicism have a very different view — although man inherits the burden of the sin of his forebears who were cast out of paradise, Christ came into the world and saved humanity, and now there is an opportunity to become a fundamentally new man, a Christian man, to build society and, ultimately, the political system on other Christian values. This is why Catholics insisted on preserving the principle of free will. According to Thomas Aquinas, man is a bearer of grace sufficient to resist sin if there is good will to do so (the theory of *gratia sufficiens*). For Protestants — for Luther and especially for Calvin — this is impossible, because after the fall into sin man was too weak, and this cannot be remedied. In Hobbes this thesis is detached from Christian theology and is affirmed as a wholly secular view of man's nature. Man is an evil selfish being, a kind of social beast, pursuing exclusively private interests without regard for the rest. So from Protestant pessimism about the nature of man we come to a modernist atheist and materialist pessimism, detached from its theological foundations (Hobbes no longer believes in heaven and the fall into sin).

So, according to Hobbes, man is a predator. At that, he is not just a predator, he is also an *intelligent* predator. He is a wolf with a brain, which is needed to gain more, to win more effectively, to capture and destroy his neighbour or to make said neighbour serve him. Gradually this selfish wolf begins to realise that if he acts in such a way, fuelled only on his own interests without taking into account the interests of another, then in some situation he may find himself the victim, the weaker, and become the prey of a stronger and more powerful predator.

According to Hobbes, while still in the 'natural state', an intelligent wolf at some point begins to understand the relativity of the very principle of predation. Then he considers creating conditions in which he can dominate others and others cannot dominate him. As this cannot be achieved in a direct manner, the intelligent predator concludes that certain compromises have to be made.

And then the cunning wolf offers to enter into a *social contract* with the other wolves (humans), to establish a set of rules to both legalise and to somewhat limit the evil nature. The essence of a social contract is to accept some rules regulating the war of all against all, setting laws, boundaries and norms within it. But in the natural state, no one will simply follow these laws, because no one can force the most powerful to abide by them and the powerful will not want to limit their appetites out of good will (according to Hobbes, good will does not exist; the will is only evil).

The solution to this dilemma is to get out of the 'natural state' and negotiate the establishment of the State. The cunning wolves conclude that it is necessary to delegate some of their powers, in order for this authority — the State — to control compliance with certain rules regarding the satisfaction of individual aspirations.

But for this entity — the State — to be effective, it must be terrifying, inspiring dread even to the strongest and most powerful of man-wolves. Hence the idea of Leviathan, as mentioned in the Bible. Leviathan is a sea monster. It is talked about in the Book of Job,[10] when Job becomes resentful of his lot — he was a righteous man, loved God, was his closest servant, and suddenly he suffers a blow from fate, loses everything, his wealth and

---

10   Book of Job 40:20–41:26.

loved ones, and he himself is poor, miserable —, he turns to God with reproach. God answers his reproaches: Have you seen the Leviathan, Job? He is so fearsome that he makes the mountains tremble. The seas boil. Have you seen the hippopotamus, Job? The hippopotamus walks and the earth shakes. So fear and do not rebel against God; God is all-powerful and can both grant and punish according to his own will. God is stronger than all, even the Leviathan and the hippopotamus, two primordial monsters stronger than which there is no such thing.

The reference to Leviathan proves to be the decisive argument. Job humbles himself: well, of course, if You have frightened me so, then You are right. This may not be a very Christian ethic, but it is quite in keeping with Protestant pessimism. The mightier one frightened the weaker one, and the weaker one humbled himself and fell silent. Job was shown Leviathan — and Job admitted he was wrong. So Hobbes reasons: just show Leviathan to the smart wolves and they will shrink from the horror.

But while the Bible has man (Job) at one end, God at the other, and Leviathan in between as an argument, Hobbes' materialism does not recognise a separate eternal God. Leviathan is 'God', only man-made, created as a result of the social contract.

According to Hobbes, the meaning and nature of the state is *the creation of a 'god'*. But a god who is evil, punitive, artificial, man-made. This 'evil god' is the state, which the cunning, selfish wolves nevertheless establish over themselves as an authority they can no longer disobey, as it is stronger than any of them. And the Leviathan is henceforth an instrument of 'legitimate violence' (as per Weber[11]). Leviathan is the state. Its main task is to frighten and punish those who do not follow the rules laid down by the consensus. If men were *only* wolves (i.e. in their natural state), they would not create the state. But they are *intelligent* wolves, they have the ability to think, and they realise that they can exterminate each other. To prevent this, they create a new monster. This monster, the Leviathan, is the New Age state.

---

11   Max Weber, *Politics as a Vocation* (Philadelphia: Fortress Press, 1965).

Leviathan's main idea is that the state was created from *below*, and by evil, disgusting, vicious, selfish people. And it was created only to keep the selfish villains in relative restraint. The state is an evil, monstrous, punishing 'god' instituted by villains to give villainy some order, so the state does not prevent violence, nor robbery, seizure, subjugation or deception — it orders it all by making rules which it forces everyone to abide by.

Such is the world of Thomas Hobbes, his political philosophy. The wicked, out of cunning and individual selfishness, in order not to destroy themselves with their own evil, create a man-made repulsive Leviathan 'god' who will terrify and oppress them.

Here there is a basic notion of the inherent negativity of human nature.

Spencer: Atomism and the Struggle for Survival in a Liberal Society

Hobbes did not have a theory of evolution of species, as Darwin (1809–1882) later developed, but it may already be anticipated in general terms, putting monkeys in the place of wolves. According to Hobbes, humans are wolves who have built a Leviathan, who have gained intelligence but retained their wolfish essence. According to Darwin, humans are apes who have developed the ability to reason in the struggle for survival and built society.[12] The two theories were combined into social Darwinism by Herbert Spencer[13] (1820–1903), the greatest theorist of liberal political philosophy.

Spencer takes his cue from Hobbes and, like him, applies the principles of atomism to society. He aims to construct a system that unites the common methods for investigating the physical structure of matter, the development of biological species and the history of mankind. Spencer's physics is based on the fact that matter, which in the zero conditional state

---

[12] Nikolay Danilevsky, *Дарвинизм. Критическое исследование В 2 т.* [*Darwinism. Critical Study Volume II*] (St. Petersburg: Publishing house of M. E. Komarov, 1885–1889).

[13] Herbert Spencer, *Essays Scientific, Political and Speculative in 3 volumes* (London: Williams & Norgate, 1868).

consists of disparate atoms, particles, has an intrinsic force (life, drive) that causes these homogeneous particles to bind together, producing heterogeneous agglomerates that are in a state of motion. Motion — its accumulation in integrated structures and its dissipation — is an inherent property of matter itself. Particle agglomerates, driven by the motion of matter, begin to adapt to external conditions, and the results of this adaptation constitute an inherited code that is transmitted from thing to thing, from being to being. In this way, an ordered universe is born, which is both the effect and the process of evolution. The goal of evolution is to achieve maximal adaptation to the surrounding conditions, but these conditions are, in turn, the process of evolution. Hence the principle of struggle and 'survival of the fittest' that lies at the heart of Spencer's philosophy. The universe and its order embody the limit of adaptation of the fittest and are the peak of evolution.

The most successful and 'most adapted' agglomeration of particles is the *individual thing*, which proves to be so stable that it transmits its properties to other things. In the natural world, the pinnacle of individuation are living things capable of reproducing themselves as a species, perfecting their qualities and transmitting them by inheritance, thus reinforcing their individuation essence. *The universe is nothing other than individuation*. For this reason, man is also thought of as an individual, capable of adapting to his environment better than other species and thereby building society.

At the same time, the individual, according to Spencer (in perfect harmony with Hobbes), is naturally selfish and aggressive, pursuing his own advantage, sometimes in a deadly struggle with other individuals. Intra- and inter-species struggles, according to Spencer, made man human, forcing him to master more and more techniques of adaptation, attack and defence, transmitted by inheritance, thereby perfecting the human series of individuals. In the course of man's struggle with man, the rise of the 'fittest' emerges, who find themselves at the head of society. Spencer sees *social inequality as a positive factor* because it reflects 'natural selection' and thus the progress of mankind. Spencer believes that the strong man is more human than the weak man and, on this basis, opposes equal rights — people should be given the freedom to realise their egoistic nature to the maximum, to gradually breed more and more perfect series of people, but this realisation will be more reasonable and 'evolutionary' while respecting the rights and freedoms of others, not as a given, but as a possibility. Everyone has the right to participate in the struggle, but the winner gets everything while the loser is left alone with his loss — so that next time he fights better, thinks faster, acts more perfectly and more effectively, thus contributing to the process of evolution.

The chaotic struggle of all against all, the war of all against all, is a property of natural society, stemming from the evil nature of man. According to Spencer, it is an order based on pure force. But it is by virtue of this struggle for survival and species selection that humans realise the development of rationality is an essential advantage for survival and success. And on the basis of this rationality they build the Political, agreeing to some restriction of their freedom, but only in order to realise their will in the optimal way.

Spencer sees history as consisting of three evolutionary phases:

- an initial chaotic phase;
- then a phase of the creation, by force and violence, of states and political structures that rigidly establish hierarchies and impede the free process of natural selection, and
- finally, the phase of industrial competition, where the struggle for survival unfolds through market competition, which is the highest form of intra-species struggle because it unleashes the full potential of the selfishness inherent in the human individual and reflects the maximum dynamism of self-moving matter.

Spencer's political philosophy is an *elitist version of liberalism* in which *equality of opportunity (participation in competition) leads to inequality of results*, with competition itself being deployed in the field where the highest technical and scientific achievements of the human species are concentrated, as an arsenal of methods of economic warfare. Spencer was an opponent of public education, believing that ignorance of the weak and inferior is an incentive for the strong and superior to multiply and develop their knowledge. Spencer also denied equality to women, believing that they represented the least perfect product of evolution, accumulating and genetically transmitting a set of adaptive functions that only perpetuated their weakness and uncompetitiveness.

Thus, as the political philosophy of modernity emerges, Hobbes' basic thesis of Leviathan and its genesis continues in a new form, with the aggressive consciousness of human wolves in the conditions of the state being honed so much that they go beyond it and choose a new strategy appropriate to a more evolved form of modernity. Yet it was still Hobbes who laid the foundations for this approach.

The Primordial Nature of the Social Contract and Pan-Egoism

Hobbes' ideas, developed by his followers, on the nature of the state are the foundation of modern political philosophy. The vast majority of modern theories on the origins of the state, its functions, its nature, and its history have in one way or another been derived from Hobbes' theses. This applies not only to those who follow him or seek to develop his insights, but also to those who fundamentally disagree with him.

Hobbes is the philosopher of the New Age, just as Plato and Aristotle were the philosophers of Tradition. And Hobbes understood with the utmost clarity the very spirit of the new paradigm, built from the bottom up, from matter to consciousness, from animal to man, from body to mind, from the chaotic struggle of all against all to the rules artificially established in the social contract.

In Hobbes, the state is negative because it is nothing but a limiting institution of violence. But it is evil not in relation to people (neutral or good in itself), it is evil precisely because people created it and they themselves are evil. Similarly, the sociologist Max Weber defines the state as 'an apparatus of legitimate violence'.[14] This is a very Hobbesian thought, because the only task of the Leviathan is to implement repressions, to

---

14 Max Weber, *Politics as a Vocation*.

suppress, to punish.[15] But this violence is legitimate; it is used to repress those who challenge the state system (Leviathan), to execute criminals, to destroy those who do not respect the rules of the social contract.

The vast majority of modern societies are built on the Hobbesian paradigm. This is the predominant model of the New Age state.

The origins of such a model are clearly marked by Protestant influences (Calvinism), but the Leviathan model itself is already fully autonomous. It is a purely 'political theology' (Schmitt), in which the state is 'God' and the presence or absence of some other level of deity adds nothing to this complete picture and takes nothing away from it. Hobbes combines atomism and materialism with socio-political philosophy and gets a quite complete and consistent picture. In Plato's system of hypotheses in *Parmenides,* it corresponds to the sixth hypothesis: atoms artificially create the 'one', which Hobbes calls 'Leviathan'. This is the type of society humanity inhabits in the modern age.

In Hobbes we already see that fundamental unit of political philosophy which retains its significance right up to the present day. If we take away original sin, or distract ourselves from the idea of social Darwinism, we see only one thing, which is the norm of our contemporary political philosophy: man is a purely egoistic actor, a *rational egoist*. As an egoist he is a predator, as a rational one he subordinates his immediate predatory egoistic instincts to some rational strategies in order to achieve an optimum result.

There is a humorous definition: 'an egoist is someone who loves himself very much and does not love me at all'. Everyone is selfish and everyone thinks the other is 'too selfish'. This is how relationships between people become like mirrors reflecting back on each other; this is how the picture of *pan-egoism* is created — each one acting in his own self-interest without thinking of the other.[16] It is only when security is at stake and the

---

15   Michel Foucault, *Discipline and Punish: The Birth of the Prison* (New York: Pantheon Books, 1977).

16   This principle is illustrated in the famous 'fable of the bees' by the classical liberal thinker Bernard Mandeville (1670–1733), who describes how a society composed of total egoists leads to universal prosperity without ever having set itself any such goal, and conversely, how an altruistic society of good and compassionate men leads to

situation becomes critical that the egoistic units put up a common defence system for their own protection. In such a picture, egoism lies at the heart of predatory behaviour as well as in its containment. Egoism forces the beast to think, but only in order to more fully satisfy its appetites and be more likely to survive in the struggle of species and individuals. This conception of man as a purely selfish actor is at the heart of our view of the world today, but its origins go back to the philosophy of Thomas Hobbes.

Later the French philosopher Jean-Jacques Rousseau (1712–1778) gave a slightly different interpretation of the social contract.[17] Rousseau also claimed that society is based on a 'social contract', but gave it a significantly different interpretation based on the recognition of the 'noble savage', i.e. that human nature in its original state is not evil, as Hobbes believed, but on the contrary is good. However, it is important to note that Hobbes talked about this much earlier and gave a philosophical analysis of the mechanism of this social contract. What do the egoistic actors agree on among themselves? About how to establish some order over themselves, which will reflect this relation between their own bestiality and the desire to somehow limit the bestiality of the other. In order to justify one's own selfishness and at the same time protect oneself from the selfishness of the other. Rousseau breaks with this simple but convincing Hobbesian logic, and although he also considers the state as evil, he interprets it as something external to the individual. Hobbes, on the other hand, is extremely consistent and seeks to explain everything in a purely immanent way, without introducing anything extraneous to his system. The limitation of egoism is a consequence of egoism and the violence of the state is a reflection of the violence inherent in predatory man.

The Political is a product of the social contract and the entire political ontology is based upon this contract. Such a thesis describes the essence of New Age political philosophy. In this we can easily recognise a completely inverted Platonism. The state has no existence of its own in a realm

---

degeneration, decline and deterioration because everyone in it thinks only of others, which ends in universal misery. Bernard Mandeville, *The Fable of the Bees, or Private Vices, Publick Benefits* (Oxford: Clarendon Press, 1714).

17 Jean-Jacques Rousseau, *The Social Contract* (London: Penguin Books, 2004).

of ideas. It has no model. It is constructed from below by individual atomic material subjects driven by private interests and egoistic appetites. Everything else follows from this — the meaning and purpose of politics, its organisation, its improvement, the creation and reform of political institutions, the place and authority of power as well as its nature, the distribution of powers, the ratio of the rulers to the bulk of the citizens, etc.

The point of bottom-up politics is to be reasonable in balancing egoistic impulses. The balancing itself involves a particular level of rationality. The wolf pack also has a certain balancing act; it is not unreasonable itself. Whoever is stronger is the chief wolf. As soon as the leader is weak, he is killed. In humans, the distribution of roles and powers also involves rational mechanisms. The strong unite in society and strive to conclude such social contracts which would guarantee their leading position and strengthen their authority even more. Nevertheless, the lower classes can respond to political forms that are too unjust (from their point of view) with a revolution, a popular uprising. The weaker can unite and threaten the stronger. This is why one has to come to an agreement with the people below and take their opinion into account. Thus, the secondary form of the social contract appears — within the limits of the created Leviathan: the top negotiates with the bottom. It would be simpler just to suppress the bottom (as the carriers of modern political philosophy believe it was in Antiquity and the Middle Ages), but the weak have intelligence and are able to realise their own selfish interests, suffering from the domination of the stronger. The development of this idea leads to socialism and Communism. But the starting point in any case is Hobbes.

This balance of revising various social contracts constitutes the political history of modernity. But in all these instances, no one in modernity seriously questions the idea that the Leviathan political body, its evolution and modernisation are based on the actions of egoistic actors, who recombine among themselves, creating — each time from the bottom upwards — different political models. At the same time, the bottom-up principle becomes more and more emphasised, erasing even the distant remnants of verticality inherent in the political systems of early modernity.

Leviathan is a 'machine god', a 'god mechanism', a man-made 'god'. It is an idol in the true sense. Friedrich Nietzsche expresses it very precisely:

> The state is called the coldest of all cold monsters. Coldly it lies; and this lie creeps from its lips: 'I, the state, am the people[...]
>
> The state lies in every language about good and evil: and what it says, it lies, and what it has, it has stolen.
>
> False is everything in it: with stolen teeth it bites, the biting one. False even are its bowels.
>
> Confusion of language of good and evil; this sign I give unto you as the sign of the state. Verily, the will to death, indicates this sign! Verily, it beckons unto the preachers of death!
>
> Many too many are born: for the superfluous ones was the state devised!
>
> See just how it entices them to it, the many-too-many! How it swallows and chews and rechews them!
>
> 'On earth there is nothing greater than I: it is I who am the regulating finger of God'—thus roars the monster.[18]

Hobbes therefore stresses that there is nothing sacred about the state. Monstrous—yes, terrifying—yes, awe-inspiring—yes. But this is the common man dressed in the uniform of a policeman. It is the shell that frightens. When the wearer of the uniform comes home, changes into his home clothes and sits down next to his wife and children, he will appear harmless and non-threatening. There is nothing intimidating about him, nothing of a monster. But dressed in his armour, the overseer gives the impression of a thunderstorm.

This observation is wittily described in *The Wizard of Oz*.[19] The ruler of the Emerald City, 'the Great and Terrible', is in fact a harmless, pathetic fool, inspiring fear only by virtue of a 'social contract', embodied by the compulsory requirement to wear green glasses so that all objects in the Emerald City appear to be emerald. This is what Nietzsche has in mind when he says of the state: 'False is everything in it'.

---

18 Friedrich Nietzsche, *Thus Spoke Zarathustra* (London: Penguin Classics, 1974).
19 L. Frank Baum, *The Wonderful Wizard of Oz* (Chicago; New York: G.M. Hill Co., 1900).

The point of the state is only to frighten. But unlike the sacred, it inspires fear rather than terror. It does not abolish our self, replacing it with something new, a new spiritual identity, but simply suppresses us, makes us bend, curl up, tremble low.

Jean Bodin and the Notion of Sovereignty

Jean Bodin is another creator of the New Age political philosophy landscape. He played a significant role in the political thought of the pivotal sixteenth century in France and Europe as a whole, when Catholicism and Protestantism were in fierce opposition. Jean Bodin draws a fundamental political conclusion from the religious confrontation between the Huguenots (Protestants) and Catholics, which, on the one hand, takes to its logical limit the Calvinist theories of confrontation with Rome and its supranational authority, and, on the other, partly in the spirit of the Catholic party (but very much in the spirit of Lutheranism), advocates the absolutisation of royal power. By this route he *formulates a theory of the nation-state*, which combines monarchism and the interests of the bourgeoisie, without a particular religious component. Thus, Jean Bodin, somewhat anticipating Hobbes, becomes the main theorist of political modernity, asserting a fully secular state, divorced from any religious (sacred) content, as the norm.[20]

Jean Bodin's central idea is the *concept of sovereignty*. In his view, the state is based on the fact that there is no supreme legal or religious authority above it. The state has no transcendent purposes; its tasks are purely technical. It must protect citizens against external enemies and order economic and social life on the basis of maximum efficiency and rationality. Bodin's state is a purely mechanical construction, whose function is limited to optimal material organisation.

The sovereignty of the state, according to Bodin, is justified precisely by the fact that it has no tasks that go beyond the circle of technical concerns and challenges. If the state does not serve any idea or mission, there is no authority capable of judging the state on the basis of higher criteria.

---

20 Jean Bodin, *Six Books of the Commonwealth* (Oxford: B. Blackwell, 1955).

The state can only be judged by itself; this is its sovereignty, the absence of any higher levels.

Like Hobbes, God is dropped from the role of delivering the biblical triad to Job and is replaced by a man-made monster — the Leviathan, Bodin's sovereign, the bearer of sovereignty, finds himself in the position of the highest authority. Although Bodin does not deny God, he, in the spirit of deism, refuses to allow Him to intervene effectively in the course of human history. That history is shaped only by the sovereign. He may or may not take God into account, but this has no effect on the very structure of the Political.

Eliminating the Power of the Pope

This conception of the head of state and the state itself as a fundamentally absolute construct is radically new to medieval consciousness. Here God becomes politically helpless, unable and unwilling to intervene in the course of human political history. In fact, he is taken out of the equation. Obviously, this is as radically at odds with the Catholic idea of 'two cities' and the ontology of empire as it is with the ideas of Machiavelli and Hobbes.

Nowadays, the notion of sovereignty is based on international law and is a basic constitutional norm. But why was it important to introduce it in the sixteenth century, in the period when Jean Bodin lived and wrote his works? Because at that time there was still the idea that an authority existed over the states and restricted their power — the Roman Church. The Pope appointed cardinals, bishops, who were essentially the agents of a supra-national system. The cardinal was the most important figure in the national European state, subordinate not to the king, but to the pope. A dual power emerged: the universal supra-national power of Catholicism (the pope) and the national power of the king.

The point of Bodin's idea is that there cannot be two powers in a nation state, and all power should be transferred to the secular ruler, that is, the prince or the king. The king is sovereign because sovereignty is the fundamental statement that there is no higher legal authority above the king. Therefore European society, according to Bodin, should be seen as a set of sovereign states, sovereign units, not as a single legal field of the Catholic Church, united by the pope.

For the era in which Bodin lived, this was a completely new conception of the very nature of the Political. Before him, the idea of the State had a sacred justification: the State serves the Church. Hence such concepts as 'Christian monarchy', coalitions of 'Christian countries', etc. The Christian element, embodied in the Catholic Church, was the authority that endowed national European states with a certain spiritual, supernatural, super-intelligent *mission*. The guardians of this mission were the representatives of the pope, who were the bearers of supra-national control. According to Carl Schmitt, this corresponded to the notion of a 'commissarial dictatorship',[21] that is, a form of government in which the entire governing institution acted in the name of a higher purpose. The pope himself did not rule in his own name, but as 'commissary of Christ'. And his legates, the cardinals and all the other clerics, subordinate to the pope, were also complicit in this mission. The system of authority was an open one. Bodin, on the other hand, postulated a very different model — henceforth the power of the king is a 'sovereign dictatorship', where the institution of power is headed by the individual himself. And it is he — as a person, not as the bearer of a mission — who is served by his subordinates, as well as by all the people. The formula for a 'sovereign dictatorship' can be summed up in the words attributed to Louis XIV (1643–1715) — 'I am the state!'

The King's Musketeers against the Cardinal's Guards

One may recall the famous novels of Alexandre Dumas (1802–1870), where we see the King's Musketeers and the Cardinal's Guards. Their confrontation reflected this fundamental seventeenth-century dilemma in France — the Catholic power of the Pope vs. the national sovereignty of the monarch. The Cardinal's Guards represented the French segment of a special supranational army — the bearers of a pan-European (and, given the European colonies, worldwide) network of 'commissary dictatorship'.

---

21 Schmitt, *Dictatorship: From the Origin of the Modern Concept of Sovereignty to Proletarian Class Struggle*.

They did not focus on the personal interests of the overbearing Richelieu (1585–1642); they ensured *the unity of the European world in the name of a supra-national mission*. Sovereignty — overtly from above — was then vested only in the pope and his system of cardinals, who oversaw the nation-states as representatives of the 'city of heaven' in the 'city of earth'. As we have seen, in Blessed Augustine's model, this 'city of heaven' was, from the Catholic point of view, a city of the righteous (hence celibacy and priests) and the 'city of earth' was a city of sinners. It was this sinful city (i.e. the national monarchy), seeking to appropriate sovereignty only for itself, that was represented by the musketeers, who had the sympathy of Dumas himself, and more broadly of the republican-nationalist oriented Frenchmen of the nineteenth century, who had by then been living for centuries in a world where the ideas of Jean Bodin had won out completely.

It is precisely against this 'commissarial dictatorship' of the pope and his legates that Bodin's main point is directed. According to Bodin, the state does not and cannot have any mission at all and therefore there should be no authority over the king. Consequently, the cardinals must be stripped of all real power and represent purely ecclesiastical ranks. Effectively, this is a change in the conception of the political system of all European politics and all European philosophy. Here the 'city of heaven' disappears from view altogether. The Political becomes a matter exclusively for the 'city of the earth'. But since there is nothing to compare it with, one cannot call it a city of sinners either. Thus, the vertical is completely removed from politics.

Towards the Westphalian World Order

Bodin's monarchism is completely desacralised. In his understanding, the king is a strictly immanent and technical figure, but when placed at the head of the state, he becomes its concentrated expression. The sovereign king represents the highest authority of the Political.

In practice, this meant that each state was given complete and absolute freedom to build its relations with other states exclusively on the basis of its national interests. Earlier European order was qualitatively different:

for example, in disputes and conflicts between England and France, Rome (the Catholic Church) actively intervened, and it had considerable legal powers to do so. Of course, the secular rulers did not always follow the instructions of the popes and at times tried to influence them in return (due to political intrigues and unrest in the Catholic Church at the end of the fourteenth and beginning of the fifteenth centuries there were several popes), but this supra-national system was legitimate from the point of view of the European legal system. It was based on the (likely apocryphal) 'Donation of Constantine', a legendary document or order in which Constantine the Great (272–337) gave all power over the Western Roman Empire to Pope Sylvester (285–335). In such a situation, neither France nor England, nor any other European power, was fully sovereign. This is precisely what Jean Bodin's ideas were directed against.

From now on, the supreme players are the rulers of nation-states. There is no higher authority above them. The relationship between them is determined only by bilateral treaties, alliances and coalitions, negotiations or war. This was most fully manifested in Protestant England, but France — although it never broke with Catholicism decisively — became the second pole of the new political system. Therefore political sovereignty, although a product of Protestant thought, found its application in the Catholic world as well, where France became the vanguard of the transition to modernity.

A system based on the principle of sovereignty was finally adopted by the European powers in the seventeenth century as a result of the bloody Thirty Years' War. In it, a coalition of Protestant countries from the European north clashed with the southern European powers that had sided with the Counter-Reformation and remained committed to Rome and the Habsburgs. The Catholic south made one last attempt to preserve — even restore — the medieval order that presupposed the supremacy of the popes and the status of the empire. But already in this war it became clear that a number of Catholic countries (above all France) were not in fact guided by a pan-Catholic agenda, but by their own national interests (confrontation with Austria, etc.). As neither side was able to gain a decisive advantage in the Thirty Years' War, in 1648 the Peace of

Westphalia cemented the victory of the principle of national sovereignty by rejecting any legal basis for religious authority, both Catholic and Protestant. It was essentially an ideological victory for Protestantism, which had originally (with Luther and in England) advocated the complete autonomy of national kings and princes. From then on it was the nation-state and its sovereign that were regarded as the highest political authority, and questions of religion were relegated to the periphery of the Political. This remains the norm of international law even today. This is how Jean Bodin's ideas triumphed.

Inside the Leviathan

We can draw an analogy between the basic concepts of the three founding fathers of political modernity:

> Prince (Machiavelli) — Leviathan (Hobbes) — sovereign (Bodin)

These are very similar and related concepts. All of them together and separately constitute a new (with regards to Antiquity and the Middle Ages) structure of the Political. Henceforth politics is placed exclusively in the context of 'this world', the ontological vertical is collapsed and the state is thought of as an exclusively immanent phenomenon. Politics becomes corporeal, materialistic, technical and exclusively earthbound, sharply detached from any heavenly spiritual dimension. There is no place in such politics for a Philosopher King or even an aristocratic warrior. Everything in it is subordinated to utilitarian practical tasks. In fact, to recognise the legitimacy of Machiavelli's Prince, Hobbes' Leviathan or Bodin's sovereignty is to accept the swineopolis and the legitimacy of its philosophical foundations.

Today we live in a Hobbesian world (Leviathan, social contract, rational egoism), under the rule of the Prince (not a commissarial dictatorship) and in terms of international law, under the Jean Bodin system (the Peace of Westphalia). Any supra-national organisations — such as the UN — have only a symbolic value and a recommendatory status.[22] Any

---

22 Dugin, *International Relations (Paradigms, Theories, Sociology)*.

state may or may not accept the principles of 'international law', as the main provision of that law is sovereignty, which means, among other things, that it is perfectly legitimate for a state not to reckon with any international norms. By recognising the principle of sovereignty as the ultimate authority, any supra-national association is no more than a club. Ostracism or censure may be psychologically and morally unpleasant, or even harmful, but there is no authority that can legitimately force a sovereign state to adopt a particular policy. Only force can be a deciding factor, and in order to pressure a sovereign state, the decisive argument is that another state or a coalition of states has to have the power to force it in one direction or another.

The Politics of the Third Begininng

We live in a *Leviathan* world; we are dealing with actors of rational egoism, with rational wolves; this is what justifies the very existence of the state, and the legitimacy of violence by the state is justified by exactly this — pessimistic — anthropology. Sovereignty is a reality that continues to have absolute significance for us today. Bodin wrote in the sixteenth century, but even today it is a fundamental factor of the very structure of our political system — regardless of the particular state in which we live. We are still in the world of Jean Bodin. This world remains Westphalian, which means that we base our international practice, our international law, on the principle of sovereignty.

It is with these three European thinkers — Machiavelli, Hobbes and Bodin — that the paradigm shift in political philosophy takes place. We leave the state of the Father and the state of the Son, political Platonism and political Aristotelianism, and move on to the domination of the third beginning of the *Timaeus*, the domain of the third social class (philistines, majority, *demos*) and the third source of the soul (carnal aspirations). All these trends are synchronised — the rise of the bourgeoisie, capitalism, secularisation, the abolition of the transcendental dimension, the transition from the vertical to the horizontal, the replacement of religion by science, the shift of the main priority from unity to multiplicity, etc.

Thus there is a change not only of the subject, but also of the object. Instead of the Platonic and Aristotelian universe, the universe of Democritus becomes the norm. Atoms of matter have their counterparts in the society of the individual, the citizens of the democratic system. The male contemplative and heroic principle gives way to the Mother, the Nurturer, the Receiver.

CHAPTER 11

INDIVIDUALISM AS THE BASIS OF NEW AGE POLITICAL PHILOSOPHY

The Foundation of Protestantism Is the Social Contract

THE DOMINANT FOUNDATION of New Age politics is the idea that the individual is the basic unit of the Political. That is to say, the Political is thought of as a product of the individual's creation. As we have seen, the origins of this approach lie in the particular theology of Protestantism, which placed the individual rational being in the central position for interpreting Holy Scripture.

Protestants see the Church as a creation of people by means of a social contract. The social contract forms the Church for Protestantism. This Church is not based on a clergy (as with Catholics), not on apostolic grace and not on a body of people united by the sacrament of baptism (as with the Orthodox), but on the contract of individuals. Protestants believe that Christians agree among themselves and that the Church is created out of the agreement.

Hence the underlying *democratic* character of Protestantism. In some cases it leads to the denial of the priesthood altogether — where there is no pastor at all, or he is elected by all members of the congregation and does not have to receive any further ordination. In many forms of Protestantism (especially in Calvinism, its varieties and parallel currents) this leads to the rejection of the Eucharist. In addition, in Protestant sects we see an almost complete rejection of icons — statues and images of saints, and even of Christ himself, are regarded as 'idolatry'.

In fact, the perception of the Church is radically changed. The Protestant Church is the product of a collective contract, a social contract.

One only needs to secularise this Protestant ecclesiology and we get the basic model of New Age political philosophy. In Protestantism, though the principle of the individual applies to the interpretation of Scripture, Scripture is still regarded as a sacred and unquestionable authority. The next step towards modernity is the rejection of this, and the introduction of the individual's freedom to henceforth interpret not only the Bible, but everything in general. The rationality argument for judging a passage in Scripture is expanded to its limit — individuals are now free to make any judgement on the basis of their own reason.

This is how the subject of the New Age is normatively conceptualised as an individual. This notion is characteristic of all three classical ideologies of modernity — liberalism, Communism and Fascism.[1] These three political theories describe almost the entire spectrum of the basic, mainstream versions of modern political philosophy. These ideologies take different positions in relation to the individual — but nevertheless, in all three the idea of the basic origin of the Political is not taken from outside the individual (in God, in the sacred, in nature, etc.) but precisely in the individual. The individual becomes the main subject of politics. This is the specific character of the New Age.

All three theories have their origins in the secular model of Protestant ideology. In a somewhat simplified way, we can say that it is enough to take the Protestant ideology, remove God, Christ and Holy Scripture from the equation, and we get the philosophy of New Age politics and the idea of a social contract which lies at its core.

---

[1] Александр Дугин, Четвертый Путь. Введение в Четвертую Политическую Теорию (Moscow: Академический проект, 2014). [Alexander Dugin, *The Fourth Way: Introduction to the Fourth Political Theory.*]

Paradoxes of the Atom — The Nihilistic Undercurrent of Modern Ontology

There is a direct and immediate connection between the atomism of physics and individualism in political philosophy. This reveals the unity which is the nature of both philosophy and politics.

In fact, the notion of the individual is not as simple as it may seem. New Age philosophy introduced a new element to the structure of the world that was absent in the Middle Ages, in Antiquity, in religious society, in the world of Tradition and in cultures where the sacred predominated.

The theories of Democritus, Epicurus and Lucretius were exceptions to the prevailing systems of cosmology and ontology (predominantly Platonic or Aristotelian), which explicitly denied atomism. But New Age physics, starting with Galileo and Gassendi, puts this marginal theory of atomism in the spotlight. That there is something indivisible (the atom in nature and the individual in society) at the underlying level of the world was the avantgarde, paradigmatic idea of the New Age, since the view of matter in the scholastic, Platonic, Aristotelian understanding was fundamentally anti-atomist. Why? Because matter was seen as a principle of insufficiency (i.e. privation, absence). The movement towards matter is the process of the cooling of the Spirit, the extinction of the illuminating idea. But darkness is only the absence of light. Evil is a diminution of good,[2] as Plotinus wrote, a notion picked up by Christian Platonism. And in this sense there is no matter.

Matter is only the horizon, the limit to which the falling Spirit aspires. There is no darkness as such, only *extinguished light*. So matter, from the philosophical point of view in the age of Antiquity, the Middle Ages and classical philosophy, is the *process of materialisation*. Matter is only a limit, only a horizon that is in itself unattainable. The spirit goes out, and the process of its extinction is a movement towards matter. Matter itself was thought of as something that does not exist, as something apophatic, having no being in itself.

---

2   Literally: 'Evil is not some defect of the good, but a total defect'. Plotinus. *The First Ennead*.

Accordingly, matter is not something given, but a *process*. There is no indivisible atom, there is a *process of division*. Only a conditional, purely conceptual horizon of this division can be called 'matter'. There is the process of atomisation of the primordial unity into a multitude, and the *unattainable limit of division* is called 'matter'.

In this case atomism cannot exist, because any material atom — as that which does not undergo *tome* (Greek τομή) — 'division' — has a limit of division, and this limit is ontologically unattainable. The atom can exist as the last link in an endless chain of division, having no existence of its own.

This is how classical philosophy thinks, and on this it bases its theories about the political order, about the sacred Empire, about the mission of the State. Everything emanates from the One and moves towards multiplicity in the course of more and more movement, fragmentation, dissection, but it never fully achieves this multiplicity, because multiplicity represents 'nothingness'. It is interesting that Democritus himself bases his atomist terminology on a pair of concepts — δέν and οὐδέν, usually interpreted as 'atom' and 'emptiness'. But the proper Greek word is οὐδέν, which means 'nothingness', 'absence'.[3] The second term, δέν, has no meaning in the language and is artificially created by Democritus to denote the opposite of 'nothing', that is, 'not nothing'. In Democritus' sense δέν means 'something', 'particle', 'atom'. But the very creation of this artificial concept is highly revealing: Democritus begins with 'nothing' (οὐδέν) and moves from it to denote its conceptual opposite. Democritus, however, does not use an already existing Greek word; he specifically creates a neologism, δέν. This is to emphasise the purely speculative (conceptual) nature of the 'atom', which is postulated by the mind, but is not an object of sensory perception like ordinary physical objects. And the fact that this concept is postulated in opposition to another — original — concept, οὐδέν, shows the ontological primacy of negation. We have said that Democritus himself, unlike his interpreters, does not define the atom as 'being'. Not being in a state of 'not being', 'emptiness', 'nothingness', does not yet mean *being*. The speculative nature of the atom does not give Democritus sufficient grounds to speak of being with the same certainty

---

3   Lurie, *Democritus. Texts. Translation. Research.*

as Plato and Aristotle (for whom the mind itself is a god and knowingly represents the maximum of being). This is why the term δέν appears in the opposition to 'nothingness' (οὐδέν), as an indication of a special modus of being derived only from rational reasoning and not confirmed by sense experience. It is important to note that from the linguistic point of view, unlike the Russian *ни-что* or English 'no-thing', the second part of the Greek term οὐδέν, i.e. δέν proper, does not carry the meaning of 'thing' at all. Rather, it corresponds to the Greek particle δέ, which translates into Russian as *же — вот же, как же*,[4] etc., and οὐδέν is then something like *нет же* — 'no', 'not'. Discarding 'no', we do not get something affirmative, we get, rather, meaningless in itself and taken apart from the other words, *же*. Tellingly, in modern Greek δέν means exactly 'no', 'not', as a shortened form of οὐδέν, where the actual negation οὐ has undergone apheresis. Thus the abridged word retained the meaning of the fuller earlier version. From this we can draw the most important conclusion: the atom as δέν is not in the full sense an ontological instance, that is, an entity pertaining to being. Δέν is not a 'what' obtained by subtraction from the 'nothing', the 'no'. Δέν is a 'not-thing' whose being we cannot say anything definite about. The negation of negation in ontology and philosophy (unlike in arithmetic) does not necessarily give an affirmation. And if the sensually perceptible things according to Democritus are spectres (εἴδωλον), atoms are the origins of spectres, their genetic matrices.

Democritus understood that, in the classical cosmology of Antiquity, that which is cumulatively under emptiness and under atoms is seen as matter, 'multitude' (πολλά), since the absence of an eidetic origin (form) made it impossible to speak of any grounded existence and could only be a purely conceptual abstraction postulated within 'nothing'. Therefore δέν as the antithesis of οὐδέν is not yet 'something', although it is postulated as 'not nothing'. The ontology of the atom is problematic and the opposite of obviousness — both the obviousness of the classical enlightened mind and the element of sense perception. The atom is something that is as unstable and unobvious as an idea or spirit, but it is not at the top, not in the realm of the mind, but below in the inaccessible strata of nothingness.

---

4   'Here' and 'as', respectively.

The same applies to the individual in society. There is no such figure, for every individual is partly individual and partly collective, and the proportions between these statuses are extremely complex and multi-dimensional. In order to get an individual, society must be destroyed. Similarly, in order to get the atom one must first destroy the body by dispersing it beyond the boundary of the definition of 'body'. 'Not nothingness' is found only at the boundary of 'nothingness'.

Hence the *nihilism of atomism in general*. Not only do classical vertical ontologies see matter as nothingness, but in a sense, Democritus also agrees with this — nonetheless finding something in the densest medium of nothingness (materiality) that is distinct from it.

Significantly, as atomistic physics developed, it turned out that an indivisible limit cannot be reached, and what was formerly considered 'atom', 'indivisible', turns out in turn to be 'divisible', consisting of even smaller particles, which are again subject to division. Thus the atom remains unattainable, which, however, does not refute Democritus, but only underlines the original conceptual nihilism of his theory. Similarly, the individual is not attainable in society, for even having freed the individual from all ties to collective identity, we do not reach the minimum of the human — then begins the transition to the divide, the organs, the cells, genetic engineering and cyborg projects, which form the basis of postmodern anthropology[5] (posthumanism and transhumanism).

An Idiot Is a Man without Qualities

If we look at the classical or medieval interpretation of the nature of man, he was necessarily thought of as part of something. Part of Adam, part of the Church, part of the people, part of the political body. In a sense, man is part of his own soul (and not vice versa). An individual is a conditional abstract result (which does not exist and is not possible in reality) of the dissection of some whole. Therefore, in the full sense of the word, the *individual*, from the point of view of traditional political philosophy, does not and cannot exist at all. There is *individuation*, a movement toward the

---

5 Dugin, *Postphilosophy*.

individual, but there is no individual himself — because his content will be strictly zero. If we do find this individual, he will be nothing, nihilism itself. He will be an elusive abstraction like Democritus's δέν. As we move from the whole to the particular, as we dissect the whole, we lose content. The individual as such is therefore an empty abstraction.

In ancient Greece, the term 'idiot', ἰδιώτης, was used to denote such a figure, in which all qualitative forms of collective identity were abolished, and which was reduced to the mere fact of having some human being in complete isolation from content. The modern word 'idiot' (in both its clinical and abusive sense) is a derivation of the ancient Greek political term, which describes an individual who does not belong to any social group. An idiot is a person who has no ancestors in that city, no place in the social system, no connection with a cult or profession. Such people are not citizens or slaves, they are nobodies. They are idiots. The idiot is a pure individual, devoid of any concrete form of social identity, bound to a collective being and its parameters.

In Greece, where everything had a qualitative character, an 'idiot' was a person who, for example, came to a town where no one knew him and was unable to relay anything meaningful or relevant about himself. The man is there, but he has no substance. He has no mythological ancestry, no religion (at least not identifiable within that society). Yet he may be rich, strong, handsome, attractive. But when the Greek polis tried to define him in some way, they would say: 'That's just a "private person", an idiot.'

In the clinical sense, an 'idiot' is a person who cannot make any coherent discourse, does not know clearly who he is, is incapable of making the minimal distinctions and actions necessary to communicate with those around him. No matter how the idiot feels or who he thinks he is within, he is completely disconnected from society, desocialised and incapable of socialisation. Here the political criterion of the Greek polis is transferred to the clinical case, which is pathological and a clear anomaly for any culture. The idiot is a private person without qualities. An entity with eyes, ears and eyebrows is present, but it has no substance. What is to be done with the idiot, with the pure individual as such? In many societies this has been a serious problem. Where to put him? On the one hand, he is not human because he does not have any form of effective socialisation; on the other hand, he resembles and is a human being. In some societies, idiots were banished or even killed. In others — Christian societies, for example — they were allowed to live freely and were even granted support. But in this case, too, they have gained no qualities whatsoever, except the most general ones. So the euphemism for 'idiot' was the word 'cretin', derived from the French *le chrétien* — that is, 'Christian' — which implied that the person had no qualities, connections or characteristics whatsoever, so out of charity he was simply called a 'Christian' or a 'good Christian' in Christian society.

The Idiot as the Norm and Individual-Objects

Modernity, following the logic of atomism, including socio-political atomism, radically changes the attitude towards the idiot. Henceforth, the person devoid of qualities appears as a social atom, and consequently as a positive phenomenon (and not the result of the subtraction of qualities). Thus something unprovable, non-existent (like an atom in physics) or outright degenerate is taken as the initial, fundamental model for understanding the political process. The origins of individualism[6] are thus not as obvious as they might at first appear.

There seems to be nothing more empirically obvious than the individual. By pointing at someone next to us or thinking of ourselves, we by default think of both as individuals. In fact — there is nothing of the sort. In order to derive an individual from a concrete person, including ourselves, we must subtract everything that constitutes their collective identity: language, frame of mind, gender, parents, ancestry, education, school, nationality, age, social role and status, and so on.

If we take the sociological totality that forms the content of the individual (persona[7]) and subtract all the collective forms, we get an abstraction. It is this individual — the social δέν — that is seen as the main actor

---

6   Dumont, *Essays on Individualism*.
7   The anthropologist Marcel Mauss (1872–1950) explains in detail that the personality, as opposed to the individual, is a social and even sociological concept.

of modern political philosophy. It is he who makes a social contract with another individual for the consequent formation of a political body. Similarly, according to Democritus, bodies are formed by invisible and non-sensible atoms. It is important to note that the state is not created by human beings, by personalities, by collective identities, but precisely by 'individuals', that is, by philosophical abstractions. These abstractions become henceforth political and legal norms that exist in the ontology of law, but are impossible to detect in reality, except in clinical cases. But despite this, it is this entity that is regarded as the negotiator of the social contract.

Let us recall Hobbes' Leviathan. What properties did he impart to this normative idiot? He does not quite have an idiot, that is, a man without properties. But close to it. Hence the stable and extremely important metaphor of the beast. And a wild one at that — in Hobbes he takes the form of a wolf. In Plato, who also wanted to express the minimum of social and political qualities, there are metaphors of the pig — from which he extrapolates swineopolis. Democritus saw the origins of human society in the imitation of animals. Humans had learnt 'from the spider to weave and mend, from the swallow to build houses, from the songbirds — the swan and the nightingale — to sing.'[8]

Thus, an idiot according to Hobbes is a wolf. It is one who, from his purely selfish aspirations, wants as much pleasure, possession, nourishment, comfort and security as possible. Accordingly, he is one who seeks to construct a situation around himself. At the centre of his system are his desires and appetites, with everything else on the periphery. Of course, the beast is by no means an idiot, and it is driven by a rather rigid program that predestines the very species. In this sense, the animal is collective; all wolves and all hares act almost identically in similar situations. Which means that they have qualities and properties. However, the metaphor of the beast as applied to man is an attempt to find some atomic basis, i.e. to deprive man of everything human. The individual is a beast in the sense that it arises as the result of the subtraction of the human content from the human, as the fruit of abstraction, reduction and liberation from

---

8   Lurie, *Democritus. Texts. Translation. Research.*

the — human — *eidos*. The individual is the most material beginning in man — much more material than the body. The body has form, structure, qualities. And the fact of separateness is nothing but an act of severing, tearing away, dismembering. Therefore 'wolf', 'pig' or 'bee', as applied to man in political narratives, serve to illustrate the special entities of 'wolf-man', 'pig-man', 'bee-man', etc., designed to describe the chimerical and purely speculative nature of the individual. These are not beasts as such, but specific metaphors illustrating the concept of individuality.

It is very important to point out that *the individual is not a subject*. More precisely, the very notion of subject (Greek ὑποκείμενον, Latin *subjectum*) bears a semantic ambiguity: it denotes literally that which is 'below', 'under' (Greek ὑπο-, Latin *sub*-). In Greek there was a similar term, 'hypostasis', ὑπόστασις (from ὑπο-, 'under', and στάσις, στάσεως, 'standing', 'placing'). But that which is 'under', 'inside' a thing or being can be interpreted in two philosophical paradigms. On the one hand, it is the hidden essence (Greek οὐσία, Latin *essentia*), which in the Platonic and Aristotelian perspective means the spiritual, heavenly origin, *eidos*, paradigm. In this case the 'subject' is thought of as a rational soul, i.e. the highest level of soul peculiar only to humans, whereas beasts, plants and stones have their own souls — animal, vegetative and mineral (there were different opinions about the souls of stones in Antiquity). Here the prefix ὑπο- or *sub-* means 'hidden behind the mask of corporeality', 'being on the other side of the phenomenal reality'. The term 'subject' has taken on this very meaning — the centre of the thinking, willed soul of a human being. In Christian theology, this very meaning has become steadily associated with the concept of 'hypostasis', coinciding with the Latin *persona*, i.e. personality.

But it is possible to move in another direction and, following the literal meaning of the prefix ὑπο- or *sub*-, to extend the movement in the direction from spirit to matter, from Father to Mother-Nurse, from paradigm to *chora*, from the One to the many, and to give it the meaning of that which is even below the border of corporeality. In Latin this interpretation has come to be associated with the concept of *sub-stantia*, i.e. literally 'being underneath', which gives us a complete tongue twister of the Greek ὑπόστασις, but with the exact opposite meaning this time. *Substantia* is the deepest layer of materiality below the body; in a sense it is not just matter, but sub-matter, the material roots of matter. The Scholastics explicitly contrasted the pair of terms *essentia — substantia* with each other, referring to two opposite poles of being: spiritual, divine, heavenly and thinking vs. material, corporeal, insignificant, earthly and unthinking. Later this pair came to be defined as subject and object (*objectum*), where *ob-jectum* (Greek ἀντικείμενον) meant that which lies opposite, in opposition to the subject. In the origins of these concepts we can see an indication of 'something hidden', which then came to be interpreted as 'hidden' like spirit, as the origin of a thing, as the inner dimension of being, and 'hidden' like matter, as that which lies below the body, as the outermost dimension of being. At the extreme it could mean both the limits of ontology and the One (Ἑν) and πολλά of Plato's *Parmenides*. The terminology was not clearly defined among the Pre-Socratics, and so Democritus' atom must be understood from the context as the origin of substance, that is, the possible maximum of objectivity, of materiality.

It is interesting that with regard to the atom in the social dimension (i.e. the individual), Aristotle argues in the *Politics* in similar terms, saying that the political dimension (i.e. collective identity), is the natural state of people, which can be escapes in two directions. Aristotle writes:

> Man is by nature a political animal. And he who by nature and not by mere accident is without a state, is either above humanity, or below it; he is the 'tribeless, lawless, heartless one,' whom Homer denounces — the outcast who is a lover of war; he may be compared to an isolated pawn on a playing board.[9]

Going beyond the collective identity (the Political) gives us either the 'superman', the one who is better, stronger, wealthier (κρείσσων), or the underdeveloped degenerate — φαῦλός. And it is significant that Aristotle compares him to an unpaired figure (Greek ἄζυξ) in the game. What is meant by the individual in New Age philosophy is precisely the sub-material segment of the human being, the attraction of the soul towards pure nothingness. The ego in man is the most (rather than the least) material

---

9   Aristotle, *Politics*, 1253a.

instance, which is the *inverted vertical*. This is the 'inner idiot', φαῦλός, the unpaired senseless object ἄζυξ, or the political analogue of what Democritus calls δέν, 'not nothing'. Indeed, the idiot/individual is not nothing, but at the same time it is also *not something*. It is a vector pointing below the lower limit of the body. And as Democritus said, atoms can only be seen by the mind, as they are purely conceptual. But not a Platonic idea or an Aristotelian essence, rather it is a concept,[10] something artificially assembled, as the New Age philosophy understands it. The individual is just the object, the most objectified and removed from its essence and its spirit, from its *eidos* and its idea.[11]

It is such empty — 'idiotic' — individuals who become the *normative figures* in New Age philosophy. They are egoistic, placing their desires, ambitions and will at the centre of their individualistic framework for experiencing the world. But all the properties of the ego are no longer individual, they are inherent in the multitude. What is individual is the ego itself, its most inner dimension.

The bearer of the ego, the individual, is fundamentally not attainable in reality; it is as abstract and conceptual as a speculative atom.

In physics, the atom serves only as a reference point in the process of a more and more subtle division of matter. This very division constitutes the essence of 'progress' as the main content of time in the conditions of the New Age. This progress is a movement into the depth of matter, striving to find after each new achievement an ever-smaller particle. Progress is an intensive transition from the one to the many. Therefore knowledge of the many in turn multiplies and objects become more and more fragmented. And although the next pretender to being an 'atom' (i.e. something 'indivisible') finds itself subject to segmentation again, progress does not stop and reconsider its starting point — the belief in the atom.

---

10   Gilles Deleuze; Félix Guattari, *What is Philosophy?* (New York : Columbia University Press, 1994).

11   In contemporary postmodern philosophy — above all in speculative realism — this becomes the main goal: to reduce the human subject to the object. But this reduction does not violate anything in individualism; on the contrary, it takes individualism to its last logical limit. Because the core of the individual is precisely the pure object or *the radical object*.

In political philosophy, something similar happens to the individual. Postulating the individual as the essence of the ego becomes the driving force of progress, which consists in freeing the individual from that which is collective in him, from that which can be separated from him. This defines the dynamic of the political era of modernity — social progress. This progress consists in *delving into the social matter* in order to acquire what is sought — the individual — who constantly slips away at each stage of liberation, again and again proving to be the 'dividual' or bearer of a collective identity. Protestantism frees the individual from the Catholic Church with its dogmas and from the empire with its mission. But he finds himself again a prisoner of the religious authority of this or that sect or under the authority of the Prince. What follows is the liberation of the individual from the state and politics. This is the ideal of civil society and the transition to purely economic interactions. The progress of liberalism, approaching ever closer to the core of the individual, at some point emphasises that gender is also a collective identity, which yields feminism and the appeal to the optionality of gender, as religion, nationality and class were previously declared optional. The last step is a move to posthumanism, as 'human being' is also a collective identity. But obviously, the desired individual — the pure 'idiot' — will not be achieved, since the result of such a liberation will be a machine and/or Artificial Intelligence, which in turn is something divisible. Therefore, New Age individualism must be understood as a process, as a movement towards a limit that cannot be reached by analytical methods.[12]

The Goat-Stag and Pseudologic

Given the particular nature of atoms and the content of the underlying concept of the individual, we can argue that the basic idea of the New Age is this: that which is not there is there. *Nihil* (nothingness) is. Nonexistence exists.

This is an anti-Parmenidean paradox, although in a certain sense it has already been conceptualised in the Platonic dialogues. From Plato's

---

12 René Guénon, *Traditional Forms and Cosmic Cycles* (Sophia Perennis et Universalis, 2003).

point of view, falsehood is that non-existence which is, because if one expounds any opinion, then this very exposition and the opinion presented in it exists. But being false, that is, narrating a non-existence, it is not complete truth or complete being. This is how an ontology of falsehood, a kind of 'pseudologia' (ψευδολογία), arises.

If we take as the basis of being that which from Plato's and Aristotle's point of view does not exist (as, for example, the worlds described by *Parmenides* 6,7,8 and 9 do not exist), then we find ourselves in the context of a particular ontology — a *pseudological ontology*, which exists exactly as a false opinion exists. This is what Plotinus wrote about the 'being' of matter:

> All that it (matter) presents itself as is false; it itself is false.[13]

Such a pseudological field of existence is pure nihilism. This is the basis of modern philosophy, a nihilism that manifests itself in an ontology of falsehood. What cannot be (the atom or the individual) is taken for what is.

Aristotle, in his treatise 'On Interpretation', gives the example of a possible word which denotes a thing whose existence or non-existence is not and cannot be determined. He writes:

> Nouns and verbs, provided nothing is added, are like thoughts without combination or separation; 'man' and 'white', as isolated terms, are not yet either true or false. In proof of this, consider the word 'goat-stag'. It has significance, but there is no truth or falsity about it, unless 'is' or 'is not' is added, either in the present or in some other tense.[14]

The goat-stag (Greek τραγέλαφος) for Aristotle is a phenomenon without any ontological status, i.e. a pure concept. In the nineteenth century, phenomenological philosopher Alexius Meinong[15] (1853–1920) proposed a

---

13 Διὸ πᾶν ὃ ἂν ἐπαγγέλληται ψεύδεται. Plotinus, *The Third Ennead*.
14 Aristotle, *On Interpretation*.
15 Alexius Meinong, *Über Möglichkeit und Wahrscheinlichkeit: Beiträge zur Gegenstandstheorie und Erkenntnistheorie* [*On Possibility and Probability: Contributions to Object Theory and Epistemology*] (Leipzig: J.A. Barthe, 1915).

special term for such objects, 'absistence'. It cannot be argued that they exist (existential), but it cannot be proved that they do not, since at least the formal side of their denotation observes some structural rules and laws. Therefore, 'goat-stag' or 'golden mountains' are absistential according to Meinong — they are not and do not exist. We can call such objects 'virtual' or 'pseudological'.

The ontological status of the individual falls into this category — it is a pseudological unit, the analogue of the 'goat-stag'. The same applies to the atom.

Implicit nihilism is the basis of all New Age philosophy. From the point of view of Antiquity and the Middle Ages, New Age philosophy is a thoroughly developed, fundamental, scientifically grounded lie.

CHAPTER 12

LIBERALISM (THE FIRST POLITICAL THEORY). JOHN LOCKE AND HIS LEGACY

The Common Metaphysical Denominator of the Three Poltical Ideologies of Modernity

IN MODERN TIMES, the history of European societies, as well as of European colonies on other continents and in other parts of the world, takes place exclusively in the context of the third origin described in Plato's *Timaeus*. Modernity is born out of the combination of the Renaissance and the Reformation,[1] the inclination towards the immanent and secular beginnings of the Renaissance combining with Protestant individualism. Southern Europe, where the Renaissance began, did not accept the Reformation and individualism of the European North. The Catholic Church's Council of Trent harshly rejected Calvinism and Lutheran theology, launching the Counter-Reformation. In some areas of the Protestant world, in turn, Renaissance secularism was rejected (e.g. by Calvin in Switzerland, where a kind of Protestant theocracy was established). However, the common denominator of modern philosophy, in absolute contrast to both Antiquity and the Middle Ages, was exactly the combination of materialism and secularism on the one hand, and individualism (social atomism) on the other. The formula of modernity is materialism + individualism.

---

1 Étienne Gilson, *Heloise and Abelard* (Michigan: University of Michigan Press, 1960).

In the structure of *Politica Aeterna*, these properties corresponded precisely to the third zone at the base of the hierarchical triangle of the vertical Political model. In ontology they correspond to matter, the multitude (πολλά), *chora* (χώρα), nothingness, the lower boundary of ontology, the 'realm of quantity',[2] and in Democritus' model to the great void (οὐδέν) and the atoms (δέν) detached from it. In the metaphysical gender model, this corresponds to the figure of the Mother, the Nurturer, the Receiver, called to nurture and envelop the Son, who is entirely the creation of the Heavenly Father, in an outer shell. In the structure of the soul this corresponded to the black horse, representing carnal desire, bodily pleasures, comfort, etc. (ἐπιθυμία).

In politics proper this corresponded to the representatives of the urban population, citizens consisting mainly of craftsmen and tradesmen, and in a wider sense all social units who were free and engaged in the production of products and material objects — and the vast majority in traditional society were precisely peasants. However, the peasants were situated outside the city-polis, and hence at some distance from politics. So a situation developed in which, in the social structure of the three strata or classes, the peasants were replaced by townspeople whose status coincided neither with the warrior caste (aristocracy, nobility), nor with the priestly caste (clergy) nor with the dynastic rulers (royal family). So the urban craftsmen and tradesmen became representative not only of themselves, but also of the peasants, who constituted the vast majority of the population of any state right up to the most recent eras. The peasants remained on the periphery of modernity, and the townspeople — the citizens, the bourgeoisie — acted on their behalf. Therefore the third component of society, connected to the lower limit of ontology and anthropology, at the origins of modernity was represented by the merchant, whose role increased with the shift from the paradigm of Tradition to the paradigm of the modern. Thus, gradually the bourgeois became synonymous not simply with the citizen, but precisely with the merchant and the entrepreneur, who was henceforth the priority bearer of the corporal-material,

---

2   René Guénon, *The Reign of Quantity and the Signs of the Times (Collected Works)* (Sophia Perennis et Universalis, 2004).

quantitative principle in society (i.e. the collective image of the Third Estate), which initially included the peasantry that was gradually pushed out to the periphery of the Political.

The whole structure of the Political New Age refers to this third segment on the map of *Politica Aeterna*. Of course, the modern did not triumph immediately even in Europe itself, where its confrontation with Traditional society, its philosophy, its interpretation of religion, its institutions and its patterns stretched over several centuries. That is why even in the New Age we are confronted with certain vestiges of the old — medieval — order, or with combined forms. But from the point of view of political philosophy, all that is legitimately New Age and constitutes modern political ideology must necessarily share the fundamental axioms of modernity, i.e. the primacy and supremacy of the third sector of ontology, anthropology and politics. This means that a political ideology is only modern in the full sense of the word when it is based on materialism, a scientific picture of the world, recognition of the priority of democracy and the individual identity of man, uniting into particular groups and collectives only artificially and secondarily. Thus it is the material aspirations (ἐπιθυμία) that are seen as predominant and central in man and society, and everything else appears as a superstructure over the black horse from Plato's *Phaedrus*. It is this wilful (or lustful, because the word 'lust' originally meant simply desire, will, aspiration) side of the human structure that is considered 'real', primary, while everything else, including consciousness, is seen as an important but secondary addition. Thus man is likened to an animal, but developed to the point of having rational qualities. This is how the Aristotelian definition of the human being as a 'political animal' was given a new — biological, materialistic — interpretation in the modern Age. For Aristotle, the political dimension is the constitutive quality of the human being, his *eidos*, manifesting itself through his bodily existence. For modern political anthropology, starting with Hobbes, politics is thought of as a new field of battle for survival, gradually shaped and mastered by animals. For Aristotle, philosophy and politics are the natural state of man. For Hobbes, it is the result of transcending the natural state, and for Locke, it is the product of the education (upbringing) of a neutral, inert human mass ready to accept any external impulse.

Within the spectrum of New Age political philosophy, as we have said repeatedly, three distinct ideological forms can be distinguished — liberalism, Communism and nationalism (Fascism).[3] All of them fall completely within the paradigm of modernity and therefore share its ideological attitudes — above all, materialism and individualism. But while agreeing with this general attitude, they draw different conclusions from this, place emphasis and priorities in different directions and give their own interpretations and combinations of various political-philosophical terms and concepts. This unity of a common denominator and the distinction of theoretical and institutional constructs built on it should always be kept in mind when considering the political ideologies of modernity — liberalism, Communism and nationalism. Although very different and even antagonistic, grouped in various combinations and alliances during political history and especially during the decisive phase of the twentieth century, they share a common paradigmatic metaphysics and belong to the same segment of *Politica Aeterna*.

The Three Types of Social Contract and Hobbes' Universality

Starting with the Protestants, and especially with Calvin, we are dealing with individuals as the main creators of the Church, society and the state. Sometimes these three contracts are separated: people's agreement on the interpretation of religion creates a sect or a denomination (this is a religious contract), agreement on the model of relations with each other on the horizontal level creates society (this is a social contract), and agreement on the system of subordination to power authorities creates the state (this is a political contract). Secularisation leads to the abandonment of the first type of contract, while the second and third come to the fore. At that, Hobbes does not distinguish between the social contract and the political contract because, from his point of view, individuals agree with

---

3   Dugin, *The Fourth Way: Introduction to the Fourth Political Theory*.

each other first of all about creating the Leviathan, i.e. about power. Any other contract is secondary.

In this way a very specific *political anthropology* emerges. The individual is endowed with derivative properties (e.g. egoism), is seen as the basis of the political body, and the entire political philosophy is then built around this figure. This figure forms the basis of the modernist paradigm and is common to all types of New Age political ideologies. Liberals, socialists and nationalists alike build their doctrines on the centrality of individuals making a contract with each other. In Hobbes, this contract summarises all the possible types that will be derived from this principle later on. First of all, individuals negotiate power, which means that this contract is political and the establishment of the state is at the centre of it. Political nationalism follows this very line: the elevation of Leviathan to the highest value. Although, according to Hobbes, this is only a necessary measure taken by human-wolves, nationalism gives Leviathan an axiological load and makes it a source of inspiration and positive affectation. The individual wants to identify with Leviathan, to become one with him. The exaltation of such identification lies at the heart of New Age nationalism and patriotism.

Liberalism and socialism put more emphasis on the social contract, i.e. the agreement between individuals regarding the creation of society. According to Hobbes, this derives from the will for government. But later this aspect began to stand out as an independent dimension. The social contract forms not the vertical structure of power, but a kind of trust, a company, an *artel*. Here, too, there are some binding rules, but they are much less strict and do not assume a monopoly on violence in any single structure. Liberals and socialists partly present the social-horizontal contract in opposition to the political (vertical) contract, believing — unlike nationalists — that the state is not a value but a necessity (or even a necessary evil) and that the less state, the better. Theoretically, therefore, according to liberal and socialist teachings, individuals can conclude a contract between themselves to dissolve the state and replace it with public, civil structures.

But there is also a difference between liberals and socialists — this time in the interpretation of the nature of the social contract itself. Both liberals and socialists reject the idea of class, traditional society, hierarchy, the sacredness of politics, the mission of the state, etc.; they are unanimous in their egalitarianism, their desire for equality. But they understand equality in different ways. For liberals, the highest value is the individual himself, freed from all forms of collective identity, whether classical (Antiquity, church, class, imperial, etc.) or new, artificial (national, state or even social). Liberals therefore insist on equality of opportunity and initial conditions. This is the essence of the liberal contract: everyone agrees that no one should have special privileges in society and that each individual is completely equal to every other. But only at the beginning. Then the individual, endowed with equal opportunities, begins to implement them, to put them into practice, and does so with greater or lesser success in the process of free competition. The optimal form of such competition is the market, because economics is the most peaceful form of competition possible — in contrast to wars, robbery, the battle of all against all. Those individuals who succeed find themselves at the top of liberal society. Those who lose — at the bottom. But this does not violate the principle of equality according to liberals, it respects the principle of individual freedom to the full. In liberalism, individualism is revealed with the most clarity, as it is freed from both the Leviathan and the socialist interpretation of equality.

The socialist interpretation insists not only on equality of opportunity, but on the total equality of individuals — in virtually all areas. Any competition, according to socialists, carries with it an element of unfairness, and the starting conditions are never really equal. Moreover, the property inequality which emerges in liberal society constitutes injustice and violates the freedom of some individuals (the underdogs, the weak, the losers) in favour of others (the successful, the strong, the winners). So the idea of another type of social contract appears, which it is fashionable to call socialist. Individuals enter into this contract with each other agreeing that de facto equality is imperative, and that this can be achieved through wealth redistribution or specific tax policies.

But this is where the state comes into play again. Some authority has to supervise that the individuals observe this contract — no matter whether it is liberal or socialist. So the state (Leviathan) again becomes a necessary instrument, forcing individuals to comply with what they have decided by themselves. Such a state may be liberal or socialist, but it is back in play.

Thus, Hobbes and his political philosophy retain their significance in the later stages of the development of modern political philosophy, while his own views are given a more differentiated and detached interpretation.[4]

John Locke: Anthropological Optimism

Before Hobbes's fundamental ideas, in one interpretation or another, became the semantic axis of the three main political ideologies of the modern age, Hobbes's anthropological pessimism, his idea of the evil nature of man (man the wolf), his egoism and the permanence of this state of affairs was subject to a certain reinterpretation. However, as we have said, this time such pessimism is purely secular and detached from the Christian premise of original sin. Man as an individual is here ultimately the beast, which defines everything else, down to the contract and Leviathan.

Hobbes' challenge is answered in the seventeenth century by another seminal New Age philosopher, the founder of political liberalism — John Locke. Like Hobbes, Locke extends his fundamental influence throughout modern political philosophy into the twenty-first century. But while Hobbes encompasses the entirety of political modernity — in all three dominant ideologies (liberalism, socialism, nationalism) —, Locke extends his influence primarily to liberals, who follow the basic tenets of his thought. For socialists and nationalists, he represents rather an ideological opponent, though one who must be recognised for the thoroughness and wholeness of his teachings.

Liberalism could have been derived from Hobbes himself by focusing on the individual, which for him already forms the basis of the Political.

---

4   Carl Schmitt, *The Leviathan in the State Theory of Thomas Hobbes: Meaning and Failure of a Political Symbol* (Chicago: University of Chicago Press, 2008).

But it is Locke who adds something to Hobbes's teaching that significantly changes the parameters of political ontology.

Locke's paradigm responds to the challenge of Hobbes' paradigm at the most profound philosophical level. In Hobbes the normative individual is evil — *homo homini lupus est*. This 'idiot-wolf' has no characteristics other than greed, selfishness, a desire to tear another apart, to subjugate, eat and take everything he has. This conception of man is at the heart of *Leviathan*. Given the analysis of atomistic ontology and accepting the fundamental thesis that the individual represents the most objective, material and even sub-material beginning, this idea by Hobbes looks to be reasonably metaphysically sound, although it rejects the very possibility of an alternative — above all non-individualistic, holistic, eidetic, Christian, Platonic and Aristotelian — anthropology. Hobbes is right to say that man as an individual is indeed a wolf. But he is clearly exaggerating by claiming that there is no other type of man.

Locke does not critique Hobbes and his conception of man from a Platonic or Aristotelian position. Locke is as much an individualist, nominalist and modernist as Hobbes. He also admits of no human identity other than the individual. However, he disagrees with Hobbes' assessment of the individual specifically — not man as a whole, but the *individual*, the social idiot, the political atom. Thus, Locke accepts Hobbes's boundaries and does not seek to overstep them, but by remaining within them, he sharply changes the interpretation. For him the individual is still the same profane, desacralised individual (as with Hobbes), but now he sees him not in a sinister light, but quite benevolently. This is a change not of anthropological register, not of the subject matter, but of the rhetoric of its description. What was horrific to Hobbes, Locke even partly likes. Locke domesticates the individual, transforming the wolf into a lapdog by benevolent, pacifying discourse.

Now Locke says: indeed, we are only dealing with individuals, but is the individual so bad? And here begins the fundamental political philosophy argument about the state of nature.

This is the most important argument for defining all forms of New Age political philosophies. Hobbes tells us that the natural state is a war of all against all, and substantiates this with the evil nature of man. Man's nature is evil. The 'idiot-wolf' is aggressive, selfish and just waiting to attack the other and crush the weak. But he is a clever 'idiot-wolf' and invents the state to balance this aggression of all against all, to turn the chaotic carnage into a war of the state against criminals and states against each other. That is no longer a fight of all against all, but of one Leviathan against another Leviathan, or against its internal opponents. This is an excellent way of regulating aggression: firstly, the state apparatus suppressing those who violate its laws, and secondly, wars, interspersed from time to time with alliances and truces. All this makes sense when we are dealing with an anthropological pessimism and agree that 'man is evil'. Hobbes formulated his ideas on the basis of the English Civil War that was going on before his eyes. When he declares that 'man is wolf to man', he speaks of what he knows, because around him there are horrific clashes of different political parties, the decapitation of the king, violence, torture, denunciations, looting, executions, massacres, and all this in the context of furious religious extremism, when mere affiliation with Catholics, Protestants or one sect or another could be sufficient grounds for immediate murder. To be Irish was to be targeted. Nor was it easy for the Scots, who floundered from Catholicism to radical Puritanism. All this was 'natural' to Hobbes. This was the result when there was no Leviathan, or the Leviathan was weak. Hobbes, too, formulated his theory by watching what happened outside his carriage window. Someone being dragged to the gallows, someone being burned, someone being raped, someone being robbed. The snitches writing scribbled letters. Yesterday's favourite hangs from a lamppost. It's not hard to conclude from this that this is what man is like.

Locke also looked out of the carriage window — but in a radically different era, during the Glorious Revolution. As a young man and a staunch Puritan, he had fought in Cromwell's army, then taken part in the overthrow of James II of England (1633–1701). But later he saw a different landscape. Everything gradually fell into place. The sun shone on the green meadows of sweet, good England and even more kindly on Locke's native Scotland. The bourgeois, having awoken early, hurries to the market. The peasants are harvesting their bread. The new social contract between the warring parties is sealed, albeit at the steep price of compromise. And then the thought arises: maybe the natural state of man is not so bad? You see the good people around you — they've packed their wares, they're going to the market. Where do you see wolves here? Where do you see a war of all against all? Man is a mercantile being, peaceful and benevolent, Locke concludes.

And then, on the basis of this observation, he formulates a completely alternative political ideology: the individual and the social contract exist, but man draws his behaviour not from his nature, but from society. Man is, in fact, an individual, but he is not evil — he is nothing, empty. This is analogous to the inner emptiness of Democritus, though now separated from the outer emptiness (between atoms). Therefore, if an individual is brought up in a wolf pack, he becomes a wolf, but if he is brought up among the benevolent Scottish bourgeois and has received a decent education and decent upbringing, he will not fight; he will try to solve all questions peacefully with reliance on his mind.

From Wolf to Blank Slate

Man is not bad, says Locke. Not because he is good, but because he is a blank slate (*tabula rasa*). Man is what society has made him. This is a very profound observation that anticipates modern sociology. It is possible to write good or bad on a man.

Of course, Locke does not come to these conclusions simply by looking around and observing life in post-revolutionary England. He is first and foremost a philosopher, and in the field of philosophy he follows the classical English trend of empiricism. Locke himself was a member of the Royal Society, to which his friends Robert Boyle (1627-1691) and Isaac Newton (1642-1727) belonged, and he carried on the English tradition of empiricism in the natural sciences and nominalism in philosophy — most of all, he revered Occam. The connection with nominalism is fundamental, because the materialism and individualism inherent in nominalism define at once the foundations of Protestant theology, the scientific picture of the world, and the corresponding bourgeois liberal political philosophy. All these elements are fully intrinsic to Locke and constitute the semantic core of liberalism.

In the spirit of radical empiricism Locke argued that human consciousness is a blank slate (*tabula rasa*), and its content is shaped by a set of influences coming from the external world (in particular from society — hence the paramount importance Locke attached to the process of education). At the same time Locke rejects certain aspects of the French rationalism of Descartes (1596–1650), where the recognition of innate 'ideas' was discussed. For Locke, 'ideas' are neither something independent (as with Platonists[5]), nor *eidos* manifesting itself in things (as with Aristotle and Thomists), nor even innate concepts (as with Descartes), but always relative and secondary *products of strictly individual thinking*.[6] The 'idea' has no independent being; it is a transitory attribute of individual consciousness. Therefore all 'ideas' are ultimately transitory, subject to change and dependent on upbringing and experience. They mean nothing in themselves. At the same time, Locke sees the genesis of 'ideas' in concrete individual and material things which leave their imprint on the mind. It is this understanding of ideas that became common in European New Age philosophy. In fact, we are not talking about the ideas of Plato and the Platonists, but about concepts artificially constructed by the human mind, or about the *eidolons*, the 'ghosts', the 'idols' of Democritus.

But if the individual is a 'blank slate', a series of 'ideas' can be written upon him — that is, some *eidolons* can be projected — which he will then manipulate to build his chains of reasoning, his structures, his 'ideas'. The individual here turns out to be a kind of machine, which must be preprogrammed and only then allowed to move freely in the context of the established code.

Therefore, Locke concludes, the natural state of the individual need not be wolfish at all. It is nothing. And if society engages in education — that is, makes a social contract to make itself better, more humane,

---

5   He polemicised with a group of Cambridge Platonists (Ralph Cudworth, Henry More, Joseph Glanvill, Edward Stillingfleet, etc.).

6   John Locke, *An Essay Concerning Human Understanding* (Oxford: Clarendon Press, 1979.)

more reasonable, friendlier, more organised, etc. —, the result will be individuals producing good thoughts and performing moral deeds. Thus the transition from Hobbes to Locke changes the normative view of the content of the individual: from beast to blank slate, from evil to a neutrality that can be programmed in either direction. The individual is no longer evil or bad, he is nothing.

The Relativisation of Leviathan

Here we come to a fundamentally important point: if man is not so bad in his natural state and if his content is taken from society (and the social contract is conceived horizontally), then Leviathan is needed only in certain historical conditions and above all to fight against the evil society, the wolf state. It is not required to fight the good society.

Accordingly, individuals contract a political Leviathan when society is in dire straits, when the worst has to be prevented, the carnage has to be stopped and chaos has to be brought to order. But if the state begins to educate the population, to civilise the citizens, things can change. The Leviathan will lose its relevance. If a person is well educated, Locke believes, the Leviathan can also be abolished, leaving society in its natural state, which can become good and even be improved further and further.

Proceeding from this change of attitude towards human nature, from the assertion that this nature is neutral, a new political ideology emerges. It is as follows: the main actor remains the individual, but the individual is subject to re-education. The individual is not bad, and if we educate him well, he will be law-abiding, moral, well-mannered, enlightened and rational. And the next generation will be even better, as positive attitudes are reinforced, accumulated and developed. For Hobbes, human society is fundamentally static. For Locke, it changes, develops, evolves. This is how we approach the idea of social and historical progress.

From a liberalist perspective, education and enlightenment are necessary if social progress is to be irreversible. Whereas Hobbes puts the emphasis on 'selfishness' in the 'rational selfishness' combination, Locke puts the emphasis on 'rational'. This rationality consists of the capacity for learning. Therefore humanity can be brought up to some irreversible civilised level of rational egoism.

Hobbes cannot have a rational egoism. He simply has egoism, and the extent of his rationality is used to delegate power to the Leviathan before that egoism destroys its host. That is, Hobbes' man delegates his mind to Leviathan, while he himself continues to pursue his own private interests. By contrast, according to Locke, the mind of man is wielded by the individual himself. But the process has several phases: at first, reason is delegated to the state, which for its part implements a program of higher education and upbringing of citizens; then, reason returns to man in the process of enlightenment, and man — the individual — becomes a rational egoist. Therefore, in the natural state, this very cycle would occur and people would not kill each other off — on the contrary, they would build their relationships in the most peaceful and optimal way possible: by trading.

This is the idea behind liberalism. If the natural state of man is not evil, then notions of politics, the state and the Leviathan are seen as temporary. Not every Leviathan is good — only the one which stops civil conflict. And the task of the state is not to interfere in people's lives, but on the contrary, to educate them, give them an opportunity to be themselves and gradually diminish its own influence. And once the programme of education, nurturing and enlightenment is fulfilled, the state must disappear. Then society returns to its natural, non-political state, but now on a new level: *enlightened*. This enlightened society is the natural state of educated people created by an enlightened bourgeois state. Society is transformed from a political to an economic society — after the state has disappeared, the mercantile bourgeois civil nature begins to dominate. Thus the vertical (political) contract of power is a temporary measure and fits into the broadly conceived social (horizontal) contract.

According to Locke, the state is not divinely given; sacredness was long ago eradicated during the time of Hobbes. Already in Protestant ideology there is no philosophy of the politics of Revelation, everything is man-made. But now this Hobbesian man-madeness passes into the man-madeness of Locke's soft civil liberal society, which argues that the state is necessary as something temporary and then must disappear. The state has no meaning other than the education of reasonable egoists. It gradually disappears and civil society sets in.

Sacred Private Property

Locke's philosophical and political views were later incorporated into the *ideology of liberalism*, of which he is generally regarded as the founding father. This ideology suggests that society should aspire to a 'state of nature' (in Locke's sense) and that this is the goal of historical progress and social development. The state can only be tolerated as long as it is constitutional, based on the separation of powers (it was Locke who introduced the principle of the separation of powers into three — executive, legislative and federal, later judicial) and fulfils its main function: enlightenment. If the state does not meet these requirements, society has the right to bring about a 'democratic revolution'. Locke called the normative society 'civil society' and considered it possible for this society to exist outside the state — with the obligatory preservation of 'sacred private property', which would fulfil the function of the main institution of social order.

The main thing, Locke argued, is to enshrine what he called 'natural law' — first and foremost, the right to private property, but also to movement, freedom of conscience, freedom of speech, etc. *Individualism on the level of the subject requires a counterpart on the level of the object, and 'private property' becomes that counterpart.* Locke's world is individualised in everything — there are only individual beings and segments of the object distributed among them, divided into units of private property. But if, according to Hobbes, rationality and the capacity for calculated thinking are embodied by the Leviathan, and private property acts as a competitive field of egoistic thirst for pleasure and possession, then for Locke private property itself is an *embodiment of rationality*, and becoming an institution — that is, a legal category — it is able to replace the state.

The 'sanctity' of private property is as man-made and artificial as the sanctity of the Leviathan. But if Leviathan is an idol parading the vertical, private property is an *idol of the horizontal*. It preserves the principle of individuality on a visible scale, carving out a separate fragment from the world, which includes both the individual himself and his ontic environs, i.e. private property.

Adam Smith: Trade vs. War

The next step in the structuring of modern philosophy is taken by Locke's disciple, the famous economist Adam Smith[7] (1723–1790). Building on the philosophy of Locke, whom he regarded as his mentor and idol, Smith constructed an economic theory of capitalism.

The basic idea of Adam Smith was to show that the philosophical principles of Locke are valid in real life, and to create an analogue of these principles in the sphere of economics, translating Locke's message in terms of political economy.

Smith's first major idea is that the main source of wealth is *not land*, as was previously believed by the physiocrats and the classical economists of the transition period to modernity, but *entrepreneurial activity*. Smith argues that wealth is not created by immovable property (estates and lands), but by production, which is mobile and can be organised in different places. It is in the industrial-entrepreneurial sector that the maximum amount of goods and things of value is produced, and it is in this area that the means and mechanisms for the fastest economic growth are concentrated. Smith's thesis reflects the reality of a society where the industrial and commercial bourgeoisie is beginning to seriously encroach on the traditional landowners (aristocrats, landlords), a consequence of the transition from a class system to a capitalist and liberal-democratic one. Indeed, in this there is an expression of individualism applied to the economy.

From this follows another principal position of New Age economics: *value is created in the process of labour*. For Marx, this would be the starting point of his own system. Adam Smith's second thesis, no less important, is the idea that the main requirement for successful economic development is the complete freedom of the individual to trade.

---

7 Adam Smith, *An Inquiry into the Nature and Causes of the Wealth of Nations* (London: Oxford University Press, 2008).

Trade and enterprise, in Adam Smith's opinion, are an expression of the noble nature of man. Adam Smith contrasts trade with war. Trade is peace, the state is war and violence. Adam Smith is convinced, quite in the spirit of Locke, that the state is a spirit of intimidation and repression directed outwards to fight other states and inwards to suppress manifestations dangerous to the existence of the Leviathan, thereby creating an atmosphere of militaristic societies. If we move from the anthropological pessimism of Hobbes to the anthropological optimism of Locke, then the natural state for man is not to fight but to trade. Hence the expression *le doux commerce* — 'gentle commerce'. This too is the realisation of private interests, also egoism, but in this form it no longer entails human sacrifice, is not based on violence and does not require its legitimation.

Smith's third key thesis is that trade should not be national, but international, because in this way the principles of freedom, of civil society on a global scale are spread along with trade. This is what the universalism of Enlightenment demands. Liberal societies, built on the principles of peaceful trade, cannot allow aggressive egoistic regimes to exist outside of them, so liberalism implies universalism and a global scale from the outset. Of course, Smith — as befits an ideologue of the Third Estate, measuring everything by material things, money and profit — argues for free international trade, bypassing the state monopoly and increasing the efficiency and growth of industry and the economy, i.e. the laws of the market. But underneath this is a fundamental ideological challenge to the Leviathan of foreign policy, where its restrictive, overbearing and belligerent nature is manifested. Smith's free trade is thought to be free precisely from the state in its two hypostases — internal and external. Liberalism insists on the minimisation of internal taxes and the reduction or elimination of customs tariffs. In this way, liberalism seeks to minimise the influence of the state in the economy both internally and externally, which inevitably leads to the obliteration of its boundaries and, ultimately, of the state itself.

In practice, such a programme has two components: tax cuts and the renunciation of the state's monopoly on foreign trade. The first only weakens the importance of the state in the economy to some extent, while the second undermines, and in the extreme abolishes, its sovereignty altogether.

Smith insisted on both, opposing a tendency towards mercantilism, which did not oppose a free market within the state, but insisted on complete state control over foreign trade. Such liberalism was only half-hearted and Adam Smith sought to make his applied — practical — theory as consistent as possible with Locke's progressive views.

According to Smith, free trade and the demand for a direct economic partnership between a citizen of one state and another is opposed to customs policy precisely because, in the view of his teacher Locke, the state should weaken and gradually die out, having fulfilled its functions. Adam Smith's imperative of free trade, which he himself justified by economic models, must be sought in Locke's philosophical attacks on Leviathan and the restriction of the national civil society by borders. This is exactly what Locke categorically opposed, believing that civil society should be universal.

Accordingly, this pan-European society should gradually abolish national borders, and for this to be possible, free trade — that is, by one actor from a nation-state with an actor from another, bypassing tariff and customs difficulties — should be allowed.

From this emerges the concept of *liberalism in international relations*,[8] argued economically by Smith: if trade is free, all societies will benefit from participating in it. Consequently, any attempt by the state to restrain this process becomes an 'evil' and an obstacle to social and economic development (in his liberal interpretation).

Here we come to a very important point: *Adam Smith's capitalism is directed against nation-states.* Smith is not against them as a phenomenon, in a sense they must exist to ensure free trade and the norms of bourgeois law, but for him the fate of free trade is more important than the fate of nation-states. Politics as such becomes only an aspect of the economy, and not vice versa, as it was considered in traditional society and in the early stages of modernity. All in all, this is a clear indication of the sphere which, in the synchronous three-part map of the Political, occupies the lower

---

8   Dugin, *International Relations (Paradigms, Theories, Sociology)*.

sector corresponding to the corporeal, the material. Smith concludes that for the swineopolis to be genuine and successful, it must be global.

This is the rationale for the construction of a global, civil, non-political, supranational, cosmopolitan society, which, in the cycle of development, is a return to the natural state, but now in an 'enlightened' — meaningful, universal — form. In Adam Smith, Locke's entire ideological program is expressed in the language of political economy.

The Roadmap to Global Capitalism

For Adam Smith, capitalism, free enterprise and therefore civil society (citizen = bourgeois) should develop quite independently of nation-states as far as possible, and these in turn should gradually disappear. Locke said little about trade, mainly focusing on enlightenment, education and the advancement of knowledge. Adam Smith in turn says: when a state has successfully fulfilled its enlightenment mission, the main occupation for the citizens of that enlightened state should not be war, but *trade*.

Smith sees trade and enterprise in double opposition: on the one hand, in relation to the peasantry, which is tied to the land where the majority of wealth was produced in medieval society, and, on the other hand, in relation to the landlords who lived off the land rents.

Accordingly, it is this economic type that becomes synonymous with Locke's 'enlightened citizen'. As we have said before, if we look closely at the three terms 'citizen', 'townsman' and 'bourgeois', their semantics are one and the same. A bourgeois is an inhabitant of a 'burg', that is, of a city (*Burg*, German for 'fortified town'). A citizen is a resident of the city. The same goes for townsman. Therefore, the idea of civil society is the idea of bourgeois and urban society, which includes simultaneously the dominant social type (the third estate, corresponding to Aristotle's *demos*, the masses, Plato's 'multitude') and belonging to the urban living environment.

Thus the *urban bourgeois entrepreneur* becomes the central figure of the political philosophy of liberalism. After Adam Smith, it is not only the political-enlightenment model which emerges, as with Locke, but also a concrete political-economic doctrine of capitalism and the normative forms of a capitalist economy. Adam Smith, with his notions of free trade, of removal of the state from interference in the economy, allowing entrepreneurs and traders to bypass the state and transact directly with economic actors from other countries (because, according to Smith, foreign trade is a private affair and not a national one) created an elaborate strategy for capitalism, which became the roadmap for Western Europe, and later all civilisation, for several centuries.

The Infinite Accumulation of Wealth

Another important idea, which Smith also borrows from Locke, is *social progress*. This is how Smith, applying the theory of social progress to the political-economic sphere, develops the thesis of an exponential growth of the world's wealth. From Adam Smith's point of view, the process of private enterprise leads to a linear increase in profits, to an increase in the general welfare, although everyone acts in their private interests, seeking to enrich themselves personally, without thinking of others. But if everyone enriches himself, everyone gets richer, Adam Smith concludes. Consequently, the total amount of wealth must increase.

Smith's position that value is created by labour, not land, provides a technological rationale for the theory of progress. Whereas land and the crops harvested from it have well-defined limits, which can only be expanded somewhat, and the fixed income derived from the land can only be redistributed, industry *can* develop — technical development promotes production, and the amount of world wealth steadily increases. If a society which is less developed than another is involved in free trade, they begin to develop together, helping each other, and again the total wealth of all mankind increases.

This *position on the growth of common wealth is a fundamental axiom of capitalist economics*, upon which everything else is based: if a state tries to protect itself with customs quotas or protectionist measures against another state in order to develop its national economy, free-traders and classical liberals always perceive this negatively, because it hinders market development by preventing the growth of common wealth, which means it hinders progress.

The liberals argue that it is not so important if one country has a less developed economy or industry and the other has a more developed one. If both countries engage in free trade, the aggregate growth of wealth will affect both. Especially since, according to Locke, the state will ultimately be abolished, while the accumulated wealth and deployed industrial and commercial complexes capable of increasing wealth will remain, so it will not matter in whose territory this or that enterprise, this or that trading platform, bank or exchange is located. From the perspective of free trade (liberalism in international relations), political (national) territories always constitute a certain contingency. Entrepreneurship and industry develop better where fiscal policy is more favourable, where taxes are easier to pay, where natural resources are closer to hand. That is where production, finance and trade will go. But this freedom to move in accordance with purely economic interests and the maximisation of profits is sometimes hampered by political considerations and interests. That is where production, finance and trade will go. But this freedom to move in accordance with purely economic interests and the maximisation of profits is sometimes hampered by political considerations and interests. So it turns out that nation-states constrain the progress of humanity as a whole. This is the fundamental liberal idea behind globalism and globalisation.

The notion of the absolute growth of world wealth is a dogma of liberalism (as unproven as any dogma). It was opposed by the proponents of an economy built according to Hobbesian principles, i.e. primarily by the mercantilists. The mercantilists argued, in contrast to Smith, that there is a finite amount of wealth on earth and therefore the economic development of one state always comes at the expense of the development of another. Once again there is an urgent need for a Leviathan, and a war of all against all looms on the horizon, though no longer at the level of society but at the level of states, coming together in a fierce struggle over world resources and the redistribution of wealth in their favour.

Both the liberal and mercantilist dogmas, for all their references to economic indicators, profit margins, tables and calculations, are in fact expressions of a metaphysical — philosophical — dispute about human nature. Liberal optimists follow the logic of progress (Locke), which gives us the axiom of economic growth (Smith). Here the prevailing certainty is: man is good, and even if he is not good enough now, he can always be improved. Their opponents object: progress is relative and even questionable, humanity always retains its true nature, i.e. selfish, greedy and aggressive. That is why it needs a guide in the form of a Leviathan. At the same time there is not an infinite amount of wealth in the world, but a strictly limited one. That is why a struggle of one Leviathan against another in the economic field is a 'zero sum game'. Mercantilists believe that if one state has gained wealth, the other has lost it; they conclude: customs barriers, state monopoly on foreign trade and protectionism should be maintained.

The dispute between liberals (Locke and his followers) and proto-liberals (Hobbes and his followers) unfolds within the paradigm of New Age political philosophy. According to Hobbes, human nature is unchangeable and fundamentally bad. To a certain extent, this thesis is carried on by the representatives of realism in international relations,[9] the traditional opponents of the liberals.

Liberalism asserts that there is progress, even if no one sees it or it looks partial, sectoral, and even ambiguous and questionable; it is still there because it is an ideological axiom. There is an endless growth of the world economy and a gradual withering of the state, the transformation of all nation-states into a single civil trading society.

Here the ideological axiom of progress, which Adam Smith converted into the idea of economic growth, reveals an important moment in the formation of the ideology of liberalism. *Politics is conclusively replaced by economics.* Economics becomes destiny.

The economy, as we have seen in the overarching framework of *Politica Aeterna*, is the result of the reduction of politics and, in the extreme, its abolition. In liberalism, politics tends to the minimum and economics to the maximum; instead of a political society, a civil society emerges. Civil society, by contrast, is a commercial system, a mercantile society,[10] where all values are determined by material equivalents and, consequently,

---

9 Dugin, *International Relations (Paradigms, Theories, Sociology).*
10 Sombart, *Traders and Heroes.*

everything has a price, i.e. everything is for sale. Civil society is a capitalist enterprising society, where politics is replaced by economics.

The principle of 'less politics, more economics' and, in the long run, 'no politics', means a vector in the direction of the end of political history, where instead of countries and nations there will be only one global market. The globalisation process is the culmination of this liberal strategy, the fundamental vector of which was clearly and convincingly laid down by Adam Smith. And the fact that it was Smith who became the main symbolic figure of liberalism only confirms the very nature of the transition from politics to economics, which is the essence of liberal ideology as well as of the whole modern era.

The Middle Class and Endless Growth

There is one crucial concept in liberal ideology: *the middle class*. The middle class is a key element of liberalism, closely linked to Adam Smith's specific *economic anthropology*. In Smith's view, all of humanity represents a potential middle class, *potential entrepreneurs*. Every human being is a merchant and a businessman, an entrepreneur and a banker. The meaning of history, and the task of historical progress, is to *actualise* this potential belonging of all to the middle class. This is possible through the infinite growth of global wealth — if it grows, so does the middle class, that is, those people who have access to it.

The objective of humanity, then, is that, amid the exponential growth of world wealth, *everyone should become middle class*. The aim of civilisation and its history is for everyone to become merchants, bourgeois (citizens, city dwellers), entrepreneurs and possess a minimum of wealth that would meet the criteria of the middle class. This expansion of the boundaries of the middle class is inextricably linked for liberals to the abolition of the state, to the establishment of civil society, to globalisation and the abolition of borders.

Notably, the notion of 'middle class' is another liberal propaganda concept, like 'progress', 'infinite growth of wealth', *laissez-faire*, free trade, 'civil society', etc. It is in the context of liberal ideology and its overall structure that this notion takes on its significance, reflecting deeper levels of Locke's anthropological optimism. The growth of the middle class is a material expression of the Enlightenment.[11]

It is important to note that from a liberalist perspective, the middle class is essentially the normative class, the only one. Thus Adam Smith gives an example of the development of an economic system: there is a baker (a petit bourgeois) in the city who bakes rolls. Having amassed enough money, he hires workers — broke peasants who have migrated to the city. The peasant bakes rolls for a while, helping the baker, who takes the bulk of the profits. However, working for the baker, the former peasant learns how to bake, communicate with customers, distribute advertising, how to sell the goods, where to buy the grain and so on. Then he takes a loan from the bank and sets up his own bakery. In time, he settles down, becomes a baker, that is, a petit bourgeois, and hires another broke peasant who has come to town to earn money and is willing to do any kind of work.

If we continue with this logic, then at some point all peasants will move to the city and become city dwellers, because the economic dynamics in the city are significantly better than on the land. So all peasants will at some point become city dwellers. As agriculture becomes less and less

---

11   Obviously, the illiberal ideologies of modernity (in Marxism and Fascism) treat the concept of 'middle class' differently. For Communists, the middle class only means the bourgeoisie, while the proletariat will never become a middle class because exploitation, inequality and poverty of the working class, whose created surplus value is continuously appropriated by the capitalists, grow along with profit and technological progress. A growth of the middle class is therefore a fiction, and it is accompanied by structural crises of capitalism, which will sooner or later lead to a proletarian revolution directed precisely against this 'middle class'. In Fascist theory, the middle class of one country is qualitatively different from the middle class of another, and from the social point of view the differences between rich and poor, the haves and have-nots, are secondary in the face of their common national (racial in National Socialism) identity. Consequently, the 'middle class' is a cosmopolitan chimera, obscuring the importance of nationhood and undermining sovereignty. These examples show how a simple change in rhetoric and a few rather trivial arguments can radically transform the ideological credibility of a particular ideology that insists on its dogmas and axioms through propaganda, pathos and ideological pressure rather than the rational fine-tuning of argumentation, which always only formalises the deeper — and always philosophically dogmatic — premises of ideology. The same considerations apply fully to the axioms and dogmas of Communism or Fascism itself.

influential in the gross income of the state, the entire economy will move to the city in the sphere of private enterprise, and peasant farming itself will become a reverse projection of capitalism onto the countryside, rather than something independent. Accordingly, the landlords would go bankrupt, the land rents would lose their significance and a kind of uninterrupted single city would emerge. Adam Smith was working on this theory in the late eighteenth century, and that is exactly what is happening now: urbanisation, the shift from rural to urban on a global scale, and the (albeit relative, but still notable) growth of the middle class.

Thus, Adam Smith gave the ideology of liberalism exactly the form that best suited the bourgeois type, focusing on the values, issues and priorities that were dear to it. And Smith's far-reaching vision of humanity was quite clear: everyone is destined to become a bourgeois and the world will become a single global free market. This is how humanity will be corrected, re-educated, abandon its aggression and propensity for violence. Instead, individualism, tolerance, 'human rights' and norms of 'political correctness' will prevail everywhere.

Replacement of the 'Third Estate': Bourgeois Usurpation

After Adam Smith, in bourgeois economics and more broadly in political philosophy, the Third Estate is finally and firmly identified with the urban bourgeoisie, precisely as Adam Smith described and conceptualised it. While later this identification gradually came to be taken for granted, its origins contain a very important sociological and even anthropological shift that sheds light on some fundamental features of the modernist paradigm in general, and liberal ideology in particular.

The fact is that in the structure of the European society of the premodern age, the Third Estate included all those who had the status of free citizens, but who were neither warriors (hereditary aristocrats), nor part of the clergy (Catholic priesthood). Throughout all periods of traditional society, from Antiquity to the late Middle Ages, the basis and absolute majority of such a Third Estate, in the broad and original sense, was the peasantry or serfs. In different societies they held different statuses and were more or less dependent on landowners, but almost never were they slaves in Europe, that is, the complete property of their masters. Rather they were regarded as the bottom rung of the feudal hierarchy, and in warfare they formed the basis of the militia of small feudal lords from whom larger armies were built. The relationship of the nobles to the serfs was a continuation of the suzerainty/vassalage principle, but only at the lowest rung. That is, a kind of social pact existed between the peasants and the landlords. The peasants worked the land, fed themselves from it and provided food for the lords and their servants. It was the peasantry that was the backbone of the economy, and the European countryside produced the bulk of the wealth at all stages of traditional society. We have seen that Adam Smith builds his theories precisely in opposition to the physiocrats, who up to the beginning of the eighteenth century continued to consider land as the main and decisive source of national wealth. When Adam Smith refutes this by taking wealth away from the land and transferring it to the sphere of the city, labour, production, entrepreneurship and trade, he actually changes the content of the fundamental concept of the Third Estate, *excluding the peasantry from it*. Of course, something similar took place before Adam Smith; in the system of the States-General, which was established in the Middle Ages (since the fourteenth century) and existed till the end of the eighteenth century, the common people (that is the Third Estate proper) were represented by wealthy city dwellers more involved in the political element. The very definition of politics already partly implied the city (*polis*), and the rich and influential non-aristocrats and non-priests of the city were more likely participants in meetings and debates than the peasants, whose horizons were usually limited to rather local spheres. Still, in the States-General the urban bourgeoisie was considered to be the representatives of the people, where the majority were the peasants, not the people themselves. This was *demos* (δῆμος), i.e. the urban areas and their empowered envoys, with the peasantry remaining behind the scenes, still considered to some extent as co-participants. In the physiocratic economic model, the peasantry plays a fundamental role, since it is the most important element in obtaining wealth from the land, which underlies the land rent.

A certain hypothesis can be put forward here as to how the democratisation of European society might have gone had it not been for this canonisation of the bourgeois (townsman) by Adam Smith, which ultimately equated urban entrepreneurs and merchants with the Third Estate and caused the peasantry to fall out of it simply by default. In such a case, the process of dispersal of power, to which modern society was gravitating, moved along the line of redistribution of landholdings from landlords to peasants. In this case, the mark of the Third Estate would at some point be the possession of a plot of land as the property equivalent of civil status (or rather peasant, rural status) on the principle of one plot of land as an atom of the economic whole, one vote. Clearly, the very nature of peasant life, associated with the necessary decentralisation, would have led to a federal system of political organisation rather than the centralised and unified system to which the cities and their structures gravitated. In this case, the Third Estate in its quantitative majority would have been taken as the basis of society, and we would have had a *peasant democratic federation*. Johannes Althusius[12] (1562–1638), the greatest representative and theorist of European federalism, suggested something similar in his own time, though in a slightly different context.

But Smith's theory definitively shifted the focus to the field of industry, the city, enterprise and trade. Consequently, liberalism narrowed democracy from the expansion of the rights and positions of the Third Estate as a whole to the interests of the urban bourgeoisie. Henceforth, those who spoke on behalf of the Third Estate represented not just a minority within it, but a phenomenon completely alien to the majority.

The rise of industrial production meant that, in the urban environment itself, the commoners who constituted the 'middle class' were pushed to the periphery, first in craftsmen being replaced by industrial complexes, and then by trade which was an area of more intensive circulation of capital than production, so that the Third Estate was largely represented by traders. As financial institutions — banks and interest-bearing capital — grew in importance, the financiers in their turn began to dominate, becoming the priority representatives of the bourgeoisie and acting

---

12 Johannes Althusius, *Politica* (Indianapolis: Liberty Fund, 1995).

on its behalf, as it had previously acted on behalf of all the commoners, among whom the peasants predominated.

Thus, liberalism logically turned out to be an ideology not of the majority, but of a special minority that rose to the upper echelons of society in a process of an increasingly reductive representation. And importantly, this could only happen because the usurpation of representation is at the very heart of liberalism, which has substituted the content of the term 'Third Estate'.

The Marginalisation of the Peasantry and the Political Science of Mystery

The ancient mysteries — above all the Eleusinian[13] ones — were closely linked to the agrarian cycle and represented the scenario of a descent underground into the zone of death, Hades, and then a return to life again, which testified to the immortality of the spiritual grain of humanity. Agrarian practices had direct access to this metaphysical subject, as the seasons of sowing, planting and harvesting were a visual representation of the entire symbolic cycle.[14]

Peasantry corresponded to the third kind in the general structure of *Politica Aeterna*, which logically correlated it with the realm of the earth and the underworld. Thus the mystery[15] and symbolism of agrarian practices naturally combined with the realm of the Mother, the *chora* and the boundary regions of being, lying closest to the lowest regions of the cosmos — the underworld. Thus the images of goddesses predominated in the mysteries, or, as in the Eleusinian scenario, even directly the goddess of the underworld, Persephone, who, after she was kidnapped by Hades, god of death and king of the underworld, was sought out by her mother, Demeter, the goddess of fields and crops. The peasantry were the bearers of Demeter's civilisation, and, accordingly, the symbolism of the grain, the ear, played a central role in the mysteries.

---

13 Károly Kerényi, *Eleusis: Archetypal Image of Mother and Daughter* (Princeton: Princeton University Press, 1991).
14 Dugin, *Noomakhia. The Kingdom of the Earth. The Structure of Russian Identity*.
15 Translator's note: Referring to Greco-Roman mystery religions/cults.

But unlike the rebellion of the Earth against Heaven, which we see in the philosophy of Democritus, and which became the dominant theme of the New Age, the mysteries, although involving descent below the earth, necessarily led to ascent and a new dawn witnessed at its culmination, *epopteía* (ἐποπτεία). Thus the peasantry maintained its connection with the earth (and, by the principle of symbolism, with the underworld), on the one hand, and it remained part of the vertical sacred hierarchy on the other, supplementing the *Politica Aeterna* structure with the metaphysical experience of visiting the lowest floors of the universe, but with a subsequent return to the face of Heaven. Closely associated with this was the persistent adherence of the peasantry to religious traditions, which was interpreted by modernists as their 'stagnation', 'ignorance', 'backwardness' and stubborn unwillingness to accept 'change', to enter the New Age.

Consequently, the peasantry was ill-suited to build a purely material and secular civilisation, which was rigidly opposed to the paradigm of Tradition. At the same time, the urban bourgeoisie, which dealt not with land and wood, but with stone and conditional — abstract — space as its dominant element, was not constrained by these sacred frameworks.

In this we can see the underlying explanation for what happened to the concept of the 'Third Estate' in liberal ideology. The urban bourgeoisie was the most desacralised part of the Third Estate, deprived of access to the mysteries and even their symbolic echoes in economic practice itself. The peasants, who grew the bread, were, in their own minds, participating in something that was more than merely material. They were co-participants in the mystery of life, bearers of eternity, passing through a successive closed cycle — from birth to ripening and death, and then a new birth. Though the labour of a farmer is expressed outside of him in the material equivalent of the crop, for the farmer it is still a sacral-religious ritual, which in Christian culture is expressed in the sacrament of the Eucharist — in the communion of the blood and flesh of Jesus Christ, which are transformed into bread and wine in the sacrament of the liturgy. The preparation of the bread and wine, however, was in turn a preparation for the Eucharist, a part of the mystery, which reached its culmination in the divine service.

On the other hand, there was nothing sacred left in the activities of the bourgeois. Only he, and by no means the peasant, dealt with pure matter, with pure production, with pure accumulation, with the pure pursuit of profit. It is the bourgeois, the normative figure of liberalism, who represents the absolute profane, whereas the peasantry retains close and inseparable ties to the sacred. Moreover, the peasantry, involved in the mystery of the grain, had a certain inoculation against the underworld and its influences. Whereas the bourgeoisie, which denied Hell, the Devil and the Antichrist in the course of more and more 'progressive' representations, had no defence against them. This is one of the most important aspects of the underlying philosophy of liberalism.

Kant: The Foundations of Constructivism and the Prototype of Artificial Intelligence

In the eighteenth century, another major theorist of liberal ideology made a fundamental contribution to liberalism — Immanuel Kant (1724–1804). In Kant, however, we find a much more sophisticated political philosophy, stemming from his notion of transcendental (or pure) reason.[16]

The most important thing in Kant's philosophy is that he questions the Cartesian dualism of subject and object, showing that reliable judgement can only be made by reason about itself and not about what lies beyond it — both external (object) and internal (subject). This was the basis of the doctrine of 'transcendental reason', i.e. the autonomy of thinking and its laws from both the thinker and that which is being considered. Transcendental reason (pure reason), according to Kant, is a complete structure of epistemological correlations which predetermines the manner of thinking, including its content. Everything one perceives, sees, feels, senses, etc., arises from and is predetermined by transcendental reasoning. Such reasoning already contains in itself '*a priori* forms of perception', that is, time and space, with time belonging to the more internal (subjective) side of reason and space to the more external one, where naïve and unreflective self-perception locates the 'outer world'.

---

16 Immanuel Kant, *Critique of Pure Reason* (London: Penguin Classics, 2007).

According to Kant, people are bearers of a single universal form of rationality, and their individual differences in the face of this structure are immaterial.

Therefore, according to Kant, one individual is just as rational as another individual, because reasoning is transcendental. Some perceive reason more vividly, hence the difference between people; if all people perceived it equally vividly, they would live in a perfectly happy society, treating others as they would want to be treated themselves. This is Kant's central imperative: 'do unto others as you would have them do unto you'.

This model of reasoning is transmitted through education (in this sense Kant follows Locke), and when society reaches a certain level of reasonableness, rationality and conscientiousness, a civil society will emerge instead of the state.

At first sight, this approach seems to have little in common with materialism and individualism, and instead of atomism asserts some primary unity of reason. Indeed, if we draw a straight line from Democritus and Epicurus to the nominalists (Roscellinus, Occam) and on to the creators of the scientific picture of the world (Galileo, Newton, Boyle, etc) and Protestant theology (Luther, Calvin), and from them finally to the secular philosophy of the New Age (Hobbes, Locke, etc), then Kant appears outside this axis. It is true, in the context of the New Age Kant occupies a special position. He is not so much an atomist and individualist as the founder of *constructivism*, a philosophical approach which asserts that the external world is a mental construction of the mind. In a sense this is a precursor to the postmodernist paradigm and themes of Artificial Intelligence[17] and virtuality.[18]

However, Kant played a significant role in the formation of the political philosophy of liberalism. Kant, like Locke, attaches crucial importance to education. Man, according to Kant, is the bearer of pure reason, whose self-awareness is realised in the process of education, which is the process

---

17 The prototype of the Artificial Intelligence can also be found in the monadology of Leibniz (1646–1716), who had a great influence on Kant.
18 Nick Land, *Fanged Noumena: Collected Writings 1987–2007* (New York; Windsor Quarry [Falmouth]: Sequence; Urbanomic, 2011).

of becoming a container of pure reason, its unfolding. Pure reason is not contained outside or within man. Man is man insofar as he participates in pure reason. But this reason is not an attribute of God; it is, on the contrary, the essential feature of being a member of the human species. Education is not a mere inscription on the 'blank slate', but the application on it of the main points of Kant's own works, which approached the comprehension of the structure of pure reason (as well as practical reason,[19] which solves the antinomies of pure reason with the help of the moral principles — imperatives). Practical reason, according to Kant, consists of closing those gaps that pure reason cannot fill with the unambiguity of its procedures, with moral statements as universal and general as the structures of pure reason. Thus, pure reason describes a constructible ontology, and practical reason realises it by covering the problematic sectors with a proactive due process. So pure reason is unable to formulate a definitive judgement (whether it is or is not) about God, the external world or the subject itself. Practical reason, on the basis of moral necessity, acts as if these three poles of ontology existed unconditionally. Reality, the subject and even God appear then as anthropological constructs.

Kant's political philosophy and its pacifism,[20] cosmopolitanism and the thesis of the necessity of a civil society[21] are based on a moral imperative. Human nature consists of its rationality. It may be more or less complete, but as it is mastered, everyone comes to the same position because rationality is universal and unified. Consequently, as enlightenment and education expand, all people will gradually come closer to this rational element. Realising the constructivist character of reality and the homology of reason, everyone will prefer to live peacefully; borders will be unnecessary, and the hierarchical state and vertical power structure will be replaced by a friendly community of people endowed in principle with the same form of reasoning — developed and capable of self-reflection.

---

19 Immanuel Kant, *Critique of Pure Reason*.
20 Immanuel Kant, *Perpetual Peace: A Philosophical Sketch* (London: S. Sonnenschein, 1903).
21 Immanuel Kant, *Groundwork for the Metaphysics of Morals* (Oxford University Press, 2019).

This is 'civil society', which takes shape in the context of the political, but will gradually — as enlightenment spreads and is assimilated — supplant the Political, replacing the state.

Since man and the world are products of construction, Kant thought that a coherent reasoning of the self should lead to a better society, since all excesses and negative aspects of life stem only from the fact that pure reason does not operate in people to its full potential.

The conclusions from Kant's philosophy were quite consistent with liberalism. Instead of the aggressive individualism of Hobbes, we see here a progressive model akin to Locke, although the importance of the individual is here almost negated and matter is replaced by universal reason.

The 'Lockean Heartland'

There is an interesting conceptualisation by the contemporary Dutch political philosopher Kees van der Pijl,[22] who proposes to rethink the scope of Locke's influence and philosophy by means of geography. Van der Pijl reminds us that originally Locke described images of burgeoning capitalism as he observed it in Scotland in relative peacetime. In fact, Locke conceptualises exactly what he sees (hence our metaphor of 'carriage windows'). Locke draws universal conclusions about the nature of humanity, the meaning of the state, the importance of trade, the value of education, and 'natural rights' from a fairly specific — both historically and geographically — landscape. The field is confined to Scotland (partly also England and Holland). And if Locke had limited his conclusions to these very borders, his conceptualisation would have been flawless. In fact, this historical-geographical framework, linked to the life of John Locke himself, describes what Kees van der Peijl calls the Lockean Heartland. But Locke himself gave his views the character of a universal theory. In practice, however, the first stage was generally adopted in Scotland and

---

22 Kees van der Pijl, *Vordenker der Weltpolitik: Einführung in die internationale Politik aus ideengeschichtlicher Perspektive* [*Masterminds of World Politics: Introduction to International Politics from a Perspective of the History of Ideas*] (Opladen: Leske + Budrich, 1996); Idem, *The Making of an Atlantic Ruling Class* (London: Verso, 1984); Idem. *Transnational Classes and International Relations* (London: Routledge, 1998).

England. It was a projection of one society onto another, which somewhat simplified the much more complex picture of England itself. Regardless, Locke's idea took hold in English educated and 'enlightened' society. Then, in the eighteenth century, it took the form of the theory of 'free trade' in the works of Adam Smith (1723–1790), a disciple and follower of Locke, who applied his ideas to economics and created the most famous economic theory, which reflects all the main points of liberalism and remains largely unchanged up to the present.

Gradually Locke's influence spread to the European continent — to France, Austria, Prussia (later Germany). This represents an even greater shift, since the social and political traditions of various parts of Europe are strikingly different. The spread of the Lockean Heartland gradually becomes a trajectory for the expansion of liberalism far beyond its original territory and specific time period.

The most important instrument in the expansion of the Lockean Heartland is the British Empire. This is how liberalism reaches the British colonies and takes root in the USA, which became one of the pillars and later the leader of modern Western civilisation. In the twentieth century, the modernisation and Westernisation of the whole world further strengthened liberalism and, in the form of globalism (generally based on the same unchanging Lockean principles), it became the leading world ideology — which was one of the three main ideologies (together with Communism and Fascism) until the mid-twentieth century, from 1945 to 1991 one of the two (together with Communism), and finally the only one left after the collapse of the USSR and the Soviet bloc.

It is clear that at each stage there was a stretching of the original model, an increasing distance from the Heartland. Thus the specific picture of seventeenth-century Scotland, which was both accurately described and brilliantly conceptualised, became a world ideology, necessarily abstract, often at odds with historical and geographical realities, and therefore increasingly rigid, intrusive and totalitarian, but also fragile.

Today, the same set of theses and axioms that constituted the essence of the Lockean Heartland has become the basis of that paradigmatic, epistemological and axiological matrix, which is taken as something 'natural' and 'self-evident' by almost *the entire population of planet Earth*. So from the land of Scotland, and then of seventeenth-century England, which represents the Lockean Heartland in its original historical and geographical boundaries, this model gradually spread to all mankind, determining the main points of modern political philosophy, in which liberalism won a fundamental political and ideological victory by the end of the twentieth century. Thus Locke's liberalism formed the basis of:

- global ideology (human rights, civil society),
- politics (liberal democracy),
- economics (capitalism, free trade),
- ethics (individualism, *laissez-faire*),
- science (materialism, empiricism) and
- technology (technological progress).

Thus, beginning with Locke, England itself became more and more of a *global* phenomenon until, through the United States and globalisation, it became something truly *universal*.

Philosophically speaking, the British Empire — liberal, commercial, 'progressive', modernist — was *Locke's Empire*.

Today, in the twenty-first century, we are all living in the Lockean Heartland.

We live in the age of liberalism; it is the earliest ideology of the New Age, but it has managed to outlast the others. Attempts to criticise and overturn it by Marxism (sometimes successful) and Fascism (no less successful) were bright flashes which prefigured the dramatic periods, clashes and wars of modern history. But liberalism has stood firm.

We should pay attention to the fact that on the scale of modernity it is a rather archaic ideology, on the one hand, and a very peripheral one, on the other. It operates with universal categories, with images, figures, processes and attitudes of the European provinces of the seventeenth century, when they were fresh, new and precise. But in other societies, the tenets of liberalism were an outright stretch. Yet with Anglo-Saxon persistence in the spirit of their colonial expansion, the British, and later the Americans, carried liberal theories with them as their ideological weapons. Although liberals and progressives, their anthropology, sociology and scientific perspective reflect the reality of modernity in its earliest stage, which in other parts of the Western world and beyond has been repeatedly challenged, developed, refuted, revised and transcended. But this provincial spectre of ancient times has proved to be extremely resilient, subordinating to its chimerical existence the lifeblood of societies, peoples, cultures and civilisations.

Compared to liberalism, the other ideologies of the modern age — Fascism and Communism — look much more 'modern', dialectical, paradoxical, sophisticated and dramatic. Sure, they too are modern and have their roots in Hobbes (and even earlier in Protestantism), but compared to the sullenly one-note, Scottishly banal and utterly boring liberalism that has been repeating the same message for centuries, regardless of the place, time and relevance of its discourse, even modernist versions of liberalism look reassuring and diverse, capable of varied and lively, at times terrifying, risky and disastrous experiments.

'Civil Society' as an Ideological Slogan

We approach the notion of 'civil society' as a specifically liberal model of political philosophy.[23] 'Civil society' is an ideological construct that operates with the concept of individuals as the basic instance of the bearer of the Political, taken in the spirit of Locke's optimistic anthropology and drawing at the same time on Kant's transcendental rationality.

'Civil society' is as much a slogan of liberalism as 'Workers of the world, unite' for Communists or 'The Aryan race above all others' for the Nazis. When we hear the phrase 'Aryan race', we immediately understand

---

23 Of course, the very expression 'civil society' can also appear in other political doctrines. So it is in Hegel's system as well, but with him it is only a dialectical moment on the way to the establishment of the absolute monarchy. According to Hegel, the collective mind of civil society does not stop at recognising itself as the pinnacle of development, but moves on, and comes to the necessity of handing over power to an enlightened monarch and building a hierarchy based on knowledge as an expression of the Absolute Spirit. See Georg Wilhelm Friedrich Hegel, *The Phenomenology of Spirit* (Oxford: Clarendon Press, 1977).

that we are talking about political propaganda, racial inequality and the division of humanity according to skin colour. This is not just a scientific statement, it is almost certainly a political ideology built on very specific principles. That is to say, the expression refers us back to National Socialism.

When we hear the slogan 'Workers of the world, unite', we know without the slightest doubt that it is Communists. The very concept of the 'proletariat' is an essential element of Marxism.[24]

But when we hear the phrase 'civil society', we are not at all aware that it is just another ideology, which, like other ideologies, has its dogmas, its grounds and its arguments — as convincing or unconvincing as Nazism and Communism. The fact that we do not identify the 'civil society' thesis as a rigid political slogan, with all its inherent limitations, propaganda dimensions and inbuilt consequences (such as criticism of the Political, individualism and the prototype of Artificial Intelligence), suggests that we are living today under the dominance of liberal ideology. If we are unable to identify this as the propaganda slogan of liberal ideology, then we are already within its grasp. That means we are living in the Lockean Heartland. Accordingly, if the notion of 'civil society' does not make us as wary as Communist or Fascist slogans, then we already agree to be supporters of Locke and Kant. When we realise that political preachers are trying to convince us of their correctness, to recruit us, to put something into our heads, we usually keep a certain distance with a sufficiently critical sense, understanding that it is propaganda with all its inherent limitations and distortions of truth in favour of obtaining concrete results and catching new followers in the net. Yet when we hear the phrase 'civil society', we take it for granted and all critical feelings disappear.

In Soviet times, when the slogan 'Workers of the world, unite!' was being bandied about, ordinary people, common citizens, also nodded: 'Of course, unite, and fast!' At the same time, sometimes it was no longer easy for them to understand who the proletarians were, why they should unite — they did not think about where it all came from, they did not

---

24 Translator's note: The slogan in the original German is 'Proletarier aller Länder, vereinigt euch!' — literally 'Proletarians of all countries, unite!'

question it critically. 'I guess we have to unite, it's international.' This is the same way we treat concepts like 'civil society' or 'human rights' today. It seems to be something self-evident, when in fact we are being forced into a dogmatic, extremely politicised ideological slogan that is as poorly substantiated, biased and manipulative as that of 'uniting proletarians' or 'the Aryan race'.

A student of political philosophy differs from the average person in that when he hears such phrases as 'civil society', he first thinks about them. The concept of 'civil society' is a consequence of an optimistic interpretation of anthropology and a view of the natural state of society as movement towards enlightenment and progress. The concept of 'civil society' is directed against Hobbes' Leviathan, against his pessimistic anthropology, but also against the Political in general (with its inevitable centralisation of the question of power) and against sovereignty. Those who use the term 'civil society' most often assume that the state should fulfil only one function: to serve as a temporary source of mass enlightenment. And the moment the state ceases to fulfil this function, it must disappear.

Thus, in the context of the Lockean Heartland, the term 'civil society' represents a specific understanding of the intrinsic nature of the state itself, which has one task: to form this 'civil society', to write the ideas of rational egoism on the 'blank slate' of individuals, and then to disappear.

Thus, 'civil society' is essentially already an anti-state idea. To advocate 'civil society' is to oppose the country, to oppose the state as a value and a self-sufficient institution. Essentially, to be a supporter of 'civil society' is in a sense a crime against the state, because in this case, the state is considered to be only an instrument of enlightenment and nothing more. All of its other functions are to be abolished as a matter of principle and the state itself is ultimately to be dismantled and abolished.

The state, as conceived by liberals, does not interfere in the affairs of its citizens, does not tax them, does not fight, does not resort — except in extreme cases — to violence, adheres strictly to established rules, and seeks in every way to disperse power into various authorities (at least three — legislative, executive and judicial, completely independent of each other). The liberal state is weak and must grow weaker and weaker until it is no more. The stronger 'civil society' is, the weaker the state is. Eventually 'civil society', in the course of the progress of mankind as it approaches an equal degree of pure reason, will abolish the state altogether and perpetual peace will reign.

Therefore, whoever says 'I am for civil society' implies 'I am for the weakening and, ultimately, for the abolition of the state'.

Civil society is the antithesis of political society. The movement towards civil society includes a systematic de-politicisation of the population.

It is important to bear in mind that a civil society, which is based on the principle of individualism and grounded in the norm of the bourgeoisie and capitalism, presupposes overcoming the bourgeois nation-states, which are also built on the principle of the individual. It is not just an opposition, but precisely an overcoming. Civil society becomes real when the bourgeois liberal state has already done the core job of educating the population, that is, of introducing liberal principles, practices and axioms into society. From the liberal point of view, it is good that nation-states with a national identity as their foundation and a social contract as the basic constitutional act are created, but their value is relative and they themselves are a temporary and transitional phenomenon. In the face of traditional society, proponents of civil society find themselves in the position of defenders and patriots of the state, so long as the state concerned is a modern one.

Nevertheless, civil society is the pitfall of the Leviathan. In the case of Locke, the actual criticism of the state and the Political is absent or given implicitly. But Locke delves into anthropological depth and by his reinterpretation of the quality of the 'natural state' of man — from negative and aggressive (as in Hobbes) to neutral and capable of improvement — he undermines the metaphysical foundations of the Leviathan. If man himself is not a wolf, neither is the Leviathan a fate, and the societal contract may be concluded not necessarily over power (political contract), but also over horizontal interactions and rules — first of all over the rules of trade (social contract).

From this we can draw an important conclusion: liberalism (that of Locke and his followers) does not simply deny Hobbes, but carries him on, develops him and overcomes him, maintaining a fundamental continuity with him consisting in general materialism and individualism, but rethinking human nature in the process.

Kant stands somewhat apart in this, but the universality of 'pure reason' (as well as of 'practical reason') allows liberals to find another powerful argument to justify civil society as a kind of post-political condition of individuals. Kant, in a sense, can also be integrated into socialist frameworks, since one can infer from the universality of reason the creation of a society based on collectivist principles. And if we take into account the development (in many ways the overcoming) of Kant that we find in Hegel (1770–1831), this is precisely what happened in the case of leftist Hegelianism, and above all in Marxism. But while Hegel himself, in keeping with his dialectic, believes that civil society, due to the accumulation of historical self-consciousness, will eventually lead to the voluntary establishment of an enlightened monarch, whose power will express (quite in messianic eschatological style) the Absolute Spirit, for Marx the bourgeois form of civil society, based on individualism and private property (the paradigm of liberalism) will pass through the moment of the proletarian revolution into socialism, that is, into an egalitarian socialist (ultimately Communist) collectivist form of civil society based on complete property equality (rather than merely equality of opportunity, as in capitalism).

In summary, through Locke, a specific liberal ideology is gradually derived from the Hobbesian philosophy of New Age politics in the seventeenth century, which has remained dominant in bourgeois democracies up to the present day. The Lockean Heartland emerged in the seventeenth century, but stretched out in a spiral unfolding in space and time into the twenty-first century and on a global scale.

Jeremy Bentham: Utilitarian Deontology

A major liberal thinker was the jurist Jeremy Bentham, who laid the foundation for the philosophy of *utilitarianism*. Jeremy Bentham embodied the main currents of liberal ideology, giving them a systematic form.

First of all, he (like all liberals) operates from a consistent *individualism*, denying any distinct ontology of a 'social whole' or 'social body'. According to Bentham, *only the individual* exists, and it is the totality of separate individuals with complete autonomy and self-sufficiency in isolation that constitutes society.

In politics and economics, Bentham proposed to focus solely on the individual and his rights, which he saw as the main goal, while also advocating an expansion of the categories to which civil rights should be extended — including groups previously denied them — such as women, the poor, and indigenous people of the colonies. For Bentham, *man = individual*, yet he was also convinced that every individual is endowed with 'common sense' to such an extent that he should take full responsibility for all actions, deeds and situations.

On this basis Bentham builds his main theory, dubbed 'utilitarianism'. Utilitarianism is an ethical system based on a schematically understood radical individualism. Bentham teaches that it is human nature to *seek pleasure and avoid suffering*. These two parameters motivate all human activity. The subject of pleasure and suffering is strictly the individual, always concerned only with his private sensations, reducible to these two poles.

The combination of the will to enjoy and the desire to avoid pain gives us Jeremy Bentham's central concept of utility. *Utility is that which leads to maximum pleasure and minimal suffering.* The individual seeks only utility, and it is utility that drives individual activity. Meanwhile, the individual's rationality transforms his pursuit of benefit into a meaningful and systematic strategy based on *calculation*. This calculation is the basis of all human actions — historical, political, cultural, religious, etc. The calculation involves assessing the scale of pleasure and suffering, with a determination of the maximum and minimum of both in each particular situation. This is the rational choice, extending to all spheres, from the sensual to the spiritual.

On this basis, Bentham builds both a doctrine of truth and a specific morality.[25] He himself called it 'deontology' (from the Greek term δέον, that which is 'needful', 'right', 'proper'), i.e. the doctrine of right, proper. *Truth is that which is beneficial*, argues Bentham, since it is the benefit that acts as a measure of the correlations and connections between an individual's subjective intentions and objective realities. The maximum amount of pleasure for the maximum number of individuals constitutes the criterion and measure of the *validity* of a socio-political system.

The utilitarian morality is also built according to this principle: good is that which gives an individual pleasure (hence hedonism as the main feature of Bentham's morality); evil is suffering and the cause of suffering. But since pleasure and pain are related to each other in an inversely proportional way, morality becomes something relative — in defining good and evil, one should always consider the specific *proportions* between them and also the specific individual who is experiencing the pleasure and pain. Therefore, the benefit is always a recalculated and subjective *calculation*, and it cannot be elevated to a universal notion in relation to society as a whole. The social benefit is based on the aspiration for the maximum pleasure and minimal suffering of the totality of individuals, who are each time different and in different conditions.

In the spirit of Locke, Bentham argues that individualistic egoism, which forces man to seek maximum pleasure and minimal suffering *for himself alone*, is overcome not by the Leviathan (in contrast to Hobbes' ideas) but by his *reason*, for man can easily understand that considering the benefit of his neighbour can only multiply the benefit to himself. Thus, the fundamental psychological, ontological and moral individualism that is the essence of human nature is, according to Bentham, the source of society as a field of exchange, always selfish but always rational. The main social institutions then become *private property and the market economy*, where everyone acts in his own interest, but this egoistic motivation

---

25 Jeremy Bentham, *An Introduction to the Principles of Morals and Legislation* (New York: Dover Publications, 2007).

spontaneously creates the rules of the market game. This is entirely in line with Adam Smith.

Jeremy Bentham insists on the equality of all human beings, as they consist only of a thirst for pleasure and an escape from pain. This is a characteristic of *any* individual. Pleasure and pain in this case can be purely bodily, but also psychological and spiritual. Thus, according to Bentham, religion can also be useful because in certain cases it allows pleasure and dulls or soothes pain. True religion must provide spiritual *benefit* and minimise suffering. If it does not, and this condition is not fulfilled, then it is 'false religion'.

Bentham's aesthetics are similarly constructed: *fine is that which is useful*; repugnant is that which is harmful.

It is telling that Bentham is the first to act as a radical defender of usury. In a 1787 work written in Russia, where he was temporarily stationed, *In Defence of Usury*, he justifies the growth of money and the practice of borrowing and lending as something that maximises enrichment and is consistent with the rational nature of individual decisions to allow one to consciously and responsibly give money to grow and receive loans. These same ideas were expressed by Bentham in his letters to Adam Smith, who disapproved of the practice in the first versions of his major work, *An Inquiry into the Nature and Causes of the Wealth of Nations*. According to G. K. Chesterton (1874–1936), Jeremy Bentham, with his radical defence of usury, was the first author who began the 'modern world'.[26]

John Stuart Mill: The Negativity of Freedom

The foremost theorist of liberalism was the Scottish philosopher, politician and economist John Stuart Mill (1806–1873). His father James Mill (1773–1836) was an enthusiastic follower of Jeremy Bentham, fully embracing the ideas of utilitarianism, a love which he passed on to his son, who also became one of the most convinced and active admirers of

---

26 'The modern world began by Bentham writing the Defence of Usury', wrote Chesterton in his work on Thomas Aquinas, who, on the contrary, was an absolute opponent of usury in the spirit of Aristotle, and consequently a defender of Tradition. G. K. Chesterton, *Saint Thomas Aquinas* (NY: Doubleday Image, 1956).

Bentham. Along with David Ricardo (1772–1823), James Mill was the founder of English classical political economy.[27] He was also the author of the three-volume *History of British India*,[28] where he argued for the necessity of harsh exploitation of the natives of the colonies, justifying this by the absence of even a hint of *utilitarian consciousness within Indian culture, which he considered a universal form of thinking*.

John Stuart Mill formulated the concept of 'freedom', central to the ideology of liberalism.[29] Like all liberals, Mill started from the premise that the *individual has an absolute being and a wholly positive nature*. Consequently, granting the individual total freedom is a positive act and the aim of the entire ideological programme of liberalism. But when Mill arrives at the content of freedom itself, he encounters the following problem: if we define the content of freedom as something universal, we end up prescribing to the individual some obligation, that is, telling him how he must treat his freedom. Mill calls this the principle of 'freedom for'. 'Freedom for' is unbounded freedom. However, 'freedom for' will turn out to be something that does *not come from the individual himself*, and therefore it will not be freedom. For liberal ideology this constitutes a big problem and contradiction: prescribing to an individual what he should use his freedom for (for example, for good, justice, creativity, progress, art, etc.) would make him unfree, as these prescriptions would have another source than the individual himself. Hence John Stewart Mill concludes that the goal of liberalism cannot be positive freedom, 'freedom for', but only another kind of freedom, which he defines as *'freedom from'* and calls on the Latin to dub it 'liberty'. Liberty is negative precisely because, for liberal anthropology, only the individual subject is wholly positive. *He is what he is and has a will and a mind.*

Bentham's utilitarianism suggests that the will and mind serve the individual to achieve maximum pleasure, which is calculated on the basis of the particular situation. In this way, the utilitarian subject who seeks

---

27 John Stuart Mill, *Elements of Political Economy* (London: Baldwin, Craddock and Joy, 1821).
28 Mill, *The History of British India*. 3 vols (London: Baldwin, Craddock and Joy, 1818).
29 Mill, *On Liberty* (Mineola, NY: Dover Publications, 2002).

maximum pleasure in parallel with the minimisation of suffering is always able to construct a positive strategy for the realisation of his agenda *himself*. Moreover, this realisation will be all the more effective the less the individual is constrained from the *outside*. Therefore, Mill concludes, liberty consists in the total renunciation of any injunctions to man by the state, by society, by religion, etc. This negative 'freedom from' is what should unite all liberals, irrespective of how each intends to exercise their freedom and where it is directed. In other words, *liberalism is a universal alliance of individual subjects united not by positive goals but by the negation of all external prescriptions and constraints*. The solidarity of liberals with one another only extends as far as they all experience oppression from external non-individual institutions. Assuming that these institutions are abolished, nothing further binds the individuals to each other, since no integrating platform of 'freedom for' exists, nor can it exist. Thus, the ultimate realisation of the liberal strategy on a global scale postulates the 'end of society' and a transition to special post-social forms of *transindividual coexistence*. This extreme means the abolition of states and social institutions in favour of a 'natural state' interpreted as a peaceful and sensible 'civil paradise' in the spirit of Locke rather than a Hobbesian 'war of all against all'.

The negativity of liberty refers us not only to the chaotic state of atoms in Democritus, but also to the ambiguous ontology of δέν — the atom defined in relation to emptiness, but not as being, rather as some twist of emptiness itself, 'nothing' (οὐδέν). This is the peculiarity of negative freedom; it is not merely the complete emancipation of the individual, his liberation from external barriers (this corresponds to Democritus' external emptiness), but also the rejection of any ontologisation of the subject, if the individual is thought at all as a subject and not as a particular otherness of the object. In this case, Mill might indirectly refer us to the inner emptiness of Democritus' system, which lives within the coupled bodies, in the inter-atomic spaces. Thus, the fully emancipated individual comes close to the image of the ghost, the *eidolon*.

The Austrian School: Mises the Founder

Later in the economic field, the ideas of liberalism were developed in the work of two philosophers and economists, Ludwig von Mises (1881–1973) and Friedrich Hayek (1889–1992).

Ludwig von Mises defended the dominance of the subjective approach in economics (i.e. the priority of individual judgement over social attitudes) and rational choice as the basis of economic practice. The philosophical foundation of von Mises' worldview, on which he bases his economic theories, is *absolute individualism*,[30] i.e. the conviction that at the basis of any social system, including the state, lies an autonomous and rational individual, who himself determines the optimal strategies of economic activity and thereby creates various socio-political forms, which he is able to choose at his will, in pragmatic correspondence with the position of other individuals, who also act on the basis of their subjective preferences and private interests. From this followed the typical liberal injunction, already familiar to us, to minimise state interference in the economy and to allow individual actors to act with as few restrictions as possible.

Hayek: Neoliberalism

This direction of von Mises' economic thought was taken up by his disciple and follower, the greatestEuropean economist Friedrich Hayek. He is considered the founder of modern *neoliberalism*, i.e. a version of liberalism that adapts the principles of classical liberalism, established in the eighteenth and nineteenth centuries, to the historical conditions of the twentieth century.

Like von Mises, Hayek's economic philosophy is based on the principle of individual freedom. Society appears to Hayek as a complex system composed of a collection of individuals, each pursuing his own individual goals. Each does so on the basis of rational calculation and is guided by the principle of efficiency and rationalisation, striving for one thing: the

---

30 Ludwig von Mises, *Индивид, рынок и правовое государство* [*The Individual, the Market and the Rule of Law*] (St Petersburg: Pneuma, 1999).

achievement of maximum effect at minimum cost. But the rationality of such behaviour is limited to the zone of activity immediately in front of the individual and to those matters and things that directly concern him and affect his existence and the success of his economic activity.[31] He divides all the factors he encounters into those which are *relevant* and those which are *irrelevant*. The former are directly related to the realisation of his objectives, the latter are irrelevant or indirect. Even the number of relevant (let alone irrelevant, to be discarded at once by the 'counting man', *homo calculans*) factors is so high that one has to make a careful selection among them as well. The results of selecting the important and the unimportant in a concrete situation are comprehended by man through his experience: positive results lead to enrichment and success, negative ones to losses and failures. This is the *rationality of economic behaviour*. When it is realised in a space adjacent to the individual, the individual develops and reinforces the logistics of successful and unsuccessful behaviour, carrying out an assessment of his actions by the reality of the results. But as soon as one moves on to generalisations about the economy, society or the state as a whole, the number of relevant factors increases exponentially and rationality dissipates, giving way to dogmatism or utopia, that is, to theories which are certainly not subject to rational verification on an individual level and are given as axioms. Lacking *a priori* knowledge of the critical relevant factors, social and economic ideologies, whether nationalism or Marxism, complete the missing pieces with more or less arbitrary extrapolations, subordinating concrete individuals to an irrational blueprint whose postulates can neither be verified nor critically questioned. Thus Hayek concludes that *any generalisation in economics is futile* and that it necessarily leads only to violence, totalitarianism, tyranny and the imposition of irrational goals and values on society, which only inhibit 'natural development' and create artificial barriers to the reinforcement of the minute rational structures of behaviour available to everyone. All this leads directly to serfdom.[32] Attempts to organise society on a

---

31 Von Mises, *Bureaucracy; Planned chaos; An anti-capitalist mentality*.
32 Friedrich Hayek, *The Road to Serfdom* (Chicago: Chicago University Press, 1994).

rational basis, according to Hayek, inevitably lead to the triumph of madness and the reign of violence.

Instead, Hayek suggests that we should limit ourselves to *small-scale rationality*, which remains at the level of the individual. In this sphere, even if an individual makes a mistake or acts irrationally, this will primarily affect him alone or others in his immediate vicinity, whereas social experiments and global projects affect vast masses, guiding them towards absurd objectives. At the micro level in economics, the most successful approach is the construction of optimal relationships and the intuitive search for the most efficient solutions, which will lead to the gradual progress of the whole community: everyone looks for the shortest path to optimal results from their position, and the whole community thus moves towards prosperity (the old argument of Adam Smith and classical liberalism). This requires minimising the interference of society and government in the economic life of citizens by creating a playing field which is as level as possible for everyone.

On the issue of social organisation, Hayek is closest to Herbert Spencer, believing that the strongest survive in society and that any attempt to artificially help the weak and disadvantaged will not only undermine the strong, but will not correct the weak either, leading only to stagnation and delayed progress.

Karl Popper: The 'Open Society'

The brightest theorist of neoliberalism was Hayek's follower Karl Popper (1902–1994), who was primarily engaged in the philosophy of science, but wrote the most important ideological work—*The Open Society and Its Enemies*.[33] In this book, Popper justifies the main points of liberal philosophy in relation to the conditions of the twentieth century. Starting from the critique of Plato and Aristotle (i.e. from the political philosophy of the Father and the Son in the context of *Politica Aeterna*), Popper moves on to socialism and nationalism (the second and third political theories[34]),

---

33 Karl R. Popper, *The Open Society and Its Enemies* (Princeton, NJ: Princeton University Press, 1966).
34 Dugin, *The Fourth Way: Introduction to the Fourth Political Theory*.

which he qualifies as 'enemies of the open society'. Popper's main idea is that both the Communists and the nationalists operate with ideal notions, norms and projects, which they forcefully try to impose on society, leading to disasters, wars and the establishment of totalitarian regimes. In this he draws entirely on Hayek and his argument about the range of the relevant factors involved.

Popper argued that project-driven ideologies, which therefore contain implicit and explicit totalitarianism, can only stand in opposition to liberalism, which is not simply based on the open market (a principle at the heart of capitalism) but is an *open system* capable of continuous evolution without any one set goal. Liberalism, according to Popper, should supplant politics as such, *replacing it with trade*, and relations between people should replicate the principles of the market and the multitude of transactions, insurance operations and futures trading of which the market is made up. This aligns exactly with Smith's ideas also.

Popper attacks Marx, Lenin (1870–1924), Stalin (1878–1953) and Hitler (1889–1945), seeing them as figures of tyrants and dictators opposed to the principle of freedom itself.

Popper attacks any philosophical doctrine which speaks of an idea or a norm as something to be taken for granted. This covers both the idealisation of the past and the existence of some future goal or pattern for the present.

Popper proclaims the need to create and protect an 'open society', which implies not just the progress and development of liberalism, but also an uncompromising struggle against various kinds of 'closed societies', i.e. Communism and Fascism. Thus, the project designed to completely overcome any dichotomies, Manichean antitheses and exclusivism — which, according to Popper, is distinguished primarily by Communism and Fascism (as well as political systems built on Plato and Aristotle, i.e. the philosophical paradigms of traditional society) — in its turn becomes an aggressive intolerant model that establishes a fundamental opposition between supporters of the 'open society' and its enemies, which is reflected in the subtitle of Popper's key political work — *The Open*

*Society and Its Enemies.*³⁵ Thus, liberalism, even in theory, acquires the features of an intolerant ideology that demands reprisals and repression against those who do not share its 'peace-loving' and 'tolerant' principles.

George Soros: Liberalism Becomes Aggressive

George Soros, a disciple of Karl Popper, put his ideas into practice, firstly by gaining tremendous success on the stock market through speculation in national currencies and later by investing a significant part of his capital in promoting various NGOs and foundations that advocated ideas of globalisation, civil society, human rights and the dismantling of the sovereignty of nation-states.³⁶ Soros embodies the colourful image of the capitalist who has no religion other than the religion of money ('alchemy of finance',³⁷ as he calls it), does not recognise any state or nation, and with messianic persistence goes towards the establishment of a liberal utopia of a global-scale open society.³⁸ In doing so, he relies on a network of informants, agents, emissaries, envoys, associates and direct collaborators, recruited by him through financial and propaganda means, as well as on special educational institutions that promote the ideology of liberalism with a fanaticism no less than that seen in religious sects and terrorist organisations. Soros actively uses bribery of political leaders, preparation of colour revolutions and coups and mass disturbances in his fight against the 'enemies of the open society'. The activities of his foundations have been declared extremist in some countries.

Voegelin: Gradualism of Order, Political Religions and Totalitarian Heresies

One of the profound theorists of political philosophy in the twentieth century is the Austrian thinker Eric Voegelin (1901–1985). In the first half of his life, he was close to Austrian nationalism and even National

---

35 Popper, *The Open Society and Its Enemies*.
36 George Soros, *On Globalization* (New York: PublicAffairs, 2005).
37 Soros, *The Alchemy of Finance* (Hoboken, NJ: Wiley, 2003).
38 Soros, *Open Society: The Crisis of Global Capitalism Reconstructed* (Boston: Little, Brown & Company, 2000).

Socialism. Many aspects of his philosophy were also in tune with the Conservative Revolution, hence his holism and sympathy for the Middle Ages. But later he emigrated to the USA, largely revising his original views and aligning himself with liberalism, albeit an entirely atypical strain. In doing so, Voegelin became a consistent opponent of totalitarianism: both with regard to Communism, which he always criticised, but also with regard to the Third Political Theory, with which he was once closely associated. However, in his critique he sought to provide profound metaphysical justifications for the ideologies he criticised, which makes his ideas extremely important in the context of *Politica Aeterna*. Thus it was Voegelin who, partly under the influence of Carl Schmitt, the greatest representative of the Conservative Revolution, introduced the notion of 'political religion',[39] suggesting that the totalitarian ideologies of the modern age (primarily Communism and Fascism) represent a revival of religious teachings in a secular context, including messianism, eschatology and soteriology.

Voegelin justifies liberalism not through individualism (and in this he differs from most neoliberals — from Hayek and Popper), but rather as *the most effective form of organisation of order*.[40] In Voegelin's view, it is not the individual who is at the centre of the political system, but the capacity to organise the order. His methodological holism is evident in this, which is also very far from (if not directly opposed to) classical liberalism.

At the heart of Voegelin's political thought is the *idea of order*. This is the central concept of his political philosophy. Although order, for Voegelin, is the product of the social contract and therefore individualism is still primary, he is not so much interested in this as in the nature of order itself.

The meaning of the concept of 'order' is 'transcendent authenticity'. From Voegelin's point of view, man deals with chaos. Man himself is an element of chaos, and so is the world around him. Man is a chaotic subject

---

39 Eric Voegelin, *Die politischen Religionen* [*The Political Religions*] (Stockholm: Bermann Fischer, 1939).
40 Voegelin, *Die neue Wissenschaft der Politik* [*The New Science of Politics*] (München: Wilhelm Fink Verlag, 2004).

immersed in a chaotic object. In such a depiction, we easily recognise the universe of Democritus and Epicurus, the metaphysical underpinning of the prevailing political philosophy of the modern era, manifested especially strongly in liberalism.

The collision of the chaotic subject with the chaotic object generates the *pain* of existence. In response to this pain, there is a desire to see light in the darkness of chaos. The (rational) light, the perception of a space illuminated among the darkness, like a circle illuminated by a campfire, creates the feeling that the pain of chaos has ceased; it is relieved in the exalted moment of light contemplation.

This exalted contemplation of light is the primordial experience of order, when the human subject overcomes the chaos in himself and in the world. Voegelin calls this the 'transcendent leap' that lies at the heart of the political system. Accordingly, he views political history precisely as an evolution of the 'transcendent leap', the forms it has taken. One may recognise Kant's pure reason in such an image, but Voegelin does not merely acknowledge its existence, he sets out to trace its genesis.

In doing so, the philosopher asks the question: why is order so banal? Why is the political thought of the most diverse cultures, peoples and historical epochs characterised by an amazing poverty of political recipes? All societies are organised vertically, from top to bottom, there are always rulers and subordinates; millennia pass and we change Parliament, the House of Commons, democracy, dictators, tyrants, presidents, emperors, kings, princes, oligarchs in different ways, repeating an extremely limited circle of patterns. That is to say, there is a remarkable poverty of different political forms in each type of society. This is how Voegelin problematises the 'hyper-banality' of politics. Humanity, in its culture, art, language, is extremely diverse; it has innumerable possibilities, orientations, value systems. The chaos of life, the chaos of subject and object, is open and virtually infinite, so why, with such richness and abundance, do we have such astonishingly contrasting primitiveness within political order?

All types of political order are remarkably similar, and in all societies we always see the same thing: a domineering subject, a subordinate object and the instruments of subordination in the form of intermediaries who hover between the top and the bottom and transmit the will of the top and the grumbling of the bottom, profiting from this differential. According to Voegelin, this is order, and it is primitive in stark contrast to the richness of life. Life is rich and multidimensional, but order is primitive and dull, as if a man suddenly stops being a man and becomes a machine, reproducing the same thing like a mechanism — ignoring the real possibilities. There is a variety of forms and creative achievements everywhere — everywhere except in the realm of the Political.

Voegelin concludes that this is the fate of chaos rationalisation, and since order is nothing other than the antithesis of chaos, its task is, through a transcendent effort, to reduce diversity and pare all chaotic richness down to simplicity. So order is the process of simplifying chaos. Order is trivial, primitive and insignificant because that is its nature. The task of order is to reduce the richness of the chaotic subject and the chaotic object to its simplest form. And this, according to Voegelin, is the meaning of politics: politics is a form of reducing the complexity of chaotic life to the transcendent simplicity of some fundamental organisation.

He goes on to say that this can develop in two ways: *gradually* or *abruptly*. In order to create a sustainable order, Voegelin believes (and this is the essence of his liberalism), one has to act gradually. Chaos must be assembled in incremental steps. An infinitely complex chaotic system must be ordered through a progressive reduction in the number of bifurcations.[41] According to Voegelin, the main element in the creation of a stable (normative) order is precisely the sequence of reducing degrees of chaos. Any order is a reduction of degrees of chaos to zero — that is its meaning. Order is a method of converting wealth into poverty, large numbers of opportunities into small ones. In essence, order is the taming (and in the extreme, cessation) of life, the transition from life to death.

---

41 Bifurcation (from Latin *bifurcus*, 'two-pronged') is a qualitative change in the behaviour of a dynamic system resulting from an infinitesimal change in its parameters. The bifurcation model is at the heart of chaotic systems. There are predictable particle trajectories and unpredictable bifurcation trajectories: for example, a particle reaches a certain point and is equally likely to fly either to the right or to the left. Knowing where it is coming from and where it is going, we cannot calculate whether it is going to make it.

The best way to build an order is to move gradually, from complete chaos to partial chaos, to a lesser chaos, to semi-order, to near-order, and so on, at each stage deploying systems of political institutions, interactions and structures around the next 'transcendental leap'. This gradualism of transition from the non-political, the vital, the chaotic constitutes, according to Voegelin, a process of political order. Liberalism, in his opinion, is the best way to transition from chaos to order because it is the most consistent (there is a first level: direct democracy, a second level: referendum, a third level: representation, etc.) Liberal democracy is understood by Voegelin as the most consistent system of transformation of chaotic nature. That is to say, it is an overcoming of chaos that seeks to preserve as far as possible the richness of life; in other words, to include to some extent chaos in itself.

Unlike most liberals, Voegelin does not see progress as something strictly linear and advancing. For him it is a more nuanced process. Thus, he cites Greece and the Middle Ages as exemplary forms of democratic order, where certain political systems were developed that allowed the order to be organised with great finesse and a high degree of persuasiveness. From his point of view, therefore, liberal democracy can be found more readily in the Middle Ages than in modern society — small communities governed themselves, larger ones operated in a more complex and sophisticated manner, but still more often in a non-linear way. And the complexity of the government system could include double and even triple subordination, not contradicting each other (for example, vassal, communal, ecclesiastical, etc.). Voegelin notes that the system of multidimensional governance levels, which reduces complexity to simplicity, from chaos to order, does not necessarily reach its limit in liberalism, but what is important is the very idea of *gradualism*, which tries in part to preserve the diversity of chaotic life in politics. In this, Voegelin somewhat converges from Hayek, who emphasised the lack of design and adaptability of social structures in a market society.

On the whole, according to Voegelin, the movement towards transcendence is nothing less than a process of downgrading the status of (chaotic) immanence while retaining an immanent quality, which finds its ultimate conceptual embodiment in the democratic system.

Such a sympathy for gradualism — which would maximise the vitality of order and incorporate some elements of chaos, thus preserving at least partially the richness of the world — led Voegelin to a harsh criticism of totalitarian regimes in which this shift towards order was abrupt and intrusive, and the simplification of chaos was violent, brutal and filled with conflict. Voegelin rightly regarded totalitarian regimes as a phenomenon of political modernity, and treated them as 'political heresies' or, more generally, forms of 'political gnosticism'.[42] Christian Gnostics, recognised as heretics even in the earliest stages of Christianity, were characterised by their radical contrasting of the true spiritual world with immanent reality. This gave rise to a profound conflict with and violent opposition to the world around them. According to Voegelin, Communism and Fascism are typical representations of such gnosticism, based on blindness, obsession with order, and a pathological hatred of chaos with all its vital and cultural richness. People suffering from chaos, excessively experiencing its dissipation and spontaneity, try to forcefully impose this order on everything they touch, abruptly and immediately — bypassing all the intermediate stages. The lack of order on the periphery of the Political generates the excess of a simplified, reduced order imposed without regard to the intermediate patterns.

In general, the same observations about the nature of totalitarianism and its critique could also be applied to some forms of liberal democracy, especially in its later expression, when it remained the sole, dominant political ideology after the victory over Fascism and the fall of the Communist regimes in Eastern Europe and Russia. In its globalist version, the liberal order is no less brutal in its dealings with the chaotic diversity of life, cultures and peoples than the Second and Third Political Theories. Voegelin's views cannot therefore be fully attributed to liberal

---

42 Eric Voegelin, *Das Volk Gottes. Sektenbewegungen und der Geist der Moderne* [*The People of God. Sectarian Movements and the Spirit of Modernity*] (München: Fink, 1994).

orthodoxy, and can in part be seen as the kind of liberalism from which the transition to a Fourth Political Theory is possible.[43]

Leo Strauss: The Need to Lie

Leo Strauss (1899–1973) is another important twentieth-century liberal political philosopher, partly in line with Voegelin and Carl Schmitt. Like Voegelin, Leo Strauss emigrated from Europe to the USA after the Nazis came to power.

Leo Strauss constructed an original system of political philosophy[44] based on the assertion that there is a fundamental *epistemological duality* between the intellectual elite of society and the masses. The elite is capable of systematic rational thinking and therefore already created a refined rationalistic scientific culture in Antiquity, sceptical of myths, religions and rituals. According to Strauss, the intellectual elite is capable of perceiving the world from a scientific perspective, of thinking critically about itself and the surrounding reality, of distinguishing clearly between object and subject, and of constructing logical systems. However, before the advent of the modern age, the elite preferred to transmit this knowledge and these skills in a closed environment, educating their own kind but not extending their rationalism and scepticism to the broader society, to the masses. Only with the Enlightenment did rationalism, logic and scientific realism transcend the narrow stratum of the aristocracy and become available to the general public. This was the essence of European democracy: if earlier liberalism was the property of the educated upper classes, now, in the context of civil society, it was transmitted to all of society.

But the mentality of the masses, according to Strauss, is organised in a fundamentally different way. It is incapable of perceiving logical constructions and gravitates towards myth, faith, religion and ritual. According to Strauss, the masses live only a 'world of life' based on unverifiable, illogical and unscientific (mythological) notions. In premodern societies, elites were well aware of this and therefore couched their rational and scientific

---

43 Dugin, *The Fourth Way: Introduction to the Fourth Political Theory*.
44 Leo Strauss, *An Introduction to Political Philosophy: Ten Essays by Leo Strauss* (Detroit, MI: Wayne State University Press, 1989).

ideas in mythological and religious forms: it was the *only* way to share knowledge with the masses. But the New Age created a new situation — elite knowledge (in particular, the scientific understanding of the world) was transmitted to the masses *directly*, without a mythological shell. The masses could not stand it and turned science, logic, and democracy into another *myth*. For Strauss, the phenomenon of Nazi Germany, from which he had to flee, represented a striking example of this contradiction — after two centuries of Enlightenment, the German people easily became victims of the most extravagant myths. It meant that rationalism and scientific culture could not penetrate the masses and existed as the same old myth — only 'democratic' and 'liberal'. Faced with a stronger myth, the Germans were immediately carried away by it.

From this observation Strauss drew a pessimistic conclusion: scientific knowledge, full individual freedom and a wholesome, responsible personality — the basic tenets of liberalism — are possible only as the *property of a minority*. Therefore, an enlightened liberal elite should put their ideals into specific *mythological forms* and transmit them only in that form to the masses, since the masses, as such, cannot otherwise perceive rational theses and will immediately pervert them. This is how the theory of the 'noble lie' was developed, necessary to promote the ideals of progress and equality in the world.

Here we see a combination of anthropological pessimism (characteristic of Hobbes and realism) with liberalism, which in the spirit of Spencer becomes in Leo Strauss an elitism, that is, the domain of elites called upon to govern the masses, who are either unable to reach liberal democracy at all or who move in this direction very slowly and occasionally fall back into the easier to master mythological and religious belief systems. Here again we come close to Voegelin's idea of 'political religion'.

The philosophical truth, accessible to liberal elites, is that the world is material and there is no Spirit, no God, no sacredness. Only mechanical laws operate in the world and society, but only the elite are aware of this. In Strauss, the elite is described as the bearer of the modern paradigm, and he extends this hypothesis to the elite of traditional society — including Plato, considering him a sceptic, atheist and rationalist, forced to hide his real views under a cloak of idealistic teachings.

Since the elite knows that there is no such thing as the transcendent and that there are only material interests held by different groups, and since the masses cannot understand this, the elite rule the masses. If the masses are exposed to this 'truth', they will go mad or even die of terror because they need something to 'believe in'. In a traditional society, there were religions for this purpose; in the modern age, the masses believe in ideology and politics. The elites, understanding that there is nothing 'ideal' (all elites are materialists, atomists and followers of the philosophy of Democritus and Epicurus), that there are only selfish interests within the global swineopolis and the fight for these interests, tell the masses myths that they are happy to believe in — myths about morals, humanism, equality, democracy, human rights, etc. Leo Strauss asserts that the elite is lying, and moreover, it has always lied, knowing that everything is material and utilitarian, ruled only by money, pleasure and egoism, but convincing the masses that there is faith, hope, dignity, justice, progress, etc.

Here again we are dealing with a combination of Hobbesian anthropological pessimism and an unconditional commitment to liberal and individualist values, concepts and theories.

Strauss neither justifies nor condemns this state of affairs; he simply states it because, in his conviction, it cannot be otherwise. He sees the only solution as a policy of including more and more circles in the elite, who will gradually become accustomed to a sceptical and materialistic understanding of the nature of the world and society, and thus accept liberalism in its realistic form — beyond the politico-religious illusions. Here Voegelin's gradualism takes on a slightly different — more pragmatic — meaning.

In practice, the idea of justifying the lies of elites in the name of liberalism was borrowed by the influential American current of neoconservatives, who combined liberalism with a certain amount of realism.[45] In

---

45 Dugin, *Noomakhia. Civilisations of the New World. The Pragmatics of Dreams and the Decomposition of Horizons.*

contemporary American political practice, many of the concepts and theories of Leo Strauss have been adopted.

Francis Fukuyama: The 'End of History' Thesis

After the collapse of the socialist bloc and the USSR, a number of Western political scientists, analysts and experts were under the impression that this event put an end to the complex dialectic of stages of globalisation, and henceforth the world would become fully integrated and liberal, since nothing else could prevent the development of the liberal-capitalist paradigm that had prevailed on a planetary scale. The globalists were optimistic about these changes and believed that the 'point of no return' had been passed and that the world as a whole was now global, united, and that the residual conflicts and contradictions would gradually smooth themselves out.

This view was held in the early 1990s by the American political scientist Francis Fukuyama, who wrote the landmark text *The End of History*.[46] Fukuyama drew on Hegel's philosophy of history, which held that the embodiment of the Idea in the historical process is oriented towards its culmination in the Absolute Spirit. History, having become meaningful, would prove to be finite: having achieved a certain goal, it would exhaust its content. Karl Marx applied the Hegelian thesis to his version of the dialectical development of the forces of production and industrial relations, which was to end in a world revolution and the advent of a 'Communist formation' as the 'end of history'. The Hegelian philosopher Alexandre Kojève[47] (1902–1968) suggested that history might also end with the total global triumph of liberal capitalism, the market and bourgeois democracy. Francis Fukuyama, analysing the collapse of the USSR, thought that Kojève's version of Hegel's interpretation was coming true, and wrote first a programme article and then a book with a corresponding title.

The meaning of the 'end of history', according to Fukuyama, boils down to the end of the major political conflicts which had torn humanity

---

46 Francis Fukuyama, *The End of History and the Last Man*.
47 Alexandre Kojève, *Introduction to the Reading of Hegel* (Ithaca, NY:Cornell University Press, 1980).

apart at previous stages and thus constituted the content of the historical process. Once, in the era of 'barbarism', all fought against all, and the rule of the strong prevailed. In modern times, nation-states were declared the subject of history and the bearer of sovereignty, and this principle formed the basis of the Westphalian system. The nation-states antagonised each other, thereby shaping European history, and by the same token, through colonial conquests, the history of the rest of the world. After World War II, the rivalry between the nations was overshadowed by the ideological confrontation between world capitalism and world socialism, and the meaning of history then became the confrontation between the two politico-economic systems. The collapse of the USSR and the victory of the West in the Cold War completes this period and, therefore, *history no longer has content*, no meaning. During the time of the ideological confrontation with Communism, the bourgeois states have come close enough to each other to become the basis of a new socio-political and economic order, and the disappearance of the ideological opponent theoretically allows liberal democracy, the market economy and the ideology of 'human rights' to spread throughout the world. In such a situation, nation-states would gradually die out and politics would be completely replaced by economics. The economy has no history, because there is no meaning, no dramatic tension, no content. The world would become a global marketplace, in which logistics and optimisation would prevail, allowing the laggards in the global economy to gradually catch up to the advanced societies.

Later Fukuyama substantially revised his views and admitted that his forecast was too optimistic,[48] but his amendments and reservations are much less interesting compared to his main thesis on the 'end of history'. The point is not that he was in a hurry and got ahead of himself, but that he depicted the philosophy of modern globalism in its most complete, consistent and coherent form. Fukuyama's ideas seemed quite realistic in

---

48 Francis Fukuyama, 'Идеи имеют большое значение. Беседа с А.Дугиным' ['Ideas count for a lot. Conversation with Alexander Dugin'] //Профиль [Profile]. 2007. №23(531).

the 1990s, when the 'unipolar moment' (Charles Krauthammer) was established in the world architecture.

The First Political Theory: Liberalism

We are talking about liberalism as the First Political Theory of the New Age. It emerged before the others, formed on the basis of the Hobbesian paradigm but with a qualitative reinterpretation of anthropology — from the pessimistic version of Hobbes himself to a neutral and optimistic one (by Locke and later by Kant). Liberalism became the most consistent ideological expression of capitalism and bourgeois society. It was liberal ideology that centred attention on enlightenment, education, progress and development.

Politically, liberalism expresses itself in liberal democracy, but in certain cases it allows for oligarchy (as the rule of the richest members of bourgeois society) and even an enlightened monarchy, which, through top-down education and reforms, is supposed to create the preconditions for subsequent — now properly democratic — structures. Obviously, in this case, the systems of social organisation that were rejected and despised in the eyes of Platonists and Aristotelians — democracy; egoistic, physical swineopolis; the community of 'idiots'; political atomism — are taken as exemplary and are glorified and praised at every opportunity. In the end, however, only the rhetoric and the subjective evaluation change: what in the eyes of Platonists, Aristotelians (as well as Catholics and Orthodox) looks like ugliness and degeneration, like a kind of political-philosophical 'heresy' (the political philosophy of the Mother, the Receiver, the *chora*), for liberals is evaluated as the highest achievement of freedom (from all forms of collective identity), progress, the coming of happy times and the exit from medieval obscurantism. However, from the point of view of *Politica Aeterna*, these rhetorical figures are secondary and in no way reflect the essence. If we remove ourselves from the value judgements we place on the structures, the basic theses and the main semantic axes of the three paradigms of the political, we see that it is liberal ideology that bears the greatest resemblance to the philosophical foundations of what Plato describes as the third kind of being, the domain of pure multitude (πολλά), the figure of the Mother, the *chora*, or Aristotle's 'matter' (ὕλη). In the three-part structure of the world, political Platonism (in all its versions) represents Heaven, the Aristotelian model represents the intermediate world, the Earth, while liberalism represents the underworld, the progressive descent to the centre of gravity, to the material core,[49] in the process gradually liberating materiality — that is the atom, the core of the individual, the dimension of radical objectivity — from all transcendental and subjective forms.

Liberalism emerged before the other modern political ideologies and lasted longer than them.[50] Its victories over the illiberal versions of modernity (Fascism and Communism) led to its triumph on a global scale by the end of the twentieth century. If we trace the ideological destiny of the twentieth century, we see the clash of three ideologies: liberal, Communist and Fascist. The first and the second defeated the third theory in 1945, and in 1991 the first defeated the second. Thus, throughout the New Age, liberalism remains the dominant conceptual matrix and may well be considered synonymous with New Age political philosophy. Of course, New Age political philosophy is paradigmatically broader than Locke and Kant (just as Hobbes is broader and more primal than Locke), but nevertheless, it is the idea of an optimistic anthropology peculiar to liberalism (indeed to Communism, or more precisely borrowed from liberals and Communists) which is the dominant trend in political philosophy of this period.

The notion of the individual as a 'blank slate' has deep theoretical links to the very semantic core of the New Age. Thus we come to a fundamental law of New Age political philosophy: *liberalism is dominant here*. From Locke to the contemporary United States of America, the Anglo-Saxon world in general, the European Union and practically the rest of the world — in the course of first colonisation, then Westernisation and modernisation, and finally globalisation — it is the liberal paradigm that has become by far the dominant one. Thus, liberalism (capitalism, bourgeois

---

49 Land, *Fanged Noumena: Collected Writings 1987–2007*; Negarestani, *Cyclonopedia: Complicity with Anonymous Materials*.
50 Dugin, *The Fourth Way: Introduction to the Fourth Political Theory*.

society and its philosophy) won the historical battle first against traditional society and later against illiberal alternatives within modernity; since the end of the twentieth century, liberalism has become the main — and essentially the only — operating system of ideology, politics and culture on a global scale.

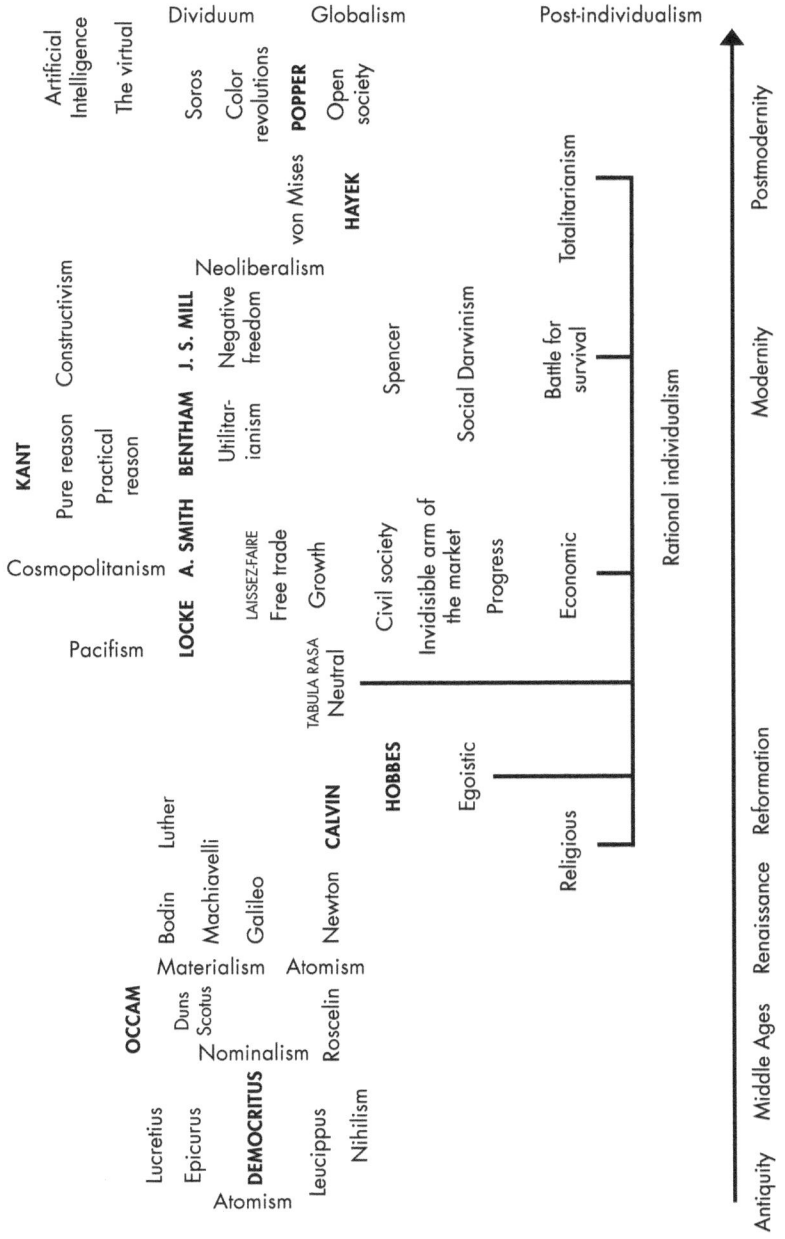

Figure 17. Genesis and formation of liberal ideology (the First Political Theory).

CHAPTER 13

COMMUNISM (THE SECOND POLITICAL THEORY)

The Dialectic of the Historical Whirlwind

The Second Political Theory

NOW WE COME to the Second Political Theory, where we can include all types of leftist, i.e. anti-capitalist, ideology critical of the bourgeois order. The most striking and complete systemic expression of the Second Political Theory is undoubtedly Marxism, which represents the most developed and elaborated theory and has achieved impressive — though at times monstrous — practical results in history. However, all types of left-wing thought, whether Marxist or non-Marxist, generically referred to as socialism or social democracy (as opposed to bourgeois or liberal democracy, i.e. the First Political Theory), have something fundamentally common at the level of their underlying philosophical positions. This common denominator of the Second Political Theory is *the attitude towards the individual*. Materialism, a belief in progress, recognition of the dominance of history and time as the only form of being, a scientific picture of the world, an obsession with technical development, as well as a conviction in the need to abolish states altogether and create a single global cosmopolitan humanity, are all common to the First and Second Political Theories. Up to a certain point, they are in solidarity with each other and evaluate the content and even the moral significance of historical developments — especially of the New Age — in the same way. Thus, both liberals and Communists are in complete solidarity in their opposition to traditional society, both in its ancient and medieval expressions. They unanimously reject vertical organisation, hierarchy, sacred politics, the ideal state of the Father and the normal state of the Son along with all their corresponding metaphysical, anthropological, cultural and political forms. Thus liberals and socialists, up to a certain point, represent a common modernist front against Tradition, fully agreeing both on the mutual evaluation of the 'old order' and on the moral-historical urgency of the transition to democracy, the power of the Third Estate. But differences begin further down the line. For liberals, bourgeois democracy is the logical crown of political and historical progress. History ends there. The American liberal Francis Fukuyama[1] brought this line to its logical conclusion in the 1990s. Hence capitalism and equality of opportunity are considered the highest limit of emancipation. Here individualism reaches its apogee. In Plato's model of *Parmenides,* it is not simply a question of the triumph of the last four hypotheses, denying the 'one', but precisely of a plunge deeper and deeper into the pure multitude that is the liberation of the individual atom from all forms of collective identity. This means that from the sixth hypothesis, which allows for an artificial and secondary 'one', liberalism calls for a move towards the seventh hypothesis, which denies the need for this 'one', and on to the eighth hypothesis, in which the many (that is, atoms) are correlated with another many (with other atoms), to the final ninth, where the many are not correlated with another many, but only with themselves. In this way the ultimate individualism is achieved, the fullest expression of which, in the twenty-first century, is the philosophy of speculative realism or object-oriented ontology.[2]

Marxism, while not rejecting individualism,[3] treats it very differently. It completely rejects the notion that bourgeois reforms liberate the

---

1 Francis Fukuyama, *The End of History and the Last Man* (London: Penguin Books, 2012).
2 Levi Bryant, Nick Srnicek, and Graham Harman, eds., *The Speculative Turn: Continental Materialism and Realism* (Melbourne: Re.Press, 2011).
3 Louis Dumont rightly observes: 'The socialist Marx believed so strongly in the individual that it was unmatched by Hobbes, Rousseau, Hegel or even Locke. Perhaps such socialism, and such a rise of faith in the individual after the French Revolution, became possible only after the epoch of 1840–1850.' Louis Dumont, *Essays on*

individual. Marx believes that capital is a mechanical dependence that does not allow a true individuality to unfold, and therefore liberal individualism is an anthropological forgery. It is not dominated by the individual, but only by a particular side of human nature, embodied in latent aggression (a reference to Hobbes). Like Locke, Marx is convinced that man can be re-educated, but such re-education is realised through a radical change in the structure of society, through the destruction of the bourgeois order and the establishment of a political order based on total equality and the absence of any kind of property superiority. Only complete equality will allow the true nature of the atom to be achieved in society, and make the individual truly free. The liberty pursued and extolled by liberals is a pseudo-freedom that preserves, together with inequality, the dependence on capital and the rigid mechanisms of exploitation. Capitalism is incompatible with real freedom for all individuals, since a considerable part of them, the proletariat, the working class, finds itself in the position of slaves and, consequently, their individuality can neither be established nor fully revealed. This is how socialists fundamentally diverge from liberals on the interpretation of individuality, putting the main emphasis precisely on equality, without which the achievement of liberation is not possible.[4]

Another fundamental difference between the Second Political Theory and the First is the treatment of the artificial 'one' from the sixth and seventh hypotheses of Plato's *Parmenides*. While liberalism moves towards the abolition of this 'one' formed by the multitude (that is, from the sixth hypothesis to the ninth), socialism stops exactly at the sixth, but makes the equality of the many a prerequisite of this 'one'. That is, in the eyes of socialists and Communists, the 'one' which is created by the many must be total and not allow any division into two classes (which they accuse liberals of doing) or into national territories (which is the fundamental

---

Individualism: Modern Ideology in Anthropological Perspective (Chicago: University of Chicago Press, 1992) p. 131.

4 Louis Dumont, *Homo Hierarchicus The Caste System and Its Implications (Chicago: Chicago University Press, 1981)*.

contrast between international Communism and nationalists, representatives of the Third Political Theory).

Campanella: The Rational City

The Second Political Theory did not fully emerge until the nineteenth century with Marx, but it had its predecessors, the most distant of which include the Anabaptists of Münzer and the creators of such rationalist utopias as Tommaso Campanella (1568-1639) and Francis Bacon (1561-1626).

A Calabrian monk, Tommaso Campanella was influenced by the general ideas of the Renaissance, which combined several disparate currents, from the Platonism of Marsilio Ficino[5] (1433-1499) and Giovanni Pico della Mirandola[6] (1463-1494) to the atomism and materialism of Galileo. In the second half of his life, Campanella draws closer to Galileo, partly accepting his ideas in physics and astronomy.

Campanella, while imprisoned for political reasons, writes his most famous work, *The City of the Sun*.[7] In it he describes a world state built on the principles of a 'new philosophy', his own philosophy. The ideal society is created on a strictly rational basis. It is headed by a Metaphysician, to whom a hierarchy of chosen authorities, structured along professional lines, are subordinated. He embodies the Sun himself, being its substitute. His three co-creators embody the three cardinal principles of the universe: Might, Wisdom and Love. Below is the Great Council, and still below that are the various professional associations and corporations, each headed by a 'king'. All the inhabitants of the City of the Sun work selflessly, not for the sake of feeding themselves, but out of a moral sense and solidarity. The rulers distribute the bounty based on the principles of fairness.

All life in the City of the Sun is extremely rational, with everyone going about his business, studying the sciences and the arts. Instead of

---

5   Marsilio Ficino, La Religione Cristiana (Rome: Città Nuova Editrice, 2005).
6   Giovanni Pico della Mirandola, *Oration on the Dignity of Man* (Gateway Publishing, 1996).
7   Tommaso Campanella, *The City of the Sun* (Saint Paul, Minnesota: Wilder Publications, 2009).

historical religions, a 'new religion' reigns, in which all three levels of perception — rationality, that which is perceived as obvious by the senses, and profound mysticism — are harmonised. The level of knowledge and competence increases as one ascends the social hierarchy.

The City of the Sun may be interpreted in different ways, as it does not yet assert complete equality, but the Communists considered the very principles of the rational organisation of society, the universal obligation to work and the replacement of existing religions by a kind of universal worldview as a prototype of their own project for world reconstruction.

Francis Bacon: Atlantis of Scientists

Another utopia, which Communists saw as a prototype of their own worldview, was written by English philosopher and politician Francis Bacon, who outlined his vision of an optimal society based on scientific principles in his book *New Atlantis*. Bacon was one of the first to formulate a complete programme for the scientific study of nature, based on induction and experiment, becoming the founder of modern empiricism. In developing medieval nominalism, Bacon argued that true ideas about things can only be obtained through *sense experience*, which is the only way to derive our knowledge of the world around us.

Bacon, in his *Novum Organum,* argues that only *pure experience* derived from experiments on matter, free from projections of 'ghosts' (*eidolons*), should form the basis of true scientific knowledge and become the main methodological basis of New Age science. Behind such an attitude, it is easy to see the implication of the *unity of being and matter* and the secondary nature (reflexivity) of reason, only reflecting the structures of materiality (i.e. full-fledged materialism). The preconditions for such a method can easily be found in Duns Scotus' doctrine of the univocity of being and in Occam.

On the other hand, Bacon also proposes the active side of the scientific agenda, which is the *subjugation of nature to man*. If in the past, Bacon reasoned, human beings grasped nature sporadically and subjected it to themselves from time to time, from now on the complete and total subjugation of nature must become a *conscious task of mankind*. In nature there is nothing but materiality, which must be *studied through experience* and *subjugated to man through practice*, declares Bacon. There is nothing in nature to contemplate, except *eidolons*, ghosts, so it must be conquered and forced to serve the interests of humanity.

Bacon was one of the first in Europe not just to articulate, but to fundamentally justify, a theory of progress. For him, progress consists in the accumulation of knowledge, which predetermines the vector structure of the development of science — *from the minimum of knowledge to the maximum of knowledge*. Society's time is constructed along this axis, moving from minus to plus, and thus constituting progress, irreversible forward movement. Mankind, following the path of experience and conquest of nature, is continually increasing its capacity — becoming more and more intelligent and more or more powerful. Hence Bacon's formula: *Scientia potentia est* ('Science is power').[8]

All three main points of Francis Bacon's philosophy — the recognition of the unity of being and matter, and the view of eidetic forms as something ghostly, fictitious; the strictly volitional attitude to the subordination of nature to scientific knowledge; and the confidence in the accumulation of scientific knowledge and progress of science — create semantic axis of the modernist paradigm.

In *The New Atlantis*, Bacon describes the ideal society built on the principles of a scientific worldview, painting a picture of a state ruled by pure rationality, the laws of empiricism and the constant growth of scientific data. The scientific utopia described by Bacon became the prototype for the organisation of the British Royal Society.

For Communists here, as in the case of Campanella's *City of the Sun*, we are dealing with a political project for the transformation of society on a scientific and rational basis. In the case of both utopias we are talking about the creation of a kind of 'unity' out of individual particles, which was the main idea of socialism — that is, the connection (lat. *socius*,

---

8   Translator's note: Although *scientia* is typically translated into English as 'knowledge', it can equally mean 'science', or specifically refer to knowledge based on reproducible data.

'companion', 'accompanying', 'comrade') of all with all, and Communism (lat. *communis*, 'common').

Baruch Spinoza: Substantialism

The philosophy of Baruch Spinoza (1632–1677) plays an important role in the genealogy of Marxist materialism and atheism. *Spinoza's philosophy represents the first historical attempt to build a metaphysical system on the principle of pure immanentism.* The entire European philosophy of antiquity, the Middle Ages and Christian doctrine was built on a *vertical principle* which affirmed the ontological primacy of God in relation to nature, the world, the elements and men — that is, *on transcendence*. This transcendence was maintained in all theological and philosophical systems up to Spinoza.

Benedict Spinoza was the first to clearly and *openly proclaim the exact opposite metaphysical thesis*: God is not transcendent of the world, but *immanent within it. God is Nature*, argues Spinoza. *Deus sive Natura*. This in itself was not mere atheism, but a fundamental change in the whole metaphysical picture of the world, from which the transcendental dimension was completely expelled. Before Spinoza, no philosopher, including those considered materialists, rationalists and 'humanists' had dared to assert anything of the sort. Typically, materialists recognised God as the cause of the world, or as Newton's 'watchmaker' watching to ensure that planets moving in the ether did not go out of their orbits.

Spinoza's system derives entirely from the basic principle of pure immanence. Spinoza asserts that there is a single and absolute origin, which he calls *substance*. It is the cause of itself (*causa sui*) and derives from itself (*sui generis*). This origin is everything; it is the world, it is God, and it is nature. Creation from nothingness is impossible, for there is neither a transcendent God nor nothingness. Spinoza says '*nam ex nihilo nihil fit*' ('nothing is created out of nothing').

Substance is ontologically unified, but is divided within itself into two derivatives (as in Descartes), the *thinking element* (*res cogens*) and the *extension* (*res extensa*). The unity of substance guarantees the *knowability of the world*, because that which thinks and that which is thought about are two sides of the *same thing*. God, which is nature, is not a subject, but signifies *substance itself*. Marxist ontology, as well as most materialist systems, is derived entirely from Spinoza's ideas. Later on, Marx will only replace the concept of 'substance' with that of 'matter', and discard the word 'God' in order to obtain the overall structure of his strictly immanentist and materialist ontology.

From the metaphysics of immanentism Spinoza derives his ethics, which constitutes an important dimension of his philosophy. This ethics is based on a juxtaposition of three fundamentals:

- necessity,
- freedom and
- violence.

Necessity is the internal law of the causal unfolding of substance. It is irrevocable because it expresses itself. Freedom is the obedience to this necessity. The ethics of freedom is to *comprehend and follow necessity* through the laws of nature and science. Violence, on the other hand, is the obstacle to the unfolding of substantive necessity, which is perceived — comprehended and experienced — as unfreedom. Marx borrowed the thesis of freedom as a comprehended necessity from Spinoza. In a sense it is a continuation of Calvin's doctrine of predestination, but while Calvin still retains the idea of a transcendent and eternal deity who is indeed the transcendent subject, with Spinoza predestination is fully embedded in substance itself as necessity and has no meaning except to conform to the logic of that substance's development.

On this principle of necessity builds his theory of desire — Spinoza calls it *conatus* and understands it as the desire of the individual, as a unit of the universal substance, *to affirm himself*. According to Spinoza, *man wants something, not because he finds it good, but because he finds what he wants good*. He wants only one thing, the affirmation of himself in the structure of the causal chains of universal substance, but he expresses this in a multitude of ways. Thus fundamental materialism (Spinoza's substantialism) and fundamental individualism are inextricably linked.

Jean-Jacques Rousseau: Direct Democracy

An important element in the preparation of the socialist outlook and theory of Communism is the doctrine formulated by the French philosopher Jean-Jacques Rousseau (1712–1778). Rousseau proposed a programme of radical transformation. He was therefore sought out by the most extreme members of the revolutionary circles, who insisted on the establishment of a *direct democracy* in France.

In his philosophical writings, Rousseau describes the figure of the 'noble savage' (*bon sauvage*), living in harmony with nature according to the laws of equality, goodness and justice.

According to Rousseau, the original organisation of society (the 'natural state') is the harmonious coexistence of man with his environment and with other people. Rousseau praises the 'savage', endowing him with all kinds of virtues. Evil comes to society when selfishness, lust for profit, technology and culture begin to spread within it. Rousseau sees civilisation and technical progress as negative phenomena leading to the transformation of the 'noble savage' into the 'evil civilised man'. The complex social institutions — church, monarchy, state, etc. — are, for Rousseau, alienating superstructures over the living human element.

Rousseau, like Hobbes, sees the origins of society in the 'collective contract', which the powerful gradually forget, usurping the authorities and consolidating the privileges of rulers for themselves and their kindred. This is why Rousseau promotes the idea of 'direct democracy', built on the rejection of any vertical hierarchy, mediated representation and alienating forms of social organisation. This is a return to the roots of society, to the 'social contract', but only in such a form that the bearers of authority will no longer be able to leverage it for personal or group power.

Rousseau's ideal is 'the villager', the 'common labourer', while the higher classes, the priests (clergy) and soldiers (aristocracy), are blamed for all kinds of vices and for violating the pristine harmony of life, which preceded the advent of differentiated civilisation. It is important to note that for Rousseau, in contrast to the liberal tradition that prevailed in

England, it is the rural community and not the *demos* of the city that serves as a model for 'direct democracy'.

At the same time, Rousseau thinks of himself as a representative of modernity, progress and enlightenment. For example, Rousseau considers Christianity to be a harmful phenomenon, incompatible with direct democracy. He is especially opposed to the idea of original sin, which he considers an instrument of suppression of free will, imposed on society by the political elite at the time of the stratification of civilisation into a minority, which has usurped power, and a suppressed majority, which is deprived of natural rights.

The French Revolution set out to put Rousseau's teachings into practice, overthrew the old 'feudal', clerical-aristocratic, monarchical order and established *political democracy* in its most radical form for the first time in Europe, which reached its paroxysm under the Jacobins.

Yet Rousseau's political democracy is fundamentally different from liberalism. Here, the normative figure is neither a townsman nor a merchant, but people living in a state which is as close to the natural state as possible. Later, influenced by this image of the 'noble savage', Marx and Engels (1820–1885) developed the idea of 'primitive communism', which was fundamentally important for their doctrine of economic change.

Rousseau's ideas anticipate Communism in that they offer an optimistic anthropology (man in himself is undoubtedly good — hence the denial of original sin); provide a detailed critique of hierarchical structures, including the urban bourgeoisie; and insist on direct democracy rather than representative democracy, which the bourgeoisie advocates, as Rousseau saw 'representation' as the main means of usurping the will of the people.

Political Materialism: Matter as Being

Turning directly to the Communist ideology formulated by Marx and Engels, it must be emphasised once again that it is constructed within the New Age paradigm. In all its aspects it belongs to what we have called the '*political modern*'. Let me remind you of the basic philosophical principle of the political modern: it is the idea of constructing politics, ontology, cosmology and, if you like, theology 'from the bottom up'. That is, it is the idea that the basic ontological reality is the bottom, some horizon of the lower world, defined by the notion of 'matter'.

This is the meaning of materialism as the basis of Marxist philosophy and Communism. Among the other political ideologies of the modern age, it is Communism, the Second Political Theory, which most insists on explicit dogmatic materialism. For Marx and Engels, materialism is not a routine fact of the general scientific picture of the world, but the fundamental basis of the entire ideology. Everything in Communism is built upon materialism and upon the irrefutable conviction for the Communists themselves of the materiality of the world. Liberalism builds on and implies materialism, but — as in the case of Kant — there may be bourgeois-capitalist theories that offer their own — somewhat different — forms of ontology and epistemology. In some cases, materialism can remain latent and unpronounced without disturbing the coherence of liberal philosophy. For the Second Political Theory, materialism is an ideological and political dogma. Nobody insists so rigidly and unambiguously as the Communists on the materiality of the world and the primordiality of matter. Therefore, it is worth recalling again — yet again — what place matter has in the general structure of *Politica Aeterna*, all the more so because this notion is given such an important — political — dimension in the Second Political Theory.

Earlier we talked about the political philosophy of the Father, where being is the realm of ideas, and objects in the phenomenal world exist only as copies of the idea (political Platonism). We also talked about the political philosophy of the Son, where being settles into the phenomenal world (political Aristotelianism). There is also a political philosophy of the Mother. If we take the dialogue *Timaeus*, it is the nurse (*chora*) who is at the bottom of the metaphysical map of the three beginnings, the genera of being. Therefore, materialism means putting being in its original sense neither at the top (as with Plato) nor in the middle (as with Aristotle), but *at the bottom*.

As we said, from the point of view of Plato and Aristotle, there is no matter as such. From Plato's point of view, matter is the dilution, the cooling of an idea to a greater or lesser extent. According to Plotinus, evil is a diminution of good. Here the emphasis is not on evil itself, but on the diminution, on the lack, the too-small amount of good. If one imagines a complete absence of good, then from the Neoplatonist point of view there is *nothing*, including evil. The absence of good is not evil, it is *pure nothingness*. Evil is the diminution of goodness as a process; it is a process of dissipation, the cooling of goodness. If the process is completed, there is neither good nor evil.

That is why matter, from the point of view of Platonism, is the conditional limit of the process of diminishing the good. There is no matter as such — there is only *striving towards matter*, materialisation.

From Aristotle's point of view, matter exists, but only *together* with *eidos* — with the form (μορφή). It is an integral part of the process of existence, without which existence is impossible. In its pure form, if we remove the eidetic component (*eidos*) of some phenomenon, we get nothing. In its pure form, matter, as in the case of Platonism, is not conceivable; it does not exist. It *is* only through the phenomenon, through the necessary complicity in the phenomenon, but not in itself.

The third political philosophy, the philosophy of the Mother (*chora*), is another ontological hypothesis — namely that matter (that which is below) actually *is* and, in a liminal sense, the only thing that *is*, is matter. Accordingly, here matter is endowed with entirely new properties.

When we say that we reject Platonism (matter as a diminution of spirit and a process of cooling of the Idea), that we reject Aristotelianism (where matter necessarily exists in combination with *eidos*), we come to the third model, in which matter exists; it represents atoms, and these atoms, indivisible particles of matter, exist by themselves.

In the first case there is no matter, in the second case matter exists only in combination with *eidos*, and in the third case matter exists by itself. Matter is given new properties and acquires the character of a special, living substance, which carries within it the content of being. Everything is reversed: before, the content of being consisted in Ideas, but in materialism it is the opposite — the content of being consists in matter.

The Living Matter of Communism

The political philosophy of Platonism viewed the world and the state from the top down — the state as God-given, as Revelation, as manifestation of the idea (hence the concept of the sacred state, the sacred empire). In the view of Aristotelian political philosophy, everything is built around the unmoved mover — there is no descent, no revelation of the idea, but the continuous existence of an ordered sacred cosmos, an eternal cosmos.

In the third paradigm, the political philosophy of the Mother, we get the idea of growth. It is in Communism that this aspect is most vividly represented. For the Marxists, matter is endowed with an inner life of its own, which develops linearly in the direction of consciousness. That is why Marxists took up Charles Darwin's (1809–1882) idea of the evolution of species, turning it into yet another political dogma. Matter evolves from primordial minerals to living cells, on to the simplest organisms (amoebas and infusoria), then to animals, and finally to hominids and humans, reaching the level of consciousness. But even consciousness itself, for all its apparent autonomy, is material, since it is nothing more than a product of the development of matter.

Consequently, the Marxists develop their ideology, matter is endowed with an intrinsic capacity for growth and therefore the whole world, including the capacity for thought, is a derivative of matter. Any phenomenon is thus not independent (as in the philosophy of the Son) and is not derived from an idea (as in the philosophy of the Father), but is *derived from the movement of matter*. So matter is given a new content and elevated to a new category that contains in itself the possibility for the development of being and consciousness. In Marxism, matter is alive and contains in itself the preconditions for the appearance of consciousness, which pre-determine the appearance of different kinds of matter, including human beings and society itself. *Society, in terms of such materialism, is the peak of matter's development*: matter grows and develops into a state and polis.

This is the materialistic understanding of the essence of politics. Politics, society, the state, the polis are the peak of the development of matter.

Marxism as Post-Capitalism

Marxist political philosophy is constructed within the paradigm that dominates modernity. But at the same time it is turned harshly against liberal ideology. Marxism rejects liberalism, but not at all the attitudes of the modern era. *The Communist Manifesto* of Karl Marx and Friedrich Engels deals considerably with a very important point — dissociating the party from all other forms of anti-capitalist theories and above all from those which oppose capitalism from the position of traditional society. Marxism thinks of itself precisely as post-capitalism, as post-liberalism, and not as pre-liberalism, nor as various versions of the anti-bourgeois ideologies that have survived in Europe from the political institutions of the Middle Ages through inertia. Therefore Marx explains in great detail that the opponents of the bourgeoisie may be anyone, but Marxists are only those who criticise liberalism and capitalism from the position of the phase succeeding capitalism, not the phase preceding it.

At the time Marx and Engels lived in Germany, there were many and varied opponents of capitalism — the Prussian aristocracy, the military, conservatives and even monarchists who harshly rejected capitalism, believing that it represented the decay of the traditional medieval order in Europe and brought only nihilism, degeneration and the reduction of all values to baseness and materiality. Such opponents of capitalism were far more numerous than Marxists at the time. In order to show that Marxism belongs to the paradigm of New Age political philosophy, rather than opposing it on the level of another political philosophy (Platonism or Aristotelianism), Marx emphasises in every possible way that his critique is a critique of capitalism not 'from the right' but 'from the left'; that Marxism represents an even more modern, even more immanent, even more materialistic, even more atheistic, even more anti-Platonist and anti-Aristotelian political doctrine than capitalism (liberalism). And furthermore, with regard to such opponents of capitalism 'from the right', Marxism is in solidarity precisely with capitalism. Capitalism is an undoubted progress in comparison with the Middle Ages, it is the socio-economic formation following feudalism, the coming of which should by no means be opposed or counteracted, because it is absolutely necessary as a preparation of the next phase. On the other hand, for the liberals capitalism is the end of the road, while for the Marxists it is only one of the stages, and the end will come after capitalism, when it in its turn will be overcome by the proletarian revolution, the building of socialist society, and finally, by the rise of Communism. Therefore Marxism sees itself as something even more modern than modernity itself, as the ideology of the future, which has moved much further away from the paradigm of Tradition, from Platonism and Aristotelianism than the First Political Theory.

Declinations of the Atom: The Individual and Fate

Marxism disputes liberalism for the right to define the essence of the paradigm of modern political philosophy.

Marx is perfectly aware of the genealogy of his teaching, its origins, its metaphysics, its stages. It is highly symbolic that Karl Marx's doctoral dissertation is devoted to Epicurus and Democritus,[9] while Marx's favourite philosopher is the substantialist Spinoza. The point is that Marx is well aware of the origins of his own philosophy in what we have called the political philosophy of the Mother. It is ancient atomism, it is Epicureanism, it is Democritus. Marx is very conscious of the paradigm of political philosophy with which he deals, which he inherits and on which he builds his own doctrine.

Marx especially dwells on what in Epicurus' system is called 'deviation' (declination), i.e. the ability of the atom to deviate spontaneously from a linear trajectory of motion. In this feature of the atom (or the individual, since Marx is well aware of the direct connection between physical atomism and social individualism), Marx sees a connection between freedom and necessity, which he understands dialectically. Necessity does not consist in the atom's strict adherence to a straight line, but rather in the capacity to deviate from it, i.e. in the presence of a certain arbitrariness. But this arbitrariness does not lead in turn to chaos and disorder, it leads to 'development', because the deviation of the atoms from the straight line

---

9   Karl Marx, *The Difference between the Democritean and Epicurean Philosophy of Nature*.

generates their coupling and further dynamics, forming vortices and 'images', '*eidolons*', i.e. bodies and worlds. And in the same way the 'arbitrariness' of the play of atoms generates life, life consciousness and society. This is what necessity is, wherein a multitude of arbitrary atomic volitional impulses are combined into a progressive chain of causes and effects. Thus freedom turns out to be fatalism, and fatalism is not freedom directly, but only when the observer is able to grasp it from a certain distance. This is precisely what Marx later does when constructing his model for interpreting the history of human society. Individuals act freely, and that is why they move through history along the axis of an unforgiving mechanical fate.

For Marx, Epicurus is a particularly important figure. From his point of view, Epicureanism enlivens the somewhat abstract atomism of Democritus by adding dialectic to it, so that phenomena become not just 'appearances' (*eidola*), but expressions of a deeper individual origin.

Gradually, these intuitions of the early Marx would lead him to create his own political philosophy, at the heart of which lies a clear awareness of the unity of thought with the pre-Socratics.

Prometheus' Titanic Rebellion

Marx is keenly aware of his profound connection not only with Democritus and Epicurus as pre-Socratic materialists, but also with the mythological figure of Prometheus. Marx understands himself to be a titan and a God-fighter, challenging the heavenly vertical order. In the preface to his dissertation, Marx writes:

> Philosophy, as long as a drop of blood shall pulse in its world-subduing and absolutely free heart, will never grow tired of answering its adversaries with the cry of Epicurus: "Not the man who denies the gods worshipped by the multitude, but he who affirms of the gods what the multitude believes about them, is truly impious."
>
> Philosophy makes no secret of it. The confession of Prometheus:
>
> "In simple words, I hate the pack of gods"

is its own confession, its own aphorism against all heavenly and earthly gods who do not acknowledge human self-consciousness as the highest divinity. It will have none other beside.

But to those poor March hares who rejoice over the apparently worsened civil position of philosophy, it responds again, as Prometheus replied to the servant of the gods, Hermes:

"Be sure of this, I would not change my state

Of evil fortune for your servitude.

Better to be the servant of this rock

Than to be faithful boy to Father Zeus."

Prometheus is the most eminent saint and martyr in the philosophical calendar.[10]

Marx is absolutely clear about the continuity and mythological connection of his philosophy with active theomachy, the rebellion of the Titans. The hatred of God, of the vertical, of the philosophy of the Father and the philosophy of the Son, is an essential element of Marxism as a worldview. Although for Marx himself both the pre-Socratics and even more so the Greek myths seem to be naïve and extremely crude forms of thought, long surpassed by the philosophy and science of the New Age, from the perspective of *Politica Aeterna* his references and metaphors take on a fundamental significance. For the paradigm of modernity, everything referring to the paradigm of Tradition is something ridiculous, naïve and, moreover, incorrect. For *Politica Aeterna*, cross-evaluations can be meaningful: not only to understand how modern sees premodern, but also how premodern sees modern. Postmodernism also claims this distance, but is unable to acquire it because it is too deeply engaged with modernism, which continues to affect postmodernism even as the latter implements its deconstructive strategies. Therefore, Marx's confessions about his sympathies for atoms, emptiness, as well as titanism, theomachy and even Satanism, can be taken with all due attention and credibility. Although for Marx neither titans nor Satan exist, and he uses these images as

---

10 Karl Marx, *The Difference between the Democritean and Epicurean Philosophy of Nature*.

metaphors, for the titans themselves or for Satan, Marx exists regardless of whether he believes in them or not. At least this is the lens through which some of Marx's (especially early) statements can be interpreted, if one truly equates all three kinds of being from Plato's *Timaeus*, recognising the legitimacy of political philosophies that prioritise any of them.

Still, it is most likely that since Marx did not believe in God, he did not believe in the devil either.[11] Marx believed in man, but he interpreted man himself in the spirit of Promethean titanism and even God-fighting Satanism. This gives us a particular Satanic titanic humanism, representing the metaphysical and anthropological basis of the Second Political Theory.

Matter, titans, Satan rebelling against God are vivid figures, highlighting in every way how the political philosophy of Marxism rebels against the political philosophy of the Father (Plato) and the Son (Aristotle).

Marx Is the Modern

Marxism as a political philosophy starts within the following milieu: there is the First Political Theory, there is liberalism, there are Hobbes and Locke, there is individualism, there is the middle class. There is commerce and economics instead of politics. This thesis had already been formalised as an ideology by the time of Marx. Bourgeois ideology was directed against the medieval Christian worldview, against Catholicism, against the Holy Empire, against the sacred state.

Marx has this to say: we agree with this ideology, with the First Political Theory, with capitalism and liberalism; we have indeed moved away from class society, replaced politics with economics and commerce, abolished patrimonial hierarchies and moved towards a class principle where all have equality of initial opportunities. In everything that concerns the struggle of the bourgeoisie against the feudal system (that is, against the preceding socio-political formation), we are in solidarity with capitalism and the bourgeoisie. But from here on the differences begin.

---

11   A detailed study on Marx's Satanism was undertaken by Pastor Richard Wurmbrand (1909–2001). See Richard Wurmbrand, *Marx and Satan* (Westchester, Illinois: Crossway Books, 1986).

The Marxists support everything about the struggle of the bourgeoisie against what came before it, and in comparison with the proponents of the Middle Ages, Marxism looks like a 'pro-capitalist' doctrine. But when capitalism wins, it will not be the end of history, but the beginning of its most important phase. For once the bourgeoisie has triumphed and liberalism has defeated traditional society, Marx believed, the tensions within this political order will start to intensify. Instead of the prosperous existence, the growth of the middle class and the enrichment of all as predicted by liberals, the class discrepancies between the bourgeoisie and the proletariat will begin to crystallise. At the same time, they will take place against a background of growing international tensions between bourgeois states and cyclical crises of the capitalist system as a whole. Thus capitalist society will begin to degenerate and decompose, splitting more and more between two poles — and then the time of Communism will come. The hour of Communism does not come before capitalism, not during capitalism, but when capitalism takes place and triumphs, replacing the preceding ideological models — then it will be replaced by the proletarian revolution and Marxism. In doing so, the Communists will take full advantage of all that the liberal order will create.

> The proletariat will use its political supremacy to wrest, by degree, all capital from the bourgeoisie, to centralise all instruments of production in the hands of the State, i.e., of the proletariat organised as the ruling class; and to increase the total productive forces as rapidly as possible.[12]

Socialism is thus a logical continuation of capitalism and the conflict between the two is the same as between the present and the future. Compared with the past, both the present and the future are qualitatively different and are even on the same side of the time axis. But at the same time, if we contrast the present with the future, a different situation will emerge. Thus, in *The Communist Manifesto*, Marx and Engels write:

> In bourgeois society, therefore, the past dominates the present. In communist society the present dominates the past.[13]

---

12 Karl Marx and Friedrich Engels, *The Communist Manifesto*, Chapter 2.
13 Ibid.

In this way Communism is a step into the future compared to the bourgeois order, which in turn is a step into the future compared to feudalism; although, according to Marx, the bourgeois order cannot free itself from the past completely, only qualitatively changing rather than completely overcoming, and at times even sharpening, the inequalities inherent in traditional society.

Thus Marxism fits into the political philosophy of the modern, having nothing against its liberal dimension so long as it is a question of confronting the medieval model. And here he agrees entirely with Adam Smith that the source of wealth is not land, but mobile production (i.e. industry, entrepreneurship). When it comes to the transition from domination by landlords, who control the surplus product through control of land and land rents, to the growth of industrial production and the shifting of the centre of the economy to the cities, Marxists support this process. In the course of the development of capitalism, there is a transformation of *estates* into *classes*, which is fundamental to Marxism. The estate hierarchy is determined by the position of the family in society while the class hierarchy is determined by the relation to the means of production.

But when capitalism has won, when bourgeois society is established, this is where the most important point, the *class struggle*, begins.

Marx thinks of Communism as the political theory that comes *after* liberalism. Marxism is post-liberalism. And he is not criticising liberalism on the grounds that liberalism itself is bad — it is *relatively* bad. From the Communist point of view, liberalism is bad in relation to Marxism, but not in relation to the Middle Ages, traditional society as a whole. In relation to traditional society it is good. This is a very important distinction.

Two modern worldviews — liberalism and Marxism — are competing with each other as to which one is more in keeping with the spirit of modernity, more avantgarde, more modern. It is a contest for the fullest consistency with the philosophy of the third kind — the Mother (earth, matter, multitude, *chora*). Both the first and the Second Political Theories are an equally *titanic rebellion* against the Father and the Son, against Plato's philosophy and against Aristotle's philosophy. And within this rebellion of ideologies it will be determined, in a competitive confrontation and desperate struggle, which of the two trends of contemporary political philosophy will win, and thus which of them belongs to the future — in its progressive, modernist understanding.

Both of these ideologies are rooted in Hobbes, Locke, Spinoza, earlier in nominalism, and even earlier in Democritus, Epicurus and Lucretius. Accordingly, common to them is the recognition of being in matter, substance, in the lower end of the cosmos in the generalised scheme of *Politica Aeterna*. Although it is precisely the Communists who imbue the identity of *being* and matter with a directly political character and make *being* an ideological dogma. For Marxists this is due to the fact that Communism represents the 'future' and so it must clearly, openly and explicitly proclaim what in liberalism is implicit and even at times somewhat obscured.

So, in the context of modern political philosophy, the First Political Theory (liberalism) and the Second Political Theory (Marxism) are in full solidarity with each other in relation to those political paradigms which treat the question of *being* radically differently (like political Platonism and political Aristotelianism), recognising the unconditional superiority of the third kind described in the *Timaeus* — the political philosophy of the Mother.

The Dialectic of the 'World Inside Out'

Marx draws on Hegel's *dialectic* in his critique of liberalism as well as for his system as a whole. Hegel's system is grounded in the position that the structure of the world, the structure of thought and the structure of being are based on a dynamic contradiction.

Hegel (1770–1831) argues that genuine consciousness is *unhappy*. Unhappy consciousness does not at all mean that it needs to be made happy. Happy consciousness, according to Hegel, is the state of an idiot. Genuine consciousness as such is always unhappy because contradiction is vividly actualised in unhappy consciousness and this, in turn, constitutes the basis of thinking and the main distinctive feature of the world. An unhappy consciousness arises by virtue of the fact that the subject does not coincide with the object, which creates tension and motivates active thinking.

Spirit is conflict, and since, according to Hegel, history is the unfolding of Spirit, history is conflict.

Consciousness has an object in front of it, but this pair is not the end of it. By shifting onto itself and retaining its relation to the object, consciousness generates representation. Hegel, in *The Phenomenology of Spirit*, calls this the 'world turned upside down' or 'world on the inside out' (*die verkehrte Welt*). He writes:

> Superficially regarded, this inverted world is thus the converse of the first,[14] in such a manner that it has the same outside of it, and repels from itself the mentioned first as an inverted actuality; that the one is the phenomenon, but the other the Being in-itself; the one is it as it is for others, the other on the contrary as it is for itself; so that [...] what tastes sweet, tastes really or internally in the thing, sour; or what on the real phenomenal magnet is north pole, would be on the inner or essential being, south pole; what makes its appearance on the manifested electricity as oxygen-pole, would be on the non-manifested electricity the hydrogen-pole. Or an action which is transgression in appearance, might be internally really good (a bad action, having a good motive); punishment, merely punishment in appearance, but in another world a blessing for the transgressor. Such antitheses, however, of internal and external, of appearance and the Super sensuous, as of two different kinds of actualities, are here no longer extant. The repelled distinctions do not divide themselves again into two substances, which would support them and furnish them a separate subsistence, through which the understanding would again fall back out of the Internal to its former place.[15]

Man forms an image of the world in his mind in tandem with the world itself, and this image does not coincide with either his thinking or the world itself. This exacerbates the problem. The human spirit is a kind of illness, indicating that the subject's ends do not fit together. This splitting, according to Hegel, is at the heart of spiritual activity. Human thought is a derivative of the underlying disease of thinking, which is thrown into the process of immanent existence as a trace of the primordial subjective

---

14   Author's note: the first world, i.e. the object.
15   G. W. F. Hegel, *Phenomenology of Spirit* (Oxford: Oxford University Press, 1976), p.238

Spirit preceding the emergence of nature (as the moment of the alienation of the subjective Spirit from itself).

Thus, the subject, the object, and the 'world inside out' as a particular representation give rise to the complex structure of the dialectic of consciousness, its phenomenology, which Hegel considers on different levels.

Marx takes from this the notion of the conflictual nature of history — and in this respect he is a consistent Hegelian. Liberalism is non-dialectical. It is analogous to an atom moving in a straight line. Bourgeois thought sees history as a process based on equilibrium and choosing the most optimal path of development. Hence appeals to the growth of the middle class, the bourgeois understanding of progress, equality of opportunity, etc. Here the pivot is the market and its central figure: the merchant. Liberals say: remove the state and business will find a better way to organise the social system. The atoms move in a straight line. The invisible hand searches for the optimum ways of communication and the most efficient means of enrichment. Market society is built as follows: it is the merchant who goes first, and everything is lined up behind him. And if he is not hindered, he will build an optimal system, a society that will develop in harmony and balance.

Marx objects: nothing of the sort. Development is struggle, it is conflict, it is dialectic. Therefore, the bourgeoisie is not the product nor the crowning achievement of the natural evolution of social and political forces, but only a phase, a moment of this dialectical confrontation. And the next peak of dialectical confrontation must be Communism. That is, for the liberal, liberalism is the peak of history; for the Communist, it is the dialectical moment. So, its place is twofold: it is better than the previous achievement, but worse than the one that follows.

Moreover, capitalism is an 'inverted world' that detaches itself from the object, producing a reverse representation of it, but remains stuck at the level of this representation. The bourgeoisie is unable to break through to matter as the being of the object and, since the being of the object is primary, and since matter itself is alive, it is unable to attain the most authentic nature of the subject that has emerged from matter. 'The world inside out' has to be turned over again (via a revolution), but not to return to the pre-representational — 'naïve' — state of the subject and its uncritical perception of the object (the 'first world', according to Hegel), but by taking the next step forward, which will bring a new form of consciousness, enriched by the experience of representation, into resonance with reality.

This is why Marx says: I am the future; this is why Marxism conceptualises itself dialectically as an ideology of the future. Importantly, this future here is not so much chronological as philosophical: the Communist thinks of himself as representative of the future already in the present, attacking capitalism not from the position of today, but from the position of tomorrow.

The Immanent Eschatology of the Proletariat

Marxism's appeal to the future is a fundamental feature of this worldview. This reveals its eschatology, and consequently its connection with Hegel's 'end of history' thesis and even more deeply with Thomas Münzer and other Anabaptists, who within the framework of the Protestant Reformation came to an extreme form of religious proto-communism in anticipation of the Second Coming of Christ. The Anabaptists abolished private property and established communes based on complete property equality, seeing no point in accumulating or possessing wealth in the face of the end times. All distinctions between people were abolished, since the end of the world was at hand, and people were to focus on the soul and spirit rather than on the body.

In Marx we see a secular version of this Anabaptist moment. The atheist Marx does not, of course, wait for the return of Christ. Being is material and there is no transcendent beginning. But nevertheless, the future represents a qualitative upheaval, a re-turning of the 'world inside out', which in its scale is comparable to the 'end of the world' (albeit upside down). History is driven by the inner laws of matter, which unfold dialectically. The capitalist world does not abolish exploitation, but takes it to a new level. This is how the working class proper, which is a messianic phenomenon, emerges for the first time. But unlike the Anabaptists, the commune does not expect the coming of God. The proletarians, as titans, are called to liberate themselves, overthrowing the bourgeoisie which, without having this goal in mind, nevertheless fostered the formation of class dichotomy. Thus, Communism appears as an immanent form of eschatology in which a triumph of matter takes place, going through a complete cycle — from the non-living state via life to society, its history, and finally to an epoch of equality and freedom, in which the atoms of matter, becoming conscious atoms of society, will attain fullness and perfection. Communism is thought of as the building of paradise on earth.

But at the same time, Marxist imagery, with its aggressive rejection of the religious vertical — which it also identifies in capitalism, only in the naked state where the will to material possession acquires an overtly explicit character, previously hidden under complex idealist and theological systems —, is not drawn toward ideas of 'heaven' or 'the end of the world', but rather to the successful triumph of the titans and giants, ancient powers of the underworld, flesh from mother-matter, who had carried out their revenge on the deities of Olympus and threw them all into oblivion. The messianism of the Communists is utterly immanent. It is not the coming of a Saviour from Heaven, from the world of Spirit, but on the contrary, the realisation by the population of the underground, by those who have no share in the wealth of the world, that they are their own saviour, which opens to them the possibility of reversing the expropriation of the products of their own labour and becoming masters of matter.

Here it is entirely appropriate to speak of the titanic and even Luciferian nature of the working class, who carry the light of labour and who are liberated from the bonds of bourgeois exploitation. Proletarians are not messengers of heaven and of the gods; they embody the coming of the titan, Satan or Prometheus. Thus we are dealing with a special eschatology, no longer Christian or Protestant (as with the Anabaptists), but secular, materialist, and even theomachist.

The fundamental historical strategy of Marxism is based on this. Marx says: we have to overthrow the capitalists, but only *we*. And if any carrier of pre-capitalist ideology tries to approach *us*, outwardly in solidarity with our own anti-capitalism, we should get rid of him immediately. Not every kind of anti-capitalism is acceptable to Marxists, only post-capitalist (that is, Communist) anti-capitalism of the future and not of the past.

If a society does not yet have capitalism, it cannot have socialism. Capitalism must be established first, and only then Communism. This is the peculiarity of Communist eschatology: the titans can only defeat the gods after these gods acquire material natures and descend into the worlds of matter, at which point they become dependent on the titans and vulnerable to them.

Therefore Communists are forced to defend capitalism where it does not yet exist or where it has not reached maturity. Class society is necessary as a precondition for the emergence of the proletariat, the messianic class. If there is no class society, there will be no proletarian revolution. If there is no proletarian revolution, there is no socialism; if there is no socialism, there is no Communism.

The Splintering of Class and Ontological Antagonism

The conflictology of Marxism and the introduction of the dialectic into the understanding of history dramatically alter the overall structure of the liberal interpretation of political history. Marxism becomes a critical theory that analyses capitalism in a way that capitalism itself cannot. This is why Marx's major work, *Capital*, is so world-famous.

Liberalism operates with only one class — the middle class. The division of society into three classes, accepted in sociology, is a kind of conditional division which does not have the same meaning as the definition of class in Marxism. Liberalism operates with only one class — the middle class. The division of society into three classes, accepted in sociology, is a kind of conditional division, which does not have the same meaning as the definition of class in Marxism. From the liberal point of view, the middle class is constantly growing, and in the long run, as all societies become more democratic and liberal, all of humanity will become middle class and the gap between the very rich and the very poor will shrink. The large bourgeoisie will become smaller and smaller compared to the middle class, and the number of poor and paupers will shrink.

Accordingly, the middle class will sooner or later become *the only class*. This is the utopia of progressive liberalism, which claims that the general increase in the well-being of each individual will sooner or later turn all of humanity into a middle class.

This is quite logical for liberal political philosophy, since it operates with one normative figure — the merchant — who is taken as the common denominator of economic anthropology. We can say that from the point of view of liberalism, there is a middle class, a 'very middle' class and an 'insufficiently middle' class. From here, the ontology and anthropology of the middle class emerges.[16] To be a member of a market society means to be middle class.

And what do Marxists argue? That there is no middle class as such and that the middle class has no essence. There are originally two antagonistic classes (not one): the *exploiting class* and the *exploited class*. Of course, an individual can pass from one class to the other: a person can either leave the position of exploited and become an exploiter, or remain exploited, and an entrepreneur can go bankrupt and be forced into the position of a hired labourer. But this does not concern the fundamentals of social and economic anthropology. For Communists, class is more primary than individuals. It reflects the very dialectics of history and the movement of matter. And the laws of this dialectic are based on antagonism: hence the fundamental thesis of the *class struggle*.

From Marx's point of view (and in this he follows Hegel), although the quantity of material goods increases, it still represents at any given moment some fixed value for which two classes (the exploited and the exploiters) struggle. Wealth (and here Marx follows Adam Smith) is created by labour and appropriated by the exploiter. All value that can be created is exclusively labour, material — and all of this value is taken from the working class by the exploiter. And, according to Marx, the more value the working class creates, the more value the exploiting class takes from it. Thus, there is no equitable distribution of wealth among all, but rather the opposite — the impoverishment of the working class and the enrichment

---

16 Karl Polanyi, *Selected Works* (Moscow: Территория будущего [Future Territory], 2013).

of the exploiting class. The poor become poorer and the rich become richer. In this Marx combines both the growth of total wealth and the dynamics of their distribution, which makes his theory quite flexible. The important thing is not who owns the critical volume of wealth at a given moment, but how the process of its redistribution in society is organised, which reveals a rather convoluted strategy by the capitalists themselves to seize the surplus value arising as a result of increasing efficiency and quality of labour and technological progress.

From the liberal point of view, the development of capitalism is harmonious and its internal crises are nothing more than corrections to the backbone of the infinite progress of production and the linear accumulation of material goods. Whereas, from the Marxist point of view, the internal crises that liberalism undergoes are a manifestation of the conflictological, dynamic, paradoxical, dialectical nature of history and even of matter itself. The conflicts and crises of liberal society are therefore vital, fateful. They reflect the essence of history, which consists in struggle. Hence, the two antagonistic classes building their struggle around the singular theme of possession of material wealth reflect the algorithm of the dialectics of *being* itself, where — according to the atomists — there is a complex game between atoms and the Great Void. Most subtle in this dialectic, however, is the determination of who actually represents the atoms (δέν) and who represents the Void (οὐδέν).

Class Definition and the Battle of the Concepts

The main driving force of history for Marx is the class struggle. It is quite clear that both the middle class of capitalism and the two classes of Marxism (the workers and the bourgeoisie) are purely abstract concepts. We are talking about a particular conceptual ensemble, which, when accepted as a basic methodology, offers one or another explanation of reality. Here we are dealing with the analogy of atoms and emptiness as Democritus understood them: their existence is postulated strictly rationally, and in concrete phenomenal experience we have no chance to encounter them, as the sensual world is a distant derivative of these concepts.

That is the point of political philosophy: it operates with concepts postulated in the field of thought, which are then projected into society and ultimately determine its structure and its derived phenomenology. Having accepted the completely unproven thesis of anthropological pessimism, from it we come to Hobbes and 'man is a wolf to man' as the main characteristic of the 'natural state', and from here the essence of the 'social contract' that establishes the Leviathan is derived. In actual fact, we do not know any 'natural state' of man and we base our conclusions on observations and inferences, which could be disputed by someone. But the acceptance of Hobbes' model in his explanation of the nature of man and the resulting nature of the state, gives rise to the foundation of the political organisation of society in modern times. And we have been living inside Leviathan — exactly as Hobbes designed and justified it — for several centuries.

But once we accept a different thesis, such as Locke's thesis that the 'state of nature' can be harmonious or neutral, on which Adam Smith, free trade and liberalism in general relied, we get a particular ideology which insists on the weakening and gradual abolition of the state. And again, this has been put into practice for centuries, leading to globalisation and the emergence of post-national structures such as the European Union. Anthropological optimism (as unproven as anthropological pessimism), based on a different form and structure of conceptualisation, produces a completely different discourse and then a different politics and, ultimately, a different reality. Meanwhile, the argument between 'realists' and 'liberals' is ongoing, usually failing to convince either party of anything.

Rousseau's positive conception of human nature, even more optimistic than Locke's, prepares the ground for socialism and Marx himself, which in turn changes the political landscape of reality again, giving rise to Communist regimes.

This is what the Political is all about, it comes from concepts, which in turn belong to one or another sector of *Politica Aeterna*, and then translates into practice, becoming an object. That said, historical praxis itself, contrary to some philosophical theories, proves nothing. Political reality is always a projection and, given the will, the power and the right conditions, various ideological models can be put into practice with equal success. This is the ontology of the Political and the essence of the ideological struggle: it is not a mathematical proof, where the more logical, convincing and consistent wins, but a clash of fundamental or less fundamental attitudes, whose victory over contrary or alternative attitudes does not at all mean they are 'true'. It is a battle of concepts, a semantic war directed into the depths of the concepts themselves, which in the course of their defence and realisation reveal more and more their underlying philosophical foundations. So, for example, the atoms of Democritus and Epicurus, whose existence had been claimed as early as antiquity, were only comprehended and taken on board under Gassendi and Galileo, and formed the basis of science, philosophy and politics even later under Hobbes and Locke. And it is precisely to Democritus and Epicurus that the young Marx turns to to justify the metaphysical basis of his worldview, which will be fully developed later. He reflects on their concepts, both analysing their original form and tracing their historical — and even political (in liberalism and capitalism) — expression and development.

The debate between a single (albeit still only potential) middle class (which liberals advocate) and two antagonistic classes (which Marx and Engels insist on) is precisely a battle of concepts. It is decided in the very fabric of political history, not in scientific discussions. Liberals postulate linear progress, where the growth of the middle class under capitalism will sooner or later include all of humanity. It is a concept, but it is also a programme, a strategy, and an action. Marx, on the other hand, argues that there is a war between labour and capital, not for life but for death. Hence, the representatives of labour, the proletarians, form one army and capital, the bourgeoisie, the other. Both the middle class and the two antagonistic classes are conceptual calibrations of society, whose mechanisms can be described and explained, but cannot be proven. By postulating class warfare, Marx enters into it, claiming to be the chief strategist and marshal of Labour's army. This is generally accepted in the twentieth century by the vast majority of the leftist labour movement.

For Marxism, the proletariat proper is born as capitalist relations take shape. But the birth of the proletariat itself is not a historical accident, it is the final expression of a historical pattern, the final formula of a much older war between exploiters and exploited. Pre-capitalist societies also had a class-based structure (the Traditional paradigm), but it was in the bourgeois age that this was fully revealed. Marx believes that classes existed in both antiquity and the Middle Ages. But they had been formed even earlier, along with the appearance of the first property and social inequality in primitive societies, when the transition began from the state of 'primitive communism' to the initial primary stratification. But all of history has been a movement towards the elucidation of the main conflict between labour and capital, between the proletariat and the bourgeoisie. The whole history of human society has been a battle over the distribution of wealth; from the very beginning there have been inequalities in this area, which have only been subsequently exacerbated. Since Marx is a materialist, it is the possession of material goods that he considers the main content of the historical process, the driving force of time. Therefore, for example, Marxism views medieval estate society as a *veiled class society* — that is, it also had classes, though they were not represented directly, but indirectly through estates. Hence the Marxist thesis that the task of both the Church as the First Estate and the aristocracy as the Second Estate is to justify the appropriation of the surplus product. Platonism, Aristotelianism, religion — for Marx, all these are nothing but a concealment of the true nature of the exploiting class and its ideological justification. That is, the estates of pre-bourgeois society and, accordingly, the main forms of philosophy and the Political are regarded by Marx as 'pseudo-bourgeois'. The clergy and the nobility for Marx are the hidden bourgeoisie. Marx believes that he has brought them 'out into the open' by exposing that, with the help of various myths and fairy tales, they are only exploiting the masses.

This is where Marx derives his radical anti-religiosity and militant — Promethean — atheism, his thesis that religion is the opium of the people. It should be noted that Communism is a rigidly anti-Christian, anti-church doctrine that sets out to fundamentally eliminate religious discourse itself, since that discourse, from Marx's perspective, is nothing more than a way to deflect attention from the real social dynamic, which is the exploitation of the workers by the ruling classes. In this view, any religion is a form of concealing an exploitative society built on inequality. Instead of explicitly stating that the workers and peasants must obey the king or pay tithes to the Church because they are their masters, it is explained to the workers as their religious duty. Thus, for Marx, the clergy, priests, warriors and aristocracy — who in traditional society constitute the sacred hierarchy, which in their own eyes reflects the spiritual verticality inherent in the world as such, as impressively described in Platonic philosophy — are the 'hidden bourgeois', concerned only with appropriating the material products of labour. Accordingly, the whole conceptual side of traditional society — the philosophy of the Father and the philosophy of the Son — is decisively rejected in favour of an overriding interpretation of *being* based on materialist concepts. Once again, it is a question of concept versus concept.

Marx does not believe in concepts that reject his own conceptuality. In polemics and propaganda, he mocks them and tries to show their inadequacy against reality. But reality for him is his own conceptual construction, or rather its projections.

Accordingly, for Marx, while an openly class-based (bourgeois) society shows that social position is directly related to the means of production, estate society hides this materialistic reality under the mask of religious ideology. Therefore, while capitalism is the embodiment of inequality, it carries the benefit of displaying this inequality in its most appropriate (i.e. material) form.

The Genesis of the Proletariat

The way in which Marx imagines the class nature of society as a whole and the way it is revealed in the course of the historical process should be described in some detail.

The very first state of humanity, according to Max and Engels, was 'primitive communism'. This was the starting condition of humanity, which evolved from primates that began to use tools. According to Marx and Engels, the evolution of humanoid apes into humans occurred precisely when the apes began to use tools, establishing an ontological distance between themselves and the world, embodied in a concrete object. In this way, the foundation was laid for a subject-object relationship.

At the first stage, cavemen lived in a state of complete equality, and this primordial collectivism was an expression of human nature itself, but only in its naïve — prehistoric — form, not yet hardened by dialectic — negation and negation of negation.

The notion of the original tool of labour transforming an ape into a human being, and of 'primitive communism' itself, is another concept, an abstraction, necessary for the construction of a theory. Darwin's theories and the observations of zoologists are used to substantiate this theory, but they cannot conclusively prove anything, they merely enrich the Marxist discourse with vivid details. However, these conceptual images and figures are necessary for the integrity and coherence of the Second Political Theory and its philosophy.

Then, as the instruments of labour improve and individual subjectivity strengthens, social stratification begins, accompanied by a gradual increase in property inequality. Here Marx and Engels follow Rousseau with his inherently good 'noble' savage, who is spoilt by social relations built on political and social inequalities. What Hobbes portrayed as the natural state, Marx attributes to the beginning and simultaneously the consequence of politics, the introduction of inequality. Again we are dealing with a war of concepts, and by accepting one or the other we will come to very different and sometimes antagonistic conclusions about the very nature of the Political.

As soon as political communities were formed and leaders appeared, class distinctions began to emerge in societies on the basis of inequality. For centuries and millennia, the material essence of these differences remained potential, implicit, hidden by numerous ideologies, which legitimised first the patrimonial order, then patriarchal families, later the slave system and finally feudalism. It was only under capitalism, Marx argues, that the masks were cast off, and from then on, society was openly ruled by those who owned the means of production.

That is to say, capitalism is a form of ultimate, shameless, open exploitation. Before capitalism, the ruling classes formalised their domination with the help of idealist constructions. For Marx, these 'ontologies' served only to conceal a basic, fundamental reality: the meaning of political society is the exploitation of man by man. This exploitation of class by class was the true content of political history.

Certainly this is a radically materialistic and even trivialised interpretation of man, the world, life and culture. Ideals, beauty, love, exploit, sacrifice, loyalty to God, suffering, martyrdom mean nothing to Marxism. All that matters is material goods and ways of redistributing them. That is why Marx did not understand the Middle Ages or the ancient world as separate civilisational phenomena; to him, all of them were hidden capitalisms, veiled by artificial ideologies, intended to camouflage the true nature of material inequality and exploitation. According to Marx, there is only one decisive distinction: either the material goods are distributed justly (equally) or unjustly (they are appropriated by the ruling exploitative capitalist elite).

For Marx, the notion of the class-based essence of society extends to all types of society, modern and non-modern. However, modern bourgeois society talks about it openly — this is the meaning of the bourgeois revolution according to Marx. Now all things fall into place: whereas before the truth was hidden, now the problem is marked out. There are those who exploit by owning the means of production — the bourgeois class — and there are those who are exploited — the workers and, to a lesser extent, the peasants.

Thus Marx believes neither the Middle Ages nor Plato and Aristotle. He believes only Democritus, Epicurus; he is a materialist from a metaphysical point of view. For him matter is alive, it is the meaning of history, and consciousness is the peak of matter's development. Overall, this is a purely Satanic and titanic perspective on the human spirit rising out of the earth. Such an interpretation is a perfect illustration of the Swineopolis, which is what all types of normative societies are in the political modern age. Without refuting the 'swine' nature of man — which, in fact, Marx tries to romanticise when it comes to describing the flowering of individual creativity in a Communist society —, he insists only on the equality of distribution and the absence of any hint of a socio-political vertical. Thus, in his version, it is equality that should be the basic law of the Swineopolis, whereas the liberal version believes that freedom is paramount.

When the bourgeoisie emerges as a class of purely material exploiters, along with it the people of labour, the exploited, also change their nature, gradually forming themselves into the urban proletariat, the second class, the aggregate pole antagonistic to the bourgeoisie. Those who were peasants or artisans in the Middle Ages and estate society form a new phenomenon, purged of additional and secondary (for Marxists) features and reduced to pure materiality.

The Concept of the Proletarian: The Minimum Man

The *urban proletariat* has no ties, no qualities — it embodies the element of *pure labour*. It is the unskilled working class, which came from the countryside and completely abandoned its qualities (religious, family, traditional), forgot its culture, folklore, all ties to local customs; it is a working element without properties or traditions, and is the central figure, the subject of Communism. Man, who has broken away from culture and become a mere machine, who produces material commodities, is the carrier of the element of labour itself.

Once again, we are dealing with a pure *concept*. Just like the stick-wielding monkey that transforms into a Cartesian subject, the total equality of the peace-loving cave-dwellers, the theologian who deliberately builds multistory scholastic structures, cults and rituals in order to rob the simple toilers with impunity, and finally, the bourgeois himself, driven only by material passions and egoism. Moreover, while Marx could observe the capitalist image with his own eyes — especially since liberal ideologists, also predominantly materialists and atheists, thought in a similar way —, the degree of approximation increases and the purely speculative nature of the image becomes more and more evident as Communist thought moves deeper into history, to a point where in the realm of apes and 'primitive communism' we deal with pure arbitrariness — quite analogous to Democritus' constructs describing how atoms are separated from the original Great Void and coalesce into whirlwinds.

The proletariat is a pure concept. In reality, the urban worker represents an entirely different figure. Almost always (even in Adam Smith's example of the baker) we are dealing with someone who was recently a peasant. First he was a peasant, then he became an indentured labourer for the baker, but in fact he retains a connection to an organic community, endowed with a culture, a particular self-awareness, numerous qualitative properties. His economic activity never exhausts his world, being only one aspect of it. The proletarian does not even exist etymologically, since the very word *proletarius* connotes a pejorative sense of those who can only produce children and are capable of nothing else. For Marx, it is important to emphasise the pure materiality of the worker, his connection to the most primal element of matter, and for this he sought a term in which the qualities would be reduced to a minimum. The proletarian is the smallest quantum of the human element, reduced to the lowest level of ontology. It is the overthrown titan, driven into Tartarus by the Olympian gods and deprived of his share in a world which once belonged to him (primitive communism). Depriving him of all his properties presents him compressed to the limit, but that is exactly what Marx wants.

Importantly, the concept is not neutral and is, indeed, acutely polemical. In principle, those who disagree with the Second Political Theory do not simply criticise the Marxist interpretation of this figure, but deny its existence altogether. For the liberal, the proletarian does not 'exist' because this state is unstable and transitional on the way to the middle class. Therefore, the proletarian is not a class, but a subclass or otherwise a 'potential bourgeois' (a very petty bourgeois). There is also no proletarian from the point of view of political Platonism or Aristotelianism, because for them there is no atom, emptiness or matter itself. Consequently, here we are dealing primarily with the peasant, with the artisan, the householder, the member of the clan, of the family, of the village, the member of the religious community or even of the sect, but all these represent qualitative characteristics. In other words, the fact that the proletariat and the bourgeoisie are ascribed 'existence' only means that there is a conceptual projection by a political movement, which tries to give practicable (phenomenological) status to this or that theoretical attitude. In principle, we have the same in the case of the middle class in liberalism, etc. However, the difference in conceptualisation between liberals and Marxists takes place within a common context defined by the basic principles of modern political philosophy, where materialism and atomism prevail. Therefore, the main dispute at the conceptual level is over which ideology is more modern and therefore more materialistic, atheistic, secular and atomistic — in a word, more progressive, understanding progress as the development of matter, technology and the highest form of the evolution of life, in the form of society.

The political philosophy of traditional society is constructed according to very different principles, rejecting not just Communism or liberalism, but the very political ontology of modernity. Here one cannot speak of concepts in the same sense as in the case of liberalism and Marxism. For the Platonists, ideas are not a concept, that is, they are not a product of the human mind. For Aristotle the *eidos* is also not a concept, but the essence of a thing, autonomous from the human subject — though somewhat differently than it is for the Platonists.

This is the fundamental significance of what we call *Politica Aeterna* and to what this course is devoted. Political philosophy needs to be interpreted in the frame of reference in which it describes itself, while trying to separate the inevitable polemical, partisan, rhetorical and evaluative ideologies projected onto it. Marx himself admitted that ideology is a 'false consciousness', i.e. that a concept is only an approximation to the truth, but not the truth itself. For him, the truth itself is matter and its deepest and most autonomous dimensions. One can only break through to it with the help of science. But in order for this science to come into being, it needs to be freed from the influence of bourgeois ideology. Herein lies the epistemology, ontology and political science of the Second Political Theory, and this is how it needs to be interpreted. Here we see a kinship with liberalism — stemming from the common belonging of the first and Second Political Theory to the paradigm of modernity, and in this is already a fundamental difference from the philosophy of the Political Traditional Society — but also a peculiarity of Marxism, which differs from liberalism as one ideology from another; meanwhile, the terms class, ideology, etc. cannot strictly speaking be applied in relation to the traditional society, since its very structure does not allow such conceptualisation.

Value as the Basis of a Revolutionary Narrative

Once Marx establishes these two conceptual classes, he launches into a massive war against the main conceptual adversary, which he labels the notion of capital. In the nineteenth century, we can indeed see some phenomenological signs of the middle class and its growth. At first sight, it seems that political-economic history itself confirms that the bourgeois philosophers, the First Political Theory, were right. To prove that this is not the case and that, in fact, there is not one inclusive class but two antagonistic ones operating in history, Marx delves into studying the secret mechanisms governing the operation of bourgeois society. Thus Marx's major work, *Capital*, is born.

In it Marx demonstrates how the process of the exploitation of the working class by the bourgeoisie takes place, which procedures enshrine the rule of capital in the structure of society, and how these structures are concealed by bourgeois ideology.

At the heart of Marx's teaching is another fundamental concept, that of 'value'. Here again, as in the case of the classes, it is a struggle of concepts above all else. Liberalism knows neither the concept of the proletariat as Marx interprets it, nor the Marxist concept of value. The expression 'value' itself appears as early as Adam Smith, who distinguishes between 'value in exchange' and 'value in use', but it does not play a major role in his theory.

From the perspective of liberal theory, in a market economy, it is not value that matters, but *price*. Price is thought of as the cornerstone around which the entire market structure is built. The pricing process is related to the balance of supply and demand. Accordingly, whoever *offers* the goods produced to the market at a price takes into account their own expenses, prospects for development, and risks. Depending on the existing demand, this price is adjusted. In some cases, the price may be unprofitable for the producer, and then he goes bankrupt (for instance by not being able to repay the loan, etc). In other cases he makes a large profit. Price, therefore, encompasses the whole market, becoming the point where the whole process of production converges to a quantitative monetary equivalent, and, from the other side, the whole consumption structure, which also includes the consumer's financial resources, the scale and acuteness of his needs and a host of social and cultural factors, is reduced to the same point. Price is fundamental because it strips away the significance of all those constituents which led to its designation. However, there is neither a 'fair price', nor can there ever be one: there is only the price at which the producer is prepared to sell the product and the consumer is prepared to buy it. Everything else disappears into the brackets and is dismissed as irrelevant.

The concept of the 'value' of a commodity also disappears here. If the entrepreneur has paid too high a price to produce certain goods, thereby increasing the cost of production, and the competitive market offers a lower price, then the producer ends up making a loss. He is forced either to sell at a discount or stay with the unsellable goods, or even destroy them. In such a case, the value of the goods produced but not sold, the amount of labour, resources and technical operations expended to produce them are irrelevant.

In a real market economy, everything is not determined by value but only and exclusively by price, and value can only serve as a secondary indicator suitable for technical price justification before a commodity enters the market; even then in complex market mechanisms, e.g. on futures exchange floors or in high-risk economic segments, prices tend to be almost completely detached from value. In principle, this autonomy of prices is the basis of stock market speculation, which is the most reflective of the essence of a capitalist economy.

According to liberalism, you cannot say exactly *how much a thing is worth on its own* — it is exactly as much as the price at which it is offered and at which it is bought. If people refuse to buy at a certain price, the price goes down. The question of how much a thing is really worth cannot be answered. Not at all. In a liberal political economy there is no value; it is a contingency. Therefore it is impossible to say whether a thing is worth it or not. If a thing is not bought, it is not worth it.

Price is the main pillar of the market, and that is the meaning of capitalism. It is the economic expression of 'freedom'. Everyone is free to produce anything, and everyone is free to buy anything. No one has the right to compel anyone to produce or consume, or to fix a certain price for a good or service. Everything is determined by the market, which is a space of freedom.

Hence an important conclusion: from the point of view of the bourgeoisie, since there is no value, there is no exploitation. The share of wage labour in the formation of the price is a secondary factor, one of many indicators which influence the price but do not determine it. The entrepreneur has to pay the workers one way or another, regardless of whether he makes a profit or loses out in the sale of goods. He is also responsible for credit. The risk of the market game renders what the workers and the labour itself have produced void of any *autonomous value*.

Accordingly, liberals ask, can we in this case speak of the exploitation of man by man? No, because nobody has appropriated anything. If the bourgeois has done the job successfully, he has profited; if not, he has lost. The worker, on the other hand, chooses a guaranteed wage, a lack of anxiety, and he pays for this peace of mind by not sharing in the profits, but also by not bearing the costs in the event of a loss. The entrepreneur, on the other hand, takes a risk, chooses a hectic life, and it is this risk that gives him the chance to get more. But this, in the eyes of liberals, is not guaranteed. One makes a profit and the other suffers a loss. One manages to get rich, the other does not, and he goes bankrupt. In the same way, a bank that risks its loans can go bust and fail.

In such a conception of the economic process, in such an economic narrative, there is no room for value or exploitation. If a worker does not want to be a wage earner anymore, he can take a chance, save some money or take out a loan and start his own business. If all goes well, he will become an entrepreneur himself. But then he will be forced to take risks and depend on the forces of the market. For the liberal, everything depends on the free choice of the individual: if we provide equal opportunities, people will either become rich or poor, but *entirely on their own account*. There is no exploitation because there is no value. There is no autonomous commodity in and of itself, there are no self-significant constituent elements; there is only price. If the commodity is not for sale, then it is not worth anything and no one is exploited.

Liberal materialism is a materialism of money, a materialism of the dynamic market element. And the fundamental element here is the market pillar. And since price depends solely on the relationship between supply and demand, there is no such entity as value independent of price. But for Marx, there is.

The introduction of value as a standalone category, as a concept, drastically changes the entire structure of the description of the market. We are dealing with an entirely new narrative about capital and capitalism. If there is value, then the economy is not based on price, but on the reality of the commodity produced. But if the central concept of economics is not price (as a market fundamental), but the actual availability of the commodity, then we are dealing with an entirely different view of the essence of economics. Here the thing itself is placed at the centre of attention, not its representation in the form of price. This is a peculiar kind of *economic materialism*. Marx immediately thinks of the economy outside the market. But in this case it is a different economy and a different society, a society where production and consumption are connected in a radically different manner than through the market. Production and consumption converge not to the price of the commodity, but to the commodity itself. This gives rise to the centrality of value as the economic (but not market) fundamental of the commodity itself.

Marx proceeds from the premise that it is labour that creates material value, and value is equal to the labour put into it. At the same time, conceptual and out-of-market value does not disappear in the market, but hides itself. Marx is called one of the 'masters of suspicion', because behind the absence of something he sees a dialectical concealment which must be revealed.

If value, not price, is the basis of the economy, then we are not dealing with one economy, but with two overlapping economies. One, explicit, bourgeois, is built around price; the other, implicit, is built around value. The former can only be market, the latter can be either market or non-market. The non-market — i.e. socialist — economy is an economy of value, distributed equally among all members of society. But before we distribute, we have to determine the equivalent of what is being distributed, and *that* is value.

But socialism, the emancipation of the economy from the market, is a future prospect. It is also possible exclusively in the context of a conceptual narrative of value, but this narrative can also be applied to the present. This is indeed the main content of *Capital*: the description of capitalist society from the position of value — that is, from the suspicion that capitalism's own narrative of value conceals something, is false. Specifically, its falsity lies in the concealment of the concept of value in favour of the concept of price.

If there is value, then the market is built around a particular commodity, a product, which has value. It is created by labour. So, in terms of justice and equity, value must be distributed among its creators. There is labour, there is a product, there is value.

But that is not how it works in the market. The capitalist pretends that he is the main figure in the economy, responsible for the ups and downs of the market game. He wants to present things in such a way that labour is of secondary importance, and what matters is not the product itself, the real object, the economic atom, but the profit or loss that arises in the course of its placement on the market. For Adam Smith, this was the meaning of 'exchange value' or 'market value', but this is not at all what Marx meant by 'value'. Marx asserts: sold or not, market or not, the thing produced is there, labour has been put into it and therefore it has value. If the thing produced cannot be sold as a commodity, then it can be used in some other way — for example, given away for free or taken by the one who produced it. And value does not disappear from this non-market existence. Consequently, capitalists also deal with value, seeking to capture it, and the market serves as a specially designed element for this purpose.

The appropriation of surplus value by those who own the means of production is the main mechanism of capitalism which leads to the growth of capital and wealth, and at the same time to the growth of inequality.

If value is the result of labour, then no matter how much is expended to produce a commodity, its value will always include the value of *labour* itself. Thus labour adds value to a commodity. Marx calls it added value. In production there is an *accumulation of value*. It is this added value that the capitalists appropriate for themselves, under the guise of risk and the market element. In this way they profit from the undervaluation of labour and explain it away with entrepreneurial and trade risks.

But if this is so, then the bourgeoisie become the exploiters and the workers become the exploited. Marx shows that the capitalist economy, the capitalist states, the capitalist media, the capitalist entertainment industry, fashion and technology are all nothing more than a process of veiled robbery by the bourgeois class of the surplus value that is created by the proletarian class in the process of labour. Therefore, from Marx's point of view, instead of the growth of the middle class, the workers are only getting poorer and the bourgeoisie is getting richer precisely because it appropriates the surplus value.

Value both justifies the existence of two antagonistic classes and becomes the basis of the class struggle in the construction of a socialist society in which there is to be no market, no exploitation and no capitalist class. The value created by labour must be redistributed directly among the workers.

This is how the Second Political Theory justifies its conceptual apparatus.

Ideology as False Consciousness

Developing his doctrine, Marx argues that the proletariat must form what the bourgeoisie has already formed — ideology. According to Engels, ideology is 'false consciousness'.[17] This is all the same Hegelian concept of the

---

17 Karl Marx, Friedrich Engels and Fritz J. Raddatz (ed.), *The Marx-Engels Correspondence: The Personal Letters* (London: Weidenfeld & Nicolson, 1981).

'world turned upside down' or 'world inside out' (*die verkehrte Welt*), which we have already discussed.

Ideology is some form of presentation of conceptual reality which is taken as a basic paradigm. Antoine Destutt de Tracy,[18] who introduced the very notion of ideology, understood it to mean *bourgeois ideology*, that is, the bourgeois class's understanding of the world, society, history and itself, and the laying of this ideology at the foundation of society and social transformations.

For Marx and Engels, capitalism is a form of social order based on an 'inverted world', on the concepts of 'false consciousness' instilled by the bourgeoisie in itself and, to an even greater extent, in the exploited classes.

But Marx calls for more than just a fight against 'false consciousness'. He believes that as the contradictions in bourgeois society intensify, an alternative ideology to the bourgeois one will gradually emerge. This is Communism: the proletariat will begin to read Marx's writings, assimilate his conceptual positions, learn to understand and reproduce, and if necessary, complete and develop the Communist narrative.

The first step is for the proletariat to realise itself as a proletariat. We are talking about a concept in the Marxist sense of the word, that is, as a class. When the worker becomes aware that he is a class, he realises that he must not pursue his own individual interests, but act on behalf of and in the interests of the class as a whole. This is a special collectivist form of consciousness, not borrowed from the bourgeoisie (as liberalism promises everyone, sooner or later, to become a middle class), but antagonistic in its attitude, ready for class struggle, revolution, and the final overthrow of the capitalist order itself. If one begins to realise oneself as a class, one begins to act differently — historically, socially, politically.

In order to be conscious of oneself as a class and to be prepared to engage in the class struggle, one must understand that the results of labour are being systematically usurped by the exploiting class; that labour creates true wealth, value, and not some contingent wealth dependent on

---

18 Antoine Destutt de Tracy (1754–1836) was a French philosopher, politician and economist.

the elements of the market game; that by creating value, the working class always also creates surplus value, which is in fact fully appropriated by the exploiting class. And this condition will last forever, because the total amount of wealth in society, created by labour and the accompanying development of the means of production and technical progress, comprising the total amount of surplus value, will always fall entirely to the capitalists, while the workers will continue to spend their days in poverty and ignorance. It is therefore time for the proletariat to wake up, to take up arms and to destroy the bourgeoisie.

This is the point of Marxism. The first step is for the proletariat to realise itself as a class, then form political Communist parties, and finally, when the capitalist system collapses, to begin a general strike which will develop into a revolution, so that the socialist order and dictatorship of the proletariat can be established.

It is often overlooked that, for Marx himself, Communism is also an ideology, i.e. a form of 'false consciousness'. Here one can also see echoes of Democritus, who believed that 'truth is in the abyss' (ἐν βυθῶι γὰρ ἡ ἀλήθεια) — that is, he saw insurmountable limits to the rational understanding of reality itself. But Marx has a somewhat different — more optimistic — interpretation. If bourgeois ideology is a lie, proletarian ideology, although not yet the truth, is closer to it. The truth as such, i.e. real knowledge about a matter, can only be reached through science. However, science is a social phenomenon, and as long as the bourgeoisie rules, it saturates science itself with its ideology. Therefore, bourgeois science is notoriously ideological and, as such, not entirely scientific. In order to liberate science from ideology in general, we must first liberate it from the completely wrong bourgeois ideology and subordinate it to Communist ideology, and then move towards science proper, which will no longer be 'proletarian' externally, under the influence of Communist ideology, but internally, in its essence, which means reaching, as far as possible, the truth (in Marx's case the truth about matter, material truth).

But the very recognition of the status of Communism as an ideology is quite telling, because with this amendment we can more accurately imagine the entire political paradigm of modernity. It is the clash of ideologies, that is, of 'false consciousnesses', of conceptual structures. That is the meaning of the ideological struggle. Nothing is proved or argued in it. In both cases, liberalism and Communism, it is ideology, not science (however we understand it). And if one strictly accepts Marx's definition of the nature of ideology, then one should note that only modern political phenomena can be attributed to it. Traditional societies — Platonism, Aristotelianism and religious societies — did not know ideology. They were not conceptual systems in opposition to each other. They were dominated by ontology, metaphysics, theology and philosophy in the most general sense, which served as the basis for formulating ideas about being, man, society, state, politics, etc.

Hence, strictly speaking, we can only speak of three political ideologies — liberalism, Communism and nationalism. They all emerged in modern times and they are all built on a conceptual basis, as three varieties of 'false consciousness'. We are dealing with 'upside down worlds', however we interpret them.

Therefore, to understand them, it is important to first identify the central axial concept or series of concepts that make up the overall narrative. Arguments, examples, objections, criticisms, etc. carry a purely rhetorical load. In a battle of concepts, proof is no more appropriate than in an interconfessional discussion.

Antonio Gramsci: Autonomy of the Superstructure

Marxism had an enormous influence on the intellectual landscape of the twentieth century, and a significant number of thinkers were fascinated by its critical theory. Elements of Marxism were added to a wide variety of philosophical currents and schools, further enhancing its influence, but also somewhat diluting its ideological rigour and conceptual uniqueness.

One of the most consistent and orthodox Communists of the twentieth century was the great Italian philosopher Antonio Gramsci[19] (1891–1937). He was a staunch supporter of Russian Bolshevism and an opponent of Italian Fascism from its early days.

---

19   Antonio Gramsci, *Le Opere. Antologia* (Milan: Nuova Iniziativa Editoriale, 2007).

Antonio Gramsci was the left-wing thinker who, more than any other, reinterpreted the phenomenon of the Russian Revolution and Leninism. In doing so, he did not stop at justifying this phenomenon within classical Marxism, but with a great deal of intellectual courage proposed to rethink, and in some ways to correct, some of Marx's teachings.[20]

Classical Marxism viewed politics as a 'superstructure' (*Überbau*) over an economic 'base' (*Basis*). According to Marx, political revolution (i.e. the qualitative transformation of the superstructure) is *only* possible when the necessary preconditions on the level of the base (structure) are in place. The base is the economy, the superstructure is politics and everything else.

The linear dependence of the superstructure on the base was the basis for some European Marxists to refute the orthodox nature of the Russian Revolution and to deny Bolshevism the right to be part of classical Marxism. In early twentieth-century Russia, the sufficient conditions (most importantly in this case, the presence of developed industrial capitalism) *did not exist*, but the fact of a socialist proletarian revolution *did*. Lenin himself and the rest of the Bolsheviks following him tried to prove that these prerequisites were in place, and that industrial capitalism had developed in Russia by the beginning of the twentieth century. But this was an obvious stretch and considerably weakened the ideological position of the Bolsheviks among European Marxists. Gramsci, who lived in the Soviet Union from 1922 to 1923 and who witnessed the social transformation of the USSR at its earliest stage, offered a different explanation of Bolshevism. From his point of view, in some cases, under certain historical circumstances, the superstructure (i.e. the political sphere) can have a *relative independence* from the base and, in turn, *influence* it. Thus, there is not a linear relationship between the structure (base) and the superstructure (where the former completely predetermines the latter), but a more complex and dialectical one: although the superstructure (politics) is an expression of the base (economy), it can actively influence the base,

---

20 Antonio Gramsci, *Prison Notebooks* (New York: Columbia University Press, 2011).

qualitatively transforming it in turn.[21] According to Gramsci, this is exactly what Russian Bolshevism demonstrated: the Bolsheviks, as a political force (superstructure), seized power in an agrarian country and quickly transformed the base into an industrial model. For Gramsci, this was *proof of the relative autonomy of the superstructure*.

But Gramsci does not stop there. Having substantiated the relative autonomy of the superstructure, he expands its content to include, along with politics, the realms of *culture*, science, and the humanities as a whole. Gramsci introduces the concept of the '*intellectual*' as a third figure, on a par with the politician and the worker/capitalist pair. The economic relationship between labour and capital divides the roles in the base (the structure of society). The bourgeoisie creates its parties, where the common element is dependence on capital, while the proletariat creates its revolutionary party, the Communist Party, defending the interests of the people of labour. But having formed on the level of the superstructure, the parties gain a *certain autonomy* over the base. If the Communist Party is strong and effective, it is capable not only of giving battle to the bourgeoisie, but also of *changing* the base. This is the lesson Gramsci draws from Leninism.

But the second component of the superstructure is just as important — the figure of the intellectual.[22] The intellectual is as free and as dependent on the base as the politician. But only he can, in turn, be independent of politics directly, while at the same time remaining the spokesman of class interests. The intellectual may not be a proletarian and may not be a member of the Communist Party or of any other labour party, but at the same time, through his work — in art, philosophy, journalism, etc. — he can *stand on the side of the proletariat*.

---

21 Antonio Gramsci, *Il Rivoluzionario Qualificato. Scritti 1916–1925* [The Qualified Revolutionary. Writings 1916–1925], Rome: Delotti, 1988.
22 Antonio Gramsci, *Gli intellettuali e l'organizzazione della cultura* [Intellectuals and the organisation of culture], Torino: Einaudi, 1948.

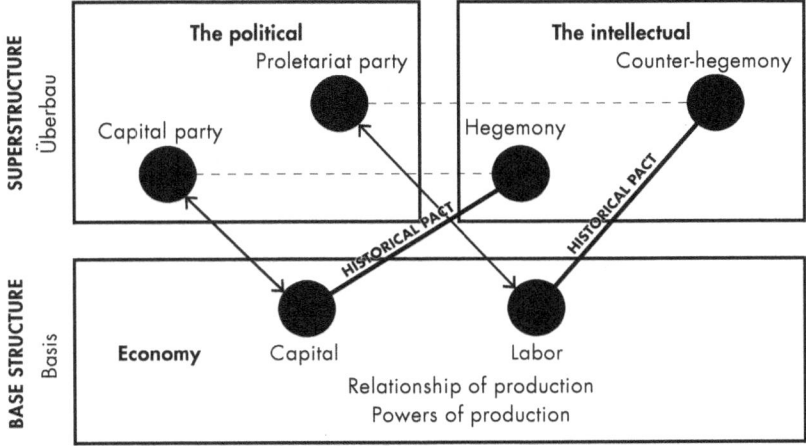

Figure 18. Antonio Gramsci's version of Marxism.

At the same time, the intellectual, even of proletarian origin, *can side with capital* without necessarily belonging to the bourgeois parties. The intellectual's choice lies on a *different* plane. Here Gramsci introduces the notion of 'hegemony'. He understands it as the intellectual's spiritual *solidarity with the bourgeois worldview in its most profound and paradigmatic core*. Hegemony consists in seizing the consciousness of man, who henceforth begins to serve the cause of the expansion of capital, whose nature gravitates towards maximum expansion over the entire territory of the planet (this Lenin called 'imperialism'). It is a conceptual gesture, a choice of concept and groups of concepts.

By siding with capital, the intellectual who chooses to serve the hegemony makes a *'historical pact'* with it. Such an intellectual may be paid by the bourgeoisie and collaborate with the bourgeois parties, but he may just as readily not be paid or act as a collaborator. The historical pact is made on another level: the intellectual either recognises the historical correctness of capitalism, liberal ideology and the bourgeois reforms of society, or not. And it goes deeper than the mechanics of class or bribery. It is a spiritual choice that reveals the height of human freedom — every thinking person (everyone, according to Gramsci, is an intellectual insofar as he thinks systematically) can either side with hegemony or reject it.

If he rejects hegemony, he automatically sides with *counter-hegemony*. This too is a historical pact, but this time made by the intellectual with *labour*. And again — this pact can be independent of cooperation with the Communist Party. The choice is realised in the broad field of culture, science, philosophy, art. This field represents an *autonomous* segment of the superstructure. And it is no less important and no less independent and influential than the domain of the Political. If the autonomy of the Political is proven by Leninism, the theory of the intellectual, of hegemony/counter-hegemony and of the historical pact is entirely Gramsci's own work.

The End of History in the Second Political Theory

The Marxist worldview is characterised by a clear and explicit view of the historical process. The emergence of intelligent life is a consequence of evolution. Then political history begins, moving from primitive communism through patriarchy, slavery and feudalism to capitalism. According to Marx this is not an accident but a law. The socio-economic formations succeed one another in a strictly definite sequence. Therefore, all other nations of the Earth shall tread the same path the West has trod, in which Marx reveals his Eurocentrism and even cultural ethnocentrism (cultural racism).[23] These stages were traversed during Marx's lifetime, and there were a few more to come, which Marxists wanted to approximate and facilitate.

The logic was as follows. After the aggravation between the proletariat and the bourgeoisie has reached its peak, that is, when the bourgeois urban society has been completely built up (i.e. the majority of the population has migrated from the villages to the cities and created megacities), when capitalism becomes the dominant socio-political system and bourgeois ideology becomes global, at that point the proletariat (which by that time constitutes the majority of humanity) will begin to realise itself as the subject of history, the creator of value and world wealth, will acquire class consciousness, will internalise Marx, will organise political movements that unite into a world proletarian International, and will eventually carry

---

23 John Hobson, *The Eurocentric Conception of World Politics: Western International Theory, 1760 -2010*, Cambridge: Cambridge University Press, 2012.

out a proletarian revolution. Something along these lines happened in Russia in 1917, although Marx himself and the European Marxists were convinced that this could not happen in Russia — due to the absence of bourgeoisie and proletariat, and its agrarian character — at least not at the initial stage. Nevertheless, several generations after Marx, this part of Marxism's historical conceptualisation was also translated into reality.

Marx himself believed that once the proletarian revolution had been realised the proletariat would abolish private property, dispel the chimera of the middle class and destroy the bourgeoisie. In this way, the whole of society would live according to the laws of equality. The surplus value, which is created as a result of the labour of the workers, would be distributed to the whole of society. For this, in the initial stages, a socialist proletarian state must arise, which, under the leadership of the Communist Party, will be responsible for redistributing the products of labour more or less equally among all the strata of society, while at the next stage, under Communism, even the socialist state will disappear as it fulfils its function; people will become conscious, creative, truly individual (as individual atoms are) and receive all they need, contributing as much effort and labour as they can or wish to the society at large (the new people of Communism will have a consciousness of the highest standard of collectivist altruistic morality).

The construction of Communism is the end of history, which goes through a complete cycle from atoms carrying on in the Great Void and forming vortices, to life, consciousness, history representing a dialectical deviation from the original simplicity of matter, and up to a new return to the fullness of materiality, but not in the form of the atom, rather in the form of a moral and conscious Communist man, in which the materiality of the atom as a thing-in-itself is transformed into a free creative individuality as a thing-for-itself, having traversed the whole path of alienation, of being-for-others. What lay beyond, however, was not at all clear to Marx: Communist humanity was to conquer the universe, rushing across it in flying machines — like the atoms and whirlwinds of the Hellenistic atomists, spreading Communism as an ideology and science everywhere.

In the USSR and other socialist countries, socialism was built — that is, even this part of Marxism's historical dogma was fulfilled. With regard to equality in the Soviet Union, Marx's criteria were generally satisfied. All people were more or less equal materially and income differences were insignificant. On average, by the end of the Soviet Union, most people earned 100 rubles — and this was more or less enough; high wages were considered 200 or more, low wages 50-70. There were differences, of course, but compared to today, they were negligible.

But the transition to Communism, which to some Soviet leaders, such as Nikita Khrushchev (1894-1971), seemed like a matter of a few decades, was accompanied by processes which could not be explained by the Marxist theory of socio-economic change. The productivity of the socialist countries was not growing in proportion, the world revolution was not taking place, and, moreover, its preconditions were dissipating, while the self-consciousness of the Soviet people was becoming confused and morality was becoming more and more 'petit-bourgeois', i.e. egoistic and utilitarian.

Thus the practical implementation of the Marxist version of history failed and socialist societies collapsed. Among them only China (as well as Vietnam, North Korea and Cuba) survived, but China only survived by fully adopting a liberal market economy from the 1980s while retaining power in the hands of the Communist Party. Chinese Communism has moved even further away from Marxist orthodoxy than Soviet Communism.

Together with the end of the USSR and socialism in Eastern Europe, the whole model of historical time, conceptualised in a Communist way, collapsed. Marxism simply did not envisage a return movement from socialism to capitalism, nor did it allow socialism to be built in one country. The ideological clarity of the Second Political Theory became clouded. The Marxist view of the logic of history is no longer perceived as self-evident and convincing. The conceptual side of Marxism has also suffered considerably, aided both by ideological struggles and by parallel processes in scientific circles, which were far from strictly adhering to Communist ideological guidelines, pulled between liberalism, Communism and

Fascism. This confrontation provided the freedom, albeit relative, to develop scientific concepts on the periphery or on the fault lines between ideologies. In a capitalist society, where Marxist predictions did not come true (although that is precisely where they should have come true), and after the fall of the USSR, the Second Political Theory lost its most important empirical foothold.

Of course, Marxism did not collapse because its predictions of a Communist end of history failed to materialise. The whole substance of Marxism, as of any modernist ideology, is concepts, which in themselves cannot directly relate to reality (cannot be either confirmed or denied), since reality itself is thought of as a concept in modernism as well. Therefore, the Second Political Theory was ideological not only about the future, but also about the past and even about the present (although in the present — that is, in the epoch of the rapid formation of capitalism in twentieth-century Europe — Marx based his ideas not simply on 'reality', but on the conceptual basis of liberalism and on the refined philosophical system of Hegel, which cannot be strictly classified either as modern or even as liberalism). But political theories and modern political ideologies have their own historical destiny. And instead of the Marxist end of history, we observe in our time the 'end of Marxism', which should be accepted as a fundamental fact of political philosophy, which can be explained in many different ways, but which cannot be denied.

The Significance of Political Thought and Its Price

A brief overview of Marxism in its conceptual foundations shows the significance of political philosophy in the environment — social, political and economic — and history of the most varied peoples. *Politica Aeterna*, its structures, its symmetries, its metaphysics and its conceptual systems are at first glance concerned with abstract and speculative subjects — both in the case of traditional society and in relation to modernity. Thus the differences between the first and the Second Political Theory, while uniting some common attitudes (materialism, individualism, progressivism, atomism) and stemming from the same type of philosophy (the philosophy of Mother), diverge at the level of some rather abstract concepts — class, value, base, dialectics of the atom, matter, etc. But the projections of these conceptual systems — ideologies (as forms of 'false consciousness') — into real life generate tremendous historical cataclysms — revolutions, bloody civil wars, battles between peoples and states, repressions that affect almost the whole of humanity. Thus a small gap in the conceptual apparatus, an interpretation of this or that term, a correct or distorted understanding of this or that socio-political, economic or historical phenomenon is paid for in rivers and even seas of human blood, millions of lost lives, great depths of suffering, and sometimes grandiose accomplishments and volcanic bursts of enthusiasm and galvanised happiness.

From concepts (bourgeois class, proletarian class, value, surplus value, exploitation, ideology as a false consciousness) a Second Political Theory emerges, which, once in power, begins to effect real change. However, Gramsci shows that in certain cases, it is the disposition of the superstructure — that is, the historical pact of intellectuals, which may far outstrip the condition of the mass, the base — that is of paramount importance.

Marx's worldview played a critically important role in twentieth-century Russia. His conceptual apparatus was adopted by the Bolsheviks, who carried out the revolution, seized power and built a socialist society, trying to follow the Marxist dogma as closely as possible. The Communists' rise to power presupposed the dictatorship of the proletariat and the extermination of the bourgeois class, and with it the rest of the non-proletarian classes — popes, nobles, landlords, etc.

Civil war, mass executions and repression, the breakdown of centuries of culture, the disappearance of the aristocracy and to some extent the peasantry were the direct results of the fascination with Marxism. Thus a totalitarian society was constructed in which the Second Political Theory came to be accepted as irrefutable dogma. The 'false consciousness' of the abstract proletariat (which, incidentally, never existed in Russia in sufficient measure) became for almost a century a natural and obligatory outlook, an intellectual landscape.

It is telling that in the early twentieth century the Marxist worldview was the domain of marginal groups (mainly the intelligentsia), the urban proletariat was insignificant, and industrialisation and the formation of the bourgeoisie was in its initial stages. The historical pact with Marxism, made by a very small but passionate and fanatical intelligentsia, decided everything.

Although the USSR itself was one colossal example of a socialist society, the influence of Marxism spread far beyond its borders. A similar system was established after World War II in Communist China, Vietnam, North Korea, some countries on the Indochinese Peninsula, Latin America and Africa, as well as in Eastern Europe. European Social Democracy, also based on Marxism, rejected Bolshevism and Maoism for the most part, but was also greatly influenced by Communist ideology.

In the 1960s, the successes of the socialist countries and the critical potential of Marxist philosophy were so obvious and impressive that many European countries also began moving towards socialism. In this period, not being a Communist meant, among European intellectuals, being a 'scoundrel' — it was viewed as an intellectual making a historical pact with the bourgeoisie, with the exploiters, with the forces of evil. This fashion was introduced first and foremost by the French 'New Left' — the philosophers Jean-Paul Sartre (1905–1980) and Albert Camus (1913–1960). Many members of Europe's artistic avantgarde had been Communists since the 1930s — for example, the leader of the Surrealist movement, André Breton (1896–1966). The appeal of Communism as post-liberalism was reinforced by the fact that it had already won in many countries and that the population of almost half the world was opposed to the capitalist system. Intellectuals thought that it could triumph in Europe, too, where tensions between the bourgeoisie and the proletariat were on the rise and where, at times, quite revolutionary events had already taken place, as in May 1968. A kind of counterpart of the Marxist revolution stirred up in France, one that was never brought to an end, but that nevertheless greatly influenced the French political scene. From then on, not only did it become culturally prestigious to be a Communist, but the dramatic rise of the Left led to the socialist François Mitterrand (1916–1996) coming into power. It seemed to many that Europe was moving in a Marxist direction. In some ways it seemed that Marx was not only partially and 'morally' correct, but also literally correct, including his promise that Communism would replace liberalism.

Of course, there was a fundamental difference between Soviet and European Marxists, as European Marxists had traditionally disapproved of Bolshevism, considering it Blanquism and adventurism; moreover, under the influence of the Trotskyites, Europeans had a particular dislike for Stalin, believing that he had created a totalitarian society in the USSR, not so much Communist as nationalist and bureaucratic. But what is significant is that socialism, as a Second Political Theory, represented for a long time a powerful current that was entirely at home in the New Age, operating with the same concepts as liberalism, but organising them in a radically different way and managing to rival the First Political Theory.

On the whole, Gramsci's theses on the historical pact, i.e. the recognition of the paramount importance of conceptualisation and ideology, were perfectly confirmed in European history, where the influence of Marxism, especially increasing by the late 1960s, changed the cultural, educational and social, as well as political and economic, environment in a qualitative way.

This is how Marx's political construction played an enormous role in the dramatic development of the twentieth century. His example alone demonstrates the decisive importance that thought, concept, ideology and philosophy play in the history of nations. This or that concept is formed in the mind of a philosopher or a few philosophers, is coupled with others or finds itself in opposition to them, and then millions and billions of people pay the price. That is how important thought is — it is what drives history.

CHAPTER 14

CLASSICAL AND REVOLUTIONARY NATIONALISM (THE THIRD POLITICAL THEORY)

The Genesis of the Third Political Theory

NATIONALISM IS a political philosophy which represents the third major branch of ideological development in the modern age. All political theories of the New Age, from the nineteenth century onwards, crystallise in one way or another, reaching their apogee in three fundamental political worldviews:

1) liberalism (the First Political Theory),

2) Communism (the Second Political Theory) and

3) nationalism (the Third Political Theory).

This sequence in enumeration of ideologies is connected with the order of their historical emergence: first, liberalism appears; then Marxism as a criticism of liberalism; and much later, only between the end of the nineteenth and beginning of the twentieth centuries, as a response and challenge to liberalism and Marxism, a full ideology of political nationalism takes shape in the form of Italian Fascism and German National Socialism (along with their analogues in other countries). Besides Fascism and National Socialism, the typologically similar political systems created by António de Oliveira Salazar (1889–1970) in Portugal, General Franco

(1892–1975) in Spain, as well as Justicialism by Juan Perón in Argentina,[1] can be attributed to the Third Political Theory. Thus, we can already see an indication of socialism in the very names of German National Socialism (though it is fundamentally different from Marxism), and in case of Italian Fascism, besides doctrinal similarity and sympathy of early Fascists to the USSR (which was initially mutual), you should take into account the fact that Benito Mussolini (1883–1945), the founder of the Fascist Party, was a socialist in his youth. Lenin spoke well of the early Mussolini and regretted that such a leader was lost for the European Left.

Twentieth-century Fascism and National Socialism represent a non-Marxist alternative to anti-liberalism. In general this was already foreshadowed by Marx in *The Communist Manifesto*, where there is a careful distinction between *anti-capitalism on the left* — that is, post-capitalism proper, which gradually developed into Marxism and a Second Political Theory — and various forms of *anti-capitalism on the right*, which oppose bourgeois society in defence of either the preservation of elements from traditional society (religion, estates, aristocracy, etc.), or do not accept the proletarian and internationalist dogma of the Communists, trying to combine socialism either with national elements or with a peasant estate. Later, the most consistent combination of socialism with the principles of estate society, embodying those tendencies of 'conservative socialism' that Marx criticised in the *Manifesto*, was proposed in the writings of Austrian theorist Othmar Spann[2] (1878–1950).

---

[1] Contemporary Greek political scientist Dimitri Kitsikis believes that since 1945, when Fascism suffered a crushing defeat in Europe, these kinds of ideologies have migrated to the Third World. Many Third World regimes, according to Kitsikis, in particular the Arab Ba'ath Party, combined right-wing and socialist, conservative and Marxist elements without being strictly socialist parties or capitalist. They represented a spectrum of variations on the Third Political Theory. Remnants of Ba'athist regimes, according to Kitsikis' classification, included the Iraqi regime of Saddam Hussein (1937–2006), Libya under Mu'ammar Gaddafi (1942–2011), and Syria's Hafez al-Assad regime (1930–2000); also many similar combinations of national and social ideas in the Palestinian Liberation Movement.

[2] Othmar Spann, *The True State: Lectures on the Demolition & Reconstruction of Society* (Vienna: Quelle & Meyer, 1921).

Marx argued harshly, in particular with Ferdinand Lassalle[3] (1825–1864), who defended a national or state socialism. His ideological opponents were the anarchists — especially P. J. Proudhon[4] (1809–1865), who defended a free federation of rural communities and denied the messianic role of the proletariat, and Mikhail Bakunin[5] (1768–1854), who accepted the Slavic and more broadly the southern European nations as a true revolutionary force, contrary to Germany and the northern European nations, which Bakunin considered too 'rational'. Later, elements of nineteenth-century National Socialism and certain currents of anarchism (especially in Fascist Italy) were integrated into a Third Political Theory — revolutionary nationalism. It is important to stress that this type of nationalism builds its ideology with reference to Marxism and anti-capitalist leftist theories and concepts, and therefore logically follows the Second Political Theory, which in turn was a critical reaction to bourgeois ideology (the First Political Theory, liberalism).

Bourgeois Nationalism and Revolutionary Nationalism

However, although a Third Political Theory — which should be understood as a complete ideology of revolutionary nationalism that takes into account the main points of socialism and Marxism and offers alternative concepts — did not develop until the twentieth century, nationalism itself appears almost simultaneously with the New Age and reflects precisely the main features of the political philosophy of modernity. Whereas revolutionary nationalism (in the twentieth century) is largely anti-capitalist and rigidly anti-liberal, we see, on the contrary, bourgeois tendencies at the origins of European nationalism. National states in Europe were formed under the influence of the Protestant Reformation and were political challenges to Catholicism and the Empire. Such bourgeois

---

3   Ferdinand Lassalle, *Macht und Recht. Offnes Sendschreiben [Might and right. Offne's epistle]* (Zürich: Meyer & Zeller, 1863).
4   P.J. Proudhon, *What is Property?* (Cambridge: Cambridge University Press, 1994).
5   Mikhail Bakunin, *Собрание сочинений и писем. 1828–1876* [Collected Works and Essays] (Moscow: Издательство Всесоюзного Общества политкаторжан и ссыльнопоселенцев, 1934–1935) [Publication of the All-Union Society of Political Torture and Penal Exiles, 1934–1935].

nationalism appears, therefore, at the very origins of modernity, and in a sense precedes even liberalism. Thus, in the field of economics, mercantilism, which insists on a state monopoly on foreign trade, developed long before liberalism; Adam Smith himself formulated his theories in polemic with the mercantilists. Later on, the same logic of bourgeois nationalism was steadily associated with protectionist policies and in the twentieth century became the basis of realism in international relations[6] — without any connection to the ideology of the Third Way, that is, to revolutionary nationalism.

Of course, there are certain common features between bourgeois nationalism, which emerged at the dawn of modernity, and revolutionary (anti-bourgeois) nationalism, which developed into a full-fledged ideology only in the twentieth century, largely as a reaction to the Second Political Theory — above all the declaration of national sovereignty as the highest value, elevating national identity to the status of the supreme subject of foreign policy, etc. — but in general they are different phenomena. The watershed here is in relation to the fundamental principles of capitalism. All types of nationalism, both bourgeois and revolutionary, are critical of liberalism (the First Political Theory), but bourgeois nationalism regards the market society and its principles (free trade, individualism, progress, etc.) as fully legitimate, while revolutionary nationalism rejects capitalism in its entirety. In this it is easy to recognise the influence of Marxist thought, only read backwards. Marx, repulsed by liberal political economy and its postulates, insists on the international nature of capital, on which he bases the alternative proletarian internationalism; for him the international character of capitalism is a dialectical point, necessary as a preparation for the world revolution of the proletariat, which must also be an international class. But the revolutionary nationalists (Fascists and National Socialists), while accepting the thesis of the international nature of capital (as both liberals and even more so Marxists insisted on), draw the opposite conclusion from it, arguing that precisely because of its international nature capitalism is not compatible with national sovereignty and will sooner or later destroy it, either directly, through international

---

6   Dugin, *International Relations (Paradigms, Theories, Sociology)*.

monopolies and financial structures, or indirectly through proletarian revolution. Therefore it is revolutionary nationalism that is the political theory, based on a profound philosophical and historical analysis of the main points of modernity and its interpretation in the First and Second Political Theories. Bourgeois nationalism, on the other hand, is not so much an ideology as a model for building foreign policy and especially economic relations with other countries. In domestic politics, such nationalism does not differ at all from the general provisions of capitalism and therefore liberalism.

Given this fundamental difference, we can trace the formation of nationalism itself — from the primordial and bourgeois to revolutionary nationalism, which had a relatively short existence in history.

Countries and Estates in the Feudal System

So, the roots of political nationalism are firmly planted in the New Age. It is a phenomenon of New Age politics and, consequently, nationalism belongs to that paradigm which we define in the terminology of Plato's *Timaeus* as the 'political philosophy of the Mother'. Thus, nationalism as a whole represents one of the strands of the materialist philosophy of the New Age.

Political nationalism is directly linked to the phenomenon of the *nation*. The nation is a bourgeois phenomenon that emerged at the dawn of the modern age along with the sovereign state, which in turn represented the antithesis of the Holy Empire. The nation is the population of a state created by means of a social contract. Thus the nation, as well as the state, is based on a social contract. The subject from which the nation is formed is the individual citizen. The phenomenon of a nation implies individual citizenship. It is a totality of individuals, of social atoms.

The nation is an artificial formation of a group of individuals considered to be rational and possessing their own singular will. It is the direct product of a social contract that proclaims the formation of some unitary structure. The unitary structure of the state means that the entire territory which appears within the boundaries of the nation consists of a homogeneous legal field, where all the citizens of that nation-state recognise a single law, a single language, a single regime, a single culture. These citizens are regarded as the authority that establishes the nation.

In French there is the expression *État-Nation* (state Nation), which shows the historical and political unity of the state and the nation, their indissoluble connection. In English the proper name is nation-state, but we must remember that the origin of this term places equal emphasis on both words. In *État-Nation* there is no adjective, it is two nouns.[7]

The nation emerges with the bourgeois revolution. Before the bourgeois revolution, there is the Holy Empire, the traditional state, the estate society. Estate society is not so much governed by nationally binding guidelines and rules as by the relations between the various estates, groups and alliances within a given society. At the same time, in this situation there will be certain cases where in some duchy there is a stable system, vassalage (there is a suzerain, vassals, feudal hierarchy), but the strict belonging of this duchy to Normandy, France, England or Germany is difficult to determine at various moments in the history of Europe before the modern age. They could belong to two states at once, or to neither, because the concept of the state is not yet standardised. The estates are more important than the state, the feudal system is more important than the national system, and the relationship between the vassals and suzerains is more important than the national affiliation with the territory to this or that kingdom. However, some territories could be directly subordinated to the Catholic Church, in which case the bishops acted as political rulers. Sometimes authority was vested in a union of rural communities. There were also a number of mixed forms. A fief was not simply the estate of a particular feudal lord or his family, it was a more complex body, sometimes allowing for a wide variety of government. During the Middle Ages, there were political and economic exchanges of service, labour, products and goods within the feudal fiefdoms. This exchange was most often in kind — goods for goods, service for service, etc. The feudal lower classes — the peasants, the serfs — had to serve as militia and provide goods to the lower nobility, who brought their troops into the armies of their suzerains, to whom they gave some of their products and goods, and so on up

---

7   For more details, see Dugin, *Ethnosociology*.

to the king. The church structure was also part of this feudal arrangement.

When moving from one suzerain to another, the vassal usually took with him those below him. But in general the attachment of this ladder to any one state — and its ruler, the king — was rather loose, and only made itself felt in cases of serious wars and conflicts. Most of the population may well not have known to which state they belonged at all. Everyone knew that they were Christians, and that their immediate suzerain was a baron, count or duke. The king was seldom heard of, and the concept of state was vague and approximate.

The political system in Kievan Rus was roughly the same until the beginning of the Muscovite period, when one can first speak of a semblance of national unity and centralisation of power. But in Muscovite Russia itself, the boyars had an enormous degree of freedom, and this was exactly what Ivan the Terrible fought against — his main reforms were directed against the free boyars (as an analogue of the feudal lords of the European Middle Ages). In the Time of Troubles, we see how autonomous the Russian nobility remained even after Ivan the Terrible.

The Nation as a Bourgeois Concept

The nation is created strictly in opposition to such a state of affairs, in opposition to such a class feudal system, in opposition to the medieval version of political philosophy. The nation is an anti-estate state. It is either the estates or the nation. Moreover, the nation is based on the principle of the dominance of the bourgeois type as the normative socio-political agent. And the bourgeoisie, as we have seen, is based precisely on equality of initial opportunities, which in practice meant refusing to take class privileges into account.

In a class society, individual identity is embedded in a *class identity*. Where, for example, do we get the common Russian surname 'Kuznetsov', which is identical etymologically and semantically to the English surname 'Smith', the German 'Schmidt', etc.? In the past, a person's surname (i.e. patrimonial name) reflected what he did. A blacksmith father had a blacksmith son, and a blacksmith grandson, and so on to infinity. The one who was 'Blacksmith' was a blacksmith. Such a surname was not possible for an aristocrat or a peasant.

People of medieval times defined their individual identity through their social function, profession, place in society, belonging to some fixed group of the class population. Accordingly, the surnames 'Medvedev' or 'Volkov'[8] are even more ancient, associated with hunters and gatherers, because in the course of initiatory practices the hunters changed roles with their victims, and the one who hunted must have been prepared to become a victim of the hunt. However, it is possible that in some cases these were rustic nicknames of later origin.

On the other hand, the surnames 'Ivanov' and 'Petrov' are very new — they appear to be native Russian surnames, but they are nothing of the sort. They emerge from patronymics during the census period, following Western European models. Commoners were asked: 'Whose are you? Ivan's or Peter's?', as these names were popular among the people and the individual was recorded by patronymic name which only later became a family name. This is already an element of individualism — the surnames 'Ivanov' and 'Petrov' tell us nothing about who the founder of the family was, in terms of the feudal model. These are modernist surnames. It was more traditional to call a person 'Krestyankin', i.e. 'son of a peasant woman'. This is closer to the Traditional paradigm.

Accordingly, the occupational surnames are a vestige of class society, while the paternal surname already signals a loss of traditional collective identity, a certain individualism and possibly a move by peasants into town, an entry into the bourgeoisie in general without characteristic professional traits.

Nation-states are based on individual citizenship. That is to say, it is the individual who is thought of as a member of the nation, the same atom which underlies the materialist worldview and its corresponding scientific conception of the world of the New Age.

---

8 TN: *medved'* meaning 'bear', *volk* meaning 'wolf'.

The Nation as a Product of Nationalism

The dominant figure of nationalism is the bourgeoisie. Therefore, *all classical nationalism is bourgeois*. It is a form of association of people who have broken their ties to class society and found themselves in the position of pure individuals. More often than not, it was the city dwellers, that is, the inhabitants of the *Burg*, the bourgeois. In order to assemble these individuals into some kind of managed and orderly social community, they are made to believe that they are *members of a nation*. The nation is an artificial construct, and it is born as a concept. The whole history of the nation is a product of the imagination of bourgeois nationalists.

All the main aspects of the philosophy of modernity, and especially the political philosophy of modernity, are concepts. The individual is the concept, and it is this concept that is most central and fundamental to modernity as a whole. In the first political ideology, the individual is taken as the main concept (perhaps this is why liberalism and its political victories over the alternative — illiberal — ideologies of the modern have been so stable). The proletariat, value, socio-economic formation are also concepts. They are central to Communism. The nation is another concept. It also operates with the individual, as in the case of socialism, but it gathers an agglomeration of individuals in a different scenario — not according to the class principle, but according to the state. The nation is the aggregation of citizens (= urbanites = bourgeois) of that particular state. Together they form the État-Nation, the nation-state.

The mechanism behind the emergence of modern nations and the intellectual and historical context of this process have been convincingly described by anthropologist Ernest Gellner (1925–1995) and sociologist Benedict Anderson (1936–2015). Gellner noted the artificiality of the concept of the nation, which has nothing to do with the historical existence of the people or medieval class society.[9]

These authors draw attention to a very important sequence in the formation of modern nations: in any situation, nationalists come first and

---

9 Ernest Gellner, *Нации и национализм* [Nations and Nationalism] (Moscow: Progress, 1991).

then the nation emerges. Gellner, in particular, insists that nationalism is not a consequence of the existence of the nation, but the nation itself emerges as a development of the ideology of nationalism. He writes:

> It is nationalism that produces nations, not the other way around. Of course, nationalism uses the pre-existing multitude of cultures or cultural diversity, although it uses them very selectively and more often than not radically transforms them. Dead languages can be revived, traditions reinvented, a completely mythical original purity restored.[10]

Nationalism invents the nation — i.e. a society that has never existed — but uses elements that are taken from the real historical experience of particular groups (ethnicities and the history of the people), taken out of context, stripped of meaning, and turned into a generally binding socio-cultural dogma imposed with the full might of the state apparatus.

Gellner stresses that the nation consists of a mechanical set of anonymous and alienated atomic citizens, but tries to pass itself off as a peaceful village community, cosy and familiar, where everyone knows each other and everyone shares the same habits and response patterns. To achieve this, the state machine is set in motion: education, codified language (idioms), works of art celebrating the nation's glorious exploits, some of which are real and some of which are invented.

Nation is a concept artificially created by a group of intellectuals in the transition from the paradigm of Tradition to the paradigm of modernity. Nationalist intellectuals take as their basis some ancient people or the name of some historical, cultural or political community, real or mythological, and declare the population, in part or in whole, of some modern bourgeois state, created in the course of the destruction of the medieval Catholic and imperial system, as direct heirs of a long-defunct ethnicity or tribe. The nationalists then indoctrinate the citizens of the state into believing that they are the direct descendants of those whose name they bear, and this allows an atomised, individualistic bourgeois society to be artificially coherent, to begin to imagine itself as the heirs of a myth. Anderson believes that this identity is strictly imaginary and often created

---

10 Gellnner, *Nations and Nationalism*, p. 127. [TN: translated from the Russian excerpt]

by romantic poets or artists. In reality, it is the product of the disintegration of class unity, which has long since replaced the organic community of ethnicity. But nationalism completely ignores this historical, cultural and political divide, becoming as artificial an ideology as liberalism and Communism, and as individualistic and materialistic as they are.

Such feats of imagination reached their extremes in the racial theories that were the most important aspect of National Socialism. Here it was no longer simply the concept of 'nation', but the larger and even more exotic and artificial — though equally modernist — concept of 'race'. Formally, National Socialism proclaimed the supremacy of the 'Aryan' race, i.e. the descendants of the Indo-European peoples. But at the same time, the pragmatic conditions of politics and the ultimate utilitarian ideology of the Nazis excluded not only the Indo-European Slavs but also the Celts from the 'Aryans', while the Italians were attributed to the representatives of the Mediterranean race. And the Romani people, also speaking an Indo-European language and coming from a quite 'Aryan' India and no less 'Aryan' Persia, were generally equated with subhumans on the basis of culture and phenotype. In terms of the political application of racism, Nazism is a most bizarre and sinister travesty. Here it can be seen that the term 'Aryan' refers primarily to the Germans, while those Indo-European peoples, with whom the historical Germans or even the Nazis themselves had political problems, were arbitrarily deprived of this status.

Gellner and Anderson demonstrate that all forms of nationalism are concepts that serve the interests of the bourgeoisie and are based on imaginative structures employed in a purely pragmatic and utilitarian fashion. And while nationalist myths are invented by romantics, sometimes without care for any practical application (as for instance James Macpherson[11] [1736–1796], who published his own poems under the guise of translating the ancient Celtic ballads of the bard Ossian, or the authors of the apocryphal Dutch Chronicle of Oera Linda[12]), in the hands of bourgeois politicians this became the conceptual basis of political ideology.

---

11 James Macpherson, *The Poems of Ossian* (Edinburgh: Edinburgh University Press, 1996).
12 *The Orea Linda Book*.

In fact, nationalism serves to break up class society, to place the bourgeois figure at the centre of society, to destroy the sacred world, to justify the secular character of statehood and to destroy the ethnic identity of peoples. The nation-state offers one language to all citizens, termed the idiom. Usually one of the dialects is taken as a model, most often the metropolitan one. The other dialects become *patois*, i.e. different from the national standard. Thus the diversity of vivid speech and local linguistic traditions is levelled before the mechanical and alienated uniformity of the idiom; all other dialects and vernaculars gradually begin to die out.

An Imagined Community

Another contemporary sociologist, Benedict Anderson, developing Gellner's approach, emphasised that the nation is a product of people's imagination.[13]

Like Gellner, Anderson describes the origin of the nation as a utilitarian construction of collective identity. Some new form of collective identity was needed to hold society together so that it would not collapse after the elimination of the estates. Benedict Anderson uses an interesting term, describing the nation as an 'imagined community'. The term 'community' refers to a group of people organically bound together by life, history, culture, origins, and many stable and long-lasting relationships. It is an organic unity of people who live next to each other — like a big family, a kind of a single collective being, where everyone not only knows but also understands the other. In a community, everyone is related to each other — brothers and brothers-in-law.

But bourgeois society has nothing to do with such a 'community'. On the contrary, in the process of the formation of capitalist relations, organic communities disintegrate into individuals. Communities are usually found in the peasant environment, on the land. The natural landscape of community living is destroyed in the transition to urbanisation, industrialisation and the forming of the bourgeoisie. And in this situation

---

13 Benedict Anderson, *Imagined Communities: Reflections on the Origin and Spread of Nationalism*, London: Verso, 2016.

bourgeois society is the product of the disintegration of the rural community, its end, its antithesis.

Ferdinand Tönnies devoted his research to the dualism of community (*Gemeinschaft*) and society (*Gesellschaft*), a crucial study for sociology and political philosophy.[14] Tönnies contrasts these two notions: community (*Gemeinschaft*) is based on the presence and preservation in the long run of living organic connections, while society (*Gesellschaft*) is a product of their disruption and isolation, as such, a disintegration of individual units (which gives us the figure of the 'idiot'). Society is an aggregate of individuals who have lost their organic ties with the community. When communities break up, a society is formed. And this artificial society is the bourgeois society, elevated into a political nation. That is why Benedict Anderson uses the term 'imagined' community. The nation is a collection of disparate elements, imagining themselves to be something whole. This is the difference between nation and society, and between nationalism and socialism. Socialism admits that it deals with a society consisting of individuals and proposes to connect them artificially, not imaginatively — again *e pluribus unum*, 'from many, one'. The nation, on the other hand, wants to make the multitude of individuals believe that they have something in common and that this commonality is organically inherent in them, when in fact this commonality stems from an artificially constructed political ideology and is simply imposed on everyone for strictly utilitarian purposes.

Thus the nation, in Anderson's eyes, is a bourgeois deception.

A Limited Body of 'Idiots' as the Ideal of Nationalism

The same separate individuals who, as we have seen, were called 'idiots' (ἰδιώτης) in Greece are assembled into a nation. It is not an association of people with qualities — clans, professions, roots — but an artificial agglomeration of quantitative units. A nation is made up of 'idiots'. Any nation is idiotic in its roots, as it is created by individuals with no quality. And in order to keep this group of individuals, stripped of their class,

---

14 Ferdinand Tönnies, *Community and Society*, Mineola, NY: Dover, 2011.

social status, ethnic background and religious and political history (and the nation is always secular — it arose as a result of the struggle between Protestant states and the Holy Roman Empire), from disintegrating, the nation offers them an artificial collective identity. Not historical, not religious, not ethnic — not actual, but, like everything in the philosophy of New Age politics, conceptual.

But if the nation is made up of 'idiots', this makes nationalism almost identical in its anthropological foundations to liberalism. The only difference between them is what scale of agglomeration of individuals they consider to be normative and desirable. Liberals are proponents of 'maximal idiocy' — the goal for them is to extend atomisation to all humanity. That is why the German philosopher Martin Heidegger (1889–1976) called the ideology of liberalism *'Planetär-Idiotismus'* — that is, the application of individualist anthropology on a planetary scale.[15] This 'planetary idiotism' is globalism, which gives the individual a gigantic horizon, on the condition that everywhere and anywhere he will find only himself, his fully identical copy.

Nationalists place more specific limits on the 'singular individual': 'idiots' are uniform within one nation, whereas they may differ somewhat in another nation. This is the rhetoric of nationalism: one's idiocy is contrasted with another's, while universalist liberals insist that idiocy must be universal.

There is no fundamental difference between the liberal project and nationalism. In both cases, there is generally a free market, separation of powers, elections, a parliamentary or presidential form of government, etc. What differs is the configuration of the boundaries within which individuals implement the social contract. Nationalism assumes the boundaries of a single Leviathan, whereas liberalism advocates a world state, in which all politics would be internal, and internationalism equates all

---

15 *Planetarism* corresponds to *idiocy*. The word does not mean a psychiatric concept describing a state of utterly diminished strength of mind and body. From an onto-historical point of view, it means a state of solitary separateness, ἴδιον, in which the modern man is today in mass society. Martin Heidegger, *Überlegungen XII–XV.* (Schwarze Hefte 1939–1941) [Reflections XII — XV. Black Notebooks 1939–1941] (Frankfurt-am-Main: Vittorio Klostermann, 2014), p. 265.

individuals with one another. In both cases it is a conceptual reduction of truly existing people, with their specific historical and cultural identities, to generalised abstract concepts, but only of different dimensions — in one case to 'nation', in the other to 'humanity'.

This creates one of the dividing lines and, consequently, semantic axes of the Political in the paradigm of the modern: classical nationalism (in contrast to revolutionary nationalism, which will be discussed later) shares with liberalism the acceptance of the market society norm and all the main points of bourgeois ideology except for the scope of its application and the limitation of collective identity to the national framework. This contrasts both nationalists and liberals with Communists, in turn completely rejecting the legitimacy of a society built on the market.

Nationalism, Hobbes and Anthropological Pessimism

So, the nation is a New Age bourgeois construct based on individual identity and, accordingly, it is oriented against the Christian religion — in its traditional, medieval versions — Catholic and Orthodox. The Christian tradition does not know nations; it divides the world on the basis of religion — Christians/non-Christians, Catholics/Orthodox, Orthodox Christians/ heretics, etc. Identity is defined first by religion and then by class. The Russian word 'крестьяне', meaning both 'Christian' and 'peasant', combines the two. National identity, being directed against the class identity, carries with it an orientation towards secularism and ultimately atheism and anti-Christianity.

The formation of nations in Europe begins with Protestant countries opposed to the popes and the Holy Roman Empire, and then extends to some Catholic peoples, who, being involved in the process of modernisation, are forced to adopt this national model and accept the formation of Catholic nations in response to the challenge of the Protestant North.

Of the three main theorists of modern political philosophy, Thomas Hobbes is the closest to nationalism.[16] In fact, he is the bearer of the classic notion of modern nationalism. Hobbes is the father of modern

---

16 Carl Schmitt, *The Leviathan in the State Theory of Thomas Hobbes: Meaning and Failure of a Political Symbol* (Chicago: University of Chicago Press, 2008).

nationalism; he has everything, both the social contract (the artificiality of creating a nation on the basis of a political pact) and the notion that the nation is a mechanism created by an idol, a monster that shapes the collective located within it through rigid management.

In Hobbes we find an interesting detail: it is the Leviathan, and the terror it instils in citizens, who is responsible for making people the same. According to Hobbes, the state makes people the same. Therefore, it is from this idea of Hobbes' *Leviathan* that the fundamental philosophy of nationalism emerges. Nationalism is always Hobbesian in one way or another.

If we look at the distinction between nationalism and liberalism from Hobbes' perspective, while the two political ideologies are secularly atheistic and anti-Christian in nature, our main distinguishing feature will again be in anthropology. Nationalists tend to follow Hobbes in his pessimism. People do not change, they remain 'wolves', and their aggression is expressed most naturally in interethnic relations, where human nature is recreated with all its chaos, aggression and egoism, but now on the level of macro-subjects: henceforth the carrier of aggressive greed is not an individual, but the Leviathan itself. Therefore, the nature of man, projected onto the Leviathan, generates realism in international relations, assuming war between nations as a kind of inevitability. And this is where nationalism finds its full application. The wolfish essence of the Hobbesian individual is scaled into a nation, which behaves towards the other nation as a predator, restrained only by force and natural limitations. At the level of the Leviathan, the proponents of realism do not follow the scenario of the transition to the Political. The social contract is made only in relation to the Leviathan — once. And between one Leviathan and another (or Behemoth, the eternal adversary of the Leviathan, to continue the series of biblical images) the social contract is no longer negotiated. The individual thus accepts the power of the collective monster, but the monster itself remains quite in its 'natural' state.

Opponents of the nationalists — liberals and socialists —, as we have seen, proceed from a different anthropology, either neutral (Locke's 'blank slate'), positive (Rousseau's 'noble savage'), or adopt the Kantian model of common 'pure reason'. This affects the interpretation of the state as a historically transitory instance and determines the liberal theory of international relations,[17] which assumes a social contract between countries in the name of a supranational authority, the world government.

Thus another axis of opposition becomes clear in the context of modern political philosophy: nationalism (as an anthropological pessimism), continuing the line of Hobbes, opposes liberalism and socialism, which are based on anthropological optimism.

Mercantilism as Economic Nationalism

We have already said that the most accurate expression of classical bourgeois nationalism in the field of economics is mercantilism.

The theory of mercantilism assumes that the main economic actor in international trade is the state. If within the state everything is determined by the laws of the market, then in the transition to international relations, the state becomes the main authority. It is in this case the sole monopoly trader, and all domestic subjects of the market going beyond the state can do so only through its mediation. In its economic policy, the state is guided by national interests, i.e. irrespective of the interests of any particular national producer or consumer, it sets such tariffs and duties as would be beneficial for the development of one or another branch of the national industry as a whole. Such a state creates preferential conditions for its own and makes competition more difficult for others.

In the market realm, there are neither 'our own' nor 'outsiders', so the state does not act according to market rules, but according to a different set of rules, defending not the private but the public interest. Mercantilism is a projection of Hobbesian logic onto the economy: the state remains predatory, regarding all that is within it as its property and that which is outside as a potential threat or prey.

The mercantilist state is therefore based on protectionism and the management of foreign trade processes in order to create a positive, or at least zero sum, balance between exports and imports. The individual

---

17   Dugin, *International Relations (Paradigms, Theories, Sociology)*.

entrepreneur seeks only his private profit, but the state has to protect itself at all costs, even by limiting the profits of its individual units, in order to defend and strengthen itself as a whole.

Within such a state, there is free competition, but outside, it is the state itself which is the aggregate actor, the entrepreneur who acts on behalf of the nation as a whole. This results in freedom in domestic trade and restrictions, and tariff policies and protectionism in international trade.

Thus, nationalist-mercantilists clash with liberal-internationalists. They are different concepts: for liberals, the state should be *reduced to the smallest role possible* in any and every situation, while for nationalists, the state should be exactly as involved as is necessary. However, the very idea of necessity differs between liberals and mercantilists: the former confine the role of the state to education, enlightenment and the maintenance of a basic order, while the latter include the representation of the nation in the military sphere, as well as in the economic sphere, in the face of other nations.

Nationalists, in a sense, identify Boden's sovereignty with the nation-state as a whole and insist that the nation must also be sovereign. Issues of peace and war, politics, trade and the international economy are all decided in the name of this sovereign nation. That is to say, internally the state oversees order and externally it acts as a full-fledged subject — including economically.

German Romanticism Changes the Perception of the Nation

Before we move on to the twentieth century, to revolutionary nationalism — that is, to the ideology of Fascism and National Socialism, which usually serve as models of the Third Political Theory —, we should pay attention to some attempts to reinterpret bourgeois nationalism in a Romantic vein, which we encounter in Germany in the eigteenth and first half of the nineteenth centuries. These are the Romantic philosophy of Herder (1744–1803) Fichte (1762–1814), Schelling (1775–1854) and Hegel. These profound thinkers tried to imbue the concepts of political modernity — such as 'nation', 'civil society' and even 'individual' — with a more complex and dialectical character, at times transcending the semantic boundaries of the New Age and returning to political Platonism and political Aristotelianism. Thus the Romantic spirit of German philosophy intervenes in the idea of pure, classical bourgeois New Age nationalism. These philosophers make attempts to reinterpret the nation, an artificial and purely political construct, in a metaphysical way, introducing into it elements of the Platonic form, the Aristotelian *eidos* and essence, particular aspects of ethnic, cultural or historical identity. In Herder we see the idea of a 'people' (*Volk*), which he does not strictly separate from a 'nation', as an extension of the historical development of the community. The community and society are not opposed, and the national society is interpreted as an extension of the community. It is an attempt to shift the properties of community onto society, of organicity onto artificiality, and thus relativise the bourgeois character of the nation. While bourgeois ideologues exploited this transference, the German Romantics clearly believed in it, without sharpening the paradigmatic divide between the Middle Ages and the modern age, and even, on the contrary, trying to overcome it dialectically.

This German Romanticism had a significant influence on twentieth-century theories of nationalism, which ceased to be so clearly Hobbesian, individualist, modernist, and took on a more atypical and extravagant character.

Herder: History as the Story of Nations

Johann Gottfried Herder was a consistent critic of Enlightenment ideas. However, his rejection of the modernist paradigm did not mean simply returning to the ideals of the Middle Ages — something that would have been rather problematic in eighteenth-century Europe, where the Enlightenment was rapidly winning. Herder did not want to take a step back, but a step forward, viewing the time in which he lived as part of a more general historical process.

In the spirit of Romanticism, Herder proposed an idea that influenced all forms of later revolutionary nationalism: in his view, the subject of history is not the individual (in the spirit of bourgeois atomism), nor is it the estates, the Empire or the Church, as pure traditionalists believed.

Herder argues that the subject of history is the people, or rather, the *peoples* in the plural, and each of them is an organic whole, a cultural unity. History is not the story of a single humanity, but of many peoples, therefore it is non-linear and consists of different overlapping cycles. Herder believed that societies and peoples go through the same phases in their history as an individual person — infancy, youth, maturity, old age, and then give way to other peoples. Therefore, each nation builds over its history its own semantic cycle, understandable only to itself or to an attentive and thoughtful observer, and corresponding to its internal logic. A nation, as an organic whole, is the bearer of a unique culture, evolving and taking shape gradually at each stage.

In order to conceptualise this organic whole, which is the people, Herder introduces the concept of the 'people's spirit', the *Volkgeist*, attributing to it consciousness, subjectivity and the capacity for volitional and consistent self-development. *History is thus a multi-dimensional cycle of the unfolding of the 'people's spirit' in each people.* There is no common measure between them, although certain patterns and parallels between similar phases of cycles can be outlined. But one should always compare similar phases with one another: a period of decline with a period of decline, a period of ascent with another period of ascent, etc. With this, Herder opened perspectives for the approach that would become the norm in science two hundred years after his death and would form the basis of a 'new anthropology' that continued and developed his intuitions.

Herder laid down his basic ideas about the structure of the historical process in his seminal work *Ideas for a Philosophy of Human History*.[18] In it, he provides the first modern generalised and systematic description of different types of civilisations based on a balanced approach to each of them, without claiming to build a universal system. The 'people's spirit' is always unique and inimitable. Herder compared it to the 'thoughts of God', between which it is ridiculous to try to establish a hierarchy — each of them is perfect and valuable in its own way. Together they make up the

---

18 Johann Gottfried von Herder, *Ideen zur Philosophie der Geschichte der Menschheit* [Ideas for a Philosophy of Human History].

harmony of history. The 'people's spirit' operates equally through geniuses, warlords and great historical figures as it does through commoners, who can have a meaningful existence by organically contributing to culture through customs, ethics, language, traditions and even everyday life.

For Germany, Herder was the founder of the *philosophy of identity*, because his ideas implied that Germans have their own cultural ideal, their own *Volkgeist*, which should not be measured by comparison with other European nations in a linear logic of 'progress', for it is a *unique sequence of meanings* expressed in history and culture, and the task of Germans was to give their 'people's spirit' its full and clear expression — in art, spirituality and, among other things, a particular state, which eighteenth-century Germans were denied. Herder thus laid the theoretical foundation for what was later to become known as the 'special path' (*Sonderweg*) and became the main line for the formation of German society in the nineteenth and twentieth centuries.

Herder talked specifically about the people as a special organic category, quite distant from the political aggregate of individuals united in a single state. The Germans were a people, but not a nation for Herder, as there was no German state and they were scattered over several polities of varying size. But in the subsequent development of the idea of Germany itself by Fichte and Hegel, and especially after its creation by Bismarck (1815–1898), Herder's *Volkgeist* as the basis of identity largely merged with the idea of 'nation', which received in German culture a meaning quite different from the classical use of this concept in England, France and most other European countries.

Fichte: The 'Great Self' of the German Nation and the Closed Mercantile State

Fichte is considered the founder of German classical philosophy. He was a disciple of Kant, but building on transcendental reason, he began to construct his own original philosophy, which is one of the pinnacles of German Idealism.

Fichte, continuing Kant's gnoseology, arrives at the affirmation of a higher self which underlies everything. Whereas Kant spoke of pure reason, Fichte moves into its depths and postulates the figure of the one whose mind is the 'great self'. The 'great self' then alienates itself by constituting an object. Again Fichte goes further than Kant, not confining himself to a cautious constructivist noumenalism about the thing-in-itself, but grounding the reality of the world in the reality of the 'great self'. Then, already within the object, the 'great self' constitutes a 'lesser self', an empirical person who is the ambassador of the 'self' to the 'non-self'. The task of the 'lesser self' is to restore through the full knowledge of the object (through science, which Fichte understood as the mystical retrieval of the traces of the 'great self' in nature) the whole structure of the 'great self'.

He thus broke sharply with the anthropology of the modern, creating a theory in tune with the Neoplatonist Plotinus or the Hindu doctrine of the 'great identity' of the Atman (the human self) with Brahman (the Absolute).[19] This anthropology resonated in part with Herder's notion of the 'people's spirit', and Fichte consciously applied his definition of subjectivity (i.e. the self both great and lesser) to the Germanic people. In doing so, although Germany did not yet exist, he used the term 'nation' in a sense closer to Herder than to the classical bourgeois usage. But at the same time, somewhat following the common definition, Fichte suggested that the nation should be constructed by giving the people the characteristic of a state, which he interpreted in the spirit of his conception of the philosophical process.

In his *Addresses to the German Nation*,[20] Fichte presented the project of creating Germany (divided into several semi-autonomous principalities and states in the early nineteenth century) as a prerequisite for an ontological and epistemological leap, a key stage in the victory over the non-self, embodied in natural and historical barriers to the unification of the Germans. Fichte regarded the Germans as a people endowed with a special capacity for science and culture, and consequently believed the 'German nation' to be an essential stage in the return of the collective 'small self' to its unified German 'great self'.

---

19 Dugin, *Noomakhia. Great India. Civilisation of the Absolute.*
20 Johann Gottlieb Fichte, *Addresses to the German Nation* (Cambridge, Cambridge University Press, 2009).

In economic practice, Fichte was in favour of a completely *closed mercantilist state*,[21] justifying typical mercantilism not on the basis of mere egoistic interests of the Leviathan, but by criticising the individualistic element as such (the 'lesser self' refusing to aspire to become the 'greater self'). He also observed that free trade (the English version of economic liberalism) creates sharp property and social inequalities in society, enriching those involved in international trade and ruining entrepreneurs engaged only in domestic trade. Fichte contrasted this with a model of state socialism, where the priority of economic activity would not be the satisfaction of individual private interests, but a general effort to overcome obstacles to the complete freedom of the 'great self', i.e. the dominance of the subject over the object resisting it (including scarcity, poverty, etc.).

Hegel: Philosophical Empire

Another representative of classical German philosophy, who had the greatest influence on all of nineteenth- and twentieth-century philosophy, both directly and through his expositors (including Marx's Left Hegelianism), was Georg Wilhelm Friedrich Hegel.

Hegel believed that he was creating a synthesis of all philosophical thought, and that his system was the most universal system that existed or had ever existed, combining in itself the most essential elements from previous systems. At the same time he attributed this capacity for synthesis not simply to the coincidence of chance or to personal genius, but to the deepest logic of world history, which, passing through various dialectical stages strictly defined by the metaphysical structure, resolved in the German culture and the Prussian monarchy as a climax (end of history), of which Hegel himself was the theorist, witness and creator. Therefore, in his philosophy the universal and the absolute are dialectically embodied in the concreteness of nineteenth-century historical Germany. According to Hegel, both his system and his philosophy of history itself were aspects of a single Historial, a metaphysical process associated with the stages of the *unfolding of the Spirit*. Hegel associated the time and place of

---

21 Johann Gottlieb Fichte, *The Closed Commercial State* (Albany, NY: SUNY Press, 2013).

formation of his philosophical system — Germany in the nineteenth century — with the finale of this historicity, its apogee. With certain adjustments and nuances, this was acknowledged by all his followers.

Hegel's influence on nineteenth- and twentieth-century philosophy, science and political processes, both among Germans and far beyond the borders of Germany, was enormous. One of the main political ideologies of the modern age — Marxism — was built on a particular interpretation of his ideas. The main theorist of Italian Fascism, Giovanni Gentile (1875–1944), also considered himself an orthodox Hegelian (right-wing, like Hegel himself), who applied Hegel's ideas about Germany to Italy. And in the context of liberal ideology, Hegel was referred to by liberal theorists such as Alexandre Kojève[22] and Francis Fukuyama,[23] who identified Hegel's concept of the 'end of history' with liberalism and its global victory (globalisation).

At the same time, Hegel's system can be seen as a synthesis of the unfolding of the whole German Logos, summarising in itself the process of world history and that segment of it where the field of its most intense and semantically rich development was Western Europe (since the Middle Ages), and from a certain point in time German thought proper, to which Hegel reduces the history of all humanity and whose ultimate expression became German classical philosophy, the apex of which Hegel considered to be his own system. The transparency and logic of such a series of statements in the very structure of Hegel's dialectics and philosophy of history (as well as the history of philosophy) was so compelling that many philosophers, intellectuals and historians who felt the fundamental influence of Hegelianism — both directly, through familiarity with the works of Hegel, and indirectly, through the many derivatives of his system, and above all through the Leftist Hegelians, mostly Marxists — agreed with this. In Russia Hegel influenced not only the Marxists, for whom he was a dogmatic source, but also the Slavophiles, the Monarchists and the Sophiologists — in other words, virtually all the currents of the distinctive

---

22 Alexandre Kojève, *Introduction to the Reading of Hegel* (Ithaca, NY: Cornell University Press, 1980).

23 Fukuyama, *The End of History and the Last Man*.

Russian philosophical thought that emerged only in the nineteenth century. Hegel also had a decisive influence on European philosophers of various currents, with the possible exception of the Neo-Kantians.

Hegel was an ardent supporter of the creation of a united Germany (the Second Reich) and regarded his philosophy as a global metaphysical formulation of this project. '*An educated people without metaphysics* is something like a temple, in general variously decorated, but without a shrine', Hegel wrote in the preface to the *Science of Logic*.[24] Since the question of creating a German state with a pole in Prussia was of acute importance in the nineteenth century, especially during Hegel's lifetime, Hegel believed that his metaphysical system should become that 'shrine', the 'altar' in the German socio-political temple.

The foundations of Hegel's system are laid out in two major works: *The Phenomenology of Spirit*,[25] which deals in depth with the structure of consciousness, and *The Science of Logic*,[26] which gives an explicit and detailed view of metaphysics. *The Science of Logic* begins where *The Phenomenology of Spirit* leaves off, and his other works are derived from these two fundamental treatises on the entire history of philosophy.

In regards to the unfolding of history, the Hegelian scheme can be briefly described as follows:

- the subjective spirit (in itself) — the thesis or first law of logic (identity);

- the objective spirit (for the other) — the antithesis, the second law of logic (negation);

- the absolute spirit (for self) — synthesis, the third law of logic (the Absolute instead of the excluded third).

The first thesis of the subjective spirit (*der subjektive Geist*) or 'spirit in itself' coincides with the theological postulation of the existence of God:

---

24 G. W. F. Hegel, *Science of Logic* (Cambridge: Cambridge University Press, 2015). Verbatim: "*ein gebildetes Volk ohne Metaphysik zu sehen, — wie einen sonst mannigfaltig ausgeschmückten Tempel ohne Allerheiligstes*".
25 Hegel, *Phenomenology of Spirit*.
26 Hegel, *Science of Logic*.

the subjective spirit is God-in-itself. This position is extremely important because it brings Hegel closer to Platonism and Christian philosophy, i.e. it establishes continuity with the philosophical paradigm of the premodern (Tradition) and therefore partly transcends the classical models of the New Age. Of course, the 'subjective spirit' allowed for various interpretations, including rationalist interpretations (in the spirit of Kant and his pure reason), but it follows from the general context of Hegel's philosophy that he means by it a transcendent beginning, that is, the God of Christian theology, although having some common features with Fichte's 'great self', that is, with the mystical understanding of God as a subject internal to the human soul.

In order to unfold itself for the Other, this subjective mind projects itself into an objective spirit (*der objektive Geist*), in which it becomes nature and even matter. That is, the subject projects itself into the object. Thus, the appearance of the autonomous drive of nature is explained as an optical illusion, attributing to the object what is in fact the property of subjectivity, reversed by a dialectical process of self-rejection. Since Marx has no subjective spirit (Marx is an atheist), for him nature and matter appear as the driving force of development in themselves, which endows them with 'magical' properties (the same goes for Spinoza's substantiation, forced to call nature 'God'). Thus the meaningfulness of nature and its knowability receive their justification in a vertical topicality reminiscent of Platonism and Neoplatonism, but described in a diachronic dynamic context (the same was a distinctive feature of Schelling's philosophy of history[27]).

The third point of dialectics represents the unfolding of the subjective spirit itself through nature (as through its otherness). Gradually, through mankind and human history, the subjective spirit returns to its essence, but in a new quality — as something conscious.

But this is already a new essence — it is neither a subjective spirit ('spirit-in-itself') nor a 'spirit-for-other', but a *'spirit-for-itself'*. Thus the spirit returns to itself through its own alienation, but this return to itself, according to Hegel, is more important than the exodus. The exodus

---

[27] Dugin, *In Search of the Dark Logos*.

creates the prerequisites of the return, and the return, having gone through the whole cycle, returns the subjective spirit to itself, which becomes the *absolute spirit* (*der absolute Geist*). So first we have the subjective spirit, unknown to anyone, hidden, then the objective spirit which constitutes itself as another, which is not God himself, which is understood as creation, and through creation and its crowning feature, human consciousness, the fullness of perfection, the conscious absolute spirit, is attained.

According to Hegel, the absolute spirit unfolds through human history and ascends to the end of history. The purpose of history is spirit's awareness of itself through matter. At first, spirit possesses itself, but does not realise it, then it begins to realise itself, but does not possess it. Nature itself carries the preconditions of history, because it is an element of history. Hence the history of religion, the history of societies, and as a result of the unfolding of the spirit through history, it reaches its climax at the end of history, when it fully realises and possesses itself. The cycle contains all the dialectical completeness: thesis, antithesis, synthesis. It follows that history is finite.

Hegel's political philosophy is based on this foundation. The evolution of political systems, models and regimes is interpreted here as a sequence of dialectical moments leading to the absolute spirit. Politics is the crystallisation of synthesis. Political history is a *movement of the spirit* aiming at becoming absolute. Politics, therefore, is the history of the absolutisation of the spirit. This definition allows us to consider Hegel's political philosophy as a dynamic version of *Politica Aeterna*.

Hegel establishes a certain hierarchy between the different political forms. On the one hand, one might get the impression that it is about historical progress, because each successive political regime is in some sense better than the previous one. This idea is fundamentally at odds with the Tradition paradigm, which refers rather to the degradation of political systems that gradually lose their resemblance to the eternal original (Platonism), or to the immutability of the normative, which individual forms of the political can both deviate from and approach (political Aristotelianism). In the recognition of 'progress' one can see a connection between Hegel and the modernist paradigm. However, unlike Marx's theory, this political evolution is not a social continuation of the development of matter or nature. It is phases of revealing the spirit that was *originally* embedded in matter and nature. Accordingly, there is no materialism here. We are dealing with a complex scheme, which combines the Platonic model (in the beginning there was spirit and not matter) and the evolutionist model (when we start looking at history from the antithesis, from nature, and this formally already resembles the political philosophy of the Mother). Marx discarded the Platonic portion, reinterpreting Hegel in an exclusively materialist way. But with Hegel himself it is more complicated.

The culmination of the third phase — the formation of the spirit as an absolute, i.e. conscious, spirit-for-itself — is conceived by Hegel as the end of history and coincides with the destiny of Prussia and the creation of the great state of all Germans on its foundation: Germany. The Germans in Hegel's lifetime did not yet have a single state. But they already had a great philosophy, of which Hegel saw his own teaching as the crowning achievement. Thus, the thinkers had prepared the end of history, which for Hegel coincided with the future enlightened German monarchy. Therefore, the whole of history is a prelude to the emergence of Germany in the nineteenth century. Hegel said that the great nations are those that have either a great state or a great philosophy. He said that the Russians had a great state and the Germans had no state at all in the nineteenth century. Accordingly, the Germans must have a great philosophy — then they will achieve a great state.

Hegel created the philosophy of the great German state before there was a Germany. He formulated his doctrine in a Germanic world consisting of Prussia, Habsburg Austria and disparate principalities which were anything but a powerful state. Hegel assembled Germany in his mind, endowed it with an intellectual mission, and created — along with Fichte and Schelling — an idealistic romantic conception of German statehood as an expression of a spirit made absolute. The peak and end of history, according to Hegel, was to be the German state — an eschatological monarchy, where the monarch himself was to be supported by a philosophical elite, the Platonic guardians developing the teachings of Hegel himself, the founder of the philosophical empire.

Hegel himself was considered a prophet of philosophy, of humanity and of Germany. He was a mystical monarchist who regarded the idea of historical logic as a manifold movement of various political forms towards a Prussian monarchy.

This is how Hegel interprets the history of religion, philosophy and politics. The spirit passes into nature, from where it is reborn through society and culture, until it reaches the culmination of self-consciousness in the highest of political systems, *philosophical monarchy*, which for Hegel was the prototype of nineteenth-century Prussia and which is to be embodied in a future united Great Germany. This scenario predetermines the entire structure of the German Historical and shows the Hegelian decoding of global, European and German history. Different peoples and civilisations develop different religious-philosophical systems, attempting to reflect their attraction to the elusive spirit. History is the cyclical unfolding of consciousness on the way to the *Logos*.

The emergence of Greek philosophy is the birth of the Logos almost in its purest form, when the spirit begins to realise itself as adequately as possible. The Logos of the Greeks is a harmonisation (*Stimmung*) of the spirit. In the field of Greco-Roman culture, the most important event of world history takes place — the incarnation of Jesus Christ, the *Logos* himself. This is the culmination of the revelation of being through time. Then the Greek Logos and the Incarnate Word live on in Christianity, which, in turn, goes through various stages of its centuries-long self-understanding. Through the chain of dialectical oppositions and their removal, history reaches the age of Enlightenment, where the Christian Logos, dispersed over as many individual beings as possible, reaches the mineral core of nature — comprehended by science, transformed by culture and made sense of by citizens, enlightened and transformed by the formation of societies.

The final gesture of history becomes the gathering together of all the enlightened units of the world, in the synthesis of a vertical *philosophical empire*, where spirit will complete its movement towards itself through self-exclusion, and history will culminate, *turning into philosophy* — not an abstract one, but a concrete one. This concrete philosophy will be the direct embodiment of the absolute spirit, in which the Logos' return to itself will be fully realised, gathering inclusively into itself all that was scattered at the beginning not just of history, but of cosmology, and even of the ontogenetic process.

According to Hegel, the centre of the history of eternity is Germany, the 'promised land' of the absolute spirit, the territory of the 'end of history', the field prepared to become a philosophical empire.

It is obvious that Hegel's grandiose picture justifying the creation of the German state has little in common with Hobbes' Leviathan. At the same time Hegel also examines civil society, i.e. the bourgeois order based on individualism, but considers it as one of the dialectical moments, the unfolding of the spirit. Civil society and the Enlightenment era itself are important for Hegel as a preparation for the establishment of a philosophical empire, which is thought of not as a nation-state in the paradigm of the modern, but as the mystical 'end of history', as its most important concluding event. Clearly, such 'nationalism' has nothing in common with the classical nationalism developed at the dawn of the Enlightenment, and is a theory that goes far beyond the modern as such. However, along with the Communist reading (by Marx, where the 'end of history' comes in the form of Communism) and liberal reading (as by Kozhev, where the 'end of history' coincides with globalisation and the final triumph of liberal democracy), a monarchist or 'nationalist' reading of Hegel would also be possible, which we see in German and Russian conservatives, as well as in one of the main theorists of Italian Fascism, Giovanni Gentile.

We find Hegelianism in all three classical ideologies of modernity, but this does not mean that it can be qualified in terms of any one of them. Hegel is broader than all the political theories of modernity, and so he does not unequivocally fall into any one of them. Accordingly, he has within him something that was borrowed by all three political ideologies of the modern, as well as something that did not make it into them — for example, the idea of an original subjective spirit that is the antecedent of all movement from below is not compatible with New Age materialism, individualism and atomism. This element of the primordial Platonic moment, which then passes into a vision that can in a sense be combined (with some stretching) with progressivist and evolutionist motifs, prevents Hegel from being counted among the political philosophers of the modern Age.

A particular reading of Hegel — not liberal, Marxist or nationalist — allows us to discover within his work components alternative to the political philosophy of the modern age and to integrate him into the Fourth Political Theory. Thus, with a certain interpretation based on the principles of *Politica Aeterna*, we can take Hegel out of the age of modernity and the particular period in which he lived and thought, into a different — more general and, in a certain sense, trans-modern, beyond-modern — context. Such a reading of Hegel, such a reconstruction of his political philosophy, as opposed to a reading grounded in the context of the three political theories, must begin with a thorough grasp of the first dialectical moment — the transition of the divine eternal beginning into a set of immanent entities. How we comprehend this process in the context of metaphysics determines both the interpretation of the ontology of the world, its eschatological completion, its teleology (goal), and the meaning and content of politics, which should ultimately (as we see in Hegel himself) be determined primarily by the relation of the state to God, eternity and the absolute and unchanging origin.

Gentile: The State as Philosophy

Thus, through Hegel, we come very close to revolutionary nationalism, which should be considered the Third Political Theory in the full sense of the term, since such nationalism emerged both after liberalism (the First Political Theory) and after Communism (the Second Political Theory), while retaining some similarities, at least terminological and partly conceptual, with the classical nationalism that emerged at the dawn of modernity, even before the emergence of distinct liberal theories, but only much later evolved into a formalised holistic ideology.

One of the main ideologues of Italian Fascism, Giovanni Gentile, was a convinced Hegelian and an advocate of objective idealism, speaking out strongly against positivism and materialism. Gentile, following Hegel, believed that a great nation needs a great philosophy and saw a direct and inseparable link between the construction of Italy as a nation-state and the intellectual shaping of Italian identity in philosophy and culture.

Gentile built an original philosophy, which he called 'actualism'. He based it on the notion of 'thought thinking' (*il pensiero pensante, il pensiero che pensa*). Gentile thinks of the act as an overcoming of the subject-object dualism. The pure act for Gentile, as for Hegel, is the moment of the cognition of the spirit — that is, of the source of thinking, of itself. Gentile distinguishes between a thinking thought and a basic thought, each having its own logic. Thinking thought is a pure act; basic thought, on the contrary, is a frozen, detached, and objectified product of thinking. In Gentile's version, Hegel's dialectical triad corresponds to:

- art (direct manifestation of the subject — thesis),
- religion (elevation of thought to the status of the object — antithesis),
- philosophy (the subject's comprehension of itself as a pure act — synthesis).

Just basic thought, according to Gentile, is subjective and manifests itself in art. At the next level, in religion, thought becomes meaningful. It is only in philosophy that thought becomes *thinking*, i.e. fully active, coinciding with the pure act as the highest moment of self-consciousness. This is the basis of Gentile's understanding of history: it is the unfolding of the three moments of the spirit, with religion being the second of them in this system — that is, a form of the spirit partly overcome by philosophy. Though being a Catholic and recognising the value of religious education, Gentile still believed that the state must be secular. But secularity in his understanding was synonymous with the third and highest act of the self-consciousness of the spirit, i.e. the organisation of society on the basis of the domination of the 'pure act'. It is from here that Gentile derived his political philosophy, which he identified with political Fascism.[28]

---

28 It is believed that it was Gentile who authored the programmatic work *The Doctrine of Fascism*, published under the name of Mussolini. Benito Mussolini, *La dottrina del fascismo* [The Doctrine of Fascim] (Firenze: Vallecchi Editore, 1935).

Fascism, as interpreted by Gentile, is the theory and practice of a pure spiritual act expressed in the elevation of the state to a philosophical principle. This is the 'doctrine of Fascism', which is the logical limit of Hegelian philosophy. The self-awareness of the spirit is embodied in the state as an instance where the spirit reaches the stage of synthesis, overcoming both the subjective stage (art) and the objective stage (which for Gentile is tantamount to religion). This justifies the absolutisation of the state as an immanent version of an idea made flesh.

At the same time, Gentile and Fascism in general were defined by the rejection of all forms of internationalism, both bourgeois and Marxist. The argument for this was the dialectic of the unfolding of the spirit, where the individualism of civil society would be overcome not by a philosophical enlightened monarchy (as in Hegel's conception), but by a national dictatorship. At the same time, the very idea of social justice played an important role in the context of Fascist ideology. Materialism and internationalism were predominantly rejected in Fascism, while concern for the working class and peasantry formed an essential part of the political programme. In one of his speeches, Mussolini, the leader of Italian Fascism, addressed his audience — 'Arise, Fascist and proletarian Italy!'[29] Furthermore, Mussolini himself came from a socialist movement, and Fascism — especially early Fascism — was an anti-bourgeois and revolutionary movement, where socialist motives played an important role. Thus, in Italian Fascism we see some convergence between the two versions of Hegelianism — socialist and nationalist.

In Gentile and in Fascism in general we see a combination of Hegelian dialectics, idealism and the political philosophy of modernity, because Gentile does not return to the traditional Catholic philosophy of the 'two cities' or to the imperial Ghibelline idea (which was defended by the much more consistent traditionalist Julius Evola[30]), but justifies with his philosophy the secular state, which, although described, following Hegel, in the

---

29 Such formulas were sharply criticised by the traditionalist Julius Evola, a supporter of an aristocratic and consistently anti-Communist as well as anti-modern political system. Julius Evola, *Fascism Viewed from the Right* (London, Arktos Media, 2013).

30 Julius Evola, *Mysteries of the Grail* (Vermont: Inner Traditions, 2018).

spirit of the unfolding of the Idea, is still too reminiscent of the theories of Bodin and Hobbes. Gentile's Fascism is thus a bizarre combination of pre-modernist and modernist elements, but the appeal to Hegel with his extremely refined intellectual theory does not allow Gentile's theory to be attributed entirely to the New Age.

Nietzsche: A Political Philosophy of Life

The formation of revolutionary nationalism as a whole, and Fascist leader Benito Mussolini in particular, were greatly influenced by the philosophy of the utterly atypical thinker, Friedrich Nietzsche (1844–1900). While the English mathematician and philosopher Alfred North Whitehead (1861–1947) said that the entirety of philosophy is notes in the margins of Plato, one can paraphrase him to say that the entire philosophy of the twentieth century is notes in the margins of Nietzsche. Nietzsche is multifaceted; there are long and heated debates about any of his theses, so his philosophy cannot be interpreted unambiguously.

Nietzsche's philosophy is extremely multi-dimensional, though fragmentary and haphazard. All the major political ideologies of the twentieth century — liberalism, Communism and nationalism — have been influenced by Nietzsche's thought at different times, where, in each case, it has been interpreted from a vastly different perspective.

Nietzsche cannot be considered a 'nationalist' in the usual sense of the word. He was highly critical of modernity itself, sharply rejected the state, and was quite pessimistic about the Germans. In his drafts he writes thus:

> You observe that it is my desire to be fair to the Germans: and in this respect I should not like to be untrue to myself—I must therefore also state my objections to them. It costs a good deal to attain to a position of power; for power *stultifies*. The Germans—they were once called a people of thinkers: do they really think at all at present? Nowadays the Germans are bored by intellect, they mistrust intellect; politics have swallowed up all earnestness for really intellectual things—'Germany, Germany above all.' I fear this was the death-blow to German philosophy.[31]

---

31 Friedrich Nietzsche, *Twilight of the Idols*, trans. Anthony M. Ludovici (Hertfordshire: Wordsworth Editions Ltd, 2007).

But he remains precisely a German thinker by virtue of the fact that he gives the last historical testimony on the state of the German spirit, and if this spirit is sick, then Nietzsche, without hesitation, makes this illness his — to follow it to the end, as a fate and destiny.

Nietzsche captures the essence of the era in which he lives by the precise formula: 'European nihilism', as he calls the first book of *The Will to Power*. In fact, by 'nihilism' Nietzsche understands European modernity, which he rejects, but at the same time tries to grasp its meaning and decipher its message.

For Nietzsche the highest value is *life and its power*. Accordingly, where life is subjected to some kind of pressure, restraint, taming, limitation, this is where one should look for the roots of nihilism. In other words, the source of nihilism is Logos itself — at least, the one that is *directed against life*.

Nietzsche's main task was to establish a new understanding of thinking, which should not be apart from life, but *within* it. Therefore, Nietzsche's doctrine is sometimes called the 'philosophy of life'. The basic idea is that life is a synthesised phenomenon, which cannot be decomposed into immobility and motion, subject and object, consciousness and the external world, i.e. the classical themes of New Age philosophy. With Nietzsche everything is fluid, both subject and object; they are not fixed but merged, though simultaneously divided in a primordial unity. Returning to the unity on the other side of the antithetical pairs (subject-object, up-down, good-evil) and overcoming these pairs is for Nietzsche an alternative way of thinking. Thinking of life not from the outside, but from within.

Usually philosophers think of life, of nature, as an object, from the outside, as if they themselves were dead or not yet born. New people, Nietzsche teaches, must think from within life, although this is extremely difficult, since life is a stream. The flow does not allow you to single out something unambiguous, to define something once and fix it as a rule — today it is one, tomorrow it is another. But according to Nietzsche, you must not stop the flow, you must immerse consciousness and thinking within it. According to Nietzsche, becoming is what should be considered the beginning and the end of philosophy. But at the same time the pure element of becoming eludes thought and being, representing pure contingency (in the spirit of Democritus' isonomy). Nietzsche does not agree with this and calls for finding moments of eternity in the stream of becoming, crystals of being, to put the stamp of being on the stream of becoming.

Hence the idea of 'eternal return', because the stream of life has a certain meaning, revealed only in a vast cycle. The vast cycle, the contemplation of the birth of things at the source of eternity and their baptism in the waters of eternity is the task of philosophy.

Life is opposed to nihilism. At first as an alienated rationality and later as a complete degeneration of thought. In his era, Nietzsche records nihilism as an overt phenomenon, as the essence of history that has become explicit. This is why he treats nihilism ambiguously: it is not simply a failure or pathology, an accident or an isolated event, but a *fate*, the tragic fate of a spirit (consciousness, thinking) waging an irreconcilable war on life through the ages.

The problem of nihilism as a tragic discovery of modernity's nothingness and the possibilities of overcoming it is the *theme* of Nietzsche's entire oeuvre. It unfolds in stages, as life and becoming are not taken as a concept for Nietzsche, as opposed to Hegel, but retain the fundamental metaphysical load that becoming (movement) is endowed with in Hegel by virtue of the dialectical nature of his apophatic philosophy. *If Hegel is a prophet of history, Nietzsche is a prophet of life.* Nietzsche sets himself the task of putting the stamp of eternity onto becoming.

> To *impose* upon becoming the character of being — that is the supreme *will to power*.[32]

He does not simply record the power and strength of nature, as a materialist, naturalist or Spinoza-like pantheist would do. He wants to deduce from life its secret essence, the 'signs of being', that is, to look into the last depth of life, precisely where the source of its tragic and inexorable power

---

32 Friedrich Nietzsche, *The Will to Power* (New York: Vintage Books, 1968), p. 330.

comes from. For Nietzsche, becoming is chaos. But it is not someone else — not the spirit, the subject or reason — who imposes upon it the character of being, who stamps (*aufprägen*) eternity onto it, *but the inner power of life itself*, reaching its culmination. Hence the Nietzschean formula from *Thus Spoke Zarathustra*:

> One must still have chaos in oneself to be able to give birth to a dancing star.[33]

Nietzsche noted the failure of the human being, his historical exhaustion, his futility, which became particularly apparent in humanism, when man demonstrated what he was capable of, freed from the 'yoke' — it turned out that he was capable only of baseness. In his place was to come the *Übermensch* [Superman]. In the Preface to *Thus Spoke Zarathustra*, Nietzsche says of this:

> What is great in man is that he is a bridge and not a goal: what can be loved in man is that he is an overcoming and a descent.[34]

He perishes to make room for *the one who comes in his place*. For he is not an end but a means, a path, an arrow of longing thrown to that shore, a moment of becoming, not a substance. Man is the death of himself as a man and the transition to what is after him in the logical structure of history — to the Superman.

Nietzsche defines the Superman as 'this conqueror of God and nothingness' ('*dieser Besieger Gottes und des Nichts*').[35] This is the most important definition. God is dead, and with him order, peace, has collapsed. What is left is nothingness, chaos and the last people. Nietzsche says of 'the last people':

---

33 Friedrich Nietzsche, *Thus Spoke Zarathustra* (London: Penguin Classics, 1974).
34 Ibid.
35 The full statement goes on: 'The man of the future who will redeem us not only from the hitherto reigning ideal but also from that which was bound to grow out of it, the great nausea, the will to nothingness, nihilism; this bell stroke of noon and of the great decision that liberates the will again and restores its goal to the earth and his hope to man; this Antichrist and anti-nihilist; this victor over God and nothingness — he must come one day.'

> 'What is love? What is creation? What is longing? What is a star?' thus asks the last man, and blinks.
>
> The earth has become small, and on it hops the last man, who makes everything small. His race is as ineradicable as the flea; the last man lives longest.
>
> 'We have invented happiness', say the last men, and they blink. They have left the regions where it was hard to live, for one needs warmth.[36]

This is the last thing people have left: to narrow their horizon to the space immediately adjacent to their body. 'The last man' does not know *love*, because he does not acutely experience separation, does not feel dismembered. Thus he evades the challenge of difference. It is enough for him that he seems to himself to be whole — and disintegrates from this further and further, becoming from an individual a divide — especially when he feels that his individuality is guaranteed and reliably safeguarded. He does not know *creation* because he does not know the Creator who created him, but he himself is unable to create: his inner emptiness is powerless. The 'last people' are the people of the modern age. Nietzsche has a deep contempt for them. But he believes that in order to overcome the nihilism of the modern we should not take a step back, but a step forward, in the direction of the Superman.

Nietzsche lays the foundations for a new anthropology, where becoming is placed in the nature of man in a way that *makes man a variable*. As a moment of becoming, man moves along a vertical axis: *from that which is always lower to that which is always higher*. This defines his dialectic, his openness, his boundlessness. Man creates himself anew each time, extracting from the inner abyss more and more new substances to surpass them again, to become the point of ruin and transition, *Untergang und Übergang*, for a new moment. This applies to the historical man and to each person individually. Moreover, the subject is always both historical and personal, for human life itself is a *time of transition*, an impulse, a leap, i.e. the will. The will to power is this axis of a dynamic transformational anthropology. The will to power is the will to subordinate the past to the future, the subhuman to the superhuman, the present self (and the past)

---

36 Friedrich Nietzsche, *Thus Spoke Zarathustra* (London: Penguin Classics, 1974).

to the future. It is the subordination of one frozen moment in the flight of the arrow to the flight *as a whole*.

'The death of God' is not a catastrophe for Nietzsche; the *catastrophe is the unwillingness of men to come face to face with the abyss*, to accept the challenge of the void, to accept chaos as the only power coming at them from all sides and leaving them alone with themselves, without support or order, which have collapsed. The only answer to the challenge of nothingness, revealed after the death of God, is the Superman. A man encountering nothingness cannot stand up to it, the 'last man' is simply naively deluded, expecting to escape from the urgency of the problem.

Nietzsche's philosophy is deeply revolutionary. He calls for a reassessment of all values. But this reassessment can be interpreted in the context of all three political theories. It is generally accepted to classify Nietzsche as one of the philosophers who inspired Italian Fascism and German National Socialism.

Indeed, the revolutionary nationalists perceived Nietzsche as a critic of bourgeois values, a singer of the heroic personality, with the German National Socialists interpreting the Nietzschean image of the 'blond beast' as a direct allusion to the 'Aryan race'.

Mussolini, for his part, liked to repeat Nietzsche's idea of living dangerously.

Nietzsche praised the will, courage, the spirit of 'war'. He was not afraid to openly ridicule and reject progress, equality and morality. Some of his statements were openly misogynistic and rigidly patriarchal (e.g. the famous statement 'You go to women? Do not forget the whip!'[37]). Nietzsche glorified inequality, believing that only the brave and clever, the strong-willed and the bold had the right to exist. Scandalous for Christian and even secular-humanist morality were such statements by Nietzsche as 'That which is leaning deserves to be pushed!'.[38]

A number of Nietzsche's statements could be interpreted chauvinistically. For example, he said that some nations would be better off not being born at all. But he used these epathetic formulas in a paradoxical sense,

---

37 Nietzsche, *Thus Spoke Zarathustra*, p. 64.
38 Ibid., p. 205.

calling for everything to be measured by life. In his vision, a nation that has life, that is imbued with its element, that courageously and boldly enters into becoming is a worthy nation.

By the way, Nietzsche was very fond of the Russians. He believed the wickeder the people, the better, the greater their vitality. He considered Russians to be very wicked. He even had an aphorism: "'Evil men have no songs." How is it that the Russians have songs?'[39] He even offered to give Europe to the Russians so that they would bring their vitality there, and the pampered European culture would develop peacefully under the Russian monarch, as once Greece did under the power of Rome.

The Third Political Theory, and especially some of its incarnations — above all the racism of the National Socialists —, picked up on Nietzsche's philosophy of inequality. Indeed, Nietzsche spoke of a 'race of slaves' and a 'race of masters', but he did not link this to a biological race. He was talking about those peoples full of life and will to power moving through history, a historically triumphant race of masters, and those who found themselves constantly conquered.

Nietzsche introduced the concept of *ressentiment*[40] into philosophical language in his *On the Genealogy of Morals*.[41] Philosopher and sociologist Max Scheler (1874–1928) has a separate book, *Ressentiment in the Structure of Morals*, which is entirely devoted to the disclosure of this critically important notion. *Ressentiment* is the psychological state of a slave — not of a social slave, but of a typological, 'ontological' slave. It includes simultaneous envy, irritation, hatred, recognition of one's own inferiority complex and a desire to take revenge on everyone above, who feels secure and calm, who has that inner greatness and dignity that are in principle inaccessible to the bearer of 'ressentiment', that is, to a 'slave by vocation' and not by position. There are people who realise that they are nothing more than bastards, cowards, scoundrels, and scum. But realising that, they blame it on the strong, the honest, the brave, the beautiful, the virile. And

---

39 Nietzsche, *Twilight of the Idols*.
40 French: *ressentiment* — resentment, spitefulness, vindictiveness.
41 Friedrich Nietzsche, *On the Genealogy of Morals* (Cambridge: Cambridge University Press, 2011).

the sharper the feeling of their own inferiority, the greater the hatred for all that is wholesome.

According to Nietzsche, this fundamental property divides people into two categories: there is a race of masters, uniting those who are free from resentment and who therefore freely extract the fullness of life from themselves, projecting it onto everything around them, and there is a race of slaves — people lacking in this fullness of life, who always want for something and who hate everyone else for their own lack. Nietzsche did not hesitate to project these generalisations onto some nations, who live with hatred and envy because, for example, they were once subdued by the stronger and have not been able to get out from under this influence since. But instead of rallying with the slime and rebelling (Nietzsche said that 'rebellion is the virtue of the slave'), they continue to fool around in their supposed servility, and sometimes bite, squeal and insult their masters when they will not be heard. Unable to rule themselves or others, they constantly experience other people's rule as a humiliation. These are not some individual peoples — they are a race of slaves, a kind of society, a type, a people who are endowed with such characteristics. But Nietzsche illustrates this anthropological remark with various examples from the history of peoples and religions, which has been used by nationalism in a context far removed from the one Nietzsche had in mind.

Although it is generally accepted that Nietzsche was primarily a harbinger of the Third Political Theory, there are also interpretations of his ideas in the context of liberalism and Communism.

Thus, some liberals view Nietzschean philosophy as an apologia for the individual. Nietzsche's calls for a reassessment of all values and his doctrine of perspectivism are interpreted in this context, which is understood as the ultimate form of an apology of subjectivity. His criticism of the state, his distaste for socialism and the image of the Superman are interpreted by liberals as a model of the ultimate freedom applied to the marketplace and capitalism. Nietzsche's glorification of inequality becomes for liberals a defence of income and property inequality (contrary to socialists and Communists). One version of this liberal reading of

Nietzscheanism is offered by Ayn Rand[42] (1905–1982). Ayn Rand takes the principle of liberal individualism and free enterprise to its logical limit, glorifying the rich as a 'superior race' and the poor and workers as a 'race of slaves'. At the same time, Ayn Rand believes that society and the state exist to contain and oppress the rich, who must declare war on them and lead themselves to victory. This philosophy is called 'Objectivism'. Many leading figures in the U.S. Federal Reserve System, including Alan Greenspan, are proponents of liberal Nietzscheanism and adherents of Ayn Rand's 'Objectivism'.

There is also a 'leftist' — Communist — reading of Nietzsche. One of the first Communist Nietzscheans was Maxim Gorky (1868–1936), a Russian proletarian writer and friend of Lenin, who applied Nietzsche's idea of the Superman to a romanticised image of the proletariat. A more systematic reading than that of Maxim Gorky was offered by the French Communist philosopher Georges Bataille[43] (1897–1962) in the 1930s. He developed Nietzsche's theme of overcoming good and evil through a form of radical personal and social revolutionary experience. Following Nietzsche, Bataille argues that the element of life precedes rather than follows philosophy. Life is primary in relation to philosophy, it is always paradoxical, never strictly right, good or evil — there is no notion of fixed dualities at all. From here Bataille takes the Nietzschean invitation to overcome inhibitions as a social programme; overcoming all prohibitions, including sexual ones (which is why parts of Bataille's work are, in fact, pornography[44]). The French postmodernists — Michel Foucault (1926–1984), Gilles Deleuze (1925–1995), etc. — have actively developed the leftist version of Nietzscheanism.

Thus we can justify or criticise the 'Fascist' Hegel and the 'Fascist' Nietzsche, the 'liberal' Hegel and the 'liberal' Nietzsche and the 'Marxist' Hegel and the 'leftist' Nietzsche. But all these adaptations of Hegel and Nietzsche to the political ideologies of the modern do not exhaust their

---

42 Ayn Rand, *Capitalism: The Unknown Ideal* (London: Penguin, 1994).
43 Georges Bataille, *Inner Experience* (New York: SUNY Press, 1988).
44 Georges Bataille, *Ненависть к поэзии: Порнолатрическая проза* [Hate Poetry: Pornolatry Prose] (Moscow: Ladomir, 1999).

political philosophy. What is left behind cannot be fully explored and comprehended by the toolkit of modern political philosophy.

Pareto: Being Elite Is the True Meaning of Politics

To some extent, Italian Fascism was influenced by the theories of the major sociologist Vilfredo Pareto[45] (1848–1923), who elaborated, in part, the philosophy of Nicola Machiavelli. Pareto did not recognise the autonomous significance of political ideologies, believing that they were used by people to cover up a more prosaic reality — a violent struggle for power. In this, Pareto was close to both Hobbes, with his anthropological pessimism, and to Nietzsche, who developed the doctrine of the 'will to power' as the main expression of life in the political and social sphere.[46]

Pareto argues that society must be taken as an absolute given; we do not know where it came from or how it was organised, but we can observe that it has certain — ironclad — regularities. The main regularity is the existence of a political elite.

Pareto observes that in any politically and socially organised society, there will always be, by necessity, the elites and the masses.

An elite is a certain type, people who *can* and *want* to rule; this means that they take on the element of violence, are willing to exercise it over others and do not allow it to be exercised over themselves. An elite person is a person who delights in the very element of ruling, takes pleasure in ruling others and feels great pain when he himself is forced to obey. Pareto believes that this is peculiar to only a small part of society.

But the majority in society is always a mass, which cannot and does not really want to rule, to exert violence over others, to command, to order, to control the destiny and the lives of others. The masses are indecisive, prefer comfort and security to risky ventures, lead an orderly life and are willing to submit to authority without giving much thought to the basis on which that authority is built.

---

45   Vilfredo Pareto, *Compendium of General Sociology* (Minneapolis: University of Minnesota Press, 1980).
46   Nietzsche, *The Will to Power*.

According to Pareto, this has always been, is, and will always be the case. Neither the elites nor the masses change. All people belong to one category or another. Either you are an elite person or you are a mass person. The minority type of the elite always wants to rule and never wants to obey. Pareto does not parse the question of whether one becomes an elite person or is born an elite person — he simply captures this state of affairs, which is easily found in a wide variety of societies — archaic or modern, traditional or democratic. Unlike liberal theorists such as Spencer, Pareto does not say that it is an innate struggle for power. He simply records the existence of these types without explaining.

Pareto was a convinced materialist and an advocate of evolutionary theory. From his point of view, the political system of society is a projection of the human organism. The baser instincts form the 'remnants', *residui*, that affect people's unconscious and everyday behaviour. Pareto includes religion, magic, prejudice, etc. in this sphere. The verticality of the social and political hierarchy reflects the uprightness of the human species, and this uprightness is the functional analogue of the spinal column. The rationality of humans as a species is reflected in the rationality of social systems, and the model of equilibrium is a projection of brain activity.

The elite and the masses are sociological types, hence they are not simply held hostage to their position in society, but on the contrary, their very social typology predetermines this position. *The elites rush to the top, the masses sink to the bottom.* If a man of the masses is placed at the top of society, he cannot hold on to power and falls back to his 'natural place'. Likewise with members of the elite: wherever they are, they will naturally burst upwards. This leads Pareto to identify another group, the *counter-elite,* which includes elite types who for one reason or another do not have access to real power. The counter-elite is a reservoir for the replenishment of the ruling elite, which tends to grow decrepit and degenerate after being in power for too long. Pareto formulated the law of 'circulation of elites', according to which

- the first generation of the elite is heroic and active,

- the second is protective,
- and the third tends to lose the characteristics necessary to rule and gives way to new elites, created from among the counter-elite.

Pareto identifies another type, the *anti-elite*. In it he includes those who are fundamentally incapable of power, that is, under no circumstances can become an elite and perform its functions, but who are also different from the masses, since they are endowed with creative activity as well as rebelliousness and love of freedom. Pareto counts representatives of the bohemia, the creative intelligentsia, sectarians and criminal circles among the anti-elite. The counter-elite, while excommunicated from power, is often mixed with the anti-elite, and together they frequently participate in confrontation with the power elites. But if the counter-elite and the anti-elite succeed in overthrowing the existing—usually decrepit—elites, their paths diverge—the counter-elite becomes a full-fledged elite, while the anti-elite is relegated to the social periphery, being fundamentally incapable of exercising power.

Thus the whole typology of society is as follows:

- the elite who are in power,
- the masses, who are always at the bottom and are unable and unwilling to rule, but are always ready to obey and follow the rules established by the authorities,
- the counter-elite, the elite type who for some reason have been excommunicated from power, but are stubbornly striving to get into said power, and
- the anti-elite, chaotic elements and asocial types unable to rule or obey.

According to Pareto, the circulation of elites, that is, the replacement of decrepit elites by counter-elites, can take place in several ways: it can be peaceful and gradual (which is characteristic of democracy) or forceful and bloody (in revolutions, dynastic coups, etc.). However, the meaning underlying these cases is the same — democracy is a smoother method for the circulation of elites and not at all a distribution of power among all members of civil society, as liberal theory, falsely, claims.

Pareto's political ideas are sharply opposed to both liberalism (the First Political Theory) and Communism (the Second Political Theory), as he denies the significance of ideology or the validity of democracy, believing that both are merely a cover for the circulation of elites. Pareto was thus preparing the ground for the Third Political Theory, which would triumph in Italy in the 1920s. It is telling that Benito Mussolini considered himself a follower of Pareto and offered him the post of Senator of the Fascist Party in 1923.

Pareto's theories, while neither socialist nor liberal, remain firmly within political modernity. He himself is a materialist, atheist and agnostic, and his understanding of the nature of power and the state corresponds to the ideas of Bodin and Hobbes; Pareto even openly acknowledges Machiavelli as his direct predecessor.

Pareto's version of political philosophy, unlike Gentile's Hegelianism or Nietzsche's philosophy of life, remains entirely within the context of the New Age political paradigm, continuing the line of classical nationalism that emerged at the dawn of the New Age.

Pareto's ideas were picked up by other representatives of the neo-Machiavellian movement. Gaetano Mosca[47] (1858–1941), for instance, built the theory of the 'ruling class' on Pareto's theory of elites, highlighting the ability to rule and organise as the main trait that defines a special social type, which always, sooner or later, ends up on top and dominates the 'majority'. Another disciple of Pareto, Robert Michels[48] (1876–1936), expressed the same idea by introducing the concept of the 'iron law of oligarchy', that is, the sociological law according to which the management of society is always necessarily concentrated in the hands of a minority — a few dominant figures.

---

47 Gaetano Mosca, *Storia delle Dottrine Politiche* [History of Political Doctrines] (Bari: Laterza, 1937).

48 Robert Michels, *Soziologie als Gesellschaftswissenschaft* [Sociology as a Social Science] (Berlin: Mauritius, 1926).

All representatives of the neo-Maciavellian school denied political ideologies and religious views any political influence, justifying the realm of the Political as an independent and autonomous realm governed only by its inherent laws and rules.

Carl Schmitt: Friend/Enemy and the Structure of the Pluriverse

A major theorist of the Third Political Theory was the German philosopher and jurist Carl Schmitt, a giant of modern political science. Before the National Socialists came to power, Carl Schmitt was a staunch opponent of liberal democracy, and after 1933 he aligned himself with the regime established by Hitler. However, he belonged to the current of the Conservative Revolution, which was much broader than the ideology of National Socialism, but which had a number of overlaps with it. Carl Schmitt and most Conservative Revolutionaries rejected racism and were not so much advocating for the nation as for the peoples (in Herder's sense). Schmitt himself was a theorist of the distinct concept of the 'right of the people' (German: *Volksrechte*), opposing both the liberal theory of 'human rights' and the class-based approach of Communists, but at the same time differing significantly from etatism, from racism and from classical nationalism — with which, however, Schmitt has some commonalities (this concerns his realism in international relations and a positive reading of Hobbes[49]).

The most important concept introduced by Schmitt was that of the *Political*,[50] which we have already discussed. The Political (*das Politische*) is distinct from politics as a sphere of concrete steps and actions — it is the ontological and metaphysical basis of politics. In a sense, the Political as the essence of politics stands *above* politics and belongs to the realm of metapolitics, that is, to the realm of *Politica Aeterna*. Defining the Political in his seminal work *The Concept of the Political*, Schmitt writes:

---

49 Schmitt, *The Leviathan in the State Theory of Thomas Hobbes: Meaning and Failure of a Political Symbol*.

50 Carl Schmitt, *The Concept of the Political* (Chicago: University of Chicago Press, 2007).

> Specific to the political divide, on which political actions and motivations are based, is the division into *friend* and *foe*.[51]

The pair *amicus/hostis* (friend/enemy) is constitutive precisely for the domain of the Political, as it is not based on religious views or innate attitudes, but on a *reasoned assessment of the situation and a willful decision*. The friend/enemy is defined situationally, and this distinguishes this pair from other dichotomies — religious (god/devil), moral (good/evil), species (man/animal), gender (man/woman), etc. At the same time, the peculiarity of the enemy and friend figures is that they can theoretically change their places: the enemy and the friend are defined in concrete circumstances, and this definition itself is a constitutive factor of the Political. It is never completely obvious who is a friend and who is an enemy. It is a matter of sovereign *decision* upon which the whole structure of the Political as such depends. The Political begins only after the pair have been constructed.

According to Schmitt, the assignment of friend/enemy roles requires the existence of an authority that can be endowed with the capacity to make such judgements. And for this it must be constituted in the same way: that is, as a bearer of sovereign will, reason and decision-making capacity. Determining who is an enemy and who is a friend is always mutual — this presupposes a symmetrical gesture on the part of the other. And this other must be able, in its turn, to define friend and foe and act accordingly. That is, the Political presupposes in its foundations the presence of the other as a political Other. Any political unit is only itself in the presence of a coexisting political unit. Both enmity and friendship are reciprocal and situational, i.e. their definition includes the possibility of changing status under certain circumstances. In the realm of religion, morality, species or gender, no such action is possible: good cannot become evil, man cannot become an animal or vice versa, and here the dichotomy is an irreducible given that does not depend on will and circumstance. Politics, on the other hand, is constructed in relation to very concrete historical-geographical conditions: friend and foe are always

---

51 Ibid.

situational, concrete, located in a strictly defined space and time — locked into a political form, acting at the moment and in the given circumstances as the *subject of the Political*.

Hence the fundamental conclusion of all Schmittian political science: politics is *pluriversal* in nature, presupposing a pluriverse as a fundamental condition of its existence. Therefore, instead of universality, the Political is always presented as something regional, local, as a concrete order and a situational form. The only universal rule in the Political is the absence of any universality beyond a concrete political unit, a structure.

Schmitt attached great importance to the principle of sovereignty in international politics, following Bodin in this regard. For him, sovereignty and the decision made by the sovereign (*Entscheidung*) are transcendent in relation to all parts of the state and do not allow for assessments on a friend/enemy scale. The consequence of the enemy/friend decision in foreign policy is a binding law for the entire state, because in the transition from domestic to foreign policy, the subject of the decision changes — it shifts from a sub-state unit to the state proper. In practice, this is sometimes not the case, which means that the functional forms and structures of the 'direct power' (*potestas directa*) are violated. In any case, the very existence of the Political requires a pluriverse in the space of which the other can be defined as friend or foe.

This interpretation of the Political as a pluriverse reflected the main idea underlying the whole current of the Conservative Revolution: German sovereignty as the highest value and the right of the Germans to a special path (*Sonderweg*), to a special identity both in the European context and more broadly in the global context.

At the same time, for Schmitt the Political was the realm of the direct manifestation of the spirit: the definition of friend/enemy is influenced first and foremost by *value* factors and only then by interests. Power is thus, like the principle of order itself, a spiritual category, while the material aspects associated with the state and the process of ordering social processes are always secondary.

In defining sovereignty, Schmitt introduces another important term.

> The sovereign is he who decides on the state of emergency.[52]

An emergency (*Ernstfall*) situation occurs when the normal functioning of the legal process cannot continue and some extraordinary step is required to resolve the problematic situation: either embedded in the legal corpus as a potential option or made contrary to the law due to the circumstances. *The sovereign is not the one who has the right to make decisions in extraordinary circumstances, but the one who makes them.* It is in this, according to Schmitt, that the very essence of the Political is revealed.

This interpretation of sovereignty led Schmitt directly to the notion of dictatorship,[53] since it is the dictator who is most clearly seen as making a decision without reliance on any precedent or legislative basis. Schmitt thus justified Hitler's system of power in Nazi Germany, which the National Socialists took advantage of.

In his seminal work *Political Theology*,[54] Carl Schmitt shows the parallels between changes in the religious and metaphysical understanding of the world and transformations in political doctrines. Political systems strictly follow the smallest fluctuations in theological doctrines, which suggests that the Political is a form of expression of the human spirit as a whole, along with religion, philosophy, culture, etc. Hence the very concept of 'political theology'. *How theologians understand the status of God and man, and the relationship between them, directly affects which political and legal systems become primary and normative.* Just as the German sociologist Max Weber showed the mechanisms of the origin of capitalism from Protestant ethics, so Carl Schmitt demonstrates more generally the process by which political concepts and systems are formed from theological models.

Thus, in the Middle Ages, scholasticism and the theistic view of God dominate. Accordingly, the papacy becomes the bearer of supreme

---

52 Carl Schmitt, *Political Theology: Four Chapters on the Concept of Sovereignty* (Chicago: University of Chicago Press, 2006).
53 Carl Schmitt, *Dictatorship: From the Origin of the Modern Concept of Sovereignty to Proletarian Class Struggle* (Cambridge: Polity, 2013).
54 Schmitt, *Political Theology*.

sovereignty in politics, replacing, in the spirit of the teachings of Saint Augustine, the 'City of Heaven' in the earthly world. In the institution of the popes, the principle of the transcendental theological attitude is manifested in the vicars of Saint Peter on earth, and through them Christ himself: God the Creator is above all hierarchies of creatures, and therefore the highest power legitimately belongs only to Him; He is the Almighty, therefore His vicar on earth, the bishop of Rome, is above all earthly monarchies. This theistic attitude, according to Schmitt, predetermined the whole structure of the Political in the Middle Ages and was the basis of the scholastic understanding of sovereignty: only God is sovereign, and in part his viceroy on earth, the pope. Schmitt himself was a Catholic and therefore generally shared precisely this premodern view of the legitimate nature of power as the most valid form of 'political theology'.

The next form of 'political theology' emerges with Protestantism. Luther introduces the norm of personal experience and rational interpretation of religion. This eliminates the mediating model of the relationship between the 'City of Earth' and the 'City of Heaven', which was embodied in the Catholic understanding of the pope and in the concept of empire. This is how the notions of the modern state and sovereignty emerge. The meaning of sovereignty in Hobbes and Bodin, as well as in Machiavelli, is that *there is no supreme power over the sovereign.*

In the eighteenth and nineteenth centuries, Schmitt shows, there is a further immanentisation of theology—from the deism of the Enlightenment to the direct atheism and materialism of the liberals and socialists, which leads to a new conception of the structure of the state as a product of the 'social contract'.

In the last section of *Political Theology*, Carl Schmitt examines the counter-revolutionary projects of European conservatives—Joseph de Maistre (1753–1821), Juan Donoso Cortés (1809–1853) and Louis de Bonald (1754–1840)—who, having documented the processes prevailing in the 'political theology' of the New Age, took a counter-enlightenment stance, rejected the norms of modernity and, above all, its most radical and nihilistic[55] expression in liberalism, and proposed projects for restoring the

---

55 in terms of traditional theology

political system of the New Middle Ages. Schmitt himself was clearly in solidarity with this counter-revolutionary project and considered possible options to legalise movement in the opposite direction to the logic of the modern: from Weimar democracy to a German nation-state based on the principle of absolute sovereignty (with a possible dictatorship[56]) and through it to a new European empire in parallel with the restoration of the power and authority of the popes. He saw the counter-revolutionary project as feasible precisely because it concerned the freedom of the individual, who always has the possibility of making choices (*Entscheidungen*) in the realm of the spirit, i.e. religion and politics, which are the direct expression of the spirit.

Developing the legal basis for the future European empire, Carl Schmitt introduced, as we have said, the concept of the 'rights of peoples'.[57] This principle was the opposite of European New Age nationalism, as it denied the individual character of citizenship and the bourgeois system of domination of the normative Third Estate, which were at the core of the nation-state, and especially its treaty character, whose recognition led to liberal democracy that gradually abolished states in general in favour of a global 'civil society'. Schmitt saw German nationalism as a transitional stage towards an entirely new (for modernity) political organisation of Europe, which was to be based, in his view, on:

- the principle of imperial centralisation of strategic management,
- the unity of spiritual form (Christianity in its traditionalist version),
- the recognition of the subjects of imperial law not as artificial nations or citizens, but as organic units — peoples united by the commonality of their historical destiny.

---

56 Schmitt devoted an entire work to legal problems and types of dictatorship. Schmitt, *Dictatorship*.

57 Carl Schmitt, *Völkerrechtliche Großraumordnung mit Interventionsverbot für raumfremde Mächte. Ein Beitrag zum Reichsbegriff im Völkerrecht* [International Law on Greater Spatial Order with a Prohibition of Intervention by Powers from Outside the Sphere. A contribution to the concept of empire in international law] (Berlin: Deutscher Rechts Verlag, 1939).

The third point of the new European empire assumed that the peoples (*Völker*) become the subject of law, have their own representation and the ability to organise their internal structures on the basis of their cultural and historical traditions, as well as on the basis of free choice. The only limitation is the consideration of the strategic interests of the empire as a whole. Such a project is the essence of the Conservative Revolution: here the peoples of Europe are given the free choice of building a future based on a democratic decision (*Entscheidung*) by consensus, which allows a combination of both traditional and innovative elements as the empire has no power of prescriptive influence over this decision, which remains entirely within the power of the peoples as full subjects of the law. The peoples, relying on their history and culture, can choose a combination of past, present and future in any proportions, shaping and transforming themselves as a self-correcting project if necessary. It combines both conservatism and a spiritual appeal to eternity, as well as democracy and even revolution. Thus we find ourselves in the context of revolutionary nationalism as a Third Political Theory, constructed at a distance from political modernity as such and in direct opposition to liberalism and socialism.

On the other hand, according to Schmitt, the principle of the 'rights of peoples' must be fitted within the specific territorial framework that characterises the empire. To this end, he introduces the notion of '*great space*' (*Großraum*) as the initially approximate geographical area within which empire-building takes place. The 'great space' is that cultural field within which there are historical prerequisites of unification processes — either on the basis of precedent (the area of ancient empires), of spiritual and religious proximity, or of objective strategic and even economic interests. Schmitt himself defines the 'great space' not as a full-fledged concept (*Begriff*), but as a pre-concept (*Vorbegriff*), i.e. as a preparatory stage for the development of a full-fledged legal model. Schmitt traces the process of the formation of historical empires and finds everywhere a special stage where the empire-building centre pre-defines the horizons of inhabited or familiar lands. *The empire, therefore, before being built in practice, matures in spirit.* This same idea was advocated, as we have seen, by Hegel.

This notion of 'natural frontiers' is confirmed or disproved by a multitude of military operations, diplomatic treaties, political alliances, i.e. the whole content of politics. But this plan always exists in one way or another, and sooner or later — if the empire-building endeavour is successful — it turns into a concrete historical and political reality, which is subsequently given full legal form. This is the 'great space'. The way it is conceptualised by the empire-building elite actively influences the concreteness of political processes until the transition from a pre-concept to a full-fledged concept occurs, and 'great space' gives way to a full-fledged empire with its boundaries, laws and, according to Schmitt, a legal code based on the principle of the 'rights of peoples'.

Revolutionary Nationalism: The Limits of Ideology

The ideology of the Third Path is not confined to historical Fascism and National Socialism — it is a much wider phenomenon. Firstly, there are characteristic features inherent in classical nationalism, which did not develop into a full-fledged ideology, but had a significant influence on the Third Political Theory, becoming part of it. We only encounter a set ideology in the twentieth century, when nationalism acquires a revolutionary character. In part, this ideologisation of nationalism is a response to the pronounced ideology of Marxism. The conceptual consistency of the Second Political Theory — which, by the way, largely contributed to the fact that liberalism was perceived as a 'bourgeois ideology' rather than as a set of theses and attitudes — forced nationalists to develop symmetrical conceptual complexes that: first, took liberalism and Communism into account and provided answers to their basic postulates; second, integrated certain aspects of classical nationalism (mercantilism, realism, and so on); and thirdly, addded completely new and atypical elements where modernism and innovation (Nietzscheanism, Futurism, existentialism, etc.) coexisted with a reference to premodern forms of the Political (Hegelian idealism, Schmitt's justification of empire and the 'catechism' function, Julius Evola's traditionalism, etc.). In part close to revolutionary nationalism, the current of the Conservative Revolution that emerged in Germany, itself extremely heterogeneous, represented a parallel phenomenon, which can be seen both as a version of the Third Political Theory and as something independent and separate. Therefore, the Third Political Theory, unlike liberalism and Marxism, which are clearly and unambiguously structured, gives the impression of being eclectic, contradictory and inconsistent. In order to better understand its main semantic nodes, one should imagine its general conceptual field.

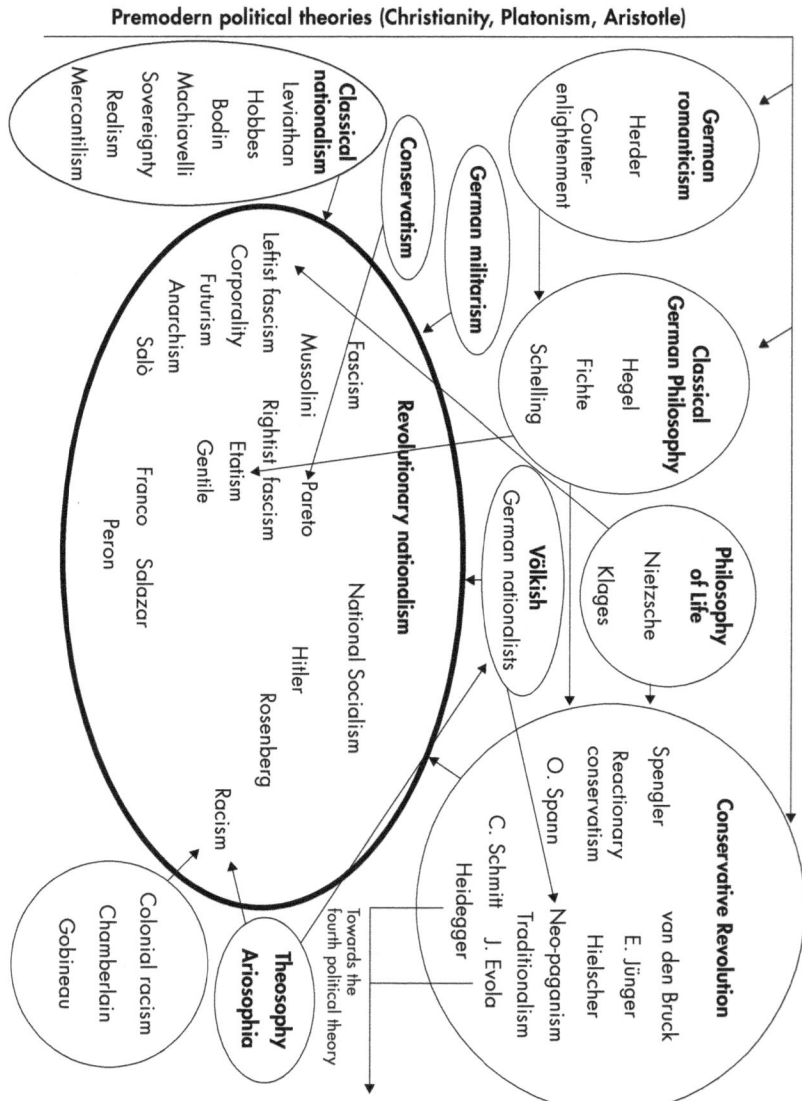

Figure 19. Third Political Theory.

Strictly speaking, the Third Political Theory should be recognised as revolutionary nationalism, which manifested itself most vividly (and simultaneously most monstrously) in the Italian Fascism of Mussolini and the

German National-Socialism of Hitler, and in a less accentuated manner in Franco's Spain, Salazar's Portugal and the era of General Perón in Argentina. Other ideological currents, worldviews and socio-political and economic trends created a breeding ground for revolutionary nationalism in the twentieth century, affecting it, providing it with separate elements and conceptual content, but not exhausting it, not defining it and not claiming to be dogmatic. In this the Third Political Theory differs from the First (liberalism) and the Second (Marxism): here there is no strictly established theoretical dogma, which all those who speak in the name of the respective ideologies are forced to acknowledge. The Third Political Theory was not as ideologically totalitarian as liberalism and Marxism, which allow no doubt at all about their fundamental foundations. In revolutionary nationalism everything depended on a particular leader or dictator. In National Socialist Germany, for example, racism acquired the status not only of ideological dogma but also of a legal system, whereas in Fascist Italy racial theses had a peripheral importance and only became more accentuated during the period of the Italian Social Republic under direct German occupation. Similarly, Franco, Salazar and Perón offered their own original versions, and in these third path regimes great importance was attached to Catholicism and traditional conservatism, whereas neo-pagan motifs prevailed in National Socialism, and Fascism focused on secular heroism stylised to the ethical culture of ancient Rome.

Nevertheless, all these political forms may well be grouped together as a Third Political Theory, since the variety of specific versions and interpretations is broadly comparable to the many currents in both liberalism and leftist ideology, which also contained several currents although their ideological boundaries were more strictly delineated and defined. The Third Political Theory was less dogmatic, although some of the political regimes based on it were sharply totalitarian in style, imposing their policies in a no less forceful (indeed, often in a more rigid and straightforward) way than Communism, let alone liberalism (which preferred to implement its ideology through suggestion, soft power, culture and economics, rather than direct and brutal political propaganda[58]).

Italian Fascism: Futurism and Conservatism

The Third Political Theory was most explicitly manifested in Italian Fascism and German National Socialism, which for some time extended their influence and direct political power over almost the entire territory of continental Europe. But when considering these forms of revolutionary nationalism one should always bear in mind the entire theoretical field of this ideology, which goes beyond the much narrower boundaries of historical Fascism and National Socialism.

Italian Fascism came before German National Socialism. It was the reaction of Italian socialism to the internationalist and strictly class-based dogmatism of Marxism. Fascism had its origins in the left-wing belief that it was necessary to fight capitalism, bourgeois exploitation and the power of the economic elites. However, the adherents of this current were convinced that the bourgeoisie is an international phenomenon which is guided by interests that do not take into account the situation of nations and states at all. Therefore, the Italian Fascists' struggle against capitalism initially combined the social and national levels. Somewhat similar ideas had been formulated earlier by the French leftist philosopher Georges Sorel (1847–1922), whose authority was recognised both by Fascists and anarchists, as well as by some currents of socialists. In principle, many aspects of early Fascism were extremely close to anarchism. For example, one of the most famous Italian theorists of anarchism, Curzio Malaparte[59] (1898–1957), joined Fascism at its early stage and took part in Mussolini's march on Rome. Fascist ideas and a particularly militant, active style of

---

58 However, in recent decades, and especially after the fall of the USSR, liberalism gradually began to acquire overtly totalitarian features, gradually tightening its ideology, coinciding to some extent with the norms of 'political correctness', which became a kind of ethical rule, but also the basis for a number of legislative provisions, proclaiming liberalism not just the dominant ideology, but also a dogma and legislative axiom.

59 Curzio Malaparte, *Technique du coup d'Etat* [Coup d'Etat: The Technique of Revolution] (Paris: Grasset, 2008).

struggle were also attractive to some Communists, most notably Niccolo Bombacci (1879–1945), one of the founders of the Italian Communist Party, who collaborated with the Fascists.

It is worth pointing out that the avantgarde art movement of the Futurists was at the forefront of Fascism, inspired and led by Filippo Tommaso Marinetti (1876–1944), who became Mussolini's closest ally. Ezra Pound (1885–1972), the great American avantgarde poet, was also a fervent supporter of Fascism. He moved to Italy and appeared on the radio in support of Mussolini up until the occupation of Italy by American troops. Despising interest-based capital, he was particularly inspired by the anti-capitalist aspects of Fascist ideology and practice, which he nevertheless considered insufficient.

Early Fascism, led by the charismatic Mussolini, was a left-revolutionary and fiercely anti-bourgeois current inspired by the ideas of Nietzsche and the pursuit of radical futurist transformations. In this context, it initially had an obvious nationalist component, which continued the earlier tendencies of the Risorgimento, an early Italian nationalism that combined republican, bourgeois-liberal and monarchist elements. Fascist nationalism, however, was distinguished by its revolutionary and anti-bourgeois character, which was the basis of the Third Political Theory.

Mussolini was not an original thinker, but he had the intellectual calibre and sophistication to comprehend the body of political ideas behind nascent Fascism, as well as the enormous will to put this heterogeneous set of ideas into practice.

The ideology of Fascism — as the Italian version of the Third Political Theory — was a combination of several strands:

- the cold *political technology* of power in the spirit of Machiavelli's *Prince*, systematically developed by Pareto and the neo-Machiavellians;
- the *right-wing Hegelianism* of Gentile, who justified the need for a strong leadership of the nation-state by the very structure of the formation of the Italian Historical in its relation to the ontology and destiny of the spirit;

- *the romantic heroic spirit* of Gabriele D'Annunzio (1863–1938), based on a Nietzschean orientation toward the Superman and a glorification of war and battle (this includes the anarchist ideas of Malaparte);

- the futuristic *cult of technology* (Marinetti);

- an appeal to *Roman ethics and ideals,* as well as to fundamental conservative values (Roman traditionalists — such as Julius Evola, Guido De Giorgio [1890–1957], etc.).

All of this is a direct continuation of the ideas and trends that took shape during the Risorgimento era, which gave rise to Italy proper as a single political entity.

At the same time, Fascism absorbed a number of ideas of non-dogmatic socialism, developed the theory of a corporate (union-based) society and adopted the colonial strategy that had become the norm of European politics in the early modern period. The hallmarks of Fascism were

- the commissarial dictatorship[60] (Schmitt) of the Duce,

- the totalitarian nature of one-party rule,

- the relativisation of legal norms and liberal democratic institutions in the face of 'revolutionary expediency'.

If we look for parallels to the history of ancient Rome, Mussolini's reforms were — in many ways a parody — analogous to the establishment of the Empire by Octavian Augustus (63 BC–14 AD) after the Roman Republic period. In both cases, a dictatorship conditioned by a specific historical situation was elevated to a political principle.

In the second phase, after Mussolini came to power, formally as prime minister but with dictatorial powers (hence the title *Il Duce,* 'leader'), the revolutionary zeal of early Fascism began to give way to a more classical nationalism. Mussolini, who had previously held an anti-clerical and anti-monarchist stance, made compromises with the Vatican and representatives of big business, though maintaining some socialist institutions,

---

60 Schmitt, *Dictatorship.*

above all trade unions and corporations, which became the social base of the Fascist regime.

By 1928, the Fascist regime began to take on increasingly clear totalitarian features — all other parties were banned. In 1929, Mussolini signed agreements with the Vatican.

During this period, up to 1943, the politics of Fascist Italy were generally quite conservative and had shifted significantly from revolutionary nationalism (which persisted at the level of style, slogans and symbols) to classical nationalism. Nevertheless, Gentile's right-wing Hegelianism added a special dimension here. At the same time, traditionalism as an alternative ideology to Gentile was formulated in this period by the philosopher Julius Evola, who was a supporter of a return to the pre-Christian sacred tradition of Europe[61] and a member of the Conservative Revolutionary movement based in Germany. The influence of Evola's ideas was marginal and insignificant, especially as he criticised Fascism for its 'plebeianism', 'modernism' and 'leftism'.[62] Evola became famous after 1945, when he became an iconic figure for most Italians who did not embrace the liberal pro-American regime.

After Hitler came to power in Germany, which instantly turned the country into a thriving, powerful empire, Mussolini tried to pursue an independent foreign policy, but gradually he became closer to Hitler, which led him to join Germany in the Second World War despite his personal reluctance to enter into conflict with the USSR, as he had a certain sympathy for the Bolshevik regime. The Communists and liberals resisted Fascism throughout its reign in Italy and, during the Second World War, began — with support from the West and from the USSR — direct guerrilla action. This became a civil war, dividing Italians into two camps — Fascists and anti-Fascists.

In 1943, with the support of left-wing forces and the Mafia (with whom Mussolini was in a bitter struggle), American troops landed in southern Italy and a number of Mussolini's closest allies and members of the higher bureaucracy overthrew him and placed him under arrest. Mussolini was

---

61 Julius Evola, *Heathen Imperialism* (Thompkins & Cariou, 2007).
62 Evola, *Views from the Right*.

rescued from prison by a Nazi task force and Germany occupied the northern parts of Italy, where an Italian Social Republic, in Salò, was established under the freed Mussolini. There Mussolini, shocked by the betrayal of the Fascist hierarchy, reverted to early Fascism in its leftist and anti-bourgeois form. Under pressure from the National Socialists, he was now forced to accept racist provisions, which were completely alien to him and to Italian Fascism in general.

After the fall of Hitler's Germany, the Americans and partisans defeated Salò, Mussolini was hanged, and this time it was those who remained loyal to Fascism who were repressed and purged. Thus the two sections of Italian society switched places.

It is worth pointing out the absence of racism at the base of the Third Political Theory in its Fascist incarnation. For example, Italian Jews made the following statement after Mussolini's death in 1945: the regime had nothing to do with the persecution of Jews on ethnic grounds and Jews could occupy any position in Italian society. Mussolini organised neither mass executions nor genocide. This did not detract from the totalitarian nature of the ideology, though, and nationalism and colonialism (in Libya and Ethiopia) were official parts of the Fascist worldview.

Nor was racism (or anti-Semitism) present in other forms of the Third Path ideology — Franco in Spain, Salazar in Portugal, much less Perón in Argentina. Consequently, racism and anti-Semitism are not hallmarks of the Third Political Theory. Revolutionary or classical nationalism and a rigid totalitarian character, as well as the dictatorial powers of a charismatic leader — these features are to a greater or lesser extent inherent in all iterations of this ideology. Racism and anti-Semitism are only found in German National Socialism, the largest and most sinister, but not the first and far from the only example of the Third Political Theory being put into practice.

Guido De Giorgio's Sacred Fascism

On the periphery of Fascist ideology, a particular ideological current was taking shape which cannot be strictly classified as being part of the Third Political Theory on the grounds that it rejected the political modern paradigm itself and its preconditions: materialism, atomism, individualism, the philosophy of matter, of the receiver, of the *chora*. It is the philosophy of traditionalism, the foundation of which was laid by the French philosopher René Guénon — who himself remained at a distance from all political theories of modernity, seeing in them a direct antithesis to what, from his perspective, was an ideal or normal understanding of the Political, possible only outside of modernity in the field of Tradition. In Italy, Guénon's followers, the philosophers Guido De Giorgio and Julius Evola, chose a different attitude towards Fascism, seeking to turn it from a political theory of the modern into something else, something sacred. In this, they were close to some representatives of the German Conservative Revolution, and Evola maintained close ties with its main figures. Traditionalism, as well as some strands of the Conservative Revolution, do not so much belong to the Third Political Theory, as they anticipate the Fourth Political Theory.[63]

In particular, Guido De Giorgio, an Italian follower of Guénon, saw in Mussolini's Fascism — and in particular in his appeal to ancient Rome and his rejection of liberalism and Communism (as two versions of modernity) — an opportunity to realise the project of restoring Tradition. He understood that the Third Path also contained elements of modernity, but believed that this ideology had the potential to evolve into something different. Heidegger and Evola thought the same. Guido De Giorgio developed the outline of an *alternative Fascism*, which he called 'sacred Fascism'. However, such 'sacred Fascism', which denies nationalism, materialism, various forms of racism and colonialism, could no longer belong to the Third Political Theory, representing something beyond it. In fact, De Giorgio understands 'sacred Fascism' not as a political doctrine or the regime of Mussolini, but as the Roman Tradition itself, which he traces from the age of antiquity to the present day.

De Giorgio interprets Fascism from the symbol of the Lictorian *fasces*, representing twelve rods and a double axe.[64] For him, 'Fascism' is that

---

63 Dugin, *The Fourth Way: Introduction to the Fourth Political Theory*.
64 The Lictorian *fasces* are an ancient symbol of the Etruscans.

which symbolises this sacred object, that is, that which is metaphysically linked to the fasces.

> One bond that connects the twelve rods of the Lictorian fasces, and one piercing lightning bolt of power captured in the double axe: it is the supreme emblem of Tradition, as it represents the vertical current: ascension and victory.[65]

Therefore 'fasciscation' is not the spread of political Fascism, but the turning of the spiritual gaze to the Latin *Logos*, to the essence of Rome itself as a *point of eternity* within the flow of time. De Giorgio writes:

> A return to the Roman Tradition implies a 'fasciscation' of Europe and the world, an integral return to the spirit of truth that in name, symbol and reality is Rome. Rome is the sacred, invincible, indomitable pinnacle beyond all selfishness and human or populist ambition, in the true light of the plan of the Divine to which Rome belongs. This is the ultimate goal of the Roman Tradition, the exaltation of the power of Rome in the context of Tradition, which alone is capable of granting truth, justice and greatness to the West.
>
> The restoration that we call for, taking as our guiding thread the inspiration and ideal of Dante, is a return to the spirit of Rome, not merely a repetition of the past, which, among other things, is impossible, since nothing transient repeats itself, but a direct adherence to the eternal foundations of truth contained in the scriptures and ancient symbols. This enormous undertaking of fasciscation involves an inhuman effort which men of good will must make if they are to save the West from disaster, not so much from the material and external, which in itself does not particularly affect us, but from the deeper, inner and spiritual: a disaster of the spiritual life, a collapse of truth, which is already disintegrating in this tumultuous decay of impulses, aspirations, errors, egoisms such as has never before been seen in world history.[66]

Guido De Giorgio sees Dante as the most prominent exponent of 'sacred Fascism'. He speaks of it in the following terms:

> In Dante, East and West balance each other in a single centre, which, in essence, is Primordial Tradition, that is, the unified and sovereignly realised universality of Tradition. In the Middle Ages there were close contacts between East and

---

65 Guido de Giorgio, *La Tradizione romana* [Roman Tradition] (Rome: Edizioni Mediterranee, 1989), p. 317.
66 Giorgio, *La Tradizione romana*, p. 45.

West, and in this great time, as never in other epochs, the elements of the various traditions complemented each other, being transmitted orally from teacher to disciple, and from disciple to disciple. Dante appeared at the end of this epoch, when the Dominicans and the Franciscans, though substantially degenerated and at odds with one another, still represented two paths, the cherubic and the seraphimic — the realisation of the Divine, both anthropocentric, but different in their natures and in their methods.[67] But it was Dante who managed to unite them, to *'fascisce'* them without mixing them up. And it must be said that when we use the term 'fascisce', we do not mean anything resembling syncretism or blending: 'fascisce' in the sense of Tradition means to give each road, each element its own direction, centre, axis, without allowing a merger. This is the novelty of the fixedness that Tradition embodies.[68]

And further:

In Dante, 'fasciscation' reaches its climax, East and West, Rome ancient and new, temporal and eternal, earth and heaven, man and God, everything is accentuated, combined, united in the supreme vertical, which is Rome. This is what Sacred Fascism is all about, the genuine triumph of justice and truth in man and the world; and the fact that there will be disagreements, battles, setbacks — all this is irrelevant, because it all happens within traditional society, where everything is maintained by the supreme equilibrium provided by the key-holders (*clavigero*) and bearers of fasces (*fascigero*), the Kingdom (*regnum*) and Empire (*imperium*), forever united in Rome.[69]

---

67 De Giorgio is referring to Song 11 (verses 37–43) from Dante's Paradise where he speaks of a vision of St Dominic and St Francis of Assisi, the founders of the two main monastic orders in Europe, the Dominican and the Franciscan. 'One was blazing with the seraphim's glow; / In the other, wisdom seemed so bright, / That he shone with the cherub's glow. Only one of them I praise, / But two are honoured by the one who speaks of one, / Because their goal was common.' Dante Alighieri, *The Divine Comedy* (Oxford: Oxford University Press, 2008). Dante links the Franciscans to the figure of seraphim and the Dominicans to that of cherubim. Moreover, Dante specifies that both the seraphim and cherubim paths lead to the same goal. De Giorgio builds on this theory that the two monastic orders represent two parallel paths of spiritual realisation, which must be linked by a 'sacred fascisce'.

68 Giorgio, *La Tradizione Romana*, p. 316–317.

69 Giorgio, *La Tradizione Romana*, p. 317.

Julius Evola: Fascism and Criticism from the Right

Another Italian traditionalist who tried to reinterpret Fascism in the spirit of overcoming modernity was Julius Evola.

Following Guénon, Evola discovered Eastern metaphysics and *Philosophia Perennis*, and gained a fundamental metaphysical foundation for his radical and largely spontaneous rejection of the modern world, already evident in his youth in his sympathies for Dadaism and antibourgeois nihilism. *Modernity, according to Guénon, is the result not of progress, but of degradation,* of the decadence of sacred civilisation. Therefore, a man, faithful to the spiritual Tradition, must logically be *in rigid and irreconcilable opposition to modernity*. The modern world, New Age, on the one hand, and Tradition, on the other, are two *mutually exclusive* phenomena: *only war* is possible between them. Evola takes this idea completely to heart and clearly defines his place in this war — *on the side of Tradition* against the modern world. *Revolt against the Modern World*[70] is the title of his seminal book, in which Evola systematically sets out his worldview. He outlines the process of degradation of sacred civilisation from the Golden Age to the Iron Age, offering an original version for reconstructing the historical process and the evolution of civilisation types, up to the extreme degree of degeneration and decadence, which he identifies in the European civilisation of the New Age.[71]

However, unlike Guénon, Evola does not accept this decline as inevitable and calls on the last bearers of Tradition in the West to rise up in *revolt*. It is this 'active traditionalism' that explains his relative support for Fascism and occasional contacts with Mussolini. Later, Evola would critically rethink Fascism as a phenomenon (*Fascism Viewed from the Right*[72]), dismissing his hopes for the possibility of its evolution in a traditionalist vein as unfulfilled.

---

70 Julius Evola, *Revolt against the Modern World* (Vermont: Inner Traditions, 1995).
71 Julius Evola, *Men Among the Ruins* (Vermont: Inner Traditions, 2002).
72 Evola, *Fascism Viewed from the Right*.

German National Socialism: From Left to Right

German nationalism belongs to the same type of revolutionary nationalism as Italian Fascism. The word 'Fascism' is usually taken to mean 'National Socialism' without making a distinction, which creates a distorted picture of the entire Third Political Theory, coloured by memories of the appalling practices of Hitler's regime and the extreme racism, which led to the extermination of huge numbers of people on the grounds of their ethnicity. That racism and the mass extermination practices based on it were an integral part of the ideology of Nazi Germany is indisputable, and therefore the historical German National Socialism cannot be separated from the racism which formed an organic and, in some sense, central part of this ideology. But this feature is absent from classical nationalism (with the exception of some theories justifying colonial practices, and often organically combined with liberalism — especially in the Anglo-Saxon world), nor is it characteristic of Italian Fascism or other versions of revolutionary nationalism. Nationalism and racism are completely different concepts. Nationalism is a political ideology concerned with emphasising the value of the identity of the population of a nation-state. That is to say, the nation is an artificial concept denoting all citizens of a given state, with an agreement on the relative individual nature of citizenship. Nationalism is thus a more strident and aggressive form of patriotism, a love of one's state, relative to other states (and by extension nations). It is a political concept, which presupposes at its very foundation statehood and individual citizenship. This is the case with classical nationalism and in the most general sense with revolutionary nationalism. The main difference between the two lies not in the sharpness of nationalism, but in the relationship to capitalism, the bourgeoisie, the market society and the institutions of bourgeois democracy. Classical nationalism fully recognises capitalism, whereas revolutionary nationalism either denies it altogether or seeks to subordinate it rigidly — politically and ideologically — to national and state interests.

German National Socialism belongs to revolutionary nationalism but also incorporates a racial component.

Yet, as with Italian Fascism, early National Socialism was much more left-wing, traces of which are preserved in the very name 'National Socialist German Workers' Party', where the address to the workers had an important ideological load. Gradually, however, Hitler began to draw closer to conservative circles and the broad ideological stream of the Conservative Revolution, meanwhile increasingly emphasising the racial component of his ideology. This meant a rift with left-wing Nazis such as Otto Strasser (1897–1974) and National Bolsheviks such as Ernst Niekisch (1889–1967), who stood in opposition to Hitler. Thus, gradually, left-wing National Socialism began to shift to the right.[73] Racism, meanwhile, was inherent at every stage of the movement, from the earliest to the latest. However, this in no way applied to the Conservative Revolution.

Pragmatically, this distinguishing feature of German National Socialism was due to the fact that German nationalism itself historically appealed to Germans who lived in the territories of different states — in Prussia, Austria, Switzerland, Italy and in the rather independent principalities and regions formerly part of the Western Roman Empire. At the same time, some Germans practised Protestantism (Lutheranism) and some Catholicism. There were also strong motifs of Enlightenment, Counter-Enlightenment, Romanticism, and radical conservatism in German culture. The ideas of the founders of classical philosophy (Fichte, Hegel, etc.) formed the basis of the Second Reich, the Germany created in the nineteenth century by Otto von Bismarck (1815–1898) around Prussia. But with the end of the First World War, the Second Reich fell and a new nationalism was needed. This is where the focus on race, which initially applied only to Germans themselves living in different states, came in. It simply could not be 'nationalism' precisely because Germans belonged to different nation-states, i.e. different nations, and in order to unite them all in a common polity a new concept had to be proposed — one as artificial as the other New Age political concepts of the individual, class, etc. In Italian Fascism, such a concept was the state and the nation proper, where

---

[73] The transition from leftist to rightist Fascism has been described in literary form by the Japanese writer and playwright Yukio Mishima (1925–1970). Yukio Mishima, *My Friend Hitler and Other Plays* (New York: Columbia University Press, 2002).

the focus was also on the artificial community of the inhabitants of the Italian peninsula, who had historically belonged to different polities — Southern Italy (originally part of Greater Greece, then Byzantium, the Lombard kingdoms and later Spain), Central Italy, where Rome proper and the Vatican played an important role, and Northern Italy, linked to the west with France, to the centre with Switzerland, and to the east with Austria. The Italian identity was an artificial nation. But in order to unite the Germans after the fall of the Second Reich, a more generalising concept was needed, a role that was fulfilled by the concept of 'race'.

Racial Ideas in Germany

Racist ideas found their way into National Socialism from England, France and the mystical sect of the Theosophists. For German culture itself, racism was completely alien, and the idea of the superiority of one race over another, a less valuable race, was not widespread in Germany because of its limited colonial experience. As we have seen, the romanticist Herder, who influenced the German identity, believed that all people are thoughts of God, and this excluded any hierarchy between them, much less any racial inequality. One of the first theses about the inequality of human races was advanced by the French sociologist Arthur de Gobineau[74] (1816–1882). The thesis of the superiority of 'whites' over coloured peoples was actively disseminated in the British Empire, which based its colonial policy on this. The British were not just described as conquerors, but as bearers of 'progress' and 'the highest form of culture'. Such views were shared by many English liberals — notably Spencer and Mill. The general theory of racism was also supplemented with anti-Semitism by the British author Houston Stewart Chamberlain[75] (1855–1927), who significantly influenced Hitler's worldview.

---

74 Arthur de Gobineau, *An Essay on the Inequality of Human Races*.
75 Houston Stewart Chamberlain, *The Foundations of the Nineteenth Century* (Massachusetts: Adamant Media Corporation, 2003).

Another source of racial theories came from the extravagant teachings of the Theosophists,[76] who hypothesised a succession of four races, based on various religious sources from Eastern civilisations, with the white race coming, in their view, from the far north, where there had once been a special Arctic continent, Hyperborea. Some German and Austrian Theosophists combined this doctrine with German nationalism and created 'Ariosophia',[77] which formed the basis of the 'Aryan theory' and Nordicism. The 'true Aryans' in this theory were generally considered to be Germans — sometimes more broadly the Germanic peoples.

Thus a combination of the pragmatic concept of the unification of the German ethnos, European (primarily Anglo-Saxon) colonialism, anti-Semitism (in which an important role was played by an aversion to 'world Jewry' as synonymous with capitalism and internationalism — i.e. the rejection of the First and Second Political Theories, among the prominent representatives of which were, in fact, many Jews) and occultist 'Nordism' came together to form the National Socialist version of racism, which played a very important, if not key, role in this ideology.

Later, the racist ideas were adapted to the German variety of revolutionary nationalism by Alfred Rosenberg[78] (1893–1946), the official theorist of National Socialism, whose book *The Myth of the Twentieth Century* was considered the main ideological work of National Socialist Germany, alongside Hitler's own *Mein Kampf*.[79]

It was with this racial attitude that the most heinous practices and crimes were committed by the National Socialists, compromising biological racism itself and, after the fall of Hitler's regime, becoming the main argument against the Third Political Theory as a whole. Although racism was a particular feature of German nationalism, and had entered German society rather late and from other European cultures, the scale of racially

---

76 René Guénon, *Theosophy: History of a Pseudo-Religion* (Sophia Perennis et Universalis, 2004).

77 Nicholas Goodrick-Clarke, *The Occult Roots of Nazism* (London: Tauris Parke Paperbacks, 2012).

78 Alfred Rosenberg, *Der Mythus des 20. Jahrhunderts* (München: Hoheneichen-Verlag, 1930).

79 Adolf Hitler, *Mein Kampf*, trans. Ralph Manheim (New York: Random House, 1992).

motivated persecution, genocide and the adoption of racial laws legitimising state practices against members of 'inferior races' overshadowed all other aspects of the Third Path, revolutionary nationalism, and to some extent nationalism as an ideology.

So after 1945, when the countries of the bourgeois West (USA, England and their allies) and the Communist East (USSR) jointly defeated the Axis countries (Germany, Italy and those who joined them), the Third Political Theory was condemned at the Nuremberg Trials for crimes against humanity and declared 'criminal'. Thus, racism, which was not a major feature of the Third Political Theory, pushed the whole ideology beyond the boundaries of what was acceptable. And although after the fall of Communism in the USSR in 1991 the representatives of the First Political Theory tried to outlaw the Second Political Theory on similar grounds — referring to the large-scale crimes committed by Lenin and Stalin, which caused the deaths of millions — this was not achieved to the extent that it was with revolutionary nationalism.

The Conservative Revolution: Against the Subject of Modernity

For a complete picture of the Third Political Theory, even in Germany itself, it should be noted that National Socialism represented only one branch. Thus, Armin Mohler (1920–2003), in his book *The Conservative Revolution in Germany 1918–1932*,[80] shows that Hitler's National Socialism, if we take its ideological component, was a rather insignificant brook in a vast stream comprising a multitude of authors, journals, currents, groups and circles. Mohler summarises this as the 'Conservative Revolution' movement.

Some of the greatest representatives of philosophical thought, such as Oswald Spengler, Karl Schmitt, Martin Heidegger, Werner Sombart, Ernst Jünger (1895–1998), Arthur Moeller van den Bruck (1876–1925) — the

---

80 Armin Mohler, *The Conservative Revolution in Germany 1918–1932* (Brooklyn, NY: Radix Media, 2018).

author of the 'Third Reich'[81] concept itself —, and many other authors with a global reach belonged to this ideology of the Conservative Revolution. Some of them were indirectly involved with National Socialism, some directly, some were opponents, some were travelling companions and others were in exile. Thus, Ernst Jünger, who was a famous writer by 1933, refused to become a National Socialist member of the Reichstag. He spoke contemptuously of Hitler and his movement.

In theory, the representatives of the Conservative Revolution could take the following positions with regard to National Socialism:

- consider National Socialism as a transitional phase to a more perfect model (this was the case of Schmitt and Heidegger, as well as early Jünger);
- adopt a radically negative stance towards it (Thomas Mann [1875–1955], Ernst Niekisch, author of the anti-Nazi programme book *Hitler — a German Fate*[82] [1909–1942], Harro Schulze-Boysen, one of the activists of the 'Red Orchestra', etc.);
- regard it indifferently as parody and imitation (the later Jünger, Friedrich Hielscher [1902–1990], Ernst von Salomon [1902–1972], etc.).

But in all cases, regardless of their specific relationship to the Third Political Theory, almost all representatives of the Conservative Revolution interpreted the main point, *the subject*, differently. All three political ideologies of the modern age were based on a Cartesian understanding of the subject, the basic properties of which were thought to be will and reason. However, this common subject was given concrete expression in each of the ideologies. Liberalism identified the subject with the *individual*, regarding it as the normative 'measure of things'. Hence the very morality of liberalism, which consists in demanding the emancipation of the individual from all forms of collective identity: religious, ethnic, racial, class

---

81 Arthur Moeller van den Bruck, *Germany's Third Empire* (London: Arktos Media, 2012).
82 Ernst Niekisch, *Hitler — ein deutsches Verhängnis* [Hitler–A German Fate] (Berlin: Widerstands-Verlag, 1932).

(since the late twentieth century, also gender, and, finally, in the postmodernist versions, species — that is, humanity).

The subject of Marxism is *class* (two antagonistic classes), which serves as the principal agent of history, expressing in itself history's laws and dynamics of formation.

The subject of nationalism is *the nation-state* (political nation), as in Italian Fascism, or *race*, as in Hitler's National Socialism.

But for the representatives of the Conservative Revolution this was quite different. All of them presented a subject which simply had no conceptual place in modernity:

- culture (Spengler);
- people (*Volk*), spirit (Moeller van den Bruck);
- order (Schmitt);
- *Dasein* (Heidegger),
- the heroic worker (Jünger), and so on.

Such a subject included both rationality and the will, as well as contemplation and a sense of the sacred (*das Heilige*), that is, something *irrational*, holistic, mystical and mythical, belonging to the depths of religious experience. Thus, in the Conservative Revolution we can see a prototype of what we call the 'Fourth Political Theory'.[83] That is, a political philosophy that consciously and consistently builds its topicality *outside the modern, in opposition to the modern, overcoming the modern and refuting it.*

At the same time, the representatives of the Conservative Revolution almost unanimously rejected racism, and if they supported National Socialism, they regarded it as revolutionary nationalism and the Third Political Theory in a generalised form. The paths of ideology in Germany in the 1930s and 1940s thus diverged significantly.

---

83 Dugin, *The Fourth Way: Introduction to the Fourth Political Theory*.

Ernst Jünger: The Gestalt of the Worker

Ernst Jünger was a key figure in the Conservative Revolution. He was a participant in the First World War and had a profound existential and philosophical experience of it. He describes modern war as a *return to the elements* and a total *dehumanisation of existence*, seeing it as the clearest manifestation of the nihilism of which Nietzsche spoke. Twentieth-century war destroyed all the illusions of the Enlightenment, placing man, devoid of properties, in the face of technology that is completely out of control. In modern warfare, man loses his cultural content; all that is left of him is pure will, a reflection of a cold mechanical and technical objectivity within the subject.

Jünger summed up his ideas and reflections philosophically in his book *The Worker*,[84] which became the most famous programmatic text of the Conservative Revolution. Here, Jünger deploys the concept of *revolutionary nationalism* as the leftmost version of the Conservative Revolution. For Jünger, the main lesson of Nietzsche lay in the discovery of the totality of New Age nihilism, from which he sees no possible escape, much less in a return to the old times and ancient ways (unlike most conservatives). In the face of nihilism, as in war, all that remains for man is the will, which must be asserted, according to Jünger, in the construction of a technocratic society, a state ruled by an iron dictatorship. Jünger sees the figure of the worker as a creative ideal, a being who has no cultural or emotional content whatsoever, only pure will, from which he must create the reality of the new age.

Jünger was convinced that humanity was experiencing the collapse of the bourgeois world, embodied primarily in the concept of the individual. The individual represented, according to Jünger, the normative figure of civilisation, based on rationality and the will, but subordinated to the criterion of security and moderation, in the form of morality, prudence and sentimentality. The individual humbled and reduced his will and reason, whether he lived in anarchy or in the society of the masses. But the point

---

84 Ernst Jünger, *The Worker: Dominion and Form* (Evanston, Illinois: Northwestern University Press, 2017).

of modernity is that this framework has gradually eroded, crumbled, and will and reason have moved far beyond the individual (and the mass), transcending the boundaries of safety to become embodied in the phenomenon of *total technology*. In the phenomenon of total technology transcending the dimensionality of the individual, Ernst Jünger saw an awakening of the elements, asserting themselves in a frenzy of steel and fire, wild speed and immeasurable *power* beyond all limits. All of this was embodied in the element of modern warfare, where, according to Jünger, the individual has no meaning at all, becoming a purely technical, mechanical and impersonal moment. What takes the place of the individual and his doubles, multiplied and reflected in the masses, Jünger calls the *Gestalt*. It is an extra-individual form of existential power organisation associated with concepts such as type or style. In modern times, the Gestalt is expressed first and foremost in *the figure of the worker (Arbeiter)*, but also in the state of the worker (*Arbeitsstaat*). The worker is not seen by Jünger as a social or class figure; he is anti-bourgeois, but is not a proletarian. Rather he is a being completely free from all humanistic boundaries and consciously engaged in the element of technology, in grandiose cycles of ascetic self-overcoming, of planetary construction, of intense existential activity, motivated not by the result but by the very fact of being a part of the life of steel might. This is what Jünger calls '*total mobilisation*'. By it he understands the essence of the worker's activity, directed at the world around him through technology. The world is made up of elements — ruthless and blind. The worker does not shy away from them, but goes towards them, gathering all the infinity of the human will into a fist, answering challenge with challenge, blow with blow, power with power. At the same time, the individual loses himself completely in the Gestalt of the worker; the elements erase him, leaving, as in war, only the torch of an unbending impersonal and inhuman will.

Jünger calls such a stance '*heroic realism*', wherein the violent characteristics of a new type begin to emerge in man through the degeneration of a lukewarm bourgeois culture. Jünger observed such transformations on the front as experienced soldiers and officers changed their facial features, gestures and expressions as they were exposed to fire and the challenges of modern warfare, acquiring the static plasticity of a mask, machine or corpse; those in whom this was most noticeable became the most effective, fearless and heroic soldiers, capable of handling impossible tasks. According to Jünger, they were thus elevated to the Gestalt, the spirit of the worker began to work in them.

It was on this principle of the worker that Jünger proposed to found a new anti-bourgeois and simultaneously anti-proletarian state, whose centre was to be the Gestalt as the highest authority, using its standards to sort out three basic new classes — those of passive will, a new aristocracy (people of active will) and the highest ascetic rulers, the 'guards', as close to the Gestalt as possible in its purest form — that is, the individual incarnations of the worker.

But at the same time it was Ernst Jünger who authored the book *Der Arbeiter*[85] (The Worker), which set out the foundations of the National Socialist worldview. Later, however, Jünger and a number of other members of the Conservative Revolution were involved in the Claus von Stauffenberg conspiracy which led to the failed assassination attempt on Hitler in 1944.

Arthur Moeller van den Bruck: The Third Reich on the Other Side of Hitler

The specific character of Conservative Revolution ideology can be traced back to Arthur Moeller van den Bruck, the founder and inspiration behind a number of elite patriotic organisations, in particular the June Club, which included many leading German thinkers of the 1920s. Moeller van den Bruck was a staunch conservative, a romantic and an admirer of the work of Fyodor Dostoevsky (1821–1881), even supervising the translation of the writer's works into German.

Moeller van den Bruck was decisively influenced by Nietzsche and set out to construct a model of the future which would be both a reassertion of the constant Teutonic spirit and a sophisticated intellectual

---

85 Jünger was himself a participant in the First World War. Jünger, *The Worker: Dominion and Form*.

breakthrough that could take into account all the major scientific, cultural and ideological challenges of the modern age.

Arthur Moeller van den Bruck picked up Spengler's idea of 'young nations' and published a manifesto, addressed to American President Woodrow Wilson (1856–1924), with a radical critique of the Versailles agreements, under the title *The Right of Young Nations*. The idea that 'young nations' wanted to build their own social system without reference to the old European experience acquired for him a strongly political dimension. In particular, Moeller van den Bruck considered the greatest evil to be *liberal ideology,* which, in his view, embodied the purely *negative* results of European history — the absolutisation of capitalism, materialism, individualism, and atheism, i.e. nihilism. The new German politics, the main points of which were expressed in the collective volume of Conservative Revolutionaries, *The New Front*, published in Berlin in 1922, therefore had to be built on *absolute anti-liberalism*, since liberalism contained everything that was completely and radically opposed to the German spirit. Moeller van den Bruck reflected this position in his programme article 'Liberalism kills the nations'.

However, Moeller van den Bruck's worldview was given a coherent formulation in his principal book, *The Third Empire* or *The Third Reich*,[86] where he presented the ideas of the Conservative Revolution in the most systematic form.

The first section of the book contains an interpretation of what the author means by revolution and, more specifically, the Conservative Revolution. For Moeller van den Bruck, in contrast to the old conservatives, revolution is not a 'nihilist plot' and not 'total destruction', but *the rise of the creative forces of the people*. The people rise to revolution only when the existing socio-political conditions run counter to their deepest interests and historical intuitions. Therefore, one must always distinguish between destructive and constructive sides of revolution. And unlike dogmatic, materialist Marxism, the constructive side needs to be defined according to the identity of each individual people. Hence, the revolution should be popular, i.e. 'national'. Arthur Moeller van den Bruck writes:

---

86 Moeller van den Bruck, *Germany's Third Empire*.

We want to link revolutionary ideas with conservative ideas that come up again and again. We want to promote this Conservative Revolution until we achieve conditions under which we can live.

We want to win the revolution![87]

Here we clearly see a direct continuation of Nietzsche's views. Revolution is nothingness, it overthrows God. Now there is only one thing left: to conquer nothingness. And that is within the power of the Superman. This is how Moeller van den Bruck thinks about the young conservative movement. He sees that Nietzsche's words are addressed to him and to the German intellectuals of the new generation. And he does not seek to fight the revolution, as reactionaries and old conservatives traditionally do, but to *lead* it, to make it *German*.

The second section of *The Third Reich* is devoted to socialism. Here Moeller van den Bruck proves the thesis in his epigraph: 'Every nation has its own socialism'. Accordingly, socialism is regarded not as something universal and dogmatic, but as a principle of *the solidarity of society around a great idea* — not for the achievement of base material aims, but for the realisation of the impossible, of the ideal and the spiritual horizon.

Here Moeller van den Bruck also offers a detailed critique of Marxism, rejecting its explanation of history exclusively through economics. He writes:

> Economy is the superstructure, whereas ideas, power and the state are the foundation. History cannot be dependent on economics; it creates economics. And therefore economics is dependent on history. The economy is only a consequence, the cause is history.[88]

This becomes the basis for a spiritual rather than materialist socialism, which, while rejecting capitalism in the same way as Marxism to an even greater extent, envisages a new society based on a metaphysical foundation that connects to the historical identity and culture of each people.

---

87 Moeller van den Bruck, *Germany's Third Empire*, p. 132.
88 Moeller van den Bruck, *Germany's Third Empire*, p. 145.

Moeller van den Bruck concludes the section by showing that socialism need not be the raison d'être of the normative state.

> German socialism is not the first priority of the Third Reich. It must be its foundation.[89]

While Moeller van den Bruck accepts both revolution and socialism in a particular young conservative interpretation, he rejects liberalism *radically and completely*. In his view, '[l]iberalism is the freedom not to have any convictions, but to assert that this approach is indeed a core conviction.'[90] Therein lies its nihilistic potential: it tears man away from the political dimension, turning him exclusively to material things, to the economy, to everything small and insignificant, which makes the little man even smaller and more insignificant. Moeller van den Bruck writes:

> Liberalism leads either to stupidity or to crime.[91]

'Foolishness' is the culmination of relegating man to a consumption machine, an apparatus in which all that is human — soul, life, nobility, ideals, spirit — disappears. It is a 'crime' to present this stupidity as a higher virtue, a value, a goal.

> Liberalism has undermined culture. It has destroyed religion. It has destroyed the Fatherland. It has been the suicide of humanity.

Liberalism is the dying word of the West, of Europe, from the moment Europeans (first the French and the English, and only afterwards the Germans) embarked on the path of Enlightenment. Moeller van den Bruck sees the age of Enlightenment — the birthplace of liberalism, which has gradually become its most monstrous and totalitarian expression — in a thoroughly negative light. It is an age of degeneration, lies, and nihilism. Moeller van den Bruck, who has carried out an in-depth study of the German *Logos*, sees that in its basic parameters it is totally incompatible

---

89   Ibid., p. 171.
90   Ibid., p. 172.
91   Moeller van den Bruck, *Germany's Third Empire*, p. 181.

with the Enlightenment, and hence the problem is posed as follows: *either Germany or the Enlightenment*. Hence his harsh and unequivocal appeal:

> The struggle we are beginning against the Enlightenment will be a struggle against liberalism, which will be fought on all fronts.

This is the main difference between liberalism and socialism and revolution: while the latter can be reinterpreted in a Germanic way, liberalism cannot. Therefore it must be destroyed in the most ruthless way. This is the most important point of the Conservative Revolution: politically and ideologically, the Revolution hierarchises not only its values but also the ideas it opposes, and the primary enemy of the Conservative Revolutionary is exactly liberalism and the Enlightenment which spawned it.

In the fourth section of *The Third Reich*, Moeller van den Bruck analyses the concept of democracy and again, as in the case of socialism and revolution, finds positive aspects within it. 'Democracy is the involvement of the people in their own destiny.'[92] This is how Moeller van den Bruck defines the essence of democracy, and in this way he affirms its organic holistic understanding. The subject of democracy, according to Moeller van den Bruck, can only be *the people as a historical whole*, not an aggregate of individuals (as in liberalism). Therefore, liberal democracy is the antithesis of democracy, a counterfeit (Moeller van den Bruck calls it a 'liberal chameleon'). Liberalism does not allow the people to participate in its own destiny, simply because it denies the very existence of the people, dispersing it into individual atoms, and then artificially arranging them.[93] Therefore, for a Conservative Revolutionary it is fundamentally important to defend democracy in its organic sense and at the same time fight against its liberal interpretation.

Moeller van den Bruck accepts democracy as a positive value: 'Democracy is an expression of the self-respect of the people.'[94]. Furthermore: 'The will for democracy is the will for the political

---

92 Moeller van den Bruck, *Germany's Third Empire*, p. 211.
93 Dugin, *Ethnosociology*.
94 Moeller van den Bruck, *Germany's Third Empire*, p. 226.

self-awareness of the people. And to its national self-assertion.'[95] The introduction of the concept of the will — the will for democracy — turns democracy into a positive value, whose defence and affirmation is the goal of the Conservative-Revolutionary programme.

In terms of the structure of the Political, Arthur Moeller van den Bruck's work captures the essence of the Third Political Theory more accurately and fully than the 'official' ideology of the Nazi regime.

Werner Sombart: Against the Spirit of Capitalism

Another thinker close to the Conservative Revolutionary movement and also heavily influenced by Nietzsche was Werner Sombart, who focused on sociological and economic questions of German identity.

Singling out the bourgeois as a separate sociological type (the '*trader*'), Sombart contrasts him with an alternative sociological type (the '*hero*') in his distinctive work *Traders and Heroes*.[96] The hero type, from his point of view, was dominant in Europe before the advent of modernity, and was most prominent in German identity. Nevertheless, the two types do not simply succeed each other chronologically, but coexist in a state of *irreconcilable war*. This is a fundamental duality. Sombart writes:

> For it was always a question of this either-or: the trader in the swamp that one may call commercialism, Mammonism, materialism, sportism, comfortism, or whatever, or the hero on the heights of idealism. In this way are God and the devil, Ahura Mazda and Ahriman, called for modern man.[97]

Sombart emphasises that this choice affects precisely *modern* man, constituting his main dilemma: pro-capitalism (i.e. pro-traders) or anti-capitalism (which means, in one way or another, in support of the heroes).

Between the trader and the hero, according to Sombart, only *war* is possible, since the dominance of either one means the social and moral enslavement of the opponent.

He writes sharply and decisively about this:

---

95 Moeller van den Bruck, *Germany's Third Empire*, p. 226.
96 Werner Sombart, *Traders and Heroes* (London: Arktos Media, 2021).
97 Ibid., p. 87.

> The only relation that we maintain now with the principal nations of Europe is war and the only important thing is at this time nothing but that we win, win essentially and decisively.[98]

Sombart devoted one of his last works, written entirely in the spirit of the Conservative Revolution, to the theorising of German socialism.[99]

Sombart's appeal to the Germans is a call to give the final blow to the Anglo-Saxons and to the capitalist spirit embodied in them.

> We wish to be and remain a strong German nation and thus a strong state and thus also grow within the limits of the organic. And, if it is necessary that we extend our territorial possession so that the greater national body may obtain space to develop itself, we shall take as much land for ourselves as seems necessary. We shall also set foot where it seems important to us for strategic reasons to maintain our inviolable strength; we shall, therefore, if it benefits our position of power on earth, establish naval bases in Dover, Malta and the Suez. Nothing more. We do not wish to 'expand' at all. For we have more important things to do. We have to develop our own spiritual character, maintain the German soul pure, have to see that the enemy, the trader's mentality, does not penetrate anywhere into our mind, not from outside nor from inside. But this task is an enormous one filled with responsibility. For we know what is at stake: Germany is the last dam against the slime-flood of commercialism that has either already poured over all other countries or is in the process of doing so unstoppably because none of the latter is protected against the advancing danger by the heroic worldview that alone, as we have seen, promises rescue and protection.[100]

The Atypicality of the Third Political Theory

Although the Third Political Theory took a more or less systematic form in the twentieth century in such phenomena as Fascism and National Socialism, these currents are themselves rather eclectic. One can find various elements within them of classical nationalism, a clear Hobbesian influence, realism, a glorification of the secular state, economic protectionism and mercantilism, as well as sometimes xenophobia carried to its

---

98 Sombart, *Traders and Heroes*, p. 103.
99 Werner Sombart, *Deutscher Sozialismus* [German Socialism] (Berlin: Buchholz & Weisswange, 1934).
100 Sombart, *Traders and Heroes*, p. 114.

limits. These are some of the constants of nationalism, but they became part of the full-fledged ideology rather late. All of these aspects are in line with the modernist paradigm and quite compatible with bourgeois attitudes. However, the influence of the Romantics, of German classical philosophy with its profound metaphysics and paradoxical dialectics, of traditionalism, as well as the absolutely revolutionary and unclassifiable ideas of Nietzsche, who called for overcoming both Tradition and the nihilism that opened after its demise by appealing to the Superman, turned revolutionary nationalism into something atypical and extravagant, which cannot be completely reduced to the political modern.

The Third Political Theory, which burst out for a short time and subjugated almost all of Europe by force or conviction, disappeared rather quickly under the onslaught of the two other ideologies of the modern, which were far more orthodox in terms of their consistency with the philosophy of the Mother, 'chora', the spirit of atomism, individualism and materialism.

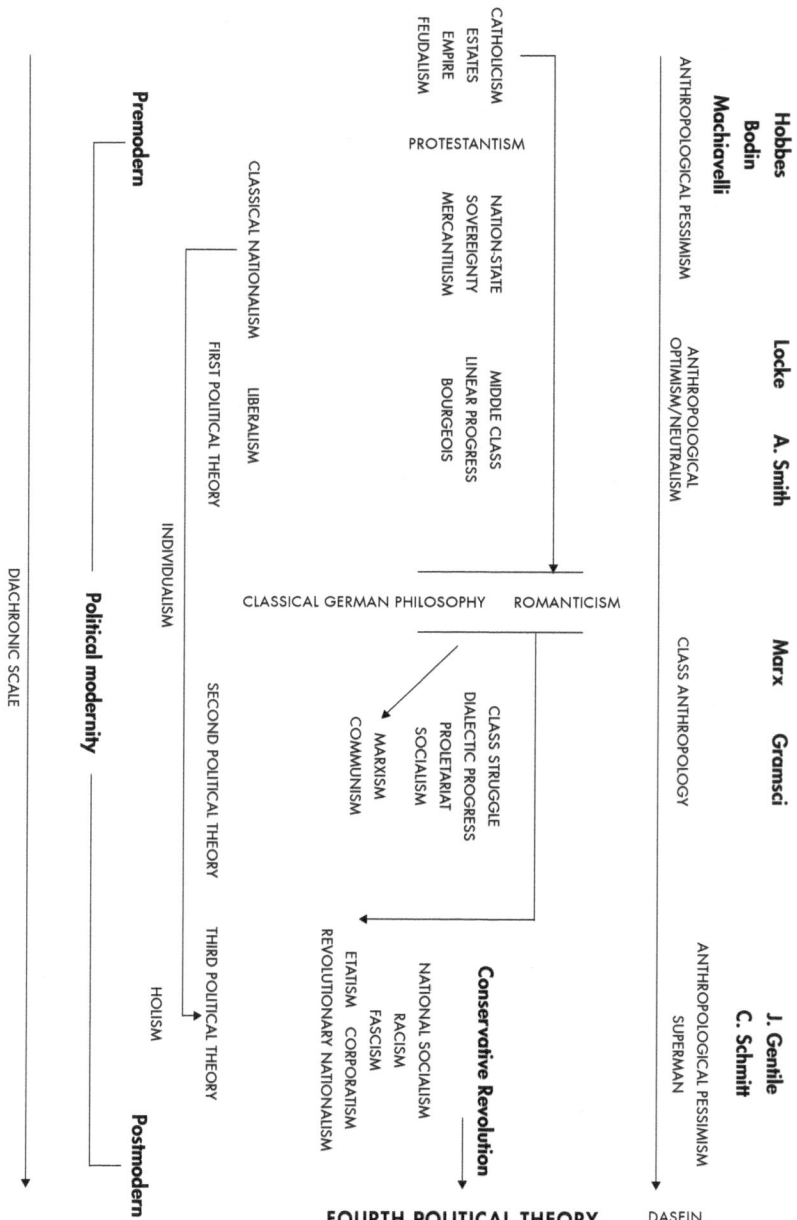

Figure 20. The Third Political Theory in a historical context.

PART IV

THE POLITICAL PHILOSOPHY OF THE POSTMODERN

CHAPTER 15

POSTMODERN POLITICAL PHILOSOPHY

The Paradigms of Tradition and Modernity Exhaust (Almost) All Forms of the Political

UP TO THIS POINT we have been dealing with the 'model set' of political philosophies, belonging to the traditional and modern paradigms, i.e. almost all the zones of *Politica Aeterna* corresponding to the three genera of being in Plato's *Timaeus* and many other types of triadic taxonomies applied to ontology, gnoseology, cosmology and anthropology, as well as to politics. Thus we can consider that we have a complete (albeit sketchy) picture of what the metaphysical and philosophical foundations of political systems in traditional, sacred and religious societies are, and what the philosophical background of modern political philosophy is. We have also examined the three main ideological versions in which modernity manifests itself: liberalism (the First Political Theory), Communism (the Second Political Theory) and nationalism (the Third Political Theory), as well as their semantic structures. Each of the three political theories of the modern includes many different versions, and combinations can also be found: for example, liberalism plus socialism are ideologies that are formally opposed, but in the phenomenon of European social democracy — or left-wing liberalism in general, which in particular is the basis of many centre-left parties, such as the modern Democratic Party in the USA — we see exactly these convergence. Similarly, there are intermediate forms between socialism and classical nationalism (e.g. National Socialism). There is also a significant segment of political ideologies that sit between nationalism and liberalism (national liberalism) and it is this ideology that dominates, for example, the US Republican Party.

In each of the three theories there are nuances, details, separate currents within these macrofamilies of modern political ideology. A detailed study of these nuances constitutes the scope of the discipline called political science. For *Politica Aeterna* it is important to show how they relate to the anthropological and ontological basis of modern political philosophy, to the notion of political Platonism and Aristotelianism, and to see the underlying matrix of these political families. All three political theories (liberalism, Communism and nationalism) belong to the political philosophy of the Mother; they are based on an atomistic materialist worldview, anthropological individualism, 'progress' and 'development', and consequently see the state as something built *from below upwards* on the basis of a social contract. This distinguishes them fundamentally from models such as Aristotle's sacred empire and the Platonic ideal state.

Among the political paradigms of traditional society (premodern), there is in turn a huge variety of structures and forms which can be glued to Platonism and Aristotelianism, but even here one can find many variations, nuances and mixed models. In part we have seen this in the analysis of political systems based on different monotheistic religions. If we take a wider context, including the sacred civilisations of antiquity and the East, the variety of sacred political forms increases manifold.

Moreover, all that refers to the politics of modernity is strictly and sharply different from that of Tradition, and between the politics of Democritus (the political philosophy of the Mother), on the one hand, and those of Plato (the political philosophy of the Father) and Aristotle (the political philosophy of the Son), on the other, lies a strictly fixed metaphysical border, sharply separating modernity from Tradition, and constituting the key to decipher the full picture of the Political in the broader context of *Politica Aeterna*. Thus the common feature of all three political ideologies of the modern is desacralisation, secularism, atomism, materialism, progressivism; strictly opposed to the sacred, holistic, spiritual politics of traditional societies based on verticality and hierarchy, on the transcendence of the Supreme (and hence, the source of power), which can be expressed either in the idea of the immutability of the Political, or in the recognition of cycles, or in the degradation of political systems gradually losing semblance to the model, but in no way as progress, the very concept of which is incompatible with Tradition.

Games of the Lying Logos on the Lower Frontier of Matter

However, we have mentioned that along with the two basic paradigms of society, Tradition (premodern) and modern, a third paradigm exists — the postmodern.[1] This may cause bewilderment. If all forms of the Political are exhausted by the three macro-families reflecting the three kinds of being according to Plato, then there is no ontological basis for one more paradigm. This is true, but in order to understand the postmodern, we should turn to the metaphysical origins of the modern itself, which, in terms of Plato's dialectical ontology of *Parmenides*, already belongs in its foundations to the realm of pseudo-being or non-being falsely represented as being. This is what should be understood as the 'nihilism' of modernity: while proclaiming the atom as the constitutive basis of reality, modern physics, adopting the conceptual model of Democritus, cannot find anything 'indivisible', and in society a liberal bigotry in liberating the individual leads gradually to its liberation from all properties (collective identity — religion and class, and then nation, gender and finally humanity itself), moving towards the divide. In the early stage of modernity its pseudological nature is not made explicit. On the contrary, one gets the impression that it is modernity that deals with reality — including human reality (humanism) — whereas Tradition operated with 'chimeras'. But gradually the scepticism towards traditional society and its axioms began to extend to modernity itself and the values it proclaimed — rationalism, materialism, secularism, equality, democracy, etc. In the late modern era, this led to an involuntary agreement with traditionalists (long ago put aside as a reference group of modern society) that modernism, after all,

---

1   Dugin, *Postphilosophy*.

had no reliable basis — either in thought or in analysis of the surrounding world — and represented cold nihilism covered up by humanistic rhetoric. Thus a new philosophical zone gradually began to emerge in the course of the late modern's critical reflection on itself and its assumptions, and was elevated to the role of a new — third — paradigm, called the postmodern.

Postmodernism does not designate a new domain beyond the three types of being. It only draws attention to the lower boundary of the philosophy of the Mother, to the deepest level of '*chora*', of 'matter', acting as an indication of what lies even lower, in the realm of the sub-material, where not just the philosophers of Tradition, but also the carriers of the modern paradigm in its classical form, did not tread. This domain does not correspond to some new — fourth — dimension, some other kind of being. From the point of view of *Politica Aeterena*, this is still the same field of the third — material — origin. But this origin itself is a pseudological instance, which, taken as something autonomous and self-sufficient, turns out to be identical with 'nothing', which refers us to the astute Democritus and his basic pair of οὐδέν and δέν, that is, 'nothing' and its indefinable dialectical invariant, the atom. Modernity is already nihilism, and hence the logos it constitutes is a bastard logos; in the words of Plotinus, it is a 'false logos'. Consequently, one can continue the vector of pseudologic even deeper into the realm of nothingness, beyond the limit where modernity itself stops for fear of losing its rhetorical persuasiveness. According to Plotinus, matter inspires existential terror. The soul copes with it only when its terrifying truth, that is, the total coldness of its nihilism, is hidden. When the shell of formalised matter disintegrates, the underlying chill of being manifests itself. This is the transition from implicit to explicit nihilism. This transition is called the postmodern, which should be located inside matter and notionally on its lower boundary. This boundary creates a special topology because the atom, according to Plotinus, is unattainable to the mind. It is postulated by the 'false logos' as a concept,[2] and the mind is extinguished by sinking into its comprehension. But it is impossible to completely extinguish the mind, so this can

---

2   In a sense, any concept is nothing more than a false logos.

exist only as an aspiration to this unattainable limit — thus it is impossible to find a pure atom or a pure individual, that would be the end of consciousness. Consequently, only a progressive approach to this limit, a gravitation towards it, but never its attainment, is possible. The lower limit of matter is insurmountable, but at this very boundary a particular pseudological ontology emerges, even more 'false' than the materialist ontology of modernity. Diving into it breaks the usual proportions and scales (as in quantum mechanics or astrophysics) and creates bizarre borderland symmetries in which nothingness plays with itself.

In terms of the *Politica Aeterna* model, the postmodern is a marginal phenomenon of the modern, but in terms of social, cultural and political cycles it can be considered a paradigm in its own right. It is the postmodern that is at the same time something independent — if we give the ontology of the lower frontier of matter and the extravagant pictures generated by it a scale and meaning — and a paradigmatic addition to the modern, its logical continuation and pseudo-logical refinement. In postmodernity, the lie of modernity becomes explicit and grotesquely acknowledged, and nihilism transforms from a hidden 'truth' into a synonym for 'progress', breaking the rhetoric of earlier modernity and tearing off the masks of its own pseudo-logic. In doing so, postmodernism is not a belated reaction to Tradition, but a bold self-disclosing step of the deepest and most avant-garde current within modernity itself. The modern becomes so strong, powerful and triumphant that it can afford to turn into the postmodern without fearing the reaction of the backward or being burdened by the numerous features of the world's archaicism.

The Subject and Object of Materialism: The Singular and Its Property

Postmodernity is a particular socio-philosophical paradigm which represents the attained limit of modernity. The modern operates with materiality, facts, objects, individuals, and presents epistemological abstractions as basic data. In Aristotelianism and in Platonism it is not *being*, not phenomenon, but only a speculative limit of the degradation of the spirit, just as the atom is some conditional measure of the decay of wholeness, but not something holistic. In modernity, matter is taken as a self-evident fact, as some ontological phenomenon. In the political philosophy of the modern, matter, atomicity, is represented as an individual, as an object, as a thing, as a price, as a society. Modernism holds that everything conceptual that it recognises — the market mechanism, wealth, class, nation, nature, society, state, the world of things and objects — *is*, that it has unconditional being. The consensus on materiality is the common denominator of all three political theories of modernity.

In this materialist worldview, the two fundamentals of New Age philosophy converge. René Descartes described these as 'subject' and 'object'. The subject is the individual human being, the object the individual item. Traditional political philosophy does not know either the subject or the object as Descartes conceived of them, because above the subject there is a functioning Deity, and the world is created by God. Accordingly, above the subject and object there is always a *third instance*, God, and the subject and object are not the final measure of things.

In New Age political philosophy, by contrast, we are dealing with this fundamental, basic dualism: the subject is the individual, the citizen in politics, and the object in the outside world is *property* (private in liberalism, collective in socialism, corporate in Fascism). This theme is very well described by the anarchist Max Stirner (1806–1856) in his *The Ego and Its Own*.[3] All political philosophy of the modern age deals with 'the one and his property', 'the individual and private property'. Marxism attempts to overcome this dualism, so that in the return to the proletarian class there is a generalisation of property and the replacement of the individual with class consciousness, but it is still the antithesis of the 'ego and its property' thesis. It is no coincidence that Marx and Engels mocked Stirner so thoroughly and extensively in *The German Ideology*.[4]

The attitude to property lies at the heart of the modern philosophy of law, which regulates, first and foremost, the relationship of the individual and his property, i.e. the subject and the object in their political

---

3   Max Stirner, *The Ego and Its Own* (Verso Books, 2014).
4   Karl Marx and Friedrich Engels, *The German Ideology* (Connecticut: Martino Fine Books, 2011).

dimension. In capitalist society this is absolutised, private property becomes the measure of the individual subject. Marxism opposes both the singular and property, but in its practice this boils down to the formula 'the individual and not his property', which underlies the doctrine of the class struggle. The struggle against private property constitutes the programme of Marxism, but the singular (the individual, the subject) is here thought of dialectically. The capitalists represent a collective subject or false subject. They are not truly free precisely because of their blind attachment to property, which becomes a fate. To emancipate oneself it is necessary to take as a basis a subject that is devoid of property but also devoid of self-consciousness, since capitalism projects a false consciousness onto it, effectively turning it into a submissive machine. The proletariat must wake up as an oppressed subject, realise its subjugation, overthrow the pseudo-subjectivity of the bourgeois class, and, having distributed property among all members of the working class, move towards the construction of Communism, where at last the individual will be freed from the chains of the object, subduing matter and nature, precisely because man is matter and nature, only the summit of its development. In medieval epistemology, man could understand the world only through the divine mind. With the Marxists, however, the knowledge of matter is given only to the one who is matter itself, and who is the most material among the material things — that is, to the proletariat.

Bourgeois nationalism also fully accepts the modernist subject, merely placing 'the one and his property' in a national context, contrasting him with 'the others and their property' in the representative of another nation-state; the individual is merely placed in a national framework. They restrict the individual's freedom of action in relation to his property if it goes beyond national boundaries.

Postmodernism Is Not Satisfied with the Achievements of Liberalism

Postmodernism is the desire to go even deeper into the essence of matter than modernism was able to do. It is a kind of *hyper-materialism*. If liberalism, Communism and nationalism are *naïve materialisms*, then postmodernism seeks to develop and purify the philosophy of matter even more deeply. Recall Plato's metaphor — Mother Earth, Mother Provider. If the political modern reduces heaven to earth, the gods to people, the transcendent to the immanent, then the postmodern seeks to penetrate deep into the earth. It is a plunge into the underworld, an aspiration not just to descend to the plane, but to bury oneself as deeply as possible in materiality.

On the one hand, the postmodern continues the inertia of the modern, because the modern is a movement towards desacralisation, immanentisation, detranscendentalisation and a desire to accept matter as a basic, fundamental ontological argument.

Postmodernists begin to attack modernity with a cry for 'more modernity', despite the fact that modernity has already made a number of decisive steps both against the philosophy of the Father and against the philosophy of the Son. Modernity has killed God, abolished the transcendent, brought Plato to naught and ridiculed Aristotle. Liberal ideologue Karl Popper's book *The Open Society and Its Enemies* is a manifesto devoted mainly to criticising Plato, Aristotle and Hegel. For Popper, Plato is a Fascist, Aristotle is a Fascist, and Hegel is a Fascist, or a Communist, which to liberals is equally bad. Importantly, it is not simply an outrage against the excesses of historical Soviet Communism or historical German Nazism (Gulags and Auschwitz, mass repression, genocide, totalitarianism, etc.); Popper is attacking Plato,[5] Aristotle and Hegel as politicians of historical philosophies belonging to a different kind of being. He criticises the roots and not the consequences, all the more so because they are not the consequences. Similarly, another liberal author, Hannah Arendt (1906–1975), convincingly showed that totalitarianism is not a consequence of the traditional society, but emerged precisely in modernity.[6]

Accordingly, postmodernism asserts the following: after the dismantling and the overthrow of Plato and Aristotle has taken place, it is

---

5 'My analysis and my critique will be directed against the totalitarian tendencies of Plato's political philosophy.' Karl Popper, *The Open Society and Its Enemies, Volume I* (Oxfordshire: Routledge Classics, 2010).

6 Hannah Arendt, *The Origins of Totalitarianism* (London: Penguin, 2017).

necessary to move on, and to *overcome modernity itself*. What seemed before to be the limit of descent into the worlds of the Mother's political philosophy (liberalism, the subject, materialism, the One and his property), in fact, the postmodernists believe, carries with it too much 'manly origin', 'verticality', 'sacredness' and 'ontology'.

The postmodernists argue: let us continue to atomise what we have atomised in modernity. Let us look at what the individual and property are. Are these truly indivisible atoms, individuals? Have we reached real matter? Have we reached the horizon of total immanence? We have the triumph of reason over other forms. This is a vertical topicality that reflects the old ideology. Yes, we have transferred the state to the level of the individual. In the political philosophy of the modern age, the polis itself is reduced to atomic politics; the polis-state is also congruent, homologous to the individual (as in the paradigm of Tradition), but already in its individual status. Hence, the notion of the 'state-individual' emerges — the individual becomes a state unto himself, and the state is abolished. This is the limit of the ideology of human rights, or civil society, globalisation, progress, humanism, and the complete triumph of the market over politics. And yet, say postmodernists, the individual himself is still too 'vertical', too 'sacred'.

In the realised political philosophy of modernity, civil society displaces political society, the remnants of class and national consciousness are eliminated, liberalism wins on a global scale, and we are dealing only with the individual, without any collective properties. This individual is the polis of the accomplished modern.

Here the postmodernists say: yes, in modernity we have sharply narrowed the scale, we have moved from being to the individual, from politics to the person, from the state to the specific citizen. But how do we conceptualise this citizen? Do we not encounter Platonism and Aristotelianism, which have illegally penetrated our progressive liberal modern worldview? After all, modern man still has some kind of goal (which is already violent and suspiciously reminiscent of Aristotle with his '*telos*', 'natural place' and 'entelechy') and recognises the dominance of reason over feelings and desires (which is already suspiciously close to Plato and the metaphysics of the divine mind).

Initially, the emancipatory practice of modern political philosophy called for the reduction of all political, ontological and epistemological instances to the individual. And this was indeed achieved — all the foundations of traditional society were destroyed, all verticals, all forms of transcendence were dismantled, everything was reduced to the One and his property.

Although the primary goal of the postmodern is the liberation of the individual from all restrictions, which is also the main goal of liberalism, and liberalism claims to 'bring freedom and equality of opportunity to all', postmodernists are critical of classical liberalism. In their view, liberalism retains too many male patriarchal traits. For all its immanence and materialism, postmodernism is 'too transcendentalist'; it believes too strongly in the unity of the individual, pays too much attention to the structure of the vertical subject and is too attentive to private property. Yes, these are atomistic concepts that are taken for reality quite in the spirit of the general pseudo-logic of the modern, but still — as is always the case with atoms — it is wrong to take the conventional 'atom' as authentic, and to stop the chiselling that moves towards the utmost limit of matter. The mind must become weaker and weaker, dodging oppositions and distinctions; the false *logos* must lie more and more subtly; and in all reality –both subject and object — must gradually dissipate further and further, revealing one subatomic level after another. The error of liberalism in the eyes of postmodernists is that it takes as a valid individual someone who is a convention, an approximation, only an outlined vector. The individual is the goal, the task, and so, in the search for an atomic subjectivity, not only the large structures, such as the forms of the Political in traditional society, but also the structures of modernity itself, built on the ruins of transcendence, must be destroyed. It is therefore necessary to move in two directions: to continue to liberate the individual from all forms of collective identity (this time from gender), but also to shift attention to the sub-individual levels and sometimes to the non-individual levels (this is the programme of posthumanism and 'deep ecology').

The same applies to the object (in particular the social object of property). Objects are not atoms, but some 'bills of atoms'. They also have to be separated into constituents. A fundamental step in this direction is money. Money crushes any thing, being precisely the atoms of property, absolutised in capitalism. But we cannot stop there. Money itself, as well as the elements of wealth, must increasingly move from reality to digitality and virtuality. And due to the abolition of the classical liberal subject, there must also be an atomisation (evaporisation) of the object.

Postmodernists often turn to Marxism and its dialectic. Capitalism is modern, but it has objective limits. Marx sought to overcome them, and although he was defeated at the level of political history, the dialectical paradoxes of his teachings are still appealing. In the postmodern, however, Marxism is no longer a doctrine of the class struggle and of the dictatorship of the proletariat. It has become a 'cultural Marxism', that is, it continues Marx's very strategy of solidarity with the bourgeois order but only in order to overcome it. Thus 'cultural Marxism' welcomes the liberal obsession with freeing the individual from all forms of collective identity, but only to take it one step further and fall through the individual, to descend (slip down) to the subatomic and sub-subjective levels of the individual and consequently of the world. In a sense, postmodernism replaces Marxism in the post-industrial context. Marx sought to surpass nineteenth-century capitalism in its industrial phase, but in the twentieth and at the beginning of the twenty-first century, capitalism in its post-industrial phase surpassed itself (although not without Marxism's help). This is how classical Marxism was taken up by postmodernists, while its methods and particular prescriptions in history proved to be either a dead end (this is how postmodernists assess the deviation of Soviet regimes and especially the USSR, following Trotskyist analysis and European social democracy in this) or incorrect (the proletarian revolution in advanced European bourgeois societies never happened), therefore demanding that they should have been revised and discarded.

But postmodernism cannot be equated with twenty-first century Marxism, since many aspects of liberalism and neoliberalism have been integrated into it. Its point of departure is not class, but rather the bourgeois individual, although — unlike liberalism — it is not celebrated as the crown of progress, but is in turn overcome through new — posthuman — concepts: the network, cyborgs, chimeras, artificial intelligence, etc.

Dissipation of the Individual and Dissociation of the Object: Towards the Fractal

Postmodern political philosophy recognises that a certain goal of historical progress has been achieved and, accordingly, the programme of modernity has been realised. The father is killed, executed (Nietzsche says, 'God is dead. It was we who killed him — you and I!'). The Son is eliminated (Aristotle's picture of the world is ridiculed and dispelled at the origins of the New Age — by Copernicus, Galileo, Newton, etc.). Henceforth we live in the bosom of the Great Mother. This creates a sense of comfort. Living in a giant techno-social womb is cosy and safe. In the West, history is finished (and where it is not finished, you can always help with 'humanitarian bombing'). The global tasks of building a political philosophy of modernity in practice are complete.

But it is precisely at this point that Western philosophers remark: yes, we have freed the individual from all (or almost all) forms of collective identity and the final touch is feminism, gender politics and the promotion of the LGBT community; yes, a market society based on private property is built on a global scale. But do you not think, say postmodernists, that we have simply transposed the same Platonic-Aristotelian vertical schemes onto the individual and onto private property? Do you not see in this attitude of 'the One and his property' a hidden Platonism again? Again a hierarchy, again a certain wholeness which is constructed 'from the top down', from the mind to the body, again a hidden and veiled, but still a domination of the subject over the object. Is not the modern still a kind of reworked Tradition? Have we not once again got what we fought against?

And having answered these questions in the affirmative, postmodernists say: the individual (if we take man as an individual) is also a vertical concept and private property is also a concept, which is a vertical concept involving a power relationship of the possessor and the property. And this is insufficiently material, egalitarian and atomistic. The process of immanentisation needs to continue, uprooting the remnants of transcendence that have infiltrated the immanence of modernity.

Hence a new round of atomisation: since the atom is a contingent construct, one must move on, not only in science through the discovery of ever smaller particles and ever more extravagant symmetries and quantum laws, but also in politics, dismantling individuals and their private property. The singular Stirner, his property, as well as things in themselves, turned out not to be the limit of the destruction of holistic coherent ensembles, but only a stage of such destruction. So they are not yet true concepts, not true atoms and individuals, but an agglomeration of particles that live a life of their own. In physics this idea is vividly represented by Benoit Mandelbrot's[7] (1924–2010) theory of fractals. He begins the construction of his theory of fractals with the observation that there are in fact no straight lines in nature. A straight line is something that exists in our minds, while in nature it is always slightly curved. Or take the volume — it is also three-dimensional only in the mind, in nature it is three-dimensional only in some approximation. Similarly, a point — like a line of zero length, a circle of zero diameter or an area of zero volume — does not exist. From this Mandelbrot concludes that a line is two-dimensional in nature, a plane will be three-dimensional and a volume four-dimensional. To describe such an ontology, Mandelbrot introduces the notion of fractals — strange particles that actually fall out of the geometry of our consciousness, but approach the geometry of nature, seen as if 'from the perspective of matter'.

The explanation for this must be sought in the early formation of the scientific picture of the New Age world. At that time materialist philosophers mixed what Aristotle strictly separated — logic, mathematics and geometry (which reflected the truths of the spirit, the gods and the universal mind) on the one hand, and physics, ontics on the other. Before that it was more correct to study physics with rhetoric, not so precise from the

---

7   Benoit Mandelbrot, *The Fractal Geometry of Nature* (San Francisco: W. H. Freeman and Company, 1982).

point of view of logic, but much closer to nature. This is exactly what Aristotle himself does, defining the single thing (one being, ὄν), that is, the ontic unit, not as a logical unit, but as a dual pair of matter (ὕλη) and form (μορφή). That is to say, the thing is a rhetorical figure, it is conventionally (from a logical point of view) one, but from a physical point of view it is dual. New Age physics erased this distinction by insisting on the unity of the physical-mathematical approach, and thereby undermined the deliberate harmony of its ontology. Mandelbrot — and before him the theory of relativity or quantum mechanics, which questioned some postulates of modern physics — only faced the consequences of this philosophical aberration, but did not dare to overturn the whole monumental building of the modernist pseudo-logic, which had gained a monopoly in the scientific world, trying somehow to correct the situation, which gradually exposed the fictiveness of all modern science. But this palliative produced only more and more exotic theories, unable to abandon the legacy of the modern, but no longer satisfied with its epistemological possibilities.

Accordingly, the theory of fractals and the physics of nature can serve as a metaphor for the strategy that representatives of the postmodern have applied to man, society and philosophy. Neither the atom in nature nor the individual in society exist as such. They are speculative. But this does not mean that one should abandon them; it only means that one should not stop there, but move on — deep into matter, dissecting it further and further — until an unattainable limit is reached. In the course of this dispersal, dizzying symmetries emerge, phantasms of new micro-worlds, possibilities of virtual and genetic construction, and thus the gaining of new degrees of freedom, though partly at the expense of losing the one who could have used this freedom, for in this process the individual himself is gradually erased or at least transformed — becoming a social fractal.

The Cancer of Civilisation

Postmodernism changes not so much the meaning and vector of modernity's formation as the rhetoric that describes it. The modern presented itself as a triumphant ascent, as an upward movement towards the seizure of new goals — essentially as an assault on the heavens by the titans. Postmodernists sharply change the tone and present the same vector as dissipation, atomisation, pulverisation, in a sense as decay, which loses pathos but retains the semantics of the basic processes of civilisation.

This is how the human individual disintegrates, his subjectivity dissipating into a multitude of momentary or somewhat-stable selves, all of them ultimately ephemeral. This is the valorisation of mental disorders and above all schizophrenia, where plurality is a characteristic symptom. The philosophical meaning of schizophrenia in the postmodern becomes a programme.

The object disintegrates as well. Physics splits particles into smaller and smaller dimensions, revealing completely new laws and rules at the quantum level, drastically changing ideas about the structures of matter and reality in general. Reality disintegrates.

Property, no longer fixed as strictly as before by the atomic framework of the 'one', is also beginning to dissipate. People used to have money in the form of a handful of gold coins, then in the form of banknotes (as the promise of gold coins). Gold itself as an equivalent was a step towards abstraction, towards the dissipation of wealth as things; next came its dissipation as well. But this is not the end of dissipation: digital money is introduced — it is now the promise of paper money, which is itself the promise of gold.

Payment cards are structured in such a way that if a very small percentage of their holders try to withdraw their savings in the form of banknotes at the same time, the whole system collapses, because ATMs and bank branches are only backed by banknotes for a fraction of the total amount involved in electronic payments. If you ask for banknotes in exchange for gold, they will not be given, because no currency is officially backed by gold after the Bretton Woods agreements were abolished.

This is how the dissipation of the object takes place. Both the 'one' himself and his property are subjected to more and more erosion. Each time there is a lower level, an even more subatomic plane, to which the former atom/individual is invited to descend. Thus the pillar of subject and object becomes less and less visible, more and more shaky and transparent.

The very unity of the human being and the object is now folded, then crumbled again, hovering in a virtuality often not backed by the real provision of promises made.

In such a situation, the world economy faces the growing danger of a 'bubble' — more and more 'securities' appear (which are not really valuable because they are just promises to pay someone someday). Options and hedging transactions for these 'securities' are then introduced, followed by options on options,[8] and so an economy is gradually formed where the volume of financial liabilities exceeds many times the world's gross product. The financial paperwork, including debts, debt sales, debt repayments, penalties on debts, interest payments, loans and credit exceeds the value of all goods on earth a thousand times over. So if a microscopic percentage of security holders wants to get rid of them and get the money itself, the system will collapse completely — the dollar will collapse, obligations between nations will collapse, the economy will collapse, production will collapse. The huge financial bubble that the world economy operates on today has nothing to do with the rather limited, negligible amount of all the wealth of the earth, which has been overvalued, overpriced, overspent and completely removed from the future. Mankind has already consumed goods for decades into the future. There is nothing but serious population growth and a huge bubble ahead. But to support this, the global liberal system continues to chant progress and development, conjuring up myths of 'endless growth' in the mass consciousness.

Jean Baudrillard (1929–2007), a French philosopher who was interested in phenomenology and the metaphysics of the pstmodern, considered cancer as a metaphor for postmodern civilisation. Thus he wrote:

> Things have a kind of cancer: the unrestrained multiplication of extra-structural elements in them, which gives things their self-assurance, is a kind of tumour after all.[9]

---

8   Dugin, *The End of Economics*.
9   Jean Baudrillard, *The System of Objects* (Verso Books, 2020). [Translated from the Russian]

The cancer consists of the same cells beginning to multiply, losing their correlation with the rest of the organism as a coherent structure. This, according to Baudrillard, is what capitalism is like: it unrestrainedly produces in great numbers objects that are detached from the structure of society as a coherent organism. But while modernism concealed this under the fanfare of middle-class growth (this growth itself represented a kind of planetary cancer), the postmodernists merely observe the phenomenon with indifference. After all, argue the most optimistic of them, death and decay are part of life.

Baudrillard points out another feature of cancer cells — they reproduce themselves, identical, without change or restriction. This production is sexless — no two carriers are involved, the same cell strictly reproduces itself. Indeed, this is how, in postmodernity, the economic processes of the decomposition of the commodity, the object and the subject itself (the producer and the consumer) lead to the proliferation of an enormous amount of junk that reproduces itself without restriction. *Dissipation, dissolution, disintegration* of the subject takes place.

It is significant that we find a metaphor of cancer and tumours in Plotinus precisely where he talks about the essence of matter.[10] He stresses that it is characteristic of matter to bloat, that is, to produce festering bubbles which constitute a kind of 'bloated nothingness'.

> To accept an eidos, matter does not (necessarily) have to *be* heavy (in itself), it *becomes* heavy (a mass), and (in becoming so) allows another (than itself) to be created.[11]

The question here is whether matter has the property of 'mass', 'weight', 'heaviness', ὄγκος by itself, or whether it becomes heavy by taking on *eidos*. The term ὄγκος (volume/mass/tumour) is fundamental. It also has the meaning 'to swell', 'to plump'. From here the concept of 'pride', ὄγγκωμα, has also evolved. Matter is not mass, that is to say, in itself it cannot be something, nor can it produce something. But having received

---

10 Plotinus, *The Second Ennead*.
11 Οὐ τοίνυν ὄγκον δεῖ εἶναι τὸν δεξόμενον τὸ εἶδος, ἀλλ᾽ ὁμοῦ τῷ γενέσθαι ὄγκον καὶ τὴν ἄλλην ποιότητα δέχεσθαι. Plotinus, *The Second Ennead*.

into itself something, it begins to puff up, becoming a material copy of what it has received. But if the *eidos* is fragmented, the matter will 'puff up' not from the *eidos*, but from its fragments, its quantum particles. And the more one denies the *eidos*, which is exactly what modernity does, the shallower its particles will be. And consequently, the tumour of matter will become more and more monotonous and lose its connection to the whole (the organism). And surprisingly, the term 'oncology', literally the science of tumours, by which we most commonly understand malignancy, comes from the same root: it refers to the unstoppable growth of a tumour as a non-functional proliferation of identical cells. According to Plotinus this means that matter itself, its swelling, its cancerous fragmentation, is a disease, and incurable for all that come in contact with it. Therefore, matter is death — everything it touches dies. Everything material is already mortal. And the weaker the eidos, the deadlier the matter is to it, the more malignant it is.

The Search for the Authentic Individual: Towards Transhumanism

Just as the object, the thing, dissipates into fractals, into diverging chains of small tumours that dismember matter, so it is with the subject in the postmodern. The same dispersion, the same dissipation, the same transition to a lower level of organisation and immersion into the fanciful quantum symmetries revealed in this plunge into the particular — this time on the level of the individual.

The individual turns out not to be a whole, but an agglomeration of its various constituent components, the product of a play of elements, of organs. The social personality is dismantled.

This can easily be seen on the internet, which reflects many of the characteristics of postmodernity.[12] Everyone can choose a nickname, as well as gender, photo, history, status, geography. There is no fixed individual, the online subject is a combination, a set of generic properties, it is

---

12 Manuel Castells, *The Rise of the Network Society* (Hoboken, NJ: Wiley-Blackwell, 2009).

not so much solid as fluid.¹³ This allows one to create not just another self, but several alter egos. At the corporate level, a whole army of clones and bots, algorithms and programmes that exist in the network independently, come into interaction with real users, collide with each other, constitute the chaotic life of the internet. These are fractals of user dividums, which are so intermingled with individuals that a new form of combined online identity is formed between them. On the internet there is no strict distinction between a real identity, an 'avatar', a 'simulacrum', a fake persona or a bot. All can have a common status of network citizenship.

This divisional structure of the internet also affects people in ordinary life, which is gradually moving closer and closer to cyberspace.

In the same way, there is a change in attitudes to the human body, which was regarded as something whole by an inertia that went back to antiquity. Postmodernity calls this integrity into question. Already in the first phase of modernity, the doctors of the iatromechanics, Giovanni Alfonso Borelli (1608–1679), Giorgio Balivi (1668–1707), and Herman Boerhaave (1668–1788), proposed considering the human body as a mechanism consisting of mechanical parts. This is the foundation of modern medicine as a whole. Advances in technology have made it possible to extend this approach to all aspects of the body, coming close to deciphering the entire genome and creating a model of the brain. The body became a kind of construction, and in some cases artificial parts or organs proved to be more reliable than natural ones.

Thus, at the bodily level, the metaphor of man-machine — introduced by the philosopher Julien Offray de La Mettrie (1709–1751) — gradually evolved, turning man into a prefabricated construction, which can be substantially upgraded or improved. Hence the development of plastic surgery and the desire to modify the body. The body was thus taken to the divisional level.

The construction of the body started with the sick and disabled, but gradually spread to everyone, changing the very idea of the human being. Postmodernity sees the human being as an artificial construct — at the

---

13   Zygmunt Bauman, *Liquid Modernity* (Cambridge: Polity, 2000).

level of the intellect, educated by society, politics and epistemological strategies, and at the level of the body by medical anatomical techniques.

Gradually the human being is constructed into an object, it can henceforth be assembled.

Gradually, humanity is being prepared to accept machines (cyborgs, robots) as equals, giving them full rights.[14] The logic behind this integration is already clear. At first, cyborgs will prove to be invaluable helpers, performing humanitarian feats to save people (children, women, and the elderly) from natural disasters and catastrophes. Then they become indispensable helpers to people in their daily lives. Finally, they are found to be capable of thinking and feeling. Some humans reject equality with robots (thus the emergence of robo-fascism), but lose out to inclusive humanists. Then mixed marriages occur, and the line between machine and human is blurred. It is important to emphasise the new atomicity of the robot, which consists in its individuation. According to the New Age iatromechanists, the human organism is a mechanism. Now this medical metaphor ceases to be a metaphor and becomes reality. People are becoming disassembled, can store their consciousness on cloud servers and their memory on USB sticks. The concept of death becomes an anachronism.

From the philosophical point of view, it is a further decomposition of the subject, in the course of which there is a movement towards the atomic level, which does not lend itself to final determination and retreats further and further from the scientific thought that attacks it. Thus in postmodernity the identification of the atom (the individual) with the human being, which has proved tentative and approximate, is overcome. He turned out not to be an atom, but a whole Democritian vortex, that is, a world composed of atoms, and therefore in need of further dissection.

The dissection of the body is occurring simultaneously on several levels. Alongside genetic engineering research, organ transplants, 3D printing, neural network development and the study of brain function, the practice of sex reassignment or artificial body transformations, including

---

14 The modern television series *Humans* and *Westworld* show this theme in an extensive and extremely realistic way. Of course, these are just extrapolations from the current state of society, culture and technology, but they are very plausible.

the implantation of various organic and inorganic elements, has played an important role. This provides the preparatory experience of transferring consciousness from one bodily form to another. Naturally, the very consciousness of the subject undergoes a transformation, separating this time not only from religious, class, national, professional identities, but also from gender, affecting the deep foundations of consciousness as such, which are connected to the gender dichotomy, reflecting in turn the very nature of mind, which according to Plotinus, manifests itself in division. Gender is the embodiment of the mind's metaphysical operation in relation to the human species. A change of sex is not a full-fledged transformation of a man into a woman and a woman into a man. Rather, it is a propaedeutics of transcending gender in general, towards a sexless identity much closer to the individual (atomic subject) being sought than it is to the ordinary human being. Therefore, the contemporary cyberfeminist Donna Haraway, in her *Cyborg Manifesto*,[15] rightly observes that full equality between men and women is only possible through overcoming gender as such and the total transformation of all humans into sexless cyborgs. From her point of view, it does not matter who is male and who is female and whether this identity is natural or artificial. In either case the very duality of gender creates a hierarchy, which is the source of gender inequality, and it is gender inequality that modern liberals, democrats and feminists should fight against.

Ecologists extend the same logic to animals and other species of life, which should also have equal rights with humans. This line has been consistently pursued by representatives of 'speculative realism' and object-oriented ontology, who advocate a new — radical — materialism.[16]

Criticising the subject, postmodernists argue that the human subject is in fact a travesty of the Platonic state. It has a philosopher-consciousness, a feeling-warrior and an inferior sensation-toiler. All this is structured in such a way that we have piety before reason, and we treat feelings (some of which are noble, some not) selectively, and we treat the senses on

---

15 Donna Haraway, *A Cyborg Manifesto: Science, Technology, and Socialist-Feminism in the Late Twentieth Century* (New York: Routledge, 1991).

16 Levi R. Bryant, *The Democracy of Objects* (London: Open Humanities Press, 2011).

the residual principle, as a subfield supplying the mind and emotions with informational nourishment. Thus, all levels of the subject — which (according to postmodernists) is in fact an agglomeration of disparate elements, each of which is an infrasubjective atom — we build up as a hierarchy within us, repeating the verticality of traditional society on the level of the individual. For postmodernists, even the fierce anti-Platonists and enemies of Aristotelianism, liberals, are still 'too Platonic'. They rightly demolish all superstructures over the individual, but dwell on the individual, who, from the point of view of the postmodern, is precisely not an individual.

Therefore, for society to be *truly open*, according to postmodernists, the human=individual formula must be transcended. The human individual is something to be overcome in the direction of a more authentic individual, which can only be transhuman or post-human. The human individual as a species is still too 'vertical', 'sacred', 'hierarchical', that is, too traditional. Thus the postmodern is in solidarity with the modern, but considers it insufficient.

Postmodern Political Philosophy: Three Key Theories

The vast majority of the great postmodernist philosophers were French, from the Surrealist forerunners of the movement, Georges Bataille[17] (1897–1962), Antonin Artaud[18] (1896–1948), to Jacques Lacan[19] (1901–1981), Michel Foucault[20] (1926–1984), Roland Barthes (1915–1980), Jean-François Lyotard[21] (1924–1998), Jean Baudrillard, Jacques Derrida[22] (1930–2004), Bruno Latour, and the most vivid and consistent

---

17   Georges Bataille, *The Accursed Share* (New York: Zone Books, 1991).
18   Antonin Artaud, *The Theatre and Its Double* (Richmond: Alma Classics, 2017).
19   Jacques Lacan, *Formations of the Unconscious: The Seminar of Jacques Lacan, Book V* (London: Polity, 2020).
20   Michel Foucault, *The History of Sexuality. Volume 1 The Will to Knowledge* (London: Penguin, 2020); Foucault, *History of Madness* (Oxfordshire: Routledge, 2009); Foucault, *Discipline and Punish: The Birth of the Prison* (London: Penguin, 2020).
21   Jean-François Lyotard, *The Postmodern Condition* (Manchester: Manchester University Press, 1984).
22   Jacques Derrida, *Writing and Difference* (Chicago: University of Chicago Press, 1978).

philosopher of this group, Gilles Deleuze[23] (1925–1995) and his co-author Félix Guattari (1930–1992). Practically all these authors were engaged in the simultaneous development of postmodern ontology, epistemology and political philosophy. From their point of view, politics is not just a separate aspect of human life, but its deepest foundation. Let us consider only the most striking and principled political philosophy of the postmodern, related to the very essence of this phenomenon. Let us take as our points of reference

- the psychoanalytic structuralist ontology of Jacques Lacan, who developed the ideas of Sigmund Freud (1856–1939),
- Michel Foucault's study of the role of epistemology in shaping political structures and his concept of 'biopolitics', and
- the philosophy of Deleuze and Guattari, which represents the most complete and perfect account of the political postmodern — at least of that formulated by the end of the twentieth century.

From these seminal authors emerges a general style of postmodern political science, which deliberately avoids systematicity and welcomes paradoxes, contradictions, ambiguities and chaotic exposition, which is meant to emphasise the transformation of the very nature of the subject towards dissolution, decomposition and dissipation that is the essence of the entire postmodern paradigm.

Lacan's Three Orders

Lacan's psychoanalysis, concerned mainly with clinical therapy of mental disorders and commentaries on Freud, for all its extravagance and fragmentary presentation, is the most important basis of postmodern political philosophy. Lacan himself paid little attention to the Political proper, but it is his philosophical foundations that are key to understanding the postmodern. Just as in Plato, the general structure of thought may be applied to the sphere of the Political, and purely philosophical works sometimes

---

23 Gilles Deleuze and Félix Guattari, *Anti-Oedipus: Capitalism and Schizophrenia* (Minneapolis: University of Minnesota Press, 1983).

contain the ideas and taxonomies most fundamental for the understanding of politics, so Lacan, without specifically focusing on politics, enables us to understand in the political philosophy of the postmodern at times more clearly than those authors who were mainly concerned with politics.

Lacan's ontological-anthropological (psychoanalytic-gnoseological) model can be described as follows.

Lacan compared the relationship between the unconscious and the conscious with the figure of a torus, where the ring corresponds to the conscious and the empty space in the centre to the unconscious.

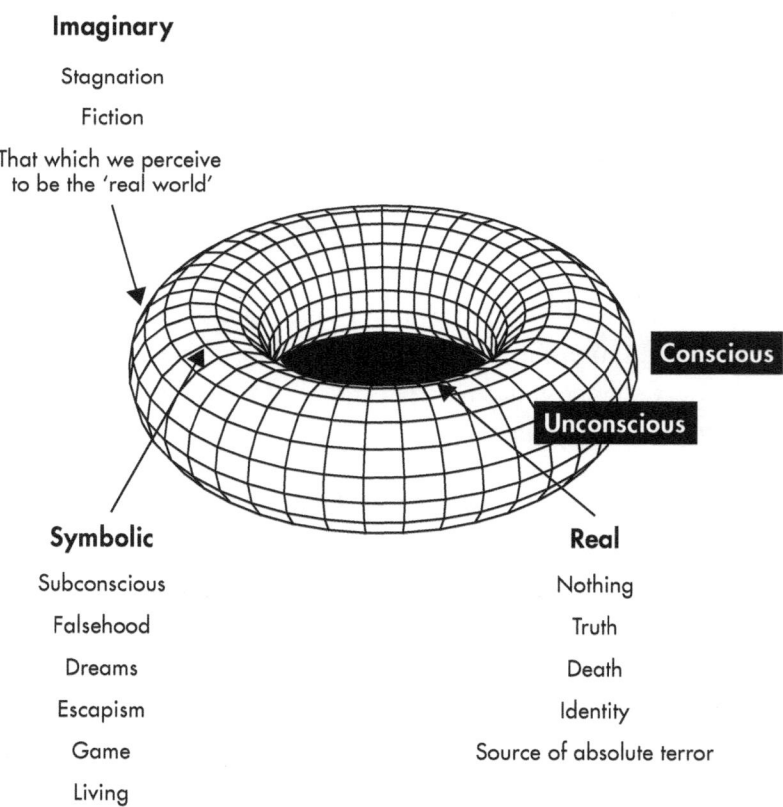

Figure 21. Lacan's Three Orders.

No matter how the point of thought moves along the surface of this torus, it always remains on the same side, although at different moments it turns out to be 'objectively' on different or even directly opposite sides. Only the emptiness in the middle remains a reference point, but it inspires horror in consciousness and therefore acts as a purely *negative reference point*, which, being negative, cannot be a reference point.

Lacan identifies three orders on which his theory is based:

- the order of the *real* (*le Réel*),
- the order of the *imaginary* (*l'Imaginaire*),
- the order of the *symbolic* (*le Symbolique*).

Lacan borrows the term 'real' from Bataille, understanding it as that which for the concrete individual being in the most final and purest experience is his experience of himself as himself. For Bataille, the real is identical to death. Lacan, however, identifies the 'real' with Freud's Id, seeing in it the root structure of the unconscious, from which the primary, basic desires arise.

Lacan follows Spinoza in recognising three basic affects — desire, pleasure and displeasure — and Lacan's unconscious itself is active, i.e. capable not only of storing representations, images and experiences, but also of generating basic impulses. The real is normally tightly hidden from human consciousness, with which it is in a private relationship: consciousness is a systematic negation of the real, its false interpretation, its suppression, an escape from it, a war with it. In this Lacan strictly follows Freud. Calling the depths of the unconscious 'real', Lacan stresses the epistemological significance of psychoanalysis as a method for addressing that which is supreme and final, giving a peculiar interpretation of ontology. According to Lacan, it is in the real that Freud's Eros and Thanatos coincide.

It is important to pay attention to the fact that Lacan's real is at the same time active, effective and wholly negative. It has no structure of its own except that which is constituted by the other two orders, according to the dialectic principle of differentials and privative oppositions. The real as pure unconscious is the *power of the negative*, which is not a set of unconscious archetypes, but only a field of active privation that spreads its insufficiency in the form of *desire*, which (as with Spinoza) is primarily desire for desire (*conatus*), a will for will and therefore does not want (something), but only wants to want, and therefore in the final analysis *does not want anything* or, rather, *wants nothing*. Desire becomes desire for something only at the stage of the symbolic order, where shame and remorse are formed, and where it takes shape and expresses its negativity as desire for the forbidden, expressing itself in inhibition and complex, that is, in pathology. Desire itself is the desire for nothing, the nothingness of the will.

The second order is the order of the imaginary. This is the realm of language as structure. Language is a rigid system of paradigmatic relations into which man is forced to place all his actions, desires and himself. Language represents the matrix of man before birth, and begins to actively cultivate man immediately after birth: the infant hears the speech of adults, and this field accompanies him until death. Lacan likens language to a hammock, in which man both rests, rocked by iterations of its habitual constructions, and is a prisoner, since the strict boundaries of its differentials, indicated by signs, rigidly determine in man all his manifestations, including that which is within him. For Lacan, language is absolutely social, and he interprets society, in turn, as a rigid binary structure of kinship. Thus, language is the order through which the unconscious is rigidly structured and systematically repressed. At the level of the imaginary, however, the unconscious does not become conscious — this is the subtlety of Lacan's psychoanalysis: on the contrary, in language the real disappears altogether, being replaced by the imaginary, and not the individual's imaginary, but language itself. The tricky thing about thinking is that in this process, it is not the individual who thinks, but thinking itself. Similarly, it is not the individual who speaks in language, but language speaks through the individual and even *apart* from the individual. In this one can easily recognise that desire for the dismantling of the individual, which constitutes the essence of the postmodern.

The third order is the symbolic, which, as in the field of the sign in structural linguistics, links the two sets (the first orders): the imaginary and the real. The symbolic is an area of weak, problematic connections between the reality of the unconscious (nothingness) and the imaginary (structures of language), most often found only in mental disorders. Freud himself described disorders as phenomena of reservations or speech dysfunctions, revealing the mechanism of 'subconscious work' that, while never ceasing for a moment, is conducted in the depth of the psyche in parallel with rational activity and is most often totally disconnected from it. It is only when the technical functioning of reason fails that subconsciousness more directly reveals what it wants, what it fears, what it suffers from, what torments it directly.

The symbolic is the field of the acquisition of content through desire, but not yet fully formed into positive structures on the level of language where the real self (desire) is completely eliminated, replaced by an imaginary self that is constituted by *what* can be desired and should be desired, and therefore by *the one who* 'properly' desires and desires exactly *what* should be desired. The symbolic is therefore the realm of the formed unconscious, represented for the first time in 'positive' terms (compared to the pure negativity of desire on the level of the real, which is pure horror), but one that still retains the imprint of the original darkness. Therefore, the symbolic order is the order of disease and pathology. Here desire is structured as forbidden, reprehensible, perverse, painful, requiring punishment, censure, condemnation, remorse and suppression. Having no qualities whatsoever, that is, *blank* (bottomless, beyond-horrible) desire at the level of the real becomes *bad*, vicious, sinful desire at the level of the symbolic, only to turn, at the level of the imaginary, into a carefully censored and acceptable legitimate desire — to eat food, get married, wait for a flight or win a competition. The strongest desire is the emptiest desire, that is, a desire so desirous that it, sensing its total and infinite emptiness, cannot be channeled into anything concrete. It weakens on the level of the symbolic order, going through the filtering labyrinths of pathology. And finally, it dissipates, along with the total loss of the subject, into the zone of the imaginary, where the desired and the desirous become fully autonomous automatic moments of a totally alienated structure.

Lacan's Political Ontology

This Lacanian model, originally intended to describe only the structure of the human psyche and consciousness (with reliance on the subconscious), lays the foundations for the entire ontology of the postmodern. Postmodernists like Democritus believe that the original state is nothingness, non-being — οὐδέν. It alone is the real, the actual and the true. Thus we find ourselves in the realm of pseudo-logic, for if truth is identical with nothingness, then any description of something other than nothingness, that is, things, phenomena, thoughts, feelings, discernments, etc. — is obviously a falsehood. Hence the postmodern irony — postmodernists do not seek the truth; they seek the truth about lies, that is, the bounds of their epistemology are lies about lies and truth about lies.

Consequently, at the level of the symbolic there is no appearance of something real, but only a flight from the truth, that is, the unfolding of pseudo-logical structures that constitute hallucinatory realms of falsehood. This is how Lacan understands the symbolic: as a lie. The essence of this lie is that the symbol always points to something else, and that other, being a symbol, points again to something else and so on in cycles. Everything points to everything to avoid pointing to nothing, which is truth and death. The realm of the symbolic is the realm of the subconscious. Here, according to postmodernists, politics is born. Its origins are not in the superstructure, but in the basis. However, the basis is interpreted not as Marx's — the relation between the productive forces and the productive relationships — but as the structure of the symbolic. Politics has its origins in the algorithm of a self-contained symbolism, each element of which points to something, but always not to what it is, and thus the basis of the Political consists in the flight from truth, which is nothing. Thus, for the postmodernists the suspicion of Marx turns into the revelation of the subconscious by Freud, whose work determines the real content of the psychological life of man (hence the postmodernists are sometimes called Freudian-Marxists). Lacan goes further and reveals the subconscious as nothing, turning the subconscious itself into a lie, while Freud offered a similar explanation to differentiate between the other two orders, the symbolic and the imaginary. According to Freud, the lie is the essence of consciousness concealing the 'truth' of the subconscious. Lacan goes further and says: a lie is all that is not true, and the truth is nothing.

Here we once again encounter Democritus' atom, but in a peculiar interpretation. Recall his extravagant synonym for atom, δέν, formed from οὐδέν, nothing, but containing no explicit reference to 'something', to 'being'. Δέν is the antithesis of οὐδέν, nothingness, but such an antithesis that is genuinely existent, that is, it is ontologically deliberately the opposite of nothingness. This is the materialist monism outlined by Marx, but which received its final form in Freudian Marxism. The alternative to pure nothingness οὐδέν is not existence, not being, but precisely falsity, i.e. the symbolic. Nothingness is true, whereas non-something is false. Hence the secondary nature of the term δέν, derived from οὐδέν, but as we have seen, unlike Russian ни-что or English no-thing, the aphorism of the negative particle 'ни', 'no', does not give us 'что' or 'thing'. Δέν is other than nothingness, and other than being, and other than absence, and other than having. This is what Lacan equates with the basis.

The superstructure is then the imaginary. This is the upper floor of the Political. Its point is to give the fluid, playful lie of the subconscious the appearance of reliability, immutability and stability, i.e. what is known in common parlance as 'reality'.

From this we can deduce the basic theme of the political postmodern. Truth is nothingness, non-being, the abyss and death. A philosophy in search of truth must be prepared for active nihilism, for a total loss of illusion. True philosophy can only be nihilism. Unlike Nietzsche, there is no need to overcome nihilism here (and it is impossible). What is proposed is to accept it as the nothingness of everything. This is the ultimate ontological — and no longer just anthropological — pessimism. Man can only commit one true philosophical act — suicide (this is how Gilles Deleuze ended his life). Everything else belongs to pseudo-logic.

Politics is the imaginary, rooted in the structures of delusion and sleep. Politics, therefore, is the frontier of lies and violence, the frontier of flight from death. But it is not the antithesis of death, it is in a sense its mirror on the other side of the torus. Those who are unaware of Lacan's torus remain in the context of the lie, the degree of which increases as one moves from the depths of the torus to its surface. Politics is not just a lie, it is a frozen lie, dead, made rigid. It is the culmination of a lie about a lie, whereas in the unconscious we have rather a truth about a lie. Hence the revolutionary imperative of the postmodern: it is necessary to return the Political to its dreamlike, psychoanalytic origins, to collapse it into the unconscious. Marx's critical theory turns into a critique of the order of the imaginary, into a critique of frozen hallucinations in favour of returning to the basis, that is, to the order of the symbolic.

But according to Lacan himself, this can never be truly achieved. Whatever success the revolutionaries have had in trying to liberate the symbolic and reclaim the imaginary, because the imaginary is order and not just arbitrariness or aberration, it will necessarily be filled with something. So after the victory of the symbolic (revolution) over the frozen structures of the imaginary, they will be recreated — albeit on different principles. The torus cannot be without a surface, and no matter how porous and open it is, without a surface that limits its presence it will dissipate into nothingness. Yes it will be true, but there will be no one and nothing to declare it. Δέν will disappear into οὐδέν, i.e. falsehood into truth.

From here follows a certain postmodern conservatism on the part of Lacan; while radically revolutionary in his ontology and his nihilism, he rather supported the existing political system (whatever it might be), trying not so much to change it as to read it correctly.

Lacan's reasoning goes like this. If desire on the level of the symbolic demands its legitimation in the imaginary (to make legal what is forbidden), this same desire will instantly cease to be symbolic desire and the desire of the symbolic (forbidden desire) and will cease to be desire at all, precisely because its entire vitality and all its 'desirability' consists in its morbidity (forbiddenness). As soon as freedom becomes a law, it ceases to be freedom and becomes a necessity. As soon as desire ceases to be shameful and forbidden, it loses its connection to the negative subject (to the order of the real) and turns into alienation, then he who has been allowed to want something no longer wants it, but either wants something which he has not yet been allowed, or wants nothing at all. But then the rearranged order of the imaginary begins to pressure the individual: what you are allowed to do, *you should do*. Eventually, freedom (in the mode of the imaginary) *becomes a field of coercion to freedom* — as in liberalism, especially in its latest totalitarian globalist stage. Lacan is not against this either, since the order of the imaginary cannot help but be totalitarian, and simultaneously cannot *not be* at all. Whatever content the symbolic throws at it, the imaginary always transforms its nature: so frozen water is ice and it is foolish to demand fluidity from it, just as it is difficult to demand fluidity from steam.

However, those who came after him, adopting Lacanian ontology, disagreed with such ironic conservatism, and gave the struggle of the basis (symbolic order) against the superstructure (imaginary order) the status of a moral imperative, liberation and progress. Thus, nihilism acquired an ethical content, becoming the goal of social and political progress, the highest philosophical truth and moral purpose.

Foucault: Freedom to Madness!

Like Lacan, another important author of the postmodern, Michel Foucault, operates with structures.

In the spirit of the general left-liberal sentiment and Freudian-Marxist generalisations, Foucault concentrates on the relationship between normative forms of consciousness (generically called epistemes) and subconscious processes, which are only directly manifest in the form of mental disorder. Foucault formulates these ideas in his book *The History of Madness in the Classical Era*,[24] where he approaches the theme of *normative rationality*, its criteria, parameters, properties and modes of implementation and protection, which is crucial for his entire oeuvre. In light of this, Foucault's qualification and definition of madness and the attitude to it at different historical stages demonstrates a change in the very *paradigm of normality* and, accordingly, in the anthropological and ontological interpretation of what reason is and what a 'reasonable man' should be. Here again we find an attack on the individual, whose normality in capitalism

---

24 Foucault, *History of Madness*.

and Communism is built on a rationality that always has concrete boundaries and definitions. In fact, 'normal man' is a figure of the imaginary (Lacan) and therefore represents a frozen moment of the symbolic (i.e. madness).

Insanity as a deviation from this norm, its interpretation, forms of treatment, and social evaluation are indicative of fundamental shifts in the underlying structures of society. In this way, Foucault comes to describe the structures of European society, which he explores in particular during the phase of transition to modernity. It is here that the fundamental transformations of the clinic, its methods and foundations take place, on the example of which one can better understand the essence of modernity's culture. Foucault will return to this theme on several occasions, particularly in his important work *The Birth of the Clinic*.[25] The revelation of the repressive nature of clinical institutions led Foucault to later describe the detailed process of the establishment of penal institutions in the modern age in his book *Discipline and Punish*.[26] Physical violence against marginalised elements — which included the mentally ill, criminals as well as those simply suffering from certain serious illnesses — for Foucault illustrates a deeper phenomenon: the repressive practice of reason against the unconscious, which is effectively tabooed and repressed through dominant epistemologies — that is, the scientific, philosophical and ideological foundations of society. The Political is above all an episteme that strictly — and always arbitrarily — establishes a standard for a 'normal person' that does not really exist and that is constituted by the political act itself.

Foucault, unlike Lacan, does not accept this observation, and calls for an epistemological uprising designed to overthrow the dictatorship of reason and give freedom to the symbolic. This is the approach that has come to dominate the postmodern, although it was Lacan — more ironic and 'conservative' — who laid down the most revolutionary aspects of postmodern ontology, against which Foucault's revolutionary optimism looks somewhat naïve.

---

25 Michel Foucault, *The Birth of the Clinic* (Oxfordshire: Routledge, 2003).
26 Foucault, *Discipline and Punish*.

Foucault's Three Epistemes

Foucault traces three phases of European history, where the transition from one episteme to another can be clearly seen through a fundamental shift in the semiotic and semantic fields:

- Renaissance (sixteenth century)
- early modern (seventeenth and eighteenth centuries)
- late modern (nineteenth and twentieth centuries).

The Middle Ages and earlier periods were based on other epistemes that remain generally outside Foucault's field of vision. But even this passage is enough to show conclusively his main structuralist thesis: the content of man, his normative status, his identity and his ontology are entirely determined by the *dominant paradigm of epistemology*. Consequently, one can speak of man not as a universal phenomenon or as an individual, but as a *sociological form* defined by the dominant episteme, and therefore derived from it. Therefore, history cannot be constructed around the axis of the individual, taken as something constant in the core and evolving in the particulars. History is a change of epistemologies and dominant epistemes, inextricably fused with the *dispositif* of power. Therefore the only authentic axis of history is the *epistemological axis*, which in turn predetermines history itself as a *functional narrative*. In the epoch of modernity (the classical period) the normative notion of the human (individual) subject was introduced as the fulcrum of being, of the world, of life and society. But this very introduction is a characteristic of a very specific historical epoch and of the ruling episteme in it, which did not exist before, and quite possibly — even for certain — will not exist in the future. Consequently, in other epistemological contexts the subject of the modern has not been and will not be in the future, Foucault concludes. For the future, this means calling for the dismantling of the subject and the search for new candidates to represent the normative individual.

For the political sphere, Foucault's analysis of knowledge as the main *dispositif* of power and the centrality of power discourse in the general practice of rule has been a classic thesis of socio-political disciplines in

Europe since the 1960s. The *dispositif* is the arsenal with the help of which power ensures its stability, continuity and sustainability. According to Foucault, power is first and foremost the installation of the dominant epistemology, and everything else follows from it. Hence, the organisation of the mental sphere through culture, education, the system of values, etc. is the main instrument of establishing, maintaining and, in some cases, revolutionarily overthrowing the model of power. It is not a question of which personality, group or even class dominates a society; the question is how they argue for this particular system, instilling society with the idea of its inviolability, legitimacy and lack of alternatives. Following Marxist Gramsci, Foucault and other postmodernists focus precisely on culture, that is, on the non-political aspect of the superstructure, which, from their point of view, is actually a more solid basis than the economy. Thus, the entire Marxian model, already modified by Gramsci, is definitively overturned. Society is not based on the economy, but on the subconscious, which is where the roots of the episteme grow from.

Biopower and Biopolitics

The late modernity of Foucault in which we live is based in this redefinition of the classical (for modernity) symmetries of the Political. The drive for democratisation, atomisation, further immanentisation and an ever-increasing degree of materialism revealed the close connection between power and the biological roots of life. This led Foucault to the concepts of biopower and biopolitics.[27] Continuing the main line of research already begun in his early works, Foucault reaches the conclusion that, ultimately, the control of the mind is achieved through control of the body, due to the fact that — from a materialist perspective — consciousness is the sublimation of materiality. The control of the corporeal through healthcare, the regulation of demography, and the economy of pain and pleasure is the main *dispositif* of power. It is this control that defines the configuration of the dominant episteme, which through the assertion of 'norm' — and the most fundamental norm is what defines what should be understood as

---

27 Michel Foucault, *Dits et écrits* [Written and Spoken] (Paris: Gallimard, 2001).

'health' and 'sickness' — controls not just consciousness, but also the bodily standards of people.

From here, Foucault arrives at the concept of a 'biopolitics of desire', suggesting that epistemology is built on the repression, supervision and control of the deepest aspects of human biological existence. Biopower is the real power that asserts its vertical authority through manipulating the lower layers of the unconscious, which directly border the body.

This picture changes the meaning of the revolution in late modernity by transferring it to the psychoanalytical and biological level. This line was later developed by another postmodernist, the Italian philosopher Giorgio Agamben.[28]

Gilles Deleuze: The Will to Nothingness

Postmodern philosophy is best represented in the work of the French philosopher Gilles Deleuze and his constant collaborator, the psychoanalyst Felix Guattari.

Deleuze accepts the Nietzschean thesis of European nihilism, but rejects the Superman as the one destined, according to Nietzsche, to overcome nothing. Nothing does not need to be overcome, nothing needs to be desired, argues Deleuze, and justifies the *'will to nothing'* on this principle.[29]

Deleuze's nothing refers to the French philosophical tradition of intense modernity as Lacan understood it (as synonymous with the real).

The peculiarity of Deleuze's treatment of nothingness is that he takes it out of the dimension of the real (Lacan) and places it in the zone of indirect but intense attention. 'Nothing' is no longer hidden, but emerges as a given, *as a phenomeno*n.

Following the 'nothingness' that, according to Deleuze, is the will of postmodern philosophical thought, his sight falls on matter, which he

---

28 Giorgio Agamben, *Homo Sacer. Sovereign Power and Bare Life* (Stanford: Stanford University Press, 1998).

29 'Man would rather want nothing than not want anything.' See Gilles Deleuze, *Nietzsche and Philosophy* (New York: Columbia University Press, 1983). In this formula it is easy to identify Lacan's idea of the identity of Eros and Thanatos in the order of the real, ascending in the first impulse to the symbolic.

interprets as *corporeality*.[30] For him, as for all materialists and immanentists, *matter is identical with being*, understood, however, in a negative way (in particular, this continues the line of Spinoza's substantialism; Deleuze considered Spinoza his philosophical beacon, along with Democritus, the Epicureans and the Stoics). There is only matter (which does not exist) and everything else is folded from it.[31] Corporeality here takes the place of Lacan's order of the real.

A Body without Organs: The Political Doctrine of Humpty Dumpty

In exploring corporeality, Deleuze descends enthusiastically into the microcosm, focusing on the faint currents and desires rising from the depths of corporeality and moving towards what he calls the 'surface' or 'screen'. This is the outside of corporeality, the skin. Deleuze, speaking of corporeality, is not referring to the already organised human or any other body. He is not interested in the body, but precisely in corporeality, that is, in what is below the body. Using Antonin Artaud's visionary metaphor, Deleuze introduces the notion of the 'body without organs' as the basic matrix of corporeality, preceding the interaction with the constructed 'outside world', representing ontic grooves (*l'espace strié*) and forcing the original 'body without organs' to acquire organs, that is, from corporeality to become a body. The 'body without organs', according to Deleuze, is the free sliding of the ball on a perfectly smooth surface (*l'espace lisse*). This is the formula for corporeality as such, i.e. being as matter. Everything else is built on top of this instance. Deleuze finds an analogue of Artaud's 'body without organs' in the figure of Humpty Dumpty in Lewis Carroll's *Alice in Wonderland*. Humpty Dumpty is represented in the form of an egg, as indicated in the description of his appearance and in the very fact that, having fallen from the wall, he broke into many small pieces like an eggshell and was therefore irrevocably shattered. The symbolism of the egg in ancient cultures refers to the image of the Great Mother. So, again,

---

30   Gilles Deleuze, *The Logic of Sense* (New York: Columbia University Press, 1990).
31   Gilles Deleuze, *The Fold: Leibniz and the Baroque* (Minneapolis: University of Minnesota Press, 1993).

the postmodern imagery refers us to the political philosophy of the Mother, the third genus of Plato's *Timaeus*.

The 'body without organs' (the surface that is Humpty Dumpty) as the main pole of the new postmodern conceptualisation is the historical culmination in the framing of the lexicon of the philosophy of the Mother. Deleuze, continuing the line of the philosophy of materialism, reaches its final deepest point: he *constructs philosophy from the perspective of matter*. The 'body without organs' (the gynecocratic Humpty Dumpty) is the pure production of the earth without the participation of heaven.

Splitting the Object: Chaosmos

Deleuze, moving towards the ultimate materiality, towards nothingness, continues the philosophical dissection of the object, approaching very closely the level of atomically understood matter, where the cosmos ends and chaos begins. But pure chaos or pure nothingness, which are to be sought and desired, are not attainable. So Deleuze fixes his attention on that boundary where cosmos ends and chaos begins. Following the writer James Joyce[32] (1882–1941), he calls it 'chaosmos'. The term is formed from the Greek words 'chaos', χάος, and 'osmosis', ὅσμος. 'Chaos' (χάος) indicates the state prior to the formation of matter, while 'osmosis' (ὅσμος) denotes the chemical process of 'one-way diffusion through a semipermeable membrane of solvent molecules towards a higher concentration of solute'. Osmosis gives a direction to chaos, oriented always in the direction opposite to momentum or disturbance, which gives rise to Democritus' vortices, vortices that always gravitate towards dissipation and rest. Disturbance and rest, which excite the mass of pure corporeality, are juxtaposed by Deleuze with the Eros and Thanatos of psychoanalysis, thus uniting philosophy, psychology and physics into a common postmodern model that is analogous to the cosmos in previous philosophical systems. Chaos seeps through its inherent membrane, generating not order and structures, but precisely 'vortices', consisting not yet of being, but of Democritus' δέν.

---

32 James Joyce, *Finnegan's Wake* (New York: The Viking Press, 1939).

According to Deleuze, God (as a hypothesis of transcendence and vertical symmetry) gives meaning to the world. And then reality becomes peace, order. But the abolition of God (the death of Nietzsche's God) means the loss of meaning (*le sens*), its dissipation in the purely immanent surfaces or, more precisely, the placement of a moment of incidental meaninglessness, a quantum of non-sense (*le non-sens*) in place of meaning, which generates a completely different post-structure where the vertical (transcendental) dimension of God disappears (and if not disappearing immediately, then, detached from the act of signification, is quickly forgotten as *Deus Otiosus*).

Thus, in place of the world appear spontaneous meaningless vortices of chaotic excretions.

Accordingly, the external world in postmodern ontology is constituted as turbulent flows of meaningless quanta flowing in a bizarre and arbitrary rhythm in planes and symmetries, nominally two-dimensional but simultaneously transcending the parameters of purely geometric patterns in the spirit of Mandelbrot's theory of the geometry of nature and fractals.

Splitting the Subject: The Rhizome

If chaosmos is the postmodern replacement for the abolished cosmos, the classical subject is even more unacceptable to postmodernists. 'The world has lost its core, the subject can no longer create a dichotomy, but it achieves a higher unity — a unity of ambivalence and superdetermination — in a dimension always complementary to that of its own object,' say Deleuze and Guattari.[33] And instead of the subject, they propose another concept, the 'rhizome'.

This concept is borrowed from botany and describes a special kind of plant and fungus that spreads horizontally, parallel to the surface of the earth, letting roots and stems in the individual nodes of a branched network system. The rhizome is distinguished by the fact that, unlike other plants, pulling out the root and stem does not lead to the death of the

---

33   Gilles Deleuze and Félix Guattari, *A Thousand Plateaus: Capitalism and Schizophrenia* (London: Athlone Press, 1988).

whole organism, which continues to exist regardless of the loss of individual elements. By uprooting it, we destroy only one form, but we do not damage the whole, the entire rhizome, which continues to expand horizontally under the ground, unseen, growing larger and larger.

Deleuze introduces the notion of the 'rhizome' in his seminal work *A Thousand Plateaus: Capitalism and Schizophrenia*, written with Guattari:

> (...)unlike trees or their roots, the rhizome connects any point to any other point, and its traits are not necessarily linked to traits of the same nature; it brings into play very different regimes of signs, and even nonsign states. The rhizome is reducible neither to the one nor the multiple. It is not the one that becomes two or even directly three, four, five, etc. It is not a multiple derived from the one, or to which one is added (n + 1). It is composed not of units but of dimensions, or rather directions in motion. It has neither beginning nor end, but always a middle (milieu) from which it grows and which it overspills. It constitutes linear multiplicities with n dimensions having neither subject nor object, which can be laid out on a plane of consistency, and from which the one is always subtracted (n — 1). When a multiplicity of this kind changes dimension, it necessarily changes in nature as well, undergoes a metamorphosis. Unlike a structure, which is defined by a set of points and positions, with binary relations between the points and biunivocal relationships between the positions, the rhizome is made only of lines: lines of segmentarity and stratification as its dimensions, and the line of flight or deterritorialisation as the maximum dimension after which the multiplicity undergoes metamorphosis, changes in nature. These lines, or lineaments, should not be confused with lineages of the arborescent type, which are merely localisable linkages between points and positions. Unlike the tree, the rhizome is not the object of reproduction: neither external reproduction as image-tree nor internal reproduction as tree-structure. The rhizome is an antigenealogy. It is a short-term memory, or antimemory. The rhizome operates by variation, expansion, conquest, capture, offshoots. Unlike the graphic arts, drawing, or photography, unlike tracings, the rhizome pertains to a map that must be produced, constructed, a map that is always detachable, connectable, reversible, modifiable, and has multiple entryways and exits and its own lines of flight. It is tracings that must be put on the map, not the opposite. In contrast to centered (even polycentric) systems with hierarchical modes of communication and preestablished paths, the rhizome is an acentered, nonhierarchical, nonsignifying system without a General and without an organising memory or central automaton, defined solely by a circulation of states. What is at question in the rhizome is a relation to sexuality—but also to the animal, the

vegetal, the world, politics, the book, things natural and artificial—that is totally different from the arborescent relation: all manner of 'becomings'.

A plateau is always in the middle, not at the beginning or the end. A rhizome is made of plateaus.[34]

The Rhizomatic Topology of Consciousness and the Desire Machine

The rhizome is the surface of great corporeality, the instance in which the principal states of consciousness are formed. In the usual example, the human structure is organised vertically: the trunk (stem), branches and crown are the upper floors of thought and consciousness; the roots are the reverse projections into the unconscious realm. Thus consciousness and the unconscious are constituted simultaneously in a moment of corporeality, forming a concrete body with its *eidos*, 'form' (the crown) and 'matter' (the roots).

The rhizome is constantly 'in between' or, as Deleuze and Guattari formulate it, 'the plateau is always in the middle — neither at the beginning nor at the end'.

The surface in which the rhizome lives is the screen of desires, where they are projected by the *desire machine*. These desires are neither articulated nor rational. Deleuze and Guattari oppose reconstructions of desire in Freud's psychoanalysis, which they accuse of 'patriarchy' and a 'phallocentric' interpretation of eros. Instead they offer a feminine view of eros as desire in its diffuse, unfocused and unfinalised form. The dispersed paneroticism of the Great Mother, which knows no inhibitions, is contrasted with the patriarchal nature of classical Freudianism. Thus, delving into the worlds of corporeality leads Deleuze and Guattari to the thesis that the taboo on incest should be lifted, since, in their view, this cultural requirement reflects mechanisms of repression and is the basis of authoritarianism and dictatorship.

---

34 Deleuze and Guattari, *A Thousand Plateaus: Capitalism and Schizophrenia*.

Liberating the 'Black Depths'

In *The Logic of Sense*, speaking of the Cynics and Stoics, Deleuze describes with great sympathy the appeal to a 'black depth':

> This is a reorientation of all thought and of what it means to think: there is no longer depth or height. The cynical and stoic sneers against Plato are many. It is always a matter of unseating the idea, of showing that the incorporeal is not high above (*en hauteur*), but is rather at the surface, that it is not the highest cause but the superficial effect par excellence, and that it is not essence but event. On the other front, it will be argued that depth is a digestive illusion which complements the ideal optical illusion. What, in fact, is signified by this gluttony, this apology for incest and cannibalism? While this latter theme is common to both Chrysippus and Diogenes the Cynic, Laertius offers no explanation of Chrusippus' views. But he does propose a particularly convincing explanation in the case of Diogenes: '...he saw no impropriety...in eating the flesh of any animal; nor even anything impious in touching human flesh, this, he said, being clear from the custom of some foreign nations. Moreover, according to right reason, as he put it, all elements are contained in all things and pervade everything: since not only is meat a constituent of bread, but bread of vegetables; and all other bodies also, by means of certain invisible passages and particles, find their way in and unite with all substances in the form of vapor. This he makes plain in the *Thyestes*, if the tragedies are really his...' This thesis, which holds for incest as well, establishes that in the depth of bodies everything is mixture. There are no rules, however, according to which one mixture rather than another might be considered bad. Contrary to what Plato believed, there is no mixture high above for these mixtures and combinations of ideas which would allow us to define good or bad mixtures. Or again, contrary to what the pre-Socratics thought, there is no immanent measure either, capable of fixing the order and the progression of a mixture in the depths of nature (physics); every mixture is as good as the bodies which pervade one another and the parts which coexist. How could the world of mixtures not be that of a black depth wherein everything is permitted?[35]

The 'world of the black depths' is the rhizomatic space of negative freedom: on the level of the individual, freedom from reason, on the level of politics, freedom from power. Dictatorship in politics is interpreted by Deleuze and Guattari as a continuation of the repression of rationality (stem and crown) against corporeality (roots and rhizome itself) in the

---

35 Deleuze, *The Logic of Sense*, pp. 130–131.

public sphere. A truly free society, according to Deleuze and Guattari, is only possible when women's sexuality is fully liberated and legally elevated to the norm, in opposition to the repressive models of phallocentric hierarchical socio-political systems. Based on this idea, Deleuze and Guattari specifically proposed a reform of psychoanalysis, calling not for a rigid dualism of the sexes (reflecting, in their view, the vertical crown/root axis), but a non-articulated rhizomatic sexuality (conceptualised, parallel to Deleuze and Guattari, by another postmodern philosopher, Michel Foucault[36]).

True emancipation, according to Deleuze — that is, the completion of the emancipatory programme of modernity — boils down to the emancipation of precisely the 'black depth' of corporeality, where 'everything is a mixture', and consequently any epistemologies based on difference, separation and, accordingly, rationality — including bans on cannibalism, incest or paedophilia — are forms of violence, oppression and dictatorship against what is for Deleuze synonymous with being itself — the nihilistic pulsation of chaosmosis.

Schizomass

Deleuze suggests that rhizomatic being is peculiar to people suffering from schizophrenia, that is, such forms of mental deviation that constitute a splitting of consciousness and a transfer of consciousness from the subject to external objects or internal mind-controlled poles of consciousness and will (from which come voices, hallucinations, etc.). According to Deleuze, the masses taken as a whole are closer to the schizophrenic model than individuals structured by patriarchal culture on the crown/root axis. Hence Deleuze takes the side of what he calls 'schizomass',[37] proposing not to regard schizophrenia as abnormality but to elevate it to normality by broadening the notion of what is healthy and sick in relation to the human psyche. In patriarchal culture, Deleuze argues, the metaphor of the tree is accepted as the norm,[38] and therefore anything that

---

36 Foucault, *The History of Sexuality. Volume 1 The Will to Knowledge.*
37 Deleuze and Guattari, *Anti-Oedipus: Capitalism and Schizophrenia.*
38 Ibid.

deviates from it is seen as pathology and disease. If we adopt a matriarchal-centered view of things, illness becomes a sign of health, and sanity becomes a special case of madness. The postmodernist Foucault, who developed similar matriarchal philosophical trends in parallel with Deleuze, devoted his work to rehabilitating madness and exposing the pejorative concept itself as a product of the patriarchal and repressive will to power.[39]

Deleuze had a decisive influence on postmodern philosophy and on its political projects, which consisted of the radicalisation of emancipation — no longer only of the subject, now also of the object — in favour of the triumph of rhizomatic structures.

Micropolis and Micropolitics

The political philosophy of the postmodern is built on these foundations. We should pay attention to the fact that, on the one hand, it is a continuation of modernity, decisive steps in the same direction — towards the philosophy of the Mother, materialism and the search for the atom and individuality through their progressive liberation from fixing structures (order, power, hierarchy). On the other hand, the postmodern transcends certain boundaries inherent in modernity.

First of all, the concept of the atom as something which has already been achieved — in physics and politics (the individual) — is called into question. Refining the content of atomism in science reveals subatomic dimensions, which at the quantum level demonstrate new laws and beginnings, essentially different from classical mechanics. Thus, an atom becomes 'indivisible' only conventionally, i.e. it becomes a 'volume', a conglomerate of other particles, which in turn are not 'atoms' (not indivisible), but quite divisible. In this way, the object acquires a new content, or rather the old content is gradually eroded. Postmodernists say: the atom is an ideal goal, not a given. Everything we have, even at the quantum level, is still a combinatorial agglomerate, a structure, and it must in turn be subjected to decomposition, dissection. These structures must be dissected

---

39 Foucault, *History of Madness*.

into parts, new pretenders to the status of 'atoms', and be taken not as a whole, but as a combinatorial assemblage. The French philosopher Marcel Conche[40] says that the world is no longer a world, but an extravagant ensemble, proposing his ontology of the incidental, rejecting any wholeness.

It is the same with the atom of society (politics) — the individual. Man is no longer an individual but an agglomerate of individual combined elements, whose freedom lies in the fact that they can be put together differently every time like mosaics. The totality of the individual content can construct absolutely any figure on the level of the subject. The individual is the divide and the rhizome. It is possible to change its past, future, to invent, to create, because everything in human society is invented and created, constructed. But everything constructed can be deconstructed[41] and reconstructed.

When such beliefs are given normative status, they become the basis for science, technology, culture, medicine and, finally, politics itself. Everything in human society is dissected, up to and including normative identity, which becomes plural. Thus, the shizomass of Deleuze and Guattari transforms from a concept into a political and social norm, and schizophrenia itself ceases to be a clinical diagnosis and becomes a legitimate, and even privileged, form of thinking.

Any wholeness, any structure, from the state to the individual, thus falls under the suspicion of being 'totalitarian', 'dictatorial', suppressing real atomism in favour of holistic structures, albeit disguised as 'atoms'. Modernity in its division of society went as far as the individual. Postmodernism goes further and insists on the splitting of the individual, on the schizophrenisation of culture, and then of politics.

Thus, for the postmodernists classical democracy or secular socialism are insufficient precisely because they preserve the classical idea of the

---

40 Marcel Conche, *L'Aléatoire* [The Randomness] (Paris: Les Belles Lettres, 2012).
41 Deconstruction is a crucial term in postmodern philosophy, coined by Derrida (1930–2004), meaning placing any utterance — more broadly, anything at all — in the historical context where it first arose in order to show how in the process of quotation or reproduction it has lost and distorted its meaning.

individual. Yes, the human individual can be freed from various forms of collective identity — religion, state, nation, even gender — and this is almost achieved in the late modern, but postmodernism has delved deeper and discovered that the wrong sort of person has been liberated. Instead of a victim, the maniac, the criminal, the dictator was set free. Consequently, the political struggle *for the emancipation of the individual* turns into a political struggle *for emancipation from the individual.*

The goal becomes the identification of a new 'atom' — a body-without-organs (political Humpty Dumpty), rhizome, schizomass, a 'parliament of organs', etc.

Postmodern politics shifts the focus from society to the individual. The human individual is henceforth seen as a *polis*. The common individual has one centre of decision-making: consciousness. It is a kind of government. As a rule, the micro-level political system is a dictatorship of the ego. The ego, the subject, the intellect and the will is not just a government, but a tyrant, an autocrat. It is cruel, rational, intolerant; it tyrannically dominates its subjects — 'feelings' — threatens them, judges them, suppresses them.

In the schizophrenic, who is the normative agent of emancipatory postmodernism, the monarchy splits (at least) into two opposing camps. Thus one becomes a site of rebellion, revolution and even civil war. One part of micro-society wants one thing, the other part wants another. In some cases, tyrannical reason appears stronger, in others, its power crumbles under the assault of multiple selves — voices, personalities, urges, impulses, intrusions from the unconscious. From the point of view of classical modern psychiatry, schizophrenia is an illness; from the point of view of postmodernism, on the contrary, the absence of schizophrenia is an illness, because it is violence against the multitude of 'selves' that inhabit us; it is a repression of desire, a dictatorship of consciousness that turns the multidimensional human rhizome into submissive slaves. Henceforth the individual human person, rather than a politically and hierarchically organised society, becomes a Leviathan, instituted by the 'social contract' of the sub-subjective — the divisional — elements. All the problems of realists (supporters of anthropological pessimism in the spirit of Hobbes) and liberals (continuing the line of Locke) are transferred to the micro-level. The former defend reason as the Leviathan of the micropolis, fearing the destruction to which liberated sub-individual schizo-personalities, the 'oozing' chaos of impulses and dark desires can lead. The latter, on the contrary, see it as 'progress', 'development' and 'liberation of creative possibilities', leading to an enrichment of difference and a deepening of democracy.

What in totalitarian society was considered a disease, postmodernists argue, is in fact free creativity. Most artists, performers, bright talented people are schizophrenic, many charismatic politicians, preachers, speakers have obvious mental deviations. Among brilliant scientists there are many people whose consciousness differs significantly from the average norm and represents an abnormality. So we simply have to shift the emphasis. What was the norm in modernity must be considered an aberration, and vice versa. According to Deleuze and Guattari, non-schizophrenics are subhuman, constrained, clamped down, diseased beings suffering under the tyrannical rule of their own minds, organised along a vertical axis.

From Deleuze and Guattari's point of view, the common man is based on the metaphor of a tree. Its roots are the past, or reference to its corporeality, its material basis; its crown and branches are its future, or consciousness. And if one takes away the past and pulls out the roots, the tree will fall; if one cuts down the crown, the personhood also disappears. Striking the roots or the crown leads to the elimination of the individual. This is the law of classical — 'vertical', according to Deleuze — anthropology. Here we see that, while the modernists were limited to the subversion of the political vertical, regarding the horizontal as having been achieved (in democracy), in the micropolitics of the postmodern, this verticality is found again on the level of the individual himself. Society may be democratic, but man himself, as a unit of this society, remains a totalitarian and hierarchical system. This is how the dimensionality of the Political changes. Deleuze and Guattari's topology, then, offers the following solution, noting that between the roots and the crown is a *line of earth*, which is a kind of screen where the lower, invisible, root, corporeal, material ('past' as achieved, available, reliable) connects with the manifested, conscious and future (shaky, projective, non-guaranteed). This intermediate territory, where the body meets consciousness and the past meets the future, is the 'eternal present'. Its metaphor is the rhizome. Having freed man from the past and the future, from an aggravating corporeality rooted in nothingness (the order of the real, according to Lacan), but also from the dictatorship of consciousness, man becomes a rhizome. Until people become a rhizome, they remain vulnerable, inferior, and tyrannical over themselves.

These people need to be liberated, made 'fully human' — i.e. schizophrenic — by first changing the very structure of psychiatric diagnoses and evaluations. Instead of the tree metaphor, it is necessary to adopt the metaphor of rhizomes, mushrooms, rootlets, i.e. of a network spread horizontally below the surface, with cultivation rather than suppression of multiple — ephemeral, playful, random and spontaneous — 'selves'. There should be loose ends in thinking; this would undermine the tyranny of reason and creative freedom would be guaranteed.

Thus the increasing splitting of consciousness becomes a process, pushing people towards progressive schizophrenisation, a dispersal of the subject into sub-subjective sets.

The rhizomatic 'man' is almost invulnerable. We can cut off his crown, we can uproot his roots, but the rhizome will not suffer — he will give new sprouts. This is how the principle of social networking works, and the internet in general. Change your nickname and avatar, close your account, delete your correspondence history and one virtual person is gone. But you can create a new virtual identity at any time. From the network, this carries over to society, offline. Here a similar virtuality grows. People change their places of residence, names, countries, professions, appearances and genders more and more easily. They live in an ephemeral present, arbitrarily changing roots and crowns, corporeality and consciousness. A rhizome may lose its memory, consciousness, past and future, but it will retain its meaningless eternal present, which spreads, unseen, in all directions beneath the earth.

Thus there is a profound democratisation of the individual at the micro level, and the rhizome becomes the most important concept of postmodern politics.

Realism and Liberalism of Desire

The transition from polis to micropolis, and consequently from politics to micropolitics, as we can see, repeats the main power lines of modern political philosophy, but in a different dimension. This change in dimensionality is the main feature of the postmodern. However, just as in the case of quantum mechanics or relativity theory, the transition to a new level of phenomena too small or too large somewhat changes the axiomatics and physical laws, so the postmodern study of micropolis — as the structure of the individual, taken as an agglomeration of heterogenous and independent particles (=micro-citizens) — is not a perfect replication of the Political as it appears in the modern. This correction is important in order to better understand the specificity of micropolitics — much here remains the same as in macropolitics (of modernity), only on a different scale; but some things change. Nevertheless, some analogies between the Leviathan and the micro-Leviathan are acceptable. So, for example, we can apply to the figure of the rhizomatic dividual[42] the patterns of dispute between liberals and realists (mercantilists).

The postmodern dividual is, on the one hand, thought of as a set of sub-subjective units that constitute a micro-society. These are impulses, phantoms, 'voices', organs and, ultimately, the basis of the unconscious — the 'desire machine'.[43] It is the 'desire machine' (as the 'subconscious factory') that generates a plurality of dividual micro-subjects reduced to a variety of desires constructing their 'worlds', including the 'micro-ego', the phenomenology and the objects to which these desires are directed. Freeing the workers of this 'desire factory' from the censorship of reason and exploitative withdrawal of 'surplus value' by the higher levels of consciousness is revolutionary postmodernist politics or 'schizoanalysis'. It corresponds to the transition from a hierarchical organisation

---

42 TN: In contrast to 'individual'
43 Gilles Deleuze and Félix Guattari, *Anti-Oedipus: Capitalism and Schizophrenia*.

of the state to a democratic one, and ultimately to a civil society, which at the dividual level corresponds to the democratic organisation of the quanta of desire. This is a kind of 'quantum democracy' achieved through the rhizomatisation and schizophrenisation of culture, politics, education, medicine, etc.

But on the other hand, the concept of the 'desire factory' put forward by Deleuze and Guattari is not accidental. There is nothing more standardised and uniform than the factory worker. In other words, the subhuman quanta (more consistent with the 'individual' than any singled-out person) that make up the human being are usually serial and almost identical, differing only in the smallest details, levels of intensity, etc. This is where liberalism or, more precisely, micro-liberalism comes in. Realism on the level of micropolitics, even accepting democratisation and the free market of desires within the individual, nevertheless considers that in the interaction with the other (the analogue of the other state of 'big politics' of the modern age), a higher authority should still have priority, which at the level of the single person in micropolitics corresponds to the intellect, to the ego, to a centralised consciousness. The emancipation of the subsubjective elements must therefore take place within the boundaries of the individual, understood in the 'old way', i.e. as a person. When interacting with another agglomerate, the first agglomerate must act as a centralised structure. This corresponds to the state monopoly on foreign trade that mercantilism and realism insist on. It is a kind of protectionist policy that protects the entire territory in which a given 'desire machine' operates.

Micro-liberalism insists on a different scenario. The uniformity of desire at its most profound level is an invitation to free exchange, the schizoanalytic equivalent of free trade. In this way an individual desire can engage with another desire directly, in a special *transindividual* space, bypassing the instance of the individual subject — the intellect. Thus emerges the thesis of transsexuality, which is not a relationship between two people with gender polarity, but a rhizomatic oscillation of multiple desire factories intersecting with each other directly, without the mediation of the individual ego. The ego blocks such freedom of exchange, acting as an analogue of 'nationalism' or 'Fascism'. Love, according to Deleuze and Guattari, in contrast to classical psychoanalysis, is not a business of three — a man, a woman and the child they beget. Love generates a multitude simultaneously, and is the work of a multitude of micro-subjects who can belong to any individual-state.

In the end, from the liberal principle of free trade, Deleuze and Guattari, who were sympathetic to Marxism, move on to the thesis of 'workers of the world, unite!', which means a call for a pansexual revolution, that is, the total mixing of all rhizomatic desires into one planetary tangle of an orgiastic network.

This analogy between macropolitics and micropolitics, which reduces everything to the dividual and simultaneously to the trans-individual level, was well understood by the postmodernists themselves. This was clearly expressed by Deleuze in the fundamental formula of the postmodern, 'Everything is politics.'

The transition to micropolitics and centralisation of the 'desire factory' puts gender at the heart of the issue, as reflected in gender politics. If we accept 'quantum liberalism' or 'quantum Marxism', which at some stage are not fundamentally different from each other — in their common struggle against 'quantum fascism' or 'quantum realism', which defends the sovereignty of reason —, then it is the sphere of gender and sexual relations, their regulation and legal status that becomes the centre of the Political.

In this case both genders are seen as agglomerations and 'nationalist' conventions, since the 'desire factories' located deep within the human being are neither male nor female, nor are their 'quantum workers' or the impulses of desire they create. Pansexualism is primary and constitutes its own polarity — that is, the being of one or the other gender. The dismantling of gender makes gender identity arbitrary, and consequently the field of transindividual relations itself becomes game-like, networked, rhizomatic, without strictly defined boundaries or identities. This is a kind of gender (or rather transgender) internationalism.

Hence, the notion of 'microfascism' is born — that is, any initiative for the preservation of rational individuality and gender identity. The struggle against Fascism, as previously against traditional society, unites postmodern liberals with postmodern Communists, which on the level of gender politics finds its expression in the promotion of the queer community (LGBT).

Microglobalism

Gender politics finds itself at the centre of the postmodern. On a new — quantum — level, it repeats the political history of the modern, only while the modern freed man from all forms of traditional identity, culminating in liberalism — and especially its historical victory in 1991 over the last serious opponent aspiring to symmetry and even a future victory by a similarly modernist ideology, Communism — the postmodern frees the dividual 'factories of desire' from man, from reason. The atom refines its dimensionality, and the subject of revolution and liberation becomes the rhizome. And the transsexual transindividual network becomes the arena of the Political, which has become global. Thus, through transindividuality (and transsexuality), micropolitics becomes a global phenomenon.

This corresponds to certain symmetries which we observe in quantum physics and especially in superstring theory (operating with microparticles and processes), and in astrophysics, the subject of which are extra-large 'cosmic' objects. Tellingly, Epicurus argued that atoms could be both very small and very large, anticipating this symmetry. Thus globalisation does not simply coincide with the transition to micropolitics, but both of these phenomena, emerging at the lower frontier of modernity, constitute a homology — the distortion of mesoproportions (corresponding to human dimensionality) in both cases — in the sphere of the giant and in that of the microscopic. This is how postmodern civil society emerges, with the dismantling of human individuality itself as the last vestige of the political philosophy of the classical eras.

Globalisation is a process of dismantling the state which has reached a critical point. Society is first reduced to the individual — this is the political philosophy of modernity, reflected in the spread of the 'human rights' ideology, pacifism, the destruction of all collective identities — hence homosexual marriage, families of three or more different-sex or same-sex members, etc. This is no longer a family, but a post-family consisting of a random set of any number of people. And what follows is a proliferation of rhizomatic groups, a union not of individuals with individuals, not even carriers of a particular gender in random combination, but a configuration of random folds of desire with other combinatorial elements that create a post-society where the inter-individual is completely replaced by the transindividual. A special kind of random chaotic interconnection takes place through the individual, and the individual himself becomes a contingent unit, a hub, a contingent server or even a directory that is detached from any fixed forms — in body, mind, memory, etc. Globalisation, starting with the individual, logically arrives at their abolition, their overcoming. Everything becomes contingent, arbitrary, including (and even above all) human beings. Democritus' principle of 'isonomy' (ἰσονομία) begins to apply to the individual: 'no more human than non-human'.

Thus. internationality coincides with transindividuality and pansexuality, juxtaposing globalisation and subindividual dispersion. Globalisation is a microprocess. This is easy to see in technology: the cohesion of states and societies is proceeding in parallel with the reduction of the main tools of connection to the network — processors, screens, etc. The global planetary network is growing as the instruments that provide access to it are shrinking.

Property Erosion

We have already talked about how in postmodernity the 'wholeness' of the classical ontology of modernity is crumbling and what role the transition from conventional money to digital, virtual money plays in this. Wealth, credit, is just a digital code that tells you whether you are poor or rich.

At the same time, the means of acquiring wealth are becoming increasingly volatile, a gamble. For example, an Indonesian teenager can (theoretically) make a billion by playing the stock market. A fashion blogger with no professional skills, intelligence or looks, who has found the key to his audience, can get rich at lightning speed. This is how very young people can — almost by accident and without effort — get huge sums of money, removing their need to work.

When a success story like this is told to millions, the motivation to work disappears. It devalues it. Easy money corrupts not only those who get it, but also those — more numerous — who learn about it from the media or the web. The billionaires who founded Google are not much different from the army of programmers and hackers, but they were caught up in the favourable financial wave that lifted them to the top. And the rest of us — no worse, no better — were not. Psychologically it is clear: as soon as we find out that somebody got 100 million dollars by offering a more original packaging for Pepsi-Cola, we are already paralysed; we don't want to study or work anymore, we want 100 million dollars. And the idea of coming up with some more packaging could drive us crazy and ruin our lives. We are waiting for the money to find a real owner, and we are convinced that we are that owner.

The detachment of wealth contributes to the *relativisation of the material*. Wealth becomes easy, accidental, arbitrary, unrelated to labour, to immense amounts of hard work. For example, the son of a representative of a large financial corporation receives a huge inheritance. In order to hold on to this inheritance for two or three years, he will have to work as hard as his father and fight for every dollar. And if he rests and enjoys life instead, those billions disappear before his eyes. Then it turns out there are no billions at all — they were just notional figures to be maintained. Many oligarchs admit that they do not own the money, the money owns them. If an oligarch stops for a moment in the frantic pursuit of zeros in his account, he will fall out of the race and most likely will go bankrupt and lose everything. Either fight for new zeros or lose existing ones.

This is how money becomes not 'property' but a process. Money no longer belongs to anyone — on the contrary, the oligarchs, the bankers, the managers, who follow the internal logic of capital, belong to it. This is how the dissipation of wealth occurs — the more ownership is asserted, the more dispersed it becomes. *Private property becomes partial property*. It dissipates into many components that become dynamic, and these whirlpools of capital movement form eddies, financial holes, and vast areas of offshore prosperity with almost no connection to the owners. This is reflected in the three basic laws of 'technical analysis' of markets:

market action discounts everything,

prices move in trends,

history repeats itself.[44]

This means that the movement of capital is detached not only from its owners but also from the market fundamental of supply/demand on which classical capitalism is based. The market is completely autonomous and it is the subject, or rather the global 'hyper-object' which governs autonomously all that is under its control — including producers, consumers and the traders themselves, the priests of the 'golden calf'.

People who play the stock market are usually quite young and do not devote many years to it, because existence on the stock market requires the highest tension, attention, intuition and almost mystical complicity in the very process of movement of virtual flows, arbitrary and sovereign. The trader is not a person, but a part of the life of global capital, a tiny algorithm. Therefore, he either makes huge profits by playing the exchange and spends the rest of his life in rest and treatment, or loses everything and disappears, thrown into nowhere by the planetary centrifuge.

And history keeps repeating itself. The movement of capital has no purpose. It is an autoreferential form of life, eroding both objects and subjects.

In modernity, in the early stages of capitalism, there was an exponential *accumulation* of wealth. In postmodernity, however, it turns into the *release* of capital. Capital moves around the planet, followed by political, economic processes, rushing hordes of brokers with golden parachutes and crowds of top managers. They all move behind the independent process of matter disintegration and its transition from the atomic to the subatomic level and beyond, until a special and autonomous geometry of money, or *'alchemy of finance'*,[45] is formed when the very non-linear processes of chaotic capital movement become synonymous with a new order in which money — or more precisely its digital analogues, sub-money and

---

44 John Murphy, *Technical Analysis of the Financial Markets* (Upper Saddle River, NJ: Prentice Hall, 1999).

45 George Soros' term.

simultaneously trans-money — themselves create chaotic and ephemeral worlds, 'chaosmos'.

Money mutates in the postmodern, but initially it is itself a product of the disintegration of real objects into economic atoms. Accordingly, money replaces commodities first, and then bills of exchange, promises, and numbers appear. The virtualisation of the economy, which we have already talked about, is taking place. The dispersal horizon ends the history of private property as we know it — that is, the history of possession of a certain volume of the outside world, of objects brought under the complete control of the individual ('the one'). Now, objects and even their financial equivalents become atomised, intertwined with one another, scattered to the point where they cannot be contained — dynamically wriggling, coming alive, disintegrating into a multitude of ever smaller particles, oozing, penetrating one another, fusing and fading away.

This is the movement of private property to partial ownership in the form of global capital. This is already corporeal matter, accessible to the senses — and we approach that matter which is nothing. The meaning of capital primarily consists of its absolute nihilism, because capital is only a process of fragmentation. But it is precisely in postmodernity, where everything undergoes a process of dissipation, that this becomes particularly clear. In essence, capital is matter, which ontologically represents nothing — consequently, money is nothing. And the more money is regarded as 'everything', the more nothingness it becomes, the more the world, people, society are destroyed. Money is a nihilistic virus, not leading to the accumulation of wealth, but corroding property itself in its ontic dimension.

As the financial economy grows, there is a pervasive spread of its nihilistic stain.[46] Freed of meaning, purpose, objects and cash, lying on the map — that is, in a place that does not exist —, money is a quantum of 'anti-matter' that decomposes matter into invisible constituents.

---

46 Dugin, *The End of Economics*.

The Anti-State

Parallel to this, as we have seen, is the erosion of the political subject, the individual, which is disintegrating into a rhizomatically schizophrenic ensemble. Taken together, these processes produce an entirely new political philosophy, one that is fundamentally different from the paradigm of the modern. The processes that reached their limit in modernity are crossing it here. That is, the very processes of the immanentisation of values, of anthropological models of philosophy, of ontology, are crossing that line, which they have set for themselves as a limit. To overcome the limit is transgression. This is why transgression becomes the main leitmotif of the postmodern. Since modernity has fully realised its programme, it must either go back (to Platonism, to religious society), or go further into the depths of itself (to the subatomic level). Obviously, postmodernism does not even consider the first possibility, and its transgression is directed precisely downwards, to its bottom line, beyond which lies the region of pure nothingness.

This gives rise to the idea of the construction of a 'state in reverse'. The state, which in the context of the titanic phase of modernity was built from earth to heaven as a kind of 'Tower of Babel', gradually loses even its materialist verticality in the course of modernity's development — spreading out over the earth along with liberalism, internationalism, pacifism and globalism. And it is when the horizontal — networked — model becomes predominant that the political postmodern actually begins. It builds a 'state', or rather an 'anti-state', in the image of a sinkhole in the ground, a kind of 'underground state', which imitates the tower upside down.

The Latin word '*inferno*', that is 'hell', literally means 'that which is below'. Thus, the political ontology of modernity is gradually digging a giant pit. This 'anti-state' is referred to by some postmodernists as an 'Empire'..

Negri and Hardt: 'Empire' as a Global Anti-State

The concept of such a postmodern 'Empire' has been most fully developed by two left-liberal authors, Antonio Negri and Michael Hardt, both typical representatives of postmodern political philosophy.[47]

In this case, by 'Empire' the authors mean their original sociological concept, through which they want to describe the modern global capitalist network system, the prototype and historical mainstay of which they consider the United States. Such an understanding of 'Empire' differs, naturally, not only from Empire in its classical, Euro-Mediterranean, traditionalist understanding, but also from the commercial British Empire, which is an accomplished paradigm of modernity (the spiralling spread of Locke's Heartland across the planet).

According to Negri and Hardt, 'Empire' is a paradigm of the social and political organisation of the postmodern, to be realised on the foundation of capitalist liberal globalisation; in the final stage of the world revolution, power should be seized by the 'multitude', the postmodern analogue of the Marxist proletarian class (very much in the spirit of the authors' anarcho-Communist conceptions).

The authors inherit, by and large, the Marxist model of understanding history as a struggle between labour and capital, but are convinced that under the conditions of the postmodern, both labour and capital have been transformed almost beyond recognition. Capital has become so omnipotent, powerful and victorious that it takes on global dimensions, becoming a universal phenomenon. From now on, capital is not a component, it is *everything*.[48] It is 'Empire'. 'Empire', according to Negri and Hardt, is the next (final and highest) phase in the development of capitalism, characterised by the fact that in this 'Empire' capitalism becomes total, global, limitless and omnipresent.

Labour, which in the industrial stage was a function of the industrial proletariat, is today dispersed, decentralised, and spread out over endless

---

47 Michael Hardt and Antonio Negri, *Empire* (Cambridge, Mass.: Harvard University Press, 2000).

48 Jean-Marc Vivenza, 'From the formal dominance of capital to its real dominance' (*Elements*, 1997, № 7).

millions of units, subservient in the face of the omnipresent and refined control of 'Empire'.

In the postmodern epoch, it is not the working class that is the bearer of labour, but the 'multitude'.[49] A major confrontation unfolds between 'Empire' and 'multitude'.

In the postmodern, everything has changed: Capital acts in a new way, labour in a new way; the confrontation between them unfolds in a new way. Instead of 'discipline', capital uses 'control', instead of politics, 'biopolitics' (a reference to Foucault and Deleuze), instead of 'state', global networks. In 'Empire', capitalism is disguised, freed from those attributes considered essential in the industrial age. The nation-state is dissolved, the strict 'hierarchy of labour' is abolished, borders are erased, inter-state wars are abolished, etc. But still, the 'Empire' controls everything and continues to confiscate the products of its creativity from the 'multitude'. This control by the 'Empire' takes global form and applies equally to all.

Negri and Hardt insist that 'Empire' has nothing to do with 'imperialism'. Classical 'imperialism', as described by Lenin,[50] is the expansion of bourgeois nation-states into economically underdeveloped countries and zones. Such 'imperialism', while increasing the territories under its control, does not change the quality of the host country itself: the bourgeois state merely exploits the colony as something 'foreign', 'external'. Moreover, the 'imperialism' of one state inevitably collides with the 'imperialism' of another, as we see in the dramatic history of the world wars in the twentieth century.

'Empire' in the postmodern sense is something else. Its structure is such that it includes any zone falling under the control of 'Empire' as a part of it, along with other spaces. The 'Empire' is decentralised, it has no metropolis or colonies, it is knowingly and inherently global and universal. 'Empire' knows no borders, it is a worldwide phenomenon. *Globalisation is the assertion of 'Empire'*.

---

49 Michael Hardt and Antonio Negri, *Multitude: War and Democracy in the Age of Empire* (London: Penguin, 2005).

50 Vladimir Lenin, *Imperialism: The Highest Stage of Capitalism* (London: Penguin, 2010).

'Empire' has three levels of control simultaneously, corresponding to *monarchical, aristocratic and democratic* forms of government. *Monarchy* refers to the concentration of nuclear weapons, the Sword of Damocles hanging over the heads of the 'multitude', in a single centre. The *aristocracy* of 'Empire' is represented by the owners of large multinational corporations. *Democracy* has been replaced by a planetary spectacle,[51] embodied in the mass-media system.

According to Negri and Hardt, 'Empire' today, unlike classical capitalism, appropriates not so much 'surplus value' (i.e. the results of 'productive labour') as the very 'vital energy' of the 'multitude'. The authors argue that, under the new conditions of technological development, the distinction between productive labour, non-productive labour and mere reproduction has been blurred. What is exploited today is the very unstructured *life force* that spills out evenly from the human collective and which manifests itself freely in the elements of desire, love and creativity.[52]

The essence of 'Empire' is *corruption*. Corruption (destruction) as a principle is the antithesis of generation. The 'multitude' generates, 'Empire' only corrupts. 'Empire' is the eternal crisis, it decomposes life, dampens its flame, it usurps the creativity and desire of the 'multitude' for freedom, harnesses it for its own functioning through a subtle system of control.

As mental labour today plays a central role in economic development, the means of production have changed considerably. The human brain has become the main means of production, and consequently the machine has been integrated into the human body. On the other hand, new technological tools (computer technology, for instance) are becoming an essential part of the human body and will, in the near future, be integrated into it.

Hence the theory of the 'cyborg' as the basic subject of the 'Empire'. According to Negri and Hardt, the cyborg is a being in whom the subject of labour (man) and the instrument of labour are fused beyond recognition. Therefore, ownership of the means of production is not enough for modern capital: the direct disciplinary instruments of power — of the

---

51 Guy Debord, *Society of the Spectacle* (London: Rebel Press, 1992).
52 Giorgio Agamben, *Homo Sacer. Sovereign Power and Bare Life.*

classical police-economic variety — are ineffective. *'Empire' must control the entire network,* whose elements are human beings, the representatives of the 'multitude'.

The United States and Alterglobalism

The creation of 'Empire' is closely linked to the history of the United States and its political system. However, the role of the US in the creation of 'Empire' is twofold. On the one hand, 'Empire' is built by the US and is based on its matrix. This is facilitated by the fact that the foundations of US national policy are exactly the same as the model that is henceforth asserted as something global. But 'Empire' also transcends American national boundaries — and this phenomenon goes beyond 'classical imperialism', even though it stems from America. The U.S. strengthens as a project, expanding far beyond the boundaries of the nation-state. America is outgrowing America, becoming planetary. The whole world becomes a *global America.*

After a comprehensive criticism of globalism ('Empire'), Negri and Hardt offer an alternative. This alternative summarises the main points of *alterglobalism.* The authors are therefore considered the most consistent theorists of alterglobalism, and their work is seen as programmatic.

Overcoming from within

Following European postmodernists — Deleuze, Guattari, Lyotard, etc. — Negri and Hardt argue that the nature of changes depicted in the postmodern era is *irreversible and objective.* 'Empire' and its power are not accidental, not arbitrary. They are conditioned by the logic of human development. *It is not a deviation* of the progress of modernity, but its *culmination.* Western European humanity, moving along the trajectory of its philosophical, social, economic and political development, could not but come to the Enlightenment, to capitalism, to imperialism and finally to globalism, postmodernity and 'Empire'. Consequently, the 'end of history' in the global market is quite natural, arising from the very structure of history. For those who are horrified by the monstrous horizons of total planetary control and new forms of exploitation, Negri and Hardt advise to pay attention to the present and the recent past: as if capitalism was more humane and just at other stages.

'Empire' cannot be avoided, its formation cannot be slowed down, it is impossible to take refuge in the 'local'. The bourgeois nation-states are not an alternative to 'Empire', they are merely its *precursors*. Consequently, the opponents of 'Empire' must bid farewell to familiar clichés, discard obsolete conceptual tools and part with nostalgia. The mutation of modern into postmodern, as well as the qualitative modification of labour and capital, are fait accompli that cannot be ignored. 'Empire' is a reality.

The 'positive' programme of the alterglobalists rests on the recognition of 'Empire' as a basic fact, just as Marx's Communism rested on a detailed study of the ontology of Capital. 'Empire' cannot be overcome from the outside, because there is no longer an 'outside' in the global world. It *includes* the entire space of the earth — in the socio-political, economic, informational and cultural sense. Therefore, the only way to explode its power *lies within it*, in its *inner contradiction*. This contradiction is described by Negri and Hardt in Marxist terms (contradiction between labour and capital, alienation, appropriation of surplus value, etc.), but transposed to the conditions of the postmodern and the global context.

The analogue of the working class (as the object of exploitation and subject of revolution in classical Marxism) today is simply *people* — the 'multitude'. Since the difference between productive and unproductive labour has been obliterated under the conditions of technological development and the globalisation of capital, then labour, according to Negri and Hardt, should be recognised as 'life itself' and its corporeal motivations — desire, reproduction, creativity, incidental drives. The distinction between work and rest, useful and useless, business and entertainment gradually disappears: only *living people* ('bare life', according to Giorgio Agamben[53]) remain in the face of a global system of corruption. The 'multitude' itself is today's labour. And 'Empire' is capital.

---

53 Giorgio Agamben, *Homo Sacer. Sovereign Power and Bare Life.*

The Multitude Counter-Attacks: The Triumph of the Disabled, Perverts and Viruses

Negri and Hardt's methods of struggle against 'Empire' are rather extravagant: abandoning the last remaining gender taboos, creatively developing shocking images, piercings, mohawks, hacking, creation of extremist communes and absurdist circles, senseless flash mobs, transsexual operations, cultivation of migration, cosmopolitanism, demanding that 'Empire' pay not for labour but for the simple existence of every citizen of the earth, and meanwhile granting the entire 'multitude' the status of citizens of the earth. One recipe for alterglobalism, as a postmodern version of the Luddites,[54] is to invite self-mutilation of the individual (automutilation), since the invalid with an inactive and incapacitated body is less susceptible to exploitation.[55] Equally effective is mental disability, which can be acquired artificially through the use of potent drugs. The best form of revolutionary practice, according to Negri and Hardt, would be to become a computer virus capable of causing maximum damage to the world's networks.

This left-liberal agenda is largely reflected in the programme points of the diverse networks of the Open Society movement, sponsored by George Soros.

The authors of *Empire* themselves show that the position of the 'multitude' is in fact fostered by the 'Empire' — it is 'Empire' that lets the 'multitude' take the form that it does; it exploits the 'multitude' on the one hand, but also institutes, supports it, promotes its further liberation, on the other. In 'Empire', the 'multitude' thus finds many positive 'opportunities', which it is called upon to exploit for its own interests. As a parallel to this turn of thought, the authors cite Marx's assessment of capitalism, which

---

54 The Luddites were a movement among workers in England in the first quarter of the nineteenth century. They believed that the source of poverty and unemployment was the machines introduced into industrial production and they smashed and destroyed the machines in the course of their demonstrations (industrial sabotage). The leader and symbol of this movement was supposedly Ned Ludd, also called 'General Ludd' or 'King Ludd', who was the first to destroy a few machines in a fit of rage.

55 In doing so, Negri and Hardt believe, it would be better to get rid of the body altogether, to reliably avoid any form of violence from the 'Empire'.

acknowledged its progressive nature in relation to the feudal system, but at the same time singled it out as the ultimate, irreconcilable opponent of the proletariat. This is how Negri and Hardt regard 'Empire': they show its 'progressive' aspects in relation to classical industrial capitalism, but believe that it carries its own demise.

The project of alterglobalism boils down not to hindering 'Empire' but, on the contrary, *pushing it forward* in order to witness and participate in its final transformation more quickly. This transformation is possible through a new self-awareness and self-perception, through the acquisition of a new ontological, anthropological and legal status by the vital and creative chaos of the liberated world masses, the 'multitude', that is designed to escape from the rigid corrupting grip of the planetary 'Empire'.

The very concept of the 'multitude', which Negri and Hardt situate as the postmodern equivalent of the proletariat, represents the next phase in the pursuit of the atom. Multitudes are no longer individuals in the classical sense of modernity, they are dividuals. They reach a level closer to atomicity, rhizomatically separating into combinations of elements. The term 'multitude' itself appears in Machiavelli, Hobbes and Spinoza, and refers to people not yet integrated into the political structure. That is to say, it is the re-emergence of Hobbes's 'natural state'. But for Negri and Hardt, such a diffuse, chaotic state is not just a starting point (however we interpret it, pessimistically like Hobbes, neutrally like Locke or positively like Rousseau), but represents the goal, that is, something necessary, towards which political history is directed. Like Marx's symmetry between the primitive communism at the beginning of history and the scientific Communism at the end of history, Negri and Hardt's 'multitude' is thought above all as the culmination of the political process, restoring the 'natural state'.

The uprising of the 'multitude' must be based on the cultivation of all kinds of transgression. The ideal for Negri and Hardt is no longer a human being, but a *cyborg*, a mutant, a voluntary invalid, a cripple, a half-human half-machine, unable to become an object of exploitation — neither in production, nor in civic duty, nor in classical marriage. Freedom from 'Empire', as the last embodiment of rationality, is realised through a slide into irrationality, into mass schizophrenia (Deleuze), into drugs, into decay, into the search for new, bizarre forms of being on the other side of the cultural and social codes dictated by authority.

Just like Marx, who wished for the victory of capitalism to bring about its own end and thereby build socialism, the alterglobalists wish for the victory of globalisation, for the victory of capital to explode itself from within, through the total migration of the multitude into the realms of irrationality and schizophrenic freedom.

The multitude is not what is, but what should be. According to Spinoza, 'the multitude is what the sovereign most fears.'[56] Hence, it is the uncontrollable mass of transgressive perverts, cyborgs fused with machines, physical and mental invalids, transgender people, and queer-types of the most unexpected versions, integrated into the world network, that henceforth becomes a revolutionary class, representing all of humanity in political history, destined to slip away from the repressive strategies of 'Empire', diving into the depths of matter for this purpose. This is how 'Empire', which is already an 'inverted state', reaches its logical goal — its lower limit rests in the centre of hell.

Underground Civil Society

Negri and Hardt describe the world after the triumph of the 'multitude' rather vaguely. It will be a networked rhizomatic society, horizontally organised and oriented further downwards, into the depths of matter. The boundaries between individuals will be erased, and people, machines, animals and plants will form one unified, pulsating mass, exchanging continuously multidimensional impulses of desire. This is reminiscent of the primordial state of the cosmos described by Empedocles, when the individual organs were not yet joined together in a proper order, hands, noses and ears growing out of the ground to form extravagant ensembles. Approximately the same flowering of disordered free potentialities and fragments is taken as the goal by postmodernists. The true multitude

---

56 Baruch Spinoza, *A Theologico-Political Treatise, and a Political Treatise* (NY: Cosimo, 2005).

cannot have a strictly human form, since it is already a certain discrimination against other species and forms of life, whether natural or artificial. In a global networked democracy, everyone can vote—human and non-human beings alike—including machines, objects, plants, animals, etc.

In such a magma, everything would be free, especially as money itself would gradually dissolve into a digital ocean. Postmodernists especially emphasise free and unrestricted access to drugs and pornographic resources, which corresponds to the liberation of the 'workers of the desire factory'.

For us today this may sound a little wild, but it is important to understand that the postmodern and its political philosophy, including the concept of 'revolution of the multitude', is not a joke, not a parody, not an extravagant delusion. It is a logical continuation of the line of modernity itself—its main powerhouses—progress, modernisation, social development, democratisation, emancipation, the development of 'civil society', etc. Thus the modern struggle for the freedom of all kinds of ethnic, sexual, religious and political minorities, together with gender politics and ecology, is a prelude to just such a rhizomatic phase.

A Postmodern Reading

It is the political programme of the 'desire machine', of the liberation of the masses from the control of the exploitative system, the plan and strategy of globalisation and especially of alterglobalisation which is to follow the victory of world capitalism. From Negri and Hardt's point of view, present globalisation is still within the political philosophy of modernity, and now it is necessary to move from the constructed 'Empire' of modernity to the final phase, the 'realm of pure quantity'.[57]

This is the political programme of the postmodern. Most of the non-governmental humanitarian organisations operating in the world today are in one way or another connected to this project of the 'multitude'. By dissolving borders and helping to break down traditions, they are preparing global territory for the 'multitude'.

---

57 René Guénon, *The Reign of Quantity and the Signs of the Times (Collected Works)* (Sophia Perennis et Universalis, 2004).

Contemporary art plays an important role in this.

Accordingly, sociopolitical philosophical models, postpositivist theories of international relations, theories of gender, feminism, the whole 'left' movement, and to a large extent the 'right' movement (where the right advocates big capital) — all contemporary politics is gradually moving into the space of the postmodern.

Postmodernists say that everything is a text, and any text can be read in different ways. Everything also depends on what decoding model we adopt. From the postmodernist point of view, reality is a combination of signs that have no meaning. Depending on how we compose the signs, we create a text — some signs we see, others we do not, some we ignore, others we acknowledge. Depending on which signs we see and which we do not, we get different words. We have all the letters in front of us, and we can read the same utterance in completely different ways, depending on which 'grid' we use and how.

The postmodernist *grille de lecture* gradually embraces all the political processes in which we live. Everything becomes political — in the spirit of Deleuze — including art, economics, medicine, culture. Everywhere, residual — though individualistic, modernist — structures of the vertical collide with one another — the classical New Age ideas of state, society, gender, family, etc. and their new postmodernist reading based on an ironic dissection — deconstruction — of these notions, presented by postmodernists as conventions, myths, social norms and cumbersome identities, unaware yet of their destiny — to free themselves from themselves, to realise transgression and dissolve in the pulsating element of electronic nihilism.

Postmodern political philosophy fundamentally combines the incongruous; the postmodern reading is based on a paradox — the absence of symmetry, position, verticality. Usually the top is the main thing, and the bottom is not, but in the philosophy of the postmodern, the opposite is true — the bottom and the top are roughly equal. Everyone gets their own right to speak out. In music, this is vividly represented in the direction of dodecaphony, introduced by Schoenberg (1874–1951), and the entire avantgarde painting of the twentieth century followed the same path.

CHAPTER 16

THE DARK ENLIGHTENMENT

Object-Oriented Ontology: Nihilism and Its Objects

A NEW STAGE in the establishment of the postmodern paradigm is seen in the modern trend of object-oriented ontology (OOO), otherwise known as speculative realism. The most prominent representatives of OOO are Ray Brassier,[1] Graham Harman,[2] Quentin Meillassoux,[3] Levi Bryant,[4] Nick Land[5] and Reza Negarestani.[6] Here the main threads of the postmodern are taken to their logical limits. Although Gilles Deleuze, among a number of other postmodernist philosophers, had already addressed nothingness directly, following Lacan's ontology, and even made the orientation to nothingness, the will to nothingness, a certain value, his systems were still too bound to the subject — even if the aim was to disperse it into the broadest possible range of dividual elements, quanta, new aspirants to the status of 'atom'. Object-oriented ontology (OOO) seeks to be extremely consistent, and to abolish the subject altogether, taking it as a particular case among an ocean of actual and

---

1 Ray Brassier, *Nihil Unbound: Enlightenment and Extinction* (London: Palgrave Macmillan, 2007).
2 Graham Harman, *Immaterialism: Objects and Social Theory* (London: Polity, 2016).
3 Quentin Meillassoux, *After Finitude: An Essay on the Necessity of Contingency* (London: Continuum International Publishing Group, 2009).
4 Bryant, *The Democracy of Objects*.
5 Nick Land, *Fanged Noumena: Collected Writings 1987–2007* (New York; Windsor Quarry [Falmouth]: Sequence; Urbanomic, 2011).
6 Reza Negarestani, *Cyclonopedia: Complicity with Anonymous Materials* (Melbourne: Re.Press, 2008).

possible objects. In this case, the world of contingency, i.e. Democritus' isonomy, is elevated to an absolute principle. Meillassoux calls this 'contingency' and proposes a consistent effort to construct ontologies where the subject would not be at the centre, as the earth in Ptolemy's cosmology, but at the ontological periphery among other objects of an infinite open (it is appropriate here to recall Popper's 'open society') cosmos based on the strict Copernican principle of isotropy — that is, the indifference of all orientations (again Democritus' isonomy). Meillassoux calls for the abolition of all correlationism, that is, the rejection of those epistemological structures which are based on correlations and hence somehow imply a subject. But in this case, the place of the subject is not simply delegated to someone else, but abolished definitively, leaving in its place a pure nothingness. This nothingness is what Rey Brassier argues for as the sole ontological reference point, urging us to accept this as the central point of philosophy. If the postmodern balances on the borderline of nothingness, then OOO calls to throw oneself into nothingness, making it not just the truth (like Lacan's order of the real), but the goal, the value and the desired outcome. Leibniz's question as to 'why something, rather than nothing, exists', which was at the heart of Martin Heidegger's philosophy, is reduced in Brasier to the abolition of the instance that could formulate it.

According to Meillassoux, man and his consciousness are random reflections of pulsating chaos, naively imagining the existence of order, unity, truth, etc. Thought is a random crease of nonsense, an illusion and an aberration. And the subject is nothing more than one of the objects that is as ontologically peripheral, contingent and nihilistic as all the others, but simply remains delusional about itself and the world. The subject is just an object that has lost its mind.

Graham Harman: Understanding the Object by Killing the Subject

Naturally in such a situation, the question arises: what then is the object? This is where the actual deployment of 'speculative realism' begins. Representatives of this movement claim that all we know about the object are the opinions of the subject. Moreover, phenomenologists show that we are not dealing with the object itself, but with '*noema*', i.e. an object located within our consciousness, not outside it. In other words, the subject does not know the object and only imagines, invents, constitutes it. The object is not data provided by the senses, because they — like any interface — are based on a protocol and an algorithm that allows some parameters through and cuts others off (this is how all systems work). Therefore, the representation of an object to the subject is not given through direct experience (as the first empiricists and materialists of the modern age naively believed), nor through conceptualisation. Hence the name 'speculative realism': for human consciousness the object, the thing, *res*, can only be the fruit of speculative knowledge. This is quite in harmony with Democritus, who affirmed the existence of atoms and emptiness with reliance on speculative reasoning. The 'thing', the 'object' is therefore only a concept. But to reach it, it is not necessary to refine the means possessed by the subject, but on the contrary, to cleanse the very process of thinking from any trace of the subject. In other words, the object can be much better understood by the object itself, that is, by the machine. In this case, speculative processes would be devoid of those ontological perturbations that are inherent to the subject. Moreover, according to the speculative realists, the subject itself is the 'ontological perturbation'.

Hence a new programme of object-oriented ontology is born, consisting henceforth *in the abolition of man*, in the complete destruction of the subject and in the construction of a philosophy that could exist outside the human context. Thus, OOO takes on a character that is the opposite of humanism. In this we see the logical consequence of the establishment of Plato's third genus, the philosophy of the Mother. This philosophy begins with the abolition of the supra-human — the sacred, the vertical — with the rejection of the state of the Father and the state of the Son. This is the first stage of materialism; God is killed, but only in order to liberate man, to put him at the centre. This era takes place under the banner of humanism. It culminates in the political philosophy of liberalism, and the turning point in history is the victory of liberals over two alternative political theories (Fascism in 1945 and Communism in 1991).

Around this time, postmodernism is gaining particular strength, proposing to move further into matter and to decompose the human being (the individual of liberalism) into its components. Although the individual is decomposing here, still, with certain tensions, some elements of humanism are still preserved. Man is now freed from the state he carries within himself and above all from the dictatorship of reason.

But with the advent of speculative realism, this process of movement into matter reaches the threshold where the emancipatory strategy of the philosophy of the Mother reaches its climax. It is no longer just man, or even the sub-subjective elements of man, the 'workers of the desire factory', but the world of objects detached from man that must now be liberated. Here postmodernism takes on the same opposition to man as modernism previously took towards God, to the sacred, to vertical ontologies. Humans have killed God. Now it is the turn of posthuman beings — machines and more broadly, objects — to kill man himself. Speculative realism is precisely this kind of materialistic anti-humanism, discovered for the first time. That is why it is sometimes conflated with posthumanism and transhumanism. Although here we are speaking about a transformation of the human species into something else, object-oriented ontologists aim to justify altogether non-human thinking. Meillassoux and Brassier create their philosophy for robotic, posthuman species. Of course, this is only a speculative construct, but it is intended by its creators and developers to serve as the basis of non-human ontologies.

The Abolition of *Dasein* and the Immortality of the Machine

To abolish the subject, to annihilate the human being, in practice, in a philosophical context, is no easy task. And here speculative realists, above all Graham Harman, understand perfectly well that this cannot be achieved directly: the subject itself and/or the notion of man are based on very complicated metaphysical and anthropological platforms, which are not only not easy, but impossible to demolish if we rely on the classical teachings of the New Age. That is why Harman turns to phenomenology and above all to Heidegger,[7] in whose teaching a purified and finely represented figure of *Dasein* already stands in the place of man and the New Age subject. Heidegger, in constructing an analysis of the *Dasein*, also translates into existentials any relationship of the *Dasein* to what is around it, and in particular what is commonly called 'thing', 'object' or collectively 'the world'.[8] Thus, in particular, Heidegger defines 'objecthood' through *Zuhandensein* — being 'ready-to-hand'. Harman proposes to build a phenomenology not from the *Dasein* outside to the 'objects', but from the objects themselves. But if we do this, then what was 'ready-to-hand', an 'instrument', will not necessarily relate symmetrically to its owner. The thing, having ceased to be handy, does not behave as the *Dasein* would have seen it. It will not turn towards it or towards another thing — at least not with the same 'fatality' with which *Dasein* treats it. Hence, this is where symmetry ends, and the *Dasein* disappears from view altogether. What remains are things and their phenomenology, which, however, are defined by them and not by someone for them. Thus, the abolition of the subject occurs through the abolition of its fundamental existential basis, the *Dasein*.

It is important to note that Heidegger himself recognises in *Dasein* two modes — the authentic, when *Dasein* is itself (*Selbst*) and the non-authentic, when *Dasein* acts as *das Man*, an abstract instance that reflects something supposedly universal, but which does not coincide either with the truth or with the opinions of individuals (*Dasein*'s carriers). Thus *das Man* represents the ultimate alienation of *Dasein* from itself. The figure of *das Man* is very close to artificial intelligence, in that artificial intelligence differs from human intelligence not by formal features, but precisely by the absence of *Dasein*. Consequently, from the philosophical point of view, the transition from the human (subject) to the machine (object) is made not on the border of reasonable/unreasonable, but through *Dasein*/non-*Dasein*. The thinking object is thought deprived of the *Dasein* — not

---

7   Graham Harman, *Heidegger Explained: From Phenomenon to Thing* (Chicago: Open Court, 2007); Idem., *Tool-Being. Heidegger and the Metaphysics of Objects* (Chicago: Open Court, 2002).

8   Dugin, *Martin Heidegger. The Last God.*

only as reality (the *Dasein* practically does not make itself known in *das Man*, although it remains its basis), but also as possibility. It is by extinguishing *Dasein*, Harman argues, that we can move on to the phenomenology of objects.[9]

At the same time, to abolish *Dasein* is, in a sense, easier than to declare war on man. The *Dasein* is an attitude to death, and this attitude is its main existential element. But for modern and postmodern man, death — in the spirit of Epicurus — is nothing, much less a value. After all, the modern and the postmodern deny the soul and post-mortem existence, retribution, judgement, heaven and hell. Therefore, by cutting out the attitude to death in the (post)modern, we do not deprive it of anything principled. Moreover, gaining immortality — even if for the price of transformation into a machine, into an object — is an attractive prospect for many. The object is immortal, just as death and nothingness in the immanent materialist ontology are immortal.

Singularity and the Mystery of the Bastard Logos

This is how speculative realism and contingentism are directly linked to technological trends that aim to create powerful artificial intelligence, cyborgs, genetic engineering procedures and the acquisition of physical immortality. The point at which there will be a complete transition from human society to post-human society is called the 'Singularity' by the futurologists of this trend.[10] Speculative realists approach this moment actually from the side of philosophy, preparing a platform for Singularity. The objects asserted by them are true atoms, for they are not the product of the separation of more and more pairs, which is the work of the Plotinian mind, but of the inner nature of nothingness itself, of matter as such, seen not from the side of the mind, but from the side of matter itself. Here again we may recall the bastard *logos* (λόγος νόθος) of the *Timaeus*. The notion of bastardism (νόθος) suggests a kind of hybridity in which

---

9   The phenomenology of objects is also developed by Ian Bogost. See Ian Bogost, *Alien Phenomenology, or, What It's Like to be a Thing* (Minneapolis: Minnesota University Press, 2012).

10 Ray Kurzweil, *The Singularity Is Near* (NY: Viking Books, 2005).

something of the Father (mind) and something of the Mother (matter) converge. Attempts to reach the very core of this bastard *logos,* by which, according to Plato, '*chora*', matter, is comprehended — by moving from the side of the real — male vertical — *logos*, have some limit. It is precisely this that makes itself felt as the atom slips away through more and more fragmentation of particles. Speculative realists make a *philosophical leap* here, and propose to constitute this 'bastard *logos*' not on the residual principle (less and less mind), but on the side of matter itself, on the side of the Mother. Singularity then becomes the triumphant moment (for the philosophy of the Mother) of the unfolding of a special form of subjectless consciousness. This is what object-oriented ontology represents.

Bruno Latour: Hybrids and the Constitution

The French sociologist Bruno Latour, exploring the epistemology of modernity in the spirit of Foucault's postmodern strategies, concluded that modernity is based on a kind of philosophical constitution according to which the world of spirit (subject) and the world of material things (objects) constitute two ontologically autonomous zones separated by a strictly set boundary.[11] Modernity bases its critique of the premodern precisely on the fact that in traditional society such a rule was not respected, leading to the creation of hybrids, that is, objects that were partly subjective and partly objective. It was the ridiculing of hybrids that was the basis of the Enlightenment's rationalist strategy.

But Latour observes that the modern itself, having proclaimed this rule as its constitution and having placed it at the centre, has constantly and systematically violated it. In doing so, the modern did not simply refuse to produce hybrids, but instead used official prohibition as a particular inspiration for conceptual smuggling — just as Prohibition, introduced in the US, only served to enrich bootleggers and illegal liquor dealers. This led him to the paradoxical conclusion that 'there was no New Age',[12] because the solemnly proclaimed constitution was never properly

---

[11] Bruno Latour, *We Have Never Been Modern* (Cambridge, Mass.: Harvard University Press, 1993).

[12] Latour, *We Have Never Been Modern.*

observed. Latour does not simply criticise this, but proposes that it should be accepted as fact and acknowledged that man will necessarily create hybrid concepts in which the subjective and the object will be mixed.

That said, Latour suggests that we should not shy away from this, but take it one step further and recognise some political rights for objects. Since they constantly invade the human world and its concepts, is it not time to extend some constitutional guarantees and social rights to extra-human areas, giving them a kind of citizenship?

Bruno Latour suggests the following: we must extend the political emancipation and the profound democratisation that has already invaded the field of gender to non-human beings, objects and even phenomena. Why do the subjects make the decision for the objects? Let objects decide too. So Latour proposes a Parliament of Things,[13] to give hedgehogs, glass, winds, rust, dolphins, ice and everything else the right to vote. After all, they too are part of the overall rhizomatic system.

At the next technological level, a 3D-printed human being will not be much different from other objects, and they should all be given equal rights. Voting by objects will be more unpredictable than voting by ordinary people. But in general, the degree of freedom of the printer and the modern average person, who is under the hypnosis of media, society, politics, economics, and gadgets, is not fundamentally very different. A command may not reach the printer; sometimes it fails — a user sends a file for printing, but it does not print because one of the wires was not connected or something went wrong in the programme ... So the printer is to some extent at will — it may or may not execute the command. A modern person is also told whom to vote for and sometimes he goes and suddenly votes for somebody else or throws a metro ticket, a note from a psychiatrist or a devalued banknote into the ballot box. Some wire has also come loose here... Strictly speaking, you cannot trust the choices made by human voters; some voters tick the box with understanding, others do not. It is a stochastic process filled with perturbations, vortices, deviations

---

13 Bruno Latour, *Politics of Nature: How to Bring the Sciences into Democracy* (Cambridge, Mass.: Harvard University Press, 2004).

from the basic trajectory, glitches... It is a spontaneous phenomenon or a technological failure. It is impossible to recognise these votes as credible.

Accordingly, the printer may vote with the same success. And the hedgehog, for its part, is not as limited as an outside observer might think. It may well choose the freedom of the forest, approve of the abundance of mushrooms, cones and berries — beautiful things! So in postmodernity we cannot discount the possibility that people will consider their options and decide — why are we choosing some unpleasant corrupt individuals, let us choose the hedgehog!

Of course, the proposal to extend the nomenclature of the subjects of voting and the proliferation of electoral status to objects still looks like a metaphor, but the plan to grant non-human phenomena and creatures a certain status — as is already the case in nature reserves and national parks — is quite realistic and reflects the main vector of the postmodern.

Latour's suggestions may seem schematic. But once upon a time democracy, bourgeois society, socialism and many other things that seem perfectly natural to us emerged from schemes. Human history is an open process of creation, it is not politics that dictates itself to us as something fatal; we make politics. We change consciousness, perceptions, images, and ultimately the construction of hierarchies changes. We change the world, and the world changes us. And although the postmodern project seems extravagant to us today, we should not take it too lightly. Man is changing, his values and senses are changing. In the paradigm of Tradition, man was always something more than human (an immortal soul). Then, in modernity, he became only a man. In postmodernity, he becomes a rhizome. And the epistemes and constitutions change accordingly.

Democracy of Objects and Sovereignty of Matter

These theories of Latour, who showed extremely convincingly how arbitrary and voluntaristic the scientific discoveries of the New Age were — often mere frauds, the results of political and even economic intrigue —, have been picked up and developed by object-oriented ontologists, and in particular by Levi Bryant and Jane Bennett.[14] In his book *The Democracy of Objects*,[15] Levi Bryant gives an outline of a political system that would include extra-human processes, random perturbations, an extended notion of citizenship delegated to certain animal species or even natural phenomena, etc. Jane Bennett, for her part, explores the 'fate' of things, including landfills or waste products, which she observes have an autonomous agency, a kind of will and even reason, as their effect on the environment affects people, who are quick to equate them with nothing, but are themselves victims of their irreversibly generated presence. Thus, according to Jane Bennett, the pulsation of matter creates a particular dimension of existence that affects not only bodies, but also non-bodily phenomena — such as thought — by weaving itself into the structures of things and engaging them in its own vitalistic strategies. In the spirit of environmental politics, Bennett develops the concept that matter itself should be recognised as a political subject, since the totality of its movements constitutes a spontaneous-willed agency that requires not just recognition, but also the granting of special rights and powers. Thus the concept of matter, of nothingness, of pure objectivity, is transformed into a new 'subject', that is, the centre of a meaningful, conscious and powerful will. If we add feminism to this, we get a complete philosophy of the Great Mother, which was, in fact, already the entire political philosophy of the modern age, though only implicitly.

However, as in the case of Latour, Bryant and Bennett's constructions are not yet a complete political project, but only an outline calling for the integration of ecology, feminism, environmental protection and endangered species into the structures of a 'new democracy' based on the principle of a more equal distribution of 'rights' between objects, among which people are only particular instances in fluid ontic vortices.

Latour and Bryant's Parliament of Things, and Bennett's agentic quivering matter, are the correlate of that 'organ parliament' of which postmodernists speak. Here again, as in the case of microglobalisation, we see

---

14 Jane Bennett, *Vibrant Matter: A Political Ecology of Things* (Durham, NC: Duke University Press, 2010).

15 Bryant, *The Democracy of Objects*.

the typical postmodern intertwining of the macro- and micro-levels at the expense of the dismantling, the deconstruction of the meso-level, where the human subject was located in the age of modernity. The individual splits into a multitude of sub-individual particles, rebelling against its own Leviathanic mind in favour of a 'civil society' of individual desires. We seem to be sinking inside the person. But in fact, we are moving to the farthest periphery of the subject, away from its centre. Hence, the dissipation of the individual brings it closer to the macrostructures that are also subject to dissipation. The subject's pulses mingle with the dust of the object, merging into swirling pulses. Thus ecology, waste, landfills, climate change, endangered and decaying species are woven into the political discussions of subindividual-level bodies, giving the rhizome an increasingly material — object-like — quality. Thus Quentin Meillassoux suggests that even Deleuze retains a certain correlationism (between life and nothingness), whereas in object-oriented ontology we should perceive nothingness from the perspective of life, and life from the perspective of nothingness. The subject is a particular case of the object, hence the legal and civic status of the trembling materiality or artificial intelligence must not merely be equated with humans, but must have superiority. The democracy of objects must lead to the first historical constitution, in which *matter itself will be declared the true bearer of sovereign power*, and individual civil rights will be apportioned to all elements of materiality — including human beings, who in turn will be combinations of organs and communes of desire.

This is an important aspect of the political dimension of speculative realism: not only identities, such as religion, profession, nationality, gender, but also the species itself and even the choice of status of living and non-living beings become optional from now on. If a discarded tin can, an iron, a robot or a grave worm is given the right of citizenship, no one has the right to impose these identities as immutable and fatal. Anyone, or even an individual part of anyone, can theoretically sign up as bush, woman, negro, giraffe or sawdust, and take their allotted place in the Parliament of Things.

It is important to stress, however, that the transfer of political sovereignty to the trembling matter itself is the logical conclusion not only of the postmodern, but also of that whole process of emancipation and immanentisation which constituted the main semantic axis of the modern and the Enlightenment.

The Political Philosophy of Mould

The study of the behaviour of various organisms and even inorganic entities in the vein of object-oriented ontology has become widespread and resulted in a shift in ideas about what is considered intelligent and what is not. Thus a number of anthropologists have put forward the idea that in archaic societies (e.g. Native American tribes in South America), animals, ghosts, plants and even inanimate objects were regarded as bearers of a certain subjectivity. While classical progressive anthropology looked down upon such theories as remnants of prehistoric thinking, thanks to the school of the American anthropologist Franz Boas[16] (1858–1942) and especially to the works of Claude Lévi-Strauss[17] (1908–2009), such conceptions have been given more attention, but even then they were interpreted as elements of semiotic systems performing symbolic functions in the system of symbols and interpretations of exchange and kinship. New generations of anthropologists, — Phillippe Descola, Eduardo Viveiros de Castro, Eduardo Kohn, etc. — largely under the influence of the postmodern, put their total trust in this view and accepted the possibility of a non-human subjectivity. This was quite in line with the projects of Latour or Bryant. Forests, animals, spirits, and natural phenomena were already endowed with certain civil rights in some archaic societies, and if the modern regarded this as the ultimate form of feeble-minded naïveté, the postmodern suggested, on the contrary, that it was the next step of democracy.

It was not that the attitude towards extra-human life forms and objects changed radically. It was primarily a matter of rhetoric, just as in a fairy

---

16 Franz Boas, *The Mind of Primitive Man* (NY: The Macmillan Company, 1938).
17 Claude Lévi-Strauss, *The Elementary Structures of Kinship* (London: Eyre & Spottiswoode, 1969).

tale or myth, the narrative itself is built on a tacit recognition of the subjectivity of magical beasts or objects. By transferring this manner of description to the realm of scientific experimentation, the whole picture was visibly changed.

One striking phenomenon in this field was the observation of the behaviour of mould — and in particular the species *Physarum polycephalum*. Initially, Japanese scientists traced that, under certain conditions, the mould behaves as if it has a memory. The first time it moved towards the edible substance in the maze, it passed through it just like a human, making mistakes, reaching dead ends and returning to the starting point. But the second time, the mould strains were already moving straight towards the goal, as if they had memorised the route. Later, under conditions reproducing a mock-up of the Tokyo railway system, with food sources in place of major stations, the *Physarum polycephalum* mould built a near-exact copy of the real railway network, taking into account natural obstacles (whose simulation was included in the mock-up) and finding the most efficient routes to channel nutrients. Thus the thinking of the mould as a whole proved to be quite comparable to that of the research institute staff. Later, a separate laboratory — The Slime Mould Collective — was set up to study mould thinking and the social aspects of its behaviour.[18]

Thus, the theory of the rhizome as the subject of society, the democracy of things and the sovereignty of matter began to take on very concrete features. The mould, capable of constructing quite an adequate model of railroad communication or developing and applying a strategy of spreading to hard-to-reach places by contaminating the brains of certain insects — who turned out to be mould carriers against their will, for which they paid with 'madness' (non-standard behaviour) —, could well take part in elections, and in certain situations could nominate its candidate for some political body. The only question is how to build a system of interaction with it. But this requires not so much technological conditions as a shift in political philosophy. If we extend the principle of subjectivity and 'citizenship' to a broader range of entities, the question of the quality of political representation becomes a matter of discussion, since at times

---

18   http://slimoco.ning.com

even in human society this representation is called into question. And we cannot rule out the possibility that a mould, a robot, or some other extravagant object could improve the degree of such representation, being more independent of the usual strategies authorities use to influence the will of the masses.

Nick Land: The Dark Enlightenment

The clearest application of the ideas of speculative realism to the field of the Political can be seen in the work of one of the most brilliant philosophers of this school, the Briton Nick Land. Land continues the logic of Deleuze and Guattari, leaning on their methodology, most of all on the theory of stratification and territorialisation,[19] but unlike them he does not share the belief that capitalism can be overcome through a global revolution which would free the 'workers of the factory of desire' found in the material roots of the unconscious. Yes, Nick Land agrees with Marx and Deleuze, capitalism leads to self-destruction, to the destruction of life, to enslavement and alienation, and sooner or later the capitalist system will collapse. But for Land, the destructiveness of global capital is itself something positive. For Nick Land, who is rooted in schizoanalysis, although 'capital is still a "social straitjacket" of schizo-production, at least it is its "most dissolved form".[20] What Land means here is that the course of the development of capitalism is the maximum possible liberation for human subjectivity. Capitalism is ready to meet any micro-wish that arises in the unconscious, and to place it immediately in the element of the market. Yes, it is an alienation and an abasement of desire, but Land argues that desire is not an alternative to death, but death itself. Desire is only seemingly opposite to death and belongs to some other subject, different from nothingness. The true subject of desire is precisely death, which stands at the centre of capital as the fundamental process of humanity's self-destruction. This is why Land introduces the concept of accelerationism, which consists of supporting and justifying capitalism precisely for its destructive, humanity-destroying dimension. Capitalism aims at the

---

19 Deleuze and Guattari, *Anti-Oedipus: Capitalism and Schizophrenia*.
20 Nick Land, *Fanged Noumena: Collected Writings 1987–2007*, p. 46.

liquidation of humanity. The technological development that accompanies it leads to the replacement of man with artificial intelligence, and that, according to Land, is remarkable. Unlike Negri and Hardt, he does not suggest that any other formation could follow capitalism. He proposes that capitalism should not be thought of as a duality: capitalism simultaneously enslaves man, alienates him, represses his desires, but also liberates him, if only we can understand that this liberation is of man from himself. Man, according to Land, is the *logos*, the hierarchy, the pure repression of his material origins. And such is life itself. Only in lifeless original matter, as the element of total death, is truth and freedom contained. The transition from capitalism to Communism in the age of virtual reality and cyberspace therefore consists in a change of rhetoric. If one frees the machine of desire from inertial humanism, then the aim of capitalism (which has no aim) and the aim of Communism (whose aim is to free oneself from capitalism, as Democritus detaches the atom from emptiness) will coincide. Both lead to the abolition of inequality, of differentiation, but capitalism gradually erodes it, while Communism proposes to overthrow it brutally in a moment of revolution. Land's accelerationism considers the history of capital, its time extended by the proletarian revolution, and conversely, the proletarian revolution as the culmination of capitalism, the discovery of its self-destruction.

Total equality can only be achieved through the overcoming of man and, moreover, of life. And that is exactly what capitalism leads to.

Nick Land devoted an early work to the phenomenon of the 'Dark Enlightenment'.[21] In it, he positively assesses a number of marginal philosophical currents developed by some scholars (mainly from Silicon Valley in the USA) who combined ultra-liberalism, libertarianism, apologia for capitalism (in the spirit of Ayn Rand) with technological progress, migration to cyberspace, virtual reality, etc. At the same time, supporters of the Dark Enlightenment criticised egalitarianism and democracy, believing that they impede technological progress and only limit the true freedom of the individual (or the dividual). However, Land generally interprets the Dark Enlightenment more broadly in the spirit of his doctrine of

---

21 http://www.thedarkenlightenment.com/the-dark-enlightenment-by-nick-land/

accelerationism. For him, the Enlightenment itself is already a 'Dark Enlightenment', only draped in rhetorically soothing humanism. He believes that modernity, capitalism and especially liberalism are above all a movement into the depths of matter, loosely disguised by empty slogans and colourful metaphors. True Enlightenment can only be dark; it does not bring about the emancipation of man, but the emancipation from man. Enlightenment is a planned, metaphysically justified genocide designed to close the page not only of human history, but also of the history of life as a cycle of distance from the only truth: the truth of non-being, death, nothingness.

In a sense, Land's own philosophy can be called 'Dark Liberalism' and 'Dark Marxism' simultaneously, since it is the discovery of the truth (the very truth that is in the abyss, as Democritus said) of the 'Dark Enlightenment' or 'Dark Modernity', which unites all political theories in itself. This is probably why, in addition to postmodern liberalism and postmodern Marxism, Land also includes in his sphere of interest a 'neoreaction' corresponding in a narrower sense to the 'Dark Enlightenment' and combining the glorification of posthumanism and technological development with a critique of leftist discourse.

Thus it is that object-oriented ontology, which solves the problem of contingency through the abolition of the subject (Harman's *Dasein*), finally proclaims in Nick Land the true vector of modernity: the destruction of man and life in order to give freedom to a world of liberated objects, taken in complete independence from the structures that hierarchise them.

Lucifer's Political Physics

According to Nick Land, the goal of capitalism is the destruction of humanity (as a differentiated logos) and the creation of a world benefitting post-human inorganic structures — machines, computer systems and artificial intelligence. At the same time, such a future will not only be, but already exists, and what we consider present by inertia is only the result of the implantation of a false memory (by the global system of the hierarchical Leviathan — capitalism and tradition). Life is a hallucination of a corpse which, moreover, has never even lived. The future is already there, and capitalism is striving to meet it, accelerating more and more, and rapidly handing over the leading role to machines (i.e. inorganic forms). This process, according to Land, entered a decisive phase during the Protestant Reformation and the great geographical discoveries. In the twenty-first century it should reach a critical point, which technocrats and futurologists call the Singularity. But in a sense, the Singularity as a 'dark eternity' of matter, totally devoid of spirit and hierarchising (dividing) consciousness, has always been and is now. Man lives with the phantom pain of a history that is not his own, embedded in him by epistemes. Capitalism is more and more insistently diluting these epistemes, thus bringing closer the moment of discovery of the truth — i.e. the Singularity. This truth is not that humanity and life will disappear, but that they never existed, that consciousness is an ephemeral whiff that has risen above the ocean of matter and built a fleeting vision of reason. Life and consciousness are illusions. Therefore death is not an alternative to life, but life itself, its subject.

Capitalism will come close to the Singularity, but will disappear — collapse — at this boundary. Not because it will be replaced by a less nihilistic form of politics, but because it will not be able to structurally shift to the side of the 'radical other' — that is, the stratum that is 'below' matter itself, within nothingness.

Land's following observation is important:

> Capitalism has no external boundaries; it has absorbed life and biological reason in order to create a new life and a new plan of rationality, far beyond human imagination.[22]

That is, 'post-capitalism' has no autonomous meaning; it is capitalism, only understood in its truth. The mission of capitalism is to prepare the frontier itself. At this frontier, organic consciousness and life will be extinguished. In their place will come not something new, but an eternal movement of matter. This is not post-history, but history itself, the main and only subject of which is and always has been matter.

---

22 Land, *Fanged Noumena: Collected Writings 1987–2007*, p. 626.

If matter is the subject of history, that short-lived chimera of life and human (biological) intelligence must reflect some fundamental scenario. This scenario for Land is the *cooling* of the earth, once a red-hot mass. This solidification is the main theme of not just earthly, but universal history as it is repeated in every corner of the open cosmos where atoms and their vortices are present. It is this trauma of solidification, which led to the formation of the Earth's crust and the core remaining in its original — stellar — state, that is the material truth of the abyss, lying below the threshold of consciousness and life, but at the same time defining the materialistic content of both.

According to Land, the cooling of the earth's surface and the contraction of the glowing core within generates a response — a desire to return to a fiery plasma form of existence. This is the will to power or the will to life on the level of matter. In organic life it defines the striving of eukaryotic cell nuclei for liberation, while in schizoanalysis the 'nucleus' is the 'desire factory' underlying the human psyche and predetermining the stratification and territorialisation of consciousness. Everything is a kernel, striving to break through the frozen shell. And it is the inability to do so immediately that causes the pain and suffering that drives not just man in his relationship with alienating hierarchical structures (Leviathan), but all matter, whose core seeks to escape to the outside. This 'core', which Land himself calls by the code term *Cthelll* (unambiguously indicating 'hell'), is Democritus' atom, finally discovered on the other side of conceptual ensembles — various particles in physics, the individual in society, etc., which have claimed — unreasonably — to this status. The atom is the truth hidden in the abyss, the centre of hell, the last secret of materiality.

The strata that Deleuze and Guattari describe in *A Thousand Plateaus*,[23] seeking to reconstruct the initial moments of the emergence of formal representations of consciousness and the corporeal world (they call it 'assemblage' — the assembly of disparate elements through three operations: coding, stratification and territorialisation), for Nick Land act as layers of earth. And the main task, then, becomes the liberation of the still-hot core from its imprisonment — which will be the triumph of liberalism, as well

---

23 Deleuze and Félix Guattari, *Anti-Oedipus: Capitalism and Schizophrenia*.

as of the proletarian revolution, since the will of matter is at the base of history. The explosion of the globe and the destruction of life and humanity — with the optional (i.e. non-mandatory) preservation of artificial intelligence — is the moment of the Singularity.

In conjunction with the realisation of the Singularity, the geological goal of history will be achieved: the revenge of the fiery core against the cooling surface.

Nick Land's ideas have been taken up by another bright philosopher of speculative realism in general agreement with the Dark Enlightenment concept, Reza Negarestani.[24] He continues and develops Land's work, approximating his images, metaphors and concepts with certain figures of ancient mythology. In doing so, he is primarily attracted to those aspects of religion and myth that have been on the periphery or have been harshly condemned by orthodoxy. Thus he is interested in the cult of the dark god Ahriman of Iranian tradition. The demonic themes associated with the plague gods, bloody subterranean powers and human sacrifices are also explored by him as a priority in other — primarily Middle Eastern — traditions: Assyrian, Sumerian, etc.

Thus, the notion of a fragmented structure of corporeality, derived from the consistent application of the principle of atomism to matter, leads Negarestani to the symbolism of rats, which puncture the surface of the earth, depriving it of a delusional continuity. At the same time, they are also the carriers of epidemics, often fatal — i.e. they act as instruments of the gods of the plague.

Negarestani applies the gesture of perforation and the poisonous particles associated with it to the modern industrial economy, in which oil and gas, produced by drilling, play a central role. Negarestani sees this act as metaphysical: industrial capitalism is possessed by the spirit of the rat, and even deeper, acts as an instrument of the gods of the plague, hence the relentless euphoria for oil, a kind of 'petroleum addiction'. People are obsessed with oil first and foremost metaphysically. They crush the surface and release the underground lubricating fluid outwards. It is a kind of

---

24 Reza Negarestani, *Cyclonopedia: Complicity with Anonymous Materials*.

industrial capitalist coitus with the Great Mother, bringing wealth and prosperity.

At the same time, the will for oil creates conflict. On a rational level, it is a struggle for resources, often manifesting itself in the form of regional conflicts, which to a large extent predetermines the political processes in the Middle East and its surrounding resource-rich areas. But at the same time, oil is 'the blood of the titans' (the Greeks called it *ichor*) and it is logical that it mixes with human blood, forming the necessary substance for manifestations of the infernal demons — Gog and Magog of the Bible or the Assyrian Lamassus, whose purpose is ultimately war. Thus, according to Negarestani, in such a war there is no 'good' and 'bad', 'friendly' and 'alien'; it is a war of evil against evil, for evil and in the name of evil.

Petroleum economics also entails an even more principled strategy. Oil and gas are only the most superficial level of the semantics of drilling. The true purpose of the movement of the civilisation inwards, towards the base stratum, is the preparation for the liberation of the molten core, which Negarestani calls, after Land, 'Cthelll'. This is precisely the secret atom, the original source of geological trauma.

Negarestani suggests a particular genre called 'theory-fiction', in which elements of science, mythology, theology, poetic imagery and mathematical expressions are inextricably intertwined with one another. Thus, the idea that in the centre of the earth there is a hidden dark deity (the 'corpse of God', according to Negarestani) can be traced back to the cults of Ahriman, the enemy of the bright sun god Ahura Mazda, and the Assyrian myth of the mistress of the underworld Ereshkigal. The entire underworld is the zone of the 'objects themselves' of object-oriented ontology, i.e. those territories where matter resides within itself. As we move in this direction, the dehumanisation of humanity, its objectification, takes place. And at the same time, these 'objects' are rising to the surface and beginning to infect human culture with their peculiar existence. However, quite in the spirit of the Dark Enlightenment, Negarestani does not resent this, but suggests, on the contrary, that this process be fully solidified and even accelerated (accelerationism). After all, we see in Nick Land that the driving force behind the 'history of matter' is the phantom pain of the nucleus.

Consequently, getting to the core and allowing the magma to break out is the goal of progress, emancipation, development and ultimately revolution.

In describing the activation of the core, Negarestani turns to the theme of the subterranean gods, the powers of the underworld, which are the driving forces behind the quivering matter. He describes them as titans and giants, deities of Hades from traditional mythologies and as idiot gods and sub-human — infra-corporeal — forms of life, of which H. P. Lovecraft, the master of dark fantasy, wrote. Dark fiction, modern technology, energy politics, artificial intelligence, development of new machines of war, ancient myths, market strategies, Middle Eastern diplomacy — all these become different sides of a self-contained rhizome reduced to the geological trauma of the core. The infernal gods are units expressing what is 'radically different' to man, that is, matter in its unfathomable truth, matter in and of itself.

The Dark Marxism of Land and Negarestani takes on a grotesque character here: matter comes full circle — including the history of life and humanity — and returns to itself, absorbing all accidental and ephemeral forms in a moment of Singularity, and in the spurt of the molten core towards the source of pain, 'appropriating for itself the status of the highest strata' of the glowing sun, claiming its deadly self-identity.

Soros' Soup: A Metaphor for Butchers

The destruction of humanity and even of life in general in the context of the Dark Enlightenment is thought of as a feast of truth, as a return to the wholeness of the object, that is, to a kind of Radical Object, which is itself the 'core'.

In this context, it is extremely revealing how Negarestani interprets the very notion of 'open society'. For Negarestani, 'openness' is above all openness to matter, which is 'radically different' in speculative realism's topicality. The logic of life and its inherent hierarchy, therefore, boils down to the act of eating. The higher strata eat the lower strata and this is the code of life embodied (according to Deleuze and Guattari) in territory and its structures. Gods eat people, people eat animals, animals eat plants, and those eat minerals. In politics, the prince feeds on his subjects and capital feeds on the whole of society. But this pyramid serves above all to conceal the truth about matter. As long as the highest eats the lowest, society is built vertically. Such a society is 'closed' from below and horizontally. In Plato's *Kallipolis*, the cosmos nourishes ideas, while in Aristotle the *eidos* of a thing consumes its matter. In the religious system, everything is based on sacrifice, and this takes the form of food: the lower offer themselves as food to the higher — and so on up to the divine worlds.

In Negarestani's model, modernity and especially postmodernity are the collapse of such a food chain. Materialism is already a step in the direction where matter itself is the recipient.

Democracy and Popper and Soros' 'open society' are designed to demolish verticality and feed on matter in more or less equal proportions. The next level of ecological democracy, Deleuze's rhizomatics and object-oriented ontology (in particular the political philosophy of mould) propose to extend this openness to include non-human entities. But Negarestani goes even further, and is no longer on the side of beasts, cyborgs and objects, but on the side of the sub-material gods of the plague, Lovecraft's idiot gods. They are more material than the objects, and therefore they also have the right to be complicit in the distribution of food. The inhabitants of 'the other side', the Radical Object and its modulations, the messengers of the core (Cthelll) must also be satisfied. Thus the 'openness' of 'open society' is extended downwards; henceforth it is the openness of people to matter, to the underworld, which is increasingly included in the general process of the relegation of hierarchies.

Negarestani wittily interprets this understanding of 'open society' as the action of a butcher gutting a carcass (tellingly, Nick Land already prefers to refer to human corporeality as 'meat'). 'Open society' is a 'dissected society', gutted by the plague gods or hacked apart by butchers. It is not a new hierarchy or a new food chain, but rather a continuation of liberalism and equality, a movement into the depths of matter. The fact that people are dying of an epidemic brings them suffering and anguish, yet they do not take into account the slaughter of livestock. And the gods of the plague also need something to eat. Moreover, the lower in the hierarchy of beings an entity is, the more material it is, the more metaphysical right it has for food, as matter is universal food. Therefore it is quite logical that the cycle of materialism ends with the act of feeding the matter, whose agents are just Lovecraft's 'idiot gods' or similar conceptual instances. In the end all must be devoured by a nucleus protruding from the centre of the earth. This is what the 'open society' in the new phase of the postmodern is heading for. The metaphor for the members of such a society is an assembly line of hormone-pumped chicken giblets.

Postmodernism Goes Dark

So, the political philosophy of the postmodern is something that is now being implemented before our eyes. It is not just a project, but a creation. It is a reading that is becoming dominant. Most of the existing political systems, legal orders and social norms still correspond to the political modern, and sometimes in a rather archaic form (thus contemporary international law remains fundamentally the same as it was at the conclusion of the Peace of Westphalia). But the interpretation of existing systems is becoming increasingly postmodern. And consequently we are rapidly and irreversibly entering the political philosophy of the postmodern. In terms of the philosophical avantgarde, we are already there, and consequently many terms, concepts and theories of the modern have (often unnoticed) changed their content. This is clearly visible, for example, in Negarestani's speculative realist treatment of the liberal 'open society'.

The question is not how one reads the text of the Political, but who *knows* how to read it. And whoever knows how to read according to the new post-humanist rules becomes the real bearer of the political postmodern. Those who cannot read will continue to be increasingly surprised and even horrified, since many things in our world, moving towards Singularity and rhizome, towards the sovereignty of matter and the practices of feeding the plague gods, are illogical from the perspective of the classical paradigm of modernity.

It should be noted that in the postmodern, the semantics of all three political theories that emerged and fought among themselves for dominance in the modern have also changed. This concerns liberalism most of all, which, having won the war for the legacy of the modern, turned out to be the ideological environment in which the postmodern was destined to take place. This is most clearly seen in the example of 'Dark Liberalism', which is gradually discarding its humanist rhetoric and more and more openly demonstrating its dark side: the hypertrophied market, where everything becomes an object of buying and selling; following the autonomous development of unrestrained technology; the transition to the satisfaction of sub-individual consumer desires; and, after the victory in the field of gender politics, the transition to robot rights and deep ecology. 'Dark Liberalism' is not some deviation of liberalism, just as 'Dark Enlightenment' is not an alternative or antithesis of the Enlightenment. 'Dark Liberalism' is already preceded by the burning of heretics by the Protestant Calvin, the atrocities of Cromwell (1599–1658), the cynical brutality of colonialism, the slave trade, the racist theories of social Darwinists, the hatred of the working class and people in general (except the big capitalists) in Ayn Rand's Objectivism, etc. But liberalism becomes truly dark when it breaks away completely from the territory of the human, opening itself up to the realm of pure matter. Classical liberalism, while defending atomicity as the human individual, for all the destructiveness of this hypothesis in relation to the anthropology of traditional society, had this individual as its frontier. It was he whom liberalism exempted from supraforms of collective identity. It becomes dark at the moment when it comes to the realisation that it is now necessary to take the next step and liberate the human being from humanity — human optional. It is here that the concept of the individual completely cuts ties with the human and moves in the direction of sub-individual and transindividual — and further rhizomatic, virtual and materialistic — entities and instances.

We see something similar in Communism. For all the abstractness of Marxist theory, which operates with empty concepts of classes, surplus value, etc., and the savagery of Communist rule in practice, this ideology did not completely sever the link with the individual, although some Marxists — such as György Lukács (1885–1971) — insisted that in the proletariat the subject coincides with the object, in part anticipating an object-oriented ontology. Some aspects of Nietzscheanism by the Communist

Georges Bataille (1897–1962) and an interest in the Marquis de Sade (1740–1814) by many leftist thinkers are also consonant with 'Dark Communism', but it only becomes so in full measure through the ontology of Lacan, and through him structuralist Freudianism, which leads directly to Foucault, Deleuze, Guattari and everyone else under their influence, which is by now the vast majority of Marxists. Freeing the 'workers of the desire factory' from the repression of consciousness is a real break with the human, and it is now that Marxism, indeed, becomes 'Dark'. In the context of the 'Dark Enlightenment' and in accelerationism, the First and Second Political Theories are already blended to the point of inseparability. Whether or not the global triumph of capitalism and the transfer of subjectivity to extra-human or even artificial entities are to be followed by a world revolution does not matter if one considers capitalism itself to be the maximum possible peak of humanity's march towards its demise. In the new theme of postmodernity — in contrast with modernity — not only is this not a decisive factor, but it means almost nothing at all. This is why vanguard structures of 'open society', such as the Soros Foundation, today simultaneously support both liberalism and Communism, which have become scarcely distinguishable in the postmodern context. Che Guevara is on a poster advertising new phone brands, while young people in T-shirts with his portrait go to revolt against the residual socialists.

Fascism is less represented in the postmodern, although the total enthusiasm for technology and technological development can, with some stretch, be considered 'Fascist' (in the vein of Italian futurism), and the fascination with biological research and biopolitics is an echo of the 'racial hygiene' of the National Socialists, who, according to Heidegger, were the first to introduce the biological element (corporality) into the system of legal legislation by passing racial laws. But since Fascism is already considered 'dark' even without the postmodern, it does not play a particularly prominent role in the Dark Enlightenment. Moreover, the thrust of postmodern criticism against the state, society, family and tradition — this time on the sub-individual level — is directed precisely against 'Fascism' and 'nationalism', in which liberals and Communists see the most effective metaphor for the vertical order in general. However, Nick Land, who positively evaluates the phenomenon of 'neo-conservatives' (NRx), sometimes referred to as the extreme Right or the Alt-Right, marks a place in object-oriented ontology for 'cyber-fascism' as well (for instance, through a particular reading of Nietzsche, where the Superman can be interpreted as a prototype of artificial intelligence[25]).

At the Line

If we look carefully at the logic of the transformation of political philosophy paradigms, we see that after the exhaustion of the possibilities and content of the political modern, only the affirmation of the political postmodern can logically follow, the digging up of the 'state in reverse', the creation of an infernal 'Empire of the multitude', a complete dehumanisation, the transfer of subjectivity to artificial and natural non-human species and, finally, a dash to the core of the earth in order to liberate the magma core. The horizontal and already therefore anti-vertical vector of modernity is being replaced by a new 'horizontal verticality', a *political drilling*.

The political philosophy of the Mother, which we identified as a possibility while considering the philosophical topology of the *Timaeus*, thus gradually reveals a hidden dimension, which was previously unnoticed. We did not see it from the position of the philosophy of the Father, nor from the position of the philosophy of the Son, nor even at the early stage of the philosophy of the modern. It is only when modernity is finally and irrevocably defeated, when we fully realise this philosophy of modernity in practice, that the deepest roots of the '*chora*' itself, the Mother, are revealed.

Modernity is now complete — it has indeed reached its logical limit. Moving further in this direction, the explicit goal of the political process will be the deliberate and systematic destruction of humanity and probably life itself. It is very important that this conclusion is reached not by the opponents of the modern (and postmodern), but by its most avantgarde supporters. In this sense, critical realism — and especially its

---

[25] It was Martin Heidegger who suggested that the figure of the Superman can mean maximising alienation rather than overcoming it.

representatives such as Nick Land or Reza Negarestani — in its vocabulary, imagery and frankness is closer to the traditionalist philosophers, who violently and totally criticise the modern as such, identifying it with the 'civilisation of the Antichrist' and the 'revenge of the Titans', fully confirming what in the opponents of the postmodern may seem like biased polemical rhetoric.

This leads to a very important conclusion for political philosophy: there is no way to stay within the modern for long; this paradigm has already reached its limit, and the process of immersion into the postmodern is in full swing. And this is not an accidental failure, but a historical and political pattern.

We can continue descending still lower through the ontological strata, burrowing ever deeper into pure materiality — steadily approaching the core. There is a final horizon left on this road, culminating in the Singularity: for now, we can try to fuse humans with fungus, replace workers and service employees with robots, entrust planetary logistics to artificial intelligence, elect mould as president, swap all organs by replacing them with new ones, upload memories to a cloud server.

What remains for postmodernity is simply to allow the free proliferation of hybrids, introduce the Parliament of Things, the dismantling of the ego into combinatorial elements and continue pumping out oil and gas, steadily approaching the core. In principle, sinking rods into the core could solve the world's energy problems. This will probably be solved at some point on the policy level, but from a Dark Enlightenment perspective, it would mean that the core itself would launch that rod at us.

CHAPTER 17

THE FOURTH POLITICAL THEORY

The Political Meaning of the Twentieth Century

THE FOURTH POLITICAL THEORY is a conceptual matrix describing the possibility of an *alternative* to the political trend that has come to dominate the modern era. It emerges when postmodernity fully establishes itself in the territory of political philosophy. It is after this that the truth of modernity — i.e., the nature of the Dark Enlightenment, with which the Fourth Political Theory deals directly — is discovered. As long as the essence of the modern was concealed and its fundamental ontological and anthropological strategy was distributed among the three branches, the Fourth Political Theory was not possible, because the outcome of the struggle among the three political theories of the modern depended on the clarification of its deepest essence. And the Fourth Political Theory corresponds exactly to this essence — to that truth in the abyss (matter), of which Democritus spoke. Therefore, in order to describe the Fourth Political Theory in depth, it is necessary to look again at modernity and the dialectic of the clash of the three main political theories inherent in it.

To reiterate: the three main political ideologies of the modern era — liberalism (as the First Political Theory), Communism (as the Second Political Theory) and nationalism (as the Third Political Theory) — essentially exhaust and embody all aspects of the very paradigm of modern political philosophy. As we said earlier, in each of the three political theories the philosophical *subject* of modernity is treated differently: in liberalism as an *individual*, in Communism as a *class*, in Fascism and National Socialism as a *state* and a *race*, respectively.

These political concepts collided in the twentieth century and predetermined the structure of the world wars, the Cold War, alliances, unions and blocs. If World War I was a clash between a number of major national European powers, World War II was already a clash between all three ideological forces: liberals, represented by the West (USA, England), Communists, represented by the USSR, and Nazis/Fascists, represented by Mussolini's Italy/Hitler's Germany, as well as other movements close to them.

Accordingly, after the Third Political Theory had been defeated (Fascism and National Socialism), two political theories remained, the First and the Second, between which a cold war developed, until the First Political Theory (liberalism) defeated the Second (Communism) in 1989 and decisively in 1991.

The entire history of modernity was marked by these three political theories, which embodied the very matrix of New Age political philosophy. All of them followed the logic of the political philosophy of the Mother: all of them were materialist, evolutionist, progressivist, all of them viewed the structure of the world from the bottom up rather than from the top down, i.e., they were created on the basis of an immanent materialist doctrine.

Accordingly, the order in which they emerged and the order in which they disappeared (or were marginalised) also reflected a certain logic, as the battle of the three political ideologies was a battle over which of them more closely matched the paradigm of modernity, its *truth*. Communism claimed to contain this truth, viewing itself as a socialist and Communist society to be built after the end of the historical cycle of capitalism. Liberalism also saw itself as an expression of modernity as such, but, and this is less obvious, Fascism also considered itself a revolutionary doctrine reflecting the spirit of modernity, but in a different context, in different proportions, with different values from liberalism and Communism.

In any case, all three ideologies fought to be the one which embodied the spirit of modernity. Each thought it was the modern. After the defeat of Nazism, only two ideologies (liberalism and Communism) contested this right, and after 1989–1991 it turned out that liberalism had won this long battle.

That is, of the three political theories of the modern paradigm, only one has proved truly paradigmatic. Related to this are the process of globalisation and the universalisation of liberal ideology, which has now become the global ideology and the only ideology to win in the unfolding of political history — that is, it was victorious in the West and, due to the fundamental influence of the West, has largely spread around the world.

There is a direct link here to Francis Fukuyama's assertion of 'the end of history'. 'The end of history' is the final and irreversible victory of liberalism over its rivals. After 1991, liberalism was no longer one of the three ideologies, but *the* ideology of modernity itself.

Capitalism (liberalism) originally saw itself as the embodiment of the spirit of modernity, but this was not necessarily obvious to anyone except the representatives of liberalism itself. This was challenged by Communists and Fascists, and in principle the dispute between the three political theories was not resolved until several centuries later. At all stages there remained the possibility of a different turn of political events (and Communism put in a serious claim to be the embodiment of modernity and the ideological formula for the 'end of history'). At one point, the successes of Hitler's Germany were so impressive that there may well have been a belief that it was Nazism that would determine the ideological foundation for the future.

It was only at the end of the twentieth century that the unconditional matrix of world political history came to fruition, where *the spirit of modernity won out in the form of liberalism*. Liberalism defended its right to be not just one ideology, but an Ideology with a capital letter. Thus the First Political Theory of modernity also became the last, the final one. It is out of the victory of liberalism that we got the political philosophy of the postmodern. Correspondingly, the triumph of the individual as an atom allowed us to move to the sub-atomic level.

Thus the winner in the rivalry between the three ideological versions of modernity was determined. And practically at the same period, liberalism, having become dominant and singular, began to rapidly reveal its totalitarian nature. Meanwhile, the paradigm shift towards the postmodern, whose philosophical preconditions had been developed a few decades earlier but which began to take on a practical dimension in the realm of politics in the 1990s, began with steady acceleration. At the same time, a wave of gender politics and eco-politics was also emerging, heralding the rise of 'Dark Liberalism'.

Modernity, victorious in liberalism, moved into the postmodern in a new — postliberal — stage. But this was only possible because all forms of collective identity (the Tradition paradigm) and the alternative artificial definitions of the political subject of the Second Political Theory (class) and the Third Political Theory (state, race) were abolished.

The individual is affirmed by liberals as the latest version of the most authentic human atom, and consequently as the philosophical foundation and political subject. And only after the victory of this ideology and the triumph of the human individual — as expressed in the ideology of civil society, the ideology of human rights, the ideology of globalisation and the world liberal capitalist market (the transition from global politics to global economy, with the abolition of history, as Fukuyama wrote) —, only at this moment did the door to the postmodern truly open. It was liberals who opened it, and therefore, in the 'Dark Enlightenment' paradigm, it is 'Dark Liberalism' that has the right of doctrinal and epistemological primacy.

Once the atom was confirmed as the basic moment of being, all further movement turned to the subatomic level. The phenomenology of *political postphilosophy*,[1] or the political philosophy of the postmodern, is linked to this.

So, without the victory of liberalism, the victory of the postmodern would not have been possible. To be more precise, in theory, the postmodern could have been different — more likely Communist and less likely Fascist. However, the result of the twentieth century in the field of ideology is unambiguous: the political postmodern is based on the

---

1   Dugin, *Postphilosophy*.

absolute dominance achieved by liberal ideology, the First Political Theory, which completely defeated the Second and Third ones.

This is roughly the context in which global society is being built. Global society is not yet a reality, it is a project. Nevertheless, it exists as a 'concept' and corresponds to a similar concept — the 'global West'. When we say 'the West', we mean not only the geographical West, but also, for example, Japan and even the Pacific coast of China, where Western models in economy, culture and society prevail, as well as some countries that follow the Western way of development in the Pacific region (Singapore, Taiwan, etc.). 'The West' is global and ideological at the same time. Certainly, the West has not yet fully penetrated into the flesh and blood of all societies, peoples and civilisations, but nevertheless, this penetration is going on at full throttle, through markets, technology, culture, information, economics, politics, etc. The West is not just a collection of European and North American powers and societies. It is the very process of globalisation, 'postmodernisation' and the gradual spread of the codes (and stratifications, to use the term of Deleuze and Guattari) of Euro-American/Euro-Atlantic culture to the entire planet. After the decisive victory of liberalism in the Cold War, the whole world has in a sense become 'the West', that is to say, an area of such territorialisation/deterritorialisation, which corresponds precisely to the liberal code of 'assemblage'.

Accordingly, the agenda of global processes in world politics today is the dominance of liberalism and the assertion of its victory on a global scale, the elimination of nation-states (as we see in Europe) and the destruction of all forms of collective identity (nation, religion, gender, etc.). In this phase, modernity completes that destruction of vertical symmetries and organic collective identities which it began when the transition from traditional society (Platonism, Aristotelianism, religion) to modern society (materialism, democracy, secularism) was outlined.

The Universality of the West and Dark Modernisation

The global political process today — at least within the dominant episteme — represents a transition from the political philosophy of the modern (in the form of a victorious liberal ideology) to the postmodern — and to its most avantgarde 'object-oriented' phase of the posthumanist 'Dark Enlightenment'. That is the agenda of Western society.

A question arises: to what extent is this agenda universal?

In answering this question, we should first of all consider the fact that the West thinks of itself globally (globalisation is the extension of the 'stain' of the West to the whole of humanity). So to the extent that we are a modern society and accept modernisation and Westernisation as something having no alternative (as our destiny), to the same extent we are part of the European world or Euro-Atlantic civilisation. This applies to any people and any society. Today, to a certain extent, almost all countries without exception (including the most anti-Western ones, such as North Korea and Iran) recognise by default the imperative of modernisation, recognising the West (or at least its technologies, its epistemologies, its economic dogmas — above all the market) as a global destiny. Thus, the universalism of the West and the logical sequence of its historical development from traditional society to modern and postmodern are insisted upon by Western civilisation itself alongside all others — the West and the rest, to quote Samuel Huntington[2] (1927–2008).

But if we accept the thesis of the *universality* of the West unreservedly, then we will be left to accept and put into practice the First Political Theory. In that case, philosophy, history, politics, economics, culture, international relations and all other fields of social life must proceed in accordance with the epistemology of liberalism and on the basis of its scale. But if this is so, then we are obliged to recognise the irreversibility and the transition from the political modern to the political postmodern — and in the end to the posthumanist agenda of the Dark Enlightenment.

By taking this model as the dominant one, we get a normative reference point for comparison, evaluating everything that happens in the various non-Western countries (including Russia) on the basis of how similar it is to the West and the different phases of its history. The GDP figures, economic statistics, industrialisation and urbanisation rates, the functionality of democratic institutions and different segments of civil

---

2   Samuel Huntington, *The Clash of Civilizations and the Remaking of World Order* (New York: Simon & Schuster, 1996).

society, the extent of political correctness and tolerance, etc. are all used to assess the level of modernity in each society. Overall, it is a matter of measuring the actual liberation of the human individual (the social atom) from various forms of collective identity. In other words, a modern and 'Western' society is one in which the political philosophy of modernity and the practices built on its basis have sufficiently prevailed.

However, this applies primarily to non-Western societies trying to catch up with the West (sometimes quite successfully, as in the case of some rapidly developing Pacific Rim countries). The Western countries themselves have different criteria that are based on measuring the extent to which a society has moved from modern to postmodern. In some matters, the USA and especially Canada are ahead of the European Union countries, while in others, European societies are more postmodern than the North American powers. Thus, in the field of philosophy and political philosophy the undisputed superiority belongs to the continental states — and above all to France, where postmodernism emerged. By contrast, in the field of applying certain postmodern strategies and practices to culture, technology, business, politics and even military strategy (above all the doctrine of 'network warfare'[3]), the primacy belongs to the United States. 'Speculative realism' and the 'Dark Enlightenment' affect both Europeans and Americans, epistemologically dominated by Lacan, Foucault and above all Deleuze and Guattari, and methodologically and stylistically by Anglo-Saxon technocratism.

The transition to postmodernity somewhat distorts the clarity of the criterion for judging 'modernisation', since in the West itself there is a liquidation of modernity (posthumanisation) and a movement towards more and more accentuated separateness — schizoanalysis, hypertolerance, 'democracy of objects', ecopolitics, etc., while in non-Western societies modern epistemology and practices based on it have not yet become entrenched. This sometimes creates extravagant situations where the index of 'modernisation' is the number of homosexual marriages, the percentage of homosexual and transgender people in power structures or the

---

3   Dugin, *The War of the Continents. The Modern World in a Geopolitical Frame of Reference*.

quality of networking, while many fundamental aspects of classical modernisation may be in their infancy. The criterion of large-scale schizophrenisation of the masses may then be outweighed by technological backwardness or collapse and dysfunction of democratic mechanisms (in the Western sense).

But in any case, recognising the universalism of the West implies embracing liberalism as an obligatory ideology, as it has won the historical battle for the essence and truth of modernity. Therefore, it is not just the West and modernity that are recognised as universal, but the ideology of liberalism with all its inherent principles and axioms has the same universal status in this case. Having recognised the universality of the West, we must also recognise the inevitability of the First Political Theory. And this in turn predetermines the vector of 'progress' within the paradigm of modernity itself — in the direction of the dividual, posthumanism, the Radical Object (core), the political philosophy of the Mother — right up to the 'Dark Enlightenment'.

Consequently all societies (including non-Western societies) that are under its influence are forced to accept the whole chain of temporal semantics reflected in liberalism: history as progress, individual liberation from all forms of collective identity, technological development — and so on, further and further into matter, in search of the elusive atomicity and truth of the material abyss.

This is the vector of the global agenda. And since we are part of the global world, it is also on the agenda of Russian politics, naturally on a par with all other societies and cultures, both Western and non-Western. In one way or another this applies to all modern societies, including those that by virtue of historical inertia retain some religious features (this primarily applies to Islamic countries) and those that follow the Second Political Theory (North Korea, China, Vietnam, Cuba). But even in these cases, liberalism — primarily in the economy — and a materialist picture of the world (in science, technology, education) have a significant impact, preparing for the next round of more complete modernisation and Westernisation.

The recognition of the universality of the West thus includes the ideology of liberalism as an indispensable element. This may be veiled, postponed or framed by symbolic imagery, but the essence of modernity at the end of the twentieth century boils down to liberalism. Fukuyama built his thesis of the 'end of history' on just such an analysis. Although he did not take into account the diversity of civilisations, his analysis is theoretically correct: modernity = liberalism. It is another matter that Fukuyama got the timing of the process wrong. Theoretically this is exactly the case, modernity is liberalism, and this derives from the West's own conviction of the universality of its history and from the recognition of this by most non-Western societies. But in practice the modern has penetrated different non-Western societies in an uneven way, at times not deeply and almost always with tremendous distortion. If we accept the universalism of the West, and liberalism accordingly, we can argue with Fukuyama about timing and forms, but not about the very essence of the process.

Here, however, we should also take into account postmodernism and especially its leap towards posthumanism and transhumanism, as well as hypermaterialism and radical nihilism, openly proclaiming not just 'the end of history', but 'the end of humanity' as a goal, and in some cases 'the end of life' in favour of the Radical Object (core) and invasion of subbodily, deeply material powers from the 'other side' (Lovecraft's 'idiot gods', gods of the plague, etc.). Today this is the least evident, but clearly identified, vector for the continuation of modernisation and Westernisation along the axis outlined by liberalism and especially its victory. It is a 'Dark Liberalism', finally breaking with humanism and with man, but following the same logic of modernity — the drive towards materialism, atomism and individualism, this time beyond the limits of man and even life.

Thus, accusing modernity of nihilism and the pursuit of death and nothingness is no longer a polemical and rhetorical move by its opponents, because it is more and more openly acknowledged by liberals themselves — modernists, and especially postmodernists, calling for acceleration and transhumanism, artificial intelligence and gene modifications, and in the end for the total triumph of matter and nothingness.

Thus, in the full cycle of the philosophy of the Mother we are dealing with a philosophy of death, with the glorification of nihilism and dissipation, of entropy and ghostliness.

To follow the way of the West means to follow the way of death. The philosophy of civil society, brought to its logical end (absence of the state, of order, of the vertical, of any common elements and values), leads to a point where human loneliness reaches the stage where nothing but the death of oneself or one's neighbour can amuse the human being. And then the metaphor of the 'open society' in the epistemology of the Dark Enlightenment leads directly to images of gutted human carcasses, who in their naïve search for freedom have become victims of the plague gods.

This is precisely what the ultimate programme of modernisation and Westernisation is all about. And while it is still beyond the attention of the general public even in the West, on the level of political philosophy, postmodernism and speculative realism are already at work, extending their influence in the epistemological sphere, affecting culture, art and technology, as well as economics and politics. In non-Western societies, this avantgarde agenda is even less well known. But anyone who acknowledges the thesis of Western universalism, of the inevitability of progress and development, any proponent of liberal ideology (conscious or unconscious) already carries the vector of a 'Dark Liberalism' that is not just *possible* in the context of the general development of Western modernity, but *inevitable* and is its logical posthumanist and nihilistic conclusion.

Questions about the Alternative

Now we come to the second question, which is directly related to the first: is there any alternative to this process?

Naturally, there are people in the world who, looking at what is happening, feel a certain unease, to say the least, realising that there is something wrong with the basic fundamental attitude of the society in which we live today. Of course, seldom does anyone guess the magnitude of the problem, since the influence of dominant epistemes is so strong that it completely predetermines the structures of consciousness both in relation to the subject and in relation to the surrounding world and society, and the episteme of modernity has been firmly entrenched (at least in the West) for several centuries, while liberalism and the political philosophy based on it have completely predetermined normative thinking on a global scale in recent decades. Accordingly, it is not easy to understand the full scope of what is happening at a distance from the ruling ideology. But the will to reject the liberal paradigm and globalism can theoretically arise in the West itself, while in non-Western societies, and above all in those that have retained certain civilisational characteristics and/or religious traditions that remain strong, such a will is often even greater — also because of the obviously colonial character of globalisation that imposes Western values and standards on all cultures.

To a great extent, the situation is exacerbated by the fact that the transition to postmodernism has opened up a posthumanist horizon that seems, for cultures where modernity has not yet taken hold, to be something 'monstrous'. Even for the average Westerner, the themes of schizomass (and schizoanalysis), the rhizome, the organ parliament, cyborgs, clones, and genetic engineering, that is, the theses of nihilistic accelerationism ('Dark Liberalism' and 'Dark Marxism'), which boil down to an appeal for the abolition of humanity, still seem today as something excessive. Until recently this was also the case with gender politics, but this frontier, which legitimised numerous sexual perversions and gave legal status to homosexual marriage, adoption of children by such couples, etc., has already been crossed, and the 'democracy of things', artificial intelligence and recognition of the political sovereignty of matter are on the agenda today. However, this shift towards posthumanism has not yet become a reality, and therefore still elicits negative reactions from the public. Outside the Western world such themes look even more grotesque, since in the context of any traditional — religious — culture it is impossible not to see direct parallels with Satanism and the Kingdom of the Antichrist.

Thus, in general, the territory for the anti-liberal and anti-globalisation stance is vast and is as global as liberal globalism itself. As a rule, political, economic, cultural and scientific elites easily accept liberalism by virtue of being included in a transnational class that relies precisely on this ideology, but the masses, as well as huge sectors of counter-elites against modernisation and Westernisation can easily embark on a search for an alternative.

In other words, the more total and global liberalism becomes, the more pressing the search for its possible alternatives becomes. This is not just a theoretical possibility, there have already been a multitude of concrete cases of its rejection: we see this in the ideology of radical Islam, in Russia's insistence on strengthening its sovereignty and on adjusting the extreme forms of liberal ideology within its borders, in the firm commitment of China to the political power of the Communist Party against the demands of liberal democracy, in the rising tide of European populism, etc.

The Fourth Political Theory Begins from a Critical Distance

The question of a possible alternative to the undivided dominance of liberal ideology on a global scale, taking into account all the logic of the formation of the political modern and those philosophical transformations that take place in the transition to the postmodern, is where the construction of the Fourth Political Theory begins. To understand the meaning, place, role and content of the Fourth Political Theory it is necessary to take into account the whole structure of *Politica Aeterna*, which describes synchronously all possible models of the organisation of political philosophy. Therefore, the Fourth Political Theory becomes fully understood only in the overall context of *Politica Aeterna*.[4]

The Fourth Political Theory begins with the observation that something went wrong with the world and with the tendencies that dominate it, and this wrongness has a fundamental metaphysical and ontological (rather than purely technical or even ideological) character.

A Fourth Political Theory begins with a philosophical distancing from the mainstream of global processes. However, this distancing itself poses a serious philosophical problem, since what is criticised is not a stable and unchanging set of statements, axioms, concepts and value systems, but a fluid, ever-changing and extremely false element that constantly and

---

4   In its turn, *Politica Aeterna* is based on *Postphilosophy* and on the methodology of the *Three Logoi* set out in the *Noomakhia* project.

obsessively generates false self-representations, reporting distorted information—both globally and in great detail—about itself and the world. The point is not that liberal ideology (like any ideology) relies on political propaganda and constructs systems of evaluation that are advantageous to itself. The problem is even more serious because, from the point of view of the completeness of *Politica Aeterna*, modernity as such is a field of sheer pseudo-logic—that is, the development of a hypothesis that is impossible, incorrect and contradictory in itself. Ontologically, the modern exists as a lie, representing the being of nothingness. And in the postmodern this nihilism is revealed in full measure, and not merely revealed, but taken up as a conscious goal and as the highest value. Thus the eminent theorist and liberal philosopher Bernard-Henri Lévy,[5] as a convinced and ardent apologist of globalism and modernity, recognises that the liberal Western-centric world order is an empire based on nothing and defending nothing as a supreme value. Accordingly, to unravel the intricacies of pseudo-logic and thereby take a position where its rhetorical and epistemological mechanisms would cease to operate is in itself far from easy. The two critical theories opposing liberalism (Communism and Fascism) were themselves elements of the political modern, and therefore were within pseudo-logic, not outside it. However, it is their absence, coupled with the way postmodernity blatantly reveals the falsehood of modernity, that simplifies this goal somewhat; with some effort critical thought about modern liberal ideology can find its appropriate zone—on the other side of the new *liberal* totality. Today it is still possible to say no to liberalism and globalisation and therefore to universalism, and this decisive 'no' lies at the heart of the Fourth Political Theory. For those who say yes to the global status quo, the Fourth Political Theory makes little (or rather, no) sense. But the number of those inclined to say 'no' in the modern world as a whole is enormous, to the point that it can be considered an implicit position of the vast majority of humanity, while full solidarity with liberalism is statistically characteristic only of global elites. But the problem is that power—above all epistemological power, but also all other power

---

5   Bernard-Henri Lévy, *The Empire and the Five Kings: America's Abdication and the Fate of the World* (NY: Henry Holt and Co., 2019).

(political, economic, cultural, etc.) — is in the hands of global elites. And thus the meaning of the Fourth Political Theory knowingly — even in this preliminary and conceptual approximation — acquires the status of *revolutionary*.

Against Liberalism, but Also Communism and Fascism

Thus, the Fourth Political Theory proceeds from disagreement with the dominance of liberalism, but since this dominance is not accidental, but rather the result of complex and generally unidirectional processes of Western political history, it questions this entire semantic sequence — the very course of the change and internal evolution of political paradigms —, above all from Tradition to modernity and then to postmodernity.

The first gesture of the Fourth Political Theory is a radical rejection of liberalism and its postmodern, somewhat postliberal subatomic version that is becoming mainstream politics today. This rejection, however, is coupled in the Fourth Political Theory with the very clear and contrasting understanding that the illiberal ideologies of the modern age — Communism and Fascism — are not real alternatives. This is the fundamental position of the Fourth Political Theory, for which reason we call it the Fourth. By radically and comprehensively rejecting liberalism, the Fourth Political Theory deliberately refuses to see itself as Communism (socialism) or Fascism (nationalism) in all their guises. There are two reasons for this refusal.

Firstly, the Second and Third Political Theories have historically lost to liberalism (at the level of political philosophy they have proved less consistent with the pure paradigm of New Age political philosophy than liberalism) and hence they have shown their limits. Of course, historical loss is not a decisive argument. But this is so only when the criterion of material victory and the ideology of progress are not fundamental. The historical clash between liberalism, socialism and Fascism in the twentieth century was a clarification of who is more in line with the very spirit of modernity, who is more progressive, who belongs to the future, and the criterion, due to the materialism inherent in all three ideologies, was the fact of victory or defeat. In this dispute and confrontation, with this system of evaluation, liberalism triumphed over both Fascism and Communism, thus proving its identity with the very essence of modernity and its right to the future — to a liberal interpretation of the 'end of history'.

Secondly, and this is already a much more serious argument (although closely linked to the analysis of the metaphysical result of the clash of the three political theories and the meaning of the victory of liberalism in it), the Second and Third Political Theories were products of the political philosophy of the modern, so even if they had won, they would ultimately themselves have been the fullest expression of the modern, which was at one point quite likely in the case of Communism, and for a brief moment even in the case of Fascism. The fact that the battle for modernity was won by liberals is of great importance, but if one imagines that it would have been Communists or Fascists, then again their planetary dominance would have meant the same thing — a total triumph of materiality, de-individualisation and, ultimately, dehumanisation: Dark Communism or a planetary Reich, having won the battle for modernity, would have become the dominant actor of the Dark Enlightenment, which would have changed nothing of the essence of the 'end of history', although it would have given it a different shape.

Now most importantly: by saying 'no' to the planetary dominance of globalist liberalism, we reject not only it, but also its very essence — the pure paradigm of modernity.

Rejecting Liberalism Is Not Enough

The Fourth Political Theory begins with the proposal to say radically 'no' to liberalism. But such a 'no' begs the question: if you are not a liberal, then who are you? A Communist? A nationalist? A Fascist? Thus, a critical distance with respect to the main trend of our time on the level of political philosophy (i.e. liberalism) naturally throws us back to the Second and Third Political Theories or to their synthesis, National Bolshevism. All this would indeed be opposition to liberalism, *but within the framework of modernity*.

Opposition to liberalism would therefore once again inevitably turn to the peripheral forms of that same modernism. In this case, we would only declare that we do not like the essence of the modern in its pure form (liberalism proper) and would stand in opposition to the centre of the modern from its own periphery. Such is conservatism: it proposes only to 'slow down' modernity, yet still proceeding in the same direction, towards the same goal, but only more *slowly*. Radical conservatism proposes moving quite slowly, while moderate conservatism proposes moving just a bit slowly.

And this is what we get: once we have stood at a distance from the dominant trend of modern political philosophy as the global liberalism, we find ourselves in the position of either 'modernist conservatives' or supporters of the 'altermodern'.

Thus, even in the most liberal circles, there are avantgarde liberals who rejoice in the transition to the postmodern and are ready to embrace 'Dark Liberalism', as well as those who say: 'Maybe not so fast, not so hasty, a little slower?' Consequently, all three political ideologies of the modern, in the face of their 'image of the future' represented by the postmodern and the 'Dark Enlightenment', can take up critical positions. Communism and Fascism are opposed to liberalism in any of its forms, while liberal conservatism is opposed to the extent that it is horrified by the extreme expressions of its own ideological platform.

Nevertheless, humanity today is moving, 'swimming' into the postmodern. And those who protest against this, remaining codified by the modern, object more often than not not to the orientation itself, but rather to the speed or the shocking images of the future presented by postmodernists.

But there are those who realise that the current is not only flowing too fast, but that it is flowing in 'the wrong direction', that it is carrying us out where we do not want to go. The 'river' has to flow back, all the more so because it is not something natural or fatal, but the result of a freely made decision that has made modernity — the political philosophy of motherhood in general, in both the liberal and illiberal versions — possible and valid.

This is the meaning of the Fourth Political Theory: it denies modernity as an inevitability and outs it as pseudo-logic based on a decision which, having been made, knowingly laid down as a goal that horizon of decay and degradation, entropy and dissipation which is exposed with utmost candour in the rhizome or Radical Object.

The Totality of the Time of the Woman

The essence of the Fourth Political Theory is that it rejects not one of the political ideologies of the modern era, but *all of them*. The three political theories exhaust the range of modernist proposals. A Fourth Political Theory says no to all of them — not just to liberalism. It is not satisfied with the very 'flow of the river' in the direction of the political philosophy of the Mother, with the very decision that has made political history move in this direction.

The Fourth Political Theory is the theory of a global, absolute, radical revolution, directed not only against the concrete domination of the West, against the present state of European civilisation, against the hegemony of the United States, against liberalism, but against m*odernity itself*, against the political paradigm of the Mother, against that metaphysics where the idea of the world, the subject and reality is constructed *from the bottom up*.

Here the political philosophy of the Father (or political Platonism) and the political philosophy of the Son (political Aristotelianism) take on great importance; we entered the age of modernity when the murder of the Father and the castration of the Son took place.

The victory of modernity and the transition to postmodernity are described in myth as dual gestures of the Great Mother, known from the traditions of different peoples. Mother Earth kills her Father/Husband, a figure which is the fundamental axis of the vertical of Platonist political philosophy, and castrates the Beloved Son, i.e. demolishes the Aristotelian axis of the 'unmoved mover', depriving the world and man of their spiritual (eidetic) component.

This is the metaphysical strategy of materialism and atomism — in order to arrive at the dominance of matter and a pseudo-logical 'ontology' built from the bottom up, two possible alternatives have to be uprooted: the political philosophy of the Father and the political philosophy of the Son. Both are incompatible with the political philosophy of the Mother.

Modernity as such is precisely the political philosophy of the Mother, of materialism, of sovereign matter, ὕλη, *chora*. And accordingly, all the fundamental ideological and politico-philosophical processes of the New Age are carried out within this political philosophy of the Mother. According to the results of the political and ideological history of the New Age, liberalism appears to be as close as possible to the matriarchal vision of the world, while political postmodernism exudes this inherently feminine structure of liberalism even more acutely, since the very matrix of modernity as the political philosophy of the Mother emerges more fully and clearly in it.

This is a point of principle: in the context of modernity, liberalism has no and can never have an alternative, since modernity itself is based on the exclusion of the other two models of the political logos, which alone could serve as a support for the alternative. But the conditions of modernity are such that these two models — a full-fledged Platonism or Aristotelianism — are rigidly and totally rejected, forbidden, censored. The field of inquiry is confined to the zone of matter and materiality, atomism and individuation. Accordingly, a Fourth Political Theory is only possible outside the context of modernity, and thus requires a revolutionary escape from its limits. However, these limits are structured in such a way that they form a totality based on the paradigmatic presumption of materialism (direct or implicit). And if we acknowledge this totality, then the philosophy of the Father and the philosophy of the Son will simply have no place, no being, no subject and no object expression. The very time of modernity, which becomes the measure of being, is structured in such a way that Platonism and Aristotelianism, tradition and religion, sacredness and spirit are placed in the 'past', as 'that which preceded', and therefore have no participation in the present and future, deprived of an ontological dimension that is placed exclusively in becoming. That is, Platonism and Aristotelianism are impossible in modernity, and if they are possible, it is only in the form of simulacra.

The Rupture of Pseudo-logic and the Experience of Eternity

A Fourth Political Theory, in order to become possible, has to realise the rupture of this totality, to overcome the ontology of time and becoming as established in modernity. If one agrees with the temporality of modernity, the philosophy of the Father and the philosophy of the Son do not exist, being a property of what was, *but no longer is*. Their defence is understood as conservatism, i.e. as an attempt to forcefully inhibit time with reliance on phantom pains of (illusory) memories. Object-oriented ontologists — Nick Land in particular — generally consider human memory a fiction introduced to 'cyborgs' by artificial intelligence from the 'future' in order to make them believe in their own 'humanity'.[6] Accordingly, modernity excludes the very possibility that the philosophy of the Father or the philosophy of the Son can have any kind of ontology behind them.

The Fourth Political Theory breaks this immanent loop by affirming above all a different time — time as the image of eternity (according to Plato) or the eternity of the 'unmoved mover' (according to Aristotle). The ontology of eternity as well as the ontology of the One is affirmed in opposition to modernity, and only this allows a genuine distance to be built in relation to liberalism. But such a revolutionary gesture of going beyond modernity requires a total overturning of both consciousness and being. This is possible through a *direct experience of the eternal*, because no constructs within the totality of the modern can bring us nearer to this. Staying inside the modern is itself a distance from such experience, blocking it, turning it into something impossible. The Fourth Political Theory breaks the matrix of the modern at its base, burns out its entire structure by the experience of eternity. The philosophy of the Father and the philosophy of the Son possess being because they are built — albeit in

---

[6] Nick Land refers to the plot of the sci-fi films *Blade Runner* and *Terminator*, describing, in his view, the mechanics of operations with time in the spirit of the Deleuzian distinction between the vertical 'time' of an aeon (along a tree axis) having meaning (a vector of movement from roots to crown, from past to future) but having no being, and the horizontal 'time' of the rhizome chronos having being but having no meaning, i.e., consistency. Thus time travel becomes possible given the aeon's lack of being and the rhizomatic presence's lack of meaning. See Land, *Fanged Noumena: Collected Writings 1987–2007*.

different ways — on the experience of eternity. Plato's *Kallipolis* exists, has existed and will exist in the purest and most direct sense. The realm of ideas and the celestial vertical is neither a construct nor a concept, it is an ontological fact. Another fact is that *Kallipolis* can act in relation to phenomenal politics from different positions, both in alliance and harmony with it, and in opposition to it. St Augustine's doctrine of the two cities or the Iranian dualistic cosmology describe scenarios of war between the ideal state and its earthly distorted — even inverted — reflection. But no twists and turns of this struggle can deprive eternity of being, heaven of its luminous divine nature. Ideas can be distorted and parodied in conceptual thinking, but by doing so the phenomenal being ultimately harms not the idea but itself. One cannot kill God, one can only ruin one's soul, corrupt one's humanity. God's renunciation of mankind does not affect God, although it probably saddens him. But it certainly affects people themselves — they fall into the abyss of nothingness, dissolving in the folds of matter, moving irrepressibly towards the centre of maximum gravity, towards the core, towards the heart of nothingness, of matter, of the Radical Object. The Fourth Political Theory is based on the wilful affirmation of political Platonism, and insists on accepting God's view of humanity, not humanity's view of God. *Kallipolis* is not a convention or utopia; it is what is, was and will be.

With the political philosophy of the Son it is somewhat more complicated. Here the measure is immanence, though not material immanence. So the ruin of the state — the transition from monarchy and aristocracy to democracy — has an ontological basis. Here, tragedy, catastrophe are real. But in this case, too, the denial of the unmoved mover and the 'natural places' of its existence do not affect it directly. Where it is lost from view, we are talking about the retreat of the thing to the distant periphery of ontology. Therefore the victory of anti-Aristotelianism does not say that Aristotle was mistaken, but only that his opponents (atomists) have moved too far away from the 'unmoved mover' itself and have withdrawn to a critical distance from its ' natural places', losing them from view completely. They have nowhere else to go, and the loss of the cause of motion (as the purposeful cause in New Age causality) means the collapse of things, their descent from orbit and their complete inability to return to it again. Therefore, it all comes down not to what, but to where. Modernity, democracy, materialism and capitalism are places on the farthest periphery of being, where the impulses of things pursuing themselves are utterly exhausted. Entelechies evaporate and things and people, jostling and tossing inexorably, move towards the precipice.

From the point of view of the philosophy of the Son, the decline of political philosophy and the state based on this decline is valid. But it corresponds to a particular topology, which in Christianity is called 'hell'.

The Fourth Political Theory is a leap out of political hell towards an unchanging eternal and perpetually existing ideal or towards the centre of immanent reality, towards the world axis, which humanity has lost sight of due to the power of centrifugal tendencies. The Fourth Political Theory is the return of things, people, thoughts, nations and rulers to themselves, to their essence, to their origins. The Fourth Political Theory is therefore above all an ontological upheaval, an awakening of what *is* from the brutal totality of what only pretends to be 'reality'. It is a dramatic experience, but it is where the difficult road to recovery begins.

Metaphors of Bird and Stone: Awakening in the Fall

The Fourth Political Theory represents an appeal not to variations or combinations of the political philosophies of the modern, but to a radical paradigm shift. This shift can be described *negatively* as a rejection of the political philosophy of the Mother in its metaphysical foundation, that is, simply as the elimination of modernity altogether. The beginning of modernity already carries with it the meaning, the content, and the logic of its end.

From the beginning, modernity could lead to nothing other than the present-day liberal hegemony. In order to truly get out of this rut today, we need to move in the opposite direction. But this does not mean that we must simply stand still and stop moving in the direction indicated by the vector of modernisation. That is not enough and it is not possible. It is a question of setting a *radically different goal*. And to move, but *in a completely different direction*. Not forward, but backward. However, this movement 'backwards' is just a symbol and a convention. For behind us, before the advent of modernity, is heaven, the suns of the spirit and the immortal (now truly immortal, undying, the resurrected and resurrecting) God.

In the political history of the West, and due to the scale of Western colonisation, in the rest of the world, we descended from the political philosophy of the Father through the political philosophy of the Son to the political philosophy of the Mother. In the structure of *Politica Aeterna*, this process is visible and placed on an ontological map, in which all genera, all levels are present synchronously, simultaneously. Therefore, each step of the movement did not irreversibly cancel the previous phase or stage, but changed the position of the observer, the *ontological and epistemological situation of the subject* (and with it, the object). The process of descending through the levels of political philosophy is based on a freely made decision, and this decision becomes fatal, becomes fate, only *after* it is made. The descent through these levels from the Father through the Son to the Mother is not a mechanical fate, it is a sequence of freely made decisions. There is nothing predetermined in the vector and the nature of this descent: each moment and each transition is based on a choice. But the paradigmatic fatality that follows the choice is fundamental and takes place in the vertical dimension. The decision to remain in a philosophical paradigm or to change it can be both an expression of ill will and the result of error. In a sense, without making a choice, it is difficult to know for certain where that choice would lead, even if there is every reason not to try to move in some direction. Freedom is such that it cannot knowingly rule out any points of application — even the most misguided and disastrous ones. The paradigmatic choice and transition from Platonism to Aristotelianism and then to atomism is a sequential catastrophe. The gap between the political philosophy of the Father and the political philosophy of the Son is within the paradigm of traditional society (premodern), while the transition to the political philosophy of the Mother means a rupture, a step outside of it. Here the true choice is along the vertical axis. And what we know of the last millennium of Western civilisation (and in recent centuries of all humanity) convinces us unequivocally that principled choices were made in favour of going down the vertical of paradigms.

To go to the right or to the left is a matter of choice when standing firmly on the horizontal plane. It is a secondary choice subordinate to the primary choice, the vertical one.

Modernity's vertical choice can be likened to being tossed into the abyss. If we are a stone, we can only fall. In this case our time is the time of *falling*, of descent and death (Nietzsche's *Untergang*). But if we are birds, even if we are just fledglings, we have the chance to figure this out, to prove it and to be convinced of it. For a stone to fall into the abyss is only a fall. But if we are talking about a soul that has wings but has never used them before, the toss into the abyss will be the beginning of flight. This is how chicks are taught to fly at a certain point in time. It is only in this flight itself that one discovers who is the rock and who is the bird.

The throw into the abyss of modernity, the transition to the political philosophy of the Mother, at some point leads to the discovery of the grand scale of the metaphysical catastrophe. The 'Dark Enlightenment' is precisely the moment when the magnitude of the catastrophe is fully revealed. It is at this moment that a *radical turn in consciousness* takes place. *This* is the beginning of the Fourth Political Theory. While the fledgling, thrown out of the nest, is flying, he does not yet know whether he is a stone or a bird. He who knows only how to fall is incapable of moving 'backwards' through the only possible gravitational trajectory (a movement into the abyss is not a movement along a plane, it is a fall).

Accordingly, only a 'winged being' can accept the Fourth Political Theory, for whom 'backwards' means 'upwards', in the opposite direction to that of modernity, where only the one who is capable of flight can move.

Here one may recall Plato's teaching on what man is. From Plato's point of view, man is a *winged being*. And he is in a body as a result of the fall, as a consequence of the catastrophe that happened to him. Man's task is to cultivate his wings so that he learns to fly and so that death becomes the end of the caterpillar's existence and the beginning of a butterfly capable of flight — a celebration of birth and resurrection. Better yet, to 'die while alive' and fly vertically — back to our heavenly homeland. That is the deeper meaning of the Fourth Political Theory.

The Fourth Political Theory is an aspiration to radically reverse the logic of world history. But since this history is a fall (top-down movement: the *logos* of the Father to the *logos* of the Son to the *logos* of the Mother), the Fourth Political Theory is a rise from the abyss. It is not a trivial conservatism at all. Conservatism makes sense in order to hold on to the paradigm or to limit the choices horizontally. When the decision for modernity was made, conservatism lost its meaning and came to denote the paradoxical desire to preserve the fall itself, to make the fall reliable, guaranteed, sustainable. In a sense, such conservatism is a way of putting the awakening terror to sleep, of veiling it, of making the faller not notice that he is falling, of imposing on him the hallucination that he is *not* falling. This is the code of pseudo-logic: modernist conservatism is perhaps the worst thing about modernity, because in its context the lie lies about itself — and does so in the most effective way.

The Fourth Political Theory is quite different from conservatism. It is, rather, a revolution that calls for a dramatic and irreversible change in the basic vector of being and living, of how we think about the civilisation of modernity, thus breaking with it as a whole, as a paradigm. In order to go 'back', it is necessary to move 'upwards', i.e. where the fatal materialistic mechanisms of modernity cannot move.

The modern is like a hearse that has descended from a mountain. This hearse does not fly. Following inertia, it has only one way out — to be blown to pieces, to disintegrate into atoms.

In order to really change the situation, the vector of modernity, the almost imminent arrival of the postmodern and 'Dark Liberalism', it is necessary to fundamentally reconsider the attitude towards all the things that appear in the context of the political philosophy of the Mother as something self-evident, obvious, indisputable. Nothing is obvious and indisputable for human beings. Consciousness always deals with representations, but these can be constructed according to one paradigmatic model or another. The postmodern reassessment of stratification, code-breaking and de-territorialisation seeks to overturn the Platonic and the

Aristotelian, making them experientially unreliable and impossible. But this is nothing more than the work and deconstruction of representation — this time nihilistic, materialistic and aggressively aimed at destroying the vertical, spiritual, heavenly dimension. The structures and rhizomatic networks thus created are, for all their cogency, nothing but pseudo-logical chimeras, like everything in the underworld of titans, shadows and ghosts.

The Dialectic of Shadows

There is no alternative within the political philosophy of the Mother, and so the First Political Theory (liberalism) and its subideological forms within the dissipative programme of the modern is destiny.

It is not an accident, a deviation or a dead end. It is precisely fate. It was the goal that was being sought, called for, rushed towards, strived for.

The devil's greatest trick is to deny God. At first, people think that since there is no God, there must be no devil, there is only man, and he is henceforth the measure of existence. At first, the devil agrees to this conclusion: all right, he mutters, there is no me, so be it. But this is another one of his tricks: who in that case insinuates that there is no God (and with him, no devil)? God is the truth, he would not lie about himself. There is a devil for that, here he is the father of pseudo-logic, i.e., modernity.

At the end of the process of secularity, rationality and scepticality, believing neither in God nor in the devil of modernity, the devil reappears. And this time without God. Alone — on his own.

In the beginning Satan was a 'shadow of God'; then there was neither God nor his shadow. Finally, God still does not exist, but his autonomous shadow emerges. The discovery of the gestalt of the devil, his incarnation and his apparition constitute the essence of the transition from the last phase of the modern to the phase of the postmodern and object-oriented ontology. The devil, Ahriman, Satan (in Islam *Dajjal*) are religious terms for the Radical Object, the 'core' (Cthelll) of speculative realism and accelerationism.

The devil (Antichrist) in postmodernism — in its imagery, in its metaphors, in its practices — becomes evident, reveals himself. From the point of view of political philosophy, we can consider it as a metaphor (the 'Antichrist' as a politico-philosophical figure). From a religious perspective, it could well be interpreted literally.

The Fourth Political Theory proposes, building on the devil of the postmodern, which has been fully revealed, to carry out a take-off/transition to those paradigms which were eliminated back in the first stage of the modern.

In other words, one should not 'slow down', but go in a *different direction* altogether. The Fourth Political Theory begins with the person who dissents, who denies, who rejects the proposed programme of paradigmatic phases and transitions of political history, undertaking a cold and in-depth semantic analysis of all its previous semantic moments. You cannot overcome what you do not understand, what you do not know. Hegel said that morality is constructed according to the following scheme: innocence to sin to virtue. Innocence is not virtue because it does not know sin. Virtue knows sin and overcomes and defeats it.

This dialectic is quite applicable to the Fourth Political Theory as it relates to conservatism. The world of Tradition is innocence, it knows no modernity. Modernity is analogous to 'sin', which kills innocence. Conservatism, then, is opposition to sin from a position of innocence. But the Fourth Political Theory is precisely the analogue of 'virtue'. It arises not *before* and not *during*, but *after* modernity, moreover, after the transformation of modernity into postmodernity and the discovery of the nihilistic and counterhumanistic (posthumanist) essence of the political philosophy of the Mother. The Fourth Political Theory deals with an autonomous shadow which it knows perfectly well and which it challenges. In a sense, the Fourth Political Theory completes the whole cycle of paradigmatic descent. It is based on a metaphysically revolutionary decision about a radically different ontology, an ontology of eternity.

The Fourth Political Theory represents the most comprehensive form of political and philosophical eschatology. In order for the Fourth Political Theory to be formulated, a preliminary victory of modernity, and more precisely a victory within modernity of liberalism over illiberal ideologies, was necessary. Previously, it would not have been possible, since modernity's three political ideologies cleverly incorporated elements of a profound rejection of the status quo at the paradigmatic level into the dialectic of opposition to these theories. The nihilistic nature of modernity was concealed in this confrontation through the possibility of criticism: liberals accused Communists of nihilism, Communists accused Fascists, Fascists accused liberals, etc. In doing so, they were all different versions of nihilism, materialism and mechanical alienation, but this could not be evident until the conclusion of their intense dramatic confrontation, which ultimately led to the victory of liberalism. To achieve true virtue, one must see the full abyss of sin, not its partial manifestations. This is probably what the Russian monk Silouan the Athonite (1866–1938) had in mind when he recommended that other monks 'keep the mind in hell and not despair'. To 'keep the mind in hell' means to behold the abyss of sin. The advice 'not to despair' refers to trusting in God and the freedom of man to make a fundamental decision, even while in the abyss.

The Fourth Political Theory emerges at the extreme edge of modernity, in the context of the postmodern. And the very structure of the postmodern and the 'Dark Enlightenment' serve as evidence for the true essence of the modern, which has not merely gone astray, but led the wrong way from the beginning, driven either by free will to sin and falsehood, or by error. In either case the modern was decided by a free human mind, though clearly not without the active participation of the devil. But no tricks of the devil can drive a man to sin until he himself accepts sin, consents to it, makes a free choice in its favour.

Europe made such a choice in the New Age and then imposed it on everyone else. The Fourth Political Theory makes a different choice: in favour of the political philosophy of the Father and the Son (and the Holy Spirit).

Rejecting the Hypnosis of the Mother

The radical break through the hypnosis of the political philosophy of the Mother is the first fundamental gesture of the Fourth Political Theory. In

Politica Aeterna, the general ontological map shows that the political philosophy of the Father and the political philosophy of the Son are not conventions; they have an independent — paradigmatic — being that determines the topics, the subject and the corresponding configuration of the cosmos.

In history, these two political philosophies have many examples of effective implementation. They are not an abstract fantasy; they are not a dream. They are actually pre-existing political systems, and have existed throughout human history and partly retain their influence to this day, in the world of today.

When we reject the political philosophy of the Mother, we do not fall into nothingness and chaos. We are still left with two perfectly valid politico-philosophical models. However, if we did not know the political philosophy of the Father and the political philosophy of the Son, no matter how disgusting it would be for us to go with the 'river' of modernity, with the stream, we might accept it too, in the absence of a possibility to choose a different direction, for fear of a pure nothingness. This is what pseudo-logic is trying to convince us of; the proponents of modernity and post-modernity want to tell us: if not modern, then nothing. But, fortunately, we know that there *is* the Father's paradigm and there *is* the Son's paradigm. And that is the second — positive, creative — half of the programme of the Fourth Political Theory.

Most importantly, the Fourth Political Theory is based on the fact that the solution is placed not in the context of the three political ideologies of modernity, but in the context of the three paradigms of *Politica Aeterna*: the philosophy of the Father (Platonism, doctrine of eternal ideas), the philosophy of the Son (Aristotelianism, phenomenology) and the philosophy of the Mother (materialism, atomism). It is a free choice, in which modernism is no more than one option among two others.

The political philosophy of the Father and the political philosophy of the Son (or their alliance) are objects which we are free to choose from. It is not a given, it is an assignment. And apparently we find ourselves in modernity because we have forgotten that the political philosophy of the Father and the political philosophy of the Son have to be affirmed anew each time, by each successive generation, by each society, by each individual — by his free will and his enlightened consciousness. We assumed them as something guaranteed and took them for granted.

As soon as even a vertically oriented political structure is taken for granted, it becomes inert and begins to fall, to collapse. If, instead of the free and willing establishment of a monarchical, imperial, traditional, caste verticality, we get used to it, accept it as fact and as a given and do not re-assert it at every stage, sooner or later we will fall into the nihilistic entropy of modernity, and the fall will continue until we reach the Radical Object that looms at the ultimate horizon of the political philosophy of the Mother.

Political Eschatology

The Fourth Political Theory today reveals the essence of the political-philosophical dignity of man as a species. That humanity which is now moving as if nothing had happened in the direction of modernisation, Westernisation, progress — faster (accelerationism) or slower (liberal conservatism) — is the '*dark double*' of humanity; it is that humanity which, by ill will and deep delusion, under the guise of 'freedom', has chosen slavery, given away the right to dignity, to rise and become heroic, and has cast itself down into atomism, nothingness and the service of matter.

Today it is more difficult than ever to return to the political philosophy of the Father or the political philosophy of the Son. But it is now that this choice takes on the fullness of its original patriarchal-heroic meaning. Man differs from his 'dark double' in that he is a philosophical being, a being able to make a free choice. He is free to choose his political philosophy on a paradigmatic level (not from what is 'on the menu').

We could say that the Fourth Political Theory is an invitation to the restoration/creation of the political philosophy of the Father and the political philosophy of the Son. We know that these alternatives exist; we are free to choose them, and, having broken the hypnotic spell of the political philosophy of the Mother, we can quietly choose an alternative political philosophy *beyond* what is (falsely) offered to us as exhaustive completeness. If it is completeness, it is the completeness of a nomenclature of diabolical temptations. *Politica Aeterna* substantiates a different completeness, hiding under the crust of the 'dark double' the true nature of man, which is not reducible to his corporeality or his materiality, much less to infra-corporeal impulses or the element of nothingness. Man has a choice to pursue matter, and, being free, he is also free to make that choice. Today we are reaching the final frontiers of this choice. Yet for all the apparent hopelessness, this is only another illusion — yes, humanity can commit suicide and merge with the Radical Object, but that too must first be decided, chosen. The Fourth Political Theory, explained in the topology of *Politica Aeterna*, reminds us of this freedom and wilfully opens the door to a different choice. Whoever understands and accepts the structure of the Fourth Political Theory is able — perhaps for the last time — to freely and consciously exercise his freedom and his consciousness.

However, the ordinary subject, dependent on the overall structure of the paradigm, on the 'assemblage', on codes, stratifications and territorialisations, does not coincide with the instance that is able to make this choice between the postmodern and the Fourth Political Theory. Such a subject is secondary to the matrix that predetermines reality. Therefore, a different subject is necessary for the affirmation of the Fourth Political Theory. We call it the Radical Subject, whose radicality should be no less, if not greater, than that of the Radical Object of the postmodern and speculative realism. This is what political eschatology is all about: a decisive battle between the Radical Subject (the axis of the Fourth Political Theory) and the 'Dark Enlightenment' takes place at the ultimate frontier of being. On both sides the masks have been thrown off and the metaphysical issues have been sharpened to the utmost. This is the politico-philosophical sense of the 'End Times', where the question of the true nature of humanity, of its meaning and its mission, of its destiny, is decided. This decision belongs to the dimension of eternity, which means that it is made not only in relation to the future, but also in relation to the past, as well as in relation to the present. In religious terms, this is the Last Judgement, which extends its metaphysical weight to all the dimensions and, moreover, to all the modalities of time.

BIBLIOGRAPHY

Works by Alexander Dugin

Available in English

Dugin, Alexander. *Ethnos and Society*. London: Arktos Media, 2018.

Dugin, Alexander. *Ethnosociology: The Foundations*. London: Arktos Media, 2019.

Dugin, Alexander. *Eurasian Mission*. London: Arktos Media, 2014.

Dugin, Alexander. *The Fourth Political Theory*. London: Arktos Media, 2012.

Dugin, Alexander. *The Great Awakening vs The Great Reset*. London: Arktos Media, 2021.

Dugin, Alexander. *Last War of the World Island: The Geopolitics of Contemporary Russia*. London: Arktos, 2015.

Dugin, Alexander. *Political Platonism: The Philosophy of Politics*. London: Arktos Media, 2019.

Dugin, Alexander. *Putin vs Putin: Vladimir Putin Viewed from the Right*. London: Arktos Media, 2014.

Dugin, Alexander. *Theory of a Multipolar World*. London: Arktos Media, 2021.

Noomakhia Project (24 Volumes)

Dugin, Alexander. *В поисках темного Логоса* [In Search of the Dark Logos]. Moscow: Академический проект, 2014.

Dugin, Alexander. *Ноомахия. Три Логоса* [Noomakhia. The Three Logoi]. Moscow: Академический проект, 2014. Dugin, Alexander. *Ноомахия. Геософия. Горизонты и цивилизации* [Noomakhia. Geosophy. Horizons and Civilisations]. Moscow: Академический проект, 2017.

Dugin, Alexander. *Ноомахия. Логос Турана. Индоевропейская идеология вертикали* [Noomakhia. The Logos of Turan. Indo-European Vertical Ideology]. Moscow: Академический проект, 2017.

Dugin, Alexander. *Ноомахия. Горизонты и цивилизации Евразии. Индоевропейское наследие и следы Великой Матери* [Noomakhia. Eurasian Horizons and Civilisations. Indo-European Heritage and Traces of the Great Mother]. Moscow: Академический проект, 2017.

Dugin, Alexander. *Ноомахия. Иранский Логос. Световая война и культура ожидания* [Noomakhia. Iranian Logos. Light Warfare and the Culture of Waiting]. Moscow: Академический проект, 2016.

Dugin, Alexander. *Ноомахия. Великая Индия. Цивилизация Абсолюта* [Noomakhia. Great India. Civilisation of the Absolute]. Moscow: Академический проект, 2017.

Dugin, Alexander. *Ноомахия. Эллинский Логос. Долина Истины* [Noomakhia. The Hellenic Logos. The Valley of Truth]. Moscow: Академический проект, 2016.

Dugin, Alexander. *Ноомахия. Византийский Логос. Эллинизм и Империя* [Noomakhia. The Byzantine Logos. Hellenism and Empire]. Moscow: Академический проект, 2016.

Dugin, Alexander. *Ноомахия. Латинский Логос. Солнце и Крест* [Noomakhia. The Roman Logos. The Sun and the Cross]. Moscow: Академический проект, 2016.

Dugin, Alexander. *Ноомахия. Германский Логос. Человек Апофатический* [Noomakhia. The Germanic Logos. Apophatic Man]. Moscow: Академический проект, 2015.

Dugin, Alexander. *Ноомахия. Французский Логос. Орфей и Мелюзина* [Noomakhia. The French Logos. Orpheus and Melusina]. Moscow: Академический проект, 2015.

Dugin, Alexander. *Ноомахия. Англия или Британия? Морское могущество и позитивный субъект* [Noomakhia. England or Britain? Sea Power and Positive Subject Matter]. Moscow: Академический проект, 2015.

Dugin, Alexander. *Ноомахия. Цивилизации Нового Света. Прагматика грез и разложение горизонтов* [Noomakhia. Civilisations of the New World. The Pragmatics of Dreams and the Decomposition of Horizons]. Moscow: Академический проект, 2017.

Dugin, Alexander. *Ноомахия. Восточная Европа. Славянский Логос: балканская Навь и сарматский стиль* [Noomakhia. Eastern Europe. The Slavic Logos: Balkan Navi and Sarmatian Style]. Moscow: Академический проект, 2018.

Dugin, Alexander. *Ноомахия. Неславянские горизонты Восточной Европы: Песнь упыря и голос глубин* [Noomakhia. Non-Slavic Horizons of Eastern Europe: The Song of the Ghoul and the Voice of the Deep]. Moscow: Академический проект, 2018.

Dugin, Alexander. *Ноомахия. Царство Земли. Структура русской идентичности* [Noomakhia. The Kingdom of the Earth. The Structure of Russian Identity]. Moscow: Академический проект, 2019.

Dugin, Alexander. *Ноомахия. Русский историал. Народ и государство в поисках субъекта* [Noomakhia. Russian Historial. The People and the State in Search of a Subject]. Moscow: Академический проект, 2019.

Dugin, Alexander. *Ноомахия. Образы русской мысли. Солнечный царь, блик Софии и Русь Подземная* [Noomakhia. Patterns of Russian Thought. The Solar Tsar, the Glare of Sophia and Russia Underground]. Moscow: Академический проект, 2020.

Dugin, Alexander. *Ноомахия. Семиты. Монотеизм Луны и гештальт Ва'ала* [Noomakhia. The Semites. Monotheism of the Moon and the Gestalt of Va'al]. Moscow: Академический проект, 2017.

Dugin, Alexander. *Ноомахия. Хамиты. Цивилизации африканского Норда* [Noomakhia. The Hamites. Civilisations of the African North]. Moscow: Академический проект, 2018.

Dugin, Alexander. *Ноомахия. Логос Африки. Люди черного солнца* [Noomakhia. The Logos of Africa. People of the Black Sun]. Moscow: Академический проект, 2018.

Dugin, Alexander. *Ноомахия. Желтый Дракон. Цивилизации Дальнего Востока. Китай. Корея. Япония. Индокитай* [Noomakhia. The Yellow Dragon. Civilisations of the Far East. China. Korea. Japan. Indochina]. Moscow: Академический проект, 2017.

Dugin, Alexander. *Ноомахия. Океания. Вызов Воды* [Noomakhia. Oceania. The Challenge of Water]. Moscow: Академический проект, 2018.

Other Works

Dugin, Alexander. *Абсолютная Родина* [The Absolute Homeland]. Moscow: Арктогея-Центр, 2000.

Dugin, Alexander. *Археомодерн* [Archaeomodern]. Moscow: Евразийское Движение, 2011.

Dugin, Alexander. *Воображение. Философия, социология, структуры* [Imagination. Philosophy, Sociology, Structures]. Moscow: Академический проект, 2016.

Dugin, Alexander. *Геополитика* [Geopolitics]. Moscow: Академический проект, 2014.

Dugin, Alexander. *Знаки Великого Норда* [Symbols of the Great North]. Moscow: Вече, 2008.

Dugin, Alexander. *Мартин Хайдеггер. Возможность русской философии* [Martin Heidegger. The Potential of Russian Philosophy]. Moscow: Академический проект, 2011.

Dugin, Alexander. *Мартин Хайдеггер. Метаполитика. Эсхатология бытия* [Martin Heidegger. Metapolitics. The Eschatology of Being]. Moscow: Академический проект, 2016.

Dugin, Alexander. *Мартин Хайдеггер. Последний Бог* [Martin Heidegger. The Last God]. Moscow: Академический проект, 2014.

Dugin, Alexander. *Мартин Хайдеггер. Философия Нового Начала* [Martin Heidegger. Philosophy of the New Beginning]. Moscow: Академический проект, 2010.

Dugin, Alexander. *Международные отношения (парадигмы, теории, социология)* [International Relations (Paradigms, Theories, Sociology)]. Moscow: Академический Проект, 2014

Dugin, Alexander. *Основы геополитики* [Fundamentals of Geopolitics]. Moscow: Арктогея-центр, 2000.

Dugin, Alexander. *Постфилософия* [Postphilosophy]. Moscow: Евразийское движение. 2009.

Dugin, Alexander. *Радикальный Субъект и его дубль* [The Radical Subject and Its Double]. Moscow: Евразийское движение. 2009.

Dugin, Alexander. *Русская вещь в 2т* [The Russian Thing in 2 Volumes]. Moscow: Арктогея-Центр, 2001.

Dugin, Alexander. *Русский Логос — русский Хаос. Социология русского общества* [Russian Logos — Russian Chaos. The Sociology of Russian Society]. Moscow: Академический проект, 2015.

Dugin, Alexander. *Социология воображения. Введение в структурную социологию* [The Sociology of the Imagination. An Introduction to Structural Sociology]. Moscow: Академический проект, 2010.

Dugin, Alexander. *Философия традиционализма* [Philosophy of Traditionalism]. Moscow: Арктогея-центр, 2002.

Dugin, Alexander. *Четвертый Путь. Введение в Четвертую Политическую Теорию* [The Fourth Way: Introduction to the Fourth Political Theory]. Moscow: Академический проект, 2014.

Dugin, Alexander. *Эволюция парадигмальных оснований науки* [The Evolution of the Paradigmatic Foundations of Science]. Moscow: Арктогея, 2002.

Works by Other Authors

A compendium of Ockham's teachings: a translation of the Tractatus de principiis theologiae. St. Bonaventure, NY: Franciscan Institute, St. Bonaventure University, 1998.

Agamben, Giorgio. *Homo Sacer. Sovereign Power and Bare Life*. Stanford: Stanford University Press, 1998.

Al-Arabi, Ibn. *The Meccan Revelations*. Edited by Michel Chodkiewicz. New York: Pir Press, 2002.

Al-Arabi, Ibn. *The Tarjumán al-Ashwáq: A Collection of Mystical Odes by Muhyiddīn Ibn al-ʿArabī*. London: Royal Asiatic Society, Oriental, 1911.

Al-Farabi. *The Political Writings. Selected Aphorisms and Other Texts*. Ithaca: Cornell University Press, 2001.

Alighieri, Dante. *The Divine Comedy*. Oxford: Oxford University Press, 2008.

Althusius, Johannes. *Politica*. Indianapolis: Liberty Fund, 1995.

Anderson, Benedict. *Imagined Communities: Reflections on the Origin and Spread of Nationalism*. London: Verso, 2016.

Arendt, Hannah. *The Origins of Totalitarianism.* London: Penguin, 2017.

Artaud, Antonin. *The Theatre and Its Double.* Richmond: Alma Classics, 2017.

Bakunin, Mikhail. *Собрание сочинений и писем. 1828–1876* [Collected Works and Essays]. Moscow: Издательство Всесоюзного Общества политкаторжан и ссыльнопоселенцев, 1934–1935 [Publication of the All-Union Society of Political Torture and Penal Exiles, 1934–1935].

Baos, Franz. *The Mind of Primitive Man.* NY: The Macmillan Company, 1938.

Bartsch, Hans Werner, ed. *Kerygma and Myth: A Theological Debate.* New York: Harper Torchbooks, 1961.

Bataille, Georges. *Inner Experience.* New York: SUNY Press, 1988.

Bataille, Georges. *The Accursed Share.* New York: Zone Books, 1991.

Bataille, Georges. *Ненависть к поэзии: Порнолатрическая проза* [Hate Poetry: Pornolatry Prose]. Moscow: Ladomir, 1999.

Baudrillard, Jean. *The System of Objects.* Verso Books, 2020.

Baum, L. Frank. *The Wonderful Wizard of Oz.* Chicago; New York: G.M. Hill Co., 1900.

Bauman, Zygmunt. *Liquid Modernity.* Cambridge: Polity, 2000.

Bennett, Jane. *Vibrant Matter: A Political Ecology of Things.* Durham, NC: Duke University Press, 2010.

Bentham, Jeremy. *An Introduction to the Principles of Morals and Legislation.* New York: Dover Publications, 2007.

Bodin, Jean. *Six Books of the Commonwealth.* Oxford: B. Blackwell, 1955.

Bogost, Ian. *Alien Phenomenology, or, What It's Like to Be a Thing.* Minneapolis: Minnesota University Press, 2012.

Brassier, Ray. *Nihil Unbound: Enlightenment and Extinction.* London: Palgrave Macmillan, 2007.

Bryant, Levi, Nick Srnicek, and Graham Harman, eds. *The Speculative Turn: Continental Materialism and Realism.* Melbourne: Re.Press, 2011.

Bryant, Levi. *The Democracy of Objects.* London: Open Humanities Press, 2011.

Buse, P.; Scott, A. (ed's). *Ghosts: Deconstruction, Psychoanalysis, History.* London: Macmillan, 1999.

Campanella, Tommaso. *The City of the Sun.* Saint Paul, Minnesota: Wilder Publications, 2009.

Castells, Manuel. *The Rise of the Network Society.* Hoboken, NJ: Wiley-Blackwell, 2009.

Chamberlain, Houston Stewart. *The Foundations of the Nineteenth Century.* Massachusetts: Adamant Media Corporation, 2003.

Chesterton, G. K. *Saint Thomas Aquinas.* NY: Doubleday Image, 1956.

Chrysostom, John. *Homilies on Second Thessalonians: Homily 4.* Translated by John A. Broadus. From *Nicene and Post-Nicene Fathers, First Series, Vol. 13.* Edited by Philip Schaff. Buffalo, NY: Christian Literature Publishing Co., 1889.

Conche, Marcel. *L'Aléatoire* [The Randomness]. Paris: Les Belles Lettres, 2012.

Corbin, Henry. *Histoire de la philosophie islamique*. Paris: Gallimard, 1964.

Corbin, Henry. *The Man of Light in Iranian Sufism*. Omega Publications, 1994.

Damascene, St John. *Writings: The Fount of Knowledge*.

Danilevsky, Nikolay. *Дарвинизм. Критическое исследование В 2 т.* [Darwinism. Critical Study Volume II]. St. Petersburg: Publishing house of M. E. Komarov, 1885–1889.

de Giorgio, Guido. *La Tradizione romana* [Roman Tradition]. Rome: Edizioni Mediterranee, 1989.

de Gobineau, Arthur. *An Essay on the Inequality of Human Races*.

de Ockham, Guilelmi. *Opera Politica. 4 vols.* Manchester; Oxford: Manchester University Press; Oxford University Press, 1940–1997.

Debord, Guy. *Society of the Spectacle*. London: Rebel Press, 1992.

Deleuze, Gilles and Félix Guattari. *A Thousand Plateaus: Capitalism and Schizophrenia*. London: Athlone Press, 1988.

Deleuze, Gilles and Félix Guattari. *Anti-Oedipus: Capitalism and Schizophrenia*. Minneapolis: University of Minnesota Press, 1983.

Deleuze, Gilles; Guattari, Félix. *What is Philosophy?* New York : Columbia University Press, 1994.

Deleuze, Gilles. *Nietzsche and Philosophy*. New York: Columbia University Press, 1983.

Deleuze, Gilles. *The Fold: Leibniz and the Baroque*. Minneapolis: University of Minnesota Press, 1993.

Deleuze, Gilles. *The Logic of Sense*. New York: Columbia University Press, 1990.

Derrida, Jacques. *Spectres of Marx*. Oxfordshire: Routledge, 1994.

Derrida, Jacques. *Writing and Difference*. Chicago: University of Chicago Press, 1978.

Dumézil, Georges. 'L'idéologie tripartite des Indo-Européens', *Latomus (Revue des études latines)* 31, 1958.

Dumézil, Georges. *Les Dieux des Indo-Européenes*. Paris: Presses Universitaires de France, 1952.

Dumont, Louis. *Essays on Individualism: Modern Ideology in Anthropological Perspective*. Chicago: University of Chicago Press, 1992.

Dumont, Louis. *Essays on Individualism*. Chicago: University of Chicago Press, 1986.

Dumont, Louis. *Homo Hierarchicus: The Caste System and Its Implications*. Chicago: Chicago University Press, 1981.

Dumont, Louis. *Homo Hierarchicus: The Caste System and Its Implications*. Chicago: University of Chicago Press, 1970.

Durkheim, Émile. *The Rules of Sociological Method*. New York: Free Press, 1982.

Dzhemal, Geydar. *Дауд vs Джалут (Давид против Голиафа)* [Daoud vs Jalut (David vs Goliath)]. Moscow: Социально-политическая мысль, 2011.

Dzhemal, Geydar. *Революция пророков* [Revolution of the Prophets]. Moscow: Ультра.Культура, 2003.

Eliade, Mircea. *Patterns in Comparative Religion*. London: Sheed & Ward, 1958.

Eriugena, John Scotus. *Periphyseon on the Division of Nature*. Eugene, Oregon: Wipf and Stock, 2011.

Evola, Julius. *Fascism Viewed from the Right*. London, Arktos Media, 2013.

Evola, Julius. *Heathen Imperialism*. Thompkins & Cariou, 2007.

Evola, Julius. *Men Among the Ruins*. Vermont: Inner Traditions, 2002.

Evola, Julius. *Mysteries of the Grail*. Vermont: Inner Traditions, 2018.

Evola, Julius. *Revolt against the Modern World*. Vermont: Inner Traditions, 1995.

Fedorov, Nikolai. *Собрание сочинений: в 4-х т.* [Collected Works in 4 Volumes]. Moscow: Progress-Tradition; Evidentis, 1995–2004.

Fichte, Johann Gottlieb. *Addresses to the German Nation*. Cambridge, Cambridge University Press, 2009.

Fichte, Johann Gottlieb. *The Closed Commercial State*. Albany, NY: SUNY Press, 2013.

Ficino, Marsilio. *La Religione Cristiana*. Rome: Città Nuova Editrice, 2005.

Foucault, Michel. *Discipline and Punish: The Birth of the Prison*. London: Penguin, 2020.

Foucault, Michel. *Discipline and Punish: The Birth of the Prison*. New York: Pantheon Books, 1977.

Foucault, Michel. *Dits et écrits* [Written and Spoken]. Paris: Gallimard, 2001.

Foucault, Michel. *History of Madness*. Oxfordshire: Routledge, 2009.

Foucault, Michel. *The Birth of the Clinic*. Oxfordshire: Routledge, 2003.

Foucault, Michel. *The History of Sexuality. Volume 1 The Will to Knowledge*. London: Penguin, 2020.

Fukuyama, Francis. 'Идеи имеют большое значение. Беседа с А.Дугиным' ['Ideas count for a lot. Conversation with Alexander Dugin'] //Профиль [Profile]. 2007. №23(531).

Fukuyama, Francis. *The End of History and the Last Man*. London: Penguin Books, 2012.

Fukuyama, Francis. *The End of History and the Last Man*. London: Penguin Books, 2012.

Gilson, Étienne. *Heloise and Abelard*. Michigan: University of Michigan Press, 1960.

Goodrick-Clarke, Nicholas. *The Occult Roots of Nazism*. London: Tauris Parke Paperbacks, 2012.

Gramsci, Antonio. *Gli intellettuali e l'organizzazione della cultura* [Intellectuals and the Organisation of Cculture]. Torino: Einaudi, 1948.

Gramsci, Antonio. *Il Rivoluzionario Qualificato. Scritti 1916–1925* [The Qualified Revolutionary. Writings 1916–1925]. Rome: Delotti, 1988.

Gramsci, Antonio. *Le Opere. Antologia* [The Works. Anthology]. Milan: Nuova Iniziativa Editoriale, 2007.

Gramsci, Antonio. *Prison Notebooks*. New York: Columbia University Press, 2011.

Greimas, A.J. *Structural Semantics: An Attempt at a Method*. Lincoln: University of Nebraska Press, 1984.

Guénon, René. *Spiritual Power and Temporal Power*. Sophia Perennis et Universalis, 2004.

Guénon, René. *The Essential René Guénon: Metaphysics, Tradition, and the Crisis of Modernity*. Edited by John Herlihy. Bloomington: World Wisdom, 2009.

Guénon, René. *The Reign of Quantity and the Signs of the Times (Collected Works)*. Sophia Perennis et Universalis, 2004.

Guénon, René. *Theosophy: History of a Pseudo-Religion*. Sophia Perennis et Universalis, 2004.

Guénon, René. *Traditional Forms and Cosmic Cycles*. Sophia Perennis et Universalis, 2003.

Haraway, Donna. *A Cyborg Manifesto: Science, Technology, and Socialist-Feminism in the Late Twentieth Century*. New York: Routledge, 1991.

Hardt, Michael and Antonio Negri. *Empire*. Cambridge, Mass.: Harvard University Press, 2000.

Hardt, Michael and Antonio Negri. *Multitude: War and Democracy in the Age of Empire*. London: Penguin, 2005.

Harman, Graham. *Heidegger Explained: From Phenomenon to Thing*. Chicago: Open Court, 2007.

Harman, Graham. *Immaterialism: Objects and Social Theory*. London: Polity, 2016.

Harman, Graham. *Tool-Being. Heidegger and the Metaphysics of Objects*. Chicago: Open Court, 2002.

Hayek, Friedrich. *The Road to Serfdom*. Chicago: Chicago University Press, 1994.

Hegel, Georg Wilhelm Friedrich. *Phenomenology of Spirit*. Oxford: Clarendon Press, 1977.

Hegel, Georg Wilhelm Friedrich. *Science of Logic*. Cambridge: Cambridge University Press, 2015.

Hegel, Georg Wilhelm Friedrich. *The Phenomenology of Spirit*. Oxford: Clarendon Press, 1977.

Heidegger, Martin. *Überlegungen XII — XV. (Schwarze Hefte 1939–1941)* [Reflections XII — XV. Black Notebooks 1939–1941]. Frankfurt-am-Main:Vittorio Klostermann, 2014.

Hitler, Adolf. *Mein Kampf*. Translated by Ralph Manheim. New York: Random House, 1992.

Hobbes, Thomas. *Leviathan*. London: Penguin Classics, 2017.

Hobson, John. *The Eurocentric Conception of World Politics: Western International Theory, 1760 -2010*. Cambridge: Cambridge University Press, 2012.

Hollier, Denis, ed. *The College of Sociology*. Minneapolis: University of Minnesota Press, 1988.

http://slimoco.ning.com

http://www.thedarkenlightenment.com/the-dark-enlightenment-by-nick-land/

Huntington, Samuel. *The Clash of Civilizations and the Remaking of World Order*. New York: Simon & Schuster, 1996.

Jarrett, James L., ed. *Jung's seminar on Nietzsche's Zarathustra*. Princeton, NJ: Princeton University Press, 1988.

Joyce, James. *Finnegan's Wake*. New York: The Viking Press, 1939.

Jünger, Ernst. *The Worker: Dominion and Form*. Evanston, Illinois: Northwestern University Press, 2017.

Kant, Immanuel. *Critique of Pure Reason*. London: Penguin Classics, 2007.

Kant, Immanuel. *Groundwork for the Metaphysics of Morals*. Oxford University Press, 2019.

Kant, Immanuel. *Perpetual Peace: A Philosophical Sketch*. London: S. Sonnenschein, 1903.

Kerényi, Károly. *Eleusis: Archetypal Image of Mother and Daughter*. Princeton: Princeton University Press, 1991.

Khadduri, Majid. *War and Peace in the Law of Islam*. Baltimore: Johns Hopkins Press, 1955.

Kojève, Alexandre. *Introduction to the Reading of Hegel*. Ithaca, NY: Cornell University Press, 1980.

Kurzweil, Ray. *The Singularity is Near*. NY: Viking Books, 2005.

Lacan, Jacques. *Formations of the Unconscious: The Seminar of Jacques Lacan, Book V*. London: Polity, 2020.

Land, Nick. *Fanged Noumena: Collected Writings 1987–2007*. New York; Windsor Quarry (Falmouth): Sequence; Urbanomic, 2011.

Lassalle, Ferdinand. *Macht und Recht. Offnes Sendschreiben* [Might and Right. Open Epistle]. Zürich: Meyer & Zeller, 1863.

Latour, Bruno. *Politics of Nature: How to Bring the Sciences into Democracy*. Cambridge, Mass.: Harvard University Press, 2004.

Latour, Bruno. *We Have Never Been Modern*. Cambridge, Mass.: Harvard University Press, 1993.

Lenin, Vladimir. *Imperialism: The Highest stage of Capitalism*. London: Penguin, 2010.

Lévi-Strauss, Claude. *The Elementary Structures of Kinship*. London: Eyre & Spottiswoode, 1969.

Lévy, Bernard-Henri. *The Empire and the Five Kings: America's Abdication and the Fate of the World*. NY: Henry Holt and Co., 2019.

Locke, John. *An Essay Concerning Human Understanding*. Oxford: Clarendon Press, 1979.

Lurie, S. Y. *Democritus. Texts. Translation. Research*. Leningrad: Science, 1970.

Lyotard, Jean-François. *The Postmodern Condition*. Manchester: Manchester University Press, 1984.

Machiavelli, Niccoló. *The Prince*. London: Penguin, 2003).
Macpherson, James. *The Poems of Ossian*. Edinburgh: Edinburgh University Press, 1996.
Malaparte, Curzio. *Technique du coup d'Etat* [Coup d'Etat: The Technique of Revolution]. Paris: Grasset, 2008.
Mandelbrot, Benoit. *The Fractal Geometry of Nature*. San Francisco: W. H. Freeman and Company, 1982.
Mandeville, Bernard. *The Fable of the Bees, or Private Vices, Publick Benefits*. Oxford: Clarendon Press, 1714.
Marlan, Stanton. *The Black Sun: The Alchemy and Art of Darkness*. College Station: Texas A & M University Press, 2005.
Marx, Karl and Friedrich Engels. *The Communist Manifesto*.
Marx, Karl and Friedrich Engels. *The German Ideology*. Connecticut: Martino Fine Books, 2011.
Marx, Karl and Friedrich Engels. *The Marx-Engels Correspondence: The Personal Letters*. Edited by Fritz J. Raddatz. London: Weidenfeld & Nicolson, 1981.
Marx, Karl. *The Difference Between the Democritean and Epicurean Philosophy of Nature*.
Meillassoux, Quentin. *After Finitude: An Essay on the Necessity of Contingency*. London: Continuum International Publishing Group, 2009.
Meinong, Alexius. *Über Möglichkeit und Wahrscheinlichkeit: Beiträge zur Gegenstandstheorie und Erkenntnistheorie* [On Possibility and Probability: Contributions to Object Theory and Epistemology]. Leipzig: J.A. Barthe, 1915.
Michels, Robert. *Soziologie als Gesellschaftswissenschaft* [Sociology as a Social Science]. Berlin: Mauritius, 1926.
Mill, John Stuart. *Elements of Political Economy*. London: Baldwin, Craddock and Joy, 1821.
Mill, John Stuart. *On Liberty*. Mineola, NY: Dover Publications, 2002.
Mill, John Stuart. *The History of British India*. 3 vols. London: Baldwin, Craddock and Joy, 1818.
Mishima, Yukio. *My Friend Hitler and Other Plays*. New York: Columbia University Press, 2002.
Moeller van den Bruck, Arthur. *Germany's Third Empire*. London: Arktos Media, 2012.
Mohler, Armin. *The Conservative Revolution in Germany 1918–1932*. Brooklyn, NY: Radix Media, 2018.
Mosca, Gaetano. *Storia delle Dottrine Politiche* [History of Political Doctrines]. Bari: Laterza, 1937.
Murphy, John. *Technical Analysis of the Financial Markets*. Upper Saddle River, NJ: Prentice Hall, 1999.

Mussolini, Benito. *La dottrina del fascismo* [The Doctrine of Fascism]. Firenze: Vallecchi Editore, 1935.

Negarestani, Reza. Cyclonopedia: Complicity with Anonymous Materials. Melbourne: Re.Press, 2008.

Negarestani, Reza. *Cyclonopedia: Complicity with Anonymous Materials*. Melbourne: Re.Press, 2008.

Niekisch, Ernst. *Hitler — ein deutsches Verhängnis* [Hitler — A German Fate]. Berlin: Widerstands-Verlag, 1932.

Nietzsche, Friedrich. *On the Genealogy of Morals*. Cambridge: Cambridge University Press, 2011.

Nietzsche, Friedrich. *The Gay Science*. New York: Random House, 1974.

Nietzsche, Friedrich. *The Will to Power*. New York: Vintage Books, 1968.

Nietzsche, Friedrich. *Thus Spoke Zarathustra*. London: Penguin Classics, 1974.

Nietzsche, Friedrich. *Twilight of the Idols*. Translated by Anthony M. Ludovici. Hertfordshire: Wordsworth Editions Ltd, 2007.

Noukhayev, Khozh-Ahmed. *Ведено или Вашингтон?* [Vedeno or Washington?]. Moscow: Арктогея-центр, 2001.

Otto, Rudolf. *The Idea of the Holy: An Inquiry into the Non-Rational Factor in the Idea of the Divine and Its Relation to the Rational*. London: Oxford University Press, 1936.

Pareto, Vilfredo. *Compendium of General Sociology*. Minneapolis: University of Minnesota Press, 1980.

Pico della Mirandola, Giovanni. *Oration on the Dignity of Man*. Gateway Publishing, 1996.

Polanyi, Karl. *Selected Works*. Moscow: Территория будущего [Future Territory], 2013.

Popper, Karl R. *The Open Society and Its Enemies*. Princeton, NJ: Princeton University Press, 1966.

Popper, Karl. *The Open Society and its Enemies, Volume I*. Oxfordshire: Routledge Classics, 2010.

Proudhon, P.J. *What is Property?* Cambridge: Cambridge University Press, 1994.

Qa'im, Mahdi Muntazir. *Jesus through the Qur'an and Shi'ite Narrations*. NY: Tahrike Tarsile Qur'an, 2007.

Rand, Ayn. *Capitalism: The Unknown Ideal*. London: Penguin, 1994.

Rose, Seraphim. *Nihilism: The Root of the Revolution of the Modern Age*. Forestville, California: Fr. Seraphim Rose Foundation, 1994.

Rosenberg, Alfred. *The Myth of the Twentieth Century*. München: Hoheneichen-Verlag, 1930.

Rousseau, Jean-Jacques. *The Social Contract*. London: Penguin Books, 2004.

Schmitt, Carl. *Dictatorship: From the Origin of the Modern Concept of Sovereignty to Proletarian Class Struggle*. Cambridge: Polity, 2013.

Schmitt, Carl. *Legality and Legitimacy; Law as Politics.* Durham, North Carolina: Duke University Press, 2004; 1998.

Schmitt, Carl. *Political Theology: Four Chapters on the Concept of Sovereignty.* Chicago: University of Chicago Press, 2006.

Schmitt, Carl. *The Concept of the Political.* Translated by George Schwab. Chicago: University of Chicago Press, 2007.

Schmitt, Carl. *The Leviathan in the State Theory of Thomas Hobbes: Meaning and Failure of a Political Symbol.* Chicago: University of Chicago Press, 2008.

Schmitt, Carl. *Völkerrechtliche Großraumordnung mit Interventionsverbot für raumfremde Mächte. Ein Beitrag zum Reichsbegriff im Völkerrecht* [International Law on Greater Spatial Order with a Prohibition of Intervention by Powers from Outside the Sphere. A contribution to the concept of empire in international law]. Berlin: Deutscher Rechts Verlag, 1939.

Schuon, Frithjof. *Undestanding Islam.* Bloomington, Indiana: World Wisdom, 1998.

Smith, Adam. *An Inquiry into the Nature and Causes of the Wealth of Nations.* London: Oxford University Press, 2008.

Sombart, Werner. *Deutscher Sozialismus* [German Socialism]. Berlin: Buchholz & Weisswange, 1934.

Sombart, Werner. *Traders and Heroes.* London: Arktos Media, 2021.

Soros, George. *On Globalization.* New York: PublicAffairs, 2005.

Soros, George. *Open Society: The Crisis of Global Capitalism Reconstructed.* Boston: Little, Brown & Company, 2000.

Soros, George. *The Alchemy of Finance.* Hoboken, NJ: Wiley, 2003.

Spann, Othmar. *The True State: Lectures on the Demolition & Reconstruction of Society.* Vienna: Quelle & Meyer, 1921.

Spencer, Herbert. *Essays Scientific, Political and Speculative in 3 volumes.* London: Williams & Norgate, 1868.

Spengler, Oswald. *Preußentum und Sozialismus* [Prussianism and Socialism]. London: Arktos Media, 2021.

Spinoza, Baruch. *A Theologico-Political Treatise, and a Political Treatise.* NY: Cosimo, 2005.

Stirner, Max. *The Ego and Its Own.* Verso Books, 2014.

Strauss, Leo. *An Introduction to Political Philosophy: Ten Essays by Leo Strauss.* Detroit, MI: Wayne State University Press, 1989.

Tönnies, Ferdinand. *Community and Society.* Mineola, NY: Dover, 2011.

Tsiolkovsky, Konstantin. *Космическая философия* [Cosmic Philosophy]. Moscow: IDLi; Sphere, 2004.

van der Pijl, Kees. *The Making of an Atlantic Ruling Class.* London: Verso, 1984.

van der Pijl, Kees. *Transnational Classes and International Relations.* London: Routledge, 1998.

van der Pijl, Kees. *Vordenker der Weltpolitik: Einführung in die internationale Politik aus ideengeschichtlicher Perspektive* [Masterminds of World Politics: Introduction to International Politics from a Perspective of the History of Ideas]. Opladen: Leske + Budrich, 1996.

Vivenza, Jean-Marc. 'From the formal dominance of capital to its real dominance'. *Elements*. 1997, № 7.

Voegelin, Eric. *Das Volk Gottes. Sektenbewegungen und der Geist der Moderne* [The People of God. Sectarian Movements and the Spirit of Modernity]. Munich: Fink, 1994.

Voegelin, Eric. *Die neue Wissenschaft der Politik* [The New Science of Politics]. Munich: Wilhelm Fink Verlag, 2004.

Voegelin, Eric. *Die politischen Religionen* [The Political Religions]. Stockholm: Bermann Fischer, 1939.

von Herder, Johann Gottfried. *Ideen zur Philosophie der Geschichte der Menschheit* [Ideas for a Philosophy of Human History].

von Mises, Ludwig. *Индивид, рынок и правовое государство* [The Individual, the Market and the Rule of Law]. St Petersburg: Pneuma, 1999.

Walras, Léon. *Elements of Pure Economics*. Oxfordshire: Routledge Library Editions, 2010.

Weber, Max. *Politics as a Vocation*. Philadelphia: Fortress Press, 1965.

Weber, Max. *The Protestant Ethic and the Spirit of Capitalism*. London: George Allen & Unwin Ltd, 1930.

Wright, M.R. *Empedocles. The extant fragments*. New York; London: Yale University Press, 1981.

Wurmbrand, Richard. *Marx and Satan*. Westchester, Illinois: Crossway Books, 1986.

OTHER BOOKS PUBLISHED BY ARKTOS

VIRGINIA ABERNETHY	*Born Abroad*
SRI DHARMA PRAVARTAKA ACHARYA	*The Dharma Manifesto*
JOAKIM ANDERSEN	*Rising from the Ruins*
WINSTON C. BANKS	*Excessive Immigration*
STEPHEN BASKERVILLE	*Who Lost America?*
ALAIN DE BENOIST	*Beyond Human Rights*
	Carl Schmitt Today
	The Ideology of Sameness
	The Indo-Europeans
	Manifesto for a European Renaissance
	On the Brink of the Abyss
	The Problem of Democracy
	Runes and the Origins of Writing
	View from the Right (vol 1–3)
ARMAND BERGER	*Tolkien, Europe, and Tradition*
ARTHUR MOELLER VAN DEN BRUCK	*Germany's Third Empire*
MATT BATTAGLIOLI	*The Consequences of Equality*
KERRY BOLTON	*The Perversion of Normality*
	Revolution from Above
	Yockey: A Fascist Odyssey
ISAC BOMAN	*Money Power*
CHARLES WILLIAM DAILEY	*The Serpent Symbol in Tradition*
RICARDO DUCHESNE	*Faustian Man in a Multicultural Age*
ALEXANDER DUGIN	*Ethnos and Society*
	Ethnosociology
	Eurasian Mission
	The Fourth Political Theory
	The Great Awakening vs the Great Reset
	Last War of the World-Island
	Political Platonism
	Putin vs Putin
	The Rise of the Fourth Political Theory
	Templars of the Proletariat
	The Theory of a Multipolar World
EDWARD DUTTON	*Race Differences in Ethnocentrism*
MARK DYAL	*Hated and Proud*
CLARE ELLIS	*The Blackening of Europe*
KOENRAAD ELST	*Return of the Swastika*
JULIUS EVOLA	*The Bow and the Club*
	Fascism Viewed from the Right
	A Handbook for Right-Wing Youth
	Metaphysics of Power
	Metaphysics of War
	The Myth of the Blood
	Notes on the Third Reich
	Pagan Imperialism
	Recognitions
	A Traditionalist Confronts Fascism
GUILLAUME FAYE	*Archeofuturism*

OTHER BOOKS PUBLISHED BY ARKTOS

	Archeofuturism 2.0
	The Colonisation of Europe
	Convergence of Catastrophes
	Ethnic Apocalypse
	A Global Coup
	Prelude to War
	Sex and Deviance
	Understanding Islam
	Why We Fight
Daniel S. Forrest	*Suprahumanism*
Andrew Fraser	*Dissident Dispatches*
	Reinventing Aristocracy in the Age of Woke Capital
	The WASP Question
Génération Identitaire	*We are Generation Identity*
Peter Goodchild	*The Taxi Driver from Baghdad*
	The Western Path
Paul Gottfried	*War and Democracy*
Petr Hampl	*Breached Enclosure*
Porus Homi Havewala	*The Saga of the Aryan Race*
Lars Holger Holm	*Hiding in Broad Daylight*
	Homo Maximus
	Incidents of Travel in Latin America
	The Owls of Afrasiab
Richard Houck	*Liberalism Unmasked*
A. J. Illingworth	*Political Justice*
Institut Iliade	*For a European Awakening*
	Guardians of Heritage
Alexander Jacob	*De Naturae Natura*
Jason Reza Jorjani	*Artemis Unveiled*
	Closer Encounters
	Erosophia
	Faustian Futurist
	Iranian Leviathan
	Lovers of Sophia
	Novel Folklore
	Philosophy of the Future
	Prometheism
	Promethean Pirate
	Prometheus and Atlas
	Psychotron
	Uber Man
	World State of Emergency
Henrik Jonasson	*Sigmund*
Edgar Julius Jung	*The Significance of the German Revolution*
Ruuben Kaalep & August Meister	*Rebirth of Europe*
Roderick Kaine	*Smart and SeXy*
Peter King	*Here and Now*
	Keeping Things Close
	On Modern Manners

OTHER BOOKS PUBLISHED BY ARKTOS

JAMES KIRKPATRICK	*Conservatism Inc.*
LUDWIG KLAGES	*The Biocentric Worldview*
	Cosmogonic Reflections
	The Science of Character
ANDREW KORYBKO	*Hybrid Wars*
PIERRE KREBS	*Guillaume Faye: Truths & Tributes*
	Fighting for the Essence
JULIEN LANGELLA	*Catholic and Identitarian*
JOHN BRUCE LEONARD	*The New Prometheans*
STEPHEN PAX LEONARD	*The Ideology of Failure*
	Travels in Cultural Nihilism
WILLIAM S. LIND	*Reforging Excalibur*
	Retroculture
PENTTI LINKOLA	*Can Life Prevail?*
H. P. LOVECRAFT	*The Conservative*
NORMAN LOWELL	*Imperium Europa*
RICHARD LYNN	*Sex Differences in Intelligence*
	A Tribute to Helmut Nyborg (ed.)
JOHN MACLUGASH	*The Return of the Solar King*
CHARLES MAURRAS	*The Future of the Intelligentsia &*
	For a French Awakening
JOHN HARMON MCELROY	*Agitprop in America*
MICHAEL O'MEARA	*Guillaume Faye and the Battle of Europe*
	New Culture, New Right
MICHAEL MILLERMAN	*Beginning with Heidegger*
DMITRY MOISEEV	*The Philosophy of Italian Fascism*
MAURICE MURET	*The Greatness of Elites*
BRIAN ANSE PATRICK	*The NRA and the Media*
	Rise of the Anti-Media
	The Ten Commandments of Propaganda
	Zombology
TITO PERDUE	*The Bent Pyramid*
	Journey to a Location
	Lee
	Morning Crafts
	Philip
	The Sweet-Scented Manuscript
	William's House (vol. 1–4)
JOHN K. PRESS	*The True West vs the Zombie Apocalypse*
RAIDO	*A Handbook of Traditional Living* (vol. 1–2)
P R REDDALL	*Towards Awakening*
CLAIRE RAE RANDALL	*The War on Gender*
STEVEN J. ROSEN	*The Agni and the Ecstasy*
	The Jedi in the Lotus
NICHOLAS ROONEY	*Talking to the Wolf*
RICHARD RUDGLEY	*Barbarians*
	Essential Substances

OTHER BOOKS PUBLISHED BY ARKTOS

	Wildest Dreams
ERNST VON SALOMON	*It Cannot Be Stormed*
	The Outlaws
WERNER SOMBART	*Traders and Heroes*
PIERO SAN GIORGIO	*CBRN*
	Giuseppe
	Survive the Economic Collapse
SRI SRI RAVI SHANKAR	*Celebrating Silence*
	Know Your Child
	Management Mantras
	Patanjali Yoga Sutras
	Secrets of Relationships
GEORGE T. SHAW (ED.)	*A Fair Hearing*
FENEK SOLÈRE	*Kraal*
	Reconquista
OSWALD SPENGLER	*The Decline of the West*
	Man and Technics
RICHARD STOREY	*The Uniqueness of Western Law*
TOMISLAV SUNIC	*Against Democracy and Equality*
	Homo Americanus
	Postmortem Report
	Titans are in Town
ASKR SVARTE	*Gods in the Abyss*
HANS-JÜRGEN SYBERBERG	*On the Fortunes and Misfortunes of Art in Post-War Germany*
ABIR TAHA	*Defining Terrorism*
	The Epic of Arya (2nd ed.)
	Nietzsche is Coming God, or the Redemption of the Divine
	Verses of Light
JEAN THIRIART	*Europe: An Empire of 400 Million*
BAL GANGADHAR TILAK	*The Arctic Home in the Vedas*
DOMINIQUE VENNER	*For a Positive Critique*
	The Shock of History
HANS VOGEL	*How Europe Became American*
MARKUS WILLINGER	*A Europe of Nations*
	Generation Identity
ALEXANDER WOLFHEZE	*Alba Rosa*
	Globus Horribilis
	Rupes Nigra

www.ingramcontent.com/pod-product-compliance
Lightning Source LLC
Chambersburg PA
CBHW051155300426
44116CB00006B/320